Georgi Ivanovitch Gurdjieff
The Man, The Teaching, His Mission

Georgi Ivanovitch Gurdjieff
The Man, The Teaching, His Mission

William Patrick Patterson

Barbara Allen Patterson, Editor

Arete Communications, Publishers
Fairfax, California

Georgi Ivanovitch Gurdjieff
The Man, The Teaching, His Mission
© 2014 by William Patrick Patterson
All rights reserved.

Design by WordPlay Consulting, New Park, Pennsylvania
korman@wp-consulting.com

Library of Congress Catalog Number: 2012934460
Patterson, William Patrick
Georgi Ivanovitch Gurdjieff: The Man, The Teaching, His Mission
Includes photos, essays, notes, chronology, references, bibliography and index

1. G. I. Gurdjieff
2. P. D. Uspenskii (Ouspensky)
3. Thomas and Olga de Hartmann
4. Jeanne de Salzmann
5. Olgivanna and Frank Lloyd Wright
6. A. R. Orage
7. Jean Toomer
8. J. G. Bennett
9. Margaret Anderson
10. Solita Solano
11. Kathryn Hulme
12. Lord John Pentland
13. Prehistoric Egypt
14. Esoteric Christianity
15. The Fourth Way

ISBN: 978-1-879514-08-9
First hardcover edition 2014

This paper meets the requirements of ANSI/NISO Z39.48-1992 (Permanence of Paper for Printed Library Materials).
Printed on Acid-Free Paper ∞

All rights reserved under International and Pan-American Copyright Conventions. No part of this book may be reproduced or transmitted in any form or by any means, electronic or mechanical, including photocopying, recording, or any information storage or retrieval system, without prior permission in writing from the publisher.

Arete Communications
773 Center Boulevard, # 58
Fairfax, CA 94978-0058

Email: Arete@TheGurdjieffLegacyFoundation.org
Website: www.TheGurdjieffLegacyFoundation.org

Other Works by the Author

Eating The "I"

Struggle of the Magicians

Taking with the Left Hand

Ladies of the Rope

Voices in the Dark

The Life & Teachings of Carlos Castaneda

Spiritual Survival in a Radically Changing World-Time

Adi Da Samraj—Realized or/and Deluded?

The Life & Significance of G. I. Gurdjieff (Film)

Gurdjieff in Egypt

Gurdjieff's Mission

Gurdjieff's Legacy

Introduction to The Fourth Way: From Selves to Individual Self to The Self (Film)

Spiritual Pilgrimage: Visiting Gurdjieff's Father's Grave (Film)

Dedicated to

the Teacher of Dancing,

and to my teacher,

Henry John Sinclair,

Lord Pentland,

and to all

who study and practice

the teaching

of The Fourth Way

Contents

Acknowledgments xv

Foreword xvii

Part I 1
Search for the Miraculous

Gurdjieff's question. Early life. Elder Brother. Sophia Padji. Dean Borsh. Bogachevsky. Yezidis. Ani. Sārmoung Brotherhood. Pre-sand Egypt. Sphinx. Professor Skridlov. Prince Yuri Lubovedsky. Initiated into Egyptian Mysteries. Christianity before Christ. Empty and abortive interval. The world will be destroyed. Sacred vow. Plan for Institute. Prince Ozay. Paul Dukes. Repetition of lives. Uspenskii's search. Nietzsche. Egypt. Anna Ilinishna Butkovskaia. India. Teaching of a more rational kind. *The Struggle of the Magicians*. Indian raja. "Glimpses of Truth." I have found the Miracle! Concept of different "I"s. St. Petersburg conditions. Group formed. Fears and sacrifices. Uspenskii's nickname. Humiliation. Yes! I believe . . . Who is Gurdjieff? The miracle began. Hearing thoughts. I knew he would not believe me. Pyotr Demianovich. Sacrifice of suffering. Noah's Ark. Creating Moon. Usually more whores here. Love between a husband and wife. You started the Quest. Oil king.

Part II 57
Higher Dimensions

Tsar abdicates. Peace, land and bread. We have only shot a thief. Gurdjieff's family. "I" and "Uspenskii." Beginning new work. Essentuki. Need for schools. Only super-efforts count. St. Petersburg conditions—Uspenskii protests. Gurdjieff's "play." Tall of stature, exceedingly finely formed. Putsch fails. Bolsheviks seize power. Anna Ilinishna Butkovskaia leaves. Institute formed. Circular letter. Forty pupils arrive. International Fellowship for Realization through Work. Study of attention, chief feature, crystallization of the soul. Plan of whole Work. Egyptian pyramids. 'Something' absolute. Dr. Black. Demand for Submission. I no longer understood. Death of Gurdjieff's father. Crossing the Caucasus. Uspenskii stays behind. He is a very fine man and she is intelligent. Institute for the Harmonious Development of Man. Letters to *The New Age*. I wish immortality. Uspenskiis arrive in Constantinople. J. G. Bennett and Mrs. Beaumont. Higher dimensions. Prince Sabaheddin. Boris Mouravieff befriends Uspenskii. Gurdjieff and students arrive. Gurdjieff and Uspenskii reconcile, work on *The Struggle of the Magicians*. The strangest eyes.

Bennett meets Gurdjieff. Stupid dirty jokes! Gurdjieff opens Institute. Tricking Karma. True religion. Russian civil war ends. Two "Gurdjieffs." Uspenskii receives copies of *Tertium Organum*. Lady Rothermere's invitation. Gurdjieff authorizes *Fragments of an Unknown Teaching*. Dalcroze's invitation. Institute closed.

Part III   103
Magicians at War

Gurdjieff to Germany, Uspenskii to England. Orage, the novice; Uspenskii, the master. Rosamund Bland. Cobbling old boots. Man serves Nature's purpose as he is. Maurice Nicoll. Hard outer shell. Gurdjieff in London. Thousands of little "I"s. Everything more vivid. Uspenskii's public humiliation. Institute opens. Gurdjieff's visa problem. Lady Rothermere and Orage lie. *The New Age*. Beatrice Hastings. Katherine Mansfield. Marmoset. Combat of ex-lovers. Le Prieuré des Basses Loges. *I knew* Gurdjieff was the teacher. Ethel Merston. This child I had conceived. Prospectus. Katherine Mansfield—If she dies here. The Ritz, Monk's Corridor, Cow's Alley. Asylum for the insane. Full immortality is quite unique. I am going to find God. Orage and Mrs. Page. Destructive elements. Denis Saurat. *London Daily News*. Institute can help one to be a Christian. I must give up the Work in London. Two kinds of love. The greatest secret. Bennett and inner barrier. Third path. Dr. Young's test. Adam and Eve. Orage to America. Political games. I wanted to save the System.

Part IV   161
Tzvarnoharno

Orage at Sunwise Turn. The most persuasive man I have ever known. Jessie Dwight. With ordinary love goes hate. First movements demonstration. I saw this man in motion, a unit in motion. Hypnotized rabbits under the gaze of a master conjuror. The Material Question. "Mystery in a Sack Suit." You will have to choose between Gurdjieff and me. It's hateful of you. I want to know everything. Jessie at the Prieuré. You *balda*. Fortune teller—heaven and earth fight. Chailly car crash. A bit of live meat in a clean bed. *Tzvarnoharno*. Manual work as chemistry. Uspenskii's principle of seniority. For me he is X. C. Daly King. The gold coin. Orage's groups grow. Olgivanna and Frank Lloyd Wright. *On Love*. Seven kinds of love.

Part V   193
All and Everything

It happened in the 223rd year. Canned food bad for stomach and psyche. Sexual foundation wrong. No shame. Orage to edit *Beelzebub's Tales*. Science of Idiotism.

Impending deaths of mother and wife. Completely unintelligible. Objective work of art, category of scripture. Toomer's chief feature. Madame Ostrowska—she live many lives, is very old soul. Freets, caretaker. Super Idiot falls in love. Mabel Dodge Luhan's $15,000 loan. Troublemaker and Miss Merston. Toomer eats watermelon. Large dolmen. American stomach. The Great Beast arrives. Orage's jealousy. Payson Loomis. Little Father. Orage marries. Nujol. Boiling oil. Bennett in jail. Man's whims. Devil and si. Ambassador from Hell. "Elsie & Allah." Sacred relic. Growing chungaree. Contact Source.

Part VI 247
The Herald

Candidate for the madhouse. Exoteric, mesoteric, esoteric. Saleswoman of Sunwise Turn. Dangerous distortion. Orage ostracized. Signing oath. Orage signs. Help thou my unbelief. Joshua Gurdjieff. Arabian Nights. Wish to fuck. I am Beelzebub. Gurdjieff and Uspenskii at Café Henri IV. New Muddle of the Universe. Thornton Wilder. Portage experiment. Nicoll to teach. "Achmed Abdullah." Russian agent. Lama Dorjieff. Salzmann and René Daumal. Auto accident. Kathryn Hulme meets Jane Heap. Broad-shouldered Buddha. *The New English Weekly*. Prieuré closed. Orage refuses Gurdjieff. Loomis leaves. Fertilizer. Young souls. *The Herald of Coming Good* finished. Prieuré sold. Rom Landau interview. The god Shiva. Madame de Salzmann directs husband's group. Three will-tasks fulfilled. Nightmare journey. Frank Lloyd Wright. Orage dies. This man ...my brother. Ruler of Africa. Russian visa. *Herald* recalled. *God Is My Adventure*. Lesbians. Emanations, attention. Three worlds of man. Lake of Hell. Damned Asiatic bugger. Knachtschmidt and Company.

Part VII 309
The Way of the Sly Man

Cigarette abstinence. Man's search for soul. Representative of The Fourth Way. Rope formed. Onanism. Emanations. Inner vision. Die to resurrect. I wish the result of my suffering. His power. Lohan. Good-wishing-for-all. High sex. Rebecca. Sophia Padji. Saint George. Understanding. Cunning. Twelve-year-old boy now. *Boolmarshano*. Krishnamurti. He was extraordinary! Escaping the treadmill. Historico-Psychological Society. God helps me. Hopeless idiot. Mystical Body of Christ. Moses, ober-idiot, make chosen, not God. God of Languages. Conjury. Kafiri. Tibet. Witch-ness. Initiate people. Alleluia. Pinder at lunch. Nearly perfect English. Electricity. Something wrong your sex. Dmitri dies. Second degree of initiatism. Second body. Toomer's Friends of Being. Victim of self-observation. Dr. Stjoernval dies. Aldous Huxley. Unknown Do. Georgette's cancer. Cinema stars. This I cannot remember. Lord John Pentland.

PART VIII 393
USPENSKII IN AMERICA

Uspenskiis leave for America; Dr. Francis Roles in charge of groups. Bennett's false starts. Claude Bragdon meets Uspenskii. Baby Garbo, the femme fatale. First talks. If he does come, I shall go to California. C. Daly King. We will die without dying. Charles Lindbergh. Carman, my beautiful darling. Marie Seton. Georgette dies. Dorothy Caruso. The Devil. Justice. Conscious evil. Sex and Evolution. *Strange Life of Ivan Osokin*. Charlatan and a thief. I am Shiva, destroyer of worlds. Violent, electric blue light. My task in life is coming to an end. Uspenskii returns to England. Gurdjieff's invitation refused. What do you want? Six meetings. I never was humble myself. Memory. Eternal recurrence. I am not going to America this time. You must make a new beginning. Uspenskii dies. A knight sets out on a great adventure.

PART IX 439
STRIKE A BIG DO

So now I love him. Cecil Lewis. South Africa. Gurdjieff is not mad. Jessie Dwight. A man who knew everything but lacked the simple understanding. He tried for such and was too intelligent to grasp it. Nicoll's refusal. Dorothy Caruso. Bennett arrives. Distinction between sensing and feeling. Auto accident. Lascaux. Lord John Pentland appointed chauffeur. I want twenty such. Gurdjieff in New York. *Fragments of an Unknown Teaching*. Very exact is. Good memory. Truth, was so. Calves for movements demonstrations. *In Search of the Miraculous* published. Mr. Bennett is like Judas; he is responsible that my work is not destroyed. You are my Paul; you will spread my ideas. First proofs of *Beelzebub's Tales*. So now I can die, because my task in life is coming to an end. Either the old world make me 'Tchik,' or I will make the old world 'Tchik.' Kenneth Walker. *Au revoir, tout le monde!* Prepare a nucleus of people. I have seen many men die, he died like a king. Strike a big do.

AFTERWORD 469

THE STRUGGLE OF THE MAGICIANS 478

ESSAYS 496

P. D. Uspenskii
Why I Left Gurdjieff
The Struggle of the Magicians: Where I Diverge from Gurdjieff

William Patrick Patterson
Gurdjieff in Egypt: The Origin of Esoteric Knowledge
Gurdjieff and Christianity
Gurdjieff, Uspenskii, Orage & Bennett
Personas & the Inner Animal
The Science of Idiotism
Images of God or Machines?

Jessie Dwight Orage
Elsie at Le Prieuré
Elsie & Allah

Solita Solano
Meeting with Rosamund Bland
Initiation

Carman Barnes
Music of the Spheres
Miracles Can Happen

Frank Lloyd Wright
Gurdjeef at Taliesin

Count Bobrinskoy
Peacock from Heaven

Notes 567

Chronology 586

References 598

Gurdjieff Students 624

Bibliography 629

Index 636

Acknowledgments

I would like to deeply thank the Sterling Library, Beinecke Rare Book and Manuscript Library, and the Music Library at Yale University, New Haven, Connecticut; Library of Congress, Washington, D.C.; Harrison Memorial Library, Carmel, California; Leeds University Special Collections Library, Leeds, England; Rare Book & Manuscript Library, University of Pennsylvania, Philadelphia, Pennsylvania; University of Rochester Library, Rochester, New York; University of Wisconsin, Madison, Wisconsin; Florence Reynolds Collection, University of Delaware, Newark, Delaware, for archiving the papers of P. D. Uspenskii, Maurice Nicoll, Thomas and Olga de Hartmann, Jean Toomer, Kathryn Hulme, Muriel Draper, Solita Solano, Janet Flanner, A. R. Orage, Carl Zigrosser, Claude Bragdon, Carman Barnes, Margaret Anderson, and Jane Heap. For the last nine years I and my research associate Teresa Adams have visited these libraries many times, and those at Yale on a yearly basis.

I would also like to acknowledge the many writers from whose material I have drawn, especially, of course, P. D. Uspenskii, Thomas and Olga de Hartmann, Anna Ilinishna Butkovskaia, Fritz Peters, Jean Toomer, Gorham Munson, Kathryn Hulme, Margaret Anderson and J. G. Bennett, and, yes, most of all, G. I. Gurdjieff. Each is listed in the Selected Bibliography. My appreciation, as well, to James Webb and James Moore for their biographies and tireless research, which provided a baseline from which to gather material and expand its horizons.

Of all the books I have written *Georgi Ivanovitch Gurdjieff: The Man, The Teaching, His Mission* has been the most demanding. It's required the most unflagging will and focus by all concerned. The indefatigable Henry Korman has provided the graphic design and painstaking inputting of text, and his wife, Mary Ellen, an author in her own right, has helped with research and proofing, as has Teresa Adams, and two late coming eagle-eyes, Mike Miller and Deborah Jacobs.

Most of all I give my wife, Barbara, my deepest and ever lasting gratitude. She's persevered, enduring the many challenges of editing all nine books on the teaching. As Lord Pentland told her, after she worked through the day and then continued through the night on kitchen duty, "You're a tough baby."

As the great poet might have said, "In my ends are my beginnings." So as this octave closes, another begins. Let the Good Lord allow it to be life-giving for everyone, and especially those about to enter the world of he who I regard as the seminal spiritual teacher of the last century and those to come, the self-named "Teacher of Dancing."

Foreword

A messiah, Shiva, solar god, charlatan, uncivilized tempter, sexist. Many are the names given Georgi Ivanovitch Gurdjieff, but for himself he was simply a "Teacher of Dancing."

Lord John Pentland, whom Mr. Gurdjieff appointed to lead the Work in America, told me when we first met, "a man like Gurdjieff comes once in a million years." I brushed off the remark, took it as hyperbole, but now I am not so sure. Madame Uspenskii, who worked very closely with Gurdjieff since his Russian days in 1916, gives the right perspective—"I do not pretend to understand Georgi Ivanovitch. For me he is X.

All that I know is that he is my teacher and it is not right for me to judge him, nor is it necessary for me to understand him. No one knows who is the real Georgi Ivanovitch."

Ultimately, how we see Gurdjieff is not important, as he himself said. What is important is what he saw the world had come to, and what Gurdjieff did about it. What he saw was: "the present period of culture...in the whole process of the perfecting of humanity, as it were, [is] an empty and abortive interval.... [and] unless "the 'wisdom' of the East and the 'energy' of the West were harnessed and used harmoniously the world would be destroyed."

What Gurdjieff did was to give a major shock to the mechanicality, rank materialism and soulessness of ordinary life. At great cost to himself, he gave his life to introducing and establishing in the West the ancient sacred teaching of The Fourth Way.[1] Never before known, this seminal scientific teaching of self-development reveals the laws, perspectives and inner practices that will enable us to develop, as he said, into "genuine, natural men, able to see the real potentialities that were proper to mankind."

The aim here is to present him, his teaching and mission as objectively as possible. So rather than a narrative, the material[2] is presented chronologically, as it happened, the only exception his and P. D. Uspenskii's[3] early life. The intent is to give as little overlay as possible, and so avoid what Gurdjieff called "bon ton literary language." My perspective I give in the Afterword and several of the Essays and occasionally in the footnotes.

—William Patrick Patterson
San Anselmo, California

---

1. There are three classical teachings of self-development: the way of the body, Hatha yoga; the way of the heart, Bhakti yoga; and the way of the mind, Jnana yoga. The Fourth Way combines them all to create a harmonious development of all three ways. Of the teaching itself, Gurdjieff says, "The teaching whose theory is here being set out is completely self-supporting and independent of other lines and it has been completely unknown up to the present time." *In Search of the Miraculous, 286.*

2. The material is supported by over nine hundred references.

3. Uspenskii is the Russian spelling of the last name. When he writes to Orage in 1919, he signs his name as "P. Uspenski." And this is the name, now with an additional 'i,' as in "Uspenskii," the Russian Theosophical Society uses when writing about him in its journal *Vestnik*.

Part I

Search for the Miraculous

Suddenly, lying on the artillery range, cannons booming and shells landing all about, Georgi Ivanovitch Gurdjieff felt "the whole sensation" of himself. "Instinctive fear in face of this inevitability," he said, "so took possession of my entire being that surrounding realities seemed to disappear, leaving only an unconquerable living terror." Working to assimilate the intensity of this primordial vibration of self, his nervous system demanding rest, he fell asleep. He was sixteen years old. It was his first breakthrough to the immersion into higher reality. Afterward, seeing people's suffering and misery, their self-love and vanity, and need for periodic reciprocal destruction, the question arose—"*What is the sense and significance of life on earth, and human life in particular?*"

Born in or near Alexandropol in 1872[1] to a Greek father, Ioannis Giorgiades,[2] and an Armenian mother, Evdokia, Georgi Ivanovitch Gurdjieff was the first born of five children, a brother, Dmitri, and three younger sisters. When Gurdjieff was a young boy his father lost his riches and several herds of cattle due to a cattle plague that spread all over Transcaucasia. The lumberyard his father opened failed and he was left with only a carpentry shop. Because of the rapid reconstruction of the nearby fortress town of Kars by Russians, and the persuasion of his brother who had a business there, the father moved his family to Kars and reopened the carpentry shop.

Ioannis Giorgiades, thirty-eight years old at Gurdjieff's birth, was an amateur *ashokh*, a storyteller and poet deeply versed in the ancient oral tradition of reciting songs, stories and legends. As Gurdjieff would later say, these legends, that of the Babylonian hero Gilgamesh in particular, formed in him "a 'spiritualizing factor' enabling me to comprehend the incomprehensible." His father also created experiences for him that would make him indifferent to fear, repulsion, and timidity, such as getting him up in the early morning to go to the fountain and splash himself with cold spring water and then having him run around naked to dry off. He came to relate to his father as an "elder brother." His grandmother, Sophia Padji, was also a strong influence. She lived with the family and was both loved and feared by all. When she lay dying, Gurdjieff says, she placed a left hand on his head and told him: "Eldest of my grandsons! Listen and always remember my strict injunction to you: In life never do as others do. Either do nothing—just go to school—or do something nobody else does."

Dean Borsh of Kars Military Cathedral, who Gurdjieff speaks of as "my second father" and "the founder and creator of my present individuality," was another early and strong influence. The seventy-year-old dean, Gurdjieff says, "was tall, thin, with a fine-looking face, of delicate health but strong and firm in spirit. He was a man distinguished by the depth and breadth of his knowledge, and his life and views were quite different from those of the people around him, who in consequence considered him peculiar." They got along well, as Gurdjieff was "very mischievous and Dean Borsh liked such rascals." The dean must have seen that "learning came very easily to me," for he advised Gurdjieff's father that his young son be home-schooled, as each of the municipal school's eight grades had to be attended for the complete year with no skipping of grades. The dean would teach some subjects and provide teachers, two candidates for the priesthood and a physician, for other subjects. Dean Borsh gave Gurdjieff religious

---
1. For discussion of the date, see Notes, "Gurdjieff's Birth."
2. In Armenian the Greek surname was "Gurdjian" and in Russian "Gurdjieff."

training and a modern scientific education, especially in astronomy and chemistry, while the other tutors taught him geography, history, scripture, Russian, anatomy, physiology and mathematics, all with the intent of preparing the young boy to be a priest and a physician.

In 1886, Bogachevsky, another influential figure, arrived in Kars after graduating from the Russian Theological Seminary. While waiting to be ordained to the priesthood, he served as a deacon at the military cathedral. For the two years Gurdjieff and he were together, Bogachevsky, soon to be known as Father Evlissi, confessed Gurdjieff and introduced him to objective morality, the basis of the formation of genuine conscience, and also awakened him to an "ever-continuing interest in abstract questions." Spiritualism, in particular, became of great interest as his first and favorite sister died that year. Table-turning, he says, "agitated me so profoundly that I decided to ask Father Borsh." "All that is nonsense," Dean Borsh told him. "Come, you little garlic-head — think! If spirits can really tap with the leg of a table, it means they have some physical force. And if they have, why should they resort to such idiotic and moreover complicated means of communicating with people as tapping with the leg of a table? Surely they could transmit whatever they wished to say either by touch or some other means!"

"In spite of my respect for the old dean," says Gurdjieff, "I doubted his views on certain problems concerning higher matters." Subsequently, "there was not a single book on neuropathology and psychology in the library of the Kars military hospital that I had not read, and read very attentively, carefully going over almost every line in my intense desire to find, through these branches of science, an explanation of the phenomenon of table-turning."

1888 was an axial year for Gurdjieff. He was sixteen years old when he saw a Yezidi boy inside a circle drawn around him in the dirt. The Yezidi belief was that Melik Tawus, their name for Satan, or one of his allies, as the name can never be uttered, was inside the circle to help the boy learn something. Only if a part of the circle was rubbed out could the boy be released, and only the Yezidi priest who had drawn the circle was to do that. Not knowing or sharing this belief, Gurdjieff rubbed out a part of the circle and freed the boy. "This so dumbfounded me," Gurdjieff relates, "that I stood to the spot for a long time as if bewitched, until my usual ability to think returned." The incident so astonished him that he says it "now compelled me to think seriously about them." Bogachevsky told him, "They are devil-worshippers,[3] and under ordinary circumstances the devil does not touch them, as they are his own. But as the devil himself is only a subordinate and is obliged by his office to impose his authority on everyone, he therefore, as you might say, for the sake of appearances, has limited Yezidis' independence in this way so that other people should not suspect that they are his servants." But did Gurdjieff incur any debt for doing this?

---

3. A belief commonly held but not true. See Notes, "Yezidis."

Known as a "master of all trades," these skills gave Gurdjieff the monies to explore his interests and make pilgrimages to most of the holy places of the many faiths in Transcaucasia. Visiting the ancient monastery of Sanaïne, he spent three months as an acolyte of the famous Father Yevlampios. He also began to drink a little. But the experience that was most decisive in his young life was his near-death experience. He was challenged by a rival to a duel in which both put themselves out on an artillery range when the firing began, all for the love of the thirteen-year-old daughter of the local vodka maker. Cannon shells bursting all about, Gurdjieff experienced "the whole sensation of myself," death seeming so inevitable that an "instinctive fear in face of this inevitability so took possession of my entire being that surrounding realities seemed to disappear, leaving only an unconquerable living terror." This primordial experiencing so grounded all the abstract and supernatural questions that concerned him that Gurdjieff devoted himself to a continual search for answers. Sometime thereafter, dates are seldom given, Gurdjieff first met his friend Sarkis Pogossian when he was finishing his studies at the Theological Seminary of Echmiadzin. Pogossian was now a priest but "suffering inwardly" and feeling "deeply distressed" once he saw "the hidden side of the life of the clergy there," but like Gurdjieff, he had come to "the definite conclusion that there really was 'a certain something' which people formerly knew, but that now this knowledge was quite forgotten."

The religion and science of their time gave no adequate answer. In studying ancient literature, they came across a whole collection of Armenian books and decided to go to the isolated ruins of the ancient Armenian capital of Ani, known as "The City of a Thousand and One Churches," a short distance from Alexandropol and Kars. There they built a hut and immersed themselves in the books. They also made excavations of the underground passages of the ruins. One day they discovered in a monk's cell a pile of parchments written in a very ancient Armenian unknown to them. They immediately returned to Alexandropol where they spent days and nights trying to decipher the parchments. Finally, it became clear that these were letters written by one monk to another monk. One letter mentioned the Sārmoung Brotherhood, the name of which, says Gurdjieff, "was a famous esoteric school ... according to tradition, was founded in Babylon as far back as 2,500 BC, and which was known to have existed somewhere in Mesopotamia up to the sixth or seventh centuries AD.... This school was said to have possessed great knowledge, containing the key to many secret mysteries."

They wanted to search for its existence, but how? Pogossian learned that the Armenian Committee was looking for several volunteers from party members to send on a special mission. The two were chosen, and joining the party they immediately set off, going into remote and dangerous areas. After some years of adventure they were given a letter to be delivered to a certain Armenian priest and, after great difficulty, found him. The priest showed them a map of "pre-sand Egypt," circa 7,500 BC. Gurdjieff wanted to buy it, but the priest declined saying a Russian prince had come and also wanted to buy it. Whatever Gurdjieff saw on the map he says appeased that "desire for knowledge which during the past two or three years had given me no rest, gnawing me within like a worm." The map showed that something existing in pre-sand Egypt still existed. Gurdjieff doesn't say what it was, but he clandestinely made a copy, and immediately broke off his search for the Sārmoung and went to Egypt's Giza Plateau alone, Pogossian deciding not to accompany him. At the Giza Plateau Gurdjieff worked as a guide and spent "all my free time walking among these places like one possessed, hoping to find, with the help of my map of pre-sand Egypt, an explanation of the Sphinx and of certain other monuments of antiquity." One day he was taken as a guide by Professor Skridlov, a Russian archaeologist. Walking from the Sphinx to the Pyramid of Cheops the professor was hailed by an old friend, the Russian Prince Yuri Lubovedsky. Several days later Gurdjieff is sitting at the foot of one of pyramids studying the map of pre-sand Egypt when the Prince approaches. It turns out he is the Russian prince who wanted to buy the map. Thereafter, "a real bond was established between us," says Gurdjieff. Later, with Professor Skridlov, the three decide to form the Seekers of Truth.[4]

What Gurdjieff is telling us in his distinctive way, one that calls on us to use our reason and intuition, is that what he saw on the map of pre-sand Egypt was the Sphinx, which would mean that it was not built in 2,700 BC as commonly thought, but long before.[5] While in Egypt he tells us he was "initiated four times into the Egyptian Mysteries." Initially, the Egyptian religion before it descended into animal worship and cults was a sacred science of spiritual self-development and conscience. It was, Gurdjieff said:

> Christian many thousands of years before the birth of Christ, that is to say, that it was composed of the same principles and ideas that constitute true Christianity.... The Christian church, the Christian form of worship, was not invented by the fathers of the church. It was all taken in a ready-made form from Egypt, only not from the Egypt we know but from one which we do not know. This Egypt was in the same place as the other but it existed much earlier.... The Christian church is—a school concerning which people have forgotten that it is a school.

Thus *prehistoric* Egypt is the source and foundation of the teaching Gurdjieff will later bring to the West, which he will call The Fourth Way, the Way of Turiya.

4. The prospectus for the Institute speaks of "Seekers After Truth," its initial capitalization in English would be SAT, in Hindu terminology, "Being." Also, the formulation is "Seekers of The Truth."
5. Says Uspenskii, "The pyramids are much more ancient than people think. What is regarded as the time of their building was actually their second restoration. Investigations show that the original purpose was not a burial place for pharaohs but some kind of astronomical instruments (not observatories)."

Though not introduced to the West until 1912, this seminal teaching thus actually *predates* all the religions, spiritual teachings and philosophies.[6]

After a stay at the Giza Plateau, Gurdjieff journeyed southward following the Nile to the Temple of Edfu and into Abyssinia where he further discovered the ideas and principles of the Society of Akhaldans, an even more ancient teaching, which existed in Atlantis before its sinking and whose survivors migrated to Abyssinia. As over time elements of the teaching had dispersed northward to Babylon, the Hindu Kush, Tibet, and the Gobi desert, Gurdjieff then made a second journey. These elements he integrated into the original Egyptian-Christian teaching and reassembled and reformulated this sacred esoteric teaching of self-development for our time. In introducing the teaching, he said:

> *The teaching whose theory is here being set out is completely self-supporting and independent of other lines and it has been completely unknown up to the present time.*[7]

Given that the present period of culture is an "empty and abortive interval" in which "the people of our civilization cannot transmit by inheritance anything of value to their descendants," and "the whole of our progress comes to be progress in the technique of murder and progress in warfare," Gurdjieff recognized that "unless the 'wisdom' of the East and the 'energy' of the West are harnessed and used harmoniously the world would be destroyed."

In order to introduce and establish the teaching of The Fourth Way in the West, Gurdjieff took a sacred vow on 14 September 1911,[8] to live "in my conscience to lead in some ways an artificial life, modeled upon a program which had been previously planned in accordance with certain definite principles," for twenty-one years.[9]

His plan was to establish an Institute to train students to become "helper-instructors" who could help in disseminating the teaching. The foundation of the Institute would be to create conditions in which "a man would be continually reminded of the sense and aim of his existence by an unavoidable friction between his conscience and the automatic manifestations of his nature" that would enable him to awaken and create a soul.

---

6. The founding of the major religions: Hinduism is 1,500 BC; Judaism, 1,100 BC; pre-Socratic philosophy, 600 BC; Buddhism, 500 BC; Islam, 620 AD; and Sufism, a mystical branch of Islam, 900 AD.

7. Note that he declares the teaching to be *completely self-supporting*, that is, contained within the self/Self. And also that it is *independent*, not eclectic. And it is *completely unknown*, truly esoteric, *up to the present time*.

8. Both Moore and Bennett misread *The Herald of Coming Good*, 11, and believe Gurdjieff takes the vow on 13 September 1911. See *Gurdjieff: The Anatomy of a Myth*, 324, and *Making a New World*, 112. The 13th is the date the vow ends.

9. Three octaves.

As he apparently spoke no Western languages[10] and didn't know its cultures, Gurdjieff felt it best to first introduce the teaching in Russia, using it as the gateway to bring the teaching to the West. And so at forty years of age, Georgi Ivanovitch Gurdjieff arrived in Russia in 1912[11] with about one million rubles (about $500,000 in U.S. dollars at that time) and two invaluable collections, one of Chinese cloisonné and the other of old and rare carpets. He did so because he felt it "necessary to be independent, at least in the material sense; the more so, since experience had already shown me that wealthy people never become seriously enough interested in these questions to support a work of this kind, and that others, even with great interest and desire, cannot do much in this respect."

In the winter of 1913 in St. Petersburg, Gurdjieff—disguised as 'Prince Ozay'[12]—meets Paul Dukes,[13] a twenty-four-year-old Englishman who worked at the St. Petersburg Conservatoire as a concert pianist and deputy conductor. Dukes is a friend of Lev Lvovitch, a professional hypnotist and healer, who apparently learned his craft while on military service in Central Asia. There he had fallen ill with an obscure malady. He spoke of his "having died" and "come

10. There is evidence that he did speak English, but whether he knew it at this time is uncertain.

11. James Moore, in his *Gurdjieff: The Anatomy of a Myth*, states that soon after Gurdjieff came to Moscow and visited St. Petersburg he met and married Julia Ostrowska, a twenty-two-year-old Polish countess. However, he cites no reference. The first time she appears in the written record is in Thomas and Olga de Hartmann's *Our Life with Mr. Gurdjieff*.

12. Is 'Prince Ozay' Gurdjieff in disguise? From Paul Dukes' description of Prince Ozay's presence, depth of occult knowledge, and behavior in his *The Unending Quest*, it certainly seems so. Moore directly asked Madame de Salzmann if this was true and she said, "Yes." James Webb, Gurdjieff's first biographer, *The Harmonious Circle*, believed Gurdjieff and the Prince are the same. Why would Gurdjieff assume the identity of Prince Ozay? Webb believes that the Prince Lubovedsky that Gurdjieff speaks about in *Meetings with Remarkable Men* was actually Prince Esper Esperovitch Ukhtomsky, a close friend of Tsarevitch Nicholas Alexandrovich. Together on a worldwide tour, Ukhtomsky and Nicholas stopped in Egypt in 1890 and visited the Giza Plateau. Gurdjieff wasn't there until 1893, but in recounting his meeting with Prince Lubovedsky he says the Prince had made "a second trip to the Egyptian pyramids." (See *Our Life with Mr. Gurdjieff*, 71, and *The Gurdjieff Journal*, Vol. 16, No. 1.) Later, when Gurdjieff comes to Russia, he speaks in *Beelzebub's Tales* of his meeting the Tsar. He could only have done so by knowing someone of a rank high enough to procure an invitation. Ukhtomsky certainly could have done that for a "Prince Ozay," and not for a commoner. It all fits together seamlessly but Dukes, however, does say two things that arouse questions. He says that Ozay claims to have been in "many churches in England and America," and that Ozay speaks better English than Russian. Gurdjieff is often given to embellishment to make a point or create an impression, and Dukes, like Gurdjieff himself, a secret agent, may be trying to hide Gurdjieff's identity. Solita Solano, author, linguist and a close student of Gurdjieff's, says that Gurdjieff knew more English words than she did, and gave an elaborate exercise in "nearly perfect English." That Ozay plays chess and Gurdjieff once said that playing chess was "pouring the empty into the void" actually supports Gurdjieff being the Prince, as this is a favorite saying of those who have seriously played "the Royal Game" and given it up.

13. Dukes was known as the "Man of a Hundred Faces." He assumed a number of identities and disguises and infiltrated numerous Bolshevik organizations, including the Communist Party, the Comintern and the Cheka, the Soviet security organization. He also learned of the inner workings of the Politburo, and passed the information to British intelligence. When he returned to Britain, Dukes was a distinguished hero who in 1920 was knighted by King George V, who called him the "greatest of all soldiers." He is the only person knighted based entirely on his exploits in espionage.

back" through the efforts of a nomadic shaman. Perhaps it was then that he met Gurdjieff. Whatever the case, Lvovitch speaks to Dukes of Prince Ozay as being a man of whom "there are but few in the world."

Dukes is led to a house at the bottom of a small street near Nikolaevsky Railway Station. Lvovitch leads him through a very plain apartment to a flat beyond that is larger and more sumptuous. It is decorated in an Oriental manner with the windows heavily curtained, carpets adorning walls, and wrought-iron lamps with colored glass hanging from the ceiling. The Prince is playing chess with another man. He is dressed in a patterned silk dressing gown and a turban. A man of medium height and sturdy build, the Prince at once notices the hole in Dukes' sock and jokes, "You believe in ventilation! Good thing—nothing like fresh air!" He holds out two closed fists, asking Dukes to choose which hand holds the white pawn. Dukes' guess is correct, but then he notices that both the pawns in the Prince's hands are white. The Prince quickly beats Dukes.

Over the course of this and many other nights, Prince Ozay tells Dukes many interesting occult facts. The Prince says, for example, that the Lord's Prayer was originally designed as a devotional breathing exercise, the entire prayer to be chanted on a single even breath. "You are a musical instrument, as a piano is," says the Prince, "and you need to be kept in tune. That's where fasting and other exercises come in; you can't possibly reflect finer vibrations when your body—or soul if you prefer—is loaded with a lot of food gurgling in the stomach, or while the blood makes a din chasing about the veins and arteries." He tells Dukes, too, that "God is achieved not through activity but through cessation of activity. Cessation to the utmost limit of diet, breath, and sex. These are the three pillars on which prayer is built. Each has to be trained and disciplined by restraint—there is no other way because they are all runaway horses. Only when the ground is cleared can true building commence. Only from that point can you begin to act consciously."

One evening the Prince asks Dukes: "Are you afraid of risks? Understand this clearly. No man can acquire this kind of knowledge without risking death. God, misapplied, is the Devil. There is only one force in creation. Good and evil lie merely in its application."

In the rising turmoil of the times, Dukes loses contact with both Lvovitch and the Prince, and at some point, perhaps late 1912 or 1913, Gurdjieff left St. Petersburg for Moscow where he established a group. Among his students were Gurdjieff's cousin, the sculptor Sergei Dmitrievich Mercourov, and the composer Vladimir Pohl, the well-known Jewish lawyer Alexei Yakovlevich Rachmilievitch,[14] Alina Fedorovna and Alexander Nikorovich Petrov. The group met at Rachmilievitch's apartment. Though the students were of high quality apparently Gurdjieff found none to have the necessary inner and outer qualities that would allow them to assist in helping to step down the teaching.

14. A hilarious sketch of Rachmilievitch at the Prieuré is given in Fritz Peters' *Boyhood with Gurdjieff*.

Reading a newspaper one day, Gurdjieff's eye came upon a series of travel articles by P. D. Uspenskii detailing his journey to India in search of a unique spiritual teaching, one unknown in the West. The maturity of observations and the keen expression were of such a quality that Gurdjieff would insist on meeting Uspenskii upon his return.[15]

Pyotr Demianovich Uspenskii's life, like Gurdjieff's, had also been one of a search for the truth. Born 5 March 1878, in Moscow, some six years after Gurdjieff, Uspenskii's parents were part of the intelligentsia, but considered themselves of no particular class. His mother was a painter with an interest in Russian and French literature, while his father, Demian, a Survey Service officer, was a mathematician, fond of music and painting, with a lifelong interest in the question of time and its Fourth Dimension.

Early on, before he was two years old, Uspenskii says he had "several quite clear mental pictures of events." At three, he began to read, and says he remembered himself "quite clearly." Literature, poetry and painting quickly became interests. By six, he was reading on an adult level and buried himself in books. Lermontov's *A Hero of Our Time*[16] and Turgenev's *A Sportsman's Notebook* made an enormous impression.

Early on, as well, a certain psychic ability also developed. He and his younger sister would sit peering out a window onto the street and play a game of what they called "remembering what would happen next." She would say, "Now will come postman," and he, "Now policeman and then milkman." This Uspenskii would later point to as the beginning of his belief in the repetition of lives.

When he was less than four years old his beloved father died. It would be the first of two severe shocks. The second occurred after he, his mother, and younger sister went to live with her parents. As he had with his father, he bonded strongly with the grandfather, a portrait painter who now painted for churches. That very same year the grandfather died. Speaking of his childhood many years later, Uspenskii said—"I did not play with toys as a child. I was less under imagination and I saw what life was like at a very early stage." In a word, life is about death. As he put it, "It is only when you realize life is taking you nowhere that it begins to have meaning."

Later, taking him to enroll at his first school, his mother lost her way. Although he had never been in the building before, Uspenskii led her to a passageway. At the end of the passageway he told her they would come to two steps and a nearby window.

---

15. While Uspenskii was in India he speaks of receiving a letter from a woman friend suggesting that he would find the teacher he was looking for in Russia. He later learned that the woman also had a friend who was in one of Gurdjieff's groups.

16. Lermontov's book is especially noteworthy because the ideas it expresses—the plasticity of time and questions of predestination, fate, and recurrence—are those which will occupy him throughout his life. That at a mere six years of age such ideas could not only be of interest but comprehended gives an indication of the rare quality of intellect that was Uspenskii's.

And from the window, he said, they would be able to see the headmaster's garden with lilies growing and, close by, the headmaster's study. All he described proved to be true. Throughout his life he would have many such remembrances. The idea of having lived a past life was not an idea but an actuality that often made its appearance.

About eight he began to dream of travels and the sea, at twelve "to feel a great interest in natural science," and at thirteen he became interested in dreams and psychology. School he found dull. "I was lazy," he says. "I hated Greek and school routine in general." Within several years he completely lost interest. "There was a dead wall everywhere. Professors were killing science in the same way as priests were killing religion." He decided never to pass any exams or take any degrees.

In his denial of the worth of ordinary life, moments appeared when he sensed the unity of all things and was overcome with its sensation. "All round me walls are crumbling," he said, "and horizons infinitely remote and incredibly beautiful stand revealed. It is as though threads, previously unknown and unsuspected, begin to reach out and bind things together. For the first time in my life my world emerges from chaos. Everything becomes connected, forming an orderly and harmonious whole." He then asked, "Why am I made to learn a thousand useless things and am not told about *'this'?*" [Emphasis added.]

At sixteen, he experienced another death, this time his mother's. He became "very anarchistically inclined"[17] and left school. Having lost his father, grandfather and now his mother, he found himself alone in life, save for his younger sister. In the depths of this aloneness Nietzsche entered his life. His *Thus Spake Zarathustra* spoke directly to him in a way no other book had. Its two seminal ideas—the development of the Overman (Superman), the superior human being, and eternal recurrence—put voice to what he had long felt but could not adequately express. Everything and everyone recurs again and again, and only the Overman could consciously live it. The development of the Overman and the understanding of eternal recurrence would be Uspenskii's life's pursuit. The idea of eternal recurrence Uspenskii would develop later in his novel, and also in his mathematical work demonstrating time not being linear, as commonly experienced, but a "period of dimensions."

But the immediate question centered on how he was to earn a living. "I mistrusted and disliked all kinds of socialism," he said, "even more than industrialism or militarism and did not believe in any kind of secret revolutionary parties with

---

17. Moore states as fact on his Internet site that Uspenskii tried to commit suicide about this time, but gives no evidence. That recognized, then Moore must base his intuition, for it can only be that, on what is written in *Strange Life of Ivan Osokin*, which in the early stages is rife with melancholy and depression. However, Uspenskii is quite unequivocal about what it means to take one's life. He says: "Suicide must build a strong momentum. In my youth I was surrounded by clouds of suicide. Weakened foundations. There are no accidental suicides. It is prepared and rehearsed for a long time. Momentum not only in the moral but also in the physical sense. Every created momentum tends to be repeated more easily. This idea can greatly change men's lives. To be aware of walking in a circle."

which all Russian 'intelligentsia' sympathized. But when I became interested in journalism I could work only on 'left' papers because 'right' papers did not smell well." By 1905, Uspenskii, now twenty-eight years old, is publishing articles in left wing papers, and between articles writing an autobiographical novel. In manuscript he titled it *Wheel of Fortune*, but when finished *Kinemadrama*, and when published *Strange Life of Ivan Osokin*.[18] In one of the novel's many evocative images, the housemaster orders Osokin to stand under a clock as punishment for an infraction. In a sense, like a card from a tarot deck, this image conveys Uspenskii's essential relationship with time and life. One had only so much time to achieve what they wished. "What is the good of beginning any kind of work," he would say, "when one doesn't know whether one will have time to finish it or not?"

The time Uspenskii found himself in was rife with revolutionary ferment. In 1879, one year after his birth, *Narodnaia Volia*, the People's Will, was formed. A secret organization, it espoused terrorism as the way to bring down the three-hundred-year-old tsarist regime of the Romanovs. Structured hierarchically and operating in a quasi-military manner, its members pledged to totally dedicate themselves to the revolutionary cause, sacrificing property and life. *Narodnaia Volia*'s mission was to assassinate government officials. Four days before Uspenskii's third birthday, on 1 March 1881, a *Narodnaia Volia* bomb killed Tsar Alexander II. Six years later, Alexander Ulianov was arrested carrying a bomb in an attempt to assassinate Tsar Alexander III. Ulianov and his co-conspirators believed in an eclectic political brew of *Narodnaia Volia*, Marxism and German Social Democracy. All were executed.

The execution imprinted Ulianov's younger brother, Vladimir Ilyich, later known as Lenin, with a deep and lasting hatred. That same year, Lenin enrolled at the university to study law, and within a short time joined *Narodnaia Volia*. Within months he was arrested and expelled. Exiled to Siberia and then deported, Lenin was living in Switzerland when on Sunday, 9 January 1905, thousands of workers led by a priest marched peacefully to St. Petersburg's Winter Palace to present Tsar Nicholas II with a petition of economic grievances. Unable to halt the surging workers, the soldiers fired point blank into the crowd, killing a hundred people and wounding several hundred more.

While the immediate threat of what became known as "Bloody Sunday" was quelled, strikes among workers and university students broke out throughout the country. Succumbing to pressure, the Tsar allowed the legalization of political parties and trade unions and set up a nationally elected Duma, or parliament. But the Tsar's image of divine rule had been irreparably damaged, and thus began the slow but inexorable erosion of autocratic rule.

18. He does not use the word "The" in the title for, the presumption is, he sees everyone's life as being strange since it may be recurring and Ivan Osokin's life is no different from theirs, but they are asleep to it.

Among those arrested on Bloody Sunday was Uspenskii's beloved sister. She died in 1908, three years after she entered Moscow's Butyrskaya prison.[19] Now, Uspenskii, thirty years old, found himself totally alone in the world. The meaning of life, the mystery of death—always nagging questions—became even more urgent.

But a year before his sister's death controls on theosophical literature, previously banned, were loosened. Uspenskii read its literature voraciously. The following year the Russian Theosophical Society registered with authorities. Uspenskii joined and rarely missed a meeting. But soon he saw its limitations:

> I found theosophical literature, Blavatsky, Olcott, Besant, Sinnett, etc., produced a very strong impression on me although I at once saw its weak side. The weakest side of which was that it had no continuation. But it opened doors for me into a new and bigger world. I discovered the idea of Esotericism, found a possible angle for the study of religion and mysticism and received a new impulse for the study of "higher dimensions."
>
> [There is] ... an unbroken line of thought and knowledge which passes from century to century, from age to age, from country to country, from one race to another; a line deeply hidden beneath layers of religions and philosophies which are, in fact, only distortions and perversions of the ideas belonging to this line.

He came to believe that this tradition of hidden knowledge, guarded and preserved by an inner circle of humanity, was responsible for all the major achievements of mankind. He integrated these esoteric ideas with Nietzsche's idea of the Overman and so intuited that mankind was only at a transitional stage of the evolution of consciousness which would ultimately lead to the appearance of the Overman.

In 1908 Uspenskii, along with his good friend Sherbakov, planned a journey to the East in search of wisdom schools of the distant past.[20] But shortly before they were to leave, Sherbakov died. Father, grandfather, mother, sister and now his best friend—all dead. Uspenskii must have felt death stalking his heels. Others might have postponed the journey, but Uspenskii set off alone.

Traveling to Constantinople, Smyrna, Greece, and Egypt, Uspenskii had many evocative experiences, some transcendent, yet none substantial, and the school he was in search of was not found. He returned to Moscow and in early 1909 left to live in St. Petersburg. He began experiments in altering consciousness through hashish and nitrous oxide. But drugs, he soon concluded, were a dead end.

During this time he began writing *Tertium Organum*, which he self-published in 1912. The book's challenge to the limitations on human consciousness, implicit

---

19. Rebuilt in 1879, the prison was known for its overcrowding, epidemics and administrative violence.
20. The very same idea that Gurdjieff had many years before.

in Aristotle's *Organon* and Francis Bacon's *Novum Organum,* was audacious, but its impressive clarity and sweep of thought attracted an erudite readership, especially among theosophical circles. Many doors now opened for him; he quickly became the darling of Russia's intelligentsia and its theosophical movement. The idealist philosopher Nikolai Berdiaev calls Uspenskii "the most independent and talented theosophical writer in Russia." Anna Alekseevna Kamenskaia, the energetic forty-five-year-old General Secretary, co-founder and head of Theosophy's powerful St. Petersburg branch, thinks of him so highly that during a lecture at the Theosophical Society, she called from the stage into the audience—"Pyotr Demianovich Uspenskii, please be so kind as to give us your opinion on this matter."

Hearing the name "Uspenskii" must have sounded like a call of fate to twenty-seven-year-old Anna Ilinishna Butkovskaia who was in the audience that night. The beautiful and talented aristocratic daughter of the counsel in the Ministry of Justice, an accomplished pianist and recently divorced, she had begun reading theosophical literature at seventeen. Recently, Anna Ilinishna had read *Tertium Organum*, and felt an immediate rapport with the author—"Here was a book which seemed to set out to answer the questions I kept asking"—but how was she going to meet him?

She watches as a squarely built man of medium height with almost albino skin and an imposing face, a pince-nez clipped on a strong nose, rises slowly from his chair. His forehead, high and broad, gives an impression of great intellect, the face reflecting both stubbornness and confidence. In the eyes peering through the thick lenses, she sees a keen sensitivity, a most uncommon visionary quality.

The lecture over, Anna Ilinishna introduces herself at once. What the thirty-four-year-old Uspenskii sees no doubt pleases him, for once the social niceties are over, he immediately connects with her, confiding that while, yes, he had attended this lecture and others, he is now withdrawing from the Theosophical Society.

Nodding toward the people in the hall, he tells her scornfully—"These ordinary members are sheep." He then looks toward the lectern and declares—"But I feel there are even bigger sheep in the 'inner circle.'"

Proud and self-confident, Anna Ilinishna meets his thought and replies—"You sound as though you are sorry there are no wolves."

"Exactly!" cries Uspenskii. "At least wolves display strength. Sheep are simply sheep, and it is hopeless for them to pretend to aspire to be the image of God, and to develop the hidden, higher faculties."[21]

Uspenskii asks Anna Ilinishna to join him for coffee the following morning at Phillipoff's, a café in Petersburg's bohemian section on the corner of Trotsky Street and Nevsky Prospekt, the city's main boulevard. As it happens, Phillipoff's

---

21. Implicit in Uspenskii's words was the declaration that he, of course, was not a sheep. But the words, too, conveyed the intellectual seduction that Anna Ilinishna was speaking with someone with the ability to develop such faculties.

is close to where they both live. Uspenskii's apartment is at Liteiny Street just off the corner of the Nevsky Prospekt, while Anna Ilinishna lives with her father on the corner of the Nevsky and Nikolaevski Street.

The next morning entering Phillipoff's, she finds Uspenskii awaiting her, three empty coffee cups in front of him. They discuss the ideas in *Tertium Organum,* especially the development of super consciousness and Uspenskii's insight that "a prolonged self-consciousness during sensation, feeling or thinking is a very rare phenomenon in man. As a rule what is called self-consciousness is simply thought, and it takes place *post factum*. True self-consciousness exists in man only as a potentiality, and if it manifests itself at all, does so only by moments."

A school, he says, is needed which emphasized this—but where is it? Nothing in the West corresponds. He tells her of his search and disappointments and his realization that what is needed is a school "of a more rational kind."

The following day at Phillipoff's the two meet again. After several coffees Uspenskii, obviously smitten by Anna Ilinishna's beauty and independence of mind, speaks directly to their relationship:

"You are attracted by the purpose of our quest—by the road that we want to travel. And a little by me, too, perhaps?... I don't think that among your other friends you have anyone as *interesting* as I am."

His words making no obvious impression and Anna Ilinishna saying nothing, he declares outright: "I came across your orbit like a comet."

Only silence.

He tries another tack: "Now, suppose you tell me of any curious experiences you have had."

"Have you ever heard of Nicholas Evreinoff, the theatrical producer and writer?" Anna Ilinishna asks.

He had seen Evreinoff's photo in the papers. "Romantic face," Uspenskii says, "like a Florentine poet of the sixteenth century."

"I had an affair with Evreinoff," she tells him.

Uspenskii, unable to control himself, shouts—"How can you do such things!"

Seeing her face, he quickly catches himself and adds: "But I am glad—it shows you are not 'a lady.'"

Anna Ilinishna, indignant, protests.

Backtracking quickly, Uspenskii says, "I don't mean in that sense." He says he means that she is a human being before she is a lady, "because you aren't afraid of things that Society would disapprove of, or what people may think of you."[22]

---

22. Like many men, Uspenskii seems a bit awkward with women. But he was quite taken with them, as evidenced in his autobiographical novel *Strange Life of Ivan Osokin* (and later near the end of his life with Carman Barnes). As many of the events in the novel parallel Uspenskii's, it is fair to suppose that Osokin's views reflected his own. For example, in the novel Osokin believed that women were for the most part more interesting than men and belonged to a higher caste. It held that an educated woman like Anna, living in more or less civilized society, would have occupied a privileged position, because "for thousands of years," said Osokin, "women have taken

Despite his arrogance, Anna Ilinishna is attracted by his "almost boyish enthusiasm and gentle, poetic radiance," and so the two continued to meet at Phillipoff's every day at noon and, later on, in the evening as well. One day, strolling along Nevsky Prospekt, the two come to the Liteiny and turn and so pass by Uspenskii's corner apartment. He invites Anna Ilinishna inside. She hesitates.

"I thought it might give you pleasure to see some of my books," he says encouragingly. "I went to your house to hear you play, now you should come to mine to look at books!"

Anna Ilinishna, who had a keen feeling for the essence of music and enjoyed sharing it, had invited Uspenskii to her home to hear her play. She had studied piano under the St. Petersburg Conservatoire's two best professors, one of them the celebrated female pianist Barinova.

Uspenskii's invitation, she knew of course, wasn't the same. And socially it was risky. A young unmarried woman, now divorced, did not frequent men's apartments. Still, she agrees.

Uspenskii's "apartment," she finds, is one very small room. The furniture consisted of a bed, chair and table, and a large bookshelf crammed with books in Russian, French and English. On the table is the final draft of *Kinemadrama*. There was also the unfinished manuscript of another of his books, *The Devil*.[23]

Afterward, their relationship deepening, Uspenskii and Anna Ilinishna sit hour after hour in coffeehouses, or at bohemian clubs like the Stray Dog, a cellar cabaret on Mikhail Louskaia Square. Dark and low-ceilinged, with walls of brick, the club perpetually smells of sweating bodies, stale smoke and urine. There, Uspenskii and Anna Ilinishna would talk and drink cup after cup of à la Varsovienne, a very strong coffee; or, because of the prohibition, teacups full of bootleg vodka cut with pineapple juice. Often they are joined by the Petersburg intelligentsia, such as Volinsky, a well-known writer, and Charkovsky, a bridge engineer, who rivaled Uspenskii in his knowledge of mystic literature, the two men talking for hours on the meaning of the various tarot cards, or Charkovsky's current passion, a circular device that organized and related forms of knowledge created by Raymond Lully, a thirteenth-century Catalan mystic and teacher.

As often as not, Uspenskii usually holds court, the words pouring forth as he talks about ancient texts such as the *Vedas* and the *Zend Avesta*, or perhaps compares, say, the different esoteric schools, relating a historical survey of each, before asking a series of rhetorical questions that he would answer himself.

The small hours of the morning arriving, the group would wander along the canals such as the Moika, where, at number 12, the poet Pushkin once lived, and

---

no active part in wars, and have rarely had anything to do with politics or government service. In this way they have avoided the most fraudulent and criminal sides of life. This alone makes women more free than men. Of course, there are different kinds of women; and undoubtedly the modern woman does everything she can to lose her caste."

23. Published as *Talks with a Devil* (New York: Alfred A. Knopf, 1973) it was comprised of two short stories, "The Inventor" and "The Benevolent Devil," originally titled "The Good Devil."

amble along the quays and past the smart hotels like the Europe or the recently built Astoria, and then past the massive granite pillars of St. Isaac's Cathedral with its golden dome, past the Mariinsky and Alexandrinsky theaters, and along the old streets of St. Petersburg.

With the coming of spring, Petersburg's lustrous "white nights" would make their appearance, a time when darkness never falls, and the group would amble amid shimmering greyish images of Petersburg's pale yellow buildings, its palaces and bridges and famous sphinxes, all the while discussing, talking, arguing, words ever pouring from Uspenskii. The first rays of a new dawn appearing, the group, ever-shrinking, now fortifies themselves with buns and tea, and perhaps more coffee, at the Nikolaevsky Station on Znamenski Square.

In Anna Ilinishna, Uspenskii sees what he admires in himself—"a driving force and a will to seek and find." For her, he comes to have two faces. One is the outer face characterized by what she calls his "arrogance of erudition." But behind is another face, that of a romantic, a "more radiant countenance filled with a youthful happiness which perhaps no one but myself ever witnessed."

Often their conversations focus on Uspenskii's search and travels. He tells her about the esoteric Schools of Builders evidenced by the cathedral of Notre Dame; of the pyramids of Egypt where he says he felt everything "as extraordinarily real, as though I was suddenly transferred into another world, which to my own astonishment I seemed to know very well . . . [where this distant past] ceased to be past, appeared in everything, surrounded me, became the present." He speaks of standing before the glance of the Sphinx, that which saw life in terms of centuries and millenniums, and feeling all at once, in that moment, "that I did not exist, that there was no I." He tells her about Ceylon and the Buddha with the sapphire eyes, which, like the Sphinx, spoke "of another life, of another consciousness, which is higher than man's consciousness," and about the Taj Mahal, where he says he had "the sensation of being in two worlds at once" and came to feel that here "before me and all around me was the soul of the Empress Mumtaz-i-Mahal," the divine feminine for whom the immense mausoleum had been built. But of all the subjects, it is always to Uspenskii's chief interest, time's fourth dimension, to which the discussion returns. For Uspenskii, along with eternal recurrence, it is the Idea of ideas, so much so that his friends called him "Uspenskii Fourth Dimension." At the age of twenty he had even published a book on the subject, *The Fourth Dimension*.

For Uspenskii the fourth dimension is not simply an intellectual idea. He had had many experiences of it, most notably perhaps in 1908. He had travelled to Constantinople and was on a ship in the Sea of Marmara on a rainy winter day standing by the railing watching the waves. He tells Anna Ilinishna:

> I was watching the play of waves with the ship, and feeling the waves drawing me to themselves. It was not the desire to jump down which one feels in the mountains, but something infinitely more subtle. The

waves were drawing my soul to themselves. Suddenly I felt it going to them. It was only a moment, maybe less than a moment. But I entered the waves and, with them, with a roar, attacked the ship. And at that moment I became all. The waves—they were myself. The violet mountains in the distance—they were myself. The wind—it was myself. The clouds, hurrying from the north, the rain—were myself. The huge ship, rolling indomitably forward—was myself. I felt that huge iron body as my body, all its movements, waverings, rollings and shudderings, the fire, the pressure of steam, the engine—all this was inside me.

Now, within a year or so of his meeting Anna Ilinishna, Uspenskii begins contemplating a second journey to the East, perhaps this time to Australia. Finally, unable to conceive of finding the teacher he seeks there, he tells Anna Ilinishna he has dropped the idea.

"But why don't you go to India, then?" she prompts, adding, "And when you come back you can tell me all about what you find there."

Fearing that Evreinoff had reentered Anna Ilinishna's life or she had become bored with him, Uspenskii wonders why she wants him to go.

Her final examination at the Conservatoire is that spring, she tells him. "If I spend all my time at Phillipoff's like this I shall never get on with my work."

His fears subdued, Uspenskii, now thirty-five years old, in June 1913 decides "to start on a long journey with the idea of searching for those schools or for the people who may show me the way."

As Uspenskii had made his living as a translator and journalist, he has little trouble convincing the three newspapers for which he freelanced to finance his trip in return for articles. His first stop is London where, drawing on his theosophical contacts, he meets Alfred Richard Orage, the twenty-five-year-old editor of *The New Age*,[24] a literary and political weekly. Orage and Uspenskii share many interests, literary and occult. Theosophy had led them both to Blavatsky's *The Secret Doctrine*, and then to the *Bhagavad Gita* and the *Mahabharata*. Uspenskii had first read Nietzsche's *Thus Spake Zarathustra* at sixteen, Orage at twenty-one. Both had developed a passion for his idea of evolution in consciousness resulting in the Overman. Proclaimed Orage—"Nietzsche was the greatest European event since Goethe." So enthused was he that six years before he had written two small books about him, *Nietzsche and the Dionysian Spirit of the Age* and *Nietzsche in Outline & Aphorism*. No record of their exchange exists, but it's likely that Orage quoted an aphorism or two—"Man is a rope connecting animal and Overman—a rope across a precipice," and "Dead are all the gods; now we will that Overman live."

From London Uspenskii slowly makes his way to Ceylon and later to Madras,

---

24. Unaccountably, Orage's biographer and others speak of *New Age*, but the logo of the weekly includes the definite article, *The New Age*.

India, where he spends six weeks at Adyar, the Theosophical Society's headquarters. He travels about India visiting such places as Benares, Bombay, Agra and Delhi. He imagines "the possibility of making contact with schools of the distant past ... and that the barriers of time and space should disappear on making such contact." He does make contact with a number of schools, but they are, he says, "either of a frankly religious nature, or of a half-religious character, but definitely devotional in tone." The sentimental moral philosophy, the shades of asceticism and spiritualism which permeated such schools, have no appeal for him. Neither do "yogi schools." Some promised a great deal but demanded, from the beginning, a complete surrender. These interest him somewhat. However ...

"Speaking sincerely with myself," admits Uspenskii, "I could not say that I was able to do this [surrender]. The price seemed too high. As I put it to myself: If I paid with my own self for what I might learn, I should have lost the object for the sake of which I wished to know." As he travels, a conviction grows that perhaps the teacher for whom he is searching will be found not in the East but in Russia, perhaps even St. Petersburg.

Though he works for a newspaper in Moscow, in November of the following year he first returns to St. Petersburg, the city where he feels most at home. Built in 1703 by Peter the Great on a marshland only a few feet above sea level, the city is the cultural capital of Russia. It is home to composers Stravinsky, Rachmaninov, and Prokofiev; painters Marc Chagall and Vasily Kandinsky; the writer Maxim Gorky and the poet Alexander Blok. Its palaces and grand homes shine with gold and silver. Cabarets, opera, and the ballet thrive, and the literacy rate is growing. The liberal newspaper *Russkoe Selo* has a circulation of 2.5 million copies.

Yet beneath Petersburg's sparkling surface, signs of discord and disintegration are everywhere. With nearly three-quarters of its population born elsewhere, the city is losing its social cohesion. One out of six of the new arrivals is from Poland or from the Baltic states, but there are also Persians, Chinese and Koreans. Few Russians come from nearby provinces, but rather from the central and northwest, bringing their peasant clothes and habits in tow. Because of the resulting housing shortage, rents have tripled and are among the highest in Europe. On average, more than three people share a room. Less than half the city's dwellings have running water.

The Neva river, necklacing the city, once beautiful, is now seriously polluted by human and industrial waste. The Neva, only forty-five miles long, flows from Lake Ladoga, the largest lake in Europe, to the Gulf of Finland, which opens onto the Baltic Sea. On the river's right bank is the working-class Vyborg district, where infant mortality reaches 25 percent. In industry, women's wages are a tenth to a third that of men's; to supplement their income, it is estimated one woman in thirty, is a prostitute. Though Petersburg's population is young, nearly half the deaths are the result of infectious diseases and epidemics, typhoid and intestinal disease spread through the city's water supply.

Search for the Miraculous

Everywhere people dabble in the occult and hold séances. Everywhere the talk is of living a life of *ogarochnyi*, meaning to burn the candle at both ends with no thought for the consequences. *Sanin*, a popular novel which glorifies vulgar self-gratification, sexual excess and experimentation, has captured the imagination of the young, many of whom live a life of "Saninism." The novelist Leo Tolstoi speaks of Petersburg as "seething and satiated . . . its people tormented by sleepless nights, stupefied and deadened by wine, wealth, and lovemaking without love. The spirit of destruction pervaded everywhere. Destruction was thought to be in good taste and neurasthenia to be a sign of refinement." At the Stray Dog, the twenty-two-year-old Futurist poet Vladimir Mayakovsky declaimed to the crowd:

> *To you who live only from orgy to orgy . . .*
> *To you who love only women and food . . .*
> *Why should I give my life for your convenience?!*
> *I'd be better off serving pineapple water*
> *To whores at the bar!*

Everywhere, too, rumors abound of the "holy devil," the man the Tsarina reverently refers to as "Our Friend," the hypnotic monk Grigori Rasputin, who increasingly meddles in affairs of state with what the Tsarina describes as his "wonderful, God-sent wisdom." She and the Tsar overlook his whoring and drinking, his blackened teeth, his long matted hair, and his beard which he uses as a napkin when wolfing down food with his fingers. He is thought to be aiding Tsarevich Alexis, the Tsarina's hemophiliac son, and that, to the Tsarina, is all that matters.

Exacerbating these conditions, the war with Germany is going badly for Russia. With early losses forcing a retreat, German forces are now on Russian territory. The war is costing forty million rubles a day, a sum financed through borrowing and the printing of rubles. This has caused the money in circulation to triple. In 1914, 2.4 billion rubles were in circulation; the amount is estimated to reach 8 billion by 1916. The price of meat has almost tripled, flour more than doubled.

"Everything was beginning to totter," says Uspenskii. "The hidden suicidal activity which has determined so much in Russian life was becoming more and more apparent." Indeed, the city's suicide rate triples, with two-thirds of those taking their life under the age of twenty-eight.

Meeting Anna Ilinishna on his return at Phillipoff's, Uspenskii exclaims—"Why on earth did I ever go to India? I found nothing there that I have not read before in books, or heard rumored in some way . . . nothing new, nothing."

Later, after another coffee, he tells her, "I have a feeling in my bones. This is not an exotic city but there must be someone here of the kind I am seeking."

His search in the East has been for what he calls "the miraculous." This he sees as "a new or forgotten road," one that would allow him to escape the lies and absurdities of ordinary life, so that he might penetrate what he calls its "thin film of false reality" to the hidden reality beyond. Though he has had glimpses of this hidden reality, he realizes his knowledge and efforts are not sufficient to maintain it.

He needs to find a genuine esoteric school. Those he has found in Russia, as well as in the East, are either lacking in real knowledge or are personally unsuitable. What he is searching for is a school of a special type, one, he keeps repeating, of "a more rational kind."

Uspenskii decides to self-publish his novel *Kinemadrama*. The novel concerns a romantic young maverick, Ivan Osokin, who has little control over his impulses, is willful, resents authority, and resists responsibility. He always sees life as too dull and boring. Through his stubbornness and rebellion, Osokin has thrown away all his chances in life. In desperation he has a magician send him back into his past so he can repair his mistakes. But, being who he is, he can only repeat them. Such knowledge in itself, he learns, can change nothing. To change, one must have the will to change.

"You must realize," says the magician, "that you yourself can change nothing and that you must seek help. And it must be a very deep realization, because to realize today and forget tomorrow is not sufficient. One must live with this realization."

The magician tells him he must sacrifice something big to gain the power and knowledge to change. "In order to know, one must learn; and in order to learn, one must make sacrifices. Nothing can be acquired without sacrifice."

Osokin maintains he has nothing to sacrifice.

The magician tells him: "You can sacrifice your life ... give me your life and I will see what can be made of you.... Twenty, even fifteen years will be sufficient. But during these years you must belong to me — I mean, you must do everything I tell you without evasions and excuses."

13 November 1914. Moscow. Uspenskii now sits at a desk in the offices of a Moscow newspaper, editing copy. Thumbing through the pages of a rival newspaper, *Golos Moskvi*, his attention is immediately taken by a headline in the coming events section — *The Struggle of the Magicians*. At once his mind is filled with associations of good and evil, images of white and black magicians waiting for souls to direct or misdirect. The notice is for a ballet which promises to give a complete picture of Oriental magic, including fakir miracles, sacred dances and so forth. Interesting, yes, but the "excessively jaunty tone" of its language is irritating, as if the writer is laughing at the reader. Suddenly the thought strikes — *the notice is not what it appears to be.* The facts give one impression, the tone another. But why? Despite misgivings Uspenskii decides to include the notice in his paper's upcoming events section, but he feels compelled to advise — "There would be everything in the ballet that cannot be found in real India but which travellers go there to see."

Though the journalist could hardly know it, this seemingly innocuous notice with its annoying double language is, in effect, the calling card of just that teacher and school for which he has so actively searched these many years. Unlike many seekers, Pyotr Demianovich Uspenskii is destined to find exactly what he has been searching for—"a new or forgotten road . . . a teaching of a more rational kind."

The year passed. Uspenskii thought no more about the notice for *The Struggle of the Magicians*. In early 1915 he gives two public lectures in St. Petersburg—"In Search of the Miraculous"and "The Problems of Death"—at Alexandroski Hall of the town Duma, or Parliament. The lectures arouse considerable interest, each attended by more than a thousand people.

The Theosophical Society's journal *Vestnik Teosofii* (*Herald of Theosophy*), its credo *Net Religni vyshe Istiny* (No Religion Higher Than Truth) emblazoned on its front page, reports:

> P. D. Uspenskii's lectures attracted a huge audience, but they evoked perplexity. The lecturer promised in the program to talk about India. In fact he talked only about disillusionment in seeking the miraculous and about his understanding of occultism at variance with its understanding by Theosophists and the Theosophical Society. With indignation he said that the Theosophists selected ethics and philosophy, not occultism, as their field of effort, and that ethics and philosophy are unnecessary to the Society and unrelated to occultism. . . . Mr. Uspenskii also accused the Theosophical Society of arrogance and sectarianism.

Easter Week, April 1915. After one of Uspenskii's lectures Gurdjieff's pupils Vladimir Pohl, a composer, and Sergei Dmitrievich Mercourov meet Uspenskii.[25] They tell him about a group they belong to that engages in various occult investigations and experiments. Does Uspenskii remember reading a notice for a ballet scenario *The Struggle of the Magicians*? At first he has a dim recollection but then it all comes back to him. Pohl and Mercourov tell him to put all reactions aside. The ballet scenario was written not by a Hindu but a Caucasian Greek, the leader of their group. About meeting this Greek who poses as a Hindu, Uspenskii is, at best, dubious, but persistent efforts by the two men finally awaken a curiosity and he relents.

The meeting's venue certainly does nothing to allay Uspenskii's doubts. He is directed neither to a meeting place of the intelligentsia nor to a café of the rich and powerful. Instead, he finds himself opening the door to a small and noisy

---

25. Moore made a number of notable discoveries, but one of them is not his claim to have discovered that the "M" Uspenskii refers to is Sergei Mercourov. James Webb had published "M"'s identity eleven years earlier. See *The Harmonious Circle*, 93.

businessmen's café on a busy Moscow side street. Entering the crowded café and seeing the man awaiting him, Uspenskii's concern could only have increased.

No two men could be more opposite in appearance. Uspenskii, thirty-seven-years old, five feet nine inches, very broad, robust and thick-set, light hair, pale skin and pale blue eyes behind thick-lensed pince-nez; the forty-three-year-old man awaiting him at a rear table of the café is five feet five inches, dark complected, bald, with a thick black mustache and strong black eyes. Uspenskii's facial features are definitely Russian, admirers describing his face as that of an emperor; the face of this swarthy, powerfully built man has a decidedly Oriental cast, his eyes the most predominant feature.

Uspenskii approaches the table with his usual self-assurance. In his mind's eye, he sees the man at the table in a white burnoose or a gilded turban. The words "Indian raja" or "Arab sheik" enter his mind. Yet the man is dressed like a common merchant—black overcoat with a velvet collar and a black bowler hat. The impression is "strange" and indefinite, as if what he sees is here and not here.

Greetings are exchanged.

"Georgi Ivanovitch Gurdjieff" is the name given. The Russian pronunciation is incorrect; the strong Caucasian accent coarse, hardly one associated with spiritual and philosophical discussions, yet the voice is full of life and force.

"Pyotr Demianovich Uspenskii." The pronunciation is that of the Russian intelligentsia, faultless, direct.

Uspenskii, very nearsighted, adjusts his pince-nez and draws up a chair. He sits facing Gurdjieff. Almost immediately an uneasy feeling arises. The man seems "disguised" in some way. And poorly at that. Uspenskii finds himself embarrassed. This stranger is not what he pretends to be, yet the odd feeling is that Uspenskii must speak and act as though he is not aware of it, and so involve himself in the duplicity.

As with the ballet notice in the newspaper, Gurdjieff has created in Uspenskii a kind of 'double-impression,' a curiosity that interests but also irritates and alarms. Uspenskii tries not to show his true inner state. And so, unwittingly, he receives a second double-impression, that of the mechanicalness of his outward expression as opposed to his inner feeling.[26]

Though Uspenskii could not know it, Gurdjieff has followed his newspaper accounts of his last journey to the East and its aims. He has also directed

---

26. From the outset, then, with only the giving of his name and perhaps a few words, Gurdjieff is acting on Uspenskii, causing him inwardly to see one thing yet outwardly having to appear as if he doesn't. The contradiction divides him, jams his mind, stops the thoughts, erases the personage of his "Uspenskii" and puts him where he rarely is with people—in question. For Uspenskii, who prides and defends himself with the power of his intellect, his control and command over himself and others, the experiencing is not only unfamiliar but decidedly uncomfortable. Momentarily, Gurdjieff has given Uspenskii the experience of having his mind stopped, his feelings opened.

his pupils to read Uspenskii's books.[27] In this way, he told his pupils, Uspenskii's level of understanding could be determined and thus it could be known what he would be able to discover.

Uspenskii, no ordinary seeker, knows a secret: *that ordinary life is meaningless, a charade, people live only to die.* This, together with his gift of a powerful intellect and thirst for the truth, enabled him to see through and free himself from many of the hypnotic societal beliefs and structures. He had entered into subtle domains of esoteric knowledge, and he was capable not only of capturing, holding, and directing the attention of others, but of bending the will of others to his own. He has experienced the change in the sensation of I, of time, and in the "long body" of man, he has been tested by "voices." He has experienced the terror and joy of life's infinity and its unity. He knows of the need to become self-conscious, to expand the space-sense. It is true that many of these experiences came from his experiments with amyl nitrate.[28] But he has come to realize, "Narcotics cannot give a man anything he has not already got. . . . All they can do, in certain cases, is to reveal that which is already in a man's soul." He has had the personal power and self-confidence to lecture in Russia's most cosmopolitan cities, St. Petersburg and Moscow, and hold the attention of thousands of people. Compared to the average man, Uspenskii is, in his own right, a magician. This meeting in a noisy Moscow café then is no ordinary meeting. Rather, it is a meeting between two magicians. And as with all such meetings the question is: *Who is the greater magician?*

So put off balance by his initial contact with Gurdjieff, Uspenskii admits he does not remember how their talk began. If Gurdjieff conducts this meeting as he does others, he will have begun with questions such as: "Why do you come to me?" "What is your secret intolerance?" "Is your life so unbearable?"

If so, Uspenskii's reply would likely follow his later expression of what he felt at this period of his life. "Ordinary life forces one to swallow customary forms of lying and living in lying," he said. "I am looking for a way to escape, a new or forgotten road. And it cannot in character be devotional. It must be more rational."

What Uspenskii does remember is that Gurdjieff speaks to him of his Work. Uspenskii's interest is psychology and Gurdjieff explains that while the character of his Work is chiefly psychological, chemistry plays a large role.[29] Uspenskii isn't certain what Gurdjieff means by 'chemistry' so he associates, telling Gurdjieff about a school in India that studied the chemistry of the human body, altering a

---

27. Having arrived in Russia in 1912, the same year Uspenskii published *Tertium Organum*, it seems likely that Gurdjieff would have read the book.

28. See *A New Model of the Universe*, "Experimental Mysticism," 308–43.

29. It is interesting that in reporting this first meeting Uspenskii does not speak of Gurdjieff's presence or power, his great being, as others do. Neither does he in any of his subsequent writings or reported conversations. Even intellectuals like C. Daly King, no friend of Gurdjieff's, spoke of the rare quality of being Gurdjieff emanated.

man's moral or psychological nature by the introduction or removal of substances.

But this 'chemistry' is not Gurdjieff's.

Uspenskii's material on the subject is slight. Instead of exposing his ignorance, he introduces into the discussion the subject of magic and narcotics.

Gurdjieff answers his questions but brings him back to the idea of chemistry saying, "To do this [to know possibilities in advance], a great knowledge of the human machine and of this special chemistry is necessary."

Despite the heavy, coarse accent, Uspenskii is deeply impressed with Gurdjieff's manner of speaking. In his answers, Gurdjieff is careful, precise, economical. More importantly, Uspenskii finds some of Gurdjieff's points of view not only new but unlike any he's ever heard.

At the end of their talk, Gurdjieff invites Uspenskii to come back to his house to meet some of his pupils. They take a carriage toward the outlying district of Sokoniki. On the way Gurdjieff gives him to understand he lives in an expensive apartment and that among his pupils are a number of well-known professors and artists. When the carriage draws up in front of a municipal school, and Gurdjieff motions him to get out, Uspenskii must have been surprised. Where is the expensive apartment? Gurdjieff leads him up to the top floor of the school. The apartment turns out to be a large empty flat. As for the pupils, Uspenskii finds them nice and decent, but they belong to a layer of Moscow society known as the "poor intelligentsia." Uspenskii cannot understand—Why is Gurdjieff so obviously creating such doubts? What is his intention?

A student begins to read aloud a story called "Glimpses of Truth." It is 12,439 words in length and takes two hours to read. At the outset the story mentions the newspaper notice for the ballet scenario *The Struggle of the Magicians*. Like a leitmotif of what Uspenskii's and Gurdjieff's relationship will be, the ballet's title is again introduced.

While the piece is read, Gurdjieff sits on the sofa, one leg crossed beneath him,[30] smoking, and drinking black coffee from a tumbler. Now and then he looks at Uspenskii. His movements, Uspenskii notices, have a kind of "feline grace and assurance." The impression slowly forms in him of Gurdjieff being someone quite rare. Though what is read covers some of the primary points of the teaching Gurdjieff will introduce—unity in multiplicity, the power of reason, law of tri-unity, structure of the universe, the octave and its notes and gaps, matter being all and everything and everywhere, and varying only in terms of qualities and place, the human body and its three foods, self-initiation—it is too much for even a mind as strong as Uspenskii's to comprehend.

When Gurdjieff asks about putting some of these ideas in print, Uspenskii focuses on the literary quality of "Glimpses of Truth." He tells Gurdjieff it is too long for an article in a newspaper, so only a monthly magazine would publish it

---

30. Just as Prince Ozay did.

and Uspenskii knows none that are suitable. He goes to leave, but suddenly the thought flashes into his mind that he must arrange to see Gurdjieff "at once, without delay." Otherwise, he might lose all contact with him.

And so the next day, and every day thereafter for the entire week, Uspenskii and Gurdjieff meet and talk at the same noisy Moscow café. What Uspenskii finds especially impressive is Gurdjieff's command of psychology, an area Uspenskii takes to be his specialty. "I saw without hesitation," says Uspenskii, "that in the domain which I knew better than any other and in which I was really able to distinguish the old from the new, the known from the unknown, Gurdjieff knew more than all European science taken as a whole."

At one point, Uspenskii introduces the subject of esoteric schools. There are no general schools, only special ones, Gurdjieff tells him. Every teacher has his specialty and all the students must study it. Uspenskii wants to know in what way Gurdjieff studied. Gurdjieff tells him of the Seekers of Truth.

"Where are they now?" Uspenskii asks.

Some are dead, some are working and "some," declares Gurdjieff, "have gone into seclusion."[31]

Seclusion. The word's inner ring has monastic reverberations. Uspenskii reacts. He experiences "a strange and uncomfortable feeling."[32]

During another talk, Gurdjieff tells Uspenskii he might learn a great deal if he knew how to read. For Uspenskii—journalist, author, translator—the remark must have been a shock. Gurdjieff intensifies it.

"If you understood everything you have written in your own book, what is it called?"—Gurdjieff makes something altogether impossible out of the book's title, *Tertium Organum*—"I should come and bow down to you and beg you to teach me."[33]

Gurdjieff tells Uspenskii of the necessity to work on oneself in a group. Uspenskii raises the question of secrecy. "I do not know," he says, "whether you exact a promise from your pupils to keep secret what they learn from you, but I could give no such promise . . . *before everything else, I am a writer,* and I desire to be absolutely free to decide for myself what I shall write and what I shall not write."[34] [Emphasis added.]

"One must not talk too much," Gurdjieff tells him. "There are things which

---

31. In the original draft of *Fragments of an Unknown Teaching*, the words are not ambiguous—"some are cloistered."

32. Gurdjieff sees the automatic reaction the word *seclusion* sets off in Uspenskii. Three years later in Essentuki all that surrounds this word for Uspenskii will unconsciously play itself out.

33. The implication is that Gurdjieff does understand *Tertium Organum* and Uspenskii does not. Therefore, he should bow down to Gurdjieff and beg to be taught. Uspenskii appears to miss this subtlety entirely. See *In Search of the Miraculous*, 20.

34. Uspenskii is here thinking of himself as a writer first, a seeker second. He is perceiving the situation not in terms of finding "the miraculous," but finding it and writing about it. His identification is understandable, of course, but "the writer" in him is also Uspenskii's "teacher," he who wants to teach others. Uspenskii's teacher-'I' will later become an issue.

are said only for disciples."

"I could accept such a condition only temporarily," answers Uspenskii. He goes on to speak of a group engaged in various scientific experiments who "made it a condition that no one would have the right to speak of or describe any experiment unless he was able to carry it out himself. Until he was able to repeat the experiment himself he had to keep silent."

"There could be no better formulation," says Gurdjieff, "and if you will keep such a rule this question will never arise between us."

At another meeting Gurdjieff tells him that the starting point is that "Man does not know himself, that he is *not*... that is, he is not what he can and what he should be." Man, he says, is a machine to which everything happens. To cease to be a machine, he must learn to study the workings of the machine, its mechanics. In this way, one begins to become responsible for one's actions.

"A *man* is responsible. A *machine* is not responsible," says Gurdjieff. The chief delusion of man is that he is convinced he can do but, in fact, everything happens to him. "*To do* it is necessary *to be*," says Gurdjieff. Everything is connected. The planets and moon are living beings. The universe is expanding, not contracting, and the moon is a planet in birth. War is the result not of economics, injustice and the like, but of planetary influences. "Everything that happens on a big scale is governed from outside, and governed either by accidental combinations of influences or by general cosmic laws. What man does have is a certain possibility of deciding the influences under which he will work."

Having spent the entire Easter week with Gurdjieff, Uspenskii must return to Petersburg. He is preparing new editions of *Tertium Organum* and *Symbolism of the Tarot*, and also *Kinemadrama*, later retitled *Strange Life of Ivan Osokin*.

Autumn 1915. St. Petersburg. Gurdjieff arrives from Moscow for a few day's visit. He telephones Uspenskii who goes to see Gurdjieff at once. Gurdjieff says he is thinking of starting group work here on a large scale, giving public lectures and demonstrations and attracting a wide variety of people of different levels of preparation. Uspenskii, always sensitive to his independence, tells him he has no interest in group work.

Afterward, Uspenskii goes straight to Phillipoff's café where Anna Ilinishna has been waiting for him. Though an hour late, he does not greet her or even sit down, but instead exclaims—"I have found the miracle!"

Nearly breathless, he says he has found the man they have been searching for, the one who can help them find "the mystic threshold." He says, "This man's knowledge goes beyond mere theory. He can teach, and give the answers to what we and so many others in different lands and times have sought. But he's very sparing—mean, almost—in communication."

This man has told him two things he has never found in any book or heard in any esoteric society. "He says that man, because he is passive, does not actually do things personally, but that everything in him is done, mechanically. A man will say, 'I do such-an-such,' but this is not the genuine I for he might have twenty-two 'I's.... What I am trying to say is, there is not one I but many."

With this as an introduction, Uspenskii takes Anna Ilinishna to the second of Phillipoff's two cafés, just across the boulevard, to meet Gurdjieff. Entering the café, Anna Ilinishna sees a man at a table in the far corner wearing an ordinary black coat and a high astrakhan cap. Introduced, she at once notices his "fine, virile features and a look that pierces right through you (though not in an unpleasant way).... His manner is very calm and relaxed, and he speaks without any gesticulation. Even to be sitting with him was very agreeable."

She finds Gurdjieff speaks Russian fluently, though in an exact and very picturesque way. He has "the gift," she says, "of assembling words expressively." Like Russian peasants, he is spare with words, "often constructing phrases as if for that time only." He uses his voice like an instrument, speaking in many tones—one lazy, another subdued, one having a glint of humor, another passionate with a kind of noble wrath. At last she feels she is "in the presence of a Guru."

He asks why she comes to him, is her life so unbearable?

"Yes! Perhaps that is the best word to define my state. *Unbearable!*"

"Then if that is so, it is better than I thought. Come! You will find me here every day from twelve o'clock onwards, at this table."

Thereafter, Uspenskii and Anna Ilinishna will arrive at the café every day at noon and meet with Gurdjieff until five or six in the evening, then parting to dine, and meeting again until late into the night.

February 1916. St. Petersburg. Gurdjieff has been ill most of the winter, but now he makes the 350-mile train trip from Moscow to Petersburg every fortnight. Says Uspenskii:

> His journeys from Moscow to St. Petersburg and back make me positively shudder. To travel with the most elementary comfort it was necessary to book several days in advance. Gurdjieff never did this. He never allowed me or anyone else to get his ticket for him. He purposely never told us the exact time he would be leaving, and driving straight to the Nikolaevsky Station would get into a second or third class carriage. Crammed full, where there was no room to move. But there was no kind of asceticism about it, no sentimentality about the people, or about the desire to suffer in common with the people—there was nothing false about it. He simply paid no attention to these things and sometimes perhaps accepted or did them deliberately as an exercise, a difficulty, a means of training himself not to depend on things and circumstances.... Gurdjieff was ill all the time and in the winter of 1916 twice nearly had pneumonia, and secondly the discomfort afterwards became unavoidable and the unavoidable is always easier to bear.

What struck one about Gurdjieff was that he had not the indifference of a man who does not understand what is good and what is bad, what is pleasant and what is unpleasant, and who does not care for external comforts simply because he does not appreciate or understand them. In Gurdjieff it was quite different. He appreciated and understood all the good things of life possibly better than anyone. But one felt all the time that he was not attached to any of these things and could at any moment give up everything without losing an atom of his energy or calm.

And in this as in all else that he did there was not any pedantry. He understood far more about every side of life than the ordinary average man. He could always choose the best, whether it was in matters of food, or pleasure or amusement, or travel, or anything.

As quite a boy he made several long journeys in the East. In the course of these journeys he came across many facts which pointed to the existence of a certain knowledge, of certain powers and possibilities.... Undoubtedly one felt in him very much that was strange. No ordinary demands could be made of him nor could one measure him on any ordinary scale. One could be sure of nothing in regard to him. He might say something today and tomorrow something altogether different, yet one could never accuse him of contradiction. One had to understand and connect everything together.

Gurdjieff takes an apartment at Pushkin Street just off Nevsky Prospekt and near Uspenskii's and Anna Ilinishna's apartments, as well as Phillipoff's café. Uspenskii and Anna Ilinishna continue to meet Gurdjieff at the café for long discussions, often going late into the night, as they have many questions. Always, Gurdjieff insists on brevity, especially of Uspenskii, who tends to talk on and on. Soon, Gurdjieff asks Uspenskii to organize groups for him in Petersburg. Uspenskii wavers but finally convinces himself:

The situation in its essence was that G refused to speak with me separately, and while not saying this, in so many words, he gave me to understand that he would answer my questions and generally speak about what interested me if I would bring people to him and organize groups. This brought me face to face with a number of questions. G interested me but I knew too little about him to be able to say anything definite. In introducing people to him and organizing groups I took a great responsibility on myself. This I saw perfectly clearly, but still there was one point about which I had no doubt. G had knowledge which it was worth risking something to acquire, and I said to myself that the people whom I brought to him would, even if the worst came to the worst, be but in the same situation as I myself.

When he next sees Gurdjieff he tells him—"Listen, Georgi Ivanovitch, I will organize these circles for you, but only on the condition that I myself do not enter them. I shall remain aside."[35]

"Why?" says Gurdjieff looking at me sideways with one of his characteristic glances.
I could not explain to him. Somehow I disliked the thought that it should be said of me that I belonged to any such circles. I had always been by myself, never belonged even to any literary groups.
Gurdjieff says nothing, only shaking his head, as if he did not understand me, or as if he were pitying me.

Says Uspenskii:

The predominant emotion in me was fear—fear of losing myself, of disappearing in something unknown. I remember a letter I wrote at that time to someone abroad. There was this phrase in it: "I am writing this letter to you, but who will write the next letter, signing it with my name and what he will say, I do not know." This was the fear. But there were many other elements in it as well; the fear of taking a wrong way, the fear of making an irretrievable mistake, the fear of losing some other possibilities. All this left me later on, when I began to gain confidence in myself on the one hand and in the system on the other.

Stuck between a "yes" and a "no," Uspenskii finds Gurdjieff suddenly acting indifferently toward him. Worse, Gurdjieff refuses to answer any serious questions. Ordinarily Uspenskii might react, becoming irritable or sulking, as that is his tendency when he doesn't get what he wants. But Gurdjieff's message is clear.
Finally Uspenskii agrees to gather people and to join a group. He tells Gurdjieff, however, that "nobody would be taken [into the group] without my consent, or remain in the Work without my consent." Uspenskii speaks of this as "the St. Petersburg conditions,"[36] a lawyer-like expression, something between two equals, not that of a student to a teacher.
Gurdjieff begins giving lectures and discussions in private houses and

---

35. Uspenskii speaks of the weakening in him of what he sees as his chief feature—"extreme individualism." And yet it is still appearing in full, as will be seen in his analysis, "*The Struggle of the Magicians:* Where I Diverge from Gurdjieff." See Essays, page 503.
36. Uspenskii's characterization—"the St. Petersburg conditions"—sounds contractual, giving a sense of a certain power and position. Uspenskii uses the word *position* a number of times in *Search* in particular ways, as when he later writes of the Essentuki period, "...my personal position in G.'s work began to change." Interestingly, the mention of "the St. Petersburg conditions" appears in the first draft of *Fragments of an Unknown Teaching* but is deleted from the published version of *In Search of the Miraculous*.

afterwards at the offices of *Apollo*, a well-known art review. The people that Uspenskii invites are, mostly, if not all, part of the intelligentsia, Petersburg's educated elite. Given that Gurdjieff asks one thousand rubles ($514[37]) to work with him, Uspenskii is amazed when people show signs of interest. Only people with private means could afford this amount, Uspenskii tells him. Gurdjieff gives a detailed answer as to why he asks for such a payment and ends by telling him—"People do not value a thing if they do not pay for it."

"Although in principle Gurdjieff put the question very strictly," Uspenskii tells us, "in practice he never refused anybody on the grounds that they had no money. And it was found out later that he even supported many of his pupils. The people who paid a thousand roubles paid not only for themselves but for others."

That spring the first preparatory group is formed. It consists of six people: Dr. Leonid Robertovich Stjoernval, a forty-four-year-old Finnish psychiatrist[38]; Anthony Charkovsky, a fifty-year-old engineer and bridge builder and Uspenskii's friend from The Stray Dog; Andrey Andreivitch Zaharoff, a thirty-seven-year-old railway engineer; Nicholas, a sixty-eight-year-old widower and member of the Senate; Anna Ilinishna Butkovskaia, thirty-one years old; and of course Pyotr Demianovich Uspenskii himself, thirty-eight years old. Later, the Petersburg group will grow to as many as thirty.[39]

Anna Ilinishna gives a picture of how she sees the group:

> Dr. Stjoernval is a business-like man, who speaks well, in his level doctor's voice, but without displaying any emotion. Charkovsky has a purity of heart, he was kind and good to everyone he met ... having a mathematical mind he had great precision of thought. Zaharoff ... was wholly unable to express anything of his inner being ... he seemed at home only with mathematics.... Andrey [Zaharoff] was a good-looking bachelor, very shy, and for a Russian, very 'frozen,' silent and reserved.... Uspenskii was all outward manifestation. In those days, before he developed, behind his quasi-scientific phrases there was no real significance or deep meaning. We could see how many facts were stored in his head: he could compare the different esoteric schools, make a historical survey of them, put rhetorical questions and then answer them himself. But in reality he was only posing the same questions in a different form ... all poured

---

37. All U.S. Dollar amounts are equivalent to the foreign currency of that time period.
38. His son, Nicholas de Val, says he first met Gurdjieff in 1915. Moore says 1914. Oddly, though his name is de Stjoernval the "de" is not used when others mention him.
39. It would seem likely that Stjoernval's 30-year-old Danish wife, Elizabeta Grigorievna, would be part of this group, but it is not mentioned. She wanted a baby but had remained childless. Hearing of Rasputin's healing powers, she has a patient of her husband's arrange a dinner to meet him. Two other times she meets with him, the last being two months before he was murdered. See de Val's book *Daddy Gurdjieff*.

forth in non-stop speech in a characteristic avalanche.

During early group meetings Uspenskii, fond of parading his knowledge, speaks too much, and doesn't keep to the point. Anna Ilinishna says, "Gurdjieff [would] look at him with a curious enigmatic smile and sometimes would stop him in full flood."

At one meeting Gurdjieff speaks about knowing oneself, or self-study. Before all else the structure, functions, and laws of one's organism must be studied. The chief method is the practice of self-observation, in which one does *not* analyze, but strives to *impartially* register the observation of the moment. This observation of oneself must be related to its given function and center, that is, the thinking, emotional, moving, and instinctive centers.

Uspenskii reports that he saw two huge trucks drive along the Liteiny. He observes they are loaded with unpainted wooden crutches, to the height of the first floor of the buildings, and imagines similar trucks moving in the streets of Vienna, Berlin, London, Paris, Rome, and Constantinople; all cities he had visited and knew well which were all separated "by new walls of hatred and crime." Says Gurdjieff, "What do you expect? People are machines. . . . Everything happens."

At the next meeting Gurdjieff asks the group what is the most important thing they have noticed during self-observation. None of the replies satisfy him. Finally he tells them that "not one of you has noticed that you do not remember yourselves. . . . You do not feel *yourselves*; you are not conscious of yourselves."

The next day, walking along the Liteiny in the direction of Nevsky Prospekt, Uspenskii attempts to remember himself. He finds he cannot keep his attention on himself. The incessant noises, the continual movement of people and cars along the street, continually distract him. Irritated with himself, he redoubles his effort and turns onto a quieter street. He reaches the following street and coming to the Nadejdinskaya realizes that his attention has wandered only for short moments. Reasoning that self-remembering is easier on less noisy streets, he decides to experiment. On the Nevsky there is a tobacconist's shop that makes his cigarettes. He will go there to buy cigarettes, all the while remembering himself. Two hours later, taking a cab to his printers, he finds himself in the Tavricheskaya when suddenly—"I remembered that I had forgotten to remember myself."

1916. St. Petersburg. The Russian Theosophical Society had focused on theosophy's belief that Russia would play a major role in bringing the East and West together. In that light, amid the deprivations of war, Anna Alekseevna Kamenskaia, editor of *Vestnik Teosofii*, writes:

> We are undoubtedly moving on to a higher level of world life. Not without purpose have all the veils been torn away, and previous illusions are burning in the fire of difficult, and, at the same time, profoundly

meaningful experiences; not without purpose are we passing through so many shocks; not without purpose are all minds and hearts opening to new ideas and inspirations. But what kind of worldview will be capable of expressing this higher level of consciousness? Only that worldview which can unify all the complex needs of human life and provide the strength to build a life on earth on the basis of brotherhood, love, and mutual assistance. Theosophy provides such a view.

February–March 1916. St. Petersburg. When in the city, Gurdjieff spends the whole day in cafés speaking with people who wish to see him. Then, and only at the last minute, he tells Uspenskii to let others know there will be a meeting that evening. Such short notice makes it difficult for many to come. Puzzled, Uspenskii inquires why. Gurdjieff tells him, "People could only value the ideas if they have to overcome obstacles."

Among the ideas Gurdjieff introduces at these early meetings are reincarnation, immortality,[40] and the four bodies of man—the physical, astral, mental, and divine. He contrasts the functioning of an automaton with one who has attained his individuality. He speaks of the absence of unity in man, that man thinks he has only one mind when, in fact, he has three minds: the intellectual, emotional, and moving-instinctive. "Man has no permanent and unchangeable I," says Gurdjieff. "To come to a real permanent I there must be a fusion of substances. For this, fire is required. A fire is built from friction, which is the result of an inner struggle between 'yes' and 'no.' Something significant must be sacrificed in the moment, if this struggle is to be evoked. The higher bodies thus formed possess qualities not found in the physical body, such as a certain electrical conductivity. It also may be possible to magnetize them."

Gurdjieff speaks of the three traditional ways to spiritually awaken: through work on the body, the emotions, or the mind. These ways are ordinarily referred to as the way of the fakir, monk, or yogi. Each demands that a man begin by doing that which is most difficult—dying to the world. There is another traditional way, as well, though not commonly known. It is The Fourth Way that Gurdjieff introduces. The Fourth Way differs from the other ways in many important and substantial respects, not all of which lend themselves to words. The Fourth Way does not focus on a specific center of body, emotions or mind as other ways do, but works on them simultaneously. Further, the pupil is not required to give up anything. One is not to withdraw from ordinary life but, on the contrary, learn to consciously use the impressions of ordinary life for one's own self-development. "A man's life and its conditions," says Gurdjieff, "correspond to what he is." The conditions of his life, its uncertainties, shocks and suffering are used to come to real life. The principal demand of The Fourth Way is for understanding, for the greater a student's

---

40. To become immortal one must create a soul which, when fully perfected, will be immortal within the solar system.

understanding of what he or she does, the greater the results. The Fourth Way is practical, immediate, and of great scale. Therefore, in contrast to the traditional three ways, the work of The Fourth Way can be more effective, more efficient. (Later he will make a further distinction, saying that unlike the other ways, The Fourth Way is not permanent, it appears and disappears and by itself has no definite aim.)

In speaking about real knowledge associated with the transformation of energies in man and the cosmos, Gurdjieff says that humanity comes into periods when the masses of men lose their reason and mindlessly destroy everything built up over time, and that these periods generally correspond to the beginning of the fall of a culture or civilization. Released at such a time is "a very great quantity of the matter of knowledge. This, in its turn, necessitates the work of collecting this matter of knowledge which would otherwise be lost."

The teaching of The Fourth Way is unusual in that it gives nothing ready-made. Though he can be totally lucid and coherent, Gurdjieff often speaks in ways that seem to confuse. Gurdjieff teaches using declarations without examples, apparent contradictions, hints, and nuances of all kinds, all of which keep the group on edge and create friction. Teaching in this way makes a demand on the group to become active, to inquire, explore, to think and act independently, to take nothing and no one for granted.

In time, Uspenskii comes to understand something about how Gurdjieff expresses himself:

> Our ordinary European logical method of thinking makes us inclined to accept everything literally, that is, if we trust the author, we suppose that with every word, he says exactly what he meant. Eastern thought, however, often uses methods of exposition totally different from ours. Eastern authors often do not define their subject as a whole. They are apt to give only one instance of the possible meaning of the given subject or phenomena without saying that it is merely an instance so that readers are left to understand their words as they like or as they can. Gurdjieff very often did the same thing.

What Uspenskii also sees and likes is the fact that "Gurdjieff not only has a total indifference to making things easy or agreeable for himself but never shirks any kind of work. Though he sometimes likes to give large dinners, he often eats and drinks very little. He is totally without any kind of affectation and shows no desire to produce an impression on others. He never pretends to any sanctity or occult powers. He enjoys a joke and has a robust sense of humor. Occasionally, he might 'act' or 'play' with people's impressions regarding himself, but rather than falseness," says Uspenskii, it "produced an impression of strength." But he adds, "Sometimes there was too much of it."

In forming a group, Gurdjieff tells Uspenskii and the others that its members must agree to engage in self-study, exchange observations and make a common struggle against their false personalities. In doing so, they must attempt to tell the whole truth to the teacher, sincerity in the group being an absolute demand. Further, members must remember why they came to a group. If they begin to express mistrust toward the teacher, lack of respect and so forth, then they can no longer work with the teacher and must leave.

As the meetings continue, Uspenskii becomes irritated. He is not getting the respect he is due. Gurdjieff, he says, "did not see me, would not give himself the trouble to understand me, that he did not wish to see that in reality I had gone much further from the ordinary outlook than he thought, that many of his ideas were much nearer and much more comprehensible to me than he would admit." Worse, Uspenskii finds Gurdjieff insisting that he give up all his knowledge and start from scratch. But many of the ideas that Gurdjieff speaks about, says Uspenskii, he has already come to himself.[41]

At that time, he was very near passing a ready judgment on Gurdjieff and his pupils. But something stops him.

> I began to realize what an immense value these ideas had for me. I became almost terrified at the thought of how easily I could have passed them by, how easily I could have known nothing whatever of Gurdjieff's existence, or how easily I could have again lost sight of him. . . . But at the same time I understood that this was only the outer aspect. The inner aspect consisted in the fact that I was necessary to him. And that he had found me and not I him. Had I not been necessary to him I should probably never have seen him. This gave a special significance to the whole system and to all that we had learnt.
>
> And at the same time, even when I thought about all this, I was dissatisfied with many things. I was necessary to Gurdjieff, but he did not know how, or did not wish, to get from me that which I was able to give him. From my point of view we were going along too slowly. Gurdjieff marked time on endless talks with unnecessary people, that is, with the sort of people from whom nothing could ever be got. At the same time if he would only slightly alter the form of his attitude, did not demand such servile subordination to his ideas from the first word, did not hammer these ideas into people's heads, I could bring people to him who were more capable of understanding his ideas than those brought to him by others, who often, in my opinion, seemed to be merely ballast. And again, I wondered: why doesn't he try to give me more of his ideas? Why does he make me sit at these often very boring lectures, instead of giving me at once as

---

41. Gurdjieff is working with Uspenskii's emotional center; he is intentionally calling up this state so Uspenskii, if he remembers himself, can impartially observe his self-love and false pride.

many ideas as possible and enable me in this way the better to help him.

But, strange though it be, many things were as I have stated. In Gurdjieff was a queer duality which I saw even then. He was both a very astute man and a very naive. He understood and saw right through many things and at the same time, many things he judged like a child. Later on I understood this better. But even then I saw that he simply did not understand our life. Did not understand Europe, did not understand Russia, did not understand St. Petersburg. In his habits, his views, and his understanding he is profoundly a man of the East. I did not doubt that there in the East he understood both the difference between type of people, and the difference in classes, professions, position in status. Everything here was all alike for him, he felt no differences. And since, in the conditions of his life in Russia up to his meeting with us, he had come into contact principally with people of the very low middle classes even though very rich as for instance Volga traders whom he had cured of hard drinking, he imagined the whole of Russian society to be on the same level. In Russia of course where the lower middle class had spread so widely and had so deeply embraced all classes, it was very difficult for a "foreigner" as indeed Gurdjieff was to discriminate. But I am not speaking now even of intellectual understanding but chiefly of attitude. Gurdjieff did not discriminate in Russian life because Russia for him was Europe. And Europe for him as a man of the East was a country of deceit, of falsehood, of immense conceit and of inner nothingness. Again, of course, he was right about many things, but still, not about everything.

In him was much of the strange: side by side with traits which attracted people to him and disposed them favorably, were other traits which I refrain from calling vulgar only by a great effort of will. Many of us noticed these traits but when we spoke of them we explained to each other that this was done *for us*, that he wished to show himself worse than he was, in order that we should value the *ideas* better. That it was "acting" and so on. And it is remarkable that in certain cases this was true and in other cases another thing was true.

April 1916. St. Petersburg. Gurdjieff gives his first lectures on the seven cosmoses. "It is with this that science and philosophy begin," he says. The Cabala and other systems speak of two cosmoses, he says, but these are "incomplete" and, as such, they are inexact. Such teachings are "merely a fragment split off from another, much fuller, ancient esoteric teaching... the full teaching on cosmoses speaks not of two, but of seven cosmoses, included one within another."

Listening to Gurdjieff lecture, Uspenskii realizes the seven cosmoses correspond to the period of dimensions and problems of space and time and higher dimensions, ideas which he has been working on for several years and are the basis of his book *Wisdom of the Gods* (later titled *A New Model of the Universe*). Declares Uspenskii: "It is not merely a coincidence of details—it is absolutely identical. I do not know how it has come about; I have never heard of seven cosmoses related to one another in the ratio of zero to infinity. Nevertheless my 'period of dimensions' coincides with this absolutely exactly."

Bewildered, Uspenskii points out to Gurdjieff passages in his own books and manuscripts where the same ideas are discussed. But Gurdjieff displays no interest. Instead, turning up the heat still more, Gurdjieff quotes verbatim to the group whole pages of Uspenskii's books.

> In speaking of man's different "I"s, he repeated word for word whole pages from my public lectures of 1912 on the Superman. He used such expressions as "Caliph for an hour," etc., and whole paragraphs from my pamphlet "What Is Yoga" [published in 1913] and many remarks and expressions from my book *Tertium Organum*.

At one point Gurdjieff says to Uspenskii, "Say what you can from your point of view, taking everything just as I said it."

Uspenskii begins by examining the idea of the ratio of zero to infinity and proceeds to work through the dimensions in a manner both comprehensive and insightful.

"There is a great deal of material in what you have just said," comments Gurdjieff, "but this material must be elaborated." He tells him to ponder that time is different in different cosmoses and ends by saying: "Time is breath—try to understand this."

Having shown no interest in Uspenskii's ideas—only to then openly plagiarize them—Gurdjieff now insists that Uspenskii give up what is for Uspenskii the Idea of ideas—"the fourth dimension." He must accept a universe of not four but only three dimensions.

For Uspenskii this is tantamount to giving up his first born. When he speaks to Gurdjieff about this, no doubt hoping for some relief or explanation, he is told instead that he must sacrifice all his knowledge. *All his knowledge!* And he must go even further. "You must not be afraid of putting everything in the fire," Gurdjieff tells him. "What is genuine is not burned up. What is burned up is not genuine, it is rubbish, waste paper. Thank God that it should be burned."

"It seemed to me," says Uspenskii, "to be absurd and unnatural. I submitted to it only because I saw clearly that unless I renounced my favorite words and ideas I should receive nothing from him."

Finally, after a great struggle, Uspenskii agrees to sacrifice his knowledge. But the cost, personally, is dear. "Naturally," explains Uspenskii, "such submission could not be achieved without great struggle with oneself, and the first result of this was that I entirely lost the power to write."[42]

At one meeting of the group Uspenskii pontificates about impressions. Finally Gurdjieff cuts him off—"Whatever is this rubbish you're talking?"

Turning to the others in the group, Gurdjieff speaks as if Uspenskii isn't present.

"I suppose he wants to show off his knowledge," Gurdjieff muses. "He's exactly like a cow going round and round a new gate without being able to find a way in. God preserve us from such people!"

Gurdjieff suggests that each of the six—in front of the others—tell the story of their lives.

Dr. Stjoernval, a private man, always holding himself in tight control, begins to make such a confession. It is soon clear he is not telling the truth. He speaks of the events abstractly, in an impersonal fashion, as though he had no hand in them.

Says Anna Ilinishna "one could sense the struggle between his desire to whitewash the action and his knowledge that it was impossible to deceive Gurdjieff."

Finally, Gurdjieff shoots a piercing look at Stjoernval that stops him in midsentence. "Another time, doctor, you will be sincere, and recall these matters accurately.... Think it over."

Later Gurdjieff gives students nicknames. Stjoernval's is "Mean," in the sense that the doctor cannot easily part with anything he possesses, be it money, words or memories. Zaharoff's is "Baba," which means in Russian "peasant woman." He is so shy and emotionally frozen that he cannot speak of his inner being. Nicholas's is "Jubilant Old Man." Anna Ilinishna's is "Wavering." Uspenskii's is "Wraps up the Thought" (ask him a question and he gives an encyclopedic answer). Later, Gurdjieff will say it is Uspenskii's name which is the fundamental feature of his attitude toward life, this and his "extreme individualism."

At another meeting Gurdjieff introduces the ideas of knowledge and being. Uspenskii says that the group divided into two camps about this. "The first camp," he says, "thought that the whole thing was from the change of being, that with the change of being we would get more from the knowledge than we already have. The second camp (to which I believe I alone belonged) said that even in our present state of being we can get much more knowledge than we have, that we are not so saturated with knowledge that we cannot absorb more. Later I understood that both are necessary."

---

42. The idea of sacrifice was not foreign to Uspenskii. In fact, in *Strange Life of Ivan Osokin*, it is the central idea. Near the end of the book the magician speaks to Osokin about sacrifice. He tells him he cannot change himself without making sacrifices and that he must sacrifice something big, not only once, but to go on making sacrifices until he gets what he wants. Osokin protests that he has nothing to sacrifice. "Everyone has something to sacrifice," says the magician, "except those who cannot be helped." And later: "A man can be given only what he can use; and he can use only that for which he has sacrificed something. This is the law of human nature." In effect, then, the book is a foretelling. What Uspenskii knows in theory, Gurdjieff leads him to explore firsthand in the reality of his own being.

Despite Gurdjieff's great being and knowledge, there are many things that Uspenskii says:

> Give rise to perplexity and doubt. The most unexpected was his eternal and continual playing. He was never simple or natural; one always felt in him some secret, hidden intent. Some people were attracted to him by this playing as one would be attracted by anything incomprehensible, strange and dangerous. . . . In connection with this play we saw perfectly clearly in him two men, and those who the one attracted did not doubt that the other was surely a mask or part adapted for some definite aim.

When Uspenskii speaks to Gurdjieff about this, Gurdjieff tells him that "play" is indispensable—that in receiving a "yes" a man must simultaneously receive "no," and that only the struggle of "yes and no" in him can create understanding. Explains Gurdjieff:

> If there were not "no," if there were only "yes," then faith would appear. "Play" is not necessary in itself, it is called for by what people are. If they are not repelled, they immediately begin to have "faith," and above all things there must not be "faith." I do not wish to infatuate people. Infatuation is always one-sided. One side is infatuated while another side knows nothing about it. A serious moment arrives and then all comes out. A man shows himself incapable of effort, of sacrifice, of serious decision. Only if a man has passed through the struggle of "yes and no" can he be relied upon, and the greater the struggle the better, and the more will he be steadfast and trustworthy from the point of view of the work.
>
> Valuation is necessary. He who at once sees only the small negative aspects, which I, it may be, show him by design, and does not see the big positive aspects, is not suitable for us. He has not and cannot have a right valuation. He would always see only the small negative things.

Uspenskii says he understands this theoretically, but in practice it often gave results quite contrary to what he expected.

> Gurdjieff's "play" on the one hand attracted to him and kept by him, people, who to my way of thinking, were not very *suitable,* who one after another went away, and who went away in most cases with an unpleasant feeling, saying about him and about all of us the most inconceivable and absurd things. And on the other hand this "play" at once drove away from him people who in my opinion could have been very useful and interesting for us, and indispensable from the point of view of the *aim* of our work as I understood it.

What often amazed us in his "play" was that sometimes it was perfectly clear that he made no effort to hide the white thread and that sometimes also he could not stop himself, "played" by habit automatically, even in circumstances where there was neither use nor meaning in it.

1916. Piatigorsk. Either before, or perhaps after, a journey to Alexandropol to see his family—the last time Gurdjieff is to see his father alive—he meets the archaeologist Professor Skridlov at the home of the professor's daughter. Along with Prince Lubovedsky, Skridlov is one of the original members of the Seekers of Truth, first formed in 1892, when the three met walking between the Sphinx and the Pyramid of Cheops in Egypt.[43] Skridlov participated in all the group's major expeditions and he and Gurdjieff have grown quite close. The two have corresponded regularly but have not seen one another since their expedition, most likely in 1896, to the monastery of the World Brotherhood in Kafiristan.

Skridlov must now be in his sixties or seventies, for his hair was slightly graying when they first met in Egypt at the Pyramid of Cheops twenty-four years before. He is entering upon the last stage of life, whereas Gurdjieff, at forty-four, has taken a vow and is embarked on a stupendous mission of bringing an ancient esoteric teaching to the West, one that has never been known before.

Meeting now, some twenty years since their six-month stay at the monastery of the World Brotherhood, the two men decide to celebrate by climbing to the summit of Mount Bechow, a nearby mountain. They of course take the most difficult and daring route, ascending the rocks from the southern side of the mountain. Though not high, Mount Bechow affords a spectacular view of the surrounding countryside. Alone on the summit, the two friends look into the broad expanse and take in the vastness of its silence.

"We saw," says Gurdjieff, "spread out before our eyes an extensive panorama of really extraordinary beauty." To the south and far away the two seekers of truth see the majestic snow-capped peak of Elbrus, the long chain of Caucasian mountains rimming both its sides. Below them sit the toylike settlements, towns and villages of nearly the entire region of Mineralni Vodi, while to the north lies the town of Zheleznovodsk.

Taking in the grandeur of the immensity about them, Professor Skridlov's eyes begin to tear. He tells Gurdjieff that after their stay at the monastery he underwent "a revaluation of all values." He had been totally absorbed only in his own pleasures and interests and those of his children. All he did, all he said, had been vanity.

"The meeting with Father Giovanni killed all this," says Professor Skridlov,

---

43. In the 1991 expanded definitive edition of *Our Life with Mr. Gurdjieff*, Olga de Hartmann records what Gurdjieff told the group in Essentuki in 1917 about the origins of the Seekers of Truth [this is the same wording in C. S. Nott's *Teachings of Gurdjieff*]: "Twenty-five years ago in Egypt, near the pyramids, three tourists met...." Gurdjieff speaks of this meeting in *Meetings with Remarkable Men*, chapter eight. The place of the group's origin is no doubt as symbolic as it is actual.

"and from then on there gradually arose in me that 'something' which has brought the whole of me to the unshakable conviction that, apart from the vanities of life, there exists a 'something else' which must be the aim and ideal of every more or less thinking man, and that it is only this something else which may make a man really happy and give him real values, instead of the illusory 'goods' with which in ordinary life he is always and in everything full."

This meeting will be the last time that the two essence friends will see one another. Gurdjieff must have spoken of his own feelings as well, but these he does not record.

1916. St. Petersburg. After his talk Gurdjieff is asked: "What is the relation of the teaching you are expounding to Christianity as we know it?"

"I do not know what you know about *Christianity*," Gurdjieff answers, emphasizing the word. "It would be necessary to talk a great deal and to talk for a long time in order to make clear what you understand by this term. But for the benefit of those who know already,[44] I will say that, if you like, *this is esoteric Christianity*." [Emphasis original.]

Later Gurdjieff makes the astonishing claim that the origin of The Fourth Way is prehistoric Egypt. "It will seem strange to many people when I say that this prehistoric Egypt was Christian many thousands of years before the birth of Christ, that is to say, that its religion was composed of the same principles and ideas that constitute true Christianity.... The Christian church, the Christian form of worship, was not invented by the fathers of the church. It was all taken in ready-made form from Egypt, only not from the Egypt that we know but from one we do not know. This Egypt was in the same place as the other but it existed much earlier."

In other words, the teaching *predates* all the known teachings and religions, even Christianity as commonly known. Still later, he speaks of four principal lines: Hebraic, Egyptian, Persian, and Hindu.[45] And of the mixtures of these lines,

---

44. This is the first record of Gurdjieff making the distinction between Christianity as commonly known and its esoteric form. In his saying, "for those who already know what Christianity is," that is, those who understand the distinction between the exoteric and the esoteric, he will say it is esoteric, that which is hidden, not openly revealed, and presented only to those capable of spiritually evolving. Sufism, Buddhism and other teachings claim The Fourth Way is derivative in that elements of the teaching can be found in their teaching. They say it is a mixture, but it is just the reverse. The Fourth Way *predates* them all as its origin is prehistoric Egypt. Over time elements of the teaching migrated northward and were mixed into these teachings. At their core, each is distinctly opposite to The Fourth Way. Sufism, for example, based in Islam, denies the Christian trinity of Father, Son and Holy Ghost. Buddhism, in its Zen, Tibetan and Vipassana variations, rejects the soul. With Hinduism, the three gunas are fixed, not interchanging. For further discussion, see the documentary trilogy *The Life & Significance of G. I. Gurdjieff* (*Gurdjieff in Egypt, Gurdjieff's Mission* and *Gurdjieff's Legacy*), as well as *The Gurdjieff Journal*, Vol. 3, Nos. 2 and 3.

45. Why the Hebraic is put first is not clear, as the Jews worshipped Set, the god of materialism, until Moses, born of Jewish parents but raised as an Egyptian aristocrat, introduced the Egyptian religion. Freud gives his intuition of what occurred later on in his *Moses and Monotheism*.

with theosophy and Western occultism.[46] Gurdjieff says that as they are mixtures, "attempts to bring them to practical realization give only negative results." Then, speaking of the teaching he brings, he declares unambiguously: "The teaching whose theory is here being set out is *completely self-supporting and independent* of other lines and it has been *completely unknown* up to the present time." [Emphasis added.]

"Some of those who attended our lectures remained dissatisfied," says Uspenskii. "Many said that there was neither love nor feeling in Gurdjieff's system, that it was nothing but cold mathematical calculation and mechanistic theories; others said that there was no morality to be found in it, no Christian principles of serving mankind, no altruism, etc."

Speaking to Gurdjieff about this, Uspenskii is told:

> It is all hypocrisy. They merely want words, behind which they can hide their vanity, their emptiness and self-love. They want love! Yet they would cut my throat because I don't believe what wonderful Christians they are. It is all a lie! They want emotional development side by side with the intellectual. But they do not know what emotional understanding means. Let them feel their own nothingness, that is, what they really are.... If they can feel this nothingness, they will understand of themselves why emotional understanding cannot be taught.... One must have conscience! Morality is only self-consolation.... We teach not morality but conscience. But they don't like it. They say we have no love. And why do they say it? Simply because we do not encourage weakness and hypocrisy but, on the contrary, take off all masks.

1916. Finland. Madame Maximovitch, a wealthy patient of Dr. Stjoernval, offers her country dacha for a weekend meeting. It is about an hour's train ride from Petersburg. Stjoernval, who has been sitting quietly, suddenly exclaims—"Yes! I believe that Georgi Ivanovitch is not less than Christ himself!"[47]

Gurdjieff forcefully cuts Stjoernval off. The meeting resumes. Again, there is a question about the origin of the teaching. Gurdjieff tells the story of the sly man who in an unknown country and an unknown time was walking by a café when he met a devil who was in a very poor way. The sly man invited the devil into the café

---

46. Were Gurdjieff alive today he would no doubt include all the New Age teachings, and particularly the distortions and deviations of his teaching given with Enneagram-psychological mysticism, beauty and third sex friendship, and eclectic diamond glitter.

47. Where Uspenskii's first impression of Gurdjieff was that of a person of power or knowledge, a raja or sheik, Dr. Stjoernval's is that of a loving and suffering Christ. Not surprisingly, Dr. Stjoernval alone of the six (despite protestations of his ever-resistant wife, Elizabeta Grigorievna) will stay with Gurdjieff through all the tumult of the ensuing years until his own death twenty-three years later in Normandy, France. Uspenskii, given his animus toward contemporary religion, must have recoiled at Stjoernval's outburst. He wants nothing to do with devotion. He wants knowledge.

and ordered coffee for him. Asked why he was in such a poor state, the devil said:

"There is no business. I used to buy souls and burn them on charcoal because they had very fat souls that I could take to hell. All my devil friends were pleased. But now all the fires are out in hell because people today have no souls."

The sly man said, "Teach me how to make souls, and I will give you a sign to show which people have souls made by me."

More coffee was ordered, after which the devil said, "Teach people to remember themselves, not to identify and imagine, and after a time they will grow souls."

So the sly man did just that, organizing groups and teaching people to remember themselves. Some students worked very seriously and did, in fact, grow souls. When they died they came to the Gate of Paradise, where on one side stood St. Peter and on the other the devil.

"Can I just ask one question?" the devil would say to each newly arrived soul. "Did you remember yourself?"

"Ahh, yes, certainly," answered the soul.

"Excuse me," the devil would smile and say to St. Peter, "this soul is mine."

This went on for a long time until word got back to earth of what was happening at the Gate of Paradise. Angrily, the sly man's students said to him: "Why do you teach us self-remembering since, when we say we have remembered ourselves, the devil takes us?"

"Did I teach you to say you remembered yourselves?" answered the sly man. "I taught you not to talk."

"But it's St. Peter and the devil," protested the students.

"But have you seen these people, the devil and St. Peter, at group meetings? Very well, don't talk. You see, I not only made an arrangement with the devil, I also made a plan to deceive him. But if you talk..."

Gurdjieff's unpredictable actions, some seemingly so irrational, continue to bother Uspenskii. Rather than suffer his reactions and identifications, the idea gradually forms in him that there are two sides, or two personalities, to Gurdjieff. One is a serious or positive side; the other "plays." People around Gurdjieff are 'sorted out' by these two sides. Some see his serious side that displays his knowledge, his disinterestedness, his Work. In them, Gurdjieff's "play" produces a struggle of "yes" and "no." Others, seeing the negative or play side, view the positive side as a pretense for getting influence and power over people. Still others are attracted by the negative side. Uspenskii believes it keeps them close to Gurdjieff because it corresponds to their own desires and predilections.

However Uspenskii sees Gurdjieff, there remains the nagging question—*Who is Gurdjieff?* It is a question with which every member of the group wrestles. They only know what he chooses to tell them. And this is very little. He is undoubtedly a man of enormous power and knowledge, in the real sense of those words—of that the group has no doubt. But, all the same, the question remains.

Says Uspenskii: "What he had been born with and what had been given him by schools, if he had passed through a school—we often spoke of this, and some of us came to the conclusion that Gurdjieff was a genius in his own domain, that he had scarcely had to learn, that what he knew could not be learned and that none of us could expect or hope to become like him."

If his history remains unknown to them, then certainly they could judge him by his behavior. But try as they may, they can't see Gurdjieff. The images he presents, his actions from day to day, are unpredictable.

"One could be sure of nothing in regard to him," declares Uspenskii. "He might say something today and tomorrow something altogether different, yet somehow one could not accuse him of contradiction. One had to understand and connect everything together."

25 June 1916. Russia. The Russian army begins a major offensive against the Austro-German armies. Despite unexpected success, the depressed atmosphere in urban areas increases as shortages of consumer goods, particularly food stuffs, grows and inflation rises.

Midsummer 1916. St. Petersburg. Gurdjieff now spends most of his time in Petersburg. Meetings are held almost every evening. Gurdjieff introduces the idea of chief fault, or chief feature. This is the psychological nucleus around which orbits a person's false personality. "Every man's personal work must consist in struggling against this chief fault," says Gurdjieff.

August 1916. Finland. The group meets again at Madame Maximovitch's country home. Uspenskii is in "a state of unusual tension." In order to give a shock to his organism, he has been doing a number of short, very intensive fasts, breathing in certain ways, and doing mental exercises to concentrate his attention.[48]

These shocks have produced a certain emotional state that Uspenskii believes "indispensable" to arriving at the facts of the hidden reality he wishes to penetrate. Gurdjieff, recognizing the change in Uspenskii's vibration and knowing the work he had done with him, begins to work with Uspenskii on a more subtle level. Earlier, in a meeting where the Last Supper was discussed, Gurdjieff had said that people who have developed a second or 'astral' body can communicate with one another at a distance. In other words, telepathy was possible.

In front of the other five students, Gurdjieff humiliates Uspenskii, repeating now openly what Uspenskii had told him "in absolute confidence" about

---

48. From Uspenskii's manner of speaking about this, it seems probable that he did this on his own and not at Gurdjieff's direction. Otherwise, why would he not have mentioned it? The exercises have caused him to be no longer so focused in his head. Sensation and feeling are beginning to function.

Dr. Stjoernval.[49] (Given the doctor's vision of Gurdjieff as Christ, it's not hard to guess what that might be.) For an intellectual of Uspenskii's stripe, the exposure of an inferior "I" had to cut deep. But Uspenskii, always in control of his feelings, reports this unmasking as merely "unpleasant."

Having created the necessary conditions, Gurdjieff now begins to show postures and physical movements. Uspenskii observes that Gurdjieff's muscles are relaxed and that he moves with "astonishing assurance and precision." At a later time, a student more knowledgeable about the body gives this impression of Gurdjieff: "I saw this man in motion, a unit in motion. He was completely of one piece. From the crown of his head down the back of the head, down the neck, down the back and down the legs, there was a remarkable line. Shall I call it a gathered line? It suggested co-ordination, integration, knitness, power.... I was fascinated by the way the man walked. As his feet touched the floor there seemed to be no weight on them at all—a glide, a stride, a weightless walk."

Following this wordless teaching of movement, control, and relaxation, Gurdjieff returns to the question of why the members of the group could not tell the story of their lives and also the thing they had done of which they were most ashamed. The tension in the room rose dramatically.

With Gurdjieff's question, says Uspenskii, "the miracle began." Gurdjieff communicates with Uspenskii wordlessly. "It all started with my beginning to hear his thoughts[50] ... suddenly I noticed that among the words he was saying to us all there were 'thoughts' which were intended for me.... After a while I heard his voice inside me as if it were in the chest near the heart."

Gurdjieff questions Uspenskii telepathically and Uspenskii replies audibly. Stjoernval and Zaharoff are visibly astonished. The "conversation" between Gurdjieff and Uspenskii continues for half an hour.

At one point, Gurdjieff tells Uspenskii there are certain conditions he has to accept or he has to leave the Work. Gurdjieff gives him a month's time to answer. Uspenskii refuses the time, so certain is he of his allegiance and ability to do what Gurdjieff tells him. But Gurdjieff, seeing the dragons with which his student will have to contend, insists on the time limit.

Later, on the verandah with Uspenskii, Stjoernval and Zaharoff, Gurdjieff again speaks to Uspenskii telepathically.

"Something he said about me affected me very strongly," says Uspenskii, "and

---

49. Why does Gurdjieff intentionally break the trust that he has so carefully nurtured? Perhaps he does so because he is preparing to introduce another level of work that demands a new level of trust. Gurdjieff's psychological "betrayal" must emotionally divide Uspenskii who is already emotional but suppressing it. Thus Gurdjieff forces a direct confrontation with the "yes" and "no" of negative emotions. The strange impression which Gurdjieff made in that Moscow café the year before, all the little buried doubts about Gurdjieff must have resurfaced now with a vengeance.

50. It is not the first time. At the end of their first meeting in Gurdjieff's apartment, Uspenskii had a "flash of thought" that he must ask to see Gurdjieff again. But, as he perhaps assumed that all his thoughts were his own, he was shut off from this recognition.

I sprang up from my chair and went into the garden." He wanders about in the forest for an hour or two, finally coming to realize that all Gurdjieff had said earlier, including his own position in the Work, is right.

He realizes "what I had considered to be firm and reliable in myself in reality did not exist." Uspenskii sees that the "I" that accepted the conditions was not real.

"But I had found something else. *I knew that he would not believe me*[51] *and that he would laugh at me if I showed him this other thing. But for myself it was indubitable and what happened later showed that I was right.*" [Emphasis added.]

Uspenskii says later, in regard to his experience in Finland: "There is something in phenomena of a higher order which requires a particular emotional state for their observation and study." In the aftermath of the experience, he also realizes that "certain very definite changes began in my views on myself, on those around me, and particularly on 'methods of action.'" These changes beggar description, but, he says: "I can only say that they were not in any way connected with what *was said* in Finland but that they had come as a result of the emotions which I had experienced there. The first thing I could record was the weakening in me of that extreme individualism which up to that time had been the fundamental feature in my attitude to life. I began to see people more, to feel my community with them more."

September 1916. St. Petersburg. Alexander Protopopov is made acting Minister of the Interior. He has no rank or bureaucratic experience, but he is an amateur occultist and a friend of Grigori Rasputin's, who has urged the appointment on the Tsarina. Protopopov, a small neurotic man with bright, wild eyes that shift all the time, gives the impression of "resembling an excited seal." Rasputin has also successfully requested that the responsibility for the organization of food supplies be transferred to the Ministry of the Interior. So Protopopov controls not only the Okhrana, the tsarist secret police, but also food distribution. He will later be accused of deliberately creating food shortages in order to provoke riots as an excuse for repression.

---

51. It is at this point that the real break with Gurdjieff begins, for here is unconsciously revealed what is characteristic of Uspenskii's personality, namely, a dividing and a hiding to preserve his I. Despite the fact that Gurdjieff had stripped Uspenskii of some of his "I"s, Uspenskii still thinks himself able to judge his teacher's understanding—"I knew that he would not believe me...." And decides that what he has found is the implacable truth—"for myself it was indubitable...."

Uspenskii unwittingly breaks a primary rule of Gurdjieff's teaching of The Fourth Way, namely, that the student cannot keep anything secret from the teacher, that he must give up his lies, identifications, and imagination. The student must continually keep questioning his motivations, perceptions, conclusions. Sincerity must be learned.

If the student is not forthcoming about all of his life, if he withholds something, then this "something" becomes the seat of his "I"-hood. It is this "I" that has to be seen. By not being totally sincere with his teacher, the student breaks the trust and bond between them. Communication thus contracts. The student is no longer open. Evaluation weakens. Rapport ends. The student's leaving only awaits a trigger event justifying his leaving. Re-hypnotized, few return.

Gurdjieff arrives from Moscow and rents quarters on the Liteiny nearer to Uspenskii. He has a severe chill and meets with people only in small groups. Uspenskii has not seen him since Finland. He is somewhat uncertain about his experience there. He asks if it is true that what Gurdjieff had said in Finland had frightened him. And, if so, why had he been frightened? Gurdjieff replies that if it's true that he was frightened, it only means he is not yet ready. Despite Uspenskii's questions, he will say nothing else.

Interestingly, on this visit Gurdjieff centers his talks around chief feature, or chief fault. He tells his pupils that they must find a way to struggle with it and to eliminate its involuntary manifestation. He points out his pupils' chief features, telling one that he is never at home; another that he does not exist at all; another has no shame; another, no conscience. In some people, he says their chief feature, or chief weakness, is so well hidden behind their various formal manifestations that its discovery is difficult. In this case, the person himself is the chief feature and in this sense Gurdjieff refers to Uspenskii's as "Pyotr Demianovich."

In a later meeting Gurdjieff tells people that they cannot go any further until they come to a definite decision about the Work and him, as "a half-serious attitude could give no results whatsoever." Of the thirty or so people who have gathered around him only two leave. "It is difficult to climb the hill but very easy to slide down it," says Gurdjieff.

October 1916. Moscow. Uspenskii visits Gurdjieff in his new apartment on the Bolshaya Dmitrovka. The walls and floors are covered with carpets and silk shawls hang from the ceilings.[52] Gurdjieff's Moscow pupils come and go. In comparison to the usual banal talking and roles people adopt when together, Uspenskii notices they are "not afraid to keep silent," some not uttering a word for hours. The silence is not heavy or psychological but supportive.

At one of the talks Gurdjieff asks Uspenskii what is the most important thing he has learned so far. "The experiences, of course, which I had in August [the telepathy in Finland]," he answers. If he could evoke such experiences at will, he believes he could discover everything else. But he sees that for this he would have to be able to create the necessary emotional state.

Gurdjieff explains that for this sacrifice is necessary. Not only must one sacrifice one's fantasies but also one's suffering.

> A man will renounce any pleasures you like, but he will not give up his suffering. This is how man is made—there is nothing he is so attached to as his suffering. And yet one must free oneself from suffering. Those who are not free from it, who have not sacrificed their suffering, cannot work. Nothing can be attained without suffering—but, at the same

---

52. The decorations accord with Paul Dukes' description of Prince Ozay's apartment in St. Petersburg.

time, one must learn to sacrifice one's suffering. In truth they must sacrifice only what they imagine they have, which in reality they have not got. They must sacrifice their fantasies. But this is difficult for them, very difficult. It is much easier to sacrifice real things.

Late October 1916. St. Petersburg. Uspenskii is mobilized and commissioned in the Guards Sappers and posted to regimental headquarters not far from his home. He will be demobilized three months later because of his acute myopia. He meets Sophia Grigorievna Maximenko, a forty-two-year-old divorcée. Whether or not they marry remains questionable, but she does adopt his last name, thereafter being addressed as "Madame Uspenskii."[53]

Sometime this year Anna Ilinishna meets an Englishman, Charles Hewitt, who had come to St. Petersburg as a representative of a British timber importing company. Anna Ilinishna's family had a room available and Hewett stayed there for several months. They will marry the following year.

November–December 1916. Moscow. Uspenskii and others begin to travel to Moscow for meetings as Gurdjieff is in ill health. Gurdjieff's teaching, Uspenskii says, "gave us a certain feeling of confidence and security. We often spoke at this time of how we should feel in the midst of all this chaos [the brewing revolution] if we had not got the system." At this period Gurdjieff, no doubt sensing the impending chaos that would soon engulf all of Russia, introduces the subject of Noah's Ark. Uspenskii had long thought this myth to be an allegory for the esoteric work. The teaching was an "ark" by which students could save themselves during the "flood."

Gurdjieff again brings up the subject of suffering and adds the idea of the emotional center. Uspenskii says he realizes that something new can come only through feeling because the mind is obviously too limited. "So how to awaken feelings?" he asks.

"The only way is by suffering," says Gurdjieff. "The emotional center is composed of two halves, one positive, the other negative, of pleasant feelings and unpleasant feelings, of joy and suffering. In the positive part our possibilities are very limited. We cannot increase the power of enjoyment. If I put a lump of sugar in my mouth, it will taste sweet, that is, pleasant. But if I put ten lumps of sugar in my mouth, it will not be ten times sweeter. It is impossible to increase the sweetness."

---

53. The likelihood is she did not marry him. Sophia Grigorievna was born in 1874 and so was four years older than Uspenskii, and much experienced having been twice married. The first marriage was to a student when she was sixteen, later to a mining engineer with whom she traveled to remote areas of Russia. A son was killed early in his life and her daughter would be old enough to give birth to a grandchild in 1919. How Uspenskii and she met and how his relationship with Anna Butkovskaia ended is not known. Interestingly, though she met Gurdjieff when he first came to St. Petersburg, she is not mentioned as a member of the group until Essentuki.

"But suffering can be increased. Our power over suffering is much greater than over enjoyment. Consequently we can intensify the work of the emotional center only by intensifying suffering."

"But you say at the same time," says Uspenskii, "that we must 'sacrifice our suffering,' free ourselves from suffering."

"Yes, at the same time it is necessary to sacrifice one's suffering," answered Gurdjieff, "but this is a very different kind of suffering. A man may suffer all his life and may get nothing from it except new sufferings. And he may suffer for a comparatively short time and receive a great deal for it."

"But how to make oneself feel more?" Uspenskii asks.

"Well this is exactly what I am speaking about," Gurdjieff answers.

"What is it that hinders it most?" Uspenskii says.

"The Moon hinders it most of all," Gurdjieff says. "It is the chief obstacle in the way of changes. It keeps everything in the state in which it actually is. A man who wants to change something in himself must free himself from the Moon."

"But how can we free ourselves from the Moon, if it controls everything living?"

"You must create your own Moon," says Gurdjieff. "The whole problem is in this."

At some point during their meetings Gurdjieff speaks of being "born." Gurdjieff says that this new growth of essence, the appearance of I, means awakening to one's nothingness, the absolute recognition of one's mechanicality and helplessness. What prevents such awakening is that man is hypnotized. He then relates an Eastern story about a very rich magician who has a large number of sheep he keeps for their flesh and skins. Not wanting to hire shepherds or build a fence to keep the sheep from being troublesome and wandering off, the magician hypnotizes them, suggesting that they are immortal and that he, the magician, is a good master who loves them all very much. He suggests to them that if anything bad was to happen to them, it would certainly not happen right then and so there is no need to think about it and, finally, he tells them that they are not sheep at all. To some he confides they are really eagles, to others, men; and to a third group . . . magicians, a code word for teacher.

16 December 1916. Restaurant Palkin, Nevsky Prospekt, St. Petersburg. The composer Thomas de Hartmann, an aristocrat and Guards officer, who lives with his wife, Olga, in Tsarskoye Selo, near the Tsar's residence, meets Zaharoff who takes him to a building near the Nikolaevsky Station. He then leads de Hartmann to the second floor where a café is hidden away. The café, an obvious hangout for prostitutes, pimps, and the trash of the city, is a shock. Seeing no one he knows, he is relieved for otherwise, as he says afterward, "I would have had to leave my regiment."

Sitting at a corner table in the rear is Gurdjieff. When de Hartmann sits down, Gurdjieff casually scans the room and murmurs, "There are usually more whores here." Several more times he tests de Hartmann. Finally he accepts him on the condition of the customary payment of one thousand rubles. He has de Hartmann contact Uspenskii, who will inform him of all that has been said in their meetings up to now. Of Uspenskii, de Hartmann says: "From the start he made a very strong impression on me. He was simple, courteous, approachable, and intelligent.... In an amazingly simple and clear way he knew how to explain the complicated scheme of worlds, planets, cosmoses, and so forth."

16–17 December 1916. St. Petersburg. Fearing Rasputin's increasing influence over the Tsarina, Prince Felix Yusupov, along with other nobles, murders Rasputin. First he poisons him and when that fails he shoots "the holy devil" three times. Rasputin's body is wrapped in a heavy linen sheet and driven to Petrovsky Island where it is dumped from a bridge through a hole in the ice. Rasputin has prophesied that if he is murdered by the nobility it will bring down the whole country. It is in December, too, that Protopopov is now made full Minister of the Interior.

Before the year's end Gurdjieff introduces the subject of religion and prayer, and what might be called religious "techniques." He goes on to say that humanity is at a "standstill" in its development and risks "a straight path to downfall and degeneration." All around, one sees the growth of personality, the artificial, the unreal, and automatism. "Contemporary culture requires automatons," says Gurdjieff. He again speaks of The Fourth Way, saying that it has no definite forms and is seemingly never permanent in that it appears and disappears.[54]

January 1917. St. Petersburg. Heavy snowfalls and a temperature of twenty-two degrees below zero. The city receives only thirty thousand pounds of flour a day instead of the normal two hundred thousand. Sugar becomes scarce, forcing working people, who suck their tea through a sugar cube, to drink it straight. A small helping of potatoes which cost 15 kopecks before the war, is now hard to find at 1.2 rubles. The Okhrana, the tsarist secret police, reports to the Tsar that "With every day the food question becomes more acute. Never before has there been so much swearing, argument, and scandal. That the population has not yet begun food riots does not mean that they will not in the nearest future."

9 February 1917. Uspenskii's apartment, St. Petersburg. Thomas de Hartmann brings his wife, Olga, to a group meeting. Both the de Hartmanns are thirty-one years old and accomplished—he a composer and conductor, she an opera singer. Dr. Stjoernval, who acts as the group's leader, asks the group of fifteen or so people whether they had given any thought to the question from the last meeting: "What is the main thing that hinders a man the most in advancing on the way in self-development?" One person answers money, another fame, another love.

54. Its appearance and disappearance is esoteric and so Gurdjieff can say it is unknown up to the present day.

Gurdjieff slips into the room, "like a black panther—bald, great black moustache and fiery black eyes," according to Olga, and sits cross legged on the sofa. He says in a low serious voice: "Yes, it is true that love is the greatest hindrance, but what kind of love? People call everything love, there are so many meanings to it. There is a kind of love for everyone, but in that you are very far away. But ordinary love, when it is only a kind of animal attraction certainly hinders. But ... love between husband and wife, if they have the same aim in life, is not a hindrance, just the contrary, it can only help."

Later, she meets with Gurdjieff alone and asks if her husband could somehow avoid going to the front. "Mr. de Hartmann is an officer so he has to go, but he should not fall under the psychosis of the war. As the war will go quickly, it will soon be over. Then revolution will begin with all its force. Try to find out where I will be and come." He tells her as well: "When you live among wolves, you have to howl like a wolf; but you should not be taken over by the psychosis of war, and inside you should try to be far removed from all this."

"What do you expect from me?" he asks. She says she is afraid he will laugh at her.

"No, tell me," he says in a very pleasant tone, like an adult speaking to a child. "I will not laugh, perhaps I can help you."

"The only thing I wish from you," she says, "is that you don't spoil my happiness with my husband."

He tells her, in effect, it would not be spoiled, only that her horizons would become much, much bigger.

At a later meeting, Gurdjieff introduces the subject of the intelligence or the consciousness of matter. He says that in nature there is nothing dead or inanimate. He relates the degree of denseness of vibration, or speed of vibration, to the degree of intelligence, while the denseness of matter corresponds to less intelligence. Later, he speaks of the Diagram of Everything Living, which shows how the kind of creature and every degree of being is determined by what it eats and what eats it.

Several days later when Thomas de Hartmann is to leave for the Austrian front in the Ukraine, he asks Gurdjieff's advice about his military service. "You are an officer and you must go to the front, but never let yourself be seized by the war psychosis. Remember yourself.... Don't forget to remember yourself."

Though de Hartmann had few meetings with Gurdjieff he had come to a mature understanding of the teaching. As he said:

> Faith in his teaching is not required. Quite the opposite is necessary, in fact. The teacher, while constantly directing and observing the pupil, at the same time changes his course, diverts him, even provokes him with apparent contradictions, in order to lead him to find out himself what is true. This is possible only if the pupil has within him the strongest urge

to persevere, a burning wish that will not permit him to be stopped by any obstacle.

14 February 1917. St. Petersburg. Ninety thousand strikers demonstrate on the Nevsky. They carry banners reading—"Down with the war! Down with the government."

18 February 1917. St. Petersburg. Because of the severe weather, throughout the country 60,000 railway cars containing food, fodder, and fuel stand frozen on their tracks. Food and fuel grow scarce. Only ten days supply of flour remains in storehouses.

20 February 1917. St. Petersburg. Rumors spread that the government plans to introduce bread rationing. Grocery shelves are quickly stripped of all available food. Having no fuel, factories begin to lay off workers and close. Worker strikes begin.

23 February 1917. St. Petersburg. Weather conditions radically change; the winter temperature soars to forty-six degrees with sunny skies. Masses of people stream outdoors to bask in the sun. With alcohol prohibited, many are drinking *khanzhn*, a homemade brew of fermented bread reinforced with cleaning fluids. Thousands of women from the Vyborg, the working-class district across the Neva from the Winter Palace, march in a parade for the International Women's Day carrying signs such as "If a woman is a slave, there will be no freedom. Long live equal rights for women."

25 February 1917. St. Petersburg. Thousands attend a meeting at Vicholayevsky Station. People call for an end to food shortages and the war. Cossack troops do not interfere and many even fraternize with the crowd. A mounted policeman is shot by a cossack and the police fire into the crowd. The Okhrana make many arrests.

26–27 February 1917. St. Petersburg. Some 160,000 soldiers of the Petersburg garrison mutiny. Riots, looting, assaults on officers. Forty people are killed at Znamenski Square.

With the smell of impending revolution hanging in the streets, Gurdjieff prepares to leave by train for the Caucasus. Before going he meets with his students and gives them the sense and feeling of being "ordained," as Anna Ilinishna puts it. "I felt myself growing in the understanding of abstract subjects," she says, "and I noticed that this development also occurred in the other members of the group."

> We had all been sitting together, deep in thought, our heads bowed, thinking hard, when something made us turn towards Gurdjieff, and we

heard him say, in a voice they had never before heard, one both solemn and abstract and with an element of love—and yet quite abstract—"You started the Quest. You are on the road. You must go on."

One of the group said: "I will go on, Georgi Ivanovitch, because you have put us on the right road."

Gurdjieff said, "I will try to hammer into your heads as much as I can of that special knowledge you are after, what Uspenskii calls 'seeking the Miracle.' There will be others coming to join our group, and they, too, will gradually progress. The only condition is that they must make the maximum effort to absorb what they hear, either from me or from one of you six."

Uspenskii and some of the group then accompany Gurdjieff to Nikolaevsky Station. After boarding the train, he comes to the window of his compartment. He is no longer the "Gurdjieff" they know. To Uspenskii he looks to be "a ruling prince or a statesman of some unknown kingdom."

Alexandr Amfiteatrov, a well-known journalist, is also on the train and a few days later he writes an article which Uspenskii reads. It is about a strange Oriental he has met on the train, a man he has taken to be an "oil king." They speak of war with Germany and the oil king notes that "everyone wants to be a millionaire."

Amfiteatrov asks, "And you?"

"We always make a profit. It [the war] does not refer to us. War or no war it is all the same to us. We always make a profit."

As Uspenskii notes, Gurdjieff is speaking of esoteric work, not oil or money. But Gurdjieff has left. He has said nothing. Left them all in question. Is he coming back or not?

Search for the Miraculous

Ioannis Giorgiades

Paul Dukes

Sergei Dmitrievich Mercourov

Georgi Ivanovitch Gurdjieff

P. D. Uspenskii as a child

Anna Ilinishna Butkovskaia

P. D. Uspenskii

Search for the Miraculous

P. D. Uspenskii in Ceylon

Dr. Leonid Robertovich Stjoernval

Elizabeta Stjoernval

Georgi Ivanovitch Gurdjieff

Thomas de Hartmann

Olga de Hartmann

Sophia Grigorievna Maximenko, later addressed as Madame Uspenskii, as a young girl (above) and as a young woman (left)

Part II

Higher Dimensions

2 March 1917. St. Petersburg. Tsar Nicholas II abdicates in favor of his brother, Grand Duke Michael, who is persuaded not to accept. The provisional government is formed with firebrand lawyer Alexander Kerensky as its head.

6 March 1917. St. Petersburg. With the fall of the tsar, all political prisoners are freed. From Siberia comes Dzhugashvili, a Georgian Bolshevik. Only five feet four inches tall, his face pockmarked, his left arm withered, the result of childhood blood poisoning, Dzhugashvili is known as "Stalin," meaning "Man of Steel."[1] He and another Bolshevik political prisoner take over *Pravda*, a local revolutionary newspaper. Much later the Bolsheviks call themselves "Communists."

March 1917. St. Petersburg. Anna Alekseevna Kamenskaia, Russia's leading theosophist, lauds the revolution.

> What a great and all-encompassing mission has been assigned our beloved Society! A free Russia will now take her honored place among enlightened peoples and soon will probably be called upon to play a great role in world history, having voiced her particularly 'Russian word' on the questions of the reorganization of social, human, and international relations. Political and social questions will naturally come to the fore and the heated work of building wisely on new lines will attract all hearts, devoted to the Motherland. The Theosophists will of course participate in this work.

24 March 1917. St. Petersburg. Uspenskii gathers the principal members of the Petersburg group at Dr. Stjoernval's home. He tells them that the short period of relative calm they are now experiencing is an illusion and everything will soon break up and collapse. As they can do nothing to help, and their own group work here would be impossible, Uspenskii declares that in his opinion, "there is no sense whatever in staying in Russia and we must go abroad." His words are taken as an exaggeration and greeted with little approval. Most, he says, do not realize the true import of what the revolution will bring. Others are "in the grip of the customary illusion that everything that happens is for the best."

Soon after this meeting Uspenskii receives a postcard from Gurdjieff written in February just before the revolution, saying he is going to Alexandropol and asking Uspenskii to "continue the work of the groups until his arrival." He promises to return by Easter.

27 March 1917. Switzerland. Lenin, the exiled Bolshevik leader, has negotiated with Germany to allow his return to Russia. The Germans believe that Lenin's lust for power is so great that he will topple the Provisional Government, take over, and withdraw Russia from the war. The German Foreign Ministry requests five million marks for "Russian work" and allows Lenin to cross its territory in a sealed train.

---

1. It was a name given to him in prison. For when prisoners had to walk between a line of guards with truncheons, everyone ducked and covered their heads except Dzhugashvili who walked upright and without flinching. Growing up, his alcoholic father had beaten him so often that he was inured to pain. Stalin was born in 1879 and there are rumors that Gurdjieff knew him. Says Bennett, "I certainly myself heard Gurdjieff say that he had known Stalin and had been at the seminary with him." But Gurdjieff is prone to say many things. Gurdjieff was *never* a student at the Tiflis Theological Seminary where Stalin was a student from 1894 until expelled in 1898.

Spring 1917. St. Petersburg. With still no word from Gurdjieff, Uspenskii begins to look through his notes of a year earlier. Again, he is struck by the similarity of Gurdjieff's presentation of the seven cosmoses to his own period of dimensions. He remembers Gurdjieff's words: "Time is breath." With this idea as key, the whole idea of cosmoses of zero to infinity opens up for him in a new way. He comes to a completely unexpected confirmation of his own ideas through defining the present as the direct sensation of the inhalation and exhalation of breath. For a man, a complete breath is three seconds; for the earth, it is eighty years. He creates a table relating the cosmoses to the period of their breath.

April 1917. Russia. Eighty percent of Russians are peasants. Land seizures rise fivefold. Prices increase dramatically. A pair of shoes that cost five to eight rubles before 1914, now costs forty rubles. A bag of rye flour which cost six rubles now costs forty rubles. A potato which cost one ruble then now costs seven rubles.

3 April 1917. Finland Station, St. Petersburg. A short, stocky forty-six-year-old man arrives — bald with a reddish beard, his slanted eyes and high cheekbones give him a feral look. He steps briskly off the train, mounts an armored car to speak to a throng of people awaiting him. His manner is brusque, often punctuated with a high, sarcastic laugh. But he utters the words the people have long waited to hear: "Peace, land, and bread." By "peace" he means not only the withdrawal from the war with Germany but also the overthrow of capitalism. By "land" he means the confiscation of the estates of the wealthy. Later at the Kshesinskaia mansion, the Bolshevik headquarters, he speaks again, insisting that the transition from "bourgeois-democratic" to "socialist" revolution be accomplished in a matter of months.[2] A member of the audience remembers:

> I cannot forget Lenin's speech, like lightning, which shook up and astonished not only me, a heretic accidentally thrown into delirium, but also the true believers. No one had expected anything like it. It seemed as if all the elemental forces had risen from their lairs and the spirit of universal destruction, which knew no obstacles, no doubts, neither human difficulties nor human calculations, circled in Kshesinskaia's hall above the heads of the enchanted disciples.

---

2. Lenin, to put himself in accord with Marxist thought, argues that Russia's economy is capitalist, not agrarian. Marx had said that economies pass through three stages: agrarianism, capitalism, then socialism. Lenin wants Russia to bypass capitalism (just as China's Mao would do later in the century).

3. Eight years later, in writing *Beelzebub's Tales,* Gurdjieff will speak of a certain Lentrohamsanin, one of the 313 *Hasnamussian*-Eternal individuals, who, among their other endearing traits, have "the irresistible inclination to destroy the existence of other breathing creatures" and "the feeling of self-satisfaction from leading others astray." Some believe Gurdjieff took Lenin and Trotsky as models for such an individual.

7 April 1917. St. Petersburg. Lenin's "April Thesis" is published in *Pravda*. Among the provisions it calls for: no backing of the war with Germany; immediate transition to the second phase of the revolution; refusal to support the Provisional Government; transfer of all power to the Soviets; confiscation of all landlord property and nationalization of all land; the creation of a single national bank under Soviet supervision; and the Soviet control of production and distribution. A German agent in Stockholm cables Berlin: "Lenin's entry into Russia successful. He is working exactly as we wish."

Easter 1917. St. Petersburg. Uspenskii still has heard no word from Gurdjieff. A week later, however, he receives a telegram. Gurdjieff says he will return to St. Petersburg in May.

21 April 1917. St. Petersburg and Moscow. The first Bolshevik demonstrations occur in Russia's two major cities.

May 1917. St. Petersburg. Uspenskii has been expecting Gurdjieff's arrival with every passing day. But to no avail.

3 June 1917. St. Petersburg. At the First All Russian Congress of the Soviets, Lenin declares "our party is ready to assume full power at any time." He calls for the arrest of "fifty to one hundred of our richest millionaires."

Early June 1917. St. Petersburg. Uspenskii receives a telegram from Gurdjieff in Alexandropol—"If you want to rest come here to me."
Within two days, Uspenskii leaves Petersburg by train.
The Caucasus lies some thirteen hundred miles south of Petersburg. With the increasing turmoil, instead of the usual three days, it takes five days to reach Tiflis. Throughout the trip Uspenskii hardly sleeps, slumbering in an armchair. The train station at Tiflis is jammed with soldiers, many wild and drunk. A glass door separates the buffet from the railway platform outside. Suddenly, from the platform, Uspenskii hears several shots.
Soldiers rush into the buffet, shouting, "Comrades, do not worry. We have only shot a thief."
The thief is said to have stolen three rubles from someone's pocket.
An hour or so passes. More shots, more cries. Another thief executed. Towards daybreak, a third shot. Another thief shot, but he turns out to be a policeman. Uspenskii peers through the glass door. Three bloodstained bodies are sprawled on the platform.
He observes that the soldiers are friendly toward the citizens. But Uspenskii knows this is only the beginning.
"Everybody was still getting bread and shoes," he says. "But it is quite clear

that as soon as there should be no bread and shoes, those with guns would get bread and shoes from those without guns."

June 1917. Alexandropol. Finally, after seven days of travel, Uspenskii reaches Alexandropol. In the Greek quarter he finds Gurdjieff setting up a dynamo for his brother, Dmitri Ivanovitch. He meets Gurdjieff's family, the Giorgiades—Ioannis, his father,[4] who is Greek; Evdokia, his mother, who is Armenian; and perhaps Gurdjieff's wife, Julia Osipovna Ostrowska.[5] They are people, Uspenskii says, of "a very old and very peculiar culture." Gurdjieff's relationship with his father impresses Uspenskii. They are obviously very close and loving. The father is "a robust old man of medium height, with an inevitable pipe in his mouth and wearing an astrakhan cap," a storyteller, an *ashokh*. An early photo of Gurdjieff hanging in the living room shows that he earned his living as a physician and hypnotist at one time. Outside, standing on a hill at a nearby ancient Armenian cemetery, Uspenskii sees in the distance the snowy peaks of Mount Ararat, the location where myth says Noah's Ark anchored during the Flood.

4 July 1917. St. Petersburg. The Bolshevik putsch is quelled by release of information about Lenin's dealings with the Germans. Lenin goes into hiding and ends up in Finland.

July 1917. St. Petersburg. At Kerensky's bidding, the Russian Army mounts an offensive against Austro-Hungarian troops in Galacia. Declares Kerensky: "No army can remain in indefinite idleness.... For the sake of her future, Russia had to perform this historic sacrifice." After initial successes, several hundred thousand men are lost. The army begins to disintegrate.

Early July 1917. Alexandropol. In the morning Gurdjieff and Uspenskii prepare to leave for Petersburg. Of the many questions he has asked his father, he now asks whether man has a soul and whether it is immortal?
"How shall I put it?" Gurdjieff's father answers. "In that soul which a man supposedly has, as people believe, and of which they say that it exists independently, after death and transmigrates, I do not believe; and yet, in the course of man's life, 'something' does form itself in him: this is for me beyond all doubt.
"As I explain it to myself, a man is born with a certain property and, thanks to this property, in the course of his life certain of his experiencings elaborate in him a certain substance, and from this substance there is gradually formed in him

---

4. Gurdjieff says, "I saw my father for the last time in 1916," *Meetings with Remarkable Men*, 45. Given what Uspenskii says, this must be a mistake.
5. Her parents are Osip Ostrowska and Marie Fédérowska Misich, according to Moore, but he gives no source. Though considered to be Gurdjieff's wife, as he refers to her, she continues to use her maiden name. It is rumored that Gurdjieff may have previously married a woman in Tibet.

'something or other' which can acquire a life almost independent of the physical body.

"When a man dies, this 'something' does not disintegrate at the same time as the physical body, but only much later, after its separation from the physical body.

"Although this 'something' is formed from the same substance as the physical body of a man, it has a much finer materiality and, it must be assumed, a much greater sensitivity towards all kinds of perceptions ... this 'something,' both before a man's death and afterwards until its disintegration, reacts to certain surrounding actions and is not free from their influence."

Leaving Alexandropol and passing through Tiflis, their train stops at one of the small stations between Baku and Derbent. While there, Uspenskii tells Gurdjieff: "Events are against us. It is now clear that it is not possible to do anything in the midst of this mass madness."

Gurdjieff disagrees. "It is only now that it is possible, and events are not against us at all. They are merely moving too quickly. This is the whole trouble. But wait five years and you will see for yourself how what hinders today will prove useful to us."

Though Uspenskii doesn't understand then, later he says, "Looked at from the point of view of 'facts,' it was difficult to imagine in what way we could be helped by events in the nature of 'civil war,' 'murder,' epidemics, hunger, the whole of Russia becoming savage, and then the endless lying of European politics and the general crisis which was undoubtedly the result of this lying.

"But looked at, not from the point of view of 'facts,' but from the point of view of esoteric principles, then what G. meant becomes more comprehensible.

"Why were there not these ideas earlier? Probably precisely because these ideas could come only in such a time when the attention of the majority is distracted in some other direction and when these ideas can reach only those who look for them. I was right from the point of view of 'facts.' Nothing could have hindered us more than 'events.' At the same time it is probable that precisely the 'events' made it possible for us to receive what we had."

During the journey, their train's departure is delayed a long time at one railway station. Taking advantage of the break, Uspenskii speaks to his teacher about the division of oneself into I and 'Uspenskii'—and asks how one can strengthen the feeling of I and strengthen the activity of I?

Gurdjieff tells him that he can't do anything about that. "This should come as a result of all your efforts," he says. By now he should have a different feeling of his I. Uspenskii says he did not have this feeling of I.

6. A student's questions, their subject matter, intent, and the clarity with which they are formulated, are important because they show the level and direction at which the student is searching. They also give a forefeeling of the future. Here, with this question, it is seen that Uspenskii now

At Mozdok, on the third day of their trip from Tiflis, Gurdjieff appears to suddenly change plans. He will remain in the Caucasus and Uspenskii is to continue alone to Moscow and Petersburg. He is to give a message to Gurdjieff's students: "Tell them I am beginning new work here. Those who want to work with me can come."

Not only has Gurdjieff dashed Uspenskii's plans for escaping abroad, he now directs him to return alone to the center of madness. Uspenskii is not afraid of the physical danger but of "acting stupidly." The future of revolutionary Russia is obvious. It's illogical, stupid, not to leave. But Gurdjieff has made this decision for him. This must really grate on him, but of this Uspenskii will only say: "Now all responsibility towards myself seemed to have been taken from me."

10 July 1917. St. Petersburg. Kerensky asks forty-seven-year-old General Lavr Georgevich Kornilov, son of a Siberian Cossack, to assume command of the armed forces.

Mid-July 1917. Essentuki. Despite the growing hazard of these days, Uspenskii and Madame Uspenskii, Anna Ilinishna and eleven others make their way to the village of Essentuki nestled in a green valley in the northern foothills of the Caucasus near Mount Elbrus. On the outskirts, Gurdjieff rents a country villa, the first of many he will rent in the Caucasus. Uspenskii and six others live here with Gurdjieff, while the rest will lodge elsewhere. Work at the villa begins early in the morning and continues late into the evening.

One day Nicholas Evreinoff, Anna Ilinishna's old lover, shows up. Meeting the group on the street, he goes up to Gurdjieff, saying: "I am a difficult, pretentious man. I am ambitious. But here, Georgi Ivanovitch, I bow to you. . . ." Evreinoff stays for a time and then leaves.

Now, in Essentuki, Gurdjieff works with the people who have come to him. For six weeks the work goes on, the people getting only four to five hours sleep a night, doing housework and chores, and the rest of the time doing exercises and listening to lectures. Among the ideas Gurdjieff communicates:

> Schools are imperative.[8] Man can never attain the necessary intensity by himself. Only super-efforts count. Another person's will is necessary. Unison of centers is chief difficulty in working on oneself. Work on the moving center. Tension among group members is indispensable.

approaches the feeling of his own I. He will come to this in Essentuki in 1918.

7. For an intellectual of Uspenskii's caliber, this had to have set up a real struggle between the "yes" and "no" in him. Emotion would have been very strong. It would thus serve to do exactly what Uspenskii asked: How to strengthen his feeling of I. As Uspenskii would answer in a meeting many years afterward: "It is necessary to create a certain particular energy and that can be created only at a moment of very serious emotional stress. All work before that is only a preparation."

8. Later when Uspenskii leaves he will argue that it was never a school. See Essay, "Why I Left Gurdjieff."

Sole possibility of other centers working in a new way is to begin with moving center. Relaxing the muscles. Yoga postures.[9] Circular sensation. Feeling the pulse throughout the body. Stop exercise. Voluntary silence. Voluntary suffering. Fasting. Breathing.[10] Fourth Way. Obyvatel. Only one thing is serious—freedom. Nothing worse than to begin to work on oneself and then to leave it and find oneself between two stools.

For Uspenskii, who from the beginning secretly kept notes of the meetings, these six weeks in Essentuki were a time of unparalleled richness. Gurdjieff provides a detailed map, as well as exercises and postures, the "new or forgotten road to the miraculous" for which Uspenskii had so long sought. Standing in the yard of the country villa in the silent early morning and looking out at the cloud-covered top of Mount Elbrus, at over eighteen thousand feet the highest of the Caucasus mountains, Uspenskii must have felt he stood at its top. And yet he says, "I always have a very strange feeling when I remember this period."[11]

He reports that all does not go well with the group. Hard feelings develop between certain members. Given the intensive nature of the work and the close quarters this is not surprising. And, as Gurdjieff has told them, a "certain tension is indispensable" for chipping away attitudes. At one point Gurdjieff brings up what Uspenskii has formulated as the "St. Petersburg conditions" in which he is responsible for the St. Petersburg students. Gurdjieff tells him that he is responsible for both the St. Petersburg and Moscow students. Uspenskii protests, it is not what was agreed upon, it's not fair, not rational. Nevertheless, Gurdjieff, stepping on Uspenskii's corns, insists he is responsible.

Friction increases, an event occurs, which Uspenskii does not specify. Uspenskii sees it as "accidental," but Gurdjieff announces he is disbanding the group and ending all work. The apparent irrationality of it all shocks Uspenskii. At first he and the others don't think Gurdjieff is serious, that he is only "playing" or "acting" as usual. Uspenskii cannot fathom Gurdjieff's actions. His confidence in Gurdjieff "began to waver." Instead of eating the shock, enduring and absorbing

9. Among the postures Uspenskii reports Gurdjieff doing are *Padmasana* (the lotus pose) and *Supta Virasana*. In *Supta Virasana* he sat on the floor on his knees, then bent backwards, reclining the torso on the floor, the arms stretched out behind the head. This posture, Uspenskii says, Gurdjieff "could adopt to perfection." (See *Search*, 350.) Gurdjieff says in *Meetings* that he did hatha yoga. Given these poses, and the one-legged, bent knee pose while smoking a cigarette that Tcheslaw Tchekhovitch reports him doing at the Prieuré, Gurdjieff had mastered hatha yoga.

10. Gurdjieff's dire warning about breathing in *Meetings*, 187, has led many people in the Work to believe that any kind of breath work should not be done. But he clearly makes a distinction between 'inflation' and breathing assisted by movements. (See *Search*, 387–88.) Both J. G. Bennett and the de Hartmanns report Gurdjieff giving breathing exercises. A careful reading of his *Beelzebub's Tales* reveals the importance Gurdjieff gives breathing in the work of self-perfection as it relates to Djartklom.

11. In the midst of his elation, the idea now emerges that he must break with Gurdjieff. He gives a number of reasons for this, but the feeling is that there is something more, something he either is not saying or does not himself know.

the suffering, he self-calms by making a fatal separation. The same pattern recurs. A year earlier in Finland with the telepathic experience, Uspenskii had hidden a part of his experience from Gurdjieff—thereby maintaining control by creating a split between what he would and would not tell Gurdjieff. He now makes the split deeper—he separates the teacher from the teaching.[12] There is Gurdjieff the man, and there are the ideas.[13]

August 1917. St. Petersburg. Lenin convinces thirty-eight-year-old Lev Davidovich Trotsky to join the Bolshevik party. Trotsky, whose revolutionary credentials extend back to 1905's Bloody Sunday, is a brilliant firebrand, gifted orator and organizer. His real name was Lev Bronstein; he took "Trotsky" from his Siberian jailer (as Vladimir Ulyanov took "Lenin" from his exile near Siberia's River Lena).

28 August 1917. Essentuki. Thomas and Olga de Hartmann arrive. For the first time they meet Gurdjieff's wife, Julia Osipovna Ostrowska. Says de Hartmann, "She was tall of stature, exceedingly finely formed: a very beautiful woman.... Our first impression was that she was rather remote from her husband's affairs. But we came to see how deeply and seriously she valued the Work of Mr. Gurdjieff."[14] Later, an epidemic raging, Thomas de Hartmann comes down with abdominal typhoid. Taken to a hospital, he did not regain consciousness until three weeks later. It would be several months until he was well enough to return to Essentuki.

Early September 1917. St. Petersburg. Accused by Kerensky of being a traitor, General Lavr Kornilov sends troops to Petersburg to topple the Provisional Government. But they desert and the right-wing putsch fails. Generals Kornilov, Anton Ivanovitch Denikin, and others are imprisoned in a converted monastery in the ancient town of Bykhov.

September 1917. Finland. From his hideout, Lenin writes a series of letters to the Bolshevik Central Committee declaring the time is ripe for the seizure of power.

September 1917. St. Petersburg. Dr. Stjoernval receives a telegram from Gurdjieff—"Terminate all your affairs and your goods and head for the south

---

12. It is tantamount to Peter separating Jesus from the Sermon on the Mount and going on to teach his own version of Christianity as the true version.
13. The act is fatal. The teacher is a living embodiment of the teaching and by splitting the teacher from the teaching, the student unconsciously creates an irreconcilable duality, one for which Uspenskii will sadly pay the rest of his life. Even many years later in writing and rewriting *Search*, Uspenskii could not admit to himself what happened, for he writes, "What the matter was and what particularly provoked me is difficult for me to define even now."
14. This is the first mention of Gurdjieff's wife.

of Russia this month." Selling what they could, he and his wife Elizabeta leave in October. Along the way their baggage is stolen.

15 October 1917. St. Petersburg. Following the teaching in Essentuki, Uspenskii leaves for Petersburg to collect his belongings. The rising famine and anarchy mean he can only pack essentials. He must leave behind his library, an intellectual's chief food. Of these last days in his beloved city Uspenskii says: "Something disgusting and clammy was drawing near. A sickly tension and the expectation of something inevitable could be felt in everything." He saw the Bolsheviks for what they were, "agents of destruction." They destroyed not so much by their actions but "by their very existence which corrupts and disintegrates everything around them. This special property of theirs explained their approaching victory and all that happened much later."

24–25 October 1917. St. Petersburg. The Bolsheviks seize power. (By the Gregorian calendar, it is November 6–7.) Peasants seize land. The economy totters.

Autumn 1917. Sochi. Returning to Sochi, Uspenskii finds that Gurdjieff has taken another country house a little over fifteen miles from the town. Ten people live in the villa, its grounds full of roses. On one side it offers a view of the sea, and on the other a chain of mountains. Despite the beauty, Uspenskii finds the atmosphere greatly changed, not at all like Essentuki.

From Dr. Stjoernval he learns that Gurdjieff and Zaharoff are not speaking. Worse, Zaharoff is preparing to return to Petersburg. The reason is that Gurdjieff had "a very absurd quarrel" with some Lettish neighbors and Zaharoff had manifested in some way so that, from then on, Gurdjieff stopped speaking to him. Uspenskii thinks the situation "pure idiocy," and convinces a reluctant Zaharoff to mend matters with Gurdjieff. Zaharoff finally does so, but Gurdjieff maintains that Zaharoff, having decided to return to Petersburg, should go. "I could not understand it. I would not have let a dog go to St. Petersburg at that time," declares an angry Uspenskii.[15]

15. Unwittingly, Uspenskii here, as elsewhere, puts himself on a level with Gurdjieff, taking himself to be awake enough to judge his teacher's actions. Zaharoff perhaps did the same. Why Gurdjieff acted as he did will never be known, but, given the mounting chaos with which the group is surrounded, the bond of trust between student and teacher had to be unshakable. Hierarchy and discipline are essential if the group is to safely walk the fault line of the psychic earthquake that the Bolsheviks had prepared. With the Letts, perhaps, Gurdjieff had acted—"With a *svolotch* [lowest of the low] I am a *svolotch*. With a good man, I am a good man," Gurdjieff said during this time—and Zaharoff, "Baba," as Gurdjieff named his chief fault, took this "acting" as real. The fact is that psychologically Uspenskii had elevated himself to the chair of the teacher. He believed he could judge Gurdjieff. It is true, however, that Gurdjieff has said to them, "By now you ought better to understand in what my aim consists and by now you ought to see whether you are on the same road as I am or not." Uspenskii may here be shoring up his decision to follow a different road by finding fault with Gurdjieff's actions, thus devaluing the road Gurdjieff is taking. It is interesting to note

November 1917. Bykhov. Facing certain execution at the hands of the Red Guards, the imprisoned generals escape to South Russia. Says General Denikin of what he experienced en route: "I saw clearly unbounded hatred everywhere. Only one desire reigned supreme—to seize and destroy. Its aim seemed to be not to better itself, but to drag down to its level anything that in one way or another stood out or seemed different."

November 1917. Tuapse. Gurdjieff, Uspenskii, and four others live twenty-five miles north of Tuapse in a house on the Black Sea.

December 1917. St. Petersburg. Anna Ilinishna Butkovskaia leaves Gurdjieff to marry the Englishman Charles Hewitt. She and her husband then leave Russia for Paris where she runs a fashionable dress salon and also deals in antiques.

Late December 1917. South Russia. Generals Kornilov, Alekseev, and Denikin form the Volunteer Army, or the White Army, to fight the Bolsheviks. Kornilov takes command in South Russia.

January 1918. Essentuki. After moving to several more villas, Gurdjieff finally returns to Essentuki in January and rents a house. It is unfinished, with all its rooms looking out onto a verandah but having no windows or doors. It was here he founded his Institute though he had yet to give it a name.

12 February 1918.[16] *Essentuki.* Over Uspenskii's signature, Gurdjieff has a circular letter sent out to his pupils in Moscow and Petersburg inviting them to come to him. Showing Uspenskii around the house he has rented, Gurdjieff reminds Uspenskii of his concern of several years before when he asked group members to pay one thousand rubles. Only "one-and-a-half persons" had paid that amount, Gurdjieff tells him, and, he declares, "I have now already spent more than was collected then."

February 1918. St. Petersburg. Anna Kamenskaia urges readers of the theosophical journal *Vestnik Teosofii* to give their support. "At this critical moment in Russian life the voice of *Vestnik* should not be silenced, the hearthfire should not go out. The Editorial Board hopes that those who warmed themselves at this hearthfire will not leave it in this difficult moment and will help to carry forward the light of Eternity into the world." In 1916 its subscription price had been seven rubles; now it is twenty-one rubles. Suffering from the paper shortage and

---

that Gurdjieff uses the word *road* here, which of course corresponds to Uspenskii's seeking what he calls "a new or forgotten road."

16. Dates prior to 1918 are according to the Julian calendar. After 31 January 1918 Russia changed to the Gregorian calendar.

rising printing costs, each issue is smaller than the preceding, until the journal ceases publication.

By the year's end, the Bolsheviks order all religious, occult, or mystical groups to cease activities. Kamenskaia and her followers go into the countryside to meet, but by spring "the Red Wave had flooded the countryside" and they return to the city.[17]

3 March 1918. Brest-Litovsk. As the Germans had predicted, the Communists sign a treaty with Germany withdrawing Russia from the war.

March 1918. Essentuki. Some forty pupils from Moscow and St. Petersburg arrive in Essentuki. From the Petersburg group, besides Uspenskii, are his wife, Sophia, and her daughter, Lenotchka Savitsky; Dr. Stjoernval and his wife Elizabeta; Charkovsky; Nicholas, the government official; Madame Bashmakova; Thomas and Olga de Hartmann; and Zaharoff, still weak from an illness, who has returned. From the Moscow group, there is, besides Gurdjieff's wife, Julia Ostrowska, Alexander Nikorovich Petrov, one of Gurdjieff's chief pupils, highly gifted in mathematics and engineering; Alexei Yakovlevich Rachmilievitch, the Moscow lawyer, one of Gurdjieff's earliest pupils; Lina Fedorovna; Zhukov and his wife; and N. F. Grigoriev. One who comes on his own initiative is P. V. Shandarovsky, a well-educated lawyer who plays the violin, a Guarneri.

Strict rules are immediately established in the house. People are forbidden to leave the grounds by day and security is posted day and night. In time, Gurdjieff asks the group to give a name for their society. Uspenskii suggests "The Society for Struggle Against Sleep," but Gurdjieff feels it is too obvious. Finally, "International Fellowship for Realization Through Work" is selected. Full members are named, the first three being Uspenskii, Petrov, and Dr. Stjoernval. A sign is made. It features two symbols, the pentagram and the enneagram. Every day notices appear on the house bulletin board. One demands that each member break all ties with everyone. There must be no identification. Another notice says that all possessions are to be given up. One notice divides the day into hours, with each hour devoted to inner exercises. Physical exercises are given that are much more strenuous, complex and varied. Movements and dances are given, also given and studied are relaxation, embodiment through sensation, refining of attention, various ways of breathing, and the "Stop Exercise."

One day after Gymnastics, Gurdjieff speaks about real confession. Real confession had no relation to confession in modern day churches. In esoteric schools,

---

17. In 1921, at the behest of Mrs. Besant, Kamenskaia would leave Russia for England. In 1922 the Bolsheviks would open their "antireligious front" in which they closed presses, confiscated literature and published numerous articles castigating occult societies. This would be followed by the exile or arrest of the more prominent members.

confession focused in essence on the necessity for a man to see his own defects, not seeing them as sinful but as hindrances to his self-development. To go to such real confession one had to make a major decision—to see one's real defects and to speak about them. This, Gurdjieff said, "was absolutely essential—especially for one to see his chief feature." Of chief feature, or chief weakness, he said it must be revealed with great care, for the truth about oneself can sometimes cause a real despair and that only a spiritual connection with the teacher can prevent this.

Many evenings are given to lectures, Gurdjieff sitting cross-legged on a sofa, the students sitting about him on the carpet. He began by discussing attention, Thomas de Hartmann remembers him saying that "If we didn't study attention—not study in the ordinary way, but putting all our attention on developing that attention—we would arrive nowhere."

Other subjects included conscience and crystallization of the soul. Of conscience, Gurdjieff says that it must guide us in our actions. It is innate. So we do not have to acquire it but only awaken it, for we are almost always asleep to it. Of the soul, de Hartmann remembers Gurdjieff saying that it "has to be awakened in us, it will be connected with the physical body by a magnetic bond. Through his work with us he temporarily took the place of our soul and so a magnetic bond had to be formed with him, which we recognized and which produced this feeling of nearness." As Gurdjieff told them, "I can lift you to Heaven in a moment, but as quickly as I lifted you up you would fall back down, because you would be unable to hold on. If water does not reach 100 degrees, it is not boiling. So in our development, by our own understanding, we had to reach the boiling point or nothing would be crystallized in us; if only one degree were lacking, we would fall back again."

Uspenskii finally asks the question that has long interested him. "Where did you acquire this knowledge yourself? Has knowledge been preserved in any other places besides those schools, utterly unknown to us, in Chitral or in Tibet? When I go over all that you have said so far in my mind, I seem to hear in your ideas the echoes of the most diverse traditions. There are ideas and even words which seem to me to be of Pythagorean origin. There are ideas which seem to me to be connected with orthodox monasteries. There are ideas with a clear Mohammedan or Sufistic flavour, there are Buddhistic ideas and others from India. But what is the chief thing. Where does it all come from?"

"We will speak of that in due time," says Gurdjieff.

It is now in this country villa that for the next six weeks Gurdjieff opens all the doors to the teaching, for the first time allowing Uspenskii and the others to see, as Uspenskii says, "the plan of the whole work." Not only does Gurdjieff reveal the links, connections, and directions of the teaching, but even the origins of its ideas. In effect, Gurdjieff entrusts them with the keys to the kingdom. He does not say why he does so now, but, given the calamitous conditions and his experiences "with stray bullets," his death is a possibility.

Gurdjieff tells them that twenty-five years before, working as a guide at the pyramids at the Giza Plateau in Egypt, he accidentally met a Russian prince and a professor of archaeology. Each had nearly the same world outlook and understanding of the meaning and aim of life. Each had been searching for that 'something' absolute which existed, but they did not have enough knowledge to come to an understanding of it. They needed a knowledge that encompassed all sides of life. To gain this they agreed to draw to themselves people having different sets of knowledge who had a like desire for this 'something.' Ultimately, some fifteen people, both men and women, joined together; they were Orthodox, Catholic, Muslim, Jewish or Buddhist and specialized in fields such as the mechanical sciences, chemistry, horticulture, astronomy, archaeology and philosophy. They went first to Persia and then in 1899 fanned out in small groups, some going to India through Kashmir, Tibet and Ceylon; others going to Palestine through Turkey and Arabia. After many years they met in Kabul. Now there were only twelve as three had died. They decided to travel to Chitral, but after some time only four, all men, met there. Three years later they returned to Kabul. This was the beginning of the Institute. Five years later they transferred their activity to Russia.

During the group's stay in Essentuki public lectures are given, first with Uspenskii reading a lecture and at another time Petrov reading from his paper about the Ray of Creation. Instead of Gurdjieff lecturing, he has the group put up posters around Essentuki announcing a lecture by the notorious "Dr. Black," a fictional charlatan depicted in satirical poems of the time.

"Why always a suggestion of charlatanism for prospective pupils at the very first meeting?" asks Thomas de Hartmann, and then explains:

> Teachers usually surround themselves with an atmosphere of great seriousness and importance, to give newcomers a good impression. With Mr. Gurdjieff it was just the opposite: everything that could repel, even frighten, a new man was always produced. A newcomer had the opportunity to meet Mr. Gurdjieff and to talk with him, but at once there was put before him some obstacle to be surmounted. On the other hand, Mr. Gurdjieff never let a newcomer go away empty-handed if he came with real questions and spoke about something that was of genuine importance to him.

But even with the older students Gurdjieff "acts" or "plays." And now, as a means of increasing the pressure on the group, he "acts" with everyone. The deceit and hypocrisy of ordinary life always rankles Uspenskii. But, theoretically, of course, as he doesn't find this "playing" always practical.

"In practice," he says, "this 'play' drove away many useful people and kept by him others that were not suitable."

It seems to Uspenskii that Gurdjieff is not always in full control of his manifestations, which is of great concern to him. "What always amazed myself and others in his 'play' was that sometimes it was too obvious not to be seen, as if he were not trying to hide the whole threads at all, or that sometimes he could not stop himself and 'played' by habit automatically, even when and where there was neither use nor meaning in it."[18]

Others, such as Thomas de Hartmann saw it differently: "As the basis of his Work was to create every kind of impression in a pupil for this transformation [to real I], he could accomplish it only through the playing of roles." He gives the example of a pupil needing the experience of injustice and so Gurdjieff plays the unjust man. "Then one had to hold back from reacting badly and not be resentful." He says, "Mr. Gurdjieff told me once that it caused him pain when I was resentful. In other words, a man had to accept intentional suffering. If he simply suffered in the usual way, it was not intentional suffering and had no value." He notes that "There is a constant temptation for the teacher to show his true self, the way he is in reality. But Mr. Gurdjieff knew full well that then everyone would run after him and become his adoring slave." De Hartmann continues, "Under the mask of bad personality, Mr. Gurdjieff became our tempter. As tempter he provoked in us a strong inner experience of feeling and sensation, which in life expresses itself as what some call 'negative emotion,' and then he strove to enable us to transform it by seeing it and reasoning about it.... When the personality is made to suffer, it produces a 'ferment'; one must not avoid this suffering, because this 'ferment,' this 'spark,' this 'fire' feeds essence. What is not good for personality is good for essence."

With the passing of days, Gurdjieff increases the pressure on Uspenskii:

> He wanted to make me submit to his will to a greater extent than was necessary for the needs of the work. From a theoretical point of view I understood perfectly well that if a man wants to become free he must sacrifice his own will, he must give up his own will. It seems to me however that I had already done that when I accepted Gurdjieff's system, the study of the three-dimensional world, which had seemed absurd to me; when I had submitted to the work in groups, contradicting my very being, and most of all when I had remained in Russia and not gone abroad.... I realized the necessity for submission or obedience in work.

---

18. Given Uspenskii's comments at the time, it seems he never appears to see Gurdjieff's "acting" in relation to himself. Like every student, he has difficulty in seeing things involving himself from any but a personal perspective. Yet, at the same time, he invariably distances himself, taking the supposedly impartial stance of the observer. His pet corn is his rejection of all which smacks of the irrational, deceit, the religious, or the cult, and Gurdjieff, of course, has acted accordingly.

> A man who directs a work leads others after him into very dangerous places or very dangerous situations and he must be certain that they will obey him without question because there may be times when he will have to take on himself responsibility for them, but on the other hand submission, the abdication of one's will must always be conscious. . . . If I submitted to him in any particular thing he very soon demanded something more of me, if I accepted this, immediately a new and still more greater demand appeared. When I refused anything it was always taken as extraordinarily tragical. In fact I always resisted everything. I could never overcome my obstinacy. I never made any effort.

Uspenskii speaks of the group disdainfully as having become a "colony." Gurdjieff, he believes, is leading the group "in fact towards the way of religion."[19] Though he does not consider this way wrong, "it is not my way."

"It became perfectly clear to me," says Uspenskii, "that there were some things in Gurdjieff and some of his demands that I could not understand. Some things accumulated [from the summer of 1917 until now] and finally, I saw that I could not remain at the Obschezitie (boardinghouse). I moved my family into a separate house and, after a long interruption in my work, I felt with relief that I was again able to write." He returns to working on the book he began seven years before, *Wisdom of the Gods*, which he will later retitle *A New Model of the Universe*. While he continues to speak with Gurdjieff, he refuses to go to the "Home."

One day Uspenskii meets Gurdjieff in the park. "You are right in one thing," says Gurdjieff, continuing the conversation they had begun about the direction of the Work. "I have tried to go along a definite path, I have tried to give knowledge to people, I have tried to help them to become free independent men. But nothing comes of all this. Now I am going to act quite differently."

"He did not explain himself but I understood what he meant to say," Uspenskii thinks.

"If you knew what I have been through," Gurdjieff says, replying exactly to Uspenskii's thoughts. At this moment one of the members of the Obschezitie appeared in the street, coming toward them. He is comparatively new amongst them but was distinguished by a special devotion to Gurdjieff and an absolute submission to what he demanded.

"I don't know what you have been through," Uspenskii says, "but I know that you have acquired many things somewhere and somehow or else from someone.

---

19. Though the civil war is all around them, Uspenskii doesn't appear to have understood the context in which Gurdjieff put forward the idea of "religion." To stay in Essentuki meant the group would be sitting ducks for the mass psychosis of the time. The group would have to be led over the Caucasus. This meant Gurdjieff would have to take them between two warring armies. A wrong gesture, a false word, and they all could be shot on sight. The situation demanded that the group put their faith and trust in Gurdjieff and do exactly as he said.

At the same time I'll stake my head that you have never been in the same relation to anyone as that man is to you."

Gurdjieff did not answer.

Says Uspenskii, "I felt right in my own eyes. I felt that to conform to the demands which Gurdjieff made as a condition of returning to his work meant for me the renunciation of the aims for the sake of which I had begun my own work. In spite of this, I did not feel quite satisfied. It was very difficult to abandon the idea of collaborating with G. and I thought that sooner or later we should meet again and continue the work we had begun in St. Petersburg."

For Gurdjieff, the pressures he has to live under at this time are extreme. The million rubles he had brought to Russia, the villa and instruments he had purchased for his Institute, the great energy he had invested—all are now gone. Uncertainty and hazard are everywhere and people are acting, he says, like "infuriated beasts, ready to tear one another apart for the slightest booty." Of this period Gurdjieff says:

> For me personally, of all that I went through in Russia, this was the period of most intense nervous strain. All the time I not only had to think and worry about obtaining the most immediate necessities of life, which had become almost unprocurable, but I was also constantly concerned about the lives of the hundred or so people who were in my care.

Spring 1918. Rochester, New York. Nicholas Bessaraboff, a young engineer, had come to America as a member of the technical mission of the Kerensky government just before the Russian Revolution. He had carried with him his treasured copy of *Tertium Organum*. Marooned here, he had begun a translation of the book into English. However, after discovering Claude Bragdon's *Four-Dimensional Vistas*, he thinks the two books so similar that he's sure Bragdon[20] will want to help, and he makes his way to Bragdon's home in Rochester. "He arrived with the book pressed to his heart," says Bragdon, "for it was his Bible." Bragdon agrees with him that *Tertium Organum* is the book that can "revolutionize human thought." Bragdon believes too that the book is the "long sought New Testament of the Sixth Race which will justify the meekness of the saint, the vision of the mystic, and create a new heaven and a new earth." The two men work on the translation together for the next year, Bragdon putting Bessaraboff's literal translation into idiomatic English.

13 April 1918. Ekaterinodar. In an attempt to capture the town, General Kornilov, commander of the Volunteer Army, is killed by a stray shell.

---

20. Along with his fellow architect Frank Lloyd Wright, Bragdon is a disciple of Louis Sullivan who believed that only an "organic architecture" based on nature could support the democratic community and values threatened by the emerging industrial capitalist mass society. In the 1930s this approach would be superseded by International style modernism.

Georgi Ivanovitch Gurdjieff

Forty-five-year-old General Anton Ivanovitch Denikin, former commander of Russia's Western Front assumes command.

15 May 1918. Alexandropol. Turkish soldiers advance into Armenia on a genocidal march. All in Gurdjieff's family flee except his eighty-five-year-old father, Ioannis Giorgiades, who loads his rifle and sits in his doorway awaiting his fate. He is later buried in the old cemetery beneath a red rock.

Mid-summer 1918. Russia. Only a few months after Russia's withdrawal from the European war, a full-scale civil war breaks out.

Mid-July 1918. Essentuki. Quite unexpectedly a cart pulls up in front of Gurdjieff's home. Inside are twenty-eight people, all relatives of his who have fled Armenia. There are his mother; his younger brother, Dmitri Ivanovitch, with his wife and a small child; his youngest sister, Sophie Ivanovna, and her fiancé, Georgilibovitch Kapanadze; another sister, Anna Ivanova Anastasieff, with her husband Feodor and their three children. They bring news that Gurdjieff's father has died protecting their home. Gurdjieff rents a house nearby where they can live.

16–17 July 1918. Ekaterinburg. Tsar Nicholas II, his family and servants are murdered.

August 1918. Germany. A regimental runner receives the Iron Cross, First Class for bravery. The medal is rarely given to a common soldier. The runner's name is Adolf Hitler.

6 August 1918. Essentuki. In the middle of a civil war, with Bolshevik and White Army soldiers on all sides, and everyone in the grip of a mounting mass psychosis with which he is very familiar, Gurdjieff decides he and his followers must do the impossible: leave Russia. Because of the danger and the rigors of the journey, Gurdjieff leaves his family behind.

To get out, the Caucasus must be crossed. The main range of Caucasus mountains is some seven hundred and fifty miles long and over one hundred miles wide. The terrain is often rugged, the roads are poor, and, besides the civil war, there are bandits. The journey seems foolhardy enough, but how to persuade the power possessing beings of the time, infected by paranoia and hatred, to allow such a crossing?

To disguise their intentions, Gurdjieff decides to say he is leading a scientific expedition to the region of Mount Induk in the Caucasus to search both for dolmens and gold. To put the plan into action, first he has Alexander Petrov, gifted in math and engineering and a master calligrapher, write a letter for Shandarovsky, a personable and persuasive lawyer, to deliver to the Essentuki Soviet's Council of Deputies. The impressive looking letter requests permission for the expedition. At the same time, as he had done earlier in placing the ballet notice with Uspenskii, Gurdjieff has a story planted about the expedition in the Piatigorsk newspapers. (It is the higher Soviet Council in Piatigorsk that had the authority to assist the expedition materially.) The story is entirely Gurdjieff's composition; he dictates all its questions and answers. The expedition intends to go to a remote wilderness, inaccessible to military activities of the civil war. Therefore this scientific work and its discoveries cannot be hindered.

Meanwhile, Gurdjieff had the women make roomy linen rucksacks with leather shoulder straps and linen hip straps. The men were to carry seventy-pound packs, the women fifty-pound packs. In the evenings, Gurdjieff had them walking, climbing steps, then racing, back and forth in the garden, their packs filled with the weight they would carry in stones. He showed them how to "walk consciously"—all the weight is put on one leg while the other touches and senses the ground—so they could navigate dark nights in the mountains. So everyone would always know their direction, he pointed out how to locate the Great Bear and North Star.

Oddly, during this time, Gurdjieff was seen holding their horse Rusty with a long rope and with the other end beating him on the belly, the horse rearing up on his hind legs. He probably did the same thing to their other horse, Dralfeet. When the soldiers from the Red Army came a few days later, they didn't touch the donkeys but led the horses away. Gurdjieff looked on without saying anything, the pupils dismayed because their lives depended on the horses. But the horses were soon returned as Rusty reared up as soon as a soldier tried to take hold of the reins, knocking the soldier over onto his back and Dralfeet bit another soldier. "Keep them," they said, "we don't need such horses!" and gave them a paper protecting the horses from later requisitions.

One night after dinner walking around the dining table as he often did, Gurdjieff says that inasmuch as he did not know exactly where the group was going, and circumstances to be encountered could not be known, he would ask for the first time for everyone's unquestioning obedience in carrying out his orders, because one person's mistake could endanger everyone and should this happen he might have to sacrifice someone's life for the good of the whole group.

Soon equipment begins to arrive from Piatigorsk. Having requisitioned and received the necessary supplies of coffee, tea, salt, potatoes, flour, tents and carpets, the group set out on their journey. Besides Gurdjieff, it includes fourteen people:[21] seven men, five women and two children—all of whom Gurdjieff says are "half-consciously or unconsciously devoted to me." Among the men are Petrov, Zaharoff, Zhukov, Thomas de Hartmann, and Dr. Stjoernval. Among the women are Madames Ostrowska, de Hartmann, Stjoernval, and Bashmakova. Notably

---

21. In her memoirs, "Across the Caucasus with G. I. Gurdjieff," Elizabeta Stjoernval says there are seventeen people. In the de Hartmann's *Our Life with Mr. Gurdjieff*, it is fourteen.

absent are Uspenskii and his family, the excuse being that Madame Uspenskii's daughter, Lenotchka, is expecting her first child. Whatever Uspenskii's outward face, he has decided to break with Gurdjieff.

7 August 1918. Essentuki. Gurdjieff and students, everyone dressed plainly like simple workers, leave at 8 p.m. They take two horses, two donkeys, four dogs, two cats and two large wagons with benches, one with a smaller Russian wagon, a telega, inside.[22] They reach Amavir, about 110 miles away, the next day. The following morning nearing Maikop they find it surrounded by Cossacks and Red Army troops, the fighting going full blaze. They await the outcome on a farm outside of town. The Cossacks finally take the town.

1 September 1918. Maikop. The group moves on by foot, heading toward the mountains, picking their way between the opposing sides. No fewer than five times they must cross either Bolshevik or White Army lines. All about them is what Gurdjieff says is an "epidemic of fanaticism and mutual hatred." The circumstances summon all of Gurdjieff's capacities. During this period he says, "miracles were being performed for us. . . . I and my companions moved under supernatural protection." After many trials and hardships, the group crosses the mountains.

Early October 1918. They reach Sochi on the Black Sea. After a few days Gurdjieff suddenly announces that the expedition is finished and advises everyone to make their own plans for the future. Only the de Hartmanns, Stjoernvals, and the Zhukovs remain with Gurdjieff and his wife. De Hartmann says Gurdjieff told them, "'Faith is the knowledge of feeling, knowledge of the heart. This knowledge burns like a bright light in the crises of life.' During this journey we experienced the truth of what he said."

Of this period Gurdjieff says:

> In my opinion, we got out safely because in the common presences of these people—although in the grip of a psychic state in which the last grain of reasonableness vanishes—the instinct inherent in all human beings for distinguishing good from evil in the objective sense was not completely lacking. And therefore, instinctively sensing in my activities the living germ of that sacred impulse which alone is capable of bringing genuine happiness to humanity, they furthered in whatever way they could the process of accomplishment of that which I had undertaken long before the war.

30 August 1918. Lenin, shot twice by a female assassin, recovers.

---

22. Another description has them leaving with two small carts and horses, all being pulled by a slow-moving train.

5 September 1918. Moscow. Red Terror officially begins. Prisoners and hostages throughout Russia are massacred. *Kulaks*, rich peasants, are hunted down and shot by the *Cheka*, Lenin's secret police.

November 1918. The First World War ends. The Russian civil war continues.

1918. Tiflis. Sometime between September and December Madame Uspenskii's daughter gives birth to a son, Leonidas, or "Lonia," Savitsky. The father is said to be the lawyer Alexei Rachmilievitch.

January 1919. Essentuki. Cossacks capture the town.

Mid-January 1919. Sochi. Gurdjieff, Madame Ostrowska, the Stjoernvals, and de Hartmanns leave by ship for Poti, then take a train to Tiflis.

February 1919. Tiflis. To make money, Thomas de Hartmann gives private music lessons and small concerts at which his wife sometimes sings. De Hartmann meets an old friend, the composer Tcherepnin, who is planning an opera festival. He learns a friend from his early days in Munich, the forty-five-year-old artist Alexander Gustav de Salzmann, is painting the scenery for the operas. De Salzmann invites the de Hartmanns to dinner. They meet de Salzmann's thirty-year-old pregnant wife, the former Jeanne Matignon, who would later give birth to a daughter, Nathalie. Born in Reims, France, and raised in Geneva, Switzerland, she had been one of Emile Jacques-Dalcroze's chief artistic assistants and one of his three principal dancers and a performer in his celebrated production of *Orpheus*. Dalcroze was the founder of Eurhythmics, a leading European school of dance, which was located at Hellerau near Dresden. It was there that she and Alexander met. They married in 1911. He designed stage sets and did the lighting. He had been born in Tiflis where his father, the State Architect, had designed most of the educational institutions, as well as the governor's residence and the Opera House.

During dinner the de Hartmanns tell them about the teaching. The two couples get together often thereafter and become good friends. Finally, the de Hartmanns ask Gurdjieff if the de Salzmanns could meet him.

Easter 1919. Tiflis. Gurdjieff and the de Salzmanns meet. Gurdjieff says: "He is a very fine man, and she—is intelligent." Of him, Jeanne de Salzmann says:

---

23. In *Meetings*, Gurdjieff explains that "intelligent" is used "not in the European sense" but how it is understood in Asia; that is, "not only by knowledge but by being." In the meeting of 22 July 1943, he says: "He who has his body enslaved is intelligent. You understand what is meant by intelligent? Intelligent means he who directs his body." In her unpublished memoir *What For?* Olga de Hartmann says Gurdjieff didn't say "intelligent" but "she is clever."

"The first impression of Gurdjieff was very strong, unforgettable. He had an expression I had never seen, and an intelligence, a force, that was different . . . a vision that could see everything."

22 June 1919. Tiflis. The school started by Jeanne de Salzmann stages the first ever performance of the movements.

Summer 1919. Tiflis. The opera *Carmen* is staged with Thomas de Hartmann conducting, Olga singing the role of Michaela (the first time she has publicly sung an operatic role), and with sets painted by Alexander de Salzmann.
Gurdjieff tells de Hartmann to give up his musical activities and so he must support himself with private lessons.
Olga has not been feeling well and is becoming weaker and weaker. A doctor tells her she must leave at once for a sanatorium.
Gurdjieff tells her to eat bacon every morning. He asks that she bring him a bottle of red wine. He keeps it for several days and then returns it, telling her to drink a little glass before eating any food. She is also to lie in the open air each day for an hour. Three weeks later she sees the doctor and he says she is cured and is glad she has taken his advice.

1 April 1919. South Russia. General Anton Ivanovitch Denikin's White Army is supplied with arms and advisors by England and France.

Early Summer 1919. Essentuki. Uspenskii and his family leave. That summer and autumn they move between Rostov-on-Don, Ekaterinodar and Novorossik. He says:

> I gathered together a small group and began lectures according to a plan which I formed the previous winter, expounding G.'s system as I understood it and what in my opinion led up to it. As far as I was concerned these lectures produced from the very first many unexpected results and gave a perfectly new explanation of my leaving G. I felt that I was able to work by myself, that I had already received something from G., something that could not be taken away from me, that the ideas themselves led me on and showed me the way. This did not mean that I do not need G. any more or that I would not have preferred to work with him. Had it been possible, I would have renounced my independent work. But as this was impossible, the independent work which I had begun was better than nothing. Again, I knew that independent work of this kind could not lead very far. Still it led somewhere.
> Gurdjieff astonished us in St. Petersburg by his capacity to see in people their hidden fundamental features. The nexus was that the whole of one's character is already wound round one particular feature or round

an axle or a reel. This capacity in him looked almost miraculous. And now I saw the same capacity in myself.

Summer 1919. Caucasus. General Denikin's White Army begins its advance toward Moscow.

25 July 1919. Ekaterinodar. Uspenskii manages to send the first in a series of five letters to A. R. Orage, editor of *The New Age,* whom Uspenskii had met in London six years before when making his second journey to the East. Uspenskii describes ordinary life amid a revolution:

> The prices of all products and necessities have risen by twenty, fifty, a hundred, or six hundred times. Workmen's wages have risen twenty, fifty, or even a hundred times. But the salary of an ordinary brain-worker—a teacher, journalist or doctor—has risen in the best cases by no more than three times and, very often has not risen at all, but has actually decreased. If you earn 2,000 rubles a month, you are considered to be doing well; but often one meets with earnings of 1,000, 800, or 600 rubles. But the cheapest pair of boots cost 900 rubles, a pound of tea 150 rubles, a bottle of wine 60 rubles, and so on. On the whole, you may reckon a ruble now as worth a pre-war kopeck, i.e., its hundredth part. . . . I honestly pity everybody who has not been here, everybody who is living in the old way, everybody who is ignorant of what we now know. . . . 'Shall we ever live again in the old way'. . . . You will surely begin to think that it is something to do with the re-establishment of the old régime or the oppression of the working classes, and so on. But in actual fact it means something very simple. It means, for example: When shall we be able to buy shoe leather again, or shaving soap, or a box of matches. . . . We know that 'war', and 'politics', and 'economic life'—in a word all those things about which one reads in papers, and in which those big two-dimensional creatures called Nations and States live and move and have their being—we know that all this is one thing, but that the life of individual men and women is quite another thing, having no points of contact with the former, except when it does not allow the latter to live. . . . We now know that the whole life of individual men and women is a struggle against these big creatures. We are able to understand without difficulty that a Nation is a creature standing on a far lower stage of development than individual men and women. . . . I personally am still alive only because my boots and trousers and other articles of clothing—all 'old campaigners'—are still holding together. When they end their existence, I shall evidently end mine.

Aware now of Uspenskii's plight, Orage contacts his friend Major Francis "Frank" Pinder, a polymath and British intelligence officer responsible for the Baku-Batum oil pipeline, who is also serving as Head of the British Economic Mission to General Denikin's White Army in Ekaterinodar. Pinder contacts Uspenskii and offers him a job on his staff writing the Mission's press summaries, paying his salary out of his own pocket.

While in Ekaterinodar, Uspenskii receives a letter from Gurdjieff, who says he has reached Tiflis and has opened there the Institute for the Harmonious Development of Man. Enclosed is a prospectus. Uspenskii sees he is listed as one of the Institute's "specialist teachers." Gurdjieff says he is preparing his ballet *The Struggle of the Magicians*, but nowhere in the letter does he mention their past difficulties. Uspenskii sees this as "very characteristic."[24] These difficulties he considers "very real." His decision to leave Gurdjieff had cost him dearly, he says, and he could "not give it up so easily, the more so because all his [Gurdjieff's] motives could be seen."

Others around Uspenskii believe that when the revolution is over they will be able to return to "the old life." Uspenskii has no such illusions. "In the face of the weakness of the intelligentsia," he says, "it [Bolshevism] began openly to wage war on culture, to destroy all cultural values, and to annihilate the intelligentsia as the representative of culture."

When he left Petersburg in 1917, he said, "the ground had fallen away behind me." He now recognizes what so many hide from themselves—there is "no way back. To no place that I had left was it possible to return."

All bridges to his past life are literally burnt behind him. There is no possibility of return to anything. His whole life, as it were, is wiped out, erased.[25]

Years before, he had foreseen all this. As he had said of the Bolsheviks as early as 1905, "Some of them are very nice people, quite sincere and terribly unselfish. But those will perish. Only scoundrels will survive." He had attended some of their meetings. "They just talked and talked: how bad everything was, how miserable everybody was, and how beautiful everything would be if there were no police, no Cossacks and no General Governors.... But when it came to having tea, it transpired that the members of the committee had eaten all the cakes and oranges, and drunk all the tea! So there was nothing left for the rest of us."

Whatever their difficulties, Gurdjieff agrees with Uspenskii about the political situation. "Marxism," Gurdjieff declares, "is satanic."

---

24. Not seeing he is identified with what happened in Essentuki, Uspenskii believes his interpretation of his impressions is accurate. Any mention of "past difficulties" by Gurdjieff, whatever tack he may take, only legitimizes Uspenskii's identification. By ignoring it, Gurdjieff forces Uspenskii to keep working with it, keep 'eating' it.

25. For a man of rare sensitivity and intelligence, this enormous sense of loss and emptiness—the virtual death of his past—must have caused a great emotional wound. But Uspenskii, however pessimistic about ordinary life, is too strong and sincere a seeker to ever totally give up.

Asked by a friend what practical results the Work had produced in him, Uspenskii says that because of it he had acquired a "strange confidence." He says, "This is not self-confidence in the ordinary sense, quite the contrary, rather is it a confidence in the unimportance and insignificance of self, that self which we usually know." This confidence stems from his realizing that "if something terrible happened to me . . . it would be not I who would meet it, not this ordinary I, but another I within me who would be equal to the occasion." He goes on to say that when Gurdjieff asked him two years before if he had felt a new I inside him, he said that he did not. "Now," declares Uspenskii, "I can speak otherwise."

16 August 1919. Ekaterinodar. Denikin captures the city. Against his orders, Denikin's men begin to rape and pillage. Jewish pogroms are mounted.

26 August 1919. Novorossiysk. Denikin captures the city.

18 September 1919. Ekaterinodar. Uspenskii writes a second letter to Orage*:*

> The armies consisting of Chinese have proved to be the hardest fighters and the most reliable force of the Bolshevik. We know, too, from trustworthy sources, that these Chinese were recruited for the Bolsheviks in China by German agents. . . . The essence of Bolshevism lies precisely in what it is not mistaken for. You think Bolshevism a political system that can be discussed, but whose existence cannot be denied. In reality, Bolshevism is not a political system at all. It is something very old, that at different times has borne different names. The Russian language of the eighteenth century knew a name, preserved until now—"pougachevchina"—which renders very well the essence of Bolshevism. Pougachev was a Ural Cossack who pretended to be the deceased Emperor Peter III, and who raised an insurrection against Catherine II, and for a time succeeded in seizing half of Russia. He plundered the estates of landowners, hanged their owners and priests, gave the land to the peasantry, etc. A classical description of the "pougachevchina" is to be found in a novel by our poet Pushkin, *A Captain's Daughter.* But Bolshevism of the twentieth century has one peculiarity—it is 'made in Germany'—and Germany knows how to make use of it. Employing Bolshevism in 1917 to break up the Russian army, Germany destroyed the danger menacing her Eastern front. . . . Germany is not annihilated or even weakened. She is energetically and cleverly preparing a *revanche*. Her chief enemy is England, and the chief trump in her pack is Russian Bolshevism.

20 September 1919. Kursk. Denikin captures the city. The White Army is now only 330 miles from Moscow. Spirits rise as victory looks obtainable.

25 September 1919. Ekaterinodar. Uspenskii writes again:

> People don't understand that if anything exists, it does so thanks to inertia. The initial push from the past is still working, but it cannot be renewed! There lies the horror. Sooner or later its energy will be exhausted and all will stop, one thing after another. Tramways, railways, post — all these are working, thanks to inertia alone. But inertia cannot last forever. . . . The man who very soon will be robbing and murdering on this very spot has not yet realized the fact that he can do it now without fear of punishment. . . . The original cause of the destruction of Russia, what led to the Revolution, was robbery — i.e., what you as a polite and cultured people call profiteering. . . . The masses wanted to have their share in the general plundering of Russia. Bolshevism sanctioned this plundering and gave it the name of Socialism.

26 September 1919. Denikin's forces surround Nestor Ivanovitch Makhno's peasant guerrillas called "The Green Forces." A charismatic guerrilla leader, "Batko" (Daddy) Makhno, a semiliterate peasant and anarchist with cunning eyes and long hair, sides with neither the Whites nor the Bolsheviks. His guerrillas, flying a black anarchist flag, somehow withstand Denikin's onslaught and defeat the Whites.

28 September 1919. Tiflis. Elizabeta Stjoernval gives birth to a son, Nikolai. Gurdjieff is the father.

No date, Ekaterinodar. Writes Uspenskii: "In the autumn of 1917 the actual traits of Bolshevism began to reveal themselves. They form the very essence of the movement, and their application consisted in the struggle against culture, against the 'intelligentsia,' against freedom of any kind. . . . The workmen were at once made equals with the intelligentsia, and were even declared superior to it. Everything in which they differed from the intelligentsia was now proclaimed unnecessary and even hostile to the interests of the people and the idea of freedom."

14 October 1919. Orel. Denikin's army takes Orel. Now Moscow is only 245 miles away. Tula is next, only 122 miles away. Victory looks assured. But in the Ukraine, Makhno's guerrillas attack Denikin from the rear, cutting supply lines and taking cities.

20 October 1919. Orel. The Red Army recaptures Orel, breaking Denikin's advance on Moscow. The Whites are sent into full retreat, while from the rear Makhno's guerilla forces continue to ravage Denikin's forces, depriving them of much needed supplies.

Late October. Ekaterinodar. In his last letter Uspenskii describes where he has been living, saying it is one of Russia's richest towns and a center for grain and other raw products. This eighteenth century town is considered the cheapest place in Russia to live. But in other ways it is a virtual hell, a foul smelling, filthy town, a soulless place without history, the streets littered now with an enormous number of dead animals. "A few days ago I was strangely struck by the fact that after half an hour's walk I had not met with any corpse. Hardly had the thought occurred to me than I tumbled over two enormous dead rats, and a few steps further was lying a little black dog on whose carcass thousands of fleas were gathering."

Autumn 1919. Novorossiysk. A second letter from Gurdjieff reaches Uspenskii, who apparently makes no reply. Both Petrov and Zaharoff show up in Ekaterinodar, both in a "negative frame of mind" about the Work. Uspenskii's advice: "It is imperative to make a distinction between the System and Gurdjieff." Near year's end Zaharoff will die of smallpox.

Autumn 1919. Tiflis. Gurdjieff decides to reestablish his Institute here. He asks Dr. Stjoernval, the de Hartmanns, and the de Salzmanns to name it. One name after another he rejects until the five offer "The Harmonious Development of Man." Rehearsals then begin at the State Theater for the staging of his ballet *The Struggle of the Magicians.* Stage sets are designed, music written, dances rehearsed, costumes made. One morning Olga enters the performance hall and sees Gurdjieff taking an axe to the decorations. She thinks he has gone mad. "Why you so astonished?" he asks. "We have done it, so don't need it anymore. Now can go to dump."

Later, her husband reminds her of what Gurdjieff has often said: "Make pupils do something that is terribly difficult and demands all attention and diligence, and then destroy it. Because, for them, only the effort is necessary, not thing itself."

At this time Gurdjieff is thought to have met twenty-one-year-old Olgivanna Lazovich Hinzenburg. Her husband, Valdemar, a wealthy architect, was designing a cabaret restaurant, the Peacock's Tail, which he co-owned with Alexander de Salzmann. Two years before she had given birth to a daughter, Svetlana. Though initially flattered by the attentions of Valdemar Hinzenburg, ten years her senior, Olgivanna came to see him as being intellectually inferior, but because of a deathbed promise to her mother she had gone through with the marriage. From the start the marriage was perfunctory, she cried at the wedding and then withdrew into philosophy. What particularly attracted her attention was Nietzsche's *Thus Spake Zarathustra.* "It struck something deep in me," she says. "I began to think there must be a supersoul in life. I understood it in the sense of an inner kingdom, of being the master of oneself. I wanted to find the way to achieve it."

One day a friend excitedly told her about a man of knowledge she had just met. Olgivanna was not interested. The friend persisted. Finally, Olgivanna sought

Gurdjieff out.[26] He asks if she has a wish. "I wish immortality," she tells him. Gurdjieff says he can help her. "Are you ready to make any sacrifice?" he asks. She says yes. He tells her to dismiss her servants immediately and learn to do everything herself. Later, Olgivanna joins the movements class.

End of November 1919. Tiflis. The young, much travelled English freelance war correspondent Carl E. Bechhofer Roberts seeks out Gurdjieff. One afternoon he meets Gurdjieff at a café sitting with a group of poets, painters and sculptors. He finds him "a curious individual, a man of striking appearance. Short, dark and swarthy, with penetrating and clever eyes; no one could be in his company for many minutes without being impressed by the force of his personality. One did not need to believe him infallible, but there was no denying his extraordinary all-round intelligence." Bechhofer Roberts brought letters of introduction but from whom he does not say. They must have been theosophical as he says Gurdjieff did not talk theosophy to him as he feared. Instead he showed him around the city, going to many obscure restaurants where he spoke Georgian or Persian to the waiters, took him to hot baths, and in the evenings, Roberts says, "I used to call at Georgi Ivanovitch's 'Institute for Harmonic Human Development' and watch him rehearsing his ballet, the movements and gestures of which he said had been handed down by tradition and paintings in Thibetan monasteries where he had been. The music, also, was of mysterious tradition. He himself could not play a note, and knew nothing of composition; but the academician [no doubt Thomas de Hartmann] who interpreted his ideas assured me that he had learned more theory of music from Georgi Ivanovitch than in any of the schools. The decorations and costumes were also his; he had even painted and sewn them himself."

1 December 1919. Rochester, New York. Bessaraboff and Bragdon complete the English translation of *Tertium Organum*. Bragdon reads the translation to Bessaraboff who at the end exclaims—"Mister Bragdon! You have left out one very important thing. You must say this is a very dangerous book." Bragdon agrees and adds a paragraph to that effect. Then, using a large part of his savings, Bragdon self-publishes it. He believes that with this book Uspenskii "has taken his place as one of the most profound and original thinkers of the modern world." With little advertising and limited means of distribution, the book sells so well that three prominent New York publishers compete for rights. Alfred A. Knopf wins. Bragdon contacts Orage about Uspenskii's whereabouts but he has lost contact and all other leads go nowhere.

---

26. A rumor is that she and Gurdjieff had already met in Moscow and that he was the father of Olgivanna's daughter Svetlana, who died in 1946. When in 1948 her second daughter, Iovanna, brought Eve Taylor, Gurdjieff's daughter, to meet her—she looking so much like Svetlana—Olgivanna cried out bitterly, "How could you do this to me? Get her out of here."

December 1919. Denikin escapes to Europe. The Red Army pursues Makhno, destroying his forces.

Mid-December 1919. The Red Army on Rostov's perimeter, Uspenskii takes his family from Ekaterinodar bringing them across the Crimea to Odessa.

Early January 1920. Odessa. Uspenskii, his wife Sophia, and her daughter Lenotchka and one-year-old Lonia, leave for Constantinople.

January 1920. Germany. Hitler becomes chief of party propaganda for the German Workers' Party. After a few months the name is changed to National Socialist German Workers' Party. Members are now known as "Nazis."

Late January 1920. Constantinople. Uspenskii and his family arrive. Twelve years earlier Uspenskii had been here. But that Constantinople, a living museum of long gone Byzantium, no longer exists. What he finds is a Constantinople not only noisier but one that looked empty despite its streets teeming with repatriated Turkish soldiers, penniless Russian refugees, an assorted flotsam of humanity. It was a city "rapidly acquiring a Western drabness and hideousness." He visits Pera, the Russian and European quarter where he had previously stayed and where many of his friends lived. But none remain. He realizes that "during these last three years, the ground had fallen away behind me. It was a quite inconceivable period, when there was no way back, when I experienced in relation to places and people the same sensation which we ordinarily feel in relation to time. To no place that I had left was it possible to return. From nobody from whom I had parted did I have any more news."

Uspenskii and his family move to a single room in a large lodging house at one of the refugee camps on the island of Prinkipo (Princes Island). It is about ten miles southeast in the Sea of Marmara and a two hour's ferry ride from Pera. Uspenskii earns money teaching English to Russian exiles and giving mathematics lessons to children in the upstairs offices of the White Russian Club, the *Russky Mayak*, in Pera. He puts up a poster—

> *The Ancient Wisdom of the East*
> *Revealed Through a New Current*
> *in Western Thought*

Lectures are held at the Russky Mayak. As he did in Rostov and Ekaterinodar, he connects the ideas of esotericism with those of psychology and philosophy. We are living in biblical times, he says, when prophecies seem to be coming to pass. "What is needed today is the emergence of a new kind of man, one who is capable of understanding the meaning of human life."

Spring 1920. Tiflis. The building promised by the Tiflis government for his Institute never materializing and the temporary quarters given unsuitable, Gurdjieff says "I finally gave up wasting my time and energy in the struggle with conditions around me. I decided not only to liquidate everything in Tiflis, but even to break with everything that up till then had tied me to Russia, and to emigrate beyond its borders and found my Institute in some other country."

He leaves for Constantinople. Leaving with him are the Stjoernvals, de Hartmanns and the de Salzmanns along with a new student, Elizabeta ("Lili") Galumnian Chaverdian. Olgivanna stays behind because of her daughter Svetlana's age but promises to join the group there soon.

Spring 1920. Constantinople. Uspenskii, looking for additional places to hold lectures, meets the buxom forty-seven-year-old Englishwoman Mrs. Winifred Elliot Beaumont, who offers him the drawing room of her Pera apartment. There Uspenskii meets twenty-three-year-old John Godolphin Bennett,[27] head of a section of British intelligence in Constantinople, who is Mrs. Beaumont's lover. She is only six years younger than Bennett's mother; they will later marry. In England he has a pregnant wife, Evelyn, whom he married only two years before. Bennett is interested in the geometry of higher dimensions, a world without bodies, so Uspenskii and he must have had much to talk about.

Lectures are held every Wednesday afternoon. Uspenskii soon finds among the audience Prince Sabaheddin, a nephew of the reigning Sultan and son of a famous Turkish reformer, and a personal friend of Mrs. Beaumont and Bennett. The Prince, slight, diminutive and delicate, has an open mind and is well-versed in the subject of self-transformation. He owns a house in Switzerland (where he and Mrs. Beaumont first met) and has traveled to the capitals of Europe. Among his many friends is Rudolph Steiner, founder of Anthroposophy. Also attracted to the lectures is Boris Mouravieff, a rather feline-looking Russian aristocrat and intellectual with a great love of books. He becomes a friend of a sort of Uspenskii's.

Summer 1920. Germany. Hitler designs the Nazi flag, its background a brilliant red and in its center a white disk with a black swastika, the *hakenkreuz*. The swastika is an ancient spiritual symbol, its one hooked line symbolizing birth, the other rebirth, and its colors—red, white and black—symbolizing the three forces or *gunas*. Hitler switches the directions of the lines and therefore its meaning.

---

27. In Bennett's autobiography, *Witness*, he tells very little of his early life, giving the implausible excuse, "My birth and boyhood seem irrelevant, as I have no memories that are different from those of any other boy I have known." He does describe his father as having an "inability to behave properly either in sexual or in financial matters" for which his mother's "puritanical New England upbringing" forced her husband out of the house. He died of fever in a "dingy boardinghouse bedroom" on the same day as Bennett's marriage.

Hitler likely got the idea from *Ostara,* an anti-Semitic magazine dedicated to racial purity, published by a defrocked monk, which uses the swastika symbol.

Summer 1920. London. Spencer Kellogg, Jr., of Rochester, a friend of Bragdon's who is quite taken with *Tertium Organum*, visits the Theosophical Society headquarters to inquire if they have copies of the book for sale. He encounters a Russian woman who is a friend of Uspenskii's and knows his whereabouts.

7 July 1920. Constantinople. Some six months after Uspenskii's arrival, Gurdjieff and his party arrive on a ship from Batum. With him are his wife Julia Ostrowska, the de Hartmanns, Stjoernvals, de Salzmanns, Major Frank Pinder (he had been captured by the Red Army in Rostov and condemned to death, but the sentence was not carried out), and assorted others. Gurdjieff rents a townhouse at 13 Yemenici Sokak[28] in Pera, the European quarter, for himself and the group.

On the first day Gurdjieff makes a poor man's stew from fat-tailed sheep for everyone. Gurdjieff asks everyone to bring sheep's heads. Thomas de Hartmann says they "could be bought cheaply, already roasted in an oven and broken in pieces, brains and all, ready for eating. Mr. Gurdjieff was very fond of sheep's head." There is also a soup and, of course, *douziko,* a strong anise-flavored Greek vodka.

His home quickly becomes a center for desperately poor Russian refugees, many former government officials. Most feel this is only an interlude and they'll soon be able to return to their homeland. Gurdjieff feeds them but says returning is an illusion. Everyone must quickly adapt to the new conditions of life. Several weeks pass. Gurdjieff tells them they need to not just take but contribute. "Everyone must help," he says. "All of you can earn some money, but first of all you must wish to do so."

Days pass. No one does anything. Finally, Gurdjieff tells them:

> I have spent nearly all my money. Tomorrow's meal is far from certain! I've had to borrow right and left to keep things going up to now. Some of you say you want to help me, but you do nothing.... Like members of Russia's ruling class, you have been nothing but parasites all your lives.... You are slaves, subject to whatever happens. If you really had no possibility of earning money, no one could blame you. But if you haven't even tried, you are less than nothing.... Those of you who are ready to do something, go to the back of the room.

Gurdjieff then leaves with some students who step into another room and then return, their arms laden with rugs and other objects. He forms the people at

---

28. Could this have been Prince Lubovedsky's house? Gurdjieff says that he met the prince in his house in Pera, not far from the Russian embassy. The house is only seven minutes or so from the Russian embassy.

the back of the room into groups of two and three, gives them rugs and objects, prices to ask, and sends them off to the bazaar.

When they leave, Tcheslaw Tchekhovitch, a twenty-four-year-old former White Army solider, circus strongman and wrestler who has been working at a restaurant, offers Gurdjieff some Turkish pounds. Gurdjieff pays no attention. Instead he takes a large red handkerchief from his pocket, carefully opens it and shows Tchekhovitch a heap of diamonds of various sizes.

"But Georgi Ivanovitch, with all these diamonds, you're very rich! You just said you haven't a penny. And here I offered you some miserable Turkish pounds!"

"Tchekhovitch, you are naïve. If you don't push people to the limit, they'll never get down to earning money."

Later, Gurdjieff also rents an apartment on Koumbaradji Street and soon sets up his "office" at the Black Rose café, a dubious haunt frequented by a cross-section of White Russians, officers, whores, alcoholics, and drug addicts. Gurdjieff contacts Uspenskii and the two meet here at the Black Rose.

Uspenskii, glad to see Gurdjieff, soon decides, as he later puts it, "in the interests of the work, all former difficulties could be set aside and that I could work with him as in Petersburg."[29] He tells the thirty or so students attending his lectures about Gurdjieff and the talks he is giving. Among them is twenty-year-old Boris Ferapontoff, a wealthy Russian aristocrat and a devotee of Nietzsche, who attends all Gurdjieff's talks, taking copious notes but remaining apart.[30] Young Bennett and Mrs. Beaumont do not attend. Uspenskii continues to lecture at Mrs. Beaumont's apartment.

Again reconciled, Gurdjieff and Uspenskii meet at the Black Rose café to work together on *The Struggle of the Magicians*. Gurdjieff had spoken to Uspenskii about his ballet scenario when they first met in Moscow in April 1915. In the intervening years it was not mentioned. Now he tells Uspenskii that the ballet is not a "mystery" but more of a beautiful spectacle with "a certain meaning hidden beneath the outward form." There are "three ideas lying at the basis," he says. It is not so much a ballet, but more "a series of dramatic and mimic scenes held together by a common plot." The dances and movements are to convey certain laws of the universe and thus are "sacred dances." Gurdjieff tells him the *same* performers will act and dance in the scenes of both the White Magician and the Black Magician; that is, he will have students dance both the aggressive, inharmonious dances of the Black Magician as well as the reconciled and sophisticated harmonies of the White Magician. Working with Gurdjieff, Uspenskii comes to see sides of Gurdjieff previously hidden—the artistic and poetical.

The Struggle of the Magicians takes place in a large commercial town of the

---

29. Setting aside and not working through these "difficulties," Uspenskii keeps in place the conditions for a future break.
30. See "The Notes of Boris Ferapontoff," *The Gurdjieff Journal*, Vol. 12, No. 2.

East. Gafar, a handsome rich Parsi, young and full of pride, falls in love with Zeinab, a twenty-one-year-old Indo-Persian beauty. Gafar tries to seduce her but fails, so he enlists the help of the Black Magician. Unwilling at first because Zeinab is a student of the White Magician, he finally puts her under a spell. When the White Magician realizes what has happened to Zeinab, he breaks the spell. Gafar, angry, goes to the White Magician who shows him two possible fates. In both he is old but in one he is happy and cheerful and much loved; in the other he is evil and dissatisfied and regarded with aversion and disgust. Seeing this creates a great inner struggle within Gafar.

The Magician tells him: "As you sow, so shall you reap. The deeds of the present determine the future, all that is good and all that is bad; both are the results of the past. It is the duty of every man in every moment of the present to prepare the future, improving on the past. Such is the law of fate." He ends with, "May the source of all laws be blessed."

The Magician then raises his right hand and, looking upwards, his voice a whisper, says as if in prayer: "Lord Creator, and all you His assistants, help us to be able to remember ourselves at all times in order that we may avoid involuntary actions, as only through them can evil manifest itself."

August 1920. Constantinople. Prince Sabaheddin telephones Bennett to ask if he might invite a newly arrived friend to Uspenskii's lectures. The Prince tells Bennett that though he had met this friend only three or four times, first in 1908 and the last in 1912, he regards him "as one of the very few men who had been able to penetrate into the hidden brotherhoods of Central Asia." The Prince tells Bennett, too, that he would be meeting "the most remarkable man he would ever know." Coming from the Prince, whom Bennett regards with respect, this is high praise.

The Prince's friend arrives at about half-past nine in the evening, long after the lecture is over and Uspenskii has departed, but he shows not the least sign of embarrassment. Bennett observes that the man—his name of course was Gurdjieff—greets "the Prince in Turkish with an accent that was a strange mixture of cultured Osmanli and some uncouth Eastern dialect."

Introduced to the Prince's friend, Bennett says: "I met the strangest eyes I have ever seen. The two eyes were so different that I wondered if the light had played some trick on me."

The difference, Bennett realizes, is not because of any kind of cast or defect in either eye but, rather, in their expression. Of Gurdjieff's general appearance, Bennett says: "He had long, black mustaches fiercely curled upwards. He wore a *kalpack*, that is, an astrakhan cap." Gurdjieff tells Bennett, perhaps for effect, that he was born in 1866, thus making himself fifty-four years old, practically twice Bennett's age.

As both Bennett and the Prince have a keen interest in hypnotism, the conversation eventually turns there. The Prince asks Bennett to relate the experiments he has been making. Gurdjieff listens attentively.

"I felt," says Bennett, "that he was not so much following my words as participating in the experience. I have never before had the same feeling of being understood better than I understood myself."

As Gurdjieff speaks about levels of experience in relation to hypnotism, it is quickly evident to Bennett that "this man had specialized knowledge of a kind I had not met with before."

At one point, Bennett speaks of his discovery of the fifth dimension[31] — he had an out-of-body experience in the caverns of Roeux, France, during the war which was, he says, "as much a birth as a death" — and his belief that it is the region of free will. "Your guess is right," answers Gurdjieff. "There are higher dimensions or higher worlds where the higher faculties of man have free play." He explains to Bennett that theoretical understanding is of no use, as one remains where they are. Even the crystallization of a finer body is not enough in that it, too, is under material laws. He tells him that he himself must change, for, "within this sphere there is no freedom. Neither your knowledge nor all your activity will give you freedom. This is because you have no *varlik*, no real being." At one point, Gurdjieff tells Bennett: "You have the possibility of changing, but I must warn you that it will not be easy. You are still full of the idea that you can do what you like."

When leaving, Gurdjieff invites Bennett and Mrs. Beaumont to a demonstration of temple dances the next Saturday evening.

Given his work with intelligence, Bennett says:

> I can personally confirm that he had an unfavorable dossier in New Delhi because, as an intelligence officer in Constantinople in 1920, I first heard of Gurdjieff in a dispatch from New Delhi warning us of a 'very dangerous Russian agent, George Gurdjieff, who was in Georgia and had applied for a permit to come to Constantinople.... His coming to Constantinople was heralded by the usual gossip of the bazaars. He was said to be a great traveller and a linguist who knew all the Oriental languages, reputed by the Moslems to be a convert to Islam, and by the Christians to be a member of some obscure Nestorian sect. He proved to be neither, and his linguistic attainments stopped short near the Caspian Sea, so that we could converse only with difficulty in a mixture of Azerbaidjan Tartar and Osmanli Turkish. Nevertheless, he unmistakably possessed knowledge very different from that of the itinerant Sheikhs of Persia and Trans-Caspia, whose arrival in Constantinople had been preceded by similar rumors. It was, above all, astonishing to meet a man, almost

---

31. Is it to be taken as just a coincidence that Gurdjieff shows up at Mrs. Beaumont's apartment? The Prince's fortunes, financial and political, are at a low ebb and Uspenskii has turned over most of his pupils. So why is Gurdjieff there? A possibility may be that he has heard about Bennett, a brilliant, ambitious, and clever young man, who has an interest in the occult — and has come to recruit him. It is interesting, as well, that Gurdjieff speaks to Bennett of his idée fixe of the moment, the fifth dimension. In Petersburg he had insisted Uspenskii abandon his notions of the fourth dimension.

unacquainted with any Western European language, possessing a working knowledge of physics, chemistry, biology and modern astronomy, and able to make searching comments on the then new and fashionable theory of relativity, and also on the psychology of Sigmund Freud.

Later, attending the demonstration of temple dances, Bennett and Mrs. Beaumont are surprised to see, of all people, Uspenskii. He had given no indication that he knew Gurdjieff. Though impressed with Gurdjieff and the dances, they do not become members of Gurdjieff's circle.

September 1920. Constantinople. Gurdjieff and Uspenskii are often working together for entire days and nights. One night the two are sitting in a café on Koumbaradji Street. Suddenly Gurdjieff begins to sing in Persian "The Song of the Dervish," afterward translating it into Russian for Uspenskii. After fifteen minutes or so of singing—when Uspenskii finds himself completely buried under forms and symbols—Gurdjieff commands:

"There, now make one line out of that."

Gurdjieff continues singing for another fifteen minutes or so before declaring—"That is another line."

So of all the ideas and feelings to which Gurdjieff alludes, Uspenskii is to sum it all up in one line of poetry.[32] By dawn, with Pera just beginning to awaken, Uspenskii realizes that he had only written five verses and had stopped at the last line of the fifth verse. He is so tired that his brain would "not turn any more."

"It was some special knowledge, very sacred," says Uspenskii. "But we were both very tired." They retire, agreeing to meet again the following night to resume the translation.

All of Uspenskii's doubts about Gurdjieff now vanish. "I felt sure I could work with him again." Uspenskii says, "That was again the real Gurdjieff."

But the next night Gurdjieff refuses to translate.

Instead he tells Uspenskii dirty jokes.

"Nothing! Nothing but dirty jokes," cries Uspenskii. "Not even good jokes. Stupid dirty jokes!"[33]

October 1920. Constantinople. Gurdjieff opens his Institute once again, this time on the ground floor of his townhouse at 13 Yemeneci Sokak, across the street and three doors down from the Grand Rabbinate and within a stone's

---

32. Gurdjieff is using one of Uspenskii's strengths—the ability to sum up, or wrap up, long elaborations of thought.

33. The teacher sees where the student is because he sees objectively. But the student, interpreting everyone and everything subjectively, cannot see the teacher. Throughout their days together Gurdjieff plays Uspenskii like a violin, plucking his strings, playing cacophony or harmony, but Uspenskii, so focused is he, so identified with acquiring knowledge, never appears to see it in any but personal terms.

throw of the Mevlevi Hanesi of the Whirling Dervishes. Here, as he did in Petersburg, Uspenskii devotes himself to helping Gurdjieff organize the Work. The movements and sacred dances are practiced, and self-remembering and self-observation are emphasized, as is work with the centers. Students are told by Gurdjieff that "effort influenced by necessity or desire is no effort. To remember oneself is effort because no external shock can force us. Effort is for the sake of consciousness. Struggle with habits gives a taste of effort. Self-remembering helps balance centers, changes chemical processes, and improves nutrition." Students also study the science of numbers, the Cabala, magical arts, and the traditions of Asian schools concerning religious myths.

Uspenskii says that working with Gurdjieff on the ballet "I gradually arrived at the same difficulties as in Essentuki and therefore when the 'Institute' opened I was unable to join it." However, so as not to be in Gurdjieff's way he ends his lectures and ceases to go to Pera. But two months later he is again lecturing there.

Olgivanna and her daughter Svetlana arrive. Gurdjieff is working on his ballet *The Struggle of the Magicians* and Olgivanna, lithe, strong-willed and intelligent, quickly becomes adept at the complex movements and sacred dances and becomes one of the principal dancers.

One morning before dawn Gurdjieff invites her to go for a walk with him in the rocky islands at the edge of Constantinople. He speaks to her of the nature of time and the unity of all life. As the sun rises she finds herself further and further away from the city, her arms full of scratches and her dress torn by branches. As Gurdjieff and she walk on, her throat becomes so parched she cannot swallow and her feet are blistering and bleeding. But still he demands they walk on.

"*Davay! Davay!*" he shouts. "Continue!" Sunburned now and filthy, she wants to die. As darkness falls, she sees some lights up ahead and smells roasting meat. Gurdjieff puts her between a "yes" and a "no." Does she want to keep walking or return to the city? Somehow, she manages to go on. She touches then a self that exists beyond the body and feels the entryway to the eternity for which she seeks here on Earth.

The subject of religion is raised at one of Gurdjieff's talks. "There are not three, not twenty, not even two, religions," Gurdjieff says. "There is simply Religion.... True religion is always and everywhere the same—it is one and unique." Then why are these religions constantly in conflict with one another? someone asks. "This is true," Gurdjieff replies. "I cannot accept or even imagine that at the heart of religion there is any division or conflict whatsoever. The essence of all the religions you've mentioned is the same. Fundamentally, they are all concerned with only one thing—evolution. The teaching of each great master enables his pupils to follow a certain evolutionary path, and to arrive at a level where contact with the highest cosmic force becomes possible. At their root, all teachings are one and the same, each having as its purpose to help us attain this possibility.... Religions are actually like mathematics: it is the elementary part, the most exoteric, that is offered to the masses, and this elementary part differs according to the religion." He then discusses the three classical ways—the body, emotions and mind. Gurdjieff then says, "There also exists a 'fourth way,' based on the sacred impulse emanating from Conscience,[34] of which a germ is deposited in each human being. This way leads to another specific form of teaching, a new approach to Religion."

Asked about eternal recurrence, Gurdjieff says:

> Even if you knew what to do, you could not do it. For it needs conditions of at least relative freedom. And even if such conditions were there, one would have to live externally submitting to Karma.[35] One has to trick Karma. It is too early for you to ask how 'not to function'. The point is not whether you wish or don't wish; but whether you like it or not. It is still very far. What you call inaction would have been precisely a real possibility of action. In doing one must not create a new Karmic chain. Food, sleep can also build a new chain inside. The chief thing is not to create this chain inside oneself; and outside a man it will be.

12 November 1920. Perekop, Russia. (Six hundred miles south of Moscow in the Crimea) Baron Wrangel's army is defeated by the Red Army. Wrangel and what is left of his army sail for Constantinople. The Russian civil war is effectively over.

Spring 1921. Constantinople. Gurdjieff invites Uspenskii to give lectures at his Institute once a week. Gurdjieff takes part, adding, when necessary, to Uspenskii's formulations. The relationship between them becomes more intimate. Gurdjieff visits Uspenskii and Madame Uspenskii in Prinkipo regularly for tea. He introduces Uspenskii to the cultural and dervish life of Constantinople. Work on the ballet moves at a furious pace as Gurdjieff rehearses the group in the subtle psychic and physical demands of his ballet.

Gurdjieff, Uspenskii notices, now dresses all in black and seems to go out of his way to provoke quarrels and misunderstandings.[36] This behavior alarms

---

34. There is no mention of Gurdjieff giving the location of conscience until he wrote *Beelzebub's Tales*. Uspenskii was never aware that it resides in the subconscious. As he said when speaking in England, "I personally consider that subconsciousness or unconsciousness, of which modern psychologists speak so much, does not exist at all."

35. It is the first and only time in Gurdjieff's written works that he mentions the word *karma*, though the idea is in his ballet scenario. It also does not appear in any of the transcribed meetings which are extant.

36. He apparently sees no connection between Gurdjieff working on the ballet with his students and, with it as a 'ground,' working on their emotions through a change in his appearance and behavior. He is, in effect, "playing with the devil," which for Uspenskii is a trigger event.

Uspenskii and, again, he begins to see his teacher as he had in Petersburg—the old sore of Gurdjieff's "playing" reopens.[37]

Says Uspenskii, "With Mr. Gurdjieff there are only two 'I's; one very good and one very bad. I believe that in the end the good 'I' will conquer. But meanwhile it is very dangerous to be near him."

For Uspenskii, there is the continuing problem of what he sees as the "two Gurdjieffs," the one who is serious and the other who plays. Says Uspenskii: "The problem of this 'play' or of the two personalities in Gurdjieff[38] . . . at times became more acute, at times seemed to disappear—we could never give a final answer to it. I am obliged to say that the majority of people who after a long period of work with Gurdjieff left him, went away because they had ceased to believe in the 'play,' and had begun to see 'reality' in many things which he did and which they could not accept as 'reality.'"[39]

Besides their struggle over the ballet, Gurdjieff and Uspenskii also do the same over the allegiance of Uspenskii's wife, Sophia Grigorievna; a curious parallel being the struggle of the black and white magicians for the soul of the beautiful and virginal Zeinab.[40] But for the worldly wise Madame Uspenskii the situation is clear: Gurdjieff is the teacher, her husband the pupil.

Life in Constantinople and also with Gurdjieff is becoming more difficult and uncertain by the day. Uspenskii begins to think of a way out. "In former Russia," he says, "even in its distant outskirts, work had become impossible and we were gradually approaching the period [here] which I had foreseen in Petersburg, that is, of working in Europe."

Uspenskii expects the plague of Bolshevism to spread to Germany and from there to all of Europe. Should England align itself with the United States, it might avoid Bolshevism. Once again, Uspenskii begins thinking of going to England. But the question is how to get there.

37. Says Shri Anirvân in Lizelle Reymond's *To Live Within*, 213, "Gurdjieff had this lightly tinted whiteness. He never stopped playing with all the colors of life; that is why fools cry out against him. Uspenskii tried to stay in the whiteness he had discovered; but if you are the disciple responsible for the kitchen, your duty is to prepare the food. If you refuse to do this, you will be sent away by the Master or you will leave of your own accord and your refusal will be a weight that will burden you for years and possibly even crush you."

38. Uspenskii imposes a duality on Gurdjieff. Gurdjieff is not two personalities but many personalities. They are all roles. "Exterior play a role, interior never," he says. What Gurdjieff may have achieved, and is not largely recognized, is he can move beyond *Nirvikalpa samadhi* to *Sahaja samadhi*. Uspenskii is still perceiving the world in terms of white and black, good and evil. Gurdjieff is beyond such duality and the ballet expresses this, if pondered.

39. See Essay, "*The Struggle of the Magicians*: Where I Diverge from Gurdjieff."

40. According to Moore, 151–52, "there ensued a sharp tussle between Gurdjieff and Uspenskii for the allegiance of Madame Uspenskii." Moore supports his view with a letter which he claims Madame Uspenskii wrote at this time but, in fact, she wrote the letter three years later at the Prieuré in the autumn of 1924. The letter's original reference is in Bennett's *Witness*, 158.

May 1921. Rochester, New York. Kellogg's information about Uspenskii's whereabouts finally reaches Bragdon. He sends two copies of *Tertium Organum* to Uspenskii who replies immediately, remarking on the "excellent translation and remarkably elegant edition."[41] Uspenskii asks help in getting him and his family to either England or America. Neither Bragdon nor Bessaraboff have the means, but Bragdon feels "such an inner assurance that the necessary help would be forthcoming" that he replies that he is sure "someone who had been spiritually awakened by his book, and possessing the necessary means, would give him help."

14 May 1921. Rochester. Bragdon receives a telegram.

Tertium Organum *interests me passionately. Desire very much to meet you if possible. Leaving for England end of the month.*
Viscountess Rothermere

The Viscountess Mary Lillian Rothermere is the wife of the Viscount Harold Sidney Harmsworth Rothermere, one of London's wealthiest newspaper moguls, who has great influence with Prime Minister Lloyd George.

Bragdon gives her Uspenskii's address and that same day Uspenskii receives a telegram:

Deeply impressed by your book Tertium Organum. *Wish to meet you New York or London. Will pay all expenses.*
Lady Rothermere

At the same time, Knopf sends Uspenskii a 100 pound check ($440) for royalties. With his relationship with Gurdjieff again ending, his pupils gone, his wife taking Gurdjieff as her teacher, there is no reason for Uspenskii to remain in Constantinople. Bennett convinces the British Consulate that Uspenskii is a highly desirable visitor and procures visas for him and his family. A new octave from the West opens.

At the same time, Gurdjieff receives an invitation from the dancing master Jacques-Dalcroze to come to Germany. The invitation has been initiated by Alexander de Salzmann who painted sets for Dalcroze at Hellerau, Germany.

May 1921. Constantinople. Gurdjieff closes his Institute. Conditions are no

---

41. In his introduction, Bragdon writes: "Uspenskii reveals at a stroke that astounding audacity which characterizes his thought throughout—an audacity which we are accustomed to associate with the Russian mind in all its phases. Such a title says, in effect: 'Here is a book which will reorganize all knowledge. The *Organon* of Aristotle formulated the laws under which the subject thinks; the *Novum Organum* of Bacon, the laws under which the object may be known; but *The Third Canon of Thought* existed before these two, and ignorance of its laws does not justify their violation. *Tertium Organum* shall guide and govern human thought henceforth.'"

longer right. Kemal Attaturk has risen to power. He is bent on secularizing the society. Islamic religious rites, including Dervish dances, and the wearing of fezzes, are banned. The Roman alphabet for the Turkish language is adopted.

Uspenskii speaks to Gurdjieff about writing a book on Gurdjieff's Petersburg lectures and talks with his own commentaries. Gurdjieff agrees and authorizes its publication. Uspenskii calls it *Fragments of an Unknown Teaching*. He says he chooses the word *fragments* because "Gurdjieff himself in the beginning used this word in reference to his teaching which, he said, could only be transmitted in fragments; and secondly, because no other word could better characterize Gurdjieff's method of exposition. This does not of course imply that the ideas were fragmentary for him or there was no coherent system behind them."

21 July 1921. Rochester, New York. Bragdon gets letters from all over the world about *Tertium Organum*. It has been a "stupefying success," he says.

26 July 1921. Moscow. Russia experiences famine. Five million starve to death. Lenin becomes ill. Any loud noise shocks him. The bells on his telephone are replaced with electric lights that flash for incoming calls.

Higher Dimensions

Gurdjieff and his dog, Philo, in the Caucasus

Gurdjieff dressed for the city

Madame Ostrowska

Georgi Ivanovitch Gurdjieff

Alexander de Salzmann

Jeanne de Salzmann

Elizabeta "Lili" Galumnian

Nicholas Evreinoff

Higher Dimensions

Prospectus for the Institute for the Harmonious Development of Man in Tiflis

Olgivanna Lazovich Hinzenburg & her daughter, Svetlana

Tcheslaw Tchekhovitch

Georgi Ivanovitch Gurdjieff

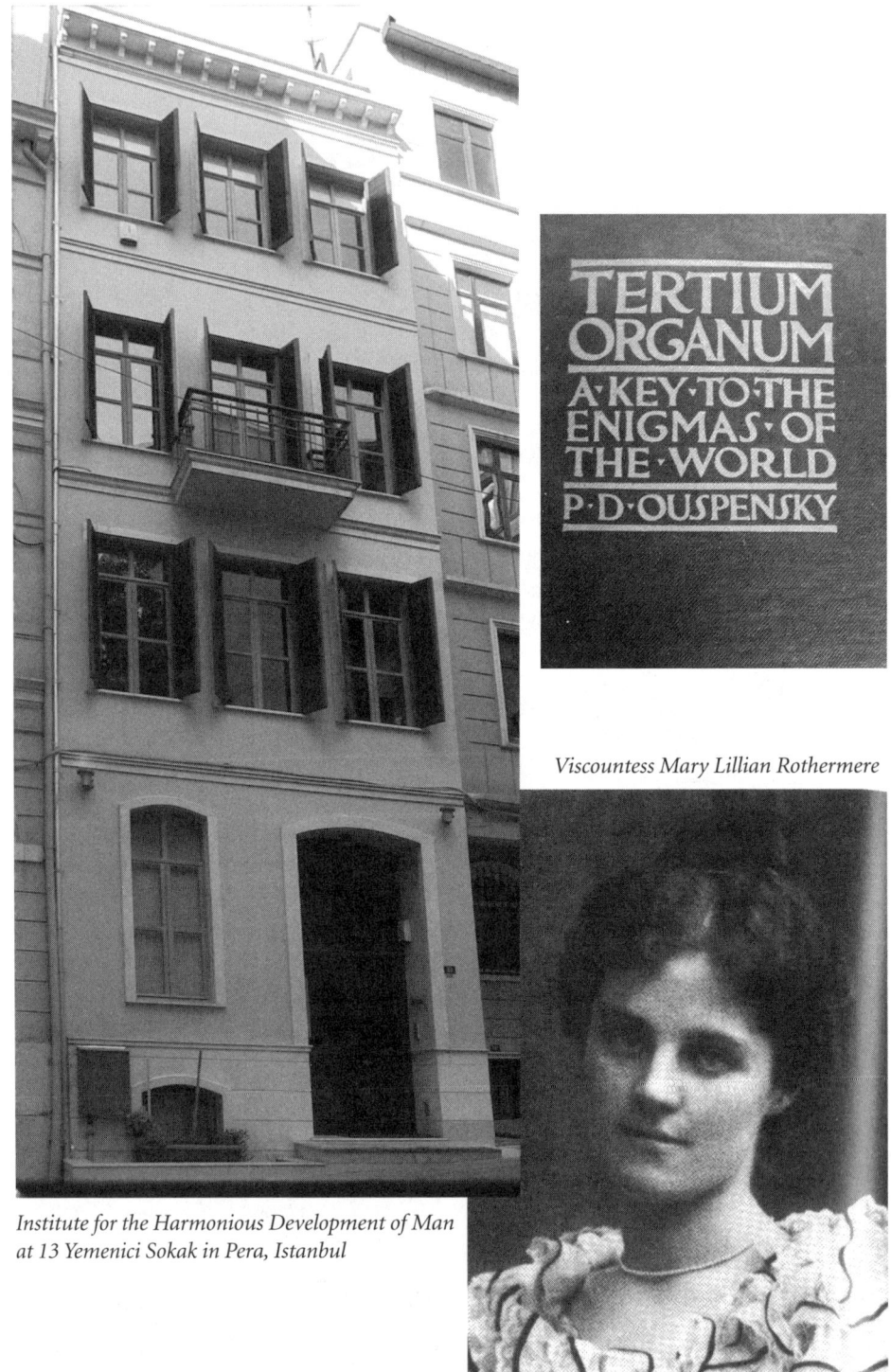

Institute for the Harmonious Development of Man at 13 Yemenici Sokak in Pera, Istanbul

Viscountess Mary Lillian Rothermere

Higher Dimensions

Prince Sultanzade Mehmed Sabâheddin

John Godolphin Bennett

Mrs. Winifred Elliot Beaumont

Part III

Magicians at War

13 August 1921. Constantinople. Gurdjieff leaves for Germany. Among Gurdjieff's entourage is Uspenskii's wife and her family. What has happened between Sophia Grigorievna and Uspenskii is not clear, but her choice of a teacher is beyond doubt. Uspenskii departs for London alone.

22 August 1921. Berlin. Gurdjieff and his students arrive. Germany is chosen because of its central geographical location and cultural level. Gurdjieff, forty-nine years old, must have a sense that time is growing short. If he is to accomplish his mission, he must move quickly. Though funds are always in question, Gurdjieff immediately rents a hall for movements in the expensive Schmargendorf district. His café of choice becomes the Romanisches, along the Kurfürstendamm.

Dr. Stjoernval and his wife have gone to Finland to sell property in order to help Gurdjieff with finances. Among those in Gurdjieff's company in Berlin are the de Hartmanns, de Salzmanns, the Zhukovs, Boris Ferapontoff, Mesdames Uspenskii and Lavrona, and the two gifted dancers Elizabeta Galumnian and Olgivanna Hinzenburg with her daughter, Svetlana. Olgivanna's husband, Valdemar, who had found his way to Constantinople, now decides to sail for America. He asked his wife to accompany him but she refused. She wants to stay with Gurdjieff.

September 1921. London. Uspenskii arrives from Constantinople. He is installed at a Bloomsbury hotel and treated like visiting royalty. Lady Rothermere introduces Uspenskii to the select of London's aristocratic, literary, and esoteric worlds. Though his command of English is far from perfect, Uspenskii's command of esoteric knowledge, his seriousness and intelligence make a powerful impression.

It's been eight years since Uspenskii and Orage first saw one another. Their ideas then were a blend of Theosophy and Nietzsche. Now Uspenskii's thinking is founded on The Fourth Way whereas Orage is still searching.

Orage, forty-eight years old, is five years Uspenskii's senior. He is taller and more angular than the square-framed, stout Uspenskii. Orage exudes an infinite poise, charm, and grace, Uspenskii tends to be reserved, brusque, no nonsense. Orage's father had died when he was one and a half years old, Uspenskii's when he was four years old. While Orage's father was a Yorkshire school teacher who had gambled away his small inheritance and left the family penniless, Uspenskii's father was of the Moscow intelligentsia.

Orage is in every sense a "self-made man," who with no powerful connections has established himself in British society as an influential editor and literary critic. He is a friend of writers like George Bernard Shaw, H. G. Wells and T. S. Eliot, who called Orage "the finest critical intelligence of our day."[1] In Russia, Uspenskii was known and honored by all the major theosophical and occult figures, here he is unknown.

Orage, like Uspenskii, is a writer possessing a formidable intellect, though without Uspenskii's mathematical prowess. However, he has a gift for quickly assimilating and articulating metaphysical complexities, and, like Uspenskii, is a magician, able to capture and sway people's attention and galvanize them to action. A close friend of Orage says, "One is not so impressed by his features so

---

1. Years later the noted American author and literary critic Waldo Frank would speak of Orage's writing as giving "to English literature a prose that ranks with Shaw's and that, for pure revolutionary thought, puts Shaw in his place as the quite proper Devil of old ladies."

much as by that which was outside and beyond his features. You were conscious of his aura; you felt his presence so much that you forgot details."

Orage no doubt expects to be Uspenskii's equal or better, but during their first serious discussion he finds himself no match at all. Uspenskii wastes no time in summarily dismissing all of Orage's views and theories as irrelevant. Remembers an intimate friend of Orage who was present at their first meeting: "Orage was shocked and hurt... [for] at every point where their views clashed, Orage had to realize that he was the novice and Uspenskii the master."

Being so easily outclassed by this Russian journalist is a shock, but Orage has a genuine thirst for real knowledge. He introduces Uspenskii to members of his psychosynthesis group, its aim being to integrate psychoanalysis with religious perspectives. Among the members are doctors Maurice Nicoll and James Carruthers Young, both associates of C. G. Jung; E. M. Eder, an intimate of Sigmund Freud; J. M. Alcock and Havelock Ellis, psychologists; Roland Kenny, former editor of the *Daily Herald;* Clifford Sharp, editor of the *New Statesman;* and Dmitri Mitrinović, a Serbian mystic and prophet, and attaché of the Serbian Legation in London.

Orage also spoke to others about Uspenskii, among them Mrs. Clifford Sharp née Rosamund Bland, who says, "He rang me up and said he had at last found a man I could believe in." In her teens, Bland had had an affair with forty-year-old H. G. Wells, and later with Orage. At Orage's behest, in order to keep their affair secret, she had married Orage's friend Clifford Sharp[2] in 1909. Now thirty-five, Rosamund mostly sees Orage as her mentor.

21 October 1921. 58 Circus Road, St. John's Wood, London. Uspenskii lectures at Lady Rothermere's studio. He speaks without notes or gestures, his words dry, economical, authoritative, having no need to convince. Though he does not read it, he hardly ever takes his eyes from the manuscript in front of him, it seemingly serving as a focal point. Occasionally, he would refer to it and then would take off his spectacles and hold the manuscript close to his eyes and then read a sentence or two. His face showed no expression of strain. It was as though he was reading something he had never seen before. The writer Rom Landau noted:

> There were none of the usual mannerisms which one so often meets with in professional lecturers. Uspenskii's movements were brisk but not hasty; the pauses and sudden halts seemed either the result of a natural reserve or merely lack of forensic gifts. There was nothing affected about them.... His command of English is serviceable but really sounds Russian, his words spoken with soft melting vowels and distinct and brisk consonants, the diction consisting of a mixture of soft cadences and

---

2. Clifford Sharp was editor of *The Crusade* and a Fabian protégé of Rosamund's father at the time. Sharp had a drinking problem and was otherwise unsuitable for marriage.

sudden abrupt stops. When the right word could not be found he simply says "or something else," or "anything you want." He leaves it at that without any sign of self-consciousness or embarrassment.... Though the speaker's manner of speech, with his clipped sentences and words that were left in the air, was at times bewildering, the lecture itself was extremely clear. The speaker's approach to his subject was very direct; the basis of his arguments painstakingly scientific, and altogether one felt that a searching mind of great independence was here revealed.

Not so impressed were two of Orage's friends, Roland Kenny and Paul Selver. Says Kenny, "When sitting in reflection or repose Uspenskii hunched himself together and looked like a dejected bird huddling in a rainstorm." For his part Selver, who wrote for *The New Age*, sees a Uspenskii who is "quite monumentally boorish. He was one of those exasperating Russians who doggedly refuse to credit any other Slav nation with artistic ability."

But Orage, long searching for a way of transcendence, saw an entirely different Uspenskii. "I may find that all I have regarded as the real me," he says, "the literary man, the artist, the philosopher, all is artificial. Perhaps my real bent is cobbling old boots."[3]

Afterward, Rosamund Bland writes a friend her impressions of Uspenskii and the meeting:

> This man, Uspenskii, isn't a psychoanalyst at all, though apparently there is something of self-analysis in his teaching. I don't really know what to call him because his teaching is not exactly religious, nor is it exactly philosophical, nor is it entirely psychological, but I suppose it takes in all three and welds them into one. He himself talks of it as purely practical, but there is the deuce of a lot of theory to be grasped before one can start the practice side of it, I should imagine.
>
> What I gathered was that there were, in various parts of the world, "schools" of this mode of thought, or whatever you call it, and that the teaching of these "schools" was practical teaching to enable the pupil to develop from being a mere automaton into something permanent and eternal. The first thing apparently that one was required to understand was that we are simply automatons and nothing more, but at the same time automatons that have within them the possibility to develop something which shall not be automatic; and the first step towards realizing one's automatism is what Uspenskii calls self-study. But self-study cannnot be done by means of analysis—analysis may come *after* one knows what one is, not as a means to *finding* out what one is. Uspenskii says that the

---

3. Gurdjieff said in one of his lectures: "There is a thousand times more value even in polishing the floor as it should be done than in writing twenty-five books."

psychoanalysts base most of their methods on the study of one form of consciousness, that is, "*sleep*," but the first thing to be able to study is the waking consciousness, because actually one is just as much asleep then as at any other time, only we think that is being awake. Being awake is something quite different, that we do not know at all. . . .

    I was thoroughly suspicious of the whole thing and its air of mystery, and also I disliked the atmosphere that the hostess [Lady Rothermere] created. It seemed as if it was "the latest thing" and she was congratulating herself on being in it and running Uspenskii as a sort of marvelous discovery. This didn't seem to me to fit with the kind of person he was nor with what I understood of his teaching and I felt all muddled up by it and uncomfortable. There seemed to be such a lot of sense in what he said in one way and at the same time there seemed to be no sense in the people there.

24 October 1921. Chinese Café, London. Orage tells Rosamund Bland that Uspenskii wishes to see her in the afternoon before the evening meeting. She is suspicious, but "finally I decided it was too interesting to miss. . . . I spent two hours with the man, and he certainly struck me as being a wonderful person. Incidentally, he has the sweetest smile in the world but that is his only attraction from an ordinary point of view, counting out his brains, of course."

2 November 1921. Baron's Court, London. Writes Rosamund Bland, "I went to see Uspenskii again yesterday at 55a Gwendwr Road in West Kensington [a modest maisonette Uspenskii has rented that will be his principal residence for the next fourteen years] and discovered that cats were his favorite animal. He said he has an awfully nice cat that comes and sits in his armchair in the evenings. He was so sweet talking about it and I felt him really human for the first time. He looks grey and severe at the meetings. His English is very charming, though, and makes me want to laugh at times."

5 November 1921. Baron's Court. Rosamund writes to her friend again:

> I told Uspenskii this afternoon about my friends: how they made it more difficult for me to realize that my personality had got to be scrapped (in the sense that one must realize how much it is just mechanical, formed by circumstances and as such quite impermanent) by clinging to it themselves and suggesting on to my belief in it their belief in it. How they feared it would change and become something they didn't like, whenever I took on some new ideas. He said that certainly this thing must change me very much and people would say how dull and boring one had become, because one was no longer

absorbed in the things one's friends were absorbed in, or in them, but that later on the friends that cared for the thing beneath personality, the essence, would see that such a change did not affect the real things they had together and would find one the same again, only possibly even better because one would have more to give to them. Of course, the people who only liked a certain *aspect of personality* probably would not stick to one, but when one had consciousness and full knowledge of oneself those people would not be important to one and so one would lose nothing.

11 November 1921. Baron's Court. Six days later Rosamund writes:

I went to see Uspenskii again on Tuesday afternoon. He was awfully nice to me and buys quantities of cream buns and cakes and makes tea for me in a little dark underground room which is rather like a tomb.... A. [Rosamund in conversation refers to Orage as "Alfred" or "Andrew" and so she uses A. when writing about him] has begun to get into trouble at meetings now. At the Monday meeting Uspenskii asked him to come to the table and explain to the group what he had said last week. He said, "Do you remember?" and A. said very gaily, "Oh, yes, I think so," and started glibly very quickly in his own way to tell us. He got pulled up every other second by Uspenskii who said, "No, I never said that. Why do you begin at the end instead of the beginning? Start again." And so on, and so on, until A. was reduced to abashed silence. It was a really dreadful exhibition and made me feel desperately uncomfortable.

15 November 1921. Baron's Court. Visiting Uspenskii again Rosamund says that at the last meeting she thinks he's been hard on Orage. Says Uspenskii—

Yes, and he will have a worse time. I will continue with him like this at every meeting now, because he does not understand anything of this. He *thinks* he understands very well and he makes no effort. He has never made sacrifice or effort in his life and he must realize this is what he must do. He cannot understand until he *feels*, and he does not feel. He only plays with it with intellect and thinks it clever, and that is not the way to understand this thing. Maybe in this way, when he finds he cannot talk at meetings he will begin to have feeling.

17 November 1921. St. Johns Wood. Rosamund writes about Orage at the Uspenskii meeting:

A. tried to be easy and rather flippant, and produced a psyche experience he has had. Personally, from the way he said it and from his face, I thought it was all made up from start to finish. I know A. when he is inventing, too well. He evidently thought that Uspenskii would think he was coming on and had done some work on himself. Uspenskii wasn't taken in for a moment. He cross-examined A. as to his feelings about it and at the end dismisses it all, telling A. in a sort of dismissing way Uspenskii has, which is terribly crushing, "That was of no importance. Perhaps a faint movement of emotional center. Quite worthless, means nothing."

A. doesn't like me at all these days, and I doubt if he will ever want to talk to me again. I can no longer look upon him as my teacher and he does not like to feel I am his equal in any way. It is obvious that he cannot stand me as things are now. I have lost him very thoroughly, and since for fifteen years I have regarded my relationship to him as the most permanent in me I shall find it there untouched when I am through this testing school, and if there is not, well, I had nothing, so how can I lose it! It may be so but it certainly does not mean that I do not *feel* as I had lost something.

21 November 1921. Baron's Court. Uspenskii earlier has told Rosamund he didn't require her to see him so much, now he says he wants to see more of her.

Things seem to be rather like that with him. Whenever you think something is decided and settled and you make plans accordingly, he reverses it — and one feels upside down. Perhaps it is done to stop one getting into ruts about this thing.... When I told Uspenskii that I felt sorry for A., but at the same time couldn't help being a little amused as well, and asked him if it was identifying with A. he said it wasn't. You know I can't really get clear about identifying. I had been thinking that when one felt pain at another's pain it was identifying, but Uspenskii says it isn't necessarily so, and that it is very important to feel for others. So now I am all muddled again about it.

You know, I am beginning to get scared about this business. B [probably Lady Rothermere who is known as "Bea"] says she is sure Uspenskii has marked me down for his own ends, and that is why he sees more of me than of the other people.

November 1921. St. John's Wood. Paraphrasing Gurdjieff, Uspenskii tells his audience straight out that man is a machine and it is because of this that they find themselves in the morass of complacency into which mankind has strayed. Worse, this machine's blind self-satisfaction, its ceaseless demand for self-gratification, has led modern civilization to the violence and crime that now breeds at every level of society. If man does not awaken to his true potentialities, and so fails to fulfill the purpose of his creation, he will become a thing of no account. Alluding to Christ, Uspenskii asserts that mankind will be the chaff that is cut down and cast into the fire.

Attending his first Uspenskii lecture is Kenneth Walker, a Harley Street surgeon. He says, "I found it difficult to follow him, partly because he speaks with so marked a Russian intonation that one had the impression that one was listening to an unknown language. He makes no use of gestures or of the other aids employed by lecturers, but this absence of all art in his delivery proved to be an asset. The very baldness of his statements added weight to them and disarmed all adverse criticism."

Walker asks Uspenskii, "Isn't this idea that man is only a machine the view of the behaviorist school of psychology? It seems to me to be only another way of saying that he is a chain of reflexes."

"For the behaviorists," answers Uspenskii, "it is only a convenient theory which they fail to apply to themselves and to their own mental constructions. They see automatism in others, but not in themselves. For us it has got to become something far more real than this. Unless we realize with our whole being that we do not possess unity, consciousness, and will, we will make no attempt to acquire them."

A question about man being a machine follows. Uspenskii answers:

> Man serves Nature's purpose as he is and, so far as the universe is concerned, there is no need for him to change. Asleep or awake, with or without will, a *machine* of a man [he emphasized the word], he does all that is required of him. If he is to change, if he is to develop his latent powers, it must be for his own purposes and by means of his own individual struggles. Nature has brought his development up to a certain point and has then left him to his own devices. She will help him no more, but she has not denied him the chance of evolving further to a yet higher stage. But if this further evolution is to occur, it will not be by nature that it is brought about, but by means of man's own conscious struggles.

Walker is impressed by Uspenskii's clarity of thought, lack of sentimentality and command of the subject. So is Maurice Nicoll, another Harley Street physician and a disciple of Carl Jung, who is also in the audience. He rushes home and shakes his wife, Catherine, out of bed, telling her, "You must come and hear Uspenskii. He is the only man who has ever answered my questions."

The interest is such that Uspenskii's lectures are moved from Lady Rothermere's studio to Earl's Court, 38 Warwick Gardens, West Kensington. An audience of forty or fifty British intellectuals, professionals and aristocrats attend his lectures, and Uspenskii is soon lecturing three and four evenings a week. A Russian émigré, Eugenie Kadloubovsky, becomes his devoted secretary.

Magicians at War

24 November 1921. Berlin. Gurdjieff gives his first lecture. The theme is man's mechanicality as seen through his habitual postures. The de Hartmanns introduce him to influential friends such as Count Valvitz and Princess Gagarin, but nothing comes of it.

Gurdjieff tries to purchase the Hellerau in Dresden, the former center of Dalcroze's Eurhythmics Institute. Here he meets Jessmin Howarth, an Englishwoman who is choreographer of the Paris Opera, and Rosemary Lillard, a twenty-one-year-old gifted pianist from Houston, Texas. Both become his lifelong pupils.

The purchase stalls, complications arise. A legal battle ensues. Germany, despite its Teutonic spirit of self-sacrifice and cultivation of virtue—traits that seemed to make it a natural base for Gurdjieff's teaching—has strangely turned a cold shoulder. Could it have been as simple a thing as Gurdjieff's dark complexion? Whatever the cause, Germany was not to be.

1 December 1921. London. Writes Rosamund:

> Uspenskii seemed rather depressed when I last saw him, and talked of going away, back to Constantinople, because things were not going well here. As far as I can make out he thinks I am the only one who takes things really seriously and who can be of use to the work from his point of view, and it is not worth his while to spend so much energy in order to perhaps get one person into a condition where they can be useful. If he is going to spend so much force, he must have more result than that.

(How her relationship with Uspenskii progressed she doesn't say, but the following year when the Institute opens at the Prieuré, she is there.)

7 December 1921. London. Rosamund had felt herself becoming more and more independent of Orage and now she finds:

> I have lost him absolutely. At the meetings now we hardly look or speak to one another, and I know he does not want to see me any more.... A. has been a great part of my life and has been so for fifteen years, and he is gone out of it, except just in so far as we have to meet to talk about Uspenskii's teaching. The old tie of my relationship with him, which I thought so deathless, is quite dead. Killed by changes in me and in him. We both know this without speaking a word.

1922. London. Anna Ilinishna Hewett, now married for five years and living in London, meets Uspenskii. "He had developed a hard outer shell," she says, "and I wondered then why he had crushed the gentle, poetic radiance of his St.

Petersburg days. Possibly he thought of this side of himself as a weakness, yet it was in this happy mood that his inspiration and vision were strongest: the intellect had nothing to do with it."

February 1922. London. Katherine Mansfield's third collection of short stories, *The Garden Party,* is published. Reviews are ecstatic. The year before she had written to Orage:

> I want to tell you how sensible I am of your wonderful unfailing kindness to me in the 'old days'. And to thank you for all you let me learn from you. I am still—more shame to me—very low down in the school. But you taught me to write, you taught me to think; you showed me what there was to be done and what *not* to do.... If only one day I might write a book of stories good enough to 'offer' you.... If I don't succeed in keeping the coffin from the door you will know this was my ambition.
> Yours in admiration and gratitude
> Katherine Mansfield

Early February 1922. London. Six months after Gurdjieff's arrival in the West, his Institute for the Harmonious Development of Man remains only an idea. Hearing of Uspenskii's success, the fate of the two men ever entwined, Gurdjieff crosses the Channel. They meet and Uspenskii's attitude becomes "much more definite." He sees again, so he believes, "all the former obstacles that had begun to appear in Essentuki." Though he doesn't believe it's possible to work with Gurdjieff, he still expects "a great deal more from Gurdjieff's work." And so he doesn't break entirely. In fact, Uspenskii decides to help Gurdjieff establish his Institute in London.

13 February 1922. Warwick Gardens, London. Gurdjieff's first talk[4] in London is at the Theosophical Hall at Warwick Gardens. Some sixty people attend. Many, including Orage, already think of themselves as Uspenskii's pupils. Gurdjieff and his translators, Frank Pinder and Olga de Hartmann, along with Uspenskii, mount the platform. Pinder translates. The audience, awed by Gurdjieff's presence, sits in petrified silence. Gurdjieff, as always, comes right to the point:

"When we speak of ourselves ordinarily we speak of 'I.' We say '*I*' did this... '*I*' think this... '*I*' want to do this—but this is a mistake. There is no such I or rather there are hundreds, thousands of little 'I's in every one of us.... We are governed by external circumstances. All our actions follow the line of least resistance to the pressure of outside circumstances."

Gurdjieff is asked if it is possible to alter one's emotions through acts of judgment. He answers:

---

4. The exact number of meetings in London and the dates on which they were held remains uncertain, given the references in the public sources from that period.

One center of our machine cannot change another center. For example: in London I am irritable, the weather and the climate dispirit me and make me bad-tempered, whereas in India I am good-tempered. Therefore my judgment tells me to go to India and I shall drive out the emotion of irritability. But then, in London, I find I can work; in the tropics not as well. And so, there I should be irritable for another reason. You see, emotions exist independently of the judgment and you cannot alter one by means of another.

At one point someone asks, "Mr. Gurdjieff, what would it be like to be conscious in essence?"

"Everything more vivid," is Gurdjieff's memorable, rapier-like reply.

After this first talk, there is no question for Orage of who the teacher is. "I knew that Gurdjieff was the teacher," declares Orage. "Uspenskii for me represented knowledge—great knowledge; Gurdjieff, understanding—though of course Gurdjieff had all the knowledge, too."

5 March 1922. Warwick Gardens. Gurdjieff returns from Germany to give a second talk. Pinder translates. At its close Gurdjieff chastises his audience:

"All the questions I have heard tonight are higher mathematics. Nobody knows elementary mathematics.[5] And so such questions are useless."

Later, speaking in private with Uspenskii, Gurdjieff finally delivers an all-out assault. He is working on the wrong lines. He is too intellectual. He lacks an understanding of the real purpose of the Work and of the purpose of himself. All his vast knowledge would be useless unless he works on himself so as to understand basic principles. If Uspenskii truly wishes to understand, he must stop teaching and begin again—work again with Gurdjieff.

It is a scorching appraisal. How could Uspenskii not hear it? Not understand his identification? How could he believe he was a spiritual equal, or near-equal, to Gurdjieff? But Uspenskii didn't hear the appraisal—he heard the assault.

Although a man of rare intellect, honest and uncompromising in his search for real knowledge, Uspenskii's blindness here and elsewhere shows the strength of buffers.[6]

15 March 1922. Warwick Gardens. Gurdjieff speaks again and, having failed to awaken his rebellious Russian pupil privately, Gurdjieff plays one of his last cards. He speaks on "Essence and Personality." And, again, instead of Uspenskii, Gurdjieff has Pinder translate.

---

5. This may be a subtle criticism of Uspenskii who is a mathematician as well as a writer.
6. Psychological 'partitions' created to lessen shocks and contradictions so that "a man can always be in the right." See *Search*, 154–55.

"Normal human beings are the exception," Gurdjieff says. "Nearly everyone has only the essence of a child. It is not natural that in a grown-up man the essence should be a child. Because of this, he remains timid underneath and full of apprehensions. This is because he knows that he is not what he pretends to be, but he cannot understand why."

Uspenskii breaks in. Pinder's translation is not accurate, he says.

"Pinder is interpreting for me—not you," answers Gurdjieff.

Gurdjieff then directly attacks Uspenskii, repeating in public now what had been said in private: *Uspenskii is neither mandated nor qualified to teach.*[7]

Later, Gurdjieff remarks to Pinder of the meeting: "Now they will have to choose a teacher." Presumably, Uspenskii will have to as well—either himself or Gurdjieff. But for all of Gurdjieff's words, and the enormity of his presence, they are without effect. Yet, despite the anger and betrayal he must have felt, Uspenskii still doesn't break completely with Gurdjieff. In fact, he helps to collect money for Gurdjieff's London Institute at Hampstead. But he does say, and unequivocally—"I had decided for myself that if the Institute opened in London I would go either to Paris or to America."

And so, since Uspenskii first broke with Gurdjieff in Essentuki, the struggle between the two continues. The Institute finally opens, but Gurdjieff has a visa problem, though the Home Secretary agrees he is no Bolshevik. Lady Rothermere promises Gurdjieff she will attempt to wield her influence and speak to the Home Secretary about visas.

Two days before she is to leave for a vacation in Spain she tells Uspenskii that the Home Secretary promised to see her on her last day. Afterward, she would meet with Orage.

When Uspenskii and she speak on the telephone she says everything is arranged. The next day Uspenskii receives a note from Orage saying that Lady Rothermere had seen the Home Secretary and he said to her that formal visa applications must be sent, and that "he would do all that is possible."

Though the applications were sent, for a long time there was no reply. It became known that Lady Rothermere did not speak with the Home Secretary personally, but instead had asked her cousin to do so.

"Orage knew it," Uspenskii says, "but he told me a lie because Lady Rothermere asked him to. So they both lied. And certainly it was my fault" [in the sense that he had accepted them into his group].

26 April 1922. Hamburg, Germany. Gurdjieff and Olgivanna Hinzenburg are on

---

7. It is a brutal disrobing. Uspenskii, the pupil Gurdjieff had staked his hopes on to help him establish his teaching, believes he is able to judge his teacher's motives, his character, and yet Uspenskii had worked little on essence. His development is only partial. To continue to teach would crystallize him at a level that would make further development impossible.

hand as her brother, Vlado, and Svetlana prepare to board the SS *Orbita* bound for America. He and his wife were childless and he hoped his niece would repair that. Gurdjieff had agreed. When Olgivanna balked he reminded her of what she had told him in Tiflis three years earlier: that she was willing to make any sacrifice to achieve immortality. Then he gestured toward her five-year-old daughter—"Even that?"

May 1922. London. It's been almost a year since Gurdjieff gave Uspenskii permission to write an exposition of the teaching with his own commentary. He now begins *Fragments of an Unknown Teaching*.

June 1922. London. Orage considers selling *The New Age*. Economic conditions are bleak, circulation has dramatically fallen, and many of the weekly's backers have withdrawn subsidies.

When he and his friend from Leeds, Holbrook Jackson, bought[8] the penny weekly in 1907 its circulation was 4,000. The first issue under Orage's and Jackson's editorship appeared May 2. The sole editorship was Orage's with the first issue of January 1908, as he and Jackson disagreed over the paper's direction, after which Jackson ran off with Orage's wife, Jean. As Orage himself had not been faithful he could have no outward complaints.

Orage opened the weekly's pages, published every Thursday, to a lively literary, social and political discussion and dissent, and within a year's time circulation had risen to more than 20,000 copies. His personality, erudition and high level of literary criticism attracted such writers as Ezra Pound, T. E. Hulme, Katherine Mansfield, H. G. Wells, Bernard Shaw, G. K. Chesterton, Edwin Muir, Wyndham Lewis, Richard Aldington and Herbert Read. Its cultural success did not carry over financially. It could only pay contributors who had no other regular income. It ran an annual deficit of over one thousand pounds ($4,400) which was met by contributions from wealthy friends.

A great help to Orage editorially and otherwise was the entrance that second year of twenty-nine-year-old, South African-born, green-eyed Beatrice Hastings (née Emily Alice Haigh; she substituting "Beatrice" for "Emily," as Orage substituted "Richard" for "James"). A feisty, erudite, feminist-anti-feminist,[9] six years Orage's junior, Hastings quickly jumped into the role of *The New Age*'s lone in-house writer-gofer, as well as bedding down with its editor, explaining it as "Aphrodite amusing herself at our expense."

---

8. Orage convinced George Bernard Shaw and his friend Lewis Wallace, a Leeds banker and theosophist, to lend the 1,000 pounds ($4,400) needed to purchase the dying weekly.

9. Hastings' *The New Age* article "The Ordinary Home Life of Women" posits that the home life "is referred to as 'domestic serfdom,' every woman is told that she is 'exploited to get nothing but her keep,' and she is jeered on to demand maternity benefits so that she may imitate the 'professional woman' who employs nurses and servants. God knows who, exactly, are to be the nurses and servants, but they would evidently be the imbecile scum of femininity."

Georgi Ivanovitch Gurdjieff

In February of 1910 Katherine Mansfield (née Kathleen Mansfield Beauchamp, daughter of a wealthy New Zealand banker), twenty-one-years-old, unpublished and unknown, found her way along with her then husband George Bowden, a professional tenor, to 38 Cursitor Street, home of *The New Age*. Leaving her husband standing on the landing, Mansfield spoke to Orage directly, and gave him her short story "The-Child-Who-Was-Tired"[10] which he ran that very month. In March he published three more stories and another two in July, these making up the Bavarian stories, published in 1911 as a book, *In a German Pension*. Mansfield became enamoured of Orage. One of Orage's biographers, John Carswell, described him:

> Orage was tall, slim, dark-haired, with a feline face, hazel eyes which were lively and challenging and in moments of excitement emitted a red glint and in whose movements there was something cat-like, he walking as though he were going to pounce on something, much as his mind pounced upon an idea or an opponent. His expression was earnest without being solemn. There was wit in his poise and manner and he was good to look at without being good-looking.

Mansfield jettisoned her husband and began to spend weekends with Orage and Beatrice Hastings at Orage's country cottage in Sussex. It was an exciting threesome for a number of years, but eventually, as Hastings wrote many years later, "Orage named Mansfield *marmoset,* thought her vulgar and enterprising and couldn't understand my putting up with her. She used to sit among us, silent and furtive, beady, obsequious, or suddenly pompous, picking up everything everyone said and did, 'grist for the sketch-mill,' as A. R. O. called her memory." Two years later, in 1912, Mansfield took John Middleton Murry as a lover and began to publish regularly with his literary magazine *Rhythm*, later renamed *The Blue Review*, its first issue appearing in June 1911, its final issue in July 1913. By 1914 Hastings had run off to Paris, indulging in a sad tale of drink, drugs and dancing on tables, and having a slew of affairs, most notably with the painter Amedeo Modigliani.[11] With Mansfield and Murry marrying, Orage began publishing negative installments on women, a negative novel about the disastrous effects of feminine influence (Hastings and Mansfield) on the masculine mind.

---

10. It was a rendering into English of Chekhov's "Sleepyhead" with many of her own changes. This wasn't realized by critics until late in her life. That said, it is generally agreed that Mansfield revolutionized the short story.

11. Though a prodigious writer with a strong masculine voice, Hastings assumed many pseudonyms in writing for *The New Age* and so was not well known. In 1936 Blue Moon Press published her forty-two-page pamphlet *The Old New Age: Orage and Others*. "Until I came in, *The New Age*, editorially, was a rag." She gives a bitter and biting character assassination of Orage and others before, at age sixty-four, committing suicide by turning on the gas in her kitchen; her pet mouse was a fellow victim.

Orage published "A Seventh Tale for Men Only" under the pseudonym of R. H. Congreve, in the same issues of *The New Age* as Beatrice's "Feminine Fables," articles about women, men, society, and literary style that she makes into fables. Readers in the know were treated to a head-to-head, war of words combat of ex-lovers.

14 July 1922. Paris. With Germany inhospitable to Gurdjieff's Institute and an English passport denied him, Britain thinking he might be a Russian spy, France is the default choice. Gurdjieff arrives from Germany accompanied by the de Hartmanns. They are met by the de Salzmanns.

Soon it is learned that a beautifully furnished château is for sale, located on the Avenue du Valvins at Avon near Fontainebleau, thirty-four miles from Paris. It is the property of the widow of Fernand Labori, the lawyer who successfully defended Captain Dreyfus, who had been accused of spying. Called Le Prieuré des Basses Loges (the Priory), it has an interesting history, having once been a Carmelite monastery and, later, the home of Louis XIV's famous mistress, Madame de Maintenon.

The château sits behind a high stone wall and heavy iron gates, and it has not been lived in since 1914. A small fountain lies within the gates of the two-story château; to the rear is a terrace with two more fountains and a long avenue of lime, maple, chestnut, and conifer trees. In the gardens there are an enormous glass orangery, a small house known as Le Paradou, and other outbuildings. The château is set in a park of forty-five acres. An additional two hundred acres, bounded by a stone wall, adjoin the Forest of Fontainebleau.

After some strong negotiating by Olga de Hartmann—Gurdjieff told her to remember herself at all times and never to forget her intention—the château is leased, fully furnished, for sixty-five thousand francs ($5,400).

16 July 1922. London. Uspenskii writes to Orage:

> I received some very strange letters from several members of the new groups. I see from these letters that somebody is frightening people out of their heads, telling them awful stories about many cases of madness in connection with the work, about danger of self-observation, about "tortures," the sexual perversity, about "sacrifices" of people going to Paris, etc., etc.
>
> I would like to know where all this nonsense comes from, and I ask you very much to find it out.
>
> I am writing about that to Mrs. Page and Wolton and ask them to help you.
>
> I hope you keep strictly to my instructions and during the meetings with the new people talk with them about themselves and about their observations and during the Thursday group meetings discuss these talks.

22 July 1922. London. Orage, who says "while Uspenskii had found what I was looking for, I *knew* that Gurdjieff was the teacher," writes to Gurdjieff :

> I wish above anything to work in the Institute with the high hopes of being allowed to work for the Institute. I want to begin at the earliest possible moment. But, even supposing that you will accept me as a pupil in anything, I, then, am tied to the following life circumstances:
> I own and edit *The New Age*, a weekly I have edited for fifteen years. It is my only source of income, about 250 pounds per annum ($1,100).
> I have no other capital. Consequently, if I can come to Paris, I should have to sell or otherwise dispose of *The New Age*.
> I probably should not get more than 100 pounds for it.
> I am willing to give up the *N. A.* and to chance the future. However, before doing anything final, I want to ask your advice.

1 August 1922. London. Uspenskii, answering for Gurdjieff, writes Orage telling him to sell *The New Age*, that "the 100 pounds will give you a year in the Institute and during that time you will become capable for a more responsible work and in that case will not have to think about your living. So arrange your plans and come if you wish."

Late August 1922. Paris. Ethel Merston sits beside Gurdjieff on a bench on the Boulevard de la Madeleine.

Merston, now thirty-nine years old, had begun with theosophy and then went into therapy with Maurice Nicoll but had ended it, as she said, "He was in too much of a hurry to break things down before having anything to put into their place, that is, before one was ready to face the void, to let go of what one knew." She then heard Uspenskii lecture on the Fourth Dimension at the Quest Society and thereafter attended his talks and heard Gurdjieff's when he came earlier in the year.

Now, hearing of the Institute's opening, she has come to Paris. She asks to be accepted at the Institute for the Harmonious Development of Man. They sit in silence for a good half-hour. "I felt he was weighing up whether to take me or not."

Suddenly, Gurdjieff says—"Come."

He then takes her to his flat for lunch and drives her to the Prieuré.

30 August 1922. London. Orage tells his friend and former mistress Katherine Mansfield, near death from pulmonary tuberculosis, about Uspenskii. She begins to attend Uspenskii's lectures. Her husband, John Middleton Murry, does as well. She finds Uspenskii "an extraordinarily sympathetic person." Murry, forever identified with ideas, says, "I don't feel influenced by Uspenskii.... I merely feel I've heard ideas like my ideas, but bigger ones, far more definite ones." Later, Murry would reflect, "I could scarcely bear to discuss the doctrines of Uspenskii and Gurdjieff with Katherine. The gulf between us was painful to us both; and living under the same roof became a kind of torture."

28 September 1922. London. Orage announces his resignation as editor and says he would "shortly be leaving London in connection with work of general and special interest."
The New Age sells for two hundred and fifty pounds.

30 September 1922. Prieuré, Avon, France. One year after his arrival in the West, his Nansen passport for Russian refugees intact, Gurdjieff buys the Prieuré for 700,000 francs ($58,300), the monies primarily supplied by Lady Rothermere and Ralph Philipson, a wealthy Northumberland coal mine owner and an admirer of Uspenskii and Orage. Here he establishes his Institute—"This child I had conceived"—which he sets up on the same basis as he had before, that is, "I wished to create around myself conditions in which man would be continually reminded of the sense and aim of his existence by an unavoidable friction between his conscience and the automatic manifestations of his nature." Always pushing things to the edge, Gurdjieff then borrows on his ownership of the Prieuré to be able to refurbish the château, the other buildings and the grounds to his liking.

He then has a prospectus for the Institute written and circulated. It begins:

The Institute for the Harmonious Development of Man by means of the system of Gurdjieff is, as it were, the continuation of the society known as the Seekers After Truth. . . .

The prospectus continues with a short history of the society and then begins its analysis of the conditions and situation which faces modern man, who, it says, has become "an uprooted being, unable to adapt to his life, alien to all its present conditions." It shows where the problems lie and tells how the Institute will help its students to correct them.

14 October 1922. Le Select Hôtel, Paris. Katherine Mansfield, after hearing Uspenskii, has come to Paris and asked for admittance to the Institute. Gurdjieff sends Dr. James Young to examine her. She is exhausted and suffering from high fever and agonising headaches and neuritis. It is obvious to Young that Mansfield has not long to live.

17 October 1922. Prieuré. Though the Institute does not officially open until November, Katherine Mansfield arrives, her face the color of chalk, her back aching with sciatica. Mansfield has tried every therapy available. She has become convinced that Gurdjieff could not only help her with her disease but with a spiritual regeneration as well. Upon seeing Gurdjieff, she thinks "he looks exactly like a desert chief."

Gurdjieff has many misgivings. "If she dies here, just imagine what malicious gossip will ensure—another pretext for slander. They are bound to say that we were the cause of her premature death." He allows her to stay for fourteen days. He gives her what she calls "a most lovely sumptuous room, a kind of glorified Garsington." Olgivanna asks to be her nurse along with her other duties as the Prieuré manager and cook. Gurdjieff agrees. Olgivanna says, "I learned that a great many prominent sanatoria had closed their doors to her under various pretexts. Hotels, of course, refused her. She was in the last stage of tuberculosis. She was soon to leave this world, probably in a few months. One of the most humane acts Gurdjieff ever did was to accept her into the Institute." Gurdjieff appoints Olgivanna and Adèle Katian, a young Lithuanian, to look after her.

Mansfield's letters give a vivid picture of her impressions:

> It's a most wonderful old place in an amazingly lovely park. About forty people, chiefly Russians, are here working, at every possible kind of thing—I mean outdoor work, looking after animals, gardening, indoor work, music, dancing—it seems a bit of everything.... A dancing hall is being built and the house is still being organized.... Mr. Gurdjieff likes me to go into the kitchen in the late afternoon and 'watch.' I have a chair in a corner. It's a large kitchen with six helpers—Madame Julia Ostrowska, the head, walks about like a queen exactly—she is extremely beautiful. Mr. Gurdjieff strides in, takes up a handful of shredded cabbage and eats it... there are at least twenty pots on the stove—and it's so full of life and humor and ease that one wouldn't be anywhere else.... The cows are being bought today—Gurdjieff is going to build a high couch in the stable where I can sit and inhale their breath! I know later on I shall be put in charge of those cows—Everyone calls them already "Mrs. Murry's cows."

24 October 1922. Prieuré. Katherine Mansfield writes to her husband:

> I want to learn something that no books can teach me, and I want to try & escape from my terrible illness. That again you can't be expected to understand. You think I am like other people—I mean—*normal*. I'm not. I don't know which is the ill me or the well me. I am simply one pretense after another—only now I recognize it.
>
> I believe Mr. Gurdjieff is the only person who can help me. It is great happiness to be here. Some people are stranger than ever but the strangers I am at last feeling near and they are my own people at last. So I feel. Such beautiful understanding and sympathy I have never known in the outside world.

November 1922. Prieuré. Students arrive, ringing the bell by the heavy iron gate of the château on Avenue de Valvins. Ushered into the courtyard, they pass the small fountain and approach a beautifully proportioned building with dormer windows set in a gray slate mansard roof. Inside they find oak paneled walls, ornate Empire mirrors, Oriental carpets, panther skins, Levantine pouffes, and other costly treasures. To the left of the entrance is a wide staircase leading to the top two floors, which have been christened by Gurdjieff "The Ritz" and the "Monk's Corridor." The attic is "Cow's Alley." To the right is a reception room and long hallway, hung with paintings, leading to an elegant formal dining room, a library which has no books, a large salon with fireplace and a Pleyel grand piano, and a study and a game room further on.

The Prieuré and the Paradou, a small two-story residence on the property, can accommodate about fifty-five people. Rooms are quickly filled with Gurdjieff's family and oldest students: the Stjoernvals, de Hartmanns, de Salzmanns, Uspenskii's wife Sophia, Elizabeta Galumnian, Olgivanna Hinzenburg, and, of course, Julia Ostrowska. Among those from London ringing the Prieuré's bell, marked "*Sonnez fort*" (ring loudly), are some very strong and successful people, such as A. R. Orage, Rowland Kenney, doctors James Carruthers Young, Konstantin Kiselev and J. M. Alcock, the diplomat Eric Graham Forbes, Misses Bland, Merston, Gordon, Crowdy and American-born Rosemary Lillard, and later, at Uspenskii's direction, J. G. Bennett. Also, either now or later, the Moscow lawyer Alexei Yakovlevich Rachmilievitch. The writer Carl Bechhofer Roberts visits from time to time but remains uncommitted.

The prospective pupils no doubt have come expecting to be initiated into the esoteric world, but, says Gurdjieff, "Everything is body." Though none realize it, no one consciously inhabits their body. The body is taken for granted, only noticed in fear, desire or disease, and quickly dismissed once these pass. The head and heart's relationship to the body is practically nil. Hard physical work helps to center and reconnect the pupils with their bodies, allowing their bodies to begin to breathe and eat normally. The pupils then learn what it is to actually inhabit a living, breathing body. Such work also allows pupils to struggle with reactions and attitudes of self-pity, sloth, superiority.

The pupils are put to work scrubbing latrines, felling trees, digging ditches, doing farm work, gardening, housework, laundry and the like. Everyone is up around four in the morning. Breakfast consists only of coffee, toast and butter. For lunch there is stew with vegetables and perhaps a pudding. There follows a late afternoon break for tea, bread and butter. In the evening everyone bathes and dresses for dinner, which is often quite lavish. Generally, guests, older students and Gurdjieff eat in the spacious and well-furnished "English" dining room, said to be where Madame de Maintenon entertained Louis XIV. There is a large table seating about twenty-five people, with two side tables seating twenty each. Gurdjieff sits in the middle of the large table facing the windows. Directly behind him on the mantelpiece rests a photo of Ioannis Gurdjieff, his beloved father. In contrast, the "Russian" dining room where the younger pupils eat is dark and bare except for a large table and benches. In good weather the pupils eat on the terrace.

After dinner Gurdjieff may give a talk, or Thomas de Hartmann may play the piano, or perhaps there are movements. Gurdjieff would often talk until midnight or later. He pours out a torrent of words lasting for several minutes, then pauses for Pinder to translate. Pinder condenses it all into a sentence or two.[12] Gurdjieff looks at him, shrugs his shoulders, and smiles sardonically.

Early Saturday evening the men take a communal Turkish bath; the women bathe earlier. With the men, Gurdjieff discusses things like "the four sources of action," these being "mother-in-law, digestion, John Thomas[13] and cash." After the men's bath there follows a feast and ritual toasts to the idiots. Except for such interludes, the physical, emotional, and mental demands are great. This unrelenting pressure creates conditions in which students can see themselves—not as they imagine themselves to be—but as they really are.

Gurdjieff, of course, does his best to add to the pressure. Says one person, "He constantly manipulated people and situations so as to provoke friction, to create negative emotions between people and give them an opportunity of seeing something in themselves."

Gurdjieff's behavior at the Prieuré raises in his students the full spectrum of emotional reactions, everything "from reverent adoration to diabolical spasms of hatred."

2 November 1922. London. T. S. Eliot's wife, Vivian, writes to Ezra Pound in Paris as to his question about Lady Rothermere: "She is now in that asylum for the insane called Le Prieuré where she does religious dances naked with Katherine Mansfield."[14] Says the writer and critic Edmund Wilson, "The Russo-Greek charlatan Gurdjieff undertook to renovate the personalities of discontented well-to-do persons . . . reducing them to a condition of complete docility."

4 November 1922. Prieuré. Dr. Maurice Nicoll, like Dr. Young,[15] has given up his lucrative Harley Street practice. He arrives along with his wife, Catherine, their young baby, and a nurse. Gurdjieff appoints Nicoll as the new kitchen boy. His work begins at 5 a.m. with lighting the boilers and lasts till 11 p.m. During that time hundreds of greasy plates, cups, glasses, and pots and pans must be washed with no soap and often no hot water. Meanwhile, his wife helps with the cooking and

---

12. This shows the level of understanding which Pinder thinks he has come to. It will be a problem for him as he later shows.
13. The slang name for penis.
14. *Ezra Pound: Selected Letters* (New York: New Dimensions, 1971), 588.
15. Both Nicoll and Young had studied with Jung in Zurich. When Freud hears they have ended up at Gurdjieff's Prieuré, he exclaims, "Ah, you see what happens to Jung's disciples!"

her sister, Léonor Champion Jones, cleans bathrooms. When anything goes wrong, Gurdjieff singles out Nicoll, calling "Nicoll!" and making a gesture of despair.

On a hillside, not far from the main house, is an old cellar dug into a massive rock. Here Gurdjieff decides to build a Turkish bath in the form of a grotto. It is hard labor. For three hours the men, including Tcheslaw Tchekhovitch, the former wrestler and the strongest pupil, have been trying to break a huge rock with heavy sledgehammers with no success.

Gurdjieff comes by. He tells the men to turn the rock. He examines all sides. "Mr. Gurdjieff makes several movements, to be sure of the best grip," Tchekhovitch says. "Then . . . a flash in the air, followed by a dry sound — crack!" Now, with the rock smashed into four pieces, Gurdjieff hands the sledgehammer back, saying, "Keep going. When force isn't enough, you must find the artist's touch."

Several weeks later Gurdjieff comes by the Turkish bath again and finds the men taking a break, amusing themselves with rudimentary acrobatics. "What! You can't even do a childish exercise like that!" exclaims Gurdjieff. He asks which leg is the more difficult to hold in the air. The left, he is told.

Gurdjieff then extends his left leg so it is parallel to the ground. Slowly, he bends his right leg, lowering himself in stages to where his whole weight is seated on his right heel. He then slowly bends his left leg and brings the sole of his left foot to his bent right knee. Maintaining that posture, he clears his throat and takes a pack of cigarettes from his chest pocket, lights up and smokes, and starts a conversation which doesn't end until he finishes the cigarette. His body then gives successive jolts upwards, the left leg continuing to rest on the right knee. Then he simply lets his left foot fall to the ground and says, "Try to sew the rest of the carpets together for tonight," and walks off.

The Turkish bath finished, Gurdjieff demands a Study House be built in a fortnight. Noticing how it is being built, Nicoll asks Gurdjieff, "Why don't you build more solidly?"

"This is only temporary," answered Gurdjieff. "In a very short time everything will be different. Everyone will be elsewhere. Nothing can be built permanently at this moment."

Gurdjieff hears some people talking about the formatory center. He reminds them, "It is not a center, it is an apparatus. It consists of a number of machines connected with the three centers. Shocks from one center pass through the formatory apparatus and if the associated thoughts, feelings, or sensations are strong enough they will set up corresponding associations in another center [mental, emotional, instinctive-sexual]. The associations between centers are conveyed through the formatory apparatus connections. The centers are of spiritized matter, so to say, the formatory apparatus not; it is machine that we are born with."

During the day, when he is not in Paris, Gurdjieff can often be seen walking around the grounds urging people on—"Must be done in half the time," he implores.

Georgi Ivanovitch Gurdjieff

He purposely places people in situations where they will experience a loss of face. Should false personality appear, Gurdjieff ruthlessly attacks it, forcing students to see and rely upon that which is real in themselves.

"I cannot change your being," he says, "but I can create conditions, thanks to which you can change yourselves."

10 November 1922. Katherine Mansfield writes to her husband.

> Until I came here I did not realize with what a little bit of my mind, even, I lived. I was a little European with a liking for eastern carpets and music and for something that I vaguely called The East. But now I feel as though I am turned to the side far more than the other. The West seems so poor, so scattered. I cannot believe knowledge and wisdom are there... In three weeks here I feel I have spent years in India, Arabia, Afghanistan, Persia. That is very odd, isn't it. And oh, how one wanted to voyage like this—how bound one felt. Only now I know!
>
> There is another thing here. Friendship. The real thing that you and I have dreamed of. Here it exists between women & women & men & women & one feels it is unalterable, and living in a way it never can be anywhere else. I cant say I have friends yet. I am simply not fit for them. I don't know myself enough to be really trusted, and I am weak where these people are strong. But even the relationships I have are dear beyond any friendships I have known.
>
> But I am giving the impression that we all live together in brotherly love & blissful happiness. Not at all. One suffers terribly. If you have been ill for 5 years you cant expect to be well in five weeks. If you have been ill for 20 years & according to Mr. Gurdjieff we all of us have our 'illness' it takes very severe measures to put one right. But the point is there is hope.
>
> I wish you could meet some of the men here. You would like them very much, especially a Mr. Salzmann, who speaks very little.

Olgivanna says Gurdjieff had a terrace built in the cow-stable right over the cows for Mansfield.

> The air was supposed to be good for her illness. Our best painter, Alexander Salzmann, painted the roof over the terrace in gay patterns of trees and flowers, animals and birds. He caricatured some of the people of the Institute in the faces of animals and birds, himself included. Stjoernval was depicted as a goat; Orage, an elephant; de Hartmann, a toucan; Pinder, a hippopotamus; Young, an ape. He painted himself as a surly, angry, fierce workman. The floor of the terrace was covered with fine oriental rugs and cushions. Katherine simply adored that place. She

would spend two or three hours of each day there.

12 November 1922. Katherine Mansfield to her husband.

> By the way I have had a great talk about Shakespeare here with a man called Salzmann, who is by 'profession' a painter. He knows & understands the plays far better than anyone I have met except you. His wife is the chief dancer here—a very beautiful woman with a marvellous intelligence . . . Since last I wrote to you I have changed my room. Now I am in another wing—another kind of existence altogether. Where all was so quiet outside the door all is noise and bustle. My other room was very rich and sumptuous. This is small & plain & very simple . . . I hope Mr. Gurdjieff does not move us again too soon. But it is a favorite habit of his to set the whole house walking. Easy to see why when one saw the emotion it aroused.

Says Thomas de Hartmann of life at the Prieuré:

> The life of a person, like a ball, is thrown from one situation to another. Our prayer was the Work, which concentrated together all spiritual and physical forces. The variety and constant change of tasks continually reawakened us. We are given minimal hours of sleep, just enough to give strength for the following day. Instead of abstinence, there is spending of forces to the utmost, attentive work renewing energies as they are spent, in the manner of a rhythmic flywheel. There is no rejection of life within the Prieuré. On the contrary, life is expanded to the utmost intensity and spirituality.

End of November 1922. Prieuré. In the evenings Gurdjieff speaks quite often in the drawing room after dinner. One evening the English students ask about the Institute and its goals. Among his answers, Gurdjieff tells them "In the Institute you have to learn how to live with your own mind, how to be active, to develop your own individuality."

He is asked about the despair that some fall into at the beginning.

> There exists a principle in the Institute about which I will tell you at once, and then this period of despair will begin to be quite clear to you.
> A man generally lives with a 'foreign' mind.[16] He has not his own opinion and is under the influence of everything that others tell him. In the Institute you have to learn how to live with your own mind, how to be active, to develop your own individuality. Here in the Institute many

---
16. It is the mechanical part of the intellectual center that is never quiet, always talking, outwardly or inwardly. Gurdjieff says, "It can't count beyond two, and sees everything in black and white."

people come only on account of their 'foreign' mind; they have no interest of their own in the Work at all.

That is why when a man arrives at the Institute, difficult conditions are created and all sorts of traps laid for him intentionally, so that he himself can find out whether he came because of his own interest or only because he heard about the interest of others. Can he, disregarding the outside difficulties that are made for him, continue to work for the main aim? And does this aim exist within him? When the need for those artificial difficulties is over, then they are no longer created for him.

The periods of despair in life are the result of the same cause. The man lives with a 'foreign' mind and his interest arises accidentally, owing to some outside influence. As long as the influence continues, the man seems quite satisfied. But when, for some reason or other, the outside influence ceases, his interest loses all meaning and he falls into despair.

What is his own, and cannot be taken away from him and is always his—this does not yet exist. Only when this begins to exist, is it possible for these periods of despair to disappear.

As to the teaching, speaking of his time in Tibet, Gurdjieff says,

From the West I wished to take the knowledge that the East could not give. From the East I took theory; from the West, practice. That which is in the East did not exist in the West and vice versa. That is why each alone has no value. Together they complete each other . . . [In Tibet all the government was in the hands of the monks.] But they couldn't put my ideas into practice, because my teaching was not known to them. My teaching is my own. It combines all the evidence of ancient truth that I collected in my travels with all the knowledge that I have acquired through my own personal work. . . . People who have a soul are immortal, but not everyone has a soul. A man is born without a soul, with only the possibility of acquiring one, and he has to earn it during his lifetime. For those who have not acquired a soul, nothing happens to them. They live and they die.[17] Individuals die, but the atoms live because in the world nothing ceases to live. But even immortal souls exist in different stages. Full immortality is quite unique.

Fritz Peters, who came to the Prieuré in June 1924 when eleven years old, speaking about conscious labor and intentional suffering years afterward, says:

For the average person, it consisted largely in a preliminary period of

---

17. See "Holy Planet Purgatory," *Beelzebub's Tales*.

joining in reasonably hard manual labor in a group.... After a while, one became conscious of being thrust into somewhat frustrating circumstances having to do with the work—such as being forced to work with someone whose temperament clashed with yours, being taken off a job as soon as you became too interested in it, etc. Most of the novice students seemed to be put through a period of purposeful frustration. Inevitably, given the reputation of the school and its stated aims, they began to wonder just exactly what was being accomplished by doing physical labor, and nothing else. The frustration would usually increase because no one, including Gurdjieff, would answer their questions—they were simply told that for the time being they were to do as they were told. When they reached some kind of breaking point, they would suddenly be given an exercise—usually being told that they should observe themselves consciously while they worked and learn about themselves. If they stayed long enough they were gradually taken into the inner circle where they attended readings or listened to lectures and participated in exercises.

Uspenskii arrives at the Prieuré. The students he describes as "a very motley company." He feels, however, "the atmosphere on the whole is very right." He speaks with Katherine Mansfield who seems to him "halfway to death." He is struck by her striving "to find the truth whose presence she clearly feels but which she is unable to touch." She tells Uspenskii:

> I know that this is true and that there is no other truth. You know that I have long since looked upon all of us without exception as people who have suffered shipwreck and have been cast upon an uninhabited island, but who do not yet know of it. But these people here know it. The others, there, in life, still think that a steamer will come for them tomorrow and that everything will go on in the old way. These already know that there will be no more of the old way. I am so glad that I can be here.

Of all the newcomers to the Prieuré, the one who is to be the most help to Gurdjieff is forty-nine-year-old Alfred Richard Orage, who had come to the devastating recognition that "my intellectual life ... was leading me nowhere." Resigning as editor of *The New Age* and asked by his secretary why he was leaving, Orage had answered—"I am going to find God."[18]

For the seven years preceding his meeting with Gurdjieff, the most influential

---

18. In an article "The Quest for God" which he wrote in 1924 for the *Commonweal*, an American magazine, Orage—perhaps hearing of this formulation—wrote: "It would be saying too much to affirm that I resigned from *The New Age* and from active participation in social reform in order to find God. I only wish that my motives could be as clearly conscious as that would imply. But at least I am clear now that no other end will end my search."

figure in Orage's life was Serbian mystic Dmitri Mitrinović, who championed the idea of a panhumanity based on a vision of a united Christian Europe. Had it not been for Mitrinović, Orage believes he could not have come to what he called "the best and hardest decision of my life—to follow Gurdjieff."

The ever fastidious Orage, now greatly overweight, finds himself relegated at night to a small room. His dawn-to-dusk labors are mostly mopping latrines and digging ditches, the latter until his hands bleed. At night, Gurdjieff has him often awakened and ordered to continue digging. This he is to do until told to stop. Once the trench is dug, he is told to fill it in. He does this with no complaint.[19] Inwardly he is in the pit of despair. "I had had no real exercise for years [and so] I suffered so much physically that I would go back to my room, a sort of cell, and literally cry with fatigue.... I asked myself, 'Is this what I have given up my whole life for? At least I had something then. Now what have I?'"

"A hatching place for eggs," is how Gurdjieff describes the Institute. "It supplies the heat. Chickens inside must try to break their shells, then help and individual teaching is possible. Until then only collective method."

Writing many years later, Orage's friend and biographer Philip Mairet says:

> It was precisely the complete submission to a will not his own that was, for Orage, the novelty and the value of the experience. He had known before what it was to be greatly influenced by others, which is quite another matter ... but this was an explicit surrender to the spiritual authority of another, in order to attain something which, by definition, one could not know at one's 'present state of development.' Such a submission opens up immense possibilities of psychic and spiritual change, either positive or negative or both. The results doubtless depend upon the spirit in which such loyalty is given, much more than the way in which it is accepted. And the spirit in which Orage gave his fealty was sincere and devout.

Experiencing the states of a "yes" and a "no," whether to go on or go back to London, and then a third in-between state of "neither yes nor no" suddenly Orage's resistance to digging ditches and then the irrationality of filling them in ends—"When I was in the very depths of despair, feeling that I could go on no longer, I vowed to make an extra effort, and just then something changed in me." He finds he is able to work manually and at the same time keep his mind occupied with the counting and other exercises Gurdjieff has given. His emotional center awakens, and a never before known life is experienced.

"Now, Orage, I think you dig enough," says Gurdjieff. "Let us go café and drink coffee."

19. Reminiscent of Milarepa's treatment by his teacher Marpa. See Lobsang P. Lhalungpa's *The Life of Milarepa* (E. P. Dutton, 1977).

Friends who visit are amazed to see a thinner, harder, more virile-looking Orage with better color, who now sometimes shows an almost childlike spontaneity.[20] In a space of months, the Prieuré has become for Orage "a house of devotion and Gurdjieff his spiritual preceptor."

Nearly every day Orage and Katherine Mansfield talk. One day Orage goes to her room and finds that "her face shone as if she had been on Sinai." Once lovers, she now speaks to him of the "Katherine Mansfield," the one he had known. She has been a camera, she says, but a selective one. Her attitude has determined what observations she selects. She has been passive, not creative. The result, she says, "like everything unconscious," has been evil. The "slices of life" she has portrayed in her short stories have been "partial, misleading, and a little malicious." She has tried to write but has torn up her work. Not one of her published stories would she dare show to God.

In the future, she tells Orage, she would widen the lens of her camera and use it for a "conscious purpose"—showing how life appeared to a "creative attitude." To illustrate what she means, she says: "Two people fall in love and marry. One, or perhaps both of them, has had previous affairs, the remains of which still linger like ghosts in the home. Both wish to forget, but the ghosts still walk. How can this situation be presented?"

She says "the late lamented Katherine Mansfield" would of course see it in terms of her "passive, selective and resentful attitude," and the result would be "one of her famous satiric sketches, reinforcing in her readers the attitude in herself."

But as she is now she would see the situation as "an opportunity for the exercise and employment of all the intelligence, invention, imagination, bravery, endurance, and in fact all the virtues of the most attractive hero and heroine." Such a story, she continues, need not have a happy ending as the problem might be too large, but the sympathy of the reader would be supported "by the continuity and variety of the effort of one or both of the characters, by their indomitable renewal of the struggle, with ever fresh invention." Her aim is to make human virtues, not human failings, interesting. She tells him she wants to be *"a child of the Sun."*

Mid-November 1922. Prieuré. Katherine Mansfield and Olgivanna have become very close, the two sharing a room in the Monk's Corridor, and Olgivanna attending to her every need. Olgivanna, who has imbibed Gurdjieff's teachings, tells Katherine, "Your body is only a medium through which you receive the thing you love most. There is no death for one like you."

Olgivanna had just seen Madame Ostrowska coming to milk the cows and

---

20. Because he had the courage to endure physical hardship and psychological despair, Orage had come to the experiencing of ecstasy—that is, his consciousness had been able to stand outside the body, knowing it and how it related to the universe.

she describes her to Katherine: "She is tall, beautifully proportioned. She wears a black dress of an old German style, tight in the waist and around the breast, with the skirt flowing down in rich folds. Her beautiful head was tied with a black scarf. A gentle smile, sad and lovely, was always on her lips. The grey-blue eyes looked into the distance with just a little touch of fear in them. A superior face. And what arms! Plastic, graceful, with the wrists softly curved into the long-fingered hands. Those hands began to milk, evenly, rhythmically; her head pressed against the cow's body. The cow stood perfectly still."

Later Katherine sees Alexander Salzmann just returning from a day's work sawing logs in the far wood. She writes in her diary: "He looks a very surly, angry and even fierce workman. He is haggard, drawn, old looking with grey hair cut in a fringe on his forehead. He dresses like a very shabby forester and carries a large knife in his belt. I like him almost as much as I like his wife. Together they seem to me as near an ideal couple as I could imagine."

Of the de Hartmanns: "They live in one smallish room, awfully cramped I suppose. But to go & sit there with them in the evening before dinner is one of my greatest pleasures. Dear precious people! She is very quick, beautiful, warm-hearted. He is small & quite bald, with a little pointed beard & he generally wears a loose blouse spotted with whitewash, very full trousers, wooden boots. He is a 'common workman' all day. But it is the life between them; the feeling one has in their nearness."

Of Gurdjieff she says, "He is the only man who understands there is no division between body and spirit, and who knows how they are related. . . . With a single blow he has got rid of all those difficulties which result from the Cartesian division of the universe into matter and mind . . . the mind-body problem has entirely disappeared. There is no longer any need to explain how two such entirely different entities as mind and body could meet and interact, for mind and body have become one."

24 December 1922. Prieuré. Writes Mansfield:

> We are going to celebrate [Christmas] in tremendous style here. Every sort of lavish generous hospitable thing has been done by Mr. Gurdjieff. He wants a real old fashioned *English* Xmas — an extraordinary idea here! — & we shall sit down to table 60 persons to turkeys, geese, a whole sheep, a pig, puddings, heaven knows what in the way of dessert, & wines by the barrel. There's to be a tree, too & Father Xmas. I am doing all I can for the little children so that they will be roped in for once. I've just sent them over colored paper & asked them to help to make flowers. It's pathetic the interest they are taking. Our pudding was made in a baby's bath, stirred by everybody & Mr. Gurdjieff put in a coin. Who

gets the coin gets our darling newborn calf for a present. The calf — 1 day old — was led into the salon to the beating of tambourines & to a special melody composed for it.

25 December 1922. Prieuré. Gurdjieff gives a large Christmas party for a hundred or so students. A pudding is served for dessert. Gurdjieff tells everyone that one serving contains a gold coin and whoever gets it will be "marked with the symbol of goodness." The winner would also get a calf that had been born two days before.

Olgivanna, who had been despondent over giving up her daughter to her brother, says, "I got the gold coin. So what?"

Gurdjieff tells her she doesn't understand what she has received. He says he saw that she was "marked" when she first entered the dining room. He has her follow him to the stables. He holds the kerosene lantern while she bends down and touches the newborn calf. Suddenly, Olgivanna is overcome with the feeling that this is a gift from elsewhere and, sensing a divine presence, feels she is now "part of the universal order."

26 December 1922. Prieuré. Katherine Mansfield writes to her husband:

> You see, my love, the question is always "Who am I?" and until that is discovered I don't see how one can really direct anything in one's self. "Is there a Me?" One must be certain of that before one has a real unshakable leg to stand on. And I don't believe for one moment these questions can be settled by the head alone. It is this life of the head, this formative intellectual life at the expense of all the rest of us which has got us into this state. How can it get us out of it? I see no hope of escape except by learning to live in our emotional & instinctive being as well and to balance all three.
>
> You see, Bogey, if I were allowed one single cry to God that cry would be *I want to be REAL.* Until I am that I don't see why I shouldn't be at the mercy of old Eve in her various manifestations forever.
>
> But this place has taught me so far how unreal I am. It has taken from me one thing after another (the things never were mine) until at this present moment all I know really, really, is that I am not annihilated and that I hope — more than hope — believe. It is hard to explain....
>
> Our cowshed has become enriched with two goats and two love birds. The goats are very lovely as they lie in the straw or so delicately dance towards each other butting gently with their heads. When I was there yesterday Mr. Gurdjieff came in and showed Lola and Nina who were milking the cows the way to milk a goat. He sat down on a stool seized the goat & swung its hind legs across his knees. So there the goat was on its two front legs, helpless. This is the way Arabs milk. He looked very like one....

31 December 1922. Prieuré. Writes Katherine Mansfield:

> I have been leading a very tame semi-existence here. My heart, under this new treatment, which is one of graduated efforts and exercise, feels decidedly stronger, and my lungs in consequence feel quieter, too. It's a remarkable fact that since arriving here I have not had to spend one entire day in bed—an unprecedented record for me! I feel more and more confident that if I can give this treatment a fair trial—as I intend to do—and stay on for six months at least, I shall be infinitely stronger in every way. More I do not venture to say.

1923. Munich. Fritz Thyssen, head of a steel trust, meets Hitler. Impressed, he donates $25,000 to the obscure Nazi Party. German newspapers print anti-Semitic tracts. The polluted atmosphere of extremism Gurdjieff found in Russia with the rise of Bolshevism now festers in Europe.

January 1923. Prieuré. Uspenskii is invited to come and talk with some English people there, some of whom had been in his London groups and had, in Uspenskii's judgment, "failed in the Work." He meant "chiefly Orage and Mrs. Page." She is a wealthy Englishwoman who had come to Gurdjieff with three suitcases and two trunks containing an assortment of gowns and dresses and a pink satin housecoat with slippers to match, as well as a blue velvet day dress and a transparent mauve negligee, both with matching slippers.

Uspenskii says, viewing the Prieuré students, he had "to begin with them from the same place where we stopped in London." Meaning he had to explain the basic principles of group work. Mrs. Page wants to know if it is necessary to speak about this group to Gurdjieff.

"Certainly not," Uspenskii tells her. "Mr. Gurdjieff has nothing to do with it; you must do it yourselves [understand the principles] in your own interests."

The next week Mrs. Page quarrels with the group. She asks Gurdjieff if this group is really necessary. Gurdjieff, who knows nothing about the group Uspenskii has set up, tells her there must be no groups. Later, Uspenskii will say, "She made out of this a big case against me, and said that I had told her to take part in a group which was organized by me contrary to Mr. Gurdjieff's wishes."

Uspenskii crosses the Channel "fairly often" to visit Gurdjieff, and on several occasions Gurdjieff invites him to live at the Prieuré. These, Uspenskii interprets as a "temptation." Though he still has an interest in Gurdjieff's Work, he sees Gurdjieff is no longer speaking as he had in Moscow and St. Petersburg about the brotherhood of seekers and an esoteric tradition, but now speaks of himself as being the repository of a new knowledge. In sum, Uspenskii says, "I could find no place for myself in this work nor did I understand its direction."

9 January 1923. Prieuré. John Middleton Murry arrives early in the afternoon for the celebration of the Russian New Year on the thirteenth. Mansfield has invited him to stay for a week. Upon seeing her he says:

"I have never seen, nor shall I ever see, any one so beautiful as she was on that day; it was as though the exquisite perfection which was always hers had taken possession of her completely. To use her own words, the last grain of 'sediment,' the last 'traces of earthly degradation,' were departed for ever. But she had lost her life to save it."

She shows Murry around the grounds. That evening they watch as Olgivanna dances The Initiation of the Priestess. It will be the last time the two women will see one another, for at ten o'clock Katherine Mansfield says good night to her husband and then climbs the staircase to her room and suddenly hemorrhages. Within a half-hour, "her eyes wide with terror," Katherine Mansfield takes her last earthly breath.[21]

12 January 1923. Avon Cemetery. Katherine Mansfield is buried in the presence of Gurdjieff, her husband, her lifelong friend New Zealander Ida Baker, her sisters, Olgivanna, and some of her Prieuré friends. Gurdjieff casts handfuls of raisins and nuts into her grave saying they contained germs of renewal. On the large grey slab that is her gravestone are carved these words from Shakespeare:

> But I tell you, my lord fool, out of this nettle, danger, we pluck this flower, safety.

Katherine Mansfield's death brings a storm of invective to Gurdjieff, many blaming him for her death. D. H. Lawrence says, "I have heard enough about that place at the Fontainebleau where Katherine Mansfield died, to know it is a rotten, false, self-conscious place of people playing a sickly stunt."

Early 1923. Prieuré. As he had in Essentuki, Uspenskii says that he finds "many destructive elements in the organization of the affair itself and [I see] that it had to fall to pieces."

Later he will say that "from the very beginning, there came into the life of the Institute many strange currents, incompatible with its ideas, aims and plans and they very soon made further development of these ideas quite impossible. In my opinion the chief cause of this was the unfortunate choice of people who Gurdjieff admitted to the Institute."

---

21. In Katherine's last entry in her journal, she writes to her husband: "When I say 'I fear'—don't let it disturb you, dearest heart. We all fear when we are in waiting rooms. Yet we must pass beyond them, and if the other can keep calm, it is all the help we can give each other. . . . And this sounds very strenuous and serious. But now that I have wrestled with it, it's no longer so. I feel happy—deep down. *All is well.*"

9 February 1923. Prieuré. Gurdjieff speaks in the salon about two spirits:

> It is said in some ancient teachings that on the day God created man he also created for each man two spirits—the spirit of good and the spirit of evil, or as they are called, an angel and a devil, and placed the angel on the right side of man and the devil on the left.
>
> Another ancient teaching says that when God sent spirits to work on the planets, the spirits asked God: "What shall we do there?" God divided the spirits according to their qualities and said: "You, on the right side, will try to lead those who live there to heaven, and you, the other half, will try to lead them to hell."
>
> Then one of the leaders asked about the means permissible to those on the one side and those on the other. God answered: "You can use any methods and means you like. But there is one essential difference. Let the weapon of those on the right be—to do through 'doing,' and the weapon of those on the left—to do through 'it happens.' The method of those on the right must be through what is active and conscious, and the method of those on the left through what is passive and unconscious."
>
> These two teachings to which I refer are ancient. At the same time, parallel with these teachings there existed another religion, another teaching and it still exists to this day.
>
> The majority of religions live, act, believe in accordance with Holy Scriptures, precepts and commandments. At the same time there has existed a teaching of learned followers who have tried to put into practice all religions, sayings, all teachings without infatuation, without faith. They did not worship blindly. Before accepting something they practiced it. What could be put into practice was accepted, what could not be was rejected. In this way a new religion was formed, although the material for it was taken from other religions. The teaching about which I speak now is the teaching of the Sufis.
>
> This teaching says the following about the angel and the devil: Every action of a man, every step, every moment, every movement emanates either from the one or from the other. Emanations from both (result) are equally deposited in the human organism in the form of certain crusts of real tangible matter which one can examine and distinguish whether the crust is of one kind or another. Each crust obeys certain laws, leads to certain consequences. And in the case of man things whispered by the devil have greater effect.
>
> [The lecture is interrupted.]

18 February 1923. Prieuré. Professor Denis Saurat, the son of peasants and now a writer and head of the Institut Français in London, visits his friend Orage. Saurat is astonished as he remembers Orage as being "rather fat, supporting his

190 lbs. on a large, bony frame." The Orage he encounters is "thin, almost gaunt, with an anxious look. An Orage who seems taller, whose movements are stronger and quicker — a healthier man, but unhappy."

Saurat walks about the grounds, noticing all the activity. He sees about seventy Russians, twenty English and no French. Saurat, asked to stay on, eventually speaks with Gurdjieff through an interpreter.

Saurat: What results are you trying to obtain here?

Gurdjieff: Better health, wider intelligence, and a complete break with people's normal routine.

S: Do you know that several people are near to despair?

G: Yes — there is something sinister in this house, and that is necessary.

S: Their ambition is to become immortal?

G: All have ambitions; few satisfy them [the tone of voice sardonic]. Each one possesses a 'me' and an essence. Many would like to transfer their 'me' into their essence and so become immortals.

S: What is the object of all this manual labor and must it go on for long?

G: To make them masters of the exterior world. It is only a temporary phase.

S: Are you trying to give them occult powers?

G: Yes, I am trying to give them all powers and other powers. The occultists of today are all wrong.

S: You do not form part of a school?

G: No, we are a group of friends. Thirty years ago, twelve of us spent many years in Central Asia, and we reconstructed the Doctrine; by oral traditions, the study of ancient costumes, popular songs and even certain books. The Doctrine has always existed, but the tradition has often been interrupted. In antiquity some groups and castes knew it, but it was incomplete. The ancients put too much stress on metaphysics, their doctrine was abstract.

S: Why did you come to Europe?

G: Because I want to add the mystical spirit of the East to the scientific spirit of the West. The Oriental spirit is right but only in its trends and general ideas. The Western spirit is right in its methods and techniques. Western methods alone are effective in history. I want to create a type of sage who will unite the spirit of the East with Western techniques.

S: Apart from questions of method, do you teach a positive doctrine?

G: Yes. Few human beings have a soul. None have one at birth. Those who do not acquire one, die; their atoms are dispersed, nothing is left. *A few make themselves a partial soul and are submitted to a kind of reincarnation which allows them to progress. And, finally, a very small number succeed in acquiring immortal souls. But this number is really very small, indeed. Most of those who have achieved any success have only managed to acquire partial souls.* [Emphasis added.]

S: Do you believe in Free Will? [Neither the interpreter, Madame de Hartmann, fluent in English, nor Gurdjieff seems to know what 'Free Will' means.]

G: Everyone does what he wants. Nothing can stop him. But men do not know how to will.[22]

Later, after reading the manuscript of *Beelzebub's Tales*, Saurat would say that Gurdjieff was an "extraordinarily highly developed spiritual teacher activated by the highest moral intentions with an exceptional moral and spiritual sensibility."

15–19 February 1923. London. The journalist E. C. Bowyer publishes a series of articles on the teaching in the *London Daily News*. He writes that Uspenskii says "he found a kindred spirit who had gone farther on the same road, and the two enthusiasts joined forces, traveling and teaching in Russia as they were driven hither and thither by the tide of war or famine." And that "Gurdjieff and Uspenskii have reached our present stage of knowledge by long and hard work in many lands. It has been much like what is going on at the present moment in the Valley of the Kings at Luxor."

Orage, after studying the articles, tells Gurdjieff that "it is evident to me that Uspenskii looked through these articles before they were published, and that they were inspired by Uspenskii with the especial intention of showing that the Institute and the whole work belongs to him equally with Mr. Gurdjieff."

28 February 1923. Prieuré. In a talk in the salon, Gurdjieff tells his students:

> The Institute can give very little. The program of the Institute, the power of the Institute, the aim of the Institute, the possibilities of the Institute can be expressed in few words: the Institute can help one to be able to be a Christian....
>
> Half of the world is Christian, the other half has other religions. For me, a sensible man, this makes no difference; they are the same as the Christian. Therefore it is possible to say that the whole world is Christian, the difference is only in name. And it has been Christian not only for one year but for thousands of years. There were Christians long before the advent of Christianity....
>
> A man who is able to do all that is demanded of a Christian, both with his mind and his essence, is called a Christian without quotation marks. A man who, in his mind, wishes to do all that is demanded of a Christian, but can do so only with his mind and not with his essence, is called pre-Christian. And a man who can do nothing, even with his mind, is called a non-Christian.

---

22. Gurdjieff says at another time: "Will is absent in ordinary man, he has desires only; and a greater or lesser *permanence* of desires and wishes is called a strong or weak will. Real will is a power, not merely composed of various often contradictory desires belonging to different 'I's but issuing from consciousness and governed by individuality of a single permanent I. Only such a will can be called 'free,' for it is independent of accident and cannot be altered or directed from without."

March 1923. London. Following Bowyer's series on the Prieuré in the *London Daily News*, Clifford Sharp, editor of the *New Statesman* runs the first of two articles, "The 'Forest Philosophers,'" making it clear that Uspenskii was Gurdjieff's disciple.

5 March 1923. Warwick Gardens. Gurdjieff speaks with Pinder translating. Uspenskii and his pupils present.

> *Question:* People talk of union with God and union with Christ. I often feel they do not know what they mean. How can one get away from the herd mind?
>
> *Gurdjieff:* Are you hypnotized by such phrases, and you wish to know how to get rid of that?
>
> *Q:* I want to get rid of the herd mind. [Laughter.]
>
> *G:* This is one of the best questions, and yet people laugh in derision.
>
> *Uspenskii:* No, not in derision; we all feel the same. Actually everyone suffers from that and the cause is a very small one. The error is because you are tranquilly assured you are already a Christian.
>
> *G:* I want to speak only of principles. You used the word, "Christian," because that was directly connected to the example you quoted, "Union with God." Let me explain the hypnotic influence. There is an undesirable quality in everybody and that is authority—"Looking to authority"—is the term—"Reliance on authority." The self reliance which varies according to the individual is due to preconceived notions which are within us, and which are linked up with faith and belief. For example, you understand that reliance on authority means reliance on someone else's authority, not on your own?
>
> *Q: Yes.*
>
> *G:* Authority that comes into you from without is erroneous. This error acts as a lever which pulls the machine, making it work wrong, perpetuating the error, and you cannot, having these erroneous conceptions, get rid of this until you have freed yourself from relying on external authority.
>
> *Q:* Is there no self love? There are plenty of people who do not admire outside authority.
>
> *G:* Why I connected your example with Christianity is that you limited it to the nature of the example you yourself put. Relying on the authority of Christians is erroneous. Christ, his disciples, their followers in subsequent centuries and followers of other religions, never said "We are Christians" but "Be Christians." It was never said and no utterance was ever given "We are such" but "Be such." Formerly two teachings went parallel, namely "Be" and "How to be." "How to be" has been rejected and though it still exists it is never used, it does not serve as guide and all that remains is "Be," "We are," "You are."

There were two independent programs of Christianity, one was absolutely discarded—thrown out of use—and now people take as a guide merely the other program that remained. People were always the same, just they are at present, so they were formerly. It is possible that formerly they were a little more complete, but on broad lines they were just the same as they are now; all nations in all times.

All nations at all times have followed, talked about and taught Religions, and these religions, if you look into them deeply, have the same aim. We cannot discern in any one of them any differences in their leading principles, only difference is in their superficial forms.

Formerly, all religions say "love your neighbor," that is regarding the second program, whereas the first said "Teach and learn how to love your neighbor." Some religions at present use both forms. The majority of people here only use the second form. If you do not take it purely as authority—an outside authority—you would not have had the quality in you which forced you on authority, but there would have been something in you which would have made you seek the missing part. You would have found "Love your neighbor," and you would have sought to know what it meant because it is impossible to love your neighbor.

Set aside now that reliance on authority, and ask yourself—is it possible—can you execute the command "Love your neighbor," and you will see it is impossible. You cannot love or hate to order. Think about it for yourself. It is possible that the teaching has gone on for thousands of years. It is seen it is impossible to carry into effect such a command. It is possible that a small crowd of persons might have been found in all that great length of time to see that it is absolutely erroneous. So if you were to examine all and look into it thoroughly and you were to decide that everyone that lived all that time, were out of their minds and at the same time you saw it is impossible to love your neighbor you would decide there must be some error somewhere. Where is the rub?

For either all people are mad or you have made a mistake that it is impossible to "love." And these two things diametrically opposed are both true—that one really can love that it is really possible to love and it is also real that you yourself cannot love. It is only by destroying your reliance on authority that you will rid yourself of that hypnotism of which you speak, and of being hypnotized by words and texts. Does this satisfy you?

Q: It is the group mind that talks like that, not the individual mind as for instance, in wartime men say "We must be heroes" etc., etc. and everyone repeats.

G: You must not look at other people, you must take your own example which was a good one. Our thralldom, our inspirations depend on ourselves and it is through them we are inspired by outside authority.

Q: We imitate the men who talk like that.

G: They are obsessions and we must start by abolishing this hypnotism and when you get rid of this you will become free. It is authority set at the very bottom and we must search to the very roots to find them. In the same way taking the example you said showed you wanted to become free and is an instance of your own observations that you could not accept it.

29 March 1923. London. Uspenskii receives a telegram from Madame Uspenskii telling him to come to the Prieuré immediately. Though still wavering in regard to his relationship with Gurdjieff, he goes to the Prieuré the next day.

At the Prieuré, Dr. James Young, who had been in Uspenskii's London group, tells Uspenskii someone was saying he told his students in London the Institute was not necessary, that it was quite possible to work in London without going to the Institute at all. Questioned rigorously, Young admits it is Mrs. Page.

"How could she say such a thing," Uspenskii exclaims, "She didn't come to my lectures."

Cornered, Young then says, "Mrs. Page told him it was Mrs. Rosamund Sharp [Bland]."

"Why didn't you tell Mrs. Page that Mrs. Sharp was lying?"

"How can I say that? I do not know," answers Young.

Later, Uspenskii reflects: "If people repeat these lies, or say that they do not know that they are lies, that shows by itself that there is nothing to be expected. Many of my words and actions were wrongly understood and wrongly interpreted—and in some cases with the evident intention to misrepresent my attitude towards Mr. Gurdjieff and towards the Institute work."

He then speaks with Gurdjieff who tells him, "Many wrong types came to your [London] Work. You were not careful enough in the choice of people."[23]

Gurdjieff pauses and then asks, "Do you understand what I just said and what you must do?"

"I understand both," Uspenskii says. "I must give up the Work in London."

"This shows," says Gurdjieff, "that you realize yourself that it gives wrong results."

After Uspenskii leaves, Gurdjieff brings all his students together and announces all work with Uspenskii is discontinued.

A year before, Gurdjieff had publicly rebuked and humiliated Uspenskii in front of his students in London. Now Gurdjieff does the same in front of the Work's senior students, Uspenskii's friends and his wife. He divides them into seven groups. In the first group he puts Dr. Stjoernval, Frank Pinder, Dr. James Young, and A. R. Orage. In the last group are Madame Uspenskii, her daughter Lenotchka,

---

23. Gurdjieff plays a variation of the St. Petersburg conditions as he did in Essentuki.

Boris Ferapontoff, Elizabeta Galumnian and Jeanne de Salzmann. Gurdjieff then declares that only the first group is to remain at the Prieuré—all others must leave. Though he personally has nothing against some people in the last group, he says he is obliged to put some people there because of their connection with Uspenskii.

As these are older students accustomed to Gurdjieff's shocks, none leave.

5 April 1923. Warwick Gardens. Uspenskii begins his lecture saying:

> There are definite and very strict rules in the Work and everyone is subject to these rules according to his place and position in the Work, and to the kind of work he is doing.... Responsibility in the Work is very big, and one has to be responsible not only for his attitude, but for all impressions he produces and not only for his own actions in regard to other people, but for all actions of other people in regard to him....
>
> If someone accuses me of having stolen his watch, which I have not stolen, it is my fault, because I should not be acquainted with him. And if he is in this Work, I am doubly responsible because I brought the wrong man to the Work.... If someone who was brought by me into this Work accuses me of something, or misunderstands me, or suspects me of something against the Work, this is considered my crime; for that means I am a fool, and one has no right to be a fool in the Work. All that I have said will help you to understand what happened in the Institute and my attitude towards it when last Thursday [29 March] I received a telegram from Madame Uspenskii telling me to come to the Prieuré immediately. [Uspenskii then relates what happened.]

Early April. Prieuré. Gurdjieff's senior students take a hard view of Uspenskii. Says Pinder,

> All that Uspenskii had of value, he got from Gurdjieff, and that only with his mind. He had a perfunctory fling at the movements; and even confessed to being lazy. Gurdjieff's main quarrel with him was that he, Uspenskii, thought he knew better, and was apt to kick over the traces.... Uspenskii apparently thought that he understood Gurdjieff and his inner teachings—which he did not, and Gurdjieff had to make him choose whether to stay with him and submit to discipline, or break away.... Uspenskii knew the *theory*, better than anyone possibly—he had the knowledge, but he did not *understand*.[24]

24. Pinder and Orage, and certainly Bennett, even Nott, are not to be taken as unbiased observers. As Uspenskii pointed out in *Tertium Organum*: "The reason why men understand one another so little is that they always live by different emotions. And they understand one another only when they happen simultaneously to experience identical emotions." Also, there is the factor of competition

For his part, Uspenskii believes the Prieuré is bound to fail because the "principle of seniority" has not been followed. "People who did not belong to groups before," he says, "like Pinder and Orage, they were given certain power over people who were much older in the Work; it did not work—it could not go on." As he will later say, "There was no lack of 'Judases.'"

Spring 1923. London. Uspenskii finishes the introduction to *Fragments of an Unknown Teaching.*[25] In a passage concerning evil, later deleted, he writes that he asked Gurdjieff if there can be conscious evil. Gurdjieff says there certainly can be, though it is possible only in a very elaborate way, and in very rare cases.

"Anything that produces big phenomena can have mind and intelligence behind it," Gurdjieff tells him, and then pauses and asks—"Why are you upset?"

"It means changing all I had thought before."

"It becomes even more interesting," says Gurdjieff. "It is one thing to have against you only mechanical forces and quite another to have intelligence; it is one thing to struggle with intelligence, and another to struggle with mechanical forces."

14 April 1923. France. Having tried to contact Olgivanna and received no response, her husband Valdemar leaves for America on the SS *Paris*.

Mid-April. Prieuré. Uspenskii sees Gurdjieff several more times. Gurdjieff tells him how the Work can be continued and invites him to return for Russian Easter, but Uspenskii refuses.

1 May 1923. Prieuré. Nicoll's father seriously ill, he leaves his wife and daughter at the Prieuré and returns to England.

May 1923. Prieuré. A large black Citroën is delivered and Gurdjieff immediately takes the wheel and with a ghastly sounds suggesting a tearing of gear-wheel cogs teaches himself to drive. Said a student later: "He drove like a wild man, cutting in and out of traffic without hand signals or even space to accommodate his car in the lanes he suddenly switched to... until he was in them, safe by a hair... he always got away first on the green light even (so it seemed) when he was one or two cars behind the starting line... the chances he took overtaking buses and trucks were terrifying."

23 May 1923. Prieuré. Gurdjieff says: "Man has three kinds of powers, which

and jealousy which breed their own special strains in any organization, especially a spiritual one.
  25. In the original draft, he writes of his personal association with Gurdjieff in one section and of the teaching in a second. Only at a later time does he interweave the two sections into one, the blending giving a more profound result.

are physical, psychic and moral. The first depends on the structure of the human machine and its tissues. The second on the quality of the thinking faculty and the material it contains. The third power is very hard to change, for it takes a long time to form. If a person has common sense and sound logic, any action may change his opinion and his will. But changing his nature, that is, his moral make-up, needs long pressure."

24 May 1923. Prieuré. Gurdjieff lectures on love saying:

> There are two kinds of love; one, the love of a slave, the other, which must be acquired by work. The first has no value at all, only the second has value, that is, love acquired through work. This is the love about which all religions speak.
>
> If you love when "it" loves, it does not depend on you and so it has no merit. It is what we call the love of a slave. You love even where you should not love. Circumstances make you love mechanically.
>
> Real love is Christian, religious love; with that love no one is born. For this love you must work. Some know it from childhood, others only in old age.... Love may be of different kinds. To understand what kind of love we are speaking of, it is necessary to define it. Now we speak about love for life. Wherever there is life—beginning with plants (for they too have life) and animals—in a word, wherever life exists—there is love. Each life is representative of God. Whoever can see the representative will see Him who is represented. Every life is sensitive to love. Even inanimate things such as flowers, which have no consciousness, understand whether you love them or not. Even unconscious life reacts in a corresponding way to each man and responds to him according to his reactions.... Whoever does not love life does not love God.

28 May 1923. Prieuré. Gurdjieff is granted official permission for his family to immigrate from Soviet Russia.

July 1923. Prieuré. A woman student vomits blood and Young, without examining her, tells Gurdjieff he believes she is suffering from an intestinal ulcer. Gurdjieff disagrees. Young is upset.

August 1923. Prieuré. Nicoll returns. Gurdjieff tells him: "When you return to Institute [you are] two men—one happy to meet friends, old associates, and so forth. The other does not begin to be felt until you arrive. Suddenly you begin to fear. He thinks of all the difficulties to be faced. He thinks seriously."

The tempo and difficulty of the work is speeded up. And, of course, doubts surface. There is much friction. As always, Gurdjieff fuels the doubts. Nicoll wonders "whether the difficulties Gurdjieff knows he creates are equal in value for work with those he does not know he creates."

August 1923. Prieuré. Twenty-seven-year-old John Godolphin Bennett arrives. Involved in a whirlwind of international business, he has spoken to Uspenskii in London about his feeling that he has lost touch with his spiritual aims. Now, despite Uspenskii's ambivalence toward Gurdjieff, he advises Bennett to go for a long visit.[26]

A visionary, highly intelligent, a leader with natural gifts of command, and a magician in his own right, Bennett is a promising candidate to fulfill the role which Gurdjieff had seen for Uspenskii of stepping down the teaching.

One day Gurdjieff takes Bennett aside and tells him, "Now only your mind is awake: your heart and body are asleep. If you continue like this, soon your mind also will go to sleep, and you will never be able to think any new thoughts. You cannot awaken your own feelings, but you can awaken your body. If you can learn to master your body, you will begin to acquire Being.... Remember yourself as two—you and your body. When you are master of your body, your feelings will obey you."

During the coming weeks Bennett makes some breakthroughs. Gurdjieff, dressed in a smart French suit, as is now his custom, invites Bennett to accompany him on a business trip to Melun. Upon their return Gurdjieff cuts off into a forest road. The two end up in a clearing overlooking the Prieuré some hundred feet below. Speaking Turkish—Bennett is the only student versed in that language—Gurdjieff confides that this view of the château is his favorite. He talks of the future, telling Bennett of his plans to buy more land. He will then build an observatory, there being many facts about planetary movements that astronomy has overlooked. The impression he creates is that there is much to do, much to learn, many opportunities.

A few days later, Gurdjieff again approaches Bennett, declaring:

> You have the possibility of learning to work.... You have seen that it is possible to be directly connected with the Great Accumulator of Energy that is the source of all miracles. If you could be permanently connected with this source, you could pass all barriers. Ever since I was a young boy, I have known of the existence of this power and the barriers that separate man from it, and I searched until I found the way of breaking through them. This is the greatest secret that man can discover about human nature. Many people are convinced that they wish to be free and to know reality, but they do not know the barrier that prevents them from reaching reality. They come to me for help, but they are unwilling or unable to pay the price.

26. Given what later happens between Uspenskii and Bennett, is Uspenskii sending him to Gurdjieff for Bennett's own good, or trying to get rid of him?

Speaking about being and knowledge (as he had to Uspenskii and others seven years before in Petersburg), Gurdjieff warns Bennett of the danger of losing everything if he relies on knowledge alone. Thinking of Uspenskii perhaps, he warns Bennett with great seriousness: "With too much knowledge, the inner barrier may become insurmountable."

Bennett asks how long will be needed before he can work alone, if he decides to stay.[27]

Gurdjieff tells him: "If you devote all your energies to the task, it may take two years before you can work alone."[28]

Gurdjieff tells him exactly what he wants to hear. Whether or not Gurdjieff meant it, Bennett, rarely doubting himself at the right time, never questions. A skilled agent of British intelligence, Bennett must sense the trap Gurdjieff has laid. He plays a last card. He tells Gurdjieff he has no money.

"I am not interested in your money," counters Gurdjieff, "but in your work. There are plenty of people who will give me money, but very few who will work. I will give you the money you need."

Gurdjieff then sweetens the pot. He offers to take Bennett with him on his forthcoming trip to America to act as his interpreter. Bennett is no doubt seeing himself sitting next to Gurdjieff, just as Pinder had in London. Gurdjieff dangles another lure. He tells Bennett that later on he will be able to give lectures himself. Gurdjieff then tells him—"At present you will have to take because you have nothing to give. Later you will be ready to give your last shirt to help the work—as I am ready to give mine."

Mid-August 1923. Prieuré. The woman who had vomited is operated on in London. She has in fact an intestinal ulcer as Young had said. For Young—who has endured a year of a "Teacher who would indulge in so much bunkum, who would produce that persistent and increasing distrust in me . . . . Gurdjieff's fantasy, cheapness, spectacular use of show, of megalomaniac hints of this and that to come"—it is simply too much.

Young spills out to Orage, his friend and roommate, all the doubts that have built up in him over the months, and now sees he is right and Gurdjieff's diagnosis was wrong! Orage, a chain-smoker who on arrival Gurdjieff had immediately forbidden to smoke and who has endured many of Gurdjieff's insults, has been sitting on the bed quietly, listening. Finally he lets his friend know it is "a test."[29]

27. To a man like Bennett, freedom—his notion of freedom, the "person's" notion—is everything. With this question it sounds like he is looking for a way out.

28. The words must have singed Bennett's brain. He had expected to hear twenty years. Mercurial, zesting after adventure, what Bennett most fears is being trapped.

29. Some years later, in another such circumstance, Gurdjieff's student Muriel Draper's son was hit by a bus and lay in a coma. Doctors felt it was dangerous to operate and more dangerous not to. She spoke to Gurdjieff who, after asking a few pointed questions, advised against operating. The doctors objected vigorously. In a few hours the boy woke up.

A test of his relationship to Gurdjieff, his valuation of the teaching, his search for truth.

Young had come to the Institute because in his work as an analyst he saw that "analytic knowledge is not necessarily effective knowledge." That is, when patients are told what their problem is they refuse to "face up to reality," that is they deflect, project, excuse, obfuscate. He saw that the teaching gave "a discipline calculated to force one to experience oneself in a new way or from a different angle.... It is needless to say that the new ways must be significant, and not trivial.... The idea of the Institute, then, was to provide an artificial milieu so arranged that the pupil would be forced to experience himself in radically new postures, both physical and psychological. The new postures were to be brought about by 'shocks' to produce sanity!"

At some point, Young had relieved his anxieties by writing to Carl Bechhofer Roberts who tells Young he sees "signs of hoofs and horns all over the place." There are only two paths of self-development, one to God, the other to Power, he says. Gurdjieff's path is a path to Power.[30]

Young leaves "with a feeling of supreme satisfaction that I turned my back finally upon the Institute and returned once more to embrace the habits of the so-called 'mechanical' life."

21 August 1923. Prieuré. Speaking to all his students, Gurdjieff declares:

> For one section of the people here their stay has become completely useless. If this section were to be asked why they are here, they would either be completely unable to answer or they would answer something quite nonsensical, would produce a whole philosophy.... Whoever does not make use of the conditions here for work on himself and does not see them—this is no place for him. He is wasting his time by remaining here, hindering others and taking someone else's place.... He who can be a conscious egoist here, can be in life not an egotist. To be an egoist here means not to give a hoot for anyone, myself included, to regard everyone and everything as something by which to help oneself. There must be no considering with anything or with anyone.... There is only one salvation: to remember day and night that you are here only for yourself and everything and everyone around you must either not hinder you or you must act so that they do not hinder you. You must make use of them as means for attaining your aims. Yet everything is done here except that. This place has been turned into something worse than in ordinary life. Much worse. All day long people are either occupied with scandal, or they blacken one another, or they think things inwardly, judge and

30. That Gurdjieff has brought a third, more ancient path, a scientific path of Understanding and Conscience, is not known and thus not considered.

consider with each other, finding some sympathetic, some antipathetic; they strike up friendships, collectively or individually play tricks on each other, concentrate on the bad sides of each other.

23 August 1923. Prieuré. Bennett, suitcase in hand, hurries past the Prieuré's flowing fountain, opens the high wrought iron gate to the street, and self-calms, telling himself, "I will go away and make money, and then I will return." Amazingly, when asked in later years why he had not followed Gurdjieff, Bennett said, "It was much rather as if Gurdjieff himself had withdrawn from me, and would not let me follow him."

October 1923. Café de la Paix. Gurdjieff tells Olgivanna to return to Chicago to bring to resolution her relationship with her estranged husband, Valdemar Hinzenburg, who has been in America since April. She leaves on the SS *Rochambeau*.

October 1923. Prieuré. Gurdjieff tells Nicoll he is sending Orage to America to prepare people for his arrival and that he is to accompany Orage. Nicoll, having been with Gurdjieff a total of nine months, always the aristocrat, graciously declines. As he has refused to do what Gurdjieff asks, Gurdjieff is no longer his teacher. Shortly afterward, Nicoll, his wife, baby, and nurse depart for London.

November 1923. Paris. Rumors of Gurdjieff's Institute having hastened the death of Katherine Mansfield has given vent to a lot of speculation. The young writer Kay Boyle sitting at a café overhears the writer-publisher Robert McAlmon tell a friend:

> The cult has been spreading among people I thought were more or less sensible.... It's mass hypnotism of some kind.... Gurdjieff started some years back in the East as a hypnotist. He gets people of various nationalities to repeat numbers and words in their own language, to repeat them over and over, and after ten minutes he asks other people, sitting in a circle, to speak in time with them, repeating "twilight," or "dawn," or "tragedy," or "labor," or "love," over and over, in their different languages. This in itself hypnotizes, of course, and they all sway as they speak, but in the middle of the circle are placed bottles of Armagnac, and the master is disturbed if these bottles are not emptied.... It sounds pretty much like what we do every night in Montparnasse.... You build houses in the forest, and you chop wood, and you live in fear that you will be turned away.... And it could be that Gurdjieff's regime is no more rigid and bleak than the routine of many a monastery or nunnery. They are all serving some master for a future that is nebulous.

November 1923. 38 Warwick Gardens. Nicoll and his wife attend Uspenskii's meetings, as does Fairfax Hall, a young Englishman who will be among Uspenskii's lifelong students. Says Hall of his first meeting, "Uspenskii was grim in his seriousness and gruff replies—off-putting. But knowing so little of the English language, how could anyone remain so still and—apparently—so unmoved by such grand questions from people who had been—and still were—members of the Theosophical Society. Then, quietly, he got up and went to the blackboard and drew what we later got to know as the 'Ray of Creation,' and—step-by-step we learned the language of *The System*."

Nicoll visits Uspenskii's flat and finds him working on "Christianity and the New Testament," a chapter in his book *A New Model of the Universe*. About the room are a number of dictionaries, as well as copies of the New Testament in Greek, German, French, Russian, and English. He writes with a pencil, of which he has many, all sharpened to a very fine point. When he speaks of a biblical passage to Nicoll, Uspenskii first looks at the translation in each of the versions, then compares it with the Greek.

8 November 1923. Munich. Hitler's beer hall putsch fails.

26 November 1923. Prieuré. Orage writes to Claude Bragdon:

> I expect to be sailing for New York on Dec. 15 to spend a few weeks preparing the way for Mr. Gurdjieff's visit in January (You know of course all about Mr. Gurdjieff and Mr. Uspenskii). Naturally I look forward to meeting you, and, in fact, I should come with even more timidity if I did not expect to find you there. I shall let you know my whereabouts instantly upon my arrival, and even perhaps I should not mind meeting you on the landing! Meanwhile, I should be most grateful if you would collect such material as might be useful to my mission. Your friends, I feel, are bound to be friends of the Institute.

27 November 1923. Warwick Gardens. Uspenskii speaks of Adam and Eve and the notion of being able to do.

> Adam and Eve were in kind of an idealistic state when they were in direct connection with higher forces and could act according to definite commandments of higher forces, but they were not satisfied. They came to a certain idea that they could decide for themselves, they thought they knew enough, that there was no need to obey this higher force so then came what is typified as the Devil and they said they knew what is good and evil and something from inside or outside told them they did not need God. They think they can *do* already. This is the original sin. It was

not decision, they attributed to themselves decision. Certainly mistakes bring a wrong state and what is interesting is that we cannot repeat same thing and all our actions are based on that association that we can *do* and first of all we must change this opinion and when understanding is sufficiently deep, when we realize that this cannot be we will look for advice, but as long as we believe we can *do*, nothing can help.

December 1923. Prieuré. Gurdjieff's family arrives from Russia. Soon living at the Paradou are Gurdjieff's mother; sister Sophie Ivanovna and her husband Georgilibovitch Kapanadze, and their daughter Lucia; nephew Valentin Anastasieff; his brother Dmitri, wife Asta, and their three daughters, Luba, Genia and Lida.

So once again Gurdjieff and his brother are together in quite different circumstances. In Alexandropol Dmitri had been quite well off, having been mayor and owning both a cinema and shoe shop. His daughter Luba remembers those days: "My father used to help my Uncle George in his traveling, you see. My father worked; he was a family man. My Uncle was all the time going somewhere. He used to come home for one or two weeks and get clothing and money and then he would go. Sometimes it was a couple of years—nobody heard anything, nobody knew if he was alive or dead and suddenly he would appear again."

While Gurdjieff and his brother were close, Luba says, "My father was not interested at all in what was going on [at the Prieuré]. He used to say [to him] 'You're talking rubbish.' My Uncle used to love my father, but they used to fight like dog and cat about everything. My father would never agree with my Uncle and my Uncle would never agree with him. You see, my father was a *bon viveur*. He used to go out all the time, play cards, drink—enjoy life. They looked very much like each other, but you'd never think it was two brothers. They didn't have at all the same ideas."

13 December 1923. Paris. First of eight public demonstrations of the sacred dances at the Théâtre des Champs-Élysées draws mixed reactions; some experience their newness and sacred quality, others believe they have no aesthetic value.

Gurdjieff chooses Dr. Stjoernval to accompany Orage to America. Gurdjieff tells them Americans have more possibilities for good than any other nation, but they are at the mercy of wrong ideals brought from Europe, and have eventually been distorted even further—they have come to power and money so easily, that their civilization may decay and rot long before it is ripe.

He has given Orage the tasks of generating interest in the teaching and raising enough money to support the stay in America. Orage is well-equipped for the first task by intellect and training, but to the second task he has a strong personal aversion. As a friend says, "his family had suffered much from poverty when he was a boy and he hated it. Equally he hated having to slave for money and almost as much he disliked asking for money for any purposes—even one not his own."

23 December 1923. New York City. On arrival, Orage unpacks his bags at the hotel and goes straight to the offices of the *Little Review* on 28th Street to speak to its editors, Margaret Anderson and Jane Heap. He asks where the best place would be to hold a talk. Both say the Sunwise Turn Bookshop next to the Yale Club Building on 44th Street and Vanderbilt Avenue, across from Grand Central Station. Orage then speaks to the architect Claude Bragdon and Herbert Croly, editor of *The New Republic,* who confirm the choice.

31 December 1923. Prieuré. Jeanne de Salzmann gives birth to a son, Mikhail ("like unto God"), though known in France as Michel. Gurdjieff is the father.

2 January 1924. Prieuré. About to go to New York, Gurdjieff says, "I found myself at the last minute in a super-unique tragi-comic situation." He has paid three hundred thousand francs ($15,100) for the Paris demonstrations, steamship tickets, the most urgent bills at the Prieuré, making provisions for those who would stay behind, and so forth, leaving no cash reserves.

He says he is "searching in my mind for a way out of the incredible situation that had arisen," when his mother comes into his room and returns an expensive brooch that he had given her for safekeeping.

Says Gurdjieff: "What occurred was one of those interventions that people who are capable of thinking consciously—in our times and particularly in past epochs—have always considered a sign of the just providence of the Higher Powers. As for me, I would say that it was the law-conformable result of man's unflinching perseverance in bringing all his manifestations into accordance with the principles he has consciously set himself in life for the attainment of a definite aim."

5 January 1924. Prieuré. Gurdjieff and his troupe of some twenty-two dancers sail to America on the SS *Paris.* Uspenskii is present at their departure. It reminds him of Gurdjieff's leaving Essentuki and "all that was connected with it." Uspenskii once again decides to break with Gurdjieff, as he had in Essentuki in 1918 and Constantinople in 1921.

"Gurdjieff had gone off the rails—become mad—and I wanted to save the System," was the reason Uspenskii gave years later.

11 January 1924. Portland Place, London. Uspenskii tells his key group at Ralph Philipson's flat[31]—"I have asked you to come because I must tell you that I have decided to break off all relations with Mr. Gurdjieff. This means that you have to choose. Either you can go and work with him, or you can work with me, but if you remain with me, you must give an understanding that you will not communicate in any way with Mr. Gurdjieff."[32]

31. The meeting is also reported as being at Warwick Gardens.
32. Uspenskii would insist on this until he died.

Philipson, who had made substantial contributions to the purchase of the Prieuré, as well as helping to underwrite Uspenskii's work in London, asks the reason behind this decision.

"Mr. Gurdjieff is a very extraordinary man. His possibilities are much greater than those of people like ourselves. But he also can go in the wrong way. I believe that he is now passing through a crisis, the outcome of which no one can foresee. Most people have many 'I's. If these 'I's are at war with one another it does not produce great harm, because they are all weak. But with Mr. Gurdjieff there are only two 'I's, one very good and one very bad."

"I believe," Uspenskii continues, "that in the end the good 'I' will conquer. But meanwhile it is very dangerous to be near him. We cannot be of any help to him, and in his present condition he cannot be of any help to us. Therefore, I have decided to break off all contact. But this does not mean I am against him, or that I consider what he is doing is bad."[33]

Uspenskii's difficulty, as Frank Pinder sees it, is that: "Uspenskii could never forget Gurdjieff's attacking him in front of his pupils." Pinder feels Uspenskii projected himself "in a role in which he saw himself as a successful religious teacher—though he may not have been conscious of this. . . . Uspenskii, for all his great brain, was, for what was real, unintelligent; and it was inevitable that Uspenskii should cut himself and his pupils off from Gurdjieff. It is strange that there can be talk of 'Uspenskii's Teaching,' and 'Gurdjieff-Uspenskii System': the Teaching is *Gurdjieff's*."

At the close of Uspenskii's remarks, someone asks—"How will we exist? Will we continue on the same line as we have been going, or by some other new line or connection with Mr. Gurdjieff's work?"

Answers Uspenskii, "We are connected with the inner meaning of the work, but as an organization we are not connected."

Kenneth Walker, a prominent Harley Street surgeon, asks, "This work can be done effectively here as in Paris, can't it?"

"Yes, practically," says Uspenskii. He speaks of the St. Petersburg conditions.

> When work was organized in Paris, it was agreed that choice of people would be my duty, nobody would be taken without my consent or remain in work without my consent. We worked on those lines in Petersburg, on those principles, but it changed when we came to the Caucasus, because some people came from Petersburg and some came from Moscow who did not know Petersburg conditions and I did not insist on these conditions. . . . But when we started again in Paris Mr. Gurdjieff said I must meet people and I must know everyone, but now there are people I do

---

33. This is sounding very much like an Uspenskiian version of *The Struggle of the Magicians*. An old soul, but still developing, his possibilities are much greater than others and so are his responsibilities. His leaving breaks the octave and many people will follow him.

not know and do not approve of. All work in Paris was without me and many wrong talks in Institute, all these are due to absence of Petersburg conditions. But people in France, they would come like you, they would be instructed, but on definite lines and I would say who could come and who could stay, that would be Petersburg conditions. But again if we made these Petersburg conditions, it would mean Institute as well, nobody would be there without my consent. So no definite connection of organization of my work in France with here could be made, only under Petersburg conditions, because I came to the conclusion — I could not speak to Mr. Gurdjieff about it, he had too many other things to do and think about before going — that I could only connect the work on basis of organization.

He then tells the group: "You must decide, do you want separate organization or one with Institute because later I will base my ideas on one decision or another."

Says Kenneth Walker, "St. Petersburg conditions worked well in Petersburg so they should work well in London."

Replies Uspenskii, "From my point of view, people [at the Institute] were taken without tests, without knowing who they were and many things went wrong."

Later Uspenskii says, "My opinion is that we must organize separately."

"What will happen," someone asks, "if Gurdjieff's struggle goes the wrong way?"

"He could go mad," answers Uspenskii. "Or else he could attract to himself some disaster in which all those round him would be involved."

Among those present is J. G. Bennett. He, along with Nicoll and many others, agrees not to communicate with Gurdjieff. Says Bennett, "Uspenskii was a brilliant and dedicated exponent of Gurdjieff's ideas, and also a man who inspired confidence by his obvious integrity and sincerity. No one else in Gurdjieff's entourage could have gained the confidence of so many wealthy and influential English people."

The octave broken, the die now cast, there will be not one Work, but two — Gurdjieff's Fourth Way and Uspenskii's "System."

And so, less than a year and a half after Gurdjieff founded his Institute at the Prieuré to establish The Fourth Way in the West, the octave is deflected, the force of the teaching halved. Uspenskii entrusts the translation of *Fragments* to Baroness O. A. Rausch de Traubenberg who lives in Paris. He asks Boris Mouravieff to supervise it.[34]

Hearing of his former student's decision to break with him and teach his version of the Work, Gurdjieff's thoughts might have returned to a time seven years

---

34. Curiously, though this break seems permanent, Uspenskii will be seen with Gurdjieff now and then throughout the years until their final meeting seven years hence on the terrace of the Café Henri IV at Fontainebleau-Avon.

earlier in St. Petersburg when supposedly exasperated at the lack of seriousness of the young group, he had stormed out of the meeting, slamming the door behind him. Uspenskii rushed after him pleading with him not to abandon the group, to have mercy on the group, for the sake of one righteous man. "But is there one righteous person among you? Who is it then?" But finally, he, ever the consummate actor, agrees to meet the next day.

Gurdjieff began by reemphasizing the central point—man had no genuine I. He was, rather, many "I"s, just acting from the "reels" of impressions each "I" had built up. "Suppose a man wants to become, say, a lecturer: it may be a good thing and lead to success because of many of the qualities of his 'reel' impressions.... One must know how to act swiftly, grasp the object [teaching] and never let go.... For will there ever be another opportunity? Probably never! And when it's been lost, a man will try to satisfy himself with some kind of imitation of what he's lost... 'Paradise lost!' According to his talent and intellect, sometimes it may work, sometimes not. But then he, too, will start trying to 'preach' about it to others. From preachers like that, Lord deliver us!"[35]

---

35. So Gurdjieff intuited early on what might happen with Uspenskii.

Magicians at War

G. I. Gurdjieff

A. R. Orage edited The New Age, *a British literary magazine noted for its wide influence, from 1907 to 1922*

Georgi Ivanovitch Gurdjieff

Katherine Mansfield & John Middleton Murry

Ethel Merston

Maurice Nicoll at the Prieuré

Magicians at War

Mr. Gurdjieff at the wheel of his Citroën

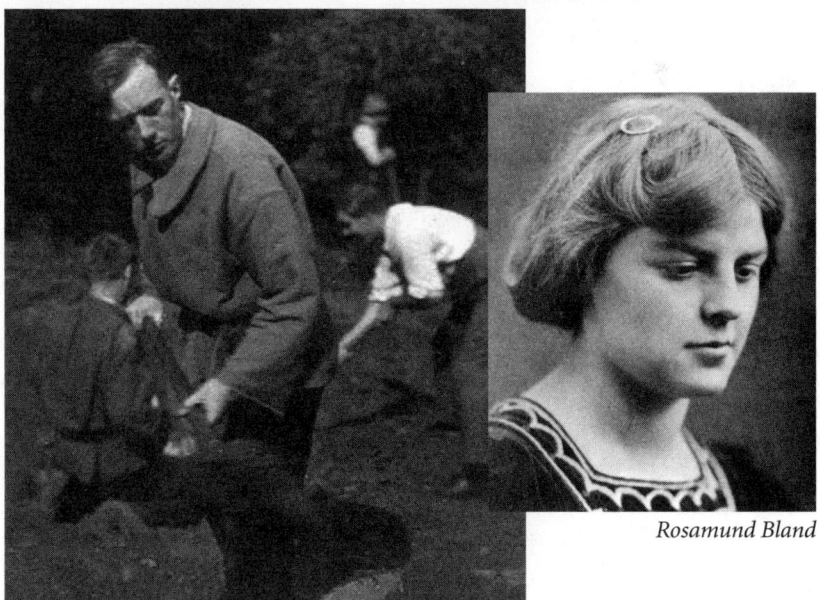

A. R. Orage shoveling soil at the Prieuré

Rosamund Bland

The Prieuré as seen from the garden

Mr. Gurdjieff supervises students working on the grounds of the Prieuré

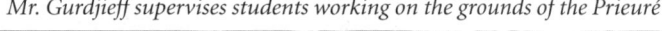

The salon of the Prieuré

Women sawing logs

Georgi Ivanovitch Gurdjieff

Framing the Study House with trusses recycled from an aircraft hangar

Thomas de Hartmann painting

The Study House enclosed and nearing completion

MAGICIANS AT WAR

Gurdjieff's sister, Sophie Ivanovna, her husband, Georgilibovitch Kapanadze, and Gurdjieff's mother, Evdokia Giorgiades

Notice of the first public demonstration of the sacred dances at the Théâtre des Champs-Elysées

PART IV

TZVARNOHARNO

9 JANUARY 1924. SUNWISE TURN BOOKSHOP, NEW YORK CITY. ORAGE, TALL, EASY OF MANNER, QUICK AND BRILLIANT OF MIND, CAPTIVATES HIS AUDIENCE, TELLING THEM THAT "THE INSTITUTE FOR THE HARMONIOUS DEVELOPMENT OF MAN, BASED ON THE SYSTEM OF G. I. GURDJIEFF, IS REALLY A CONTINUATION OF THE SOCIETY CALLED THE 'SEEKERS OF TRUTH.'"

ORAGE THEN SKETCHES THE HISTORY OF THE INSTITUTE FROM ITS FIRST FORMATION IN RUSSIA BEFORE THE REVOLUTION TO ITS FOUNDING AT AVON NEAR FONTAINEBLEAU IN FRANCE.

THEN HE STATES:

> The life of our time has become so complex that man has deviated from his original type.... Our civilization has taken away from the natural and essential qualities of his inherited type, but it has not given him what was needed for the harmonious development of a new type, so that civilization, instead of producing an individually whole man adapted to the nature and surroundings in which he finds himself and which really were responsible for his creation, has produced a being out of his element, incapable of living a full life, and at the same time a stranger to that inner life which should by rights be his.... The world perception of man of our time and his way of living are not the conscious expression of himself as a complete whole; but, on the contrary, are the unconscious manifestation of only one of the three parts of him [intellectual, emotional, instinctive-moving].... Each truly conscious perception and expression of man must be the result of simultaneous and coordinated working of all three centers, each of which must take its part in the whole task.

Orage's talk makes a strong impression. Many in the audience are part of the New York literati, two of the most well-known are Margaret Anderson and Jane Heap, co-editors of the *Little Review*, a lively review of the arts.[1] Says Anderson after the talk, "[Orage is] the most persuasive man I have ever known."

The following morning a fateful meeting occurs. Returning to the Sunwise Turn, Orage spies an attractive young woman and remembering that while she had attended his talk she listened with a certain dismissiveness, he asks, "How did you enjoy the talk?"

"Not at all," she immediately answers.

Her interest in his talk is marginal, but she is attracted to Orage and so the two soon fall into chatting. He learns that her frankness and independence are bred from a long line of Connecticut clergymen and scholars; she is a direct descendent of the Connecticut Wit and president of Yale University Timothy Dwight, and the well-connected first cousin of Dwight D. Eisenhower. Five-foot-five, beautiful and educated, the chestnut-haired Jessie Richards Dwight, springing from a wealthy New York family, is also one-third owner of the bookstore.[2]

Orage thanks her and gives his attention to an employee of the bookshop who had also attended his talk. He asks what his impressions were.

---

1. The *Little Review*, founded in 1914 by Margaret Anderson, who defined it as "A Magazine of the Arts, Making No Compromise with the Public Taste," published the avant-garde of its day, many of them steered to its pages by poet Ezra Pound, the magazine's "foreign correspondent." Among its writers: James Joyce, Ernest Hemingway, William Butler Yeats, T. S. Eliot, Jean Cocteau and Gertrude Stein.

2. What a great help she could be to him in the task Gurdjieff gave him—establishing the teaching in America. What man, indeed a stranger in a strange land, facing such a monumental responsibility, would not feel with Orage that this enchanting young woman is heaven-sent?

"None at all. I could not get the hang of it," replies the young Englishman C. S. (Charles Stanley) Nott.

"Never mind," Orage says. "Gurdjieff is arriving in a week's time with some twenty pupils to give demonstrations of sacred dances and exercises. Why don't you come?"

Later Nott reflects, "It was as if I were meeting someone whom I had known intimately and had liked, and from whom I had been separated for a very long time."

15 January 1924. New York. Gurdjieff and his dancers arrive.

16 January 1924. New York. The author William Seabrook had traveled extensively in the Middle East and beyond, meeting Bedouins, Druses, Whirling Dervishes and Yezidis and several years hence would write about his experiences, *Adventures in Arabia*. Probably at Orage's invitation, Seabrook says of Gurdjieff:

> I was taken to meet him, privately, on the night after his arrival, in a palatial suite in an old-fashioned uptown hotel, and was so deeply impressed by his brains and brute strength that we sat talking until nearly dawn. Whether his power lay simply in the fields of hypnotism and auto-suggestion, or went beyond it into authentic telepathy and clairvoyance, or even further into the Tibetan and Yoga fields of alleged occult miracle-working, I never became convinced—for the reasons that I've never yet become convinced that power in these latter categories can exist at all. But whatever category Gurdjieff's power may have lain in—I can testify of my own knowledge that Gurdjieff knows more about dervish mysticism and magic than any man I have ever met outside a dervish monastery.

Middle of January 1924. New York. At a meeting of those interested in the teaching, Gurdjieff is asked, "What place has love in your system?"

> With ordinary love goes hate. I love this, I hate that. Today I love you, next week or next hour, or next minute, I hate you. He who can really love can *be*; he who can be, can *do*; he who can do, *is*. To know about real love one must forget all about love and must look for direction. As we are we cannot love. We love because something in ourselves combines with another's emanations; this starts pleasant associations, perhaps because of chemico-physical emanations from instinctive center, emotional center, or intellectual center; or it may be from influences of external form; or from feelings—I love you because you love me, or because you don't love me; suggestions of others; sense of superiority; from pity; and for many other reasons, subjective and egoistic. We allow ourselves to be

influenced. We project our feelings on others. Anger begets anger. We receive what we give. Everything attracts or repels. There is love of sex, which is ordinarily known as "love" between men and women—when this disappears a man and a woman no longer "love" each other. There is love of feeling, which evokes the opposite and makes people suffer. Later, we will talk about conscious love.

23 January 1924. New York. Gurdjieff's troupe makes its first appearance at Manhattan's Leslie Hall on West 83rd Street. The program says the movements that will be performed are based on the enneagram and had been taken from the Aisors, a Christian sect tinged with Sufism, located near Mount Ararat. Seabrook was there and says:

> The demonstrations, I imagine, were to show the extent to which the Gurdjieff Institute in Fontainebleau had taught them supernormal powers of physical control, co-ordination, relaxation, etc. And there was no fake about it, regardless of whether it was supernormal or not, because if they hadn't learned supreme co-ordination, they'd have broken their arms and legs, and maybe their necks, in some of the stunts they did. But what I felt the demonstrations showed, even more than their control over themselves, was the terrific domination of Gurdjieff, the Master.
>
> Gurdjieff himself, a calm, bull-like man, with muscles as hard as steel, in immaculate dinner clothes, his head shaven like a Prussian officer's, with black luxuriant handle-bar mustaches, and genially smoking expensive Egyptian cigarettes, stood casually down in the audience, or off to the side beside the piano, which was not on stage. He never shouted. He was always casual. Yet always in complete command.... Among his other qualities, he was a great showman, and a climax came one night which literally had the front rows out of their seats.
>
> The troupe was deployed extreme back stage, facing the audience. At his command, they came racing full tilt toward the footlights. We expected to see a wonderful exhibition of arrested motion. But instead, Gurdjieff calmly turned his back, and was lighting a cigarette. In the next split second, an aerial human avalanche was flying through the air, across the orchestra, down among the empty chairs, on the floor, bodies pell-mell, piled on top of each other, arms and legs sticking out in weird postures—frozen where fallen, in complete immobility and silence.
>
> Only after it had happened did Gurdjieff turn and look at them, as they lay there, still immobile. When they presently arose, by his permission, and it was evident that no arms, legs, or necks had been broken—no one seemed to have suffered even so much as a scratch or bruise—there were storms of applause, mingled with a little protest. It

had been almost too much.

25 January 1924. New York. C. S. Nott attends the performance and is taken with the sacred dances and the music. The highlight for him is a series of movements called the "Big Seven" or "Big Group." Orage returns with Dr. Stjoernval to the Sunwise Turn where Nott works. He says:

> At once I sensed that I was a mere youth in the presence of these adult men. Very soon I made another and more striking comparison; Gurdjieff arrived, very impressive in a black coat with an astrakhan collar and wearing an astrakhan cap. With a twinkle in his eyes he began to joke with the others. Then he walked round, and I found him standing beside me. I looked up, and was struck by the expression of his eyes, with the depths of understanding and compassion in them. He radiated tremendous power and "being" such as I had never in all my travels met in any man, and I sensed that, compared with him, both Dr. Stjoernval and Orage were as young men to an elder.

2 February 1924. New York. The troupe's second performance is given at the Neighborhood Playhouse on MacDougal Street in Greenwich Village. The audience responds favorably to Gurdjieff's presentation of sacred dances and a large amount of money is collected. Among those present at the performance is the thirty-year-old writer Jean Toomer whose novel *Cane* had been an instant critical success the year before. Toomer is familiar with German and Swedish gymnastics and had studied the Alexander Technique [a body work] and has a keen sense of the body. When he first saw Gurdjieff he says:

> I saw this man in motion, a unit in motion. He was completely of one piece. From the crown of his head down the back of the head, down the neck, down the back and down the legs, there was a remarkable line. Shall I call it a gathered line? It suggested coordination, integration, knitness, power.... I was fascinated by the way the man walked. As his feet touched the floor there seemed to be no weight on them at all—a glide, a stride, a weightless walk.... His complexion is swarthy, his dark eyes wide-spread, his nose finely modelled and even delicate compared with the rugged four-square lower face, and he has a tigerish black moustache.
>
> Gurdjieff seemed to have everything that could be asked of a developed human being, a teacher and a master. Knowledge, integration, many-sidedness, power—in fact, he had a bit too much power for my comfort.... I held back, Gurdjieff's power disturbed me. I was not sure of it, and I wanted to be sure before I placed myself wholly in his hands.

In his diary Toomer comes closer to his impression of Gurdjieff:

"Power[3]—something more than strength of body, something in addition and other than strength of mind. Though he contained it, it came out of him, this deep, pervasive, unfathomable power. I soon became sure that I had never seen any other man with power of this kind. But how was he using it? For good? For evil? How would he use it on me should I become one of his pupils? From this time on I had no peace until I had finally settled this question so far as I was concerned.

Says British author Llewelyn Powys:

The famous prophet and magician Gurdjieff appeared in New York accompanied by Mr. Orage, who was acting for him as a kind of Saint Paul. . . . I had the opportunity of observing Gurdjieff while he stood smoking not far from me in the vestibule. . . . His general appearance made one think of a riding master, though there was something about his presence that affected one's nerves in a strange way. Especially did one feel this when his pupils came onto the stage to perform like a hutchful of hypnotized rabbits under the gaze of a master conjurer.

15 February 1924. New York. Gorham Munson, writer and literary disciple of Waldo Frank, attends a demonstration by Gurdjieff and his troupe:

The sensation in New York for the past month has been the visit of Gurdjieff, Orage, and a troupe of pupils from Fontainebleau. They came unheralded, give out no addresses, assign no purpose for their visit, and put on quite suddenly demonstrations for invited audiences. It is the very devil to find out when and where they are demonstrating, and it is the very devil to get admitted. At last, however, Lisa [Munson's wife] and I were placed on their list. I have seen two demonstrations and heard three lectures. The dancing is quite undreamed of. Ritual dances from the East, temple dances of esoteric cults, monastic experiences: I have never seen so much complexity, contradiction, and detailed variety held together in an unaccountable unity. It is a dance of design (of complicated geometry) rather than of motion. Strictly impersonal. Also there are demonstrations of tricks, semi-tricks, possibly thought-transference, and these have been concentration tests. Gurdjieff is the most powerful man I have ever seen: God or Satan himself—almost. Everyone is talking—literati, society, little girls—amazing rumors spread.

3. For Toomer, the difficulty is Gurdjieff's power. For Uspenskii, it is Gurdjieff's "playing" and his use of devotional methods. For Bennett, it is the demand for commitment. For Orage, a woman.

Margaret Anderson gives a potent first impression of Gurdjieff.

> I had just time to look carefully at a dark man with an Oriental face, whose life seemed to reside in his eyes. He had a presence impossible to describe because I had never encountered another with which to compare it. In other words, as one would immediately recognize Einstein as a "great man" we immediately recognized Gurdjieff as the kind of man we had never seen—a seer, a prophet, a messiah? . . . We looked upon this man standing in the wings as a messenger between two worlds. . . . I think I really thought of Gurdjieff, at first, as a sort of Hermes, teaching his son Tat. . . . What philosophers have taught as 'wisdom,' what scholars have taught in texts and tracts, what mystics have taught through ecstatic revelation, Gurdjieff would teach as a science—an exact science of man and human behavior—a supreme science of God, world, man—based on sources outside the scope, reach, knowledge or conception of modern scientists and psychologists.

26 February 1924. Munich. Correspondents from the world press and leading German newspapers cover thirty-four-year-old Adolf Hitler's trial for treason. It lasts for twenty-four days. Hitler's speaking ability and nationalistic spirit transform the defeat of his putsch into a triumph. His aim is to get rid of the Reich government. Of himself, Hitler declares:

> The man who is born to be a dictator is not compelled, he wills it. He is not driven forward, but drives himself. There is nothing immodest about this. Is it immodest for a worker to drive himself toward heavy labor? Is it presumptuous of a man with the high forehead of a thinker to ponder through the nights till he gives the world an invention? The man who feels called upon to govern a people has no right to say, "If you want me or summon me, I will cooperate." No! It is his duty to step forward.

March 1924. Boston and Chicago. As he did in New York, Orage drums up interest, giving newspaper interviews and talks, and Gurdjieff and his troupe of dancers follow with demonstrations.

1924. London. Writers Aldous Huxley and Gerald Heard attend Uspenskii's lectures. The occult writer A. E. Waite also comes. Listening to Uspenskii discourse on the need for man to realize he is a machine, Waite walks out crying—"Mr. Uspenskii, there is no love in your system."

Spring 1924. New York. Orage, the consummate lecturer, attracts larger and larger audiences to his exposition of Gurdjieff's teaching. Besides Margaret Anderson, Jane Heap, and Jean Toomer, he draws into his orbit authors, poets, critics, actors, and budding psychologists. Among them are: Waldo Frank, his wife Margaret Naumburg, Muriel Draper, Rebecca West, Zona Gale, Gorham Munson with his wife Elizabeth, Carl Zigrosser, Schuyler Jackson, Edwin Wolfe, John O'Hara Cosgrave, and the philanthropist Mabel Dodge Luhan.

Says thirty-five-year-old Waldo Frank, the literary lion of the time: "Orage blights the claims of humanness. With valedictory sentiment, wipes sentiment off the slate. With logic swift as a machine, he discredits logic. With courteous manner, drops spiritual bombs into the laps of ladies who adore him."

Says Claude Bragdon, "It was Orage, the perfect disciple, the Plato to this Socrates, who was responsible for most of the success which attended the movement in America. His charming manner and brilliant mind did much to counteract the bewilderment in which Gurdjieff so often left his auditors."

For Gorham Munson what stands out is Orage's intelligence. He and his wife are introduced to Orage by Jean Toomer and Margaret Naumburg. Says Munson: "I felt that this man's note was intelligence, and I have never met a man who struck it with as much clarity.... He gave no sign of middle age. No hint of grey in the dark hair, and only a slight recession of the hairline near the part on the left. No sign of corpulence."

Munson's wife, Elizabeth, a former dancer, later recounted: "I felt his alertness and his relaxation. I felt in Orage something always in motion but not hurried, not tense, not forced—an easy swiftness which could change its course deftly and resume the original direction with perfect sureness. Quick intelligence, quick feeling and understanding, and an extraordinary speed of perception—a sort of lightning functioning."

3 March 1924. Carnegie Hall, New York. The auditorium was packed with only a few of the expensive front-row seats empty. Gurdjieff, who for the first time had charged for tickets, waves the people from the back seats forward.
"I have ventured to come to this 'dollar-growing country,' and here, breathing this air saturated with the vibrations of people who sow and reap dollars in a masterly fashion, I, like a thorough-bred hunting dog, am on the scent of certain and good game."

1 April 1924. Germany. Adolph Hitler is convicted of treason, sentenced to five years' imprisonment at the old fortress of Landsberg, high above the River Lech.

8 April 1924. New York. The day of the opening of the New York branch of the Institute for the Harmonious Development of Man. With Muriel Draper's

Manhattan apartment as its center, groups are now also active in Westchester County. After a dinner in honor of Mr. Gurdjieff at a Russian restaurant, he and friends, and several pupils of the French branch, retire to the apartment of a Mrs. Juliet Rublee, wife of a prominent New York lawyer, for coffee and liqueurs. Gurdjieff is asked about finances and replies at length, the account forming the final chapter in the *Second Series* of *All and Everything*, "The Material Question."

With Gurdjieff's visit a success, Orage has no trouble raising monies. He tells Nott: "Gurdjieff says that the attitude to finance is all part of the dream state that we live in. If men could wake up it would very soon be changed. Gurdjieff's attitude to money is different from that of anyone I have met.... Gurdjieff may appear to be throwing money about, but he calculates and uses it for certain non-personal ends."

23 April 1924. Gurdjieff says the Feast Day of St. George the Victor, Warrior of God, Knight of Christ, is to be regarded as the Institute's "Coronation Day."

June 1924. Darien, Connecticut. Toomer is invited to spend a weekend at the home of Waldo Frank and his wife, Margaret Naumburg. Frank had become Toomer's mentor and friend, having written a highly complimentary foreword to *Cane*. Toomer rejected author Sherwood Anderson's offer to write a foreword since he insisted on calling Toomer a "Negro." Frank's foreword used "African-American." For both personal and artistic reasons Toomer rejected all traditional racial classifications.

Physically white in appearance, the six-foot-one, lemon-skinned Toomer, grandson of a former governor of Louisiana, is racially mixed, his ancestry including not only African-American but Indian, Jewish, German, French, Dutch, and Welsh blood as well. America, Toomer believes, was in the process of forming a new race, and that he was "one of the first conscious members of this race." He thinks of himself as "the first American." He speaks of himself in the third person. "Toomer has a long slim body with long tapering fingers. He has the sensitivity of an artist, the lips of a sensualist, the eyes of a fanatic."

Frank's wife, Margaret Naumburg, dark-haired, powerful and self-assured, is a psychologist, artist and a professional educator who had founded the well-regarded Walden School in New York, which taught children to trust in themselves. She had a mystical view of the world, as did her husband, but they had long been at odds. The birth of a son the previous year had failed to reconcile them.

Toomer, magnetic, charming and learned, had a natural ease and affability with women; he provided the shock needed for dissolution of the marriage. After that weekend they began seeing one another and by October Naumburg had taken an apartment in the city. Though Toomer did not exactly move in with her, he could always be found there. By December she informed Frank she was going to Reno for a divorce.

Caught in the middle between Frank and Toomer was Gorham Munson, a friend of both men. He refused to take sides. Of Toomer, Munson says: "His sex nature was sweet and pure, and I imagine that he was a genuine lover and genuine person in his sex contacts."

Orage's meetings are held first in the apartment of a psychoanalyst, then at 24 East 11th Street, Jane Heap's apartment in the Village, and finally in Muriel Draper's more spacious Murray Hill apartment at 24 East 40th Street. Draper is a writer, social activist and close friend of both Henry James and Gertrude Stein; she will later become the architectural critic of *The New Yorker*. "Mrs. Trapper," Gurdjieff delights in calling her, much the same as he will later refer to Jane Heap as "Mees Keep."

Soon at Orage's meetings an attractive, shapely young woman is seen sitting adoringly at Orage's feet. He has long recognized his weakness for women, but if Orage is a "super idiot," as Gurdjieff will call him, she is a "superwoman," American style. Before long the fifty-year-old Orage succumbs to the twenty-two-year-old Jessie Dwight, but not without a bit of resistance perhaps. For in England he had spoken of the need to free himself from the desire for female companionship. As he had written earlier in *The New Age*:

> Long after the liability to complete subjection to female illusion is over, men sometimes continue to experience perturbations of their equilibrium in the presence of women. In few instances are these perturbations violent enough to overthrow the mind entirely, but for the moment they undoubtedly do cause the judgment to reel and stagger and the resulting conversation and actions to become distorted. These residual phenomena, however, are to be distinguished from the similar phenomena of adolescence by the fact that they no longer inspire hope but disgust or, at least, annoyance.[4]

But Orage must also deal with what Philip Mairet, his friend and biographer, calls "a feminine element." As Mairet points out:

> The acute sensibility and responsiveness of mind in which lay so much of Orage's personal magnetism was due to a feminine element in his character of which he was well aware, though he could never wholly accept it. He feared it, as men often do, and made matters more difficult by additional efforts to stiffen his character and harden his mental texture, which, as is usually the case with such efforts, especially if undertaken in mature years, were far from achieving their object but brought

---

4. Like Uspenskii's Osokin, Orage sees his situation clearly enough but has not the requisite self-remembrance and will to change it.

on tortured and precarious feelings. He became unable to miss a shot at golf without glancing round anxiously in fear that some stranger had noticed the blunder.

Settling in Manhattan, Orage moves into a tiny apartment in Chelsea. He works steadfastly to build interest in Gurdjieff's teaching and to form groups. Some two hundred people, many drawn from New York's intelligentsia, will show interest in joining Orage's groups. Soon Jessie Dwight leaves the Sunwise Turn to become his personal secretary. She subsidizes Gurdjieff's trip to Boston, and arranges with her banking contacts to loan Gurdjieff much needed money. Except for a tendency to drink, Jessie is far more emotionally stable than Beatrice Hastings or Katherine Mansfield. Jessie Dwight is a woman who knows what she wants and will sacrifice to get it; the "sacrifice" in this case being to appear to align herself with Gurdjieff's teaching.[5] For his part, Orage seems to be at right angles to himself. Intellectually, he is opposed to granting women independence, but emotionally strong-willed, independent women are his great attraction.

The New Yorker publishes Waldo Frank's portrait of Orage, "Mystery in a Sack Suit":

> Here were true intellectuals who despise Greenwich Village. Here were socially elect who looked down on Park Avenue as a gilded slum. Here indeed were men and women dry and fresh, smart and solemn, rich or merely famous—perpendicular extremes of our extremely perpendicular New York. And now if you looked still closer, you saw that they were listening with passionate concern to a man they call Orage and Orage was most intempestuously sitting in an upholstered armchair, smoking a cigarette and cavalierly smiling. He seems a proverbial schoolboy, slightly damaged by the years, yet on the whole intact—as he sits enwreathed in all those seeking brains and eager eyes. He has a hard body in a tight drab suit. He has hair like a cap drawn close upon his skull. The finger tips are yellow with tobacco. The face is gray with thought. And its prominent part is the nose. The nose is the pinnacle of Orage. Intense brow, willful jaw, keen eyes, ironic mouth—they all converge upon this proboscidean symbol of pertinence and search.... He talks more of Behaviorism, Astronomy and Mechanics than of what is commonly called religion. And he believes in literally nothing. Nothing that is, I mean. This is what makes him so detached. He knows all the scriptures from the *Mahabharata* to Hart Crane, and he is detached from them all. Even Buddha believed in the world enough to cry against it, to invent harsh disciplines to combat it. Not Orage. He despises the world so well that he is at peace with it wholly.... His sensuous

---

5. It may be that a part of her is interested in the teaching, but from her original comment to Orage and her later battle with Gurdjieff, that part never grew substantially.

hospitality is the sign of his contempt. Even so, his boy face is the counterfeit of candor; and his language, which for fluent clarity has few peers in England, weaves a mist about him. Orage knows not alone the Pali Canon, but as well the Jesuits and Machiavelli. He barbs you with his words; he swathes and soothes you with his perhaps too unctuous manner—and himself glides by.... The Puritan Socialism of Bernard Shaw—dear Shaw who takes liquor, meat, tobacco, coffee, tea and women so seriously that he does not take 'em at all—was not for Orage. Shaw stayed on in England: Orage—who takes 'em all—has come to our wider land.

Many in New York want to go to the Prieuré, among them the young Englishman C. S. Nott. But there is a problem. Nott tells Orage that a young American woman he is seeing has "become resentful" of his interest in the Gurdjieff system. She has refused to go to any more meetings and blames Nott for a loss of interest in what they had both worked for—"social reform and the good of others." When he told her of his plans to go to the Prieuré, she declared—"You will have to choose between Gurdjieff and me."

Replies Orage, who soon will be no stranger to the problem:

You must remember that American women, more than any others, are spoilt. Of course, all women want their own way but one of the tragedies of American life is that women have succeeded in getting it to the extent of dominating men. The passive force has become the active. One of the consequences is the enormous number of divorces here compared with Europe. Gurdjieff blames men for the deterioration in the status of women in America. The strange thing is that Americans regard it as a sign of "progress."... In a real civilization woman understands her function and has no wish to be other than a woman.

June 1924. New York City. Orage and Jessie see Gurdjieff off at the dock. Jessie had no interest in coming to the Prieuré, especially without Orage.

Gurdjieff tells her, "Very important you come Prieuré. Very important you come now."

"I am coming in Fall," Jessie says.

"Fall—too late. Very important come at once. You remember! Fall—perhaps no Prieuré."

"It's hateful of you," she tells him, close to tears.

June 1924. Prieuré. Upon Gurdjieff's return he finds that Pinder, perhaps still working as a secret agent, has rifled through his files and personal papers hoping to find perhaps some fraudulence. Finding nothing, he flees, leaving Gurdjieff's bedroom in disarray.

June 1924. Prieuré. Arriving for a stay are Jane Heap, Margaret Anderson and her two young nephews, Fritz and Tom Peters, and Georgette Leblanc, an actress and classical singer, and former companion of Maurice Maeterlinck, the playwright and poet.[6] One evening at dinner they are surprised to see Uspenskii, since they had heard he had left the Institute.

"Uspenskii," says Margaret Anderson, "sat at Gurdjieff's left and acted like a small boy, laughing more than he meant to, saying what he meant not to, flushing with the Armagnac forced upon him.... Though Uspenskii must have taken part in this ceremony a hundred times, I always felt that he had never discovered its significance; that he knew ideas but didn't know people."

Margaret speaks with Gurdjieff, who tells her: "I cannot develop you. I create conditions; you develop yourself."

The three women and the two boys become residents of the Prieuré. The women will live off and on at the Prieuré for two years.[7]

Georgette says to Margaret, "We have spent our lives walking about under parasols." Thinks Margaret, always highly imaginative, "Yes, white parasols, like those used by Catholics in midnight Mass at New Year's."

Georgette's impression of Gurdjieff is that "he resided on the earth as on a planet too limited for his own needs and function. Where did he manifest his real existence?... I was not astonished that he was little known, that he was not surrounded by thousands of followers. Neither money nor influence could open the doors of the Prieuré—Gurdjieff created all possible obstacles to discourage any idler-spirits who might push their way into a world where they did not belong."

While in New York, Olgivanna had lived with Jane Heap and the two had become intimate. Earlier, in New York, Olgivanna had declined Orage's advances. He told her that you are "in the power of a despot which is the sum of your personalities which says 'Won't' to everything." Olgivanna told a friend, "I'll have to give 'Olgivanna up.'" The proud, aristocratic Montenegrin and daughter of Ivan Lazovich, first chief justice of the country, her mother, the imperious Melena

---

6. Of their twenty-year relationship and its breakup see her *Souvenirs: My Life with Maeterlinck* (New York: E. P. Dutton & Co., 1932).

7. Though Margaret and Jane had been longtime companions, their relationship was no longer what it was. Still, Georgette becoming close with Margaret might have caused sparks. "No greater contrast can be imagined," says Margaret, "than that between the natures, characters, temperaments, personalities and behavior of my first two great friends. In the beginning it seemed impossible that any bond could be established between them. Of course, they finally became the greatest of friends. No one could resist being a friend of Georgette's after hearing her talk seriously. But at first Georgette had to find a key to communication. As she explained, 'When I am face to face with Jane, for me it is as if she were two persons. I don't address myself to her human side, I see facing me only an astonishing mind, so astonishing that its superiority can be separate totally from the human being that she is. I have the impression that this separation is not total for you. You think of the other side—of the person you know—as much as you think of the person you are listening to. It is this that creates a latent discord between you.'"

Milianova who had been raised as a boy by her father, Marco Milianov, the country's heroic general who had rid Montenegro of the Turks—Olgivanna bowed to no one save Gurdjieff.

Mid-June 1924. Prieuré. Eleven-year-old Fritz Peters is interviewed by Gurdjieff on the terrace. The boys' mother has been hospitalized for a year in a mental institution, and their aunt Margaret Anderson and her companion Jane Heap have legally adopted the boys.

Told that Gurdjieff is a prophet or someone very close to the second coming of Christ, the young boy dreads the meeting. He is relieved when he meets Gurdjieff.

"The actual meeting," says Peters, "did not measure up to my fears. 'Messiah' or not, he seemed to me a simple, straightforward man."

Among the questions Gurdjieff asks him is what he wants to know.

"I want to know everything," Peters replies.

"You cannot know everything. Everything about what?"

"Everything about man."

Gurdjieff sighs and tells him, "You can stay. But your answer makes life difficult for me. I am the only one who teaches what you ask. You make more work for me."

Peters is put to work from 6 a.m. to 11 p.m. cleaning out the stable and taking care of the horse and donkey. Not only is he differentiated from others there by his age but also he is, understandably, not searching for anything. He is also there, as he says, "against my will—in the sense that any child is at a boarding school against his will—or at least, hardly by choice."

Besides Fritz and his brother Tom, the children at the Prieuré include Dr. Stjoernval's son, Nikolai; Tolik Mercourov; Madame de Salzmann's daughter, Boussique, and later two sons, Michel and Claude; as well as Gurdjieff's niece, Luba, her sisters Genia and Lida; and nephew, Valya. There are some nine children in all and they are able to attend the readings and lectures, if they wish.

29 June 1924. Prieuré. Jessie Dwight arrives. Orage has assured her he will come in September and told her, "You see, I am dedicated to this. I have given up everything for this. You must go now without me." She is given the best room in the best part of the château. Then she is taken to see Gurdjieff who tells her, "Very good, miss, you come." They have tea together and then he leaves. She lights up a cigarette but is told women should smoke only in their rooms. She laughs. Dinner is a trial. It is outdoors. She manages a dead fly in her dish, but when a young Russian sits down next to her and begins "wolfing down his food with loud gurgles and tearing his bread with black filthy hands," she can eat no more. For work the next day she dresses in knickers and a flannel shirt. Seeing her, Gurdjieff says to someone, "She dress like man—she work like man." Says Jessie on hearing this—"Why not?" She writes Orage, "The Prieuré is a most extraordinary place."

Jessie is there nearly two weeks when she mentions she is going to Paris and tells Gurdjieff of her intention.

"Very good," he says, and, in accordance with her suspicions: "I also go to Paris. You come to my apartment this evening for supper. I motor you back."

"Okay," answers Jessie, "but I must bring Mary, as she is going with me."

"You *balda*,"[8] shouts Gurdjieff. "You spoil everything."

"Sorry," Jessie laughs.

Later, Gurdjieff discovers her reading letters from Orage and immediately delivers a shock, ordering that all mail must first be given to him. Jessie now posts her letters outside the gate and checks the concierge's mail box daily.

In one of his many letters trying to console her, Orage writes, "I unfortunately did not go to the Institute in my youth, but the investment of a single year there has yielded me a handsome profit in renewed health [Orage was obese, pallid and chain-smoking when he arrived], in courage, in self-confidence, and in the capacity and the astonishing good fortune to fall so divinely in love.... I should never have known what love is if I had not sloughed off several skins of Orage in the Institute.... I swear on my faith... that one day and in this very life, you will thank God for your voluntary sacrifice."

Jessie will later write two short stories "Elsie at the Prieuré" and "Allah."[9]

Summer 1924. Germany. Adolph Hitler begins dictation of *Mein Kampf (My Struggle)* to his cellmate, Rudolph Hess. Hitler's book gives his rationale for what has gone wrong with European civilization and his plans to change it.

8 July 1924.[10] *Chailly, France.* Gurdjieff and Olga de Hartmann are in Paris and are expected to return today to the Prieuré. A day or so before Olga had gone to a fortune teller who has been accurate in what she has told her previously. She brought the fortune teller Gurdjieff's handkerchief. The cards were dealt. Suddenly a look of fright appeared on the fortune teller's face. "No," the woman said, "I will tell you nothing. Here heaven and earth fight, and I don't wish to be harmed."[11]

8. Damn fool, or blockhead.
9. See Essay, "Jessie Dwight Orage."
10. The exact date is uncertain. Both Olga de Hartmann and Fritz Peters say it is Saturday, 5 July. Bennett says 6 July. Jane Heap, writing to her friend Florence Reynolds, says the accident was on Tuesday, 8 July. See Florence Reynolds Archives, University of Delaware, Newark, DE.
11. In the winter of 1886 when Gurdjieff was 14 years old, the half-witted Eoung-Ashokh Mardiross came to Alexandropol and his aunt had him foretell the young boy's future. Some of what he predicted had already happened but one was yet to happen. He was "in danger of a serious accident from a fire-arm." About a week later, he and some friends went duck hunting and Gurdjieff was accidentally shot in the leg. Gurdjieff's interest aroused, when the fortune teller came again, Gurdjieff asked more predictions. "And one day, without fail," Gurdjieff writes in *Meetings with Remarkable Men*, "I will relate how these predictions were fulfilled." Later in life Gurdjieff

Olga doesn't tell Gurdjieff about this, but he seemingly senses something wrong, for he tells her, "Telephone the garage and ask them to look very carefully through the car, especially the steering wheel." On this day, too, he signs papers giving her power of attorney should anything happen to him. Though they usually return together, he tells her he will drive alone, she is to take a train.

Once out of Paris, Gurdjieff's small black Citroën speeds at 115 kilometers an hour (71 m.p.h.), he cuts the speed to 90 kilometers (56 m.p.h.) in towns. Near the hamlet of Chailly, his Citroën approaches a crossroads where the road from Paris to Fontainebleau meets the N 168 road from Versailles to Choisy-le-Roi. Suddenly, a car darts out from the N 168 road. Gurdjieff swerves the Citroën violently, shoots off the road, veers past a signpost, and heads straight into a grassy area between some trees and a stone embankment. The Citroën hits the embankment head on, snapping the steering wheel, and comes to a dead stop against a tree. The immense force of the impact crumples the front axle and fenders, crushes the radiator, throws the engine off its seating, and smashes the windows and doors.

A passing policeman finds Gurdjieff, unconscious and bloody, his head lying on a car cushion. Gurdjieff has a severe concussion. He has either been thrown from the car, somehow crawled out, or the driver of the other car pulled him out and left. He is taken to a hospital. After the gendarme has brought the news to the Prieuré, Olga de Hartmann finds him. He is brought back to the Prieuré on a stretcher, his head wreathed with bandages, still unconscious. He is carried up to his second floor bedroom. For five days he lies unconscious in his corner room beneath two large paintings, one of Christ, the other of Buddha. Doctors come and go at intervals. Tanks of oxygen are delivered and removed.

Madame de Hartmann takes over the running of the château while Madame Ostrowska and Dr. Stjoernval nurse Gurdjieff. Everywhere, there is a hushed atmosphere as if everyone is involved in a silent prayer for his recovery. Finally, he awakes only to find himself, as he says, "a bit of live meat in a clean bed."

Uspenskii believes he had foreseen some accident like this. He says, "Gurdjieff lost contact with the source after Essentuki. His behavior goes contrary to his teaching. He drives a car as if he were riding a horse."

Some days after the crash Uspenskii and his friend Boris Mouravieff[12] visit

---

would be shot three times. One of the definitions of "fortune" is "things that happen or are to happen to a person." The opposite of "fortune" is "misfortune." In *Beelzebub's Tales* he uses the word 59 times, twice in reference to his 1924 motor accident; in *The Herald of Coming Good* the word is used twice; in *Life Is Real Only Then, When "I Am"* 16 times. In its Prologue, Gurdjieff speaks about "law abidingly arisen misfortune," and in the Introduction he speaks of the 1924 motor accident as his "misfortune." Afterward, he had a number of motor accidents, the last in 1948.

12. Mouravieff has a strong animus toward Gurdjieff and does all he can to fan Uspenskii's concerns about his former teacher. His viewpoint and the accuracy of quoted material are to be taken accordingly. Gurdjieff answers why the accident happened in *The Herald of Coming Good*.

Tzvarnoharno

the crossroads where Gurdjieff's Citroën had hit the tree. Mouravieff says that Uspenskii was "despondent and crushed." After a prolonged silence, Uspenskii says:

> I'm frightened... this is dreadful.... Georgi Ivanovitch's Institute was established to escape from the influence of the law of accident under which men spend their lives. Well, see how he himself has fallen under the influence of this very law.... I still wonder whether it's really a pure accident?—Gurdjieff used always to make light of honesty together with all the rest of human personality. Has he not gone too far?—I tell you, I'm terribly afraid!

All the talk at the Prieuré is of the motor accident. But for Gurdjieff it is no accident at all. That, he says, is "their usual superficial understanding."

"As I supposed from the first when I recovered my senses," he says, "and as I am now quite convinced—it was the last chord of the manifestation toward me of that 'something' usually accumulating in the common life of people, which... was first noticed by the Great, really Great King of Judea, Solomon, and was called '*Tzvarnoharno.*'"

21 July 1924. New York. Orage writes Jessie at the Prieuré to explain Gurdjieff's accident.

> The law of accident is not very easy to understand, but it does not mean that such accidents—even fatal ones—*cannot* happen! All it means is that we suffer our own individual 'karma.' But no collective Karma. When a man is in partnership with others, he sinks or swims *with them*. His own exertions may be little or great, but his return will be the average of the collective business: that is, it does not depend solely upon himself, but on the "accident" of his associates. On the other hand, if he is in business on his own, anything may still happen to him; but it will not be "accident" (in this sense) but karma. G. is always taking risks. They would not be risks if he were insured against the possibility of injury. But he *does* feel sure—probably from astronomy or some similar calculations—that he will not die before he has finished his task. And within that field he can not only take risks, but undertake to extract advantage from one result or another. How a thing turns out is all the same if one way such and such a course is possible, if another way, another course.

Late July 1924. Prieuré. Jean Toomer arrives from America. Margaret Naumburg had also wanted to come but has to stay because of divorce proceedings. For Toomer, he has finally seen that his concern for all the power that emanated from Gurdjieff is "a deep-seated unwillingness to put my life under the direction of anyone other than myself, and a stubborn belief that I could make my own way, unaided by such help as I would receive in the course of ordinary life."

Now ready to work with Gurdjieff, Toomer finds him incapacitated, with no one allowed to see him except those caring for him. A great gloom hangs over the Prieuré. Toomer finds there is little to no work going on, and what there is is done half-heartedly. In New York he has heard about the benefits of manual work from Orage, and so soon begins working in the vegetable garden and helping to uproot tree stumps, saw logs, and make roads.

Gurdjieff, slowly recovering from the accident, is seen now and then walking with effort along the paths with a cane, his head bandaged, his swollen eyes concealed behind dark glasses, a shell image of this once amazingly powerful man. With him are Madames Ostrowska and de Hartmann. It is the height of summer and the weather is quite warm, but Gurdjieff is bundled in his thick black coat and astrakhan hat. Students approach him; he does not recognize them, his sight is so impaired. He does not speak. Against doctors' warnings, he has made a tremendous effort to get out of bed. Slowly, only taking a few steps at a time before stopping, he has made his way down the staircase and out onto the terrace. Always behind him carrying a chair for him to sit upon, is eleven-year-old Fritz Peters, his designated "chair-carrier." After fifteen minutes or so, his wife and Madame de Hartmann take him back to bed. Each day Gurdjieff forces himself to stay outside a little longer. He has bonfires built and he would gaze into the flames for an hour or more, drawing strength from the blaze. Despite his physical condition, as Nott observes, "One could still sense and feel the undiminished force of his being."

Gurdjieff soon is directing the work from a bench or chair. He seldom speaks and has not smiled since the accident. One day a fallen tree is being hoisted from a watery ditch. Thomas de Hartmann and Nott are up to their knees in water. The tree falls back into the ditch hitting Nott on a leg he has previously injured. Instantly, Nott cries out, "Damnation!" Everyone stops and stares at him. "It's all right," says Nott, "no harm done, just uncomfortable."

Gurdjieff, watching, starts to smile and everyone begins to laugh. Says Nott, "A new feeling, almost of joy, emanated from everyone," and from that day forward, Gurdjieff begins to talk a little. Toomer, who has taken to the physical work, finds that with Gurdjieff's return "things begin to hum.... It is perfectly amazing what his presence does. Extra life, extra zest, extra power, extra will springs up in us. Everybody works hard all day long and sometimes into the night."

The hard physical work, consciously done, redirecting the attention from the mind to both the body and the work at hand, begins to have an effect on Toomer and soon puts him "in simply wonderful shape, feeling that I could continue on and on, wanting no other life than this. All other life seemed, by contrast, flat, undynamic, unstretching, ungrowing and, above all, unreal, a mere dream-life of vague surfaces and a stir of words." And Toomer learns the real value of manual work as a means of transformation:

Manual work is usually done for the sake of outward results, for the products, that is a farmer works to grow crops, a carpenter to build a house. Here at the Prieuré we were to work chiefly for the sake of purification, growth, increased ability and consciousness. Each job, to be sure, was to be done as well as we could do it. Work standards were anything but lax. Each of us was to improve as a workman, acquiring competence and skill. Tools and materials were to be cared for as real craftsmen care for them. But we were not to be attached to the fruits of our labor. The aim was the same as that expressed in the Bhagavad Gita, "Be free from attachment to results." People who became overly egotistical about their accomplishments were likely to find their pet projects mysteriously disrupted.

Toomer gets a new sense of manual work as chemistry:

> When you work the way we did, the blood is drawn down from the head into the body. The blood, pumped vigorously through the body by this intellectual and sustained activity, is purified. The purified blood revitalized, well-nigh regenerates the body. Then there is a surge upwards into the brain. After several weeks the purified blood courses back into the head, revitalizing and well-nigh regenerating the mind. The total result is a recharged body-mind, a body purified, energized, strengthened, a mind able, lucid, with greatly increased power to grasp and comprehend.

Toomer is reading the aphorisms on the wall of the Study House. When he reads—*Remember you come here having understood the necessity of struggling with yourself—only with yourself. Therefore, thank everyone who gives you the opportunity*—he says:

> The saying took instant hold of me, found purchase in my very roots; for it crystallized a practice that I had engaged in, none too consistently at all, but very earnestly, off and on, ever since that boyhood illness.[13] The new slant was the unmistakable pointing to oneself, the emphasis put on contending with oneself, not with others. The entirely new angle was the allure of actually thanking those who gave us the opportunity. I could remember, on several occasions in the past, being spontaneously grateful to those who had made me face myself and see things I didn't want to see, so that I had to struggle to overcome them. But thank everyone who calls out your faults, your anger, your impatience, your egotism; do this consciously, voluntarily; make determined practice of it—here indeed was

---

13. At ten years of age Toomer was stricken with severe stomach ailments that greatly altered his life. He says: "I had been strong. Now I was weak. I was compelled to exert efforts to get strong again. Life had taken away from me what it had given, and I was forced over years to obtain it by exertion."

an entirely new effort, an effort whose value struck me at once but whose full significance was to become clear only after years of application.

As Gurdjieff's physical strength slowly returns, he takes more and more part in the Institute's activities and begins to answer questions and explain various aspects of the teaching. Says Toomer: "Each day was a full day. Indeed, more effort and more experience are packed into a day at the Institute than in an ordinary month. It gives you a measure of man's reserve power, a standard of human capacity."

20 August 1924. New York. Orage writes to Jessie at the Prieuré. "I'm so glad you kept your sense of humor and feet during the recent maneuver. G's motive is a little obscure, but, in general, when he wants to get rid of one or two people he usually makes a sweep or, at least the gesture of a sweep. He cannot 'liquidate,' I think, and really has no intention of doing so. He may be fed up with the personnel of the Institute temporarily: but, as you rightly say, he cannot give up his life's work at the very moment that he has actually paid for the estate of the parent school."

26 August 1924. Prieuré. Gurdjieff has students assemble in the Study House. He sits in his armchair in the center of the floor. Earlier he had dictated to Olga de Hartmann the speech he wished to give. In a quiet voice, he begins to read the dictation:
"I was very ill. Now, thank God, I feel better and continue to be better. . . ."
Gurdjieff stops. He hands the pages to Olga, telling her to read.
"What happened to me, how it happened, I do not know. I remember nothing. I went to the place where it happened and imagined how it happened. There are not many people who could speak with you like this after such an accident. In principle, I had to die, but accidentally I stayed alive."
Later, in speaking before the assembled students, Gurdjieff apologizes if he offended anyone in the weeks after the accident, as his memory was weak. He says only three or four days ago his memory came back to him and "I can live as before, not as an animal." His first thoughts were: "Did die or not? How will everything be now? And what about the Institute? I saw that I was alive. . . ." He has, however decided to close the Institute.
"First of all," he says, "there are very few people who understand. I gave all my life for my Work, but the result from other people in general was not good and that is why I think it is not necessary for those few to sacrifice their lives here." People can leave immediately or stay on as guests for two weeks. He will sell the Prieuré, but, he says, "All the same, I cannot throw away all my Work. . . . In two weeks I will begin a new work. The names of those who may stay will be posted. Others will have to leave."

Gurdjieff gives some organizational instructions and then returns to his main point: "Again, I repeat that the Institute is closed. I died. The reason is that I was disenchanted with people after all that I have done for them and I have seen how 'well' they have paid me for it. Now, inside of me everything is empty."

Besides his "disenchantment" with his students, Gurdjieff says, "the second reason is that I wish to live for myself. I have to rest and use all the time for myself. I don't wish to continue as before, and my new principle is—everything for myself."

Everything for myself. These last words have a quality of uncharacteristic self-pity if taken in an ordinary way, but Gurdjieff is a teacher, always teaching, and in this case mirroring how everyone lives.[14]

Some thirteen years before, on 14 September 1911, Gurdjieff had taken a special oath binding himself for twenty-one years, he writes, "in [my] conscience to lead in some ways an artificial life, modeled upon a program which had been previously planned in accordance with certain definite principles."

So, nearly thirteen years later, Gurdjieff appears to end his oath. He no doubt took his mission to be a failure. To establish the teaching in the West, he needed to put someone in his place. He needed to find and prepare a student with a Western mentality who could step-down the teaching. Otherwise, it would never take root. He had failed with Uspenskii, with Bennett, and, perhaps at this juncture, he saw Orage was a question mark.[15]

Gurdjieff's sudden closure of the Institute is a thunderbolt whose reverberations are felt for many days. Toomer wrote of this sometime later:

> Most of us were shot straight into the air, and stayed there, suspended, an uncomfortable length of time. Day after day you would see people, sometimes in twos and threes, sometimes alone, in conference with Gurdjieff, talking over their future course of life, where they would go, what they

14. The closing of the Institute seems to alter his original plan in which the Institute would train helper-instructors who would then open "clubs" in major cities in the West.

15. Despite his understanding and being, Gurdjieff had been unable to make any of his students sufficiently aware of their identification with the properties of what he calls *Kundabuffer*, the blind egoism that puts man-in-quotation-marks at the center of the universe. The car crash has opened him to what he probably had known but would not admit for some time. Namely, none of his would-be students at the Prieuré could break through this identification either. In the summer of 1923, Bennett says, "He certainly was under some special kind of obligation, that in the particular work he had to do, he should not assume a position of being a great teacher, with a large number of pupils depending upon him. It was often very obvious that with the greatest of ease, if he had chosen to do so, he could have exercised the power he had to attract people. He could have had thousands of people round him . . . ." Ten years later, Bennett, able to see the larger picture, would add, "They (his old and intimate pupils) saw him as their teacher, concerned with the spiritual progress of his pupils, whereas he was concerned with the impact which his work and ideas could have on the world over a long period of years. This is why he so frequently refers to the realization of his aims after his death."

would do. I had such a conference. Gurdjieff said I might stay on, if I wished. I thought it over. Not much work would go on. But had I come here only to go away in a few months? Where would I go? What would I do? Finally, after quite a struggle, something clicked in me and I decided to return to New York.

August 1924. London. Uspenskii tells students, "Gurdjieff's work at the Prieuré failed simply because the principle of seniority was not followed.... People who did not belong to groups before, like Pinder and Orage, they were given certain power over people who were much older in the Work; it did not work—it could not go on."

20 August 1924. Prieuré. Orage arrives from New York and reunites with Jessie. Gurdjieff immediately meets with Orage, as he had not done initially with Toomer, who had wandered about the grounds for a month before being befriended by Bernard Metz, a small, furtive English Jew and Gurdjieff's unofficial valet. Gurdjieff and Orage spend a great deal of time with one another. A month will pass before Orage and Jessie return to New York.

August 1924. Prieuré. The car crash and Gurdjieff's later actions fuel the swirl of questions and rumors around him as to who he is. For Madame Uspenskii it is not an issue: "I do not pretend to understand Georgi Ivanovitch," she declares. "For me he is X. All that I know is that he is my teacher and it is not right for me to judge him, nor is it necessary for me to understand him. No one knows who is the real Georgi Ivanovitch, for he hides himself from all of us. It is useless for us to try to know him, and I refuse to enter into any discussions about him."

Lists were posted every day as to who was to stay on at the Prieuré. Olgivanna Hinzenburg notices her name is missing. Indignant, she tells Gurdjieff it is unfair. He tells her she had failed, not worked hard enough. Worse, he says those who became her friends were enemies of the Institute. She leaves. The only work she can find in Paris is working in a women's lavatory.

16 September 1924. Philadelphia. Jessmin Howarth gives birth to a daughter, Cynthia Ann, called "Dushka" ("darling" in Russian). Gurdjieff is the father.

Autumn 1924. New York. Through the door of the Sunwise Turn[16] steps C. Daly King. A light-skinned African-American, graduate of Yale, living on private income, King has a keen interest in Egyptology and psychology. The bookshop is

---

16. The Sunwise Turn plays a prominent role in Orage's life. Not only is the bookstore the venue of his first American talk, but it is here that he meets Jesse Dwight, C. S. Nott and now C. Daly King, all of whom become significant figures in his life. Gurdjieff even mentions the bookstore and Jesse Dwight in his *Third Series* of *All and Everything*.

where twenty-nine-year-old King buys all his books. The previous January he and his wife had attended two performances of Gurdjieff's troupe and found the dances "totally unusual and impressive to a degree." In the ensuing months Jessie Dwight had often invited him to attend Orage's meetings, but he had always declined, picturing it as a group of "fanatics meeting privately to discuss strange notions."

Finally, bowing to Jessie Dwight's persistence, King reluctantly attends a meeting. Intellectual to a high degree, King expects "a proselytizing harangue." He goes armed with an incredulous attitude, ready to object to every point. But he finds that the tall slender Englishman in the inconspicuous dark business suit presents the teaching with "complete and utter *rationality*." Moreover, Orage makes clear that no starry-eyed believers or woolly thinkers are countenanced.

"My incredulity was not admitted," says King. "Instead, it was demanded that I adopt skepticism toward what I heard, that is, that I should neither believe nor disbelieve."

Upon his return to New York, Jean Toomer, without authorization and unable to resist his desire to be a teacher, however premature, sets up his own Gurdjieff study group, imitating Gurdjieff, affecting his mannerisms, even using Russian words. Says his friend Gorham Munson: "Jean had a lot of nerve to do that; he was really not qualified to do it." The group only lasts five or six meetings. He then returns to Orage's group.

Orage is quick to recognize the young man's possibilities and begins to work closely with Toomer. At one point after a question about will, Orage tells Toomer: "Work hard while you feel like it, and then, when you no longer want to, work twice as hard. It is the work done after wish ceases that really counts. When desire ends, then and then only can will come into play. When your automatic activity slows down and stops, then is your chance for voluntary, non-habitual action."

October 1924. Café de la Paix, Paris. Gurdjieff tells Olgivanna it is time to start a new life. She should go to New York and reconnect with Orage and members of the Institute. Then she should go on to Chicago and help set up the group there. "I have taught you everything I have to teach you. You will never be lost now. Make a new form of life for yourself. I will see you again." Later, he tells her, "You are my true student. You remember the gold coin you found at Christmas? I told you then you were the chosen one. But still you must make your own decisions."

21 October 1924. Le Havre. Olgivanna and her daughter, Svetlana, who has returned with her to the Prieuré, board the SS *Rochambeau* bound for New York.

Late October. New York. Orage moves into Jessie's apartment on East 56th Street.

2 November 1924. New York. Orage gives the first of a new round of public lectures, "The Past, Present and Future of the Gurdjieff Institute." The quality and number of those attending the lectures and joining study groups is exceptional by any standard. These include the writers Jean Toomer, C. S. Nott, Caesar Zwaska, Muriel Draper, Gorham Munson and his wife, Lisa, Schuyler Jackson, William Seabrook, Carl Van Vechten, Waldo Frank, Israel Solon and John Riordan, literary critic Van Wyck Brooks, poets Melville Cane and Edna Kenton, architects Claude Bragdon and Hugh Ferris, psychologist C. Daly King, concert pianists Carol Robinson and Rosemary Lillard, Broadway actress Rita Romilly and actor Edwin Wolfe, art curator Carl Zigrosser, editors Margaret Anderson and Jane Heap, Herbert Croly, John Cosgrove O'Hara, and T. S. Matthews (later editor of *Time* magazine) and his sister Peggy (Flinsch), Juliet Rublee and Larry Morris, five-and-dime heiress Blanche Grant, businessmen Sherman Manchester and Stanley Speigelberg, and the endocrinologist Louis Berman. By the year's end two hundred people have joined groups, each paying $10 per month.

30 November 1924. Eighth Street Theater, Chicago. The architect Frank Lloyd Wright is sitting in a box seat for the performance of the great Russian ballerina Karsavina dancing to Mozart's "Elopement." Just as the ballet begins, says Wright: "An usher quietly showed a dark, slender gentlewoman to the one empty seat in the house. I secretly observed her aristocratic bearing, no hat, her dark hair parted in the middle and smoothed down over her ears, a light small shawl over her shoulders, little or no makeup, very simply dressed." At intermission, she and Wright spoke. "I was in love with her," the fifty-eight-year-old architect says. "It was all as simple as that. When Nature by hand of Fate has arranged her drama all else is besides the mark. It is as it should be."[17] For twenty-six-year-old Olgivanna, Wright was her wish come true. "God had heard my earnest wish," she says, "to meet a man whom I could love and respect."

3 December 1924. New York. Orage's essay "On Love" appears in *The New Republic*. It had been written at the Prieuré after Gurdjieff talked to Orage a long time on love and its different qualities. Love is of seven kinds, Gurdjieff says, but he will only speak of three: instinctive love, emotional love, and conscious love.

> Instinctive love obeys the laws of chemistry or biology and proceeds by affinities.
> Emotional love is an aberration. It is not rooted in biology but is often

---

17. In New York, before Olgivanna left for Chicago, the American painter Jerry Blum, who knew many of the Gurdjieff students in New York, had met and become friends with her at Waldo Frank's. Wright and Blum were friends but had not seen one another for ten years when Blum unexpectedly shows up at Wright's room at the Congress Hotel. They chat, and Blum suggests that they see Karsavina, as he just happened to have tickets for the sold-out performance.

opposed to biology in its direction and character. Often it is a mutual attraction of biological incongruities.

Conscious love, rarely attained, is the only true form of loving.

A conscious lover works on himself in order to help the loved one achieve perfection, the aim being to bring about rebirth.

Afterwards Orage says, "I went to my room and wrote till four in the morning."

Two months after "On Love" is published *The Atlantic Monthly* publishes his "New Standards in Art and Literature." Throughout the year Orage publishes a number of articles in *Psychology* and other magazines. Also, demand increases for him to lecture on writing; he receives some $250 per lecture.

Georgi Ivanovitch Gurdjieff

Margaret Anderson

Jean Toomer

Gorham Munson

The Sunwise Turn Bookshop

TZVARNOHARNO

RECORD OF ALIENS HELD FOR SPECIAL INQUIRY

LIST OR MANIFEST OF ALIEN PASSENGERS

S.S. "PARIS" Passengers sailing from LE HAVRE

HEAD-TAX STATUS	Family name	Given name	Age Yrs.	Sex	Married or single	Calling or occupation	Read	Able to—Read what language	Write	Nationality	Race or people	Last permanent residence Country	City or town
TRANSIT	POLD	Walter	34	M	M	Artist	Y	Engl-French-Dutch	Y	Dutch	Scandinavian		New York	
TRANSIT	-"-	Stella	31	F	M	None		French-Dutch	"	"	"	"	"	
	DAVIDSEN	Ore	46	M	M	Director	"	Engl-Swedish		Dane	"	Denmark	Copenhague	
	SGUEGLIA	Joseph	43	M	M	Merchant	"	French-Engl-Italian		Italian	Italian North	U.S.A	Worcester	
TRANSIT	SAJURI	Ugo	42	M	M	Engineer	"	French-Italian		"	"	Italy	Turin	
TRANSIT	PEREZ	Fidel	38	M	S	Merchant	"	Spanish		Spanish	Spanish	U.S.A	New-York	
	STRAUSS	Martin	44	M	M	-"-	"	Engl-French-German		German	German	"	"	
TRANSIT	HASLER	Marie	40	F	S	Cook	"	French-Austrian		Austrian	Austrian	France	Paris	
	GURDJIEFF	George	47	M	M	Overall	"	Russian-Engl-Greek		Russian	Greek	France	"	
TRANSIT	OLIWIC	Hipolit	45	M	M	Diplomat	"	French-Polish-German		Polish	Polish	Poland	Varsovie	
TRANSIT	CHALHOUB	Joseph	31	M	M	Merchant	"	French-Spanish	"	Syrian	Syrian	Equateur	Guayaquil	
TRANSIT	DE ZAYAS	Marius	43	M	M	Journalist		Engl-Spanish		Mexican	Mexican	U.S.A.	New-York	
TRANSIT	DOMINGUEZ	Gustave	29	M	S									
TRANSIT	LASRUA	Simon	40	M	M									
	PEREZ	Isabel	32	F	M									
TRANSIT	KAJAI	Rokuro	30	M	S									
TRANSIT	MACHIDA	Shiro	40	M	M									
TRANSIT	OKINOGI	Shuzo	35	M	M									
	MILCHAS	Kosmas	33	M	M									

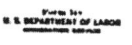

This page from the Ellis Island passenger list of the SS Paris records Gurdjieff's arrival in America for the first time

Georgi Ivanovitch Gurdjieff

Another page from the Ellis Island record shows some of the members of Gurdjieff's entourage

Tzvarnoharno

C. S. Nott

Uspenskii at the Prieuré

Tom Peters, Jane Heap, Fritz Peters at the Prieuré

Georgi Ivanovitch Gurdjieff

William Seabrook

Waldo Frank

Claude Bragdon

C. Daly King

TZVARNOHARNO

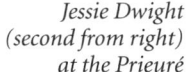

*Jessie Dwight
(second from right)
at the Prieuré*

*58-year-old Frank Lloyd Wright and
26-year-old Olgivanna Hinzenburg meet
and are smitten with one another*

The crossroads where Mr. Gurdjieff had his accident, near the hamlet of Chailly, where the road from Paris to Fontainebleau meets the N 168 road from Versailles to Choisy-le-Roi

Part V

All and Everything

16 December 1924. Prieuré. *It was in the year 223 after the creation of the World, by objective time-calculation, or, as it would be said here on the "Earth," in the year 1921 after the birth of Christ.*

Through the Universe flew the ship Karnak of the "transspace" communication ....

Gurdjieff has called Olga de Hartmann to his room and begins dictating in Russian what will be his magnum opus, his *Legominism*, *All and Everything: Beelzebub's Tales to His Grandson.*

"Since I had not," he says, "when in full strength and health, succeeded in introducing in practice into the life of people the beneficial truths[1] elucidated for them by me, then I must at least, at any cost, succeed in doing this in theory, before my death."[2]

20 December 1924. Germany. Hitler is released from Landsberg prison. The following year his seven hundred-page, two-volume *Mein Kampf* is published. Written in the agitprop style of a political pamphlet, Hitler calls for a *völkisch* nationalist alternative not only to Marxism and social democracy, but also to parliamentary democracy, monarchy, and the church. International Jewry is described as a force committed to a global conspiracy to dominate the world and reduce Germans to their underlings. He asserts that rootless, cosmopolitan Jews were behind Bolshevism, as well as American-style capitalism. He argues for Germany's rearmament, the annexation of Austria, the rejection of the Versailles peace treaty, and the necessity of a *Rassenkrieg* (racial war) to win *Lebensraum* (living space) for Germans in Eastern Europe.

22 December 1924. Prieuré. "All nations are like people, like individuals, same law," says Gurdjieff. "Some born to live one hundred years; some ten, some one year. America now a baby, as far as I can see cannot grow old. Canned food very bad for stomach and psyche. Sexual foundation wrong. No shame."

1925. Prieuré. Gurdjieff, though pale and weak and walking with difficulty, wills himself to keep writing *Beelzebub's Tales to His Grandson*, either dictating to Madame de Hartmann in Russian or scribbling in pencil in Armenian in notebooks. The Armenian is first translated into Russian by Elizabeta "Lili" Galumnian, an Armenian pupil, then given to Thomas de Hartmann who, with the help of Bernard Metz, makes the translation into French, which Ethel Merston then translates into English and sends to Orage. Besides writing the book in Armenian, Gurdjieff dictates it in Russian and a pidgin French, as he says no

1. In his *Life Is Real Only Then, When "I Am"* Gurdjieff says he began to dictate *Beelzebub's Tales* on 1 January 1925, and not as Olga de Hartmann said 16 December 1924. But this date Old Style corresponds with January 13 New Style, the date he gives as his birthday. He mentions the book as early as August–September 1924. The date she gives corresponds to when she first met Gurdjieff seven years before. Ethel Merston places Gurdjieff beginning dictation in July of 1924. She writes: "Very shortly after regaining consciousness and while still in bed, he began dictating a book. It was the story of Beelzebub. He still had no memory and the interesting thing about the writing of the book was that, for the first two or three weeks of dictation of it in his childhood Armenian-Russian, he would say, 'Take down.' 'I am being told.' 'I hear,' as though someone were dictating to or telling him. Only when he recovered complete consciousness did he claim the writing as his, claiming the book as his own. And to me the book is indeed in two distinct parts, the one definitely inspired, the other very much Mr. Gurdjieff, the man with his tongue in his cheek." See Mary Ellen Korman, *A Woman's Work* (Fairfax, CA: Arete Communications, 2009), 19.

2. Gurdjieff viewed contemporary writing as "bon ton literary writing," calling attention to itself, or mere journalism. He had a particularly low regard for science fiction. So why did he choose this form? Perhaps it has something to do with how he saw the future.

single language could give him sufficient freedom of expression for his complicated ideas and theories. It is for Orage to shape the words into appropriate English form, making literal what is to be taken literally, and symbolic what is to be taken symbolically. To be rightly assimilated, Gurdjieff's ideas had to enter the psyche in a form that forces the reader to have to work to extract substance.

Early on, Gurdjieff introduces "The Science of Idiotism" and the ritual of toasting the idiots. In Greek *idiot* meant a private person, one who possessed something of his own, but Gurdjieff uses it in terms of a fundamental form of thought that lives one, an overlay on reality. There are twenty-one categories of idiot such as Original, Superior, Arch, Hopeless, Compassionate and so forth.[3] In drinking, men were supposed to drink the glass in three toasts, one-third per glass per toast; women in seven.

1925. London. J. G. Bennett and Mrs. Beaumont marry.

1925. Prieuré. Gurdjieff sits on a bench in the garden writing his book. His wife and aged mother frequently come and sit on either side of him. "One of them always adored by me was my old mother and the other, my uniquely and sincerely beloved wife." His mother has a chronic liver condition, his wife cancer. Like his mother, his wife, once tall and beautiful, now stooped, walks with a cane.

Accompanying his mother on her walks to his bench are four animals. A cat walks in front of her, two peacocks at her side, and behind a dog. It is obvious from the condition of these two women—"uniquely nearest to my inner life," says Gurdjieff—that both will soon die. To his mother's death he is reconciled, as this is "the normal destiny of every person of esteemed age." But the prospect of his wife's early death calls up a strong feeling of "implacable revolt against the injustice of casual, self-willed destiny." Seeing them, he feels every kind of association of suffering and so as not to "experience this unpleasant process, [I] immediately buried myself in the question of writing."

1925. New York. Toomer has written to Orage that he "would like to learn from you, to work with you, more than formerly.... Substances in me are turning to Gurdjieff, and, more immediately to you." Toomer had seemed to quickly grasp "the method," so Orage gives him permission to form a group in Harlem and the group meets regularly with Orage and his assistant, the short story writer Israel Solon. Students in Harlem don't have the time or the money to commit and so Orage sends Toomer to Chicago to assay the interest there.

31 January 1925. Taliesen, New Spring, Wisconsin. Olgivanna moves into Wright's home. Only a day's drive from Chicago, it would make a perfect location

---

3. See Essay, "The Science of Idiotism."

to establish a "Prieuré" in America. Olgivanna has introduced Wright to many of Gurdjieff's ideas and he feels a kinship with them, but he resists Taliesen becoming a center for Gurdjieff's teaching.

Spring 1925. London. Uspenskii finishes the first draft of *Fragments of an Unknown Teaching.* He will then revise it again in 1926, and continue to revise it until the late thirties.

March 1925. New York. Orage receives some translated chapters of *Beelzebub's Tales*. Orage sends the chapters back, declaring—"It is completely unintelligible. I've no idea what it is about."

A few weeks later a revised version arrives. "This is entirely different," says Orage. "Now I begin to smell something very interesting."

Later Orage says of the book: "It is really an objective work of art of the highest kind; it is in the category of scripture. . . . It is consciously designed to have a definite effect on everyone who feels drawn to reading it. Anyone who tried to rewrite it would distort it."

C. Daly King has continued to attend meetings. Orage sees his promise and the two men often have lunch together. Says King of his mentor: "I have never encountered any other mind of the shining clarity which Orage's achieved nor have I met any other teacher who so completely understood that no human being can ever be taught anything, that the true teacher's task is to assist another to learn."

20 March 1925. New York. At a meeting whose theme is chief feature, Toomer, now back from Chicago, decides that his chief feature is the desire for power. "Orage thought that this came pretty close to the mark," Toomer writes. And Orage adds, "We say that the chief feature must die. Meanwhile, observe it in all acts." He told him that he was "too much given to forcing things. Too much cerebral domination." Further, he was self-observing these qualities and others "without self-criticism or aim or improvement."

20 April 1925. Taliesen. Wright's home burns to the ground.

May 1925. Prieuré. Gurdjieff has nearly fully recovered from the car crash, though his eyes continue to trouble him. Because of his inactivity, he has begun to put on weight. But, says Nott, "He is also radiating more 'light.'"

Life at the Institute has returned to its usual course with movements in the Study House, meals in the English dining room, and Turkish baths on Saturdays. Gurdjieff again is giving tasks in the forest and gardens, but, reports Nott, he does "not take much active part himself." Another small black Citroën has been purchased. Gurdjieff resumes his trips to Paris.

Wherever he goes, Gurdjieff carries with him a supply of cheap exercise books and pencils. No matter where he is he writes. Often, it is an effort and he must, through a variety of means, compel his organism to allow him to write. Once he asks Nott to meet him at the Café de la Paix at 11 a.m. They drink a glass of Armagnac together. For the next two hours Gurdjieff writes, not saying a word, stopping only to order coffee or drinks. He has been writing "A Letter to a Dervish." He shows it to Nott:

> The sign of a perfected man and his particularity in ordinary life must be that in regard to everything happening outside him, he is able to, and can in every action, perform to perfection externally the part corresponding to the given situation; but at the same time never blend or agree with it. In my youth, I too . . . worked on myself for the purpose of attaining such a blessing . . . and . . . I finally reached a state when nothing from outside could really touch me internally; and so far as acting was concerned, I brought myself to such perfection as was never dreamed of by the learned people of ancient Babylon for the actors on stage.

"All the time I am sitting there," says Nott, "it is as if I am being charged with electricity, magnetized with energy from Gurdjieff; as if a force is passing between us. Although I have felt listless and tired when I arrived, and had sat for two hours apparently doing nothing, I am now charged to the brim with bubbling energy, like a battery."

At one o'clock Gurdjieff finally finishes and closes the exercise book.

"You see," he tells Nott, "what a lot I have done. Very good work this morning. Now take this back to the Prieuré and ask Madame de Hartmann to have it typed."

15 June 1925. Prieuré. Margaret Naumburg arrives. Toomer has given her a letter of personal introduction to Gurdjieff. In the one private meeting she has with him he pretends not to know who Toomer is. Finally, he asks if she is his wife. When she says no, Gurdjieff asks when they are going to be married. When she returns at the end of the summer she wonders what it was all about. "I can't see two inches ahead of me anymore," she says.[4]

Late June 1925. Prieuré. Gurdjieff's mother dies. Gurdjieff buys a plot in the Avon cemetery among the graves of World War I's French soldiers. He places a dolmen over her grave with the words in French saying, "Here lies the mother of him who, by this death, finds himself forced to write the book entitled 'The Opiumists.'" Some time later, the epitaph is removed.

---

4. Naumburg is a strong, intelligent woman interested in the teaching. Why would Gurdjieff treat her like this? Like Jessie, does he see her as a distraction, a possible threat?

All the while, Madame Ostrowska's cancer grows worse. She takes to her room permanently.

Summer 1925. Prieuré. Fritz Peters and his brother Tom had left in October. They now return. He finds Gurdjieff, sitting on the terrace at one of the marble-topped tables shaded by a striped umbrella, writing *Beelzebub's Tales*. Gurdjieff makes Fritz his "caretaker." He is to clean his room, bring him food, and so forth.

Gurdjieff speaks to "Freets," as he calls Fritz, about the work he is doing with his wife. It is extremely difficult, he says, "because I try to do thing with her which almost not possible. If she alone, already she be long time dead. I keep alive, make stay alive, with my strength; very difficult things. But also very important—this most important moment in life for her. *She live many lives, is very old soul; she now have possibility ascend to other world.* But sickness come and make more difficult, make impossible for her do this thing alone. If can keep alive few months more will not have to come back and live this life again."[5] [Emphasis added.]

July 1925. Prieuré. Orage returns with Jessie Dwight. It is Orage's delicate job to edit *Beelzebub's Tales* in a way that makes it clear and yet remains faithful to Gurdjieff's intention. "Although I've talked over the chapters with Gurdjieff and discussed the sense of them, he will never explain the meaning of anything." While Orage edits, Jessie helps with the typing of the manuscript. Gurdjieff outlines for Orage the contents of *Meetings with Remarkable Men* but says nothing about the *Third Series* of *All and Everything*.

Orage, now in the full bloom of "falling in love," is more and more under Jessie's influence. Like Uspenskii and Bennett before him, he is blind to his identification and its significance. Gurdjieff, ever watchful over his "super idiot," notes Orage's growing infatuation and tries to make him see what is happening, what Jessie represents in terms of the teaching.

One wet morning Orage and Nott are sitting in the dark, empty Russian dining room having tea. Gurdjieff appears wearing a light grey suit and carrying a walking stick and, as Nott observes, "looking very handsome." He stops by their table, lights a cigarette and begins to talk about his accident. Nott does not understand the meaning behind his words but intuits that Gurdjieff is "speaking in parables, conveying something to Orage."

Gurdjieff tells them that it was his habit when driving from Paris to the Prieuré to put his hand out of the window to pick an apple off a row of trees that grew near the spot where his car crashed. He did so on this occasion and the wheel

---

5. Gurdjieff's statement "live this life again" directly refers to Uspenskii's idea of eternal recurrence. As Gurdjieff told Uspenskii in St. Petersburg, "This idea of repetition is not the full and absolute truth but it is the nearest possible approximation of the truth.... But what you say is very close to it. And if you understand why I do not speak of this, you will be still nearer to it. What is the use of a man knowing about recurrence if he is not conscious of it and does not change?" *Search*, 250.

of his car must have bumped into something. He remembered nothing. He must have unconsciously taken a cushion from the Citroën and put his head on it.

Nott can make nothing of the rest of the story.

Gurdjieff pauses, lights another cigarette, and continues, "You know, Orage, when you give something to a man, or do something for him, the first time he will kneel and kiss your hand; second time, he takes his hat off; third time, he bows; fourth time, he fawns; fifth time, he nods; sixth time, he insults you; and the seventh time, he sues you for not giving him enough."[6]

Gurdjieff then glances at Nott, but says—"You know, Orage, we must pay for everything."

After Gurdjieff leaves, Nott asks Orage what he had meant.

"He is probably getting at us for not knowing how to give," answers Orage. "Neither of us, it seems, has yet learnt. Perhaps Gurdjieff himself has had to learn how to give."

After luncheon one day, Fritz Peters delivers a tray of coffee and brandy to Gurdjieff's room on the second floor. Opening the door, Peters finds Orage standing by one of the windows, impassive and very pale. Gurdjieff stands by his bed, raging. In order to put the tray on the table Peters must walk between them. Doing so, he feels "flayed by the fury in Gurdjieff's voice."

Says Peters: "Orage, a tall man, seemed withered and crumpled as he sagged in the window, and Gurdjieff, actually not very tall, looked immense—a complete embodiment of rage.... Suddenly in the space of an instant, Gurdjieff's voice stopped, his whole personality changed, he gave me a broad smile—looking incredibly peaceful and inwardly quiet—motioned me to leave, and then resumed his tirade with undiminished force."

Peters feels great pity and compassion for Orage. Yet upon leaving the room, he says, "my feelings were completely reversed. I was still appalled by the fury I had seen in Gurdjieff; terrified by it. In a sense, I was even more terrified when I left the room because I realized that it was not only *not* 'uncontrollable' but actually under great control and completely conscious on his part."

Peters does not say, if he indeed knew, the subject of Gurdjieff's anger, but it likely had to do with Jessie Dwight.

Days pass and, given Gurdjieff's accident and Orage's skill at attracting students, Orage is given a de facto mandate to teach the Work in America

29 July 1925. Prieuré. Gurdjieff begins a period of intensive work and collaboration with Thomas de Hartmann on music for the movements.

July 1925. Prieuré. One morning Gurdjieff, rather sardonically, asks Fritz Peters if he still wants "to learn everything," or has he changed his mind?

6. Interestingly, Gurdjieff repeats this in its entirety—"Such is the nature of man that for your first gift... "—in the *Third Series* of *All and Everything*, 56.

Peters says he hasn't changed his mind.

"Freets, why you not ask about this then, if not change mind?"

He didn't mention it, he says, because he assumed Gurdjieff had not forgotten his request and that he didn't think Gurdjieff would have time since he was so busy.

"If you want something, must ask. You must work. You expect me to remember for you; I already work hard, much harder than you can even imagine, you wrong if also expect me always remember what you want." He then added: "If I busy, this is my business, not your affair. If I say I teach, you must remind me, help me by asking again. This show you want to learn."

With this begins weekly lessons at ten o'clock Tuesday mornings.

23 September 1925. Prieuré. Orage leaves for New York. Now having the bulk of the book he begins a concerted effort of putting the book into publishable condition. Toomer helps Orage with the translation through the spring of 1926.

Fall 1925. Prieuré. Gurdjieff leaves the Prieuré for a time. Miss Merston, as the Prieuré's director, is to be in complete charge. Jane Heap arranges for Fritz and his brother to visit with Gertrude Stein and Alice B. Toklas in Paris every Thursday, beginning with Thanksgiving, even though she knows Stein is hostile to Gurdjieff and his teaching. Soon, Gertrude and Alice are taking the boys on guided tours of Paris in Gertrude's Model-T Ford. In time, Fritz and Tom come to meet James Joyce, Ernest Hemingway, Constantin Brancusi, Jacques Lipschitz, Man Ray, and Paul Tchelitchev.

24 October 1925. New York. Orage moves out of Jessie's apartment and into another a block away. The reason is not clear, but her jealousy along with her drinking may be reasons.

Mid-November 1925. New York. Orage and Toomer dine with Mabel Dodge Luhan, a forty-six-year-old heiress. Long on a search for a new spiritual way of living, Mabel has immersed herself in the teachings of Tiwa Pueblo Indian culture through her fourth husband, Antonio Luhan, "Tony," a full-blooded Pueblo Indian and a leader of his tribe. Then her interest waned and he was left in limbo. Most recently, D. H. Lawrence has attracted her affections. She first heard Gurdjieff speak in February 1924. Later, she heard Orage at Jane Heap's studio. Since then, whenever she has been in town (she keeps a house in Croton-on-Hudson and an apartment in New York) she has attended Orage's lectures. Now, for the first time, she meets Jean Toomer. Like many women, she is mesmerized.

Winter 1925. Prieuré. Madame Ostrowska's cancer becomes more acute. Says de Hartmann, "I was aware that her life had been full of suffering, but we all were witness to an extraordinary change in her during her last years."

1 December 1925. New York. After several meetings with Toomer, Mabel Dodge Luhan invites him to spend the Christmas holidays with her and her husband at their home in Taos, New Mexico. During his stay, much to her Indian husband's displeasure, she offers to give Toomer a loan of $15,000[7] to enable Gurdjieff to open his institute on her property in Taos. Of this amount, Toomer is to keep $1,000 for himself.

2 December 1925. Chicago. Daughter Iovanna is born to Olgivanna and Frank Lloyd Wright.

28 December 1925. New York. Orage opens the meeting saying that readings of *Beelzebub's Tales* will begin on January 1. He speaks of the chapter on Purgatory and says he has read thousands of books and nothing in philosophy, not Plato or Plotinus, compares in lucidity, concentration and subtlety to this chapter. "It leaves all philosophy behind," he says.

January 1926. London. At some point in the year Uspenskii writes some thirteen pages in *Fragments* (which he later deletes) as to why he left Gurdjieff in Essentuki in 1918. Gurdjieff had been his teacher up until that time, but he says "some very essential change took place between G. and myself. While a teacher cannot cease to be a teacher, the man [interestingly, Uspenskii does not use the word *student*] without abandoning his work, can leave the teacher if there are changes in the teacher's work." Nevertheless, he realizes:

> There is a general rule of which I was aware even before I met G., and namely, that a man who leaves one teacher because he could not overcome certain difficulties or refuses to submit to certain demands, meets under another teacher (if he succeeds in finding one) *literally* the same difficulties and *literally* the same demands, possibly even in an intensified form. There cannot be the slightest misunderstanding, because the character of the demands made upon him and the nature of the difficulties on his way are determined by the man's own features and qualities. But this rule is valid only in the case of a perfect school. If a man was forced to leave through lack of organization in the school or through wrong demands made upon him, this does not at all mean that the same demands will arise again.

Gurdjieff, he says, never called his groups an esoteric school, though he gave many new ideas and particularly many new ideas about schools "it would be

---

7. This was the beginning of a money problem between Toomer, Orage and Gurdjieff. The figure is given as $14,000 in Lois Palken Rudnick's *Mabel Dodge Luhan: New Woman, New Worlds* (University of New Mexico Press, 1984), 228.

utterly wrong to see in everything that took place an already existing school." That aside, he admits "I knew something had failed. Why it had failed was another question, and I preferred to leave it unanswered." He then gives "the formal reason" as to why he left, which was his not accepting the demands Gurdjieff was making on him. From the first, he had accepted demands:

> The first of these demands was the fact that I had to work in a group with people who seemed to me quite unprepared for work; then, the fact that I had to accept theories which seemed absurd at first; the next was the fact that I had to introduce people to G. and to take upon myself the responsibility for doing so without the slightest idea of what he intended to do with them. Further, my work with G. actually demanded that I should abandon my own work, that I should remain in Russia after the revolution, in spite of my thinking it absurd, and so on. Besides this, at a certain definite moment in 1916 I had to accept a series of demands of a very difficult personal character. All this was not at all easy, but I realized perfectly that everything I received from G. was only due to my submitting to his demands.

He then speaks of two categories of demands, the first being demands that "were insignificant in themselves, but which forced me to do things that went very much against my nature." There were several instances that the demands "touched upon those sides of my nature which I was unable to overcome." Of the second category of demands he says Gurdjieff once said, "One must ridicule oneself," not directly referring to these demands, but in connection with them. "I understood that submission to these demands would have given me a remarkable chance of 'acting.' And yet, I did not submit to them."

5 January 1926. New York. Orage receives the chapter "The Holy Planet Purgatory." He writes to Jean Toomer: "I haven't plumbed the depths of Gurdjieff's thought and probably never shall; but at least certain meanings and interpretations of the colossal parable I now begin to understand."

17 January 1926. New York. Orage begins a series of talks on *Beelzebub's Tales*. He says:

> Gurdjieff proposes in the book to show the steps by which he has recovered his own reason. Experiences have made him different. His Beelzebub is understanding just as his Christ is love, and there is wisdom in each. In referring to his own odyssey on the track of truth, Gurdjieff said, "I would

gladly spare any human being the fruitless efforts I have gone through."[8] Hassein is that part of you that is open to the suggestions of another part of you not yet actualized. Tuluth (Hassein's father), Beelzebub's favorite son, is an emanation of Gurdjieff himself, and so I am Tuluth to you. Remember, Philosophy means not only love of wisdom, but wisdom of love.

26 January 1926. Chicago. Toomer writes to Gurdjieff to tell him of Luhan's offer of a loan and sends the money.

February 1926. New York. Toomer and Margaret Naumburg break up. Now he is in need of money, but, as his friend Gorham Munson observed, all his life he was "successful in getting people to support him." He takes up with thirty-year-old Edith Taylor who has attended some of Orage's talks and knows Jessie. Taylor, like Jessie, is something of a "modern woman." Having lived in Europe, on and off, since 1914, she has an apartment in Paris and speaks fluent French. Vivacious, clever, worldly wise, full of energy and bisexual, she had met Scott Fitzgerald in the south of France and Paris and flirted with the lesbian-homosexual and artistic set of Djuna Barnes, Gertrude Stein, Natalie Barney, Man Ray and Marcel Duchamp. In 1922 she had attended Gurdjieff's talks in London and several talks he had given at the Prieuré the following year.

11 February 1926. Prieuré. Olga de Hartmann writes to Toomer saying Gurdjieff is too busy to reply, that he is not interested in setting up an institute in Taos, but he accepts the money. She encloses a letter from him to Luhan thanking her for the money, the amount not mentioned. Olga accepts the whole $15,000 and thanks Toomer for his $1,000 donation.

1 March 1926. New York. On a visit to the Sunwise Turn where Jessie is working, Orage meets Ilonka Karasz, a Hungarian textile designer, illustrator and painter, who introduces him to her husband, Wim Nyland. Both become members of Orage's group.

April 1926. Prieuré. Martin Benson was at the dock when Gurdjieff was leaving and told him he would come that spring. In April he wrote to him saying he would be there in mid-April. Gurdjieff had someone send him a telegram saying, "Do not come, I do not wish to see you." When Benson got to Paris he sent a telegram — "I am on my way." Someone met him at the train station when he got to Paris telling him, "He really does not want you to come."

The next day Benson showed up at the Prieuré and Gurdjieff says, "Oh, you

---

8. This is a reference to Blavatsky's *The Secret Doctrine*.

have come." "Yes, I have come," answers Benson. At dinner that evening Gurdjieff tells him "You have to leave right away." Benson leaves but the next day shows up at the gate. Gurdjieff says, "I believe deeply you wish to stay—but this is a crazy place and you may not like it.... Stay." He was made the gatekeeper.

6 April 1926. New York. Orage tells Toomer: "What we say aloud is personality. What we say to ourselves is essence. The aim is to speak what we now withhold, and withhold what we now speak." Further, he advises him: "We are not entitled to entertain ideas of development or reform for another person. We should not have them. Eliminate them from the man-woman relationship." Being more explicit, Orage tells him: "The only types of sexual relations possible are with someone who is as advanced and capable as oneself. In either case, there will be no feeling of responsibility in regard to progress in the work to interfere. Such a feeling of responsibility should not cut across a sexual relationship. Real sex is impossible if it does."

Spring 1926. Prieuré. Gurdjieff returns. A general meeting is called. Miss Merston, who he has left in charge of the Prieuré, reads all of the 'offences' that have occurred during his absence. Fritz Peters, who had rebelled against Ethel Merston's authority, has a long list of black marks. Gurdjieff calls him forward and asks if he admits to everything. Peters does so. Gurdjieff then enumerates the offenses, peels off an equal number of ten franc notes and hands them to Peters. Then the next offender is called forward. At the end of the 'punishments,' Gurdjieff turns to Miss Merston and gives her one ten franc note for her "conscientious fulfillment of her obligations as director of the Prieuré." Miss Merston shows no obvious reaction and even thanks Gurdjieff for her reward.

Says Peters: "We were all aghast; we had been taken completely by surprise, of course. But the main thing we all felt was a tremendous compassion for Miss Merston. It seemed to me a senselessly cruel, heartless act against her."

A few days later Peters tells Gurdjieff that he didn't understand why he was rewarded for not doing his tasks and causing Miss Merston so much trouble.

"What you not understand," says Gurdjieff, "is that not everyone can be troublemaker, like you. This important in life—is ingredient, like yeast for making bread. Without trouble, conflict, life become dead. People live in status-quo, live only by habit, automatically, and without conscience. You good for Miss Merston. You irritate Miss Merston all time—more than anyone else, which is why you get most reward. Without you, possibility for Miss Merston's conscience fall asleep. This money should really be reward from Miss Merston, not from me. You help keep Miss Merston alive."

13 May 1926. New York. After dinner with Wim and Ilonka Nyland, Orage and Jessie go to a party. She writes in her diary, "I got really drunk... when I got home I was going to kill myself, but Orage grabbed the gun... I am frightened."

For his part, Orage has resumed the smoking he gave up at the Prieuré. Now he is again chain-smoking.

15 May 1926. SS France. In advance of Toomer, Edith Taylor sails for France along with art gallery owner Betty Parsons, who has become interested in the teaching.

28 May 1926. Prieuré. Toomer arrives along with Edith; she has met him at the boat-train in Paris with a car she has borrowed for the summer. As the only student with a car she is soon acting as Gurdjieff's chauffeur, doing deliveries, and picking up special guests.

Toomer, for his part, now having a personal recommendation from Orage, is soon seeing Gurdjieff daily. Once during a discussion of the teaching, Toomer asks, "For whom are you doing all this work?" Gurdjieff answers, "I will live for coming generations. It is for them."

June 1926. Prieuré. At lunch, Gurdjieff calls Toomer "Mr. Half-Hour-Late," presumably referring to his habit of speaking slowly. Sensing Toomer's sensitivity to race—"When I live with the blacks I'm a Negro. When I live with the whites, I am white, or, better, a foreigner. My concern is with the art of literature. Call me what you like"—Gurdjieff begins to play with what he calls Toomer's "African nature." He promises to make him "Ruler of Africa."[9] But first, of course, the initiation, the stepping on corns.

Noticing Toomer eating a watermelon (no doubt it was no mistake that it was served), Gurdjieff asks, "Mister you like such fruit?"

"Why yes, very much," Toomer answers.

"Then eat like, how you say, black baby ... special name, eh? Yes, picaninny; you know how picaninny eat?"

"You mean with both hands?"

"Good, I see you know very much."

Toomer picks up the piece of melon and eats it. Putting the rind down when he finishes, he gives Gurdjieff a satisfied smile.

"You finish, mister?" Gurdjieff says. "You not finished. Eat *all*, even white part."

Puzzled but obedient, Toomer again picks up what is left of the melon and eats it down to the green and then puts the rest back on his plate.

"Get up, you finished. Go back to garden. Work like you eat. When you finish in garden I send you to America where big picaninny live. You show them very special picaninny you are. You live there, work there, enlighten such men how you live. If you fulfill, I give substantial commission."

---

9. This means a ruler over himself.

Before meeting Gurdjieff, Toomer had already recognized that there is an "I" and a "not-I" in himself. Writing, he had believed, was a means to unifying himself, but had found that not to be true. Years later in writing one of his unpublished autobiographies he wrote: "Writing, real writing, it now seemed to me, presupposed the possession of the very thing I knew I lacked, namely, self-purity, self-unification, self-development. I wasn't fit to write. I felt and felt strongly that one ought to be something before one essayed to say something. I felt and felt deeply that a man ought to be a Man before he elected to write." But he never stopped writing. After *Cane*, he wrote three novels, *The Gallonwerps, Transatlantic*, "Portage Potential," a documentary of sorts, and *Caromb*, a fictionalization of his Carmel experience; plays such as *The Sacred Factor*; as well as many poems, "Blue Meridian" being the most well-known. All were rejected and none published. *Essentials*, a book of aphorisms, he self-published.

Recognizing Toomer's seriousness, intellect, power of expression and no doubt the Mabel Dodge Luhan gift, Gurdjieff tells Toomer he wants him to go to Washington, D.C., to form a group which will help with the monetary situation Gurdjieff faces for the upkeep of the Prieuré, along with housing and feeding all the refugees. Toomer convinces him Chicago would be a more lucrative location.

June 1926. Prieuré. Toomer, grafting his experience and understanding of self-development onto Gurdjieff's, decides to use Edith and their relationship to explore how a man and woman could come into a harmonious relationship, this being exactly what Orage had warned against.

Except with Margaret Naumburg, his intellectual equal, Toomer will "teach" all his mistresses and the two women he marries.

17 June 1926. Prieuré. A week or so earlier, Jessie had arrived and now Orage arrives, having first gone to England to speak with his wife's attorney about a divorce. In 1894 Orage was only twenty-three years old when he married Jean Walker, a Scottish student at the Royal College of Art. The marriage was childless. Orage had a number of dalliances and his wife went off with his best friend. As Orage had paid no alimony for twenty years, her attorney demanded double payment plus a cash settlement.

At the Prieuré, Orage continues editing Ethel Merston's English translation of *Beelzebub's Tales*. Orage generally comes for only a few months of the year, and Gurdjieff tries to spend as much time as possible with him, but this year though Jessie will leave in mid-October, Orage won't return to New York until January.

Gurdjieff interacts with Orage in a way quite different from the way he acts with other pupils. The two can often be seen joking with one another and having a great deal of fun. Often, Gurdjieff uses this as a means of teaching. "Few knew better how to joke and have fun with him," says Nott, "without exceeding the bounds between master and pupil."

Every day Gurdjieff works as usual on his book, rewriting and revising. He works in cafés and at the Prieuré, and, when traveling, dictates in Russian to Madame de Hartmann, who sits in the back seat of the Citroën furiously writing. In the evening after dinner chapters are read aloud in the salon. Gurdjieff watches the expressions on people's faces and other physiological signs.

C. Daly King is in Europe vacationing with his family and one day arrives at the Prieuré. At the gate he rings the bell marked "*Sonnez fort.*" He is not admitted.

Of this King says, the words sounding rather laconic, "I found nobody of much authority about when I sought entrance and, not insisting, was turned away."

Doubtless he was of many minds about putting himself under Gurdjieff's eye. While he holds Orage in high regard, Gurdjieff remains a bewilderment. King is put off by what he takes to be Gurdjieff's bullying, his manner, the irrationality of his method of teaching. As he will later say:

> No doubt for many years to come there will be discussion regarding the character and personality of Mr. Gurdjieff.... I do not hesitate to say that in my opinion he is not a teacher, and I have seen him both privately and at the meetings conducted by him many times. He is evasive, and I have never yet heard him give a direct answer to any inquiry.... When not evasive, he blusters; in these bullying moods there is more of contempt for his followers than of animosity, but in any case it is scarcely an attitude conducive either to loyalty or to successful instruction. It may well be that he does not wish to instruct—others besides myself have received the idea that he knows much but isn't telling—and my own view is that, insofar as he desires to assist anyone, his principle is that this cannot be done through intellectual information.

Unlike King, Gorham Munson from the Orage group arrives at the Prieuré and is admitted. Margaret Anderson and Jane Heap arrive and converse with Orage. Margaret reflected:

> Orage spoke of Eliot's *Waste Land* and Joyce's *Ulysses* as the two high points of contemporary expression—the artist's statement of the present human bankruptcy.... As he talked, Orage seemed to be simultaneously performing several other feats—taking a complete inventory of our mental and emotional equipment, forcing us to lay our cards on the table, realizing that we might not enjoy this, courteously turning his back that we might recover our bearings, but directing every phrase of the conversation as toward a preconceived intention and result. I tried to discover the intention and became baffled. I felt such admiration for

Orage's expertness, such sudden panic as I reflected it was a faculty I might never possess, that I became slightly hysterical. I wanted to shake Orage and shout, Tell me what it is you know that I don't! Next I wanted to weep, as a token of admiration. Then I decided it would be better to discuss my reactions than to scream or weep. So we did. Orage told of what he had been seeking for all his life, what he had found, what he was working at, what its object was. He made careful distinctions between subjective and objective states of being, the former receiving his taboo. He asked me about my life.

"What is your object in playing the piano?"

"As nearly as I can define it, playing the piano is the logical way to recapture continuously that state of ecstasy without which life is not worth living."

"That is not an object," corrected Orage. "If you say you are playing the piano to make money or to give concert tours you have named objects."

And then he added five words that have changed my outlook upon life:

"Act," said Orage, "don't be acted upon."

26 June 1926. Prieuré. At four o'clock in the morning, Madame Ostrowska dies. Says Olga de Hartmann:

> She had been ill for some time. Mr. Gurdjieff often came to see her and sat near her window in an armchair. She could no longer swallow, not even liquids. Once, I had just entered the room when Mr. Gurdjieff told me: "Give me half a glass of water." He held it in his hands for about ten minutes and then told me to give it to her to drink. "But you know she cannot swallow," I said. He repeated what he said. So I lifted her head and gave her a drink and she drank it all, and after that, perhaps for nearly a month, she was able to swallow liquids. Once, when the doctor came to see her and stayed to dinner with us, he sat near me and told me, "She should have died a month ago. I cannot understand how she continues to live."

But once he knew she was dying, Gurdjieff did not come to see her. When Olga de Hartmann asks him why, he replies:

> You have seen that I helped her to the utmost, but that it was not possible to prevent her death. Dying people take very much magnetic force from everything surrounding them and I certainly would give her all the force I could if she were alive, but I could not prevent her death, and I need all my force for all of you.

28 June 1926. Avon Cemetery. Julia Osipovna Ostrowska is buried beneath a large dolmen facing Gurdjieff's mother. Uspenskii attends the funeral. The two men do not speak. Gurdjieff goes to his room where he stays for two days. Within two years of his car crash he has lost his wife and mother, and closed his Institute.

Said Tcheslaw Tchekhovitch, a pupil with Gurdjieff since Constantinople:

> Monsieur Gurdjieff had succeeded in conquering the heart of this Polish woman when she, a young woman, was unaware of anything extraordinary in him. With a smile she one day spoke to us of the surprise and astonishment she felt when she understood the reality. After several years of marriage, her husband revealed himself suddenly as a man whose mission was to change the face of the inner life of humanity. Until that day, Julia Osipovna was a wife who only saw in her husband the businessman, shelter, affection, and protector and father of a future family, a family life in which she sought personal happiness. From the moment when she saw in her husband the man considered by all around him as the promised messiah, she completely changed her attitude toward him. From that day, being already more advanced than the other students in the teaching of Georgi Ivanovitch, she took a place that was unassuming.

Summer 1926. New York. Toomer has been practicing diligently what Orage had taught him of the teaching and now, while awaiting a subway at the 66th Street subway platform, he suddenly finds himself "borne above the body into a world of psychological reality.... In my private language I shall call this experience the Second Conception.... All I had formerly thought and felt about a larger being and a higher consciousness became for me a living reality of higher experience... which became unbearable... but it left an unforgettable taste."

Later in one of his autobiographies, *From Exile into Being*, he describes it:

> I was startled by an uncommon inward event. It was as though I had been touched from within in an extraordinary quiet way that stilled my functioning and momentarily suspended me between what had been and what was to come. My very life had been stopped, so it seemed, and yet I was about to live again, live anew, and strangely. Somehow I understood I was going to be moved, regardless of my wish or will, into a nameless experience.

Of his sensations, Toomer wrote that they "could not have been more strange had my body left the ground and soared into the air." Not only his body but the totality of his presence changed. "My body and my life were in the power of a Power.... I was losing my life. It was being taken away by a noble creation.... There was Being, Consciousness, and Existence so large and deeply powered—that it would surely absorb me as a particle." He has the feeling of having "a second body, a body in addition to the physical, composed of subtler matters, having its own forces and appropriate functions." And when he looked at his body "It seemed removed from me, placed 'out there,' and below me, as though there were space between myself and it. Though I knew I was still attached to it, or it to me, I felt no relation to it whatsoever. It could have walked off and gone about its business, vanished, and I would not have missed it. I had been torn above the body. To me the body was an object."

When Toomer awakes the following morning the experiencing is still active. "There was no filter between myself and things, no buffer between myself and men." In walking, "the impression of walking-bodies-sleeping-beings was so sharp that I had a sense of moving in a crowd of somnambulists."[10]

8 July 1926. Prieuré. Gurdjieff drives to Orléans with Orage, Jessie, Dmitri, Olga de Hartmann and Stjoernval. After a two-day stay he drives on to Biarritz. Discovering a four-day-old jar of caviar among the provisions in the picnic baskets, Gurdjieff persuades Orage to eat it. Orage gets sick; Gurdjieff attributes it to his having an "American stomach." Gurdjieff then asks Jessie to drive. Upset at Gurdjieff, she promptly sideswipes a small hackney coach nearly destroying it, the horse fortunately is unhurt.

22 July 1926. Prieuré. Arriving back, they have dinner, Gurdjieff augmenting the food with copious amounts of alcohol. He continues to poke fun at Orage's "American stomach." After dinner, angry and addled from all the drink, Jessie rushes up to the "Ritz" where she and Edith have rooms, Orage being relegated to the "Monk's Corridor" above. She goes into Edith's room, takes her pistol, and heads down the corridor toward Gurdjieff's room, Edith restraining her just in time.

Mid-July 1926. Paris. C. S. Nott has lunch with Aleister Crowley, a black magician, self-styled "The Great Beast." Nott says, "He had magnetism and the kind of charm which many charlatans have; he also had a kind of dead weight that was somewhat impressive. His attitude was fatherly and benign, and a few years earlier I might have fallen for it."

Nott says they talked about publishing (the reason for the lunch) and then talked of black magic. "To make a success of anything," Crowley tells him, "including publishing, you must have a certain combination. Here you must have the

---

10. Most spiritual experiences last minutes or an hour or so at most. That Toomer's experience lasted so long one wonders if it was due in part to marijuana. The lead character in *Cane* is named "Kabnis," whom Toomer has identified as himself. The name could be a diminutive of cannabis. It is odd that when Toomer speaks almost daily to Gurdjieff at the Prieuré several months later he does not speak about this experience, or, at least doesn't record it.

Master, here the Bear, there the Dragon—a triangle which will bring results." Having established a connection, Crowley then shows his hand—would Nott get him an invitation to the Prieuré? Nott demurs.

Late July 1926. Prieuré. Aleister Crowley arrives, perhaps sensing that with the death of his wife Gurdjieff may be at a low point and vulnerable. He has tea with Gurdjieff. Several boys are about and Crowley tells one he is teaching his son to be a devil. Gurdjieff immediately gets up and speaks to the boy. Gurdjieff ignores Crowley thereafter.

After Sunday night dinner when Crowley had gathered his things and was at the front door about to leave, Gurdjieff, who was standing above him on the balcony stairway, calls out—

"Mister, you go?"

Crowley nods.

"You have been guest?" says Gurdjieff. "Now you go, you no longer guest?"

Crowley, somewhat perplexed at Gurdjieff's words, nods, saying he is on his way back to Paris.

Now Gurdjieff, first having let Crowley know he had not violated the traditional rules of hospitality, shouts—

"You filthy, you dirty inside! Never again you set foot in my house!"

White-faced and shaken, The Great Beast trundles off into the night, his tail between his legs.

Nott watched the two interacting and he said he "got a strong impression of two magicians, the white and the black—the one strong, powerful, full of light; the other also powerful but heavy, dull, and ignorant."

Fall 1926. Chicago. Jean Toomer sets up a Gurdjieff study group. He again begins to imitate Gurdjieff, passing himself off as an Eastern mystic or mystery man. Of this Gorham Munson will later say:

> ... a good deal of Jean's life after he went to Chicago was the leading of a life of lying, lying, lying.... Jean pretended to be more than he was. He assumed the development and psychology beyond the point that he had ever reached; he ascribed to himself powers and knowledge which he had not really attained. Some would say he had a fantasy which he truly believed about himself as a master of psychological teaching, psychological knowledge. It doesn't seem to me that he could have deceived himself to that extent. He play acts as a spiritual leader.

21 October 1926. Prieuré. Orage writes to Jessie: "We 'men' [Orage, Salzmann, Hartmann] sat and drank G into a state of sleep (Mme H said he didn't sleep a wink the two days he was away); and in the meanwhile H and I translated; and you'll be as surprised as pleased to know that we've finished the 3rd descent."

22 October 1926. Prieuré. Orage writes, "I've got one or two very good things from G today, including a psychological definition of *Kundabuffer*! Psychic action by association, i.e. not originating in essence. Also some other ideas that I have absorbed. You were referred to again today as the author of two famous words in the book: fishy and brat. I claim 'brat,' but 'fishy' is yours! Nothing else, is there? Oh yes, Salzmann turned up tonight a cripple, so to speak. He'd been knocked down by a taxi in Paris, and had a lame shoulder, arm and leg. Michel has had a fever, but is better. We occasionally work in Mme S's room and Michel's behavior is angelic. The Dr. always asks after you: he apparently thinks you are already in America: and by the way Michel is always asking Where Miss Jessie? Miss Merston is next me now, and works 'on book' all day. She certainly has given herself no time to worry; and I equally think she is not dis-enjoying herself."

23 October 1926. Prieuré. Along with Lili Galumnian, Orage has been tirelessly working on editing *Beelzebub's Tales*, sometimes as many as twelve hours a day, and then giving it to Miss Merston to type. He writes to Jessie, "It's really a 'Bible,' for the 'Bible' is also a parable with 'history' as its material, and the Biblical history is much less plausible than G.'s. I told this to G. tonight and he said he had purposely made it fit history when he could—which was a broad hint. I hope to get hold eventually of some of its 'keys,' but so far I am baffled."

November 1926. New York. Olgivanna visiting, asks a friend from the Gurdjieff days about Julia Ostrowska. Hearing that she was dead, she says, "I got a blow right in the middle of my forehead and then a sharp pain in my heart and tears, tears—all in one second—I was there, right there. I that was lost saw everything that passed for the past two years clearly and simply, saw it together with my dear friend. She was with me with all her love and understanding. Such happiness and quiet she brought to me.... She woke up the life within myself.... It was the first time in my life, my first experience—I knew, felt, understood, that she did not die. She stayed with me a few days . . . and left leaving the life and light."

2 November 1926. Prieuré. Orage writes: "Yesterday being All Saints Day, G and everybody went to the cemetery where a service was held over the graves of his mother and Mme Ostrowska. A special lunch was prepared for the Great Priest, and in the afternoon G and Hartmann gave a 'concert.' You know G's piano accordion. He made three quite marvelous 'noo moosics.' Evening—at the café, G having been persuaded not to go to Paris. We sat in his room until about 2.30 a.m."

4 November 1926. Prieuré. Orage writes: "Back to the 'osses'—G said today he wished to finish the first book in another week; and then to go by car-trip to Dijon and to spend a few days there arranging for the printing. I hope he does so and that he and Mme H etc. make themselves responsible for all the details of paper, type, etc. We will guarantee the English text bill—but I shall be immensely relieved by the anticipated transfer of the detailed job. It will be another string cut for Xmas."

9 November 1926. Prieuré. "Yesterday might have been a day of it," writes Orage, "but for the fact that I had your letters. After sitting up late, G took H and me to coffee early in the morning, and we worked there until 2, at which hour G suddenly decided not only to go to Paris hurriedly but to take me and H to translate en route. We scrambled down lunch, and then G said that we would stay the night in Paris to translate more. Well, just as I was in the car, Fritz gave me your letters—and after that anything could happen. In fact, everything went quite all right. We translated, we had dinner, we translated again, and finally I was given a room at the neighboring hotel, when I read my Jessie's letters over and over again until I know them nearly by heart. We pottered about the Paix this morning and all came back this evening. I've a heap of translation and re-translation to do, and Lili is going over everything with Miss M and disputes are referred to me. I'm away with G most of every day. However, one must pay the postage, and though I cannot yet get 'real hold' of the book, I'm a little nearer to sensing some of its ideas, and they really are earth-shattering. God knows if ever I'll be able to talk kindergarten again; but at the moment—once more—I feel too humble and stupid for anything!"

10 November 1926. Prieuré. Orage writes: "The book is going; and G is nearly up to the final chapter on 'Art.' In fact, he said today that we should go to Dijon next week and arrange about printing."

11 November 1926. Prieuré. Writes Orage: "I'm thirsting to have your letters, sweetheart. Nothing will make me feel really at home here, and though G, as I've said, is very considerate, I'm always a fish out of water. Language is a terrible barrier; and hours of *nothing* but Russian are wearying. And you know I am now nearly always the only English-speaking present! But I cling to the book and the music as *real*—and for the book I am not paying too dearly, I feel—though the price is high! I've been quite unhappy without you, my darling, occasionally almost intolerably—today for instance. But I'll try to think of you only with happy love. Bless you, sweetheart."

26 November 1926. Prieuré. "Oh yes, I forgot," Orage says, "Miss Gordon's question about 'food.' *Air is taken in at the lungs, as food is taken in at the mouth; but just as the transformation of food begins only in the stomach, so the transformation of air begins only in the liver. The liver is the air's stomach!* You were quite right!"

27 November 1926. Prieuré. Orage tells Gurdjieff he needs to leave so as to be in New York for Christmas with Jessie. The translation into English considered finished, Orage writes to tell her:

> The book is too colossal. Suppose "God" were to begin observing himself, reviewing his past, and trying to put Himself normal — that is, what Beelzebub seems to me to be doing. He is God — coldly, rationally, reviewing himself — but, of course, his "past" extends back to creation. Beelzebub is a "brain-cell" of God, depicted, on the strength of his dislike of God, to make God's review of himself — seems to me to be rather an interesting idea and appears confirmed by many things G. says of both B and himself. Also, there should be, as there are, many analogies in consequence between God's self-observation etc., and any one's person.

28 November 1926. Prieuré. Orage writes to Jessie again, concerned now that he has read her letter speaking of Toomer's humor at a luncheon and a meeting afterward.

> In criticizing "Jean" in these days, I know I'm risking your reaction. I always said you were fond of him, you know! And I was not in the least surprised, except by *your* surprise to hear you had rung him up *from Edith's* [Taylor] to come there, and take you home to talk or that your heart to heart talk left you liking him "immensely" and in relations you are sure Gurdjieff would like. In fact, my darling Jessie, if "Jean" were only white, I should consciously advise you to go to Chicago [where he will set up a group] and cooperate with him there. You would be a thousand times happier in equal association with a being of your own age. . . . I have not the least suspicion, darling, that your frank and heart to heart talk with "Jean" travelled outside Institute business to your personal relations; but I merely take note of the fact that in your desperation you *could* forget all about Edith and "Jean" and time and place and so on . . . . Well, so much for one unpleasant trifle. I shall only add that if "Jean" calls you "Dwight" again, I shall take the occasion "to kavatar." [Meaning unknown.]

Orage's jealousy of Toomer who, like Orage, has a way with the ladies, could have scorched their relationship, but a few days later Toomer leaves New York for Chicago with Edith Taylor in tow.

Christmas 1926. Prieuré. Gurdjieff, in reflecting on his productivity in regard to writing, realizes that it "strictly corresponded in its duration with the length and quality of the, so to say, 'degree of contact,' between my consciousness and the suffering proceeding in me on behalf of my mother and wife." He had written before with Olga de Hartmann, Dr. Stjoernval, and C. S. Nott sitting beside him, acting as a sort of negative pole in the 'battery' setup. But with his wife and mother Gurdjieff had suffered unconsciously. And so he elicits the use of unconscious suffering as well as conscious. While "watching the children around the Christmas tree and their unrestrained joy," Gurdjieff says he comes to the recognition "of the full possibility of attaining [my] aims through the forces of the inner-world struggle."

27 December 1926. Prieuré. Orage, writing to Jessie, tries to console her that he has missed Christmas.

January 1927. Prieuré. Twenty-six-year-old Payson Loomis arrives. He is here to help Gurdjieff with the English translation of his *Meetings with Remarkable Men*. Earlier, Loomis had been hired as an amanuensis for Grand Duchess Marie of Russia who was writing her memoirs. Loomis, who had graduated from Yale with honors in Russian and French, had read "everything," particularly in comparative religion: the Gitas, Gilgamesh, the Apocrypha, the Koran, Confucius, and Madame Blavatsky, whom he believed had brought to the West priceless wisdom texts from the Orient. The Grand Duchess had told him of Gurdjieff, they had met, and Loomis, entranced, agreed to help with translation.

January 1927. Taos, New Mexico. Mabel Dodge Luhan, whose ardor for Toomer has cooled, writes telling him she now has recognized she would continue to live with her husband "difficulties included," but also offers him space in Taos if he wants to write there. Then, she adds, "Do you still love yourself as much as ever with that half-pitying-half-patronizing but quite considerate love you felt two years ago? I wonder." She had written him a year earlier: "You see, Jean, I am trying to subjugate your will to mine—it is my talent—my whole mechanism works together to this end—to seduce your spirit—as I have always been doing. Why, I wonder? They are all around me—the ones I did succeed with and I don't like it at all, really! Why should I want to keep it up and up? And yet how defeated I will feel if I don't."

Toomer proposes marriage to Edith but is rejected.

January 1927. Prieuré. Gurdjieff, recognizing Jane Heap's seriousness and quality of mind, asks her to form an artists group in Paris.

14 January 1927. Prieuré. Orage, still distressed over Toomer and Jessie, finally sets sail for New York.

22 February 1927. New York. Orage's divorce from Jean Walker is granted. A six-month waiting period and then it is final.

23 February 1927. Prieuré. Solita Solano arrives. She is a writer, literary critic, and companion of *The New Yorker* writer Janet Flanner. She has heard from her friends Margaret Anderson and Jane Heap that in Gurdjieff she "will see not one man, but a million men in one." She rejects Gurdjieff on all counts.

"I hoped for a demigod, a superman of saintly countenance, not this 'strange' écru man about whom I could see nothing extraordinary except the size and power of his eyes."

Solita listened to the reading from his "vaunted book," and declares, "It bored me." And so she rejects him intellectually, "although with good humor." Later she hears the "famous music" played. That she also rejects, "almost from the first measures."

A week later, Solita goes with Margaret and Jane to a restaurant to dine with Gurdjieff and twenty or so others. She is seated next to him. "For two hours [he] muttered in broken English. I rejected his language, the suit he was wearing and his table manners; I decided that I rather disliked him."

March 1927. New York. Orage publishes *Psychological Exercises*, a book which combines the talks he has given on Gurdjieff with a series of psychological exercises focused upon logic, mathematics and spatial perception that he had been working on before he met Gurdjieff. Gurdjieff is furious when he hears of this, as it shows Orage's lack of understanding and true valuation of the sacredness of the teaching.

March 1927. New York. Toomer and Edith break up and within a month he is having an affair with one of his Chicago students. For her part, Edith, bi-sexual, enters into an intense but brief lesbian affair.

Spring 1927. Prieuré. Gurdjieff is now receiving $1,000 a month from the American groups. But the demand for money continues. Says Orage, "Gurdjieff is really quite extraordinary about money—but not, unfortunately, unique; we've known many people at college and in life equally extraordinary. However, I'm giving him still the benefit of the doubt, and I'm only sorry I cannot give him a million if only to see if he could be impecunious within a month or so of receiving it."

Spring 1927. Prieuré. Lili Galumnian, who first met Gurdjieff in Tiflis eight years ago, gives birth to a son, Sergei. Gurdjieff is the father.

1 May 1927. Prieuré. Having composed some three hundred pieces of music, Gurdjieff ends his collaboration with Thomas de Hartmann.

Early Summer 1927. Canada. Jessie, fighting to hold Orage, has found an ally in C. Daly King, who also believes his mentor is too much under Gurdjieff's thumb. The two men have now become quite close, frequently lunching and dining together during the week, with Orage often visiting as King's house guest on weekends. King has just published a book, *Beyond Behaviorism*, which seeks to show the relationship between scientific psychology and Gurdjieff's teaching. Like Uspenskii, King is enamored of the teaching, but sees Gurdjieff as a "dubious messiah, even if an extremely sophisticated one."

Customarily, Orage spends his summers at the Prieuré but this summer, no doubt at the behest of King and Jessie, he asserts his independence. Orage does not go the Prieuré. Instead he vacations in Canada with Jessie and Daly King and his wife, the conversation likely turning on the need for fifty-four-year-old Alfred Richard Orage to establish his independence.

Summer 1927. Sidlesham, England. Maurice Nicoll has become Uspenskii's closest pupil and friend. He begins to spend every other weekend at Nicoll's Alley Cottage at Sidlesham. Besides the System they would talk about the esoteric meaning of the New Testament. At other times he would be silent for almost a whole day, even at meals, and heavily preoccupied. He did like to go to the local Crab and Lobster Inn and sit among the farm hands. Drinking, he says, was like borrowing—as something borrowed from tomorrow. Speaking of his childhood, Uspenskii says, "I never could properly deceive myself with toys." He realized many things which people do not realize till late in life, if ever. "I saw many illusions," he says, "quite clearly and naturally."

13 July 1927. Prieuré. Payson Loomis invites twenty-year-old Lincoln Kirstein to meet Gurdjieff. He was a Harvard sophomore come to Europe to meet Ezra Pound and T. S. Eliot for a college literary magazine. After being taken to the Study House to see the movements exercises, Loomis introduces Kirstein to Martin Benson, the gatekeeper, and departs. Kirstein is quite taken with Benson, "it was like a match struck, something flared." Kirstein sees Benson as "a classic prototype of an American farmer." Loomis returns and takes Kirstein to the Bath House where he first sees Gurdjieff lying on his stomach while a young boy jogs on his back. When he rises, Kirstein says he sees he is not as old as he had looked.

> The man was no beauty with his Mongol features, moustaches of dank ferocity, balding, though hairy epaulets and matted paunch . . . . [later in the salon] Heavy set, impassively glowing with tigerlike moustachios crisply curled . . . . [during dinner] Wine was poured, red, and there were small brandy glasses at every place. Following the hors d'oeuvres, two large platters were brought in, and then additional smaller ones. On the first were steaming carcasses which I guessed were suckling pigs, but which turned out to be whole baby lambs. Mr. Gurdjieff, whetting a small sabre, sliced the meat with professional ease; plates were passed

around, and a maid passed what else was available. There was no mint jelly to go with the lamb. I noted its absence. Instead there was a green sauce or soup of thickened fresh mint. What somewhat bothered me was that bare skulls of the sheep were still attached to the rest of the roast. They were split down their centers, with the grey brain glistening, and the eyes withered to black raisins.

At the end of the sumptuous meal, Gurdjieff begins the Toasts to the Idiots. When he gets to the toast "To all compassionate idiots," he looks straight at Kirstein and adds, " ... and, incidentally, Monsieur, to you." Kirstein lasts until the ninth toast, now drunk, he is guided away by Martin Benson, as Gurdjieff says, smiling kindly, "Sleep well, Little Father."[11] Benson helps Kirstein upstairs, takes off his shoes and socks, undoes his belt and Kirstein passes out.

The next morning in the salon Metz says, a trace of cockney in his voice, "I bet you didn't sleep a wink." Kirstein asks him what "idiot" means. "Oh, we're all idiots," Metz tells him. "That's his oldest joke. It takes people down. You're an idiot to get drunk; you're an idiot to be here. You're an idiot to be alive. The whole kit-and-caboodle is idiotic."

After breakfast Kirstein is taken to Gurdjieff's study. Gurdjieff is seated at a very large desk, piled with papers in orderly stacks. Beside the desk is a small table and typewriter, where Loomis sits editing the manuscript. Gurdjieff questions "Little Father" on why he is leaving.

Gurdjieff. So, Little Father, you go?

Kirstein. Mr. Gurdjieff, I want to thank you so very much for allowing me to come to the Prieuré.

G. Very nice. What you want?

K. I just want to thank you.

G. Mister, I ask you what you want.

K. (*nervously*) I just want ...

Loomis. (*quietly*) What do you want to do, or *be* ...

K. (*confused*) Now I have to get back to Paris ...

G. Ah — important appointment.

K. Well, yes; it's important to *me*.

G. Important? How?

K. Loomis has arranged for me to meet a very great poet.

G. Oh — poet. Very important.

K. Well, at least, *I* think he is.

G. What kind poet??

K. Perhaps, actually, for the present our greatest living poet.

---

11. Kirstein is tall and has an imperial bearing and posture, so perhaps Gurdjieff uses the term in the sense that Russian peasants used it as a tongue-in-cheek endearment when referring to the Tsar; he being the "Little Father" on Earth, the "Big Father" being God the Father.

G. What language?
K. English, of course...
G. English, of course. Not Hungarian?
K. Hungarian? I can't read Hungarian...
G. Not read Hungarian. Too bad.
K. I mean to say the greatest living poet in the English language.
G. What kind poem he write?
K. He writes *every* kind.
G. Every kind. He writes sex-poems?
K. Sex-poems?
G. No. I mean fuck-poems.
K. No, Mr. Gurdjieff. It is Ezra Pound. He also writes wonderful translations. He has taught me a lot.
G. Ah. Translation. Already good. Maybe great. What language he translated?
K. From the Anglo-Saxon, Chinese. From the Greek. And Egyptian.
G. No Russian?
Loomis. I don't think Mr. Pound speaks Russian.
G. No speak, but read?
L. He must read it in translation...
G. But he speak Anglo-Saxon, Chinese, Egyptian. Get him for me. I need good translator. I pay.
K. (*to the rescue*) His are *poetic* translations. He takes original texts and makes them more beautiful...
G. Ah — translator also magician. Takes texts; makes more beautiful...
K. Mr. Gurdjieff, it's very hard to explain this in English.
G. But easy in Anglo-Saxon or Egyptian.
K. (*Realizes G. is unfair, but holds his tongue.*)
L. Mr. Gurdjieff, he is talking about Ezra Pound's talent.
G. Yes, I know very well — for long time. He likes my soup.
K. (*incredulous*) He likes your soup?
G. Very much he like my soup.
K. What sort of soup?
G. When you grow up I give recipe. Then *you* make soup.
K. (*deeply hurt*) Mr. Gurdjieff, I am sorry if I have offended you. I just wanted to thank you. I don't want to waste your time.
G. Little Father not offend. Not waste my time. You waste your time.
L. Mr. Gurdjieff has known Ezra Pound for many years.
K. (*amazed, to Loomis*) You mean, he really *does*?
G. Really does. You know what Ezra Pound call my soup?
K. Not really...
G. You know painting?
K. (*modestly*) A little bit.

G. You know Rembrandt?

K. Of course.

G. Of course. You know Piero della Francesca?

K. (*back on his heels*) Yes, certainly . . .

G. Ezra Pound say my Persian-melon soup, compared to borscht, has tone of Piero della Francesca. You know borscht?

K. (*firmly*) I *like* borscht.

G. You like borscht. Pound say my melon soup is clean like Piero della Francesca, compare to shit-color Rembrandt. Now, what you want?

K. (*silenced*)

G. Mister. I tell you what you want. You want pay me.

K. Pay — you — for what?

G. Three things. One thing: Turkish bath. Two thing: Martin Benson. Three thing: eyes-of-sheep.

K. Pay? How much do you charge?

G. I not charge. Pay what you think worth.

K. I don't happen to have much money with me . . . I've got to get back to Paris, and it's Sunday and the banks are . . .

G. No need banks. Give me anything in your pocket. Loomis lend your ticket.

K. I've less than a hundred francs.

G. Oh. Less than hundred. Too bad. Better than nothing.

L. I have plenty of money.

G. Loomis, lucky; he have money. Loomis wash hand with ticket. Now, *dear* Little Father. You go.

K. (*Dazed, hands over francs. Turns to go.*)

G. Wait.

K. (*Looks pleadingly at Loomis.*)

G. Mister. You wait. You come here. You curious. Very interesting. You have bath. You shock. You meet Benson. Nice man. Benson. Honest workman. You get good food. Very shock: food. Even you see, maybe: dance. *Stop!* All this — worth something?

K. I gave you all I have.

G. Not yet.

K. I will send you the rest, just tell me how much.

G. You pay *now*. If you stay here — you don't need pay.

K. But Mr. Gurdjieff, I've got to . . .

L. I'll phone Pound; you've missed the train.

K. But Loomis made my appointment *weeks* ago. I need to, I must see Mr. Pound . . .

G. You need many thing, Mister. You go now, you never come back here, and Loomis, you too; Loomis never speak to you again.

K. (*to Loomis in utter confusion, Loomis turns traitor by his silence.*) I don't understand. You don't understand. I must see Mr. Pound ...

G. I understand very well. Now: you go.

K. (*Helpless, wordless, turns to go, reaches door*)

G. Wait, Little Father; come here.

K. (*idiotically*) But I don't know ...

G. That's right. You don't know. Here: your ticket to Paris. Five hundred francs. I keep one hundred. Save rest for ticket back to Prieuré. You like that?

K. Yes, Mr. Gurdjieff. Thank you very much.

G. Not thank me. Thank Loomis.

K. (*recovering*) I thank Loomis for many things.

G. I also thank Loomis for many things.

K. (*firmly*) I thank Loomis for *many* things.

G. Very polite. Many thanks. Now you go. On train you think many things. You think bath. You think Benson. You think sheep-eye. Maybe you think ballet. What?

K. I'll try to.

G. Already good. You try. You know who you are?

K. You said I was a compassionate idiot.

G. Already good: also square idiot, round idiot, zigzag idiot. You, something else.

K. (*taking the game as a joke*) Also sheep to be shorn.

L. Come along now, or you'll miss your train.

G. Goodbye Little Father: *Do svidaniya. Au revoir. Arrivederci. Hasta la vista. Auf Wiedersehen.* Maybe you learn Hungarian.

Summer 1927. Prieuré. Gorham Munson and his wife, Elizabeth, arrive and are given a simple room on the third floor, the Monks Corridor. Earlier, Waldo Frank and his new wife, Alma, had arrived, along with Carl Zigrosser, Schuyler Jackson, and Edwin Wolfe. C. S. Nott also arrives with his new bride, Rosemary Lillard Nott. Munson finds Toomer showing Frank around the property. The two men seem to be getting on. The group runs into Gurdjieff coming down the walk. He invites them to "the Russian bath" that evening. The group has coffee on the terrace. Then Gurdjieff drives them in his Citroën to the Café Henri IV where he at once orders a round of Armagnac and proposes a toast: "Health — candidates for idiots." Then Gurdjieff takes another table and begins writing a chapter of *Beelzebub's Tales* in Armenian in a cheap notebook. Frank, a self-important doyen of American letters who expected red carpet treatment, is put off and tells Gurdjieff he acts like a jovial headmaster.

"Health — candidates for idiots," Gurdjieff calls out, raising a glass to a second round of Armagnac.

Munson remembers that Thomas Carlyle had once criticized Jesus for his incompleteness, saying, "He had no Falstaff in him."

"On the biggest scale," thinks Munson, observing Gurdjieff write amid the café noises and passings to-and-fro of waiters and clientele, "he is all that a writer should be: indefatigable, living life to the fullest, inspired with the highest aim in literature—the writing of modern scripture."

Despite Gurdjieff's disclaimer that he no longer was teaching, Munson says he was teaching all the time. A few times he hears Gurdjieff speak perfect English. "I believe," he says, "it was a deliberate part of his pedagogy to speak broken English. By making himself hard to understand, Gurdjieff obliged his listeners to give full attention. In order to get his meaning, they had to be active instead of passive toward him."[12]

In the late afternoon the men go to the bathhouse, but Gurdjieff demands no anecdotes, as these are for special occasions only. Then Gurdjieff rushes the group back to the château for the evening meal. About sixty people assemble in the English dining room, Gurdjieff sits in the center of a long table, everyone eating and toasting to the twenty-one different types of idiots.

The toasts go as high as eight or nine idiots. Sometimes Gurdjieff toasts with a glass of water: "Health—wise man." Gurdjieff then examines the display of dishes before him and carefully picks the eye out of the sheep's head before him and tosses it across the table to Alma and says, "Blondine, eat! Very special properties it has, necessary for you." To Frank, he says, "You not marry Blondine, why you tell me so? Better you stay with Jewish wife, for Jewish man only Jewish woman corresponding. In bed he use her like handkerchief, truth I tell, woman squirm, she know truth I tell."

After dinner Gurdjieff invites everyone into the drawing room to hear a chapter of *Beelzebub's Tales* read. It becomes clear to Munson that Gurdjieff "is writing to produce intended effects upon an intended audience, and he is checking on the production of designed effects." Gurdjieff had once remarked, he says, "To write my book for conscious men would be easy but to write it for donkeys—very hard."

A day or so later, Gurdjieff is at the Café de la Paix seated at a front table on the terrace. Waldo Frank, seeing him, comes up to his table, shaking with rage. He raises a fist, shaking it at Gurdjieff, and yells—"Go back to your hell, you devil, and leave us alone." Gurdjieff looks up with a child's innocent eyes. "What angry man say? I not understand."

August 1927. Prieuré. Now Orage arrives, notably alone, to continue work on *Beelzebub's Tales*. He informs Gurdjieff he must leave on September 1—before his divorce is finalized on September 9—he has "promised Jessie." He explains it by telling himself, "I ran out on my first marriage. I will never do so again."

Gurdjieff—who set great importance on completing the translation—"naturally" suddenly can never find the time to work on it.

12. Munson, Jean Toomer and Solita Solano are writers, keen observers and listeners, who all note examples of Gurdjieff speaking perfect English.

Ten days pass. No work.

Then, the very evening of Orage's departure, Gurdjieff announces translation work will begin the next day. Orage says he has given Jessie his essence-promise to return to New York.

Gurdjieff storms at Orage for leaving his work at the Prieuré "to return to nonentities in New York."

Orage leaves Gurdjieff and returns to Jessie Dwight.

24 September 1927. New York. Despite his teacher's expressed disapproval, Orage marries Jessie Dwight. As an exasperated Alexander de Salzmann once told her in her early days at the Prieuré, "If only you'd admit that you're a squirming idiot,[13] what a marvellous initiate you'd be!" Gurdjieff will later characterize Jessie as "a sales woman of the 'Sunwise Turn,' a young American pampered out of all proportion to her position." Their marriage he sees as being representative of "that abnormality at the basis of family life, crystallized in the life of contemporary people... which consists in the fact that the leading role in the household belongs to the woman."[14]

But Orage, "in love," describes the situation this way: "He [Gurdjieff] regarded me as someone who had, so to speak, come with him from another planet with a task to carry out. But I fell in love with a native, and this interfered with his aim."

6 November 1927. Prieuré. Gurdjieff writes: "The sole means now for the saving of the beings of the planet Earth would be to implant again into their presences a new organ... of such properties that every one of these unfortunates during the process of existence should constantly sense and be cognizant of the inevitability of his own death as well as of the death of everyone upon whom his eyes or attention rests."

After three years of writing, Gurdjieff completes the first draft of *Beelzebub's Tales,* only to realize that for anyone not personally associated with him, the book will be unintelligible. The three series of books that comprise *All and Everything* are his *Legominism* that is to be understood and actualized in a future time. It is his last means of completing his mission—and this, *Beelzebub's Tales,* for most people is unreadable!

The shock of all the intentional effort he has made since his auto accident—the thought of now having to rewrite the whole book—suddenly strips him of the one thing that has never failed him—self-remembering.

Gurdjieff no longer has the full sensing of the whole of himself.

There is nothing to do but to begin again. But his health is bad. He has a

---

13. Gurdjieff later said of squirming idiots, "Such people can never can stay same, never I know how find them one day from next, inner state is such." A squirming idiot is someone with a particularly unpleasant personality trait.
14. Gurdjieff says that if in relationship the man is one, the woman is two. But if the woman is one, the man is zero. Gurdjieff is talking about forces. This needs to be pondered deeply.

foreboding that time is running out. He wrestles with the idea of suicide. Gurdjieff finds himself at what is conceivably the lowest point in his life.

Finally, freeing himself from these dark thoughts, he decides to begin rewriting *Beelzebub's Tales.*

Christmas 1927. Prieuré. A tree is cut from the surrounding forest, placed in the main salon and decorated with hundreds of candles. Presents are hung from the tree.

Just as it is beginning to get dark, Gurdjieff sends for Fritz Peters and tells him that he is to act as the concierge that evening, that he is expecting a long distance phone call and that it must be answered. Gurdjieff tells him he has chosen him because he trusts him and that he speaks English, French and enough Russian to be able to cope with any call that might come. Peters is crestfallen, as this is the first Christmas at the Prieuré when Gurdjieff is present. So Peters must watch from the small unheated concierge house outside as the Christmas festivities take place, including the giving of gifts. Unable to control himself, Peters goes up to the window of the château and peers in. Gurdjieff sees him and sends for him. "Why not at concierge? Why you here?" he angrily demands. Peters gives some lame answer and he is directed to return. At the end of his shift, he says, "I went back to my room, hating Gurdjieff, hating the Prieuré, and by this time I was almost feeling proud of my 'sacrifice' for him. I vowed that I would never mention that evening to him or to anyone else; also, that Christmas would never mean anything to me again."

Gurdjieff doesn't mention what happened, but Peters says, "He no longer spoke to me as if I were a child, and my private 'lessons' came to an end."

Sunday after Christmas, 1927. Prieuré. Since mid-morning Peters has been drinking with some Americans. They are all angry with Gurdjieff about a recent incident and fourteen-year-old Peters, for the second time in his life, is drunk. By late afternoon Gurdjieff, who is preparing to leave for Paris, sends for him. He and Madame de Hartmann are in his car by the front gate. He asks Peters to go to his room and get a bottle of Nujol, a medicine, explaining that he had locked his door and now cannot find the key and Peters, his "caretaker," had the only existing key. Though Peters has the key in his hand, he lies to Gurdjieff declaring that he has also lost his key.

"Gurdjieff became very angry," says Peters, "began to shout at me, talking about my responsibilities and saying that losing the key was practically a crime, all of which only served to make me more determined."

Gurdjieff orders Peters to go to his own room and search it. Still gripping the key, Peters tells him that he "would gladly search my room but that I knew I would not find the key because I remembered losing it earlier in the day."

He does go to his room, makes a search, and returns to the car to report that the key is still missing.

"Gurdjieff went into another tantrum," Peters says, "saying that the Nujol was very important—that Madame de Hartmann had to have it while she was in Paris."

She could buy some more at a drugstore, Peters tells him.

Gurdjieff, furious, says that as there was some in his room he was not going to buy any more and, further, that the drugstores were closed on Sunday.

Peters says that "even if there was some in his room, we could not get it without his key or my key, which were both lost, and that since even Fontainebleau had a 'pharmacie de garde' open on Sundays, there must be a similar one in Paris."

With that, Gurdjieff, accompanied by Madame de Hartmann, drives off in a rage. Peters staggers back to his room.

The next evening Gurdjieff returns and Peters, fearing he would lose his job as Gurdjieff's "caretaker," goes to his car.

"I went," he says, "like a lamb to slaughter."

Gurdjieff says nothing to him. Peters carries his luggage to his room, opening the door with his key. When they are alone, Gurdjieff holds up the key, shakes it at Peters, and says: "So, you find key."

"Yes," says Peters, who then, unable to contain himself, admits that he never lost his key.

Gurdjieff asks where the key had been when he had asked for it.

It had been in his pocket all the time, Peters says.

Gurdjieff shakes his head and looks at the young boy incredulously... and then laughs. He says he will tell him later what he is going to do with him. Peters leaves with the key.

At dusk Gurdjieff sends for him. They meet on the terrace of the Prieuré. Gurdjieff says nothing. Finally, he holds out his hand.

"Give key," he says flatly.

Peters, holding the key in his hand, does not hand it over. His eyes plead with Gurdjieff. With his hand Gurdjieff makes a firm gesture. The young boy gives up the key. Gurdjieff puts the key in his pocket and starts to walk down the path.

Peters watches until Gurdjieff is almost out of sight. Then he jumps on a bicycle and races down the path after him. When he is within a few yards of him, Gurdjieff turns and looks back. Peters gets off the bike and rushes up to him. The two stare at each other for a very long time. Finally, Gurdjieff asks, very quietly and seriously—"What you want?"

Peters, his eyes full of tears, holds out his hand. "Please give me the key," he pleads.

Gurdjieff shakes his head. Very slowly but firmly he answers—"No."

"I'll never do anything like that again," Peters cries. "*Please.*"

Gurdjieff puts his hand on Peters' head, a very faint smile on his face.

"Not important," he says. "I give you other work. But you now finished with key."

Gurdjieff then takes the two keys out of his pocket and holds them up.

"Have two keys now," he says. "You see, I also not lose key."
With that, he turns away and continues down the path.

January 1928. Prieuré. Edith Taylor has had an affair with a married man. He is willing to leave his wife but not to marry her. Gurdjieff consoles her and at some point they become intimate.

7 January 1928. Prieuré. Orage and his new wife arrive. Gurdjieff kisses Orage's wife saying—"You are now half mine, whether you like it or not." At dinner one evening Gurdjieff makes sure the Armagnac is poured more liberally than usual. In time, Gurdjieff appears very drunk. But, at one moment, he snatches a small object, a watch or locket, from Jessie. He plays with the object. Orage, sitting next to him, waits, a tiger-like look on his face. Suddenly Orage lunges. But Gurdjieff yanks the object just beyond Orage's grasp. This play with Orage in front of Jessie is dangerous, as before with the "American stomach" incident it almost leads to physical violence.

Sometime thereafter Gurdjieff takes Orage and Jessie on a tour, this time with Edith Taylor driving. And as before he makes things pleasant and unpleasant by turns. The pressure builds with the days and Jessie often quarrels with her new husband over his putting Gurdjieff's interests before hers.

One day as they picnic, Gurdjieff rants about Americans, their smell, their love of money, and so forth. At dinner he looks at Edith and says he was talking about her. That night Jessie writes in her diary: "He was superb during the outburst. I sat near him and stared. His eyes were never angry, obviously he was playing a role. Afterwards he came up to me and said he was sorry but he had drunk too much. I said, 'Don't apologize, you were delightful.'"

Not long afterward, Edith discovers she is pregnant.

27 February 1928. Paris. At Gurdjieff's apartment before the newlyweds leave, he transfixes Jessie with his gaze, warning her—"If you keep my super-idiot from coming back to me, you burn in boiling oil."[15] Interestingly, Orage had used that same metaphor when he wrote to Jessie four years earlier from Chicago where Gurdjieff was giving movements demonstrations.

Speaking of Gurdjieff, Orage told her, "It must be all to the good to be boiled in oil for a period, to come out brown and crisp for some god's table. We have to be eaten, and better cooked for the sun than raw for the moon. Life in the big sense is as terrible as it is beautiful."

29 February 1928. Orage and Jessie sail back to New York carrying a fresh

---

15. In her diary, Jessie said that Gurdjieff had told her she was a squirming idiot and a candidate for a harmful one, and if she kept Orage from being one of his inner circle then she would burn in Hell.

typescript of *Beelzebub's Tales* in need of editing, this version replacing the 1927 version.

Spring 1928. Prieuré. Gurdjieff is asked about the lack of understanding between Oriental and Occidental mentalities. This is caused in part, Gurdjieff says, by the lack of energy in the East and lack of wisdom in the West. He went on to predict that the importance of the Eastern world would grow to where it would "become a threat to the momentarily all-powerful, all-influential new culture of the Western world." Among the purposes of all messengers from the gods, messiahs and leaders, there is one that is fundamental: "to find some means by which the two sides of man, and, therefore, the two sides of the earth, could live together in peace and harmony.... Time is short—it is necessary to achieve this harmony as soon as possible to avoid complete disaster." The only way this can be accomplished is through the individual development of man into a genuine, natural being. One even *partially developed* individual can influence many others. [Emphasis added.] History, Gurdjieff says, has proven that politics, religion, and any other organized movement which treated man in the mass—and not as individual beings—were failures. The separate, distinct growth of each individual in the world was the only possible solution.

Spring 1928. Athens. Bennett is incarcerated in Athens' central jail, accused of bribing an official to fabricate title deeds relating to an imperial Ottoman property in which he has a concessionary interest. Bennett receives a telegram:
Sympathy to Bennett under ninety-six laws.
—*P. D. Uspenskii*
To win his release, Bennett drinks iodine to fake appendicitis. He is removed to a municipal nursing home. Later, defending himself in Greek, he is acquitted with costs awarded against the government. When Bennett returns to London that autumn, Uspenskii refuses all communication.

Later, Bennett learns why. Apparently when the Greek police searched his Athens flat they found several letters from Uspenskii. As his name was Russian, they thought he might be a Communist. This information was forwarded to the Home Office in London which questioned Uspenskii about his political leanings.

Cut off by his teacher, with less than five years as a pupil of Uspenskii, Bennett forms his own study group. He has reservations, not feeling it is "right for me to set myself up as an expositor of Gurdjieff's System without permission either from him or Uspenskii." He resolves the question by sending Uspenskii a full transcript of each meeting. Bennett says, "I wrote to say that if he disapproved he had only to tell me and I would stop."[16]

---

16. A neat move, given that Uspenskii has told him he does not want to talk to him.

23 April 1928. St. George's Day. Prieuré. Edith, now three months pregnant with Gurdjieff's child, confronts him about his assuming some responsibility, to which Gurdjieff gives only a wry smile and a murmur. Later, he advises her to marry Caesar Zwaska, another of his students, which she eventually does. Ten years later they divorce.

Seeing that Jessie is troubled about Gurdjieff's treatment of her friend Edith, Orage tells her how Gurdjieff sees male-female relations:[17]

> Women are collaborators with men. They nourish men and bear their children, but no man should put his domestic relations before his work for self-actualization. Some women, whose proper roles are collaboratively spiritual and moral, need not bear and raise children in the interests of men, but others should do so to provide Earth with more seekers for truth. Jessmin Howarth and Edith were chosen by Gurdjieff for this role, and Jessie to fulfill hers with him [Orage]. Something had blocked Jessmin's and Edith's bodies from the proper childbearing process. Since they did not realize this and did not know how to remedy the situation, Gurdjieff worked for them, not as potential husband or father in the usual sense of those words but as a guide. Edith had made the mistake of demanding husbandly affection and outward fatherly signs of care. By her demands, she had put into peril Gurdjieff's projects for his children.

Rachmilievitch, one of Gurdjieff's oldest pupils from the Moscow days, raises his glass and addresses Gurdjieff— "God give you the strength and the manhood to endure your lofty solitude." Gurdjieff looks at him kindly, but without smiling, and begins the toasts to the idiots.

6 May 1928. Prieuré. To stimulate his writing, Gurdjieff decides "to remove from my eyesight all those who by this or that make my life too comfortable" and imposes on himself three "will-tasks." One, to rewrite all his books in a new form which he now understood after the first draft of *Beelzebub's Tales*. Two, to make clear to himself "the very deep questions concerning the common psyche of man." And three, to renew his physical body and spirit so that upon the completion of his writings he "can direct the spreading of them myself, with the energy and persistence which was peculiar to me in my youth." He sends Madame Uspenskii to England and the de Salzmanns to Germany. He cables Orage in New York that he needs him to raise $10,000 within three months.

Mid-May. New York. Orage says he "set to work, though not with much enthusiasm; and, marvelous to say, I got the money guaranteed in a couple of days." He

---

17. To begin to understand his point of view one must first understand the cosmos and our place in it as organic receiver-transmitters of energy.

doesn't mention this to Jessie, because "she is really at such odds with Institute that she loses her head when money's mentioned in connection with it." The translation of *Beelzebub's Tales* is now complete. Writes Orage:

> Ten million people may say the book is nonsense; but I shall still say, because I cannot do otherwise, that is the profoundest, most illuminating book that I have ever seen or can imagine. My only disgust with it, in fact, is not that nobody can understand it, but that I cannot; and I get so angry and desperate about it, just because I fail to grasp it, and G. seems quite maliciously to have made it not difficult but impossible to understand. And what is worse, I cannot see him giving me any clues, except at a price I am not prepared to pay merely for the off-chance. My only consolation is that I *have* done my best, and the rest I must leave. We'll see what G. does next, but I *think* I can say that I'll not be at the institute again until G. promises to make it really worth my while.

Summer 1928. London. Madame Uspenskii visits Uspenskii. It will be the first of successive summer visits.

15 June 1928. New York. To take a honeymoon and no doubt to distance themselves from Gurdjieff's continual demand for money, Orage and Jessie leave on a cross-country trip, arriving in San Diego some six weeks later in early August. They then drive to Carmel and visit the poets Lincoln Steffens and Robinson Jeffers, neither of whom is responsive. A study group is formed in Carmel. By the end of August Orage and Jessie arrive in San Francisco.

Late Summer 1928. Prieuré. Gurdjieff works on the first of what will be three revisions of *Beelzebub's Tales*. In writing the book, he says he came to hate pencil and paper and the very idea of writing—that he has to force himself every day to begin. Nevertheless, he perseveres.

Of the book, Orage says, "It is to be read from the real heart, that is, with emotional understanding." About the book's unusual use of language, he says, "Gurdjieff will not use the language of the intelligentsia—ideas in the book will not be presented in our habitual thought patterns. Our intellectual life is based on chance associations which have become more or less fixed. Only when these are broken up can we begin to think freely." Of values, he says:

> The book destroys existing values; it compels the serious reader to revalue all values, and, to a sincere person, it is devastating.... For myself, I realize now that for two years I tried to use these ideas, tried to assimilate them into my own set of values, hoping to enrich the values without giving them up. I thought that the new ideas would widen the scope and

extend the perspective of the old and give variety to the content. There comes a time to almost everyone in this work when he asks himself, "Shall I lose the old values that gave incentive, and shall I then be able to go on to new ones, ones of a different order?"

There is in the book as a whole, a parallel with the Bible, in that it opens with a cosmology and a cosmogony, an account of how and why the world was created, and of the fall of man.... The anomalies that seem to us incongruous and absurd may be a text within a text, which, when rooted out, may comprise an alphabet of the doctrine.

Late Summer 1928. Prieuré. Gurdjieff writes:

> Only such a sensation [the constant sensing of one's death and that of the death of all whom one sees] and such a cognizance can now destroy the egoism completely crystallized in them [human beings] that has swallowed up the whole of their Essence and also that tendency to hate others which flows from it—the tendency, namely, which engenders all those mutual relationships existing there, which serve as the chief cause of all their abnormalities unbecoming to three-brained beings and maleficent for them themselves and for the whole of the Universe.

With these words Gurdjieff finishes his revision of *Beelzebub's Tales*. Olga de Hartmann is sitting with Gurdjieff at the Café de la Paix. "I must confess," she says, "that I was so emotional by the last words of Beelzebub that I could hardly write. He noticed it and told me, 'We have a whole other book to write, so be peaceful.' Almost that very day he began to dictate to me about his father, about his first teacher, Father Borsh, and other remarkable people he met during his travels when he was young. When he came to the part about Father Giovanni, he dictated to me something and then told me, 'Leave it, it will come later.'"

She kept the page, but 'later' never came. The page reads in part:

> Our language, which is the only means to express our understanding, is so limited and so badly adapted to it, that even a thousandth part of our subjective understanding we cannot transmit to others by our talk.
>
> Understanding is not our thoughts; understanding is the essence that we receive from the material we possess.... That is why I have said that I wish my old friend Father Giovanni could know not what I say but what I think.[18] If he could know, he would be very happy and at the same time very astonished. He would be happy that I now finally understand what I did not understand then, thirty years ago,[19] when he told me this—and

---

18. See *Meetings with Remarkable Men*, Brothers Ahl and Sez, 241–42.
19. If this is true, then Gurdjieff met him in 1897. Gurdjieff speaks of the 'World Brotherhood'

astonished that I have actually reached this point, the impossibility of which he many times argued during our conversation.

Having written one book he has profited by the experience and says that now, "I had become more adroit in the art of concealing serious thoughts in an enticing, easily grasped outer form, and in making all those thoughts which I term 'discernible only with the lapse of time' ensue from others usual to the thinking of most contemporary people, I changed the principle I had been following and, instead of seeking to achieve the aim I had set myself in writing by quantity, I adopted the principle of attaining this by quality alone."[20]

25 August 1928. La Jolla, California. Olgivanna Hinzenburg and Frank Lloyd Wright marry.

Late September 1928. San Francisco. Jessie experiences morning sickness and several days later her pregnancy is confirmed. The following month Orage lunches with the photographer Ansel Adams who takes his portrait. Orage and Jessie then take a train to Los Angeles to visit Charlie Chaplin, and Orage gives a talk on the teaching. Afterward, a young man approaches Orage angrily, declaring—
"How dare you say we can't think—that our minds need exercising? Now you repeat backwards what I have just said. Can you do that?"
"Certainly I can," Orage replies quietly.
"Do it then!"
"Certainly I won't."
"Well, what can you do with all your superior thinking that I can't?" cries the young man.
"I can keep my temper," Orage replies, and with a snort of rage the young man flees.
From Los Angeles Orage and Jessie take the train back to New York. When students ask Orage about his impressions of California, he says, "Jesus Christ was not a Californian."

13 November 1928. Rouen, France. Edith Taylor gives birth to a daughter. Gurdjieff is the father. He names the baby Evdokia, his mother's name, which is shortened to Eve. Edith calls her "Petey."

---

to which Father Giovanni belonged not only in *Meetings with Remarkable Men* but in a disguised way in *Beelzebub's Tales*, 447.
20. Gurdjieff withheld one chapter, "Prince Nijeradze," the narrative concerning a betrayal of trust. That Leon Trotsky refers to Stalin as using the cover name of 'Nizheradze' has caused speculation. Stalin did attend the Tiflis Theological Seminary from October 1894 until he was expelled 27 May 1899. Some think that Stalin boarded with Gurdjieff's family, but the seminary insisted all pupils be housed within.

Fall 1928. New York. Orage gives C. Daly King permission to teach two groups, one in New York City, another in New Jersey.

December 1928. Prieuré. Fritz Peters receives two letters. One from his mother in Chicago telling him it is time to return home. In it there is also a note from his stepfather saying that he would be welcome and that he would assume the cost of sending Fritz to college. The second letter is from Jane Heap inviting him and his brother to spend Christmas with her in Paris. In the past his relationship with Jane had been explosive; two months before he arrived at the Prieuré he said she had hit him with a board with nails in it because he refused to do as she asked.[21] Fritz saw Jane, as did Margaret, as someone who needed to dominate, have power over others, and who created a continual and compulsive melodrama. Lately, they have reconciled. When told about his desire to leave the Prieuré, she is strongly against it. As Jane Heap and Margaret Anderson had adopted Fritz and his brother, he could only return to America if the adoption was legally broken. Knowing what a rare opportunity it was to be with Gurdjieff at so early an age, Jane vehemently argues against his leaving. Her arguments bring others to her side. But to no avail.

23 January 1929. New York. Gurdjieff arrives and reviews Orage's reediting of *Beelzebub's Tales*. This was the least of it for Orage. "Gurdjieff is more himself than ever," he says, "that is to say, he is more impossible than ever. But certainly New York needed a shaking up; and I too must have needed it." Around this time, and perhaps before, Orage feels he needs a new initiation from Gurdjieff.

"I told Gurdjieff that I'd come to the end of my patience," he says, "and that, without a new initiation, I was as good as dead about the Prieuré."[22]

Orage would probably beg off responsibility for his action by siding with Uspenskii's Ivan Osokin, who says to the magician: "The whole trouble is that we never know for certain what is coming. If we know definitely what would be the result of our actions, do you suppose we should do all that we do?"

"You always know," says the magician, looking directly at Osokin. "A man may not know what will happen as a result of other people's actions or as the result of unknown causes, but he always knows all possible results of his own actions."

In one conversation, the question of what Gurdjieff calls "a man's whim"[23] — his true desire in life — arises. Asked what his whim is, Gurdjieff

---

21. Says C. S. Nott, "She had the most stimulating and penetrating mind of any American woman I have ever met, and like all people with strong positive vibrations, her negative ones were equally strong. She could be quite ruthless and regardless of friend or foe when she wanted something. She had a strong masculine side; as she said to me, 'I'm not really a woman.'"

22. Does Orage understand that in disobeying his teacher and in marrying Jesse Dwight he has, in effect, divorced himself from Gurdjieff? Initiation can only take place when there is rapport, not a rupture, between student and teacher.

23. Gurdjieff's use of the word *whim* is indicative of the care with which he uses words. The dictionary definition of the word is "a capricious or eccentric and often sudden idea or turn of mind,"

answers, "to live and teach so that there should be a new conception of God in the world, a change in the very meaning of the word."[24]

Orage, asked the same question, answers that his whim is to produce and edit the best weekly journal in England.

If Orage is joking, Gurdjieff doesn't laugh.

There is a conversation that goes very close to the heart of the difficulty between Orage and the teaching.

"Gurdjieff once told me," recounts Orage, "that he knew my ambition. He said I wanted to be one of the 'elder brothers' of the human race, but that I had not the ability it required."

Then Gurdjieff added: "You not know how to give. You only let others take. Let them take, you do no good: you lose and they get dependent. Not easy to give. Learn how to give, then you make other people free."[25]

5 April 1929. New York. Gurdjieff departs for France. Orage dances on the quay. "Thank God I'm free again!" he cries.

Upon his return to the Prieuré, Gurdjieff tells Thomas de Hartmann to not dedicate his life any longer at the Institute but to find a house in Paris and have his wife's parents come to live with them. A house is found in Courbevoie, near Paris, on the outskirts of Neuilly.

19 April 1929. New York. Jessie delivers a son, Richard Dwight Orage.

June 1929. Prieuré. One morning the de Hartmanns are having coffee with Gurdjieff at a café, which they often do. Gurdjieff asks Olga de Hartmann to go and telephone someone. When Olga returns she says, "I saw my husband, quite pale, jump up from the table and run away. I only had time to shout, 'Thomas!' but he did not stop, but kept running like he was mad." Gurdjieff tells her to "Go and see what has happened to him." She finally finds him on a nearby street, "his heart beating like mad." They take a taxi home to Courbevoie. "Only when we entered our room," she says, "did he stop and tell me, 'Can you swear never to insist that I see that man again? He will always be my Teacher, and I will follow his teaching, but I never wish to see him again.' I certainly did not ask him then what had happened, as I only wished that his heart not beat so fast, so I told him, 'Yes.' I gave him some medicine to appease his heart and insisted that he lie down until it stopped beating so rapidly. After he had calmed down he said, 'I will certainly

---

and we come to a deeper insight into the terms "I" and real I; and why, too, Gurdjieff's whim is to make a change in the very meaning of the word.

24. Note what Frank Pinder says after Mr. Gurdjieff passes about "striking a big Do."

25. Orage insisted on being loved by people. He "gave," so that by giving, letting people take, he would gain their love. Gurdjieff understood that there are circumstances in which only by *not* giving does one give.

never change my attitude toward him as my Teacher, but help me never to see him again. You, please, continue to go to the Prieuré, you know it cannot exist without you.' I did not know what had happened in the café, but I never asked my husband so as not to make him nervous again. He had almost had a nervous breakdown, but happily, his music and perhaps also myself, in my happiness to arrange our new house, helped finally to pacify him."

June 1929. Prieuré. Louise Goepfert arrives from New York. Jeanne de Salzmann has been translating Orage's English version of *Beelzebub's Tales* into French, and now the Swiss-born German, this twenty-nine-year-old professor of art, is to do the same for German.

Gurdjieff introduces Goepfert to "Jeanna," his name for Madame Jeanne de Salzmann. Then he tells Miss Goepfert, the woman he will come to call "Sausage," to take a bath.

"Take time," says Gurdjieff, "wash off American dirt, then see."

She chooses a room on the third floor of the château, the austere Monks' Corridor. It is painted in ocher and oxblood red. There is a skull and crossbones painted above the door to her room, which is simply furnished with bed, table and chair.

Dr. Stjoernval says to her, "May I say something to you? How to explain it? Mr. Gurdjieff tries something that no one has tried. He tries to put people born under certain stars under another constellation. And that, in general, is impossible."

Within a week of her arrival, Gurdjieff drives Louise Goepfert to Chailly, the scene of his near-fatal auto accident. As he had done to Dr. Stjoernval in Finland, he reveals himself to her in the image of the suffering Christ. Gurdjieff begs her "to help him, to translate for him." She says: "I am overwhelmed—on my knees before Him who reveals his suffering to me."

She finds that Gurdjieff drives every morning to Paris to the Café de la Paix where he drinks Armagnac or coffee with lemon and revises *Beelzebub's Tales.* One day she asks him why he doesn't stay at the Prieuré with its fresh air and beautiful surroundings.

Says Gurdjieff: "I always work in cafés, dance halls, places where I see people, how they are; where I see those most drunk, most abnormal. Seeing them I can produce impulse of love in me. From that I write my books."

Early Summer 1929. France. Madame Uspenskii, living near Courbevoie in Asnières since 1924, only three miles from Paris, had visited her husband the year before but had no taste for the English and returned. Now she crosses the Channel again. But again she returns to France.

Summer 1929. Prieuré. Fritz and Jane Heap remain at loggerheads over the issue of his leaving. Gurdjieff is asked to resolve it. He asks Peters if he "had considered and evaluated my relationships to my mother, to Jane, and to himself and the school conscientiously and if, having done so, I still wanted to go back to America. I said that I thought I had. I felt that I belonged in America."

With that Gurdjieff agrees. Freets should leave.

3–4 August 1929. Nuremberg. Nazis mount an impressive Party Congress. Thirty trains bring two hundred thousand members and sympathizers. Sixty thousand SA men (known as Brownshirts) parade before Hitler, their Führer (leader).

October 1929. Prieuré. Fifteen-year-old Fritz Peters leaves for America. Having met Gurdjieff at the age of eleven, he has spent four and a half years at the Prieuré as a resident student.

At the gate Gurdjieff shakes his hand and, with a smile on his face, says rather sadly, "So you decide to go?"

Said Peters later, "I was only able to nod my head at him. Then he put his arm around me, leaned over and kissed my cheek."

Gurdjieff said, "Freets, must not be sad. Sometime maybe you will come back; remember that in life anything can happen."

Said Peters: "At that moment, for the only time in many months, I regretted my decision. Whatever had taken place at the Prieuré, whatever I had or had not experienced or learned, my affection for Gurdjieff had remained essentially undiminished. I realized, although not immediately, that if he had at any time put the question of my departure on a personal, emotional level—the end of my personal association with him—I probably would not have left. He did not; as I have said, he always seemed to me to play fair."

At Cherbourg, Jane Heap gives him a copy of a document dissolving the adoption and says, "You may be shocked when you read this but try to realize my position and remember that it was very difficult to break the adoption without some reason that would be legally valid."

Peters *is* shocked when he reads it. "The essence of the document," he says, "was that I was being 'expelled' from the Gurdjieff school because I was 'morally unfit.'"

Boarding the *Leviathan*, the world's largest ocean liner, at Cherbourg, he sets off for Chicago to see his mother, stepfather and seven-year-old half sister. During the voyage Peters hears of the Wall Street Crash.

In Chicago he finds his mother has been hospitalized for nervous collapse. His stepfather, a lawyer, confronts him with the disadoption document and a letter from Jane Heap amplifying the meaning of the words "morally unfit." Peters says that according to the letter, "I was some sort of sexually depraved delinquent given, principally, to the practice of corrupting other, smaller, children."

His stepfather wants to hear his side of the story.

Peters says that it seems to him, in general, that people believe what they want to believe. Therefore, if he admits to the letter's allegations, he would be believed. But if he denies them, inasmuch as the charges had been voiced, the stepfather would always wonder if he was telling the truth or not. "I said further that since I had no way of proving my 'innocence' the only course left to me was to say nothing. That I would leave it up to him—not to decide which one of us, Jane or myself, had been telling the truth—but simply to decide whether or not Jane had been honest." For the next three hours, despite persistent pressure from his lawyer-stepfather, the young boy resolutely refuses to speak about the subject.[26]

Though his family is affluent despite the stock market crash, Peters' idea of going to college is deemed out of the question and he is enrolled in high school as a senior.

Autumn 1929. London. Bennett returns to England and telephones for an appointment to see Uspenskii. He is told that Uspenskii will not see him and had forbidden his pupils to see or speak with him on any pretext. It is only the following year that Bennett learns it is because of the telegram Uspenskii sent him in Greece, "Sympathy to Bennett under ninety-six laws," referring to Bennett's actions putting him in the Moon world.

October 1929. Berlin. Gurdjieff asks Olga de Hartmann to accompany him to Germany. He does not speak the language and needs her to translate. She doesn't want to go but her husband insists.

Once there, Gurdjieff tells her, "You are quite blind about your husband; you don't even see that he is a pederast."[27] She says he tells her:

> He had never seen such an idiot as me, and that I didn't understand that my husband wasn't interested in me, but only in young boys.
>
> I just laughed, and told him that I regretted that he was telling me such nonsense, thinking that I would believe him. And then I took the opportunity of asking him what he had said to my husband in the café to make him so unhappy. "Nothing special. I told him that he had not to be so proud of you." He said that I was too attached to my husband and that I couldn't even see what was going on. I told him again, laughing,

---

26. The maturity and keenness of Fritz Peters' mind and his resolute will are amply demonstrated by this event. Whatever his faults, he was always known to be honest. In his book *Gurdjieff Remembered*, 18, in speaking of Chicago's Gurdjieff group which he meets two years after his confrontation with his stepfather, he will say, "Having had, up to that point in my life, no sexual experience … " In an interesting and unconscious way, perhaps, he is practicing the Way of Blame which Gurdjieff spoke about many times. But given what Gurdjieff will say about de Hartmann to his wife are Peters' leaving and de Hartmann's leaving connected?

27. When they had first met she said to Gurdjieff, "The only thing I wish from you is that you don't spoil my happiness with my husband."

"Don't you think that I am so stupid. I know my husband better than you. Why did you hurt him so much? I am not important. I never pay attention to these things. I know the truth, so you can say what you wish." He never answered.

1930. Germany. Hitler travels the country courting German businessmen. He meets with many of them at the mansion of piano manufacturer Carl Bechstein, whose wife is much enamored of Hitler. Between now and his election to Chancellor in 1933, industrialists from companies like I. G. Farben, the giant chemical cartel, will contribute two million marks a year to the Nazi Party.

January 1930. Café de la Paix. "If you acknowledge your sin," Gurdjieff says, "and feel remorse of conscience for having done wrong, your sin is already forgiven. If you continue to do wrong, knowing it to be so, you commit a sin that is difficult to forgive."

Early 1930s. 38 Warwick Gardens. Uspenskii speaks about evil and the devil. One cannot do evil consciously, he says. Some actions require people to be conscious, but evil requires a man to be mechanical, asleep. To discover evil, one must aim to be conscious. Then whatever is an obstacle for that aim is evil. "You can only understand evil in relation to yourself."

Uspenskii says for him the devil is "real, quite real. It is not the System; it is my opinion." The devil works through imagination, negative emotions, inner considering and the like. What he wants is man's soul. The devil cannot exist on the level of the sun but "maybe [speaking of the lateral octave] the devil can have his roots in si. Si is bigger than la, sol, fa. Not all si. But maybe when man was invented, the devil was invented also," he says. The devil of which he speaks is not the conception of medieval demonology, that of a concrete image or figure. His idea is that the devil is abstract and general so that the name "devil" can be applied to any who slander, tempt, and so forth.

February 1930. Paris. The evening before Gurdjieff is to sail for America, he asks Olga de Hartmann to come to his new flat in the rue du Commandant Marchand. He asks her to give him the key to his little chest of drawers that she keeps for him. Gurdjieff opens it and proceeds to burn all his personal papers, correspondence, certificates, passports — anything that might throw light on his past.

The next morning she returns to the flat and they have what she describes as a "wonderful talk ... a talk that could occur only in exceptional moments." Then they go to the railway station and sit in a café where Gurdjieff tells her she is "the only person who never had done what he demanded without wishing it" [for themselves]. Gurdjieff then tells her he needs her and her husband, Thomas, in New York in a week's time. Her husband is much too sick she tells him and she will not leave him. The train whistle blows. Gurdjieff mounts the steps to the dining car. He stops on the car's platform. Olga looks up at him.

"Come in a week's time," Gurdjieff says, "or you will never see me again."

"Then . . . I will never see you again," says Olga Arkadievna.

She, who had served him loyally for thirteen years as his secretary, she, who as he would later say was "the first friend of my inner life," looks silently on as her teacher's train slowly pulls away and disappears from sight. "In my thoughts," she says, "I saw before me Prince Lubovedsky going away and leaving Mr. Gurdjieff alone. When he was dictating this chapter of *Meetings with Remarkable Men* to me I always wondered about this tragic moment in his life and dreaded that it might happen to me."

The 'death' that Gurdjieff experienced with the Prince, she now experiences. She goes home and goes to bed. Four days pass before she is able to get up and resume her life.

13 February 1930. New York. Orage receives a telegram:

If love not dissipated arrange bath and party.
— Grandson and Unique Phenomenal Grandmother

A second telegram follows:

Bremen brings thousand kilos disillusion, hundred kilos momentary happiness and ten pounds retribution.
— Ambassador From Hell

"Confess, Orage, that your heart sinks when you hear that I am coming!" Gurdjieff had once told him. There was always a good-natured banter between the two — only Orage and Alexander de Salzmann were capable of making Gurdjieff really laugh — and Orage had likely riposted. But there was more than a kernel of truth in Gurdjieff's remark.

18 February 1930. New York. When Gurdjieff's ship, the *Bremen*, docks Orage is not there to greet his teacher. His absence appears to be making a "statement." The issues between them are money, initiation, and independence. The first, Gurdjieff demands; the second, he withholds; and the third is premature.

Nevertheless, Orage meets with Gurdjieff regularly in the mornings at Childs, Gurdjieff's favorite "office," and weekday evenings at his apartment, and on Saturdays he and Gurdjieff go to the baths. By month's end, all this time spent away from her, Jessie's frustration reaches the boiling point. She tells Orage as he leaves one morning that if goes to see Gurdjieff, it will be the last time he sees her. Orage appeases her and stays.

"Interesting thing, Orage," Gurdjieff later tells him, "whole group sheep, but Jessie not sheep—she dog. Sheep follow Orage because he too much like them—a bigger sheep."

Besides Jessie, money is an issue. Orage writes Nott that Gurdjieff is again in search of funds. "I doubt whether this time he will get much," says Orage. "His coming has, of course, bust up my group meetings and left me desperately placed for income, but I must be 'clever,' I suppose and find a substitute."[28]

20 March 1930. New York. Gurdjieff gives Orage a selection of chapters from *Beelzebub's Tales* to either get published or to publish himself. Orage has managed to squirrel away enough money in a special bank fund subscribed to by American pupils to pay for the publication of Gurdjieff's book. Alfred Knopf, the publisher of Uspenskii's *Tertium Organum*, is interested. But when Knopf approaches Gurdjieff about publishing, Gurdjieff tells him certain things are necessary.

"And what are your conditions, Mr. Gurdjieff? I'm sure we can meet your requirements. What would you wish us to do?"

"Not conditions," Gurdjieff replies. "One condition. One small thing."

"And that is?"

"First clean house, your house, then perhaps can have my book!"[29]

28 March 1930. New York. Knopf turns the book down. Orage next tries Doubleday but, again, the same result. "I share your opinion," Orage finally tells Toomer, "that no publisher will accept it.... The situation is anything but bright and I confess to a little fatigue with Gurdjieff and his ways. Perhaps that is because I've just had to find over two hundred dollars with which to discharge the debts he failed to remember!"

31 March 1930. New York. Hearing what Gurdjieff had said about her—"Jessie not sheep—she dog"—Jessie writes the longest entry since she began keeping a diary in 1924. Later, Jessie makes it into a short story, "Elsie & Allah."[30]

11 April 1930. New York. Leaving for France, Gurdjieff returns a gift of an expensive harmonium to its original donor. After he is gone, he says, the world would

---

28. The Work works by pressure and Gurdjieff knew how to press the 'corns' of people. If it wasn't hard manual labor, it was eccentric, even outrageous behavior, or the massive quantities of alcohol consumed during his toasts to the idiots. And always there was the material question—the demand for money. Nothing stops the formatory apparatus in its tracks, creates projection and doubt like a ceaseless demand for money. America, Gurdjieff said, was a "dollar growing country." And he came often to shear the sheep. Certainly he had need of money to keep the Prieuré afloat. But he never worshipped money. When he spent, he spent lavishly; perhaps, from an ordinary perspective, foolishly. But it was also—and this is missed by most of his critics—a direct way of teaching.

29. Perhaps Gurdjieff is alluding to Knopf having published Uspenskii's book. Otherwise, it is difficult to make sense of his remark.

30. See Essay, "Elsie & Allah."

take note of this event and the harmonium would by then have become ... He searches for the right English word. Finally he asks a pupil, who suggests "souvenir." Not satisfied, Gurdjieff turns to Orage, asking what he would say.

"Sacred relic," answers Orage with a "sacred" intonation.

Gurdjieff breaks into laughter that sounds like "a giant child's delight."

Nott later writes, "Orage's mind is more nimble than Gurdjieff's and to be with these two is better than a play."

Gurdjieff made many voyages to America. Certainly without American dollars he would not have had the time to write *Beelzebub's Tales* or been able to maintain the Prieuré. The English had given initially and had enabled Gurdjieff to purchase the Prieuré. But that was long ago. The Institute had been established on French soil only because Germany and England proved untenable. As he sometimes gave animal names to people to indicate their chief feature, he did this as well with national character. The Russians he called "turkeys," the Germans "jackals," the English "sheep," the Americans "burros" and the French "donkeys." Too Cartesian and self-adoring, the French did not begin to take an interest in the teaching until the 1930s and were never a financial factor until long after the war.

Besides their generosity, Gurdjieff was interested in America because, as he told Fritz Peters, "Americans more receptive because not closed up inside yet; they naive, stupid, perhaps, but still real. Americans, particularly, have more chance grow properly as men because have not yet become—like you say—'phony' men." Gurdjieff will also tell him: "Impossible to do my work with all energy if also concerned with money. But all these things very difficult for your contemporaries. Not only cannot do. Cannot even understand why this question of money important. Such people will never understand real teaching or real possibility of learning anything."

What is to happen between Orage and Gurdjieff is foreshadowed in a cab ride Orage takes with C. Daly King. Orage suddenly tells him:

"It is necessary to make these things your own, so that you may never need to rely upon others for them. You must be prepared, for example, to hear Gurdjieff himself deny the validity of the Method."

13 May 1930. New York. Orage calls the groups together and, as he has so often done in the past, says that the most fortunate event in his life was his meeting with Gurdjieff. He says he is leaving with his wife and one-year-old son, Richard, to spend the summer in Rye in East Sussex, England. He plans to write essays and articles for a number of American magazines. If he returns, as he hopes, there would be a new kind of Work. He then speaks about the difference between a group and a circle. "The latter meet for themselves individually, to help each other and to help a common cause, 'to make the world safe for consciousness.'" He says that even after six years of attending groups very few of them have a sense of three conscious responsibilities. These three form a triangle which, when functioning, distinguish a circle from a group. The first part of the triangle is individual responsibility toward consciousness and development in one's own everyday life. The second is consciousness "toward our neighbors, the members of our tribe also striving for consciousness." The third center of gravity is consciousness toward some in the group as "elders." He speaks of returning in January and says, "I shall have to be independent of the group financially—no one will have to pay anything again to attend a group of mine." He continues speaking about what he envisions when he returns, saying that to be a member of this new group [whose sole aim is to transform itself into a circle] people must work so hard that one comes to a momentary experience of feeling "you are losing your body and your life.... You will have known the fact of death. This is the kind of evidence I shall require for membership in a group." He goes on to say that "I am too tender-hearted to force the pace as Gurdjieff and Uspenskii can so ruthlessly do. But unless you are serious, I cannot be serious—you can hold me back." He then speaks about the five points of objective morality [five being-*obligolnian*-strivings] and ends with "Now having perhaps unfortunately listened to this, you are capable of sin—of refusal to convert verbal form into formal understanding."[31]

14 May 1930. New York. Writing to Nott, Orage says:
"We had a farewell group meeting last evening and it would have done your heart good to witness the scene. I love the group; and I couldn't bear the thought of being long out of touch with them."

---

31. At the Prieuré, Orage had experienced the 'death' of which he speaks. During his time there, the physical exhaustion and the elimination of all his spiritual dreams and expectations had brought him to the depths of despair. In fact, he was being tested. He might have easily turned tail and run, as so many did, but he persisted and had his first initiation. Such 'death,' however, is not undergone once, but many times. Now, though he does not appear to realize it, he is entering a time of a new testing. Having become prematurely independent of Gurdjieff through his marriage to Jesse Dwight, Orage now finds himself being drawn more and more into family life. Marriage and raising a family, of course, seems natural enough. But it is merely biological and, given the mission Gurdjieff has entrusted him with, as a "messenger of my new ideas," as well as his own stated aim of "finding God," it is a 'temptation' to which Orage, given his chief weakness, has blithely and blindly succumbed. Now he comes to another crossroads in which, one, he finds himself psychologically worn down with Gurdjieff's incessant (and what look more and more to him as irrational) demands for money; and, two, having come to the end of what he is able to teach. He needs a new initiation—that recognition is pulling him one way. Pulling him another way is 'familism.' Once again, though he appears to have no presentiment of it, Orage is going to experience the octave of 'death.' Die he must. His choice is: *will he choose to die on an ascending or descending octave?* Will he die for being or die for 'love'? Orage is now capable of sinning; that is, he has sufficient knowledge and will to act as he wishes. Using his own words to his group, will he or will he not refuse "to convert verbal form into formal understanding"? Orage's choice will be difficult, for he still looks at the world, as Gurdjieff says, "topsy-turvy." A careful reading of Philip Mairet's otherwise splendid biography, *A. R. Orage: A Memoir*, shows such a viewpoint. What he says seems so sensible, rational, understanding—until one realizes what is at issue.

11 June 1930. Rye, England. Orage writes to an American student:

> I told Gurdjieff in New York that I'd come to the end of my patience and that, without a new initiation, I was as good as dead about the Prieuré; furthermore, that I proposed to try the effect of 'growing chungaree' by myself—his reply was so unsatisfying that I shall carry out my plan. In other words, I shall stay here in England doing my best to get a new understanding of the Book on my own resources—in despair, frankly, of Gurdjieff doing anything more for me than he has done for Stjoernval, de Hartmann, etc., however faithfully they have given up all to follow him.... One thing remains unshakably true—the ideas are all the world to me, and I shall always be ready to cooperate in their spread provided I myself continue to increase in their understanding. What I cannot do any longer is to continue teaching without also learning—and Gurdjieff has ceased to teach *me*.

Fall 1930. Chicago. Fritz Peters' mother and stepfather separate and sue for divorce. In the spring, Peters' stepfather had hired him as a clerk in his law office. When his mother and half sister go to Europe his stepfather lets him go.

October 1930. 38 Warwick Gardens. Uspenskii decides to expand his work. It is now seven years since he left Gurdjieff. He has been working in strict secrecy with forty or fifty pupils. He will begin a new lecture series, "The Search for Objective Consciousness," at Warwick Hall. Bennett, whom Uspenskii has refused to communicate with since his jailing in Athens two years before, is invited back into the fold. Soon he is given the responsibility of deputizing, that is, reading the lectures aloud in Uspenskii's presence. Later, the two men talk and when the conversation comes to what has become for Uspenskii the perennial question and thorn in his side—Gurdjieff!—he tells Bennett:

> I waited for all these years [to expand the work] because I wanted to see what Mr. Gurdjieff would do. His work has not given the results he hoped for. I am still as certain as ever that there is a Great Source from which our System has come. Mr. Gurdjieff must have had a contact with that Source, but I do not believe that it was a complete contact. Something is missing, and he has not been able to find it. If we cannot find it through him, then our only hope is to have a direct contact with the Source.... Our only hope is that the Source will seek us out. That is why I am giving these lectures in London.

All and Everything

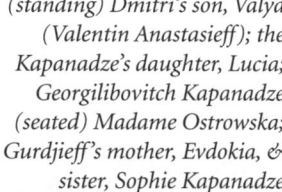

Madame Ostrowska & Gurdjieff

(standing) Dmitri's son, Valya (Valentin Anastasieff); the Kapanadze's daughter, Lucia; Georgilibovitch Kapanadze (seated) Madame Ostrowska; Gurdjieff's mother, Evdokia, & sister, Sophie Kapanadze

Georgi Ivanovitch Gurdjieff

Jessie Orage & son, Richard

J. G. Bennett & Mrs. Beaumont

Mabel Dodge Luhan in Taos

CHAPTER XXXIX

THE HOLY PLANET PURGATORY

The next day, the ship set off for its final destination in the direction of the Planet Karatas, where Beelzebub is now dwelling. Shortly after the ship had started, Hassein sat down as usual at Beelzebub's feet, and said, "Grandfather, dear grandfather, please explain to me, why, as we have been told, on this holy planet Purgatory, on which we have just been, Our All-Comprehensive Endlessness so often appears?"

At this question, Beelzebub thought a little longer than usual and then said: "It is a pity, my dear Hassein, that it is impossible at the moment to reply at length to this question of yours, because we shall soon be arriving on our planet. For a complete understanding, that is, such an understanding as I would like to give you of this holy planet, Purgatory, I should be obliged to talk a very long time. But do not fail to remind me of it, on a more convenient occasion when I may be able to explain it all to you. The understanding of the holy planet Purgatory is the most important thing for your education, and sooner or later, it will become decidedly necessary for every being, of whatever nature or form, to know of it.

"Nevertheless, my dear boy, as we shall not be arriving home at once, in order to shorten the time, I will try my best to reply in brief to your question, "Why Our Endlessness appears so often on that holy planet?" Then Beelzebub spoke as follows:

"Our Endless Creator appears so often on that planet, unfortunate souls from e Universe. The souls uffer as nothing and

First page of Chapter XXXIX from the 1931 typescript of Beelzebub's Tales

A. R. Orage

The de Hartmanns after leaving the Prieuré

PART VI

THE HERALD

13 NOVEMBER 1930. NEW YORK. GURDJIEFF ARRIVES. IT IS HIS FOURTH VISIT. ORAGE IS NOT AT DOCKSIDE TO GREET HIM, AS HE AND HIS FAMILY ARE IN ENGLAND ON HOLIDAY. TO GURDJIEFF, THE FACES OF ORAGE'S STUDENTS WHO GREET HIM HAVE THE LOOK OF WHAT HE CALLS "A CANDIDATE FOR THE MADHOUSE."

28 NOVEMBER 1930. STUDIO 61, CARNEGIE HALL, NEW YORK. BETWEEN NOW AND DECEMBER 19 GURDJIEFF GIVES FIVE TALKS TO THE ORAGE GROUPS. IN HIS FIRST TALK HE SPEAKS OF INITIATION — ORAGE'S QUESTION — AND MAKES THE DISTINCTION BETWEEN THREE GROUPS, OR LEVELS, OF UNDERSTANDING. THE FIRST GROUP IS EXOTERIC, OR OUTER; THE SECOND, MESOTERIC, OR MIDDLE; AND the third, esoteric, or inner. The exoteric group is for those who have newly entered the Work and do not yet merit belonging to the other two groups. The mesoteric group is for those initiated into a theoretical understanding of "all the questions not accessible to the average man." The esoteric group is to be initiated not only theoretically and practically into all relevant questions, but will be introduced to all means for a real possibility of self-perfecting.

Gurdjieff speaks about the exercise of self-observation which enables a person to cognize the "exaggerated importance given to his individuality" and the individual's "almost complete 'nullity.'" He speaks of his so-called "motor accident," which he regards as the action of *Tzvarnoharno,* and notes that though some of his students "decided to 'proselytize'" his ideas, they all belonged only to the exoteric group. He ends by noting that each nation has its own idée fixe regarding the teaching. For Americans, it is self-observation.[1]

Having set the foundation with his first talk, Gurdjieff in his second talk launches a full-scale attack on the students' beloved teacher, Mr. Orage. He speaks of Orage as being the consequence of "that abnormality at the basis of family life, crystallized in the life of contemporary people . . . which consists in the fact that the leading role in the household belongs to the woman." He says that at first Orage was "not yet completely under the influence of his 'left-shoulder Angel,'" a not too subtle reference to Jessie Dwight, but that his marriage to "a saleswoman of 'Sunwise Turn,' a young American pampered out of all proportion to her position," had resulted in the need to meet excessive expenditures. Once the knowledge which he had received at the Institute was used up, Orage had to "manipulate in every way" his very limited knowledge. This led to the practice of self-observation becoming "the center of gravity for the mentation of man," and so a dangerous distortion.

Gurdjieff then asks his secretary, Louise Goepfert, to read aloud a letter addressed to the absent Orage. He then demands that the "Orage people" sign what he calls an "obligation," or oath, vowing not to have any further contact with Orage unless Gurdjieff so instructs.

> I, undersigned, after mature and profound reflection, without being influenced by anyone else at all, but of my own free will, promise under oath not to have, without instructions from MR. GURDJIEFF or a person officially representing him, any relations whatsoever, spoken or written, with any of the members of the former group existing till now under the name of 'Orage's group' of the followers of MR. GURDJIEFF's ideas and also not to have any relations without special permission of MR. GURDJIEFF or his substitute with Mr. Orage himself.

---

1. The appearance of the students can be the result of only one thing: a distorted understanding of the practice of self-observation.

A number of Orage's pupils balk, one telling Gurdjieff that Orage was not only his teacher and mentor but his "own loving father."

Louise Blinken blurts out—"If Orage made a mistake or did not know how to go on, it was your fault. He taught us what he learned from you, and you did not give him the additional material he needed."

To which Gurdjieff, pleased at the open expression of resistance, replies: "Bravo!"

C. Daly King, the most adamant of the Oragean diehards, says:

> The charge against Mr. Orage's activities is that they were intellectually lopsided, placed undue stress upon mental activities at the expense of emotional and practical activities, and that thus, far from being of objective benefit to the pupils who sat under Mr. Orage, it could be guaranteed to render them even more abnormal, objectively, than they had been in the first instance.
>
> It is difficult to speak of this charge in moderate and serious terms. It is brash and blatant nonsense, though a few in the group think Gurdjieff's assessment correct.

Years later King's assessment of Gurdjieff is this:

> While I have received no impression that Mr. Gurdjieff is by any means as outstanding intellectually, emotionally or practically as his faithful disciples suppose him to be, I am convinced by my personal experience of him that he possesses another quality that may be more important than any of the foregoing. This quality he possesses to a degree not merely superior to that of any other man whom I have ever encountered but to a degree greater than it would have ever occurred to me to exist, had I not met Mr. Gurdjieff. It is the quality, not of mind or feeling or of successful accomplishment, but simply of *being*. I have never failed to experience this in his presence; one (or I) cannot 'put one's finger on it' but it is most certainly there. It has always prevented the slightest show of impertinence toward him upon my part but, more than that, it has always prevented my (otherwise frequently demonstrated) ability to challenge him even upon those grounds to which he constantly lays himself open to the most obvious challenge. I cannot account to myself for this, in other ways, inexplicable respect in which I hold him than by my admiration of the remarkable degree of being with which I am always impressed when in personal contact with him.

Georgi Ivanovitch Gurdjieff

Gurdjieff's third talk[2] is a masterpiece. It gives a glimpse of the rare level of understanding which he possesses. He speaks of the difficulty of liberation and the need for "the entire sensing of the whole of oneself" and speaks about the use of attention.

The talk is given at the first general meeting of those who have signed the paper, the "first meeting on new principles," replacing the former "meetings for collective titillation." Gurdjieff advises to "cease entirely, at least for three months, the reading of your newspapers and magazines" and instead to study the *First Series* of *All and Everything*, which elucidates most questions arising for contemporary man in a "confrontative form" which will accustom readers to active mentation and bring them to what is "most important and unfailingly required for the possibility of further work upon oneself, namely, the ephemeral nature of former conceptions and understandings."

As students are not yet familiar with the *First Series* so that he could simply refer to it, Gurdjieff has his secretary read extracts from "The Addition" in the last chapter.[3] The passages speak of the possibility for liberation from a man's entire slavery to Great Nature. Gurdjieff then gives a brief explanation of the dividing of the river into two streams, one into the nether regions serving only nature's need and the other into the ocean for one's evolutionary movement. Those present are still in the first, but there is hope. The reading then continued, warning of the difficulties of crossing streams and advising of the necessity of the great intensity necessary for the struggle against one's crystallized habits that form and support our inner "Evil-God."

Gurdjieff again interrupted the reading to speak about the path of "evolutionary movement" and data needed for the acquisition of one's own I. There are seven data indispensable for attaining this, but he will speak only of three and how to obtain data for each of the three impulses, for which names are absent in the English language, there being only approximations: can, wish, and the entire sensing of the whole of oneself.[4] He then gives a "simple" soil-preparing exercise for developing these impulses, dividing that attention into three parts, and also

---

2. Gurdjieff's *Life Is Real Only Then, When "I Am,"* in which the talk appears, works on so many different levels with such comprehensive understanding that summarization is impossible. This is generally true of most of Gurdjieff's writings.

3. The passages differ both from the 1931 draft by Orage and Jane Heap, of which 102 copies were made, and from the final that Gurdjieff approved for publication and published in 1950.

4. The emphasis in Orage's talks throughout the years has been on self-observation and this alone, as Gurdjieff says, makes one a "candidate for a madhouse," as it keeps the attention in the head, not the body. Only first self-remembering, withdrawing the attention from the ongoing automatic momentum, becoming consciously embodied in physical reality, dividing the attention, creates the basis for real self-observation, observing one's "I-of-the-moment" with the intent of observing impartially, can lead to the being and self-knowledge which comprise genuine understanding. In reading Daly King's *The Oragean Version*, his resume of Orage's talks, so little is said of self-remembering that one wonders if Gurdjieff ever explained it to him at the Prieuré. Did Gurdjieff purposely hold this back? Orage kept saying he needed another initiation. Was this it?

explains the difference between "sensing" and "feeling."

12 November 1930. New York. In the classified section of the *New York Times* this notice appears: "Lost. Portfolio Brown marked G. Gurdjieff containing typewritten mss left in taxi Tuesday midnight. Reward offered. Return to 204 W. 59th St."

10 December 1930. New York. Orage and family return from England. He at once asks to see Gurdjieff, who directs Miss Goepfert to ask Orage to sign the obligation proposed to Orage's groups. Orage, always deft intellectually, comes at once to Gurdjieff's apartment and signs the letter.[5] His apology, from Gurdjieff's description, is ornate and what Gurdjieff terms "philosophizing." This gives Gurdjieff what he calls a "'touchy emotion' . . . right in the center between the two hemispheres of the brain."

12 December 1930. New York. Orage attends the fourth general meeting. Gurdjieff describes Orage and several of his "'first-rank' defenders" as those who sit with their "'tails between their legs' and facial expressions of unchangeable 'plasto-oleaginous' traits."

As with Uspenskii eight years before—and in front of an audience which included Orage—Gurdjieff now attempts to wake Orage up to his situation by a shock technique. He openly humiliates him in front of his students, speaking of the group's "'loving father,' that is to say, Mr. Orage" and his "philosophizing." This tactic did not work with Uspenskii, neither does it work with Orage.[6] And as with Uspenskii, all the years of work with Orage appear to result in nothing. Unable to assimilate and learn from the shock, Uspenskii left to teach his own groups. Orage leaves as well, not to teach but to begin again where he left off—the editing of a magazine-newspaper propagandizing for the economic theory of Social Credit.

When Uspenskii left, Gurdjieff still had a number of promising students. With

---

5. How should Orage have acted? He had defied his teacher in marrying Jesse Dwight. He had broken his promise to Gurdjieff to come to the Prieuré. He had "invented" parts of the teaching and so led his students astray. Wanting to be loved, he had given his students too much of himself, despite Gurdjieff's many warnings against it. If he allowed himself to take the full weight of the shock, it would have opened him, and his relationship with Gurdjieff could have begun again on fresh ground with a new understanding. Instead, Orage deflected it with his always facile intellectual center.

6. It would seem that Gurdjieff expected Orage to absorb the shock to his chief feature, and continue. But the shock for Orage, as it was for Uspenskii, was too great. It was the moment of truth for each pupil. But neither could totally surrender. They did not wholly trust Gurdjieff and, therefore, reserved the right to judge him. In so doing, they judged themselves. Gurdjieff's action seems a desperate attempt to save both students, not for themselves, not for him—but for his mission. Given their breaking with Gurdjieff, it seems fair to conclude that neither really understood his mission. Despite Gurdjieff's knowledge and being, despite the many experiences Uspenskii and Orage had through Gurdjieff and his teaching, in the end they could only follow their teacher part of the way. They could not do as Jesus' apostles did. They could not step out of the web of their lives.

Orage's leaving, there is only Jean Toomer. Orage wore many hats for Gurdjieff. He was editor, fund raiser, teacher and, yes, "John, the Baptist."

29 December 1930. England. Learning of the storm Gurdjieff has created, Orage writes to a student:

> I came to New York as an agent of G. and the Institute idea—not at all in my own right or on my own responsibility. Certainly, however, G. may say I have only titillated—I have done my best both for the group and for G. But if after these years G. himself comes along and, declaring that I have failed him, as a good servant, proposes to take over the group himself, *or* to nominate a new agent in my place, I certainly have no complaint to make... I have not been, in relation to the New York group, *just* an agent of G. Perhaps that has been my failure from his point of view. I should, perhaps have regarded the group as simply material for G.'s use in all respects, and had no such feelings about you all as would give me a qualm at whatever he might do. It *may* be, perhaps, that I should have treated you all like dogs (I don't mean harshly, of course), or, better to say, like a flock of sheep whose wool and mutton were of value to G. and one or two of whom might conceivably one day attain a higher state of being, *through* being used as wool and mutton by a presumed superman. Maybe it is so, and maybe any other attitude on my part (or that of any of G.'s agents) is titillation. My reply is simply that I couldn't either feel or pretend to feel in that relation. I, if you like to say so, fell in love with the group personally[7] and so far from being willing to carry out my commission if it involved seeing the group shorn and encouraging it to grow wool, I found the shearing one prolonged agony; and in the end, I was more disposed to side with the group than with my master!
>
> It is obvious that my unwillingness to go to all lengths for G., with the group and with myself, indicates an insufficiency of what shall I say?—faith in him? trust? radical conviction that he can do no wrong? Well, to be explicit, that is the fact. I have not that absolute faith. If I were Nahom and G. commanded me to slay my first born, I wouldn't do it. I realize that this degree of faith is perhaps essential to full participation in G.'s teachings. I realize that any degree of belief, short of this makes all services to him ultimately conditional and therefore, except within limits, not to be counted upon.... "Lord," I can say, "I believe"; but I have to add, "Help thou my unbelief." Because, in truth, my belief is not absolute.... I can see clearly that from his point of view, believing in himself so absolutely, my half or three-quarters belief in him is titillation, and results only in the titillation

---

7. Is this an example of Orage's unconsciousness of his "feminine element"?

of others. He *cannot* but wish either that I shall be absolutely faithful, or cease to be regarded or to regard myself as his chief "minister" in America. I accept this without reproach. But what I pray for is that my own friends, the best I have on earth, the New York group, may not only not suffer on my account, but that, through me, like another Moses, they may find themselves led to the Jordan and transported across by Joshua Gurdjieff!

1931. New York. Jean Toomer self-publishes *Essentials,* a collection of nearly three hundred aphorisms and definitions largely influenced by Gurdjieff's teaching.[8]

23 January 1931. New York. Orage, having quietly celebrated his birthday the day before—he is now fifty-eight years old—calls a meeting of the New York group and in an emotional address tells them that they were nearly a real brotherhood, well past that of a group, and on the way to becoming a school.

January 1931. Henry Hudson Hotel, New York.[9] The adventurer and author William Seabrook, who first met Gurdjieff in 1924 and has become friendly with him, receives a call one day from Gurdjieff who asks him to invite selected friends for a reading from *Beelzebub's Tales* and "to enjoy an Arabian Nights collation afterward." Seabrook, feeling Gurdjieff wants to meet only his most intelligent friends, invites the behaviorist John B. Watson, journalists Lincoln Steffens, George Seldes, and Carl Helm, philosopher William Pepperell Montaigue, and several Harvard psychologists. Among the women are Irita Van Doren, the editor of the *Herald Tribune,* Claire Spencer, daughter-in-law of Mabel Dodge Luhan, Virginia Hirsch, and novelist Blair Niles. For his part, Gurdjieff invites Fritz Peters and Edwin Wolfe. He wants Peters to help him prepare the meal and Wolfe to put things in order. During the preparation he asks Peters to teach him American words for the various parts and functions of the body "that were not in dictionary." For two hours, he has Peters repeat every four-letter word and obscene phrase he can think of.

When the guests arrive at 11:30 in the evening at the luxurious apartments Gurdjieff has rented at 204 West 59th Street, they find a young girl sweeping the well-worn floor with a carpet sweeper and Wolfe and another man setting up

---

8. The aphorisms are linked together, such as in aphorism XL: • Each of us has in himself a fool who says I'm wise. • Most novices picture themselves as masters—and are content with the picture. This is why there are so few masters. • When I speak I am persuaded. • People mistake their limitations for high standards. • Ordinarily, each person is a cartoon of himself.

9. William Seabrook dates the event as January 1931 in his book *Witchcraft: Its Power in the World Today*. Fritz Peters dates it as the fall of 1933 in his *Gurdjieff Remembered*, 30–36. Edwin Wolfe, who recounts the evening in his *Episodes with Gurdjieff*, gives no date other than the early thirties. What appears here is a compilation of what the three write. Seabrook's date is cited as his book was published in 1940, only nine years after the date he gives, whereas Peters' book was published in 1965.

rows of steel-framed chairs which look on a shabby brown couch with sagging cushions. Several of the men are in black tie and two women, grande dame types in their fifties, are elegantly dressed in evening gowns beneath mink coats. Some fifteen or so in all, many in their thirties, a few older. Peters serves drinks while they stand about looking as though they might be at the wrong party.

About a half hour after their arrival, Gurdjieff appears from the small bedroom in the rear and slowly walks to the couch and sits down with a sigh. Toying with the heavy gold watch chain across his waist, he smiles at his guests. He is very apologetic for the late hour and crudely flatters the women about how beautiful they are and how everyone does him so much honor in agreeing to be "the guests of a poor, humble man like himself." Peters can't believe that everyone accepts this flattery.

"So, who will read my book?" Gurdjieff inquires. "I write book, *Beelzebub's Tales to His Grandson*. But who here can read?"

Seeing Edwin Wolfe in the back row he motions him forward. Wolfe sits down in a chair at the end of the couch. The young woman who had been sweeping the floor hands him the manuscript.

"Now read America chapter from beginning," Gurdjieff tells him. "Slowly and loudly. Read."

For a full hour Wolfe reads "Beelzebub in America" before Gurdjieff has him stop. John B. Watson, who has been sitting in the front row before Gurdjieff now moves and sits alongside him.

"I enjoyed very much hearing your book read, Mr. Gurdjieff," says Watson. "And by the way of appreciation I wish to send you a copy of my book, *On Behaviorism*."

Gurdjieff only smiles and nods pleasantly, then waves a hand toward the grand piano upon whose closed top was spread an array of liquors and glasses.

Everyone gathers about the piano, drinking, relaxing, becoming more animated, free now from having to hear about Beelzebub, until Gurdjieff suddenly ends it all, saying—"Now read some more."

Watson, after a few minutes of this, tells Gurdjieff:

"Either this is an elaborate and subtle joke whose point is completely over our heads, or it's piffle. In either event, I don't see much that can be gained by hearing more of it. I propose, if Mr. Gurdjieff is agreeable, that we now converse for a while."

Dinner is then served: superb Algerian melons, stuffed eggplant, stuffed grape leaves, along with great cook pots of stewed goat. The mood becomes mellow and relaxed. Questions are politely asked about Gurdjieff's Work and his reasons for coming to America.

Says Seabrook:

> Mr. Gurdjieff was more brilliant, and more witty, than the manuscript had been. He was so agreeable, so keen, and so affable, that Watson,

Steffens, Montague and the rest took him into their complete confidence and explained unanimously their conviction that — unless he was trying to put over a cosmic joke of some sort whose point had not yet become manifest — his future did not lie in the field of authorship. Gurdjieff suggests that his purpose might be too deep for our limited comprehension.

A bit more conversing and then Gurdjieff's tone of voice suddenly changes, and he gives Peters a sly wink. He says that humanity is in a very bad condition because people — "especially Americans — are never motivated by intelligence or good feelings, but only the needs — usually dirty — of their genital organs." He uses, of course, all the four-letter words and phrases Peters had earlier taught him.

Turning to one well-dressed, attractive woman, Gurdjieff profusely compliments her on every aspect of her appearance, then, saying they could be honest with each other, tells her she dressed so because she "wish to fuck" a certain person. She is tormented by this sexual urge, Gurdjieff tells her. She is very imaginative and she can already picture herself performing various sexual acts with this man — "Such as, how you say in English? Sixty-nine?"

He then launches into a description of his own sexual abilities following it by a detailed description of the sexual habits of various races and nations. After some two hours of such talk, with everyone's behavior becoming completely uninhibited, Gurdjieff eggs them on into having an orgy. When in full swing, Gurdjieff suddenly says "in loud, stentorian tones" that they have already confirmed his observations of the decadence of the Americans and that they need no longer demonstrate for him.

He points at various individuals, mocks their behavior and tells them that if they are now partly conscious of what sort of people they really are, it was an important lesson for them. As this is thanks to him, Gurdjieff says he deserves to be paid for this lesson and he would gladly accept checks and cash from them as they leave the apartment. To Peters' surprise, Gurdjieff collects several thousand dollars. He rebukes Seabrook afterward telling him he found the intelligence of his friends "distinctly in the nine-minute-egg category."

28 January 1931. New York. Interviewed by Isabel Rose, a writer for the *New York Herald Tribune,* Gurdjieff declares — "I am Beelzebub traveling the solar system, telling my grandson the history of all the countries we pass. We begin with Atlantis and end with a picture of the America of the future."

1 March 1931. New York. Orage writes to Nott: "Gurdjieff's going may or may not change things for the better, his effect here having been to kill the interest of at least three out of four of the old members. I don't know whether they will ever return, *even* if I should be disposed to try to reassemble them. G. talks as if he expects me to carry on as before; but in spite of my constant association with him, I'm not feeling even warm about group work."

5 March 1931. New York. At a meeting of the esoteric group which Orage attends, Gurdjieff explains that because of his accident he was forced to let Orage teach in New York, though he was not sufficiently instructed. Self-observation which he taught was based on something else and were the group to continue its members would become psychopathic. Gurdjieff says:

"So for seven years he, Orage, a conscious being, has allowed his followers and believers to become one-sided and entertain a misconception—not to mention those who have been made unhappy and desperate at the seeming futility of things and those who have given up the whole thing as hopeless...."

He then said he was prepared "to give Orage the necessary instruction to carry everyone on." But Orage was to do so only for the rest of the spring.

13 March 1931. New York. Orage to Nott: "Gurdjieff sailed last night, leaving behind him an almost hopelessly scattered and hostile group. He has given the impression, as never before, that he cares for money only and thinks of the NY people in that light alone.... Of course it is not so; but I despair of pointing to any evidence in support, except evidence that he has alienated the rich members as well as the poor."[10]

14 March 1931. New York. On the "Religion" page of *Time* magazine is a long article, "Harmonious Developer." It gives a quick history of the Institute and Gurdjieff's beliefs, picturing him as "a clever man, he acts sometimes like a lunatic, sometimes like a genius, sometimes like a child. He loves to laugh, apparently enjoys being angry."

Spring 1931. Chicago. Jean Toomer meets Margery Bodine Latimer, a writer and student of Orage's. Initially, she is put off by Toomer and writes to a friend: "Toomer I couldn't bear to look at. He sat at the head of the table and I was next to him. I felt he was so tainted with his master, Gurdjieff. I felt he was consciously being G. and also unconsciously being him." But few women could withstand the magnetic personality of Jean Toomer and Latimer is soon captivated.

---

10. As Gurdjieff worked with Uspenskii, pressing his corns over "the St. Petersburg conditions," he works in like manner with Orage about money. He will also use money with Jean Toomer. And through Orage and Toomer, he of course works on his American students who form their groups. His continual pressing for more and more money evokes anger and doubt. He seems venal, but it really is Gurdjieff applying what he calls the "Divine principle," see *Third Series* of *All and Everything*. It is for the student, not the teacher, to resolve and reconcile the contradiction Gurdjieff's behavior creates, to impartially absorb the heat. Many of Gurdjieff's imitators who have never been in The Fourth Way but picked it up from books or rogue teachers, point to this in defending the tithing and heavy money demands they make on students.

April 1931. New York. At Gurdjieff's direction, Orage dutifully makes one hundred copies of his English version of *Beelzebub's Tales* from his typescript (the only one besides Gurdjieff's). Missing is chapter 35, "A Change in the Appointed Course of the Falling of the Transspace Ship Karnak," the change due to the radiations of Zilnotrago (the poisonous gas cyanic acid) of the solar system Salzmanino. It is this manuscript which will be read and revised over the coming years. When published in book form in 1950 it will include chapter 35. These are sold for ten dollars apiece. Fifty copies are quickly sold, the remainder taking nearly ten years to dispose of, the last going in 1940 for one hundred dollars.

May 1931. New York. J. G. Bennett, who was not present for Gurdjieff's talks to Orage's groups but who had many contacts, said that during this time Gurdjieff introduced "new methods of work, of which most of his groups had previously no idea. Indeed, the new exercises that were being introduced in 1930 and in the early part of 1931 seem to have been different from the exercises which he had shown people individually at the Prieuré between 1924 and 1929."[11]

1 July 1931. New York. Having said goodbye to his students, Orage, Jessie and their son Richard sail to England.

Summer 1931. Café Henri IV, Fontainebleau. Uspenskii comes to the Prieuré but is not admitted. He is told that Gurdjieff will meet him at the café. They sit together on the terrace, with its charming view of the historic gardens of Fontainebleau with its roses, goldfish pond and carefully trimmed trees. Sixteen years have passed since the two first met in a noisy Moscow merchants' café. To any but the most knowledgeable eye, their situations have totally reversed.

Here now is the former student, fifty-three years of age, fit and in excellent health, an accepted teacher and magician in his own right with a large number of pupils, many quite wealthy, and one who enjoys a stainless and growing worldwide reputation as a teacher, serious author, and investigator of the Fourth Dimension and eternal recurrence.

And facing him is his former teacher, the once great teacher and magician, now fifty-nine years old, growing fat, his health in question, attacked as having contributed to Katherine Mansfield's death, his reputation in ruins, heavily in debt, having only a few pupils, and the author of what is commonly taken as a windy, exasperating, unpublished tome of unreadable spaceship fable and myth.

What passed between the two is not known.[12] Whatever their exchange, this

---

11. Having spent only six weeks at the Prieuré in 1923, what Bennett says can only be secondhand, but it does bolster the argument that Gurdjieff withheld self-remembering, only telling people to "separate I from it."

12. The idea has recently been put forth that Gurdjieff approved of Uspenskii's separation "and may have even suggested it himself." There is absolutely no evidence, direct or indirect, to support

is their final meeting, their great octave's outward ending.[13]

Soon after, Sophia Grigorievna Uspenskii, perhaps sent by Gurdjieff, makes peace with her husband and joins him in England.

Summer 1931. London. Uspenskii's *A New Model of the Universe* is published; its original title was *Wisdom of the Gods.*

Summer 1931. Prieuré. Gurdjieff, shown a copy of Uspenskii's book, turns his back and makes a scornful remark. Says Dr. Stjoernval: "Uspenskii does not understand. He does not know what Mr. Gurdjieff's aim is. We who are working with Mr. Gurdjieff have gone beyond such books. It only adds to the sum of ordinary knowledge, of which there is already too much. Uspenskii ought to have gone beyond it."

Orage calls it "A New Muddle of the Universe."

Some weeks later at the Café de la Paix, Nott finds Gurdjieff, who, he reports, is in a "worked-up state." Nott tells him that Orage had spoken of Gurdjieff bringing his pupils just so far and then seemingly leaving them up in the air.

With a sardonic grin, Gurdjieff tells him: "I needed rats for my experiments."

"What?" cries Nott.

"I needed rats for my experiments," repeats Gurdjieff.

Nott, who suffered from inferiority feelings, is crestfallen.

Easing the shock, Gurdjieff invites him to lunch at his apartment where they speak of many things. At the end, with a look of compassion, he tells Nott—"You're a good man."

"What is good?" Nott asks, still despondent. "It seems to me that goodness is often a name for weakness. Sometimes I see myself as what I really am—*merde de la merde*."

A slow smile spreads over Gurdjieff's face.

Sometime later Orage tells Nott, "A man named Rom Landau has telephoned me. He's writing a book about certain 'philosophers' and wants information from me about Gurdjieff. I can't be bothered. He's a lightweight, a fluent writer but not a serious thinker."

Says Nott: "Landau was 'a representative of contemporary art,' an artist with a wide range of knowledge but with no understanding of 'inner teaching.' I gave him some superficial information about Gurdjieff, which he used in *God Is My Adventure*, but being only a writer about philosophy he never could understand Gurdjieff or his teaching."

---

this. And if the rupture between them wasn't true why did Uspenskii refuse to see Gurdjieff when he returned to London in January 1947? There is a lot of revising of history and repositioning going on that is both unfortunate and transparent in its intent, but also with explanations for revising Gurdjieff's *Legominism, All and Everything.*

13. Whatever contact they might have hereafter could only occur telepathically.

The Herald

Some days later Thornton Wilder, the much celebrated author of *The Bridge of San Luis Rey*, notices Gurdjieff, who is sitting on the terrace of the Café Henri IV drinking coffee and cognac and working on a translation of *Beelzebub's Tales*. Introduced, Gurdjieff grunts and motions him to sit down and have coffee and cognac.

Gurdjieff's face looks to him like someone who is "at once sly and jovial, arrogant and clownish." He asks Wilder a number of questions. To every answer, Gurdjieff laughs inordinately. He looked, says Wilder, "like a very intelligent Armenian rug-dealer."

Gurdjieff orders more coffee and cognac and tells Wilder, "In the world, everybody idiot. Twenty-one kinds of idiot: simple idiot, ambitious idiot, compassionate idiot, objective idiot, subjective idiot—everybody one kind of idiot."

Wilder tells him he thinks he is a subjective idiot.

"No," answers Gurdjieff, laughing uproariously. "One mustn't go too fast. One must search.—But you are idiot type twenty: you are idiot without hope."

Wilder is not offended and Gurdjieff asks him to come to dinner at the Prieuré. Says Wilder, "I had begun to like him, and his eyes rested on me affectionately."

Gurdjieff holds his glass toward Wilder and says—barely able to speak for laughter: "I idiot, too. Everybody idiot. I idiot twenty-one." Gurdjieff holds his forefinger emphatically pointed skyward—"I the unique idiot," breaking into convulsions of laughter.

At the Prieuré Gurdjieff greets Wilder with what he describes as "buffoon joviality" and introduces him to an American lady.

"Smell him and see if he have money," Gurdjieff tells her, sniffing at Wilder. "Yes, I smell him. I think he have money."

Wilder sees this as "brilliant," for he suspects Gurdjieff of pressing people for money.

There are some twenty-five people at dinner, all served at one vast table. Before each place is a bottle of cognac. The principal dish is a sheep brought in on a large platter, its head still on, and lying in a bed of cooked fruits.

Gurdjieff is noisy and clowning, and constantly toasting Wilder with cognac. The other guests are muted, meditative and withdrawn.

"Gurdjieff and I," says Wilder, "were the only happy people at the table."

After dinner Gurdjieff offers to let him read *Beelzebub's Tales*, telling him that when it is published it will cost five thousand dollars.

"I give you five thousand dollars," Gurdjieff says.

After a question from Wilder, Gurdjieff tells him: "You no square idiot, you round idiot." Wilder is given the English typescript of the first chapter of *Beelzebub's Tales*, which fails to impress him.

Before he leaves, Gurdjieff tells him, "You come here and stay. You come three days, three months, or three years."

"I'd like to," replies Wilder, somewhat hesitantly. "But I can't come now. I can come in November."

Gurdjieff suddenly flies into a rage, lashing his arms and stamping his foot—"Not November, now! I no live November. I live now."

Wilder, a keen if conventional observer, says of the rage that "It was terrific and it passed as suddenly as it came. It was not a loss of control; it was a pedagogic emphasis."

Late Summer 1931. Portage, Wisconsin. Toomer, Margery Latimer, and six other unmarried people from his Chicago groups experiment with communal living in a small cottage. On weekends, the number may rise into the thirties. Toomer tries to apply, in his own way, some of the principles practiced at the Prieuré, with himself as the center of all events. Toomer's aim is to see if artificial societal barriers can be transcended through living in close quarters and the sharing of work and play. Through a combination of work assignments, exercises, games and discussion, Toomer brings to life what he regards as the essentials of the Gurdjieff teaching. By summer's end, Toomer feels the experiment is a success. "I am satisfied that it is entirely possible," he says, "to eradicate the false veneer of civilization, with its unnatural inhibitions, its selfishness, petty meanness and unnatural behavior, under proper conditions. Adults can be re-educated to become as natural as little children, before civilization stamps out their true or subconscious instincts." Toomer's experiment causes a scandal with the Portage citizenry. Rumors of Communism, nudity, and sexual license abound.

20 August 1931. 38 Warwick Gardens. Shortly after his last meeting with his former teacher, Uspenskii finds himself having to deal yet again with what must seem like a dog that will never die.

In a group meeting, a student says: "As I understand it, one of the principles of esotericism is that the teaching must be passed from one conscious being to another ... after the general principles of the work are received it is necessary to keep the line unbroken. I ask this because it seems to us as if the line was broken when you left Gurdjieff."

"What has all this to do with Gurdjieff and me?" answers Uspenskii. "I was working with Gurdjieff until I saw a difference in him. This has nothing to do with esotericism. When I found that I could not work with him any longer I left him. That is all. . . . The idea is that one can have only such a teacher as one deserves. But only so long as he is teacher. If he ceases to be teacher—well—then why talk about it? I went to Gurdjieff in 1915, but in 1918 I found that I could not continue to work with him. In 1920 again I started to work with him, and again I came to the conclusion that it was impossible to continue, and in 1924 you remember that I spoke to you about this and said: 'I may be wrong but I had to part with him.'"

Later, in the same meeting, Uspenskii says, "How can I say what number man Gurdjieff is? I know only one thing; that he knows more than I of certain principles. He changed all these principles and I parted from him."

Still later he is asked—"Was it because of the system that you left Gurdjieff?"

"What do you mean by this?" Uspenskii asks, and then upon reflection adds, "In a sense, yes."

"Then you must have believed something."

"There is no question of belief; it is a question of fact. I saw. I saw that things had changed...."

9 September 1931. 38 Warwick Gardens. "Nicoll, you had better go away...." Uspenskii pauses then adds "... go away and teach the System."

About this time Uspenskii begins to make use of his senior students, such as Dr. Francis Roles and J. G. Bennett. He deputizes them and later Henry John Sinclair, Lord Pentland, a journalist, aspiring politician and former president of the Cambridge Union Society, to answer basic questions and to do readings. Uspenskii also begins to speak more about his personal ideas, such as the role of the devil in preventing human evolution. At some point, he moves into "The Dell" at Sevenoaks and Madame Uspenskii permanently settles in England.

Autumn 1931. Hampstead Heath, London. Orage and his family set up housekeeping. He lays plans to return to journalism either as a co-editor of *The New Age* or of a new paper. His days with Gurdjieff, he feels, are over, but he says he still practices the teaching and says he holds it in high regard.

Fall 1931. Chicago. Fritz Peters, alone in the world, working as a file clerk and French translator, joins Jean Toomer's Fourth Way study group. Meetings consist of readings from Orage's English version of *Beelzebub's Tales* followed by a discussion in which the ideas are related to one's personal life. Peters has many reservations about the approach.

"Since the writings were obviously critical of ordinary values, standards and social morality," Peters says, "the group members usually interpreted these criticisms as meaning that any values which ran counter to the prevailing morality were worthwhile. With this view of life, such things as free love, adultery, or any radical social behavior became almost automatically justified." Most irritating of all is Toomer's affecting a Russian accent in answering questions.

Late October 1921. Portage, Wisconsin. A few days before his marriage to Margery Latimer, Toomer writes:

> There is a new race in America. I am a member of this new race. It is neither white nor black nor in-between. It is the American race, differing as much from white and black as black and white differ from each other. It is possible that there are Negro and Indian bloods in my descent along

with English, Spanish, Welsh, Scotch, French, Dutch, and German. This is common in America; and it is from all these strains that the American race is born. But the old divisions into white, black, brown, red, are outworn in this country. They have had their day. Now is the time of the birth of a new order, a new vision, a new idea of man. I proclaim this new order. My marriage to Margery Latimer is the marriage of two Americans.

Understanding perhaps that few are ready to accept such a new order, Toomer lists himself as white on the marriage certificate. Racially, Toomer was more white than Negro. But he is going against the social conviction that a drop of black blood makes a person a Negro.

After the initial success of his 1923 novel *Cane*, Toomer has continued to write novel after novel but is unable to get any published. He now commences to write at breakneck speed about the experiment in living he conducted with group members at Portage, Wisconsin, which he calls "Portage Potential." His writing has become a 'teaching' and his once fluid and poetic style is now didactic. Gorham Munson, his friend and fellow Gurdjieffian, points this out, but Toomer does not see it.

He has heard that Gurdjieff is not pleased about his impending marriage, believing that marriage is a stage in a man's life and that stage is past. But while Latimer is not wealthy, she does have enough money to make for a comfortable life giving Toomer time to write and teach without financial worry.

30 October 1931. Portage. Jean Toomer, thirty-six years old, a descendant of Louisiana's Governor Pinckney Benton Stewart Pinchback, first Negro to become governor of any state, marries thirty-three-year-old Margery Latimer, whose ancestry can be traced back to the Puritan preacher Cotton Mather.

Autumn 1931. New York. Gurdjieff arrives from France. Following Orage's ouster, Gurdjieff now seems open and approachable. Money is collected as usual.

16 November 1931. New York. Rom Landau attends a dinner party given in Gurdjieff's honor at the Colony Club by John O'Hara Cosgrave, former Sunday editor of the *New York World*. Among the twenty guests and sitting beside Landau is Alexander Nicholayevitch Romanoff who now writes books under the pseudonym, "Achmed Abdullah."[14] He was formerly an acting colonel in Younghusband's Expeditionary Force that invaded Tibet in 1903 and later a British spy. Says Landau:

---

14. Oddly, Moore believed his name was Nadir Khan, who was king of Afghanistan until assassinated in 1923.

When Gurdjieff entered the room Achmed Abdullah turned to me and whispered: "I have met that man before. Do you know who he really is? Before the war he was in Lhasa as an agent of the Russian Secret Service. I was in Lhasa at the same time, and in a way we worked against each other."

Much later Romanoff—"Achmed Abdullah"—writes Landau a letter:

> As to Gurdjieff, I have no way of proving that I am right—except that I know I am right.
> When I met him thirty years ago in Tibet, he was, besides being the young Dalai Lama's chief tutor, the main Russian political agent for Tibet. A Russian Buriat by race and a Buddhist by religion, his learning was enormous, his influence in Lhasa very great, since he collected the tribute of the Baikal Tartars for the Dalai Lama's exchequer, and he was given the high title of *Tsannyis Khan-po*. In Russia he was known as Hambro Akvan Dorzhieff; to the British Intelligence as Lama Dorjieff. When we [Younghusband's Expeditionary Force in which Romanoff served] invaded Tibet, he disappeared with the Dalai Lama in the general direction of outer Mongolia. He spoke Russian, Tibetan, Tartar, Tadjik, Chinese, Greek, strongly accented French and a rather fantastic English.[15] As to his age—well—I would say ageless. A great man who, though he dabbled in Russian imperialistic politics—did so—I have an idea—more or less in the spirit of jest.
> [Meeting him at that dinner party] I was convinced that he was Lama Dorjieff. I told him so—and he winked. We spoke Tadjik.
> I am a fairly wise man. But I wish I knew the things which Gurdjieff has forgotten.

It is certain that Gurdjieff was in Tibet. He says he was collecting taxes for the Dalai Lama. His wink when Romanoff addresses him as Lama Dorjieff isn't necessarily a confirmation, as Gurdjieff is given to supporting people's impressions of him. Old photographs of Dorjieff and Gurdjieff don't clear up the question. Madame Alexandra David-Neel, who spent many years in Tibet, writes an article disputing that Gurdjieff is Lama Dorjieff.[16] Claude Bragdon, however, who was also at the dinner, says that later "Gurdjieff, through Orage, acknowledged that he had been in Lhasa, saying that his political activities had been but a cloak to his religious interests: he was there studying Buddhist theology."

Orage later explained that Gurdjieff told him that "in Tibet he was not a

---

15. If Gurdjieff was speaking a "fantastic English" in 1903, then he had nine years to perfect it when, as "Prince Ozay," he spoke to Paul Dukes in Russia.

16. See *Les Nouvelles Litteraires*, "Gurdjieff et Dordjieff" (Paris, 22 April 1954).

foreign agent; he got himself appointed collector of dues from the monasteries for the Dalai Lama, and in this role was able to go into any monastery. He discovered instances of abnormal development, 'high elevations', what are called 'magical powers', but he says that he found little, apart from something in certain dances and ceremonies, which could be described as objective knowledge." Most of the powers developed by certain monks were diversions from the normal—interesting, but not useful for a method of self-development for people of the Western world, such as he had in mind. So Gurdjieff was there but whether or not he was "Lama Dorjieff," like so many things with Gurdjieff, who can say?

In 1949 Bennett says Gurdjieff told him that at the Tibetan frontier "he gave his name and papers made out in Russian. He said that there is no letter 'g' in Tibetan and so they pronounced his name 'Dorjieff' and gave him a pass in Tibetan with his name on it." He said that his eldest son had become a lama and had made such spiritual progress that at a relatively early age he had been appointed the abbot of an important lamasery. The Dorjieff story cannot be taken literally.

1932. Rouen, France. The Stjoernvals open a simple rooming house and raise chickens and geese for sale.

1932. Paris. Alexander de Salzmann, who left the Prieuré as things ran down, has earned his living in Paris, first as an interior designer and then an antique dealer. He is sitting, as has become his custom, in a café on the Boulevard Saint Germain, drinking a concoction of beer and calvados and smoking from a long cigarette holder. He draws what looks like Oriental calligraphy. René Daumal, the avant-garde poet and writer,[17] who at that time was, as he said, "close to madness and death," is introduced to de Salzmann. Daumal is suddenly rejuvenated and writes to his friends that de Salzmann is "a former dervish, former Benedictine, former professor of jujitsu, healer, stage designer, not a tooth left in his head, an incredible man." Eventually, at Daumal's urging, a group springs up around de Salzmann.[18]

1932. England. C. S. Nott returns and says:

> I was astonished at the change since my departure less than four years before. Shops were empty of customers, streets unswept, shabbiness everywhere; soup queues, bread lines. Twenty million people without money to buy food lined up each day to receive a dole to keep their families from starving. It was as if a terrible war or famine or plague had

---

17. Daumal will later write an unfinished novel, *Mount Analogue*, which gives his understanding of the Work. He dedicates the book to de Salzmann, who is believed to be the prototype for Pierre Sogol, the book's wisdom figure.

18. Whether Gurdjieff knew of the group at the time is a question.

passed over the country.

It was a blinding example of how life is organized by the power-possessing beings on this planet. In America alone twenty million were going hungry while food was being destroyed. Wheat was being used as fuel, fruit dumped into the sea by thousands of tons a week. Farmers were being paid not to produce wheat and pigs, and all because there were not enough dollar bills, printed pieces of paper, being distributed with which to buy them. The big banks were bursting with money, while the small banks failed right and left.

The monetary system first broke down in America; from America it spread to Canada, then to Europe, to Australia and to every country where the gold standard operated. It was an extraordinary example of how the minds of power-possessing beings become fixed along a certain line, and rather than depart from this line they will let millions suffer. Only the big banks and big business did not suffer.

1932. England. John Buchan's novel *The Gap in the Curtain* is published. Its main character is Professor August Moe, a powerful and brooding man of Central European or perhaps Scandinavian extraction, whose idée fixe is time and who casts an intellectual spell over five people at a weekend house party. Professor Moe is the first of three fictionalized depictions of Uspenskii.

1932. London. Orage, perhaps putting his best English face on his rift with Gurdjieff, speaks to Nott in glowing terms about him, saying: "We can never understand the being of man who is on a higher level than our own. Gurdjieff is a kind of walking god—a planetary or even solar god."

15 January 1932. Paris. Gurdjieff returns to Paris. At some point Gurdjieff travels to Vichy and has another auto accident, this time because he avoided hitting a chicken. Dr. Stjoernval and some others were traveling with him. When they arrive back at the Prieuré, Martin Benson says Gurdjieff looked "like a battlefield"; he is cut all over and doctors put clips on his wounds. Stjoernval has a hole in his ankle, but refuses to go to a hospital. Instead, he sits in his room drinking a bottle of Vieux Marc that Gurdjieff had sent to everyone's room.

Meanwhile, Gurdjieff, stitched up with metal clips, sits naked on his bed and orders Benson to take off the clips. Having no tools, Benson sterilizes a pair of pliers and a screwdriver and tears up sheets and makes tourniquets. As the clips are taken out, Gurdjieff drinks Vieux Marc. Oddly, he does not bleed. He sleeps for an hour, then sets out to walk up the hill to Fontainebleau to a café to finish the "My Father" chapter in *Meetings with Remarkable Men.* Benson sees him and tries to convince him to take a cab. Gurdjieff tells him: "Benson, I'll tell you something, my aim is to finish *All and Everything* [the Three Series], and not even death will stop me."

23 January 1932. London. Orage writes to an American student:

> I'm disappointed that you and others found G.'s deprecation of self-observation discouraging, since his reason for his statement was familiar to you all. I never at any time said that there is, ready-made, an actual I that can observe; but I always said—following Gurdjieff—that by feeding this conception I on self-observations (or, rather by its own feeding) it develops as an embryo develops.[19] The whole point of the method lay in its being a means to self-development; not, of course, to self-conception, this latter having been done for us, so to speak, and evidenced by the fact that our planetary body becomes fully formed. The *method* was to be practiced by the conceived but not yet developed I; and it had to start from 'nothing,' since only self-developed individuals rank as individuals....

1932. Carmel. Toomer completes the manuscript for "Portage Potential." Margery, his wife, says of the book, "It is really a remarkable thing, not involved with people's pains and frustrations but with their growth. I hope there are enough people in America interested in growth rather than the opposite to make its publication and success outstanding."

1 February 1932. Carmel. Clifton Fadiman, a highly regarded literary critic and editor, writes Toomer regarding "Portage Potential":

> There are very definite reasons for the rejection; but I hardly know how to list them in a letter. I believe very deeply that since *Cane* which had genius in it, you have traversed the wrong road. Perhaps this post-Gurdjieff period is necessary for your development. In that case, I prefer to look upon books like *Portage* as mere entries in your personal journal rather than as works of art destined for an audience. Unless I speak with you at length, it is difficult to explain. Be assured that I read—and with close attention—every word of *Portage*. I am sorry it is no go with us.

February 1932. Jane Heap's apartment, Montparnasse, Paris. Solita Solano introduces Kathryn Hulme, and her companion Alice Rohrer, to Jane Heap. Since 1927 Jane Heap has supervised an "artist's group" interested in the Work. Says Hulme, "Jane Heap in appearance was as formidable as her literary reputation—a

---

19. He does not mention the term "self-remembering."

handsome, heavy-set American with dark cropped hair, that revealed the size and sculpture of a remarkable cranium. Her warm brown eyes softened the austerity of her masculine countenance, as well as the bright lipstick she wore on her generous mouth. Her personal magnetism was almost visible."

Others attending are Margaret Anderson and Georgette Leblanc when they are in town, and, from time to time, Janet Flanner, who writes a "Letter From Paris" for *The New Yorker* under the pseudonym "Gênet." Earlier, Hulme and Rohrer by chance had seen Gurdjieff at the Café de la Paix and spoken with him. When they left, Hulme glanced back, "With one leg pulled up beneath him Oriental-fashion on the banquette, he looked from a distance like a broad-shouldered Buddha radiating such power that all the people between him and me seemed dead."

29 February 1932. New York. Gorham Munson writes to Toomer saying, "I could not resist a rapid reading of the manuscript ["Portage Potential"], and though my opinion is unsolicited, I feel I must give it. Gurdjieffian writings fall into two classes, writings for students and writings for the world.... It is very interesting material for the followers of Gurdjieff, but for the world it won't do."

4 March 1932. New York. Gorham Munson writes to Toomer again about "Portage Potential":

> I wish I could work up an enthusiasm for the book and allay some of my fears about it, but I can't. One thing I will mention are the occasional traces in it of the influence of Mr. G.'s style on you. These I think unfortunate, and I have been hoping in the past that you would see for yourself that G.'s "sublime egoism" at moments is unapproachable by us when we write, and that you would see the difference between his vernacular raciness and what I must call your lapses into a wooden colloquialism. But the main consideration is that the book is not crafty enough to disarm the hostile readers who abound while winning the innocent readers whom we don't know about. Many people are waiting to pounce on the first avowed Gurdjieff exposition that comes along, so we must beware, lest we ourselves work harm to the system of ideas we love.

28 March 1932. New York. In a story headlined "Just Americans," *Time* magazine runs a story on Toomer's Portage experiment and his marriage:

> No Negro can legally marry a white woman in any Southern State. But Wisconsin does not mind, nor California. Last week at Carmel, Calif., "Provincetown of the Pacific Coast," there was an intellectual charivari. A parade of Carmel artists and authors marched to the cottage of

Jean Toomer, 36, Negro philosopher (*Cane*), psychologist, and lecturer, and novelist Margery Bodine Latimer (*This Is My Body*), 33. It had just been revealed that they were married four months ago at Portage, Wis. Bridegroom Toomer, who has a small moustache and few Negroid characteristics, told the story of their romance... "Americans probably do not realize it," Bridegroom Toomer told his callers, "but there are no racial barriers any more, because there are so many Americans with strains of Negro, Indian and Oriental blood. As I see America, it is like a great stomach into which are thrown the elements that make up the life blood. From this source is coming a distinct race of people. They will achieve tremendous works of art, literature and music. They will not be white, black or yellow—just Americans.

10 April 1932. Germany. A runoff election for president gives Hindenburg 19.5 million, or 53 percent, of the votes; Hitler is second with 13.5 million, or 37 percent.

21 April 1932. London. Backed by American friends who contribute one thousand pounds ($3,350), Orage publishes the first issue of *The New English Weekly*. Its purpose is to champion Social Credit, a monetary system designed to replace money with a kind of barter and distribute tax money to the poor.[20]

1 May 1932. Café de la Paix, Paris. Unable to meet mortgage and coal payments, Gurdjieff orders the Prieuré's kitchen closed and the château boarded up. On Tuesday, Louise Goepfert goes to the Café de la Paix to say good-bye to Gurdjieff. When they see one another she says "a sharp electric spark passes between us."

She tells him why she is there.

"You are very kind," says Gurdjieff. "I know now there in the Prieuré some hate me. Make worst man of me, I do so and so. They not know how much they cost me, even their shit. To take away their shit, five thousand francs a year."

A week later she will ask him: "Can I do anything for you?"

"Now only money, money. One hundred thousand francs I need at once."

11 May 1932. Paris. Gurdjieff closes the Prieuré and moves to Paris. The upkeep of the Prieuré he can no longer afford. It has fallen into disrepair, its gardens neglected, the orangery in ruins, the Study House deserted, and some of the precious carpets damaged by rats and mice. According to Nott, Gurdjieff is able to keep going only because of the support of Orage's old New York group of about thirty, the small group of Americans in Paris, and several English students.

20. It is interesting to recall in this connection Orage saying, "There comes a time to almost everyone in this work when he asks himself, 'Shall I lose the old values that gave incentive, and shall I then be able to go on to new ones, ones of a different order?'"

The Herald

Only one or two French show any interest.

August 1932. Hampstead Heath. Orage receives a letter from Gurdjieff asking him to come to Paris for a day. Replies Orage—"There was a time when I would have crossed oceans at your bidding. Now I would not even cross the Channel."[21]

16 August 1932. Chicago. Jean Toomer's daughter is born but his wife dies of complications. Toomer names the baby Margery, after her mother. He calls her Argie.

9 September 1932. Little Gaddesden, Hayes, England. The Uspenskiis move here from Sevenoaks to a large Victorian mansion on seven acres of land near Hayes in Kent, less than an hour's drive from the center of London.

13 September 1932. Café de la Paix. The day his twenty-one year vow ends Gurdjieff begins writing his appeal to contemporary humanity, *The Herald of Coming Good.*

October 1932. Taliesin. With debts mounting and little architectural work, Wright decides to start The Taliesin Fellowship program for aspiring architects.

Autumn 1932. Prieuré. Payson Loomis, who has been helping with the translation of *Meetings with Remarkable Men* and *The Herald of Coming Good*, and acting as Gurdjieff's secretary and chauffeur, enters his office. Gurdjieff is sitting working on papers. Loomis doesn't sit down but stands before him. He tells him he is leaving.
"This is alright, only I give you exercise," says Gurdjieff. Loomis declines. He insists he is leaving.
Gurdjieff reaches down and opens a bottom drawer of the desk and pulls out a large black revolver. He offers it to him.
"Take this and shoot me . . . . Or shoot yourself," says Gurdjieff.
Loomis turns and walks out. He returns in the late 1930s for lunch with Gurdjieff but never resumes an active student relationship. He ends his career writing sermons on "The Power of Positive Thinking" for the Reverend Norman Vincent Peale.

Winter 1932. New York. Gurdjieff arrives. He demands money and his followers react. Jean Toomer reports several are driven away "with disgust and anger and the conviction that he was using his power merely in order to obtain money,

---

21. Nott reports Orage saying, "Time was when I would have gone to the ends of the earth at your wish. Now I must know exactly why you want to see me."

money and more money without cease." But Gurdjieff knows what they cannot—the bank threatens to foreclose on the Prieuré.

Winter 1932. New York. Fritz Peters, now nineteen years old, visits Gurdjieff at his request. Gurdjieff tells him that because of his childhood association with him he had certain problems and struggles others would never experience. Says Gurdjieff:

> You not wish to come to see me tonight, so necessary for me—very busy man—to take time to send for you. This because you now have struggle between real self and personality. You not learn my work from talk and book—you learn in skin, and you cannot escape. These people must make effort, go to meetings, read book. If you never go to meeting, never read book, you still cannot forget what I put inside you when you child. These others, if not go to meeting, will forget even existence of Mr. Gurdjieff. But not you. I already in your blood—make your life miserable forever—but such misery can be good thing for your soul, so even when miserable you must thank your God for suffering I give you.

Gurdjieff tells him that he had been studying the American language and instead of the word "fertilizer," he would now use "sheet" as it was a real word. He tells Peters that he, like most young people, looks at the world upside down. For example, Gurdjieff tells him that he assumes that anyone he meets is good, honest, upright, and so forth. So, when he learned the truth about people, he becomes disillusioned. This attitude is a long, slow and improper process.

Gurdjieff says:

> You must learn to look right side up. Every person you see, including yourself, is shit. You learn this and then when you find something good in such shit people—some possibility not to be shit—you will have two things: you will feel good inside when you learn this person better than you think, and you will also have made proper observation. Just so, when you can observe self, if you already think self is all shit then when see something good in self will be able to recognize at once and will also feel joy. Important that you think about this.

At a later meeting Peters tells Gurdjieff of his experience with the Chicago group. Ordinarily Gurdjieff has no taste for opinions or gossip about others, says Peters, but this time he listens. Peters is concerned with the group's "phony reverence" and its "tendency to use his work as an excuse for sexual promiscuity or at least a good deal of talk about sexual promiscuity."

"America is still very young, strong country," Gurdjieff says. "Like young people everywhere, all Americans very interested, very preoccupied with sex things.

So very natural for them talk and act this way. And not bad thing they do. I tell many times that all work must start with body; like I tell many times that if wish observe self must start from outside, by observing movements of body. Only much later can learn how observe emotional and mental centers."

Gurdjieff goes on to tell him:

> When you come Prieuré first time you not yet spoiled, have not learn to lie to self. Already even then you can maybe lie to mother or father, but not to self. So you fortunate. But these people very unfortunate. Like you, when child, they learn lie to parents, but as they grow up also learn lie to self and once learn this is very difficult to change. Lying, like all other things, become habit for them. So when I say even ordinary thing, because they wish have reverence for their teacher — this reverence can be very bad thing, but is necessary for their good feeling — and because also wish not disturb their inside sleep, they find other meaning for what I say.

"In that case," Peters asks, "how can they ever learn anything from you — or from anyone else?"

"Maybe they not learn anything new."

"Then why bother to try to teach them?"

Gurdjieff smiles, indulgently. "Because is possibility, even if very small, may learn."

1933. Chicago. Toomer completes the final draft of his novel *Transatlantic*. He no longer writes in the rich lyrical style of *Cane,* with which he sought answers to human problems. Instead, using Gurdjieff's teaching, Toomer becomes a social critic and spiritual reformer. He cannot find a publisher for the book or any of the books that follow. Still, he doggedly continues to write, here and there publishing an essay or poem. He writes a number of plays as well, but none are staged, with the exception of one produced by a university.

Many years hence, Charles R. Larson, a literary critic, cuts to the heart of Toomer's problem with writing:

> Toomer's own writing became a problem of distance. In *Cane* he wrote as if by possession about a way of life that fascinated yet threatened him. He had touched the forbidden subject yet managed to wriggle away. Thereafter, his subject was not culture in all its song and movement but an individual turned in on himself. The gobbledygook characters and situations in the post-*Cane* works, which were intended to be satirical, more often collapse under their ideological weight. As he pushed Gurdjieffian thought — forced it, one might say — into his fiction, his characters became one-dimensional and bloodless. Thus, race and Gurdjieff both

ruined and propelled his work—race, because he couldn't accept his blackness after *Cane* was completed, and Gurdjieff, because the master's philosophy helped Jean [22] to deny his former self.

Spring 1933. New York. Gurdjieff telegrams his followers declaring he is "absolutely destitute" and the Prieuré is about to be sold.

1933. Little Gaddesden, Hayes. Uspenskii has come to the habit of sitting up half the night drinking claret and reminiscing about his early days in Russia. To Bennett he appears as if he is "obsessed with the need to put himself back into the life he was living before he first met Gurdjieff in 1915." At one such drinking bout, Bennett is suddenly "quite outside myself." He finds himself hearing his own voice and even watching his own thoughts, as if they were going on in someone else. "I saw myself as completely artificial," he relates, "neither my thoughts nor my words were my own. 'I'—whoever at that moment 'I' might be—was a completely indifferent spectator of the performance."

Bennett tells Uspenskii that he now knows what self-observation is.

Replies Uspenskii: "If only you can remember what you have just seen you will be able to work. But you must understand that no one can help you in this. If you do not see for yourself, it is impossible for anyone else to show you."

The conversation turns to Uspenskii's theory of eternal recurrence. Bennett is of two minds about it. He believes it contains an important element of truth but does not think it literally true.

Uspenskii tells Bennett: "You are like Madame [Uspenskii]. Both of you have young souls. You have not the experience of living many times on this earth."

Early on in their St. Petersburg days Uspenskii had spoken about eternal recurrence many times to Gurdjieff, who would merely listen and make no reply. Finally, he did agree to reply and so Uspenskii put it to him flatly—"Is there any truth in this, or none at all. What I mean is, do we live only this once and then disappear, or does everything repeat and repeat itself, perhaps an endless number of times, only we do not know and do not remember it?"

"This idea of repetition," said Gurdjieff, "is not the full and absolute truth, but it is the nearest possible approximation of the truth. In this case truth cannot

---

22. Entering into an authentic teaching of self-transformation like The Fourth Way is like handling a poisonous snake. For transformation can lead in either direction—to understanding and wisdom, or personal power and heavy karma. One must *learn* to be sincere, as Gurdjieff says, work against self-will and, as one verifies the tenets of the teaching, be ever vigilant to any personal elements "owning" the teaching, and using it to mask, rather than reveal, one's self-love and vanity. The practices seem simple enough, but ignorance of the depth, complexity and interlocking principles that lie behind them make a descent inevitable if one does not have a teacher in the lineage, or is being their own teacher. We see with Toomer how his mixing his premature understanding of the teaching with his literary career and his "Portage Potential" experiments and later setting up his own institute shows what he acknowledged to Orage—his desire for power. Still, Toomer was a man of exceptional intelligence, talent and vision.

be expressed in words. But what you say is very near to it.... What is the use of a man knowing about recurrence if he is not conscious of it and if he himself does not change?... All laws can be seen in one life. Knowledge about the repetition of lives will add nothing for a man if he does not see how everything repeats itself in one life, that is, in this life, and if he does not strive to change himself in order to escape this repetition."

7 March 1933. Paris. With *The Herald of Coming Good* finished, Gurdjieff now writes a bizarre "Supplementary Announcement." Though the *First* and *Second Series* of *All and Everything* are written but not published, Gurdjieff publishes *Herald*. With the exception of Nott and some others, it strikes many as a very strange book. Some, like Uspenskii, think it shows he has lost his mind.

May 1933. Prieuré. Gurdjieff is unable to meet mortgage payments, and so the château and its grounds are sold and all its contents auctioned off. Says Martin Benson:

> At the end I was the only one there. A fifty-eight room house and Rex, the colored boy, whom Mr. Gurdjieff brought over. I didn't have a penny. I was in charge of the gate, and then I was in charge of the whole goddamn place. It was a fifty-eight room chateau, on fifty acres! Walled in.
> That's why Madame de Salzmann asked me, "Frankly, tell me honestly, were you the last one at the Prieuré?" Yes, I was the last one. I had everything in my possession: All the manuscripts, all the paintings of de Salzmann, all of the music—every goddamn thing. I tried to borrow five hundred dollars. They didn't know what five hundred dollars was. This was during the Depression.... I couldn't borrow five cents from anybody.
> And then I left.... I closed it as much as closing the gate. And then, Mr. Gurdjieff gave me a champagne party in Paris. And I invited ... I didn't know who to invite, because everybody was living in London. There was Tom Peters, brother of Fritz Peters, who was a decent person. And Tom?—he came. There was Nick Putnam, who was a descendent of General Israel Putnam; he owned the Putnam stores, which were worth a fortune.... When I left, the only person who came to the boat train to Le Havre was the Old Man. He didn't want me to leave.

Midsummer 1933. New York. Gurdjieff has come once again. He stays with Fred Leighton, a wealthy friend and student of Orage.

September 1933. Hampstead Heath. Jessie gives birth to a daughter, Ann.

September 1933. New York. Rom Landau interviews Gurdjieff for the book he is writing, *God Is My Adventure.* Gurdjieff offers him a cigarette. Landau thanks him but says he does not smoke. Gurdjieff keeps insisting. Gurdjieff, he feels, is trying to hypnotize him. Landau says he was not easily influenced by "telepathic" enticement, was not a good medium and no doctor or hypnotist has ever succeeded in hypnotizing him. Intentionally, he avoided Gurdjieff's eyes, looking at and talking to a student who was present. Suddenly Landau notices:

> I began to feel very queer. I was beginning to feel a distinct weakness in the lower parts of my body, from the navel downwards, and mainly in the legs. This feeling grew steadily every second. After about twenty or thirty seconds it became so strong that I knew I should hardly be able to get up and walk out of the room.... The feeling inside my stomach was one of acute nervousness, amounting almost to physical pain and fear.... My legs were suffering from the sensation similar to that which people experience before a trial at court, an examination, or a visit to the dentist.

Landau concentrates more and more on the student and after a couple of minutes he says "I had definitely left Gurdjieff's 'magic circle.'"

The interview goes nowhere. At the end Gurdjieff gives him a copy of *The Herald of Coming Good*.

Returning to his hotel room, Landau has a strong desire to wash his hands. "I washed them in very hot water for about five minutes, and then felt better." He then picked up *Herald*.

> The little book is an amazing publication. It gave you in many instances the impression of the work of a man who was no longer sane. And yet it was impossible to sweep aside Gurdjieff's statements as the self-adulation of an insane mind.... The style itself exhibited the same signs of strangeness, amounting almost to insanity, that were manifest in the subject matter. Reading the *Herald* was like the progress of a cart over cobblestones. Most sentences ran on endlessly. The first sentence contained no fewer than two hundred and eighty-four words.

Back in London and still perplexed, Landau seeks out a former follower of Gurdjieff's. Landau's account does not surprise him at all. He tells him:

> Even to me certain things about Gurdjieff were always inexplicable as they must be to anybody unaccustomed to his wanton methods. And yet he has brought me — and many other people — nearer to the truth than anybody else.... You would be wrong to judge his conduct according to ordinary human standards. There seems to be a richness within Gurdjieff which allows him to do things that would be wrong for our own limited selves. In a way he reminds me of the god Shiva, you know

the destroyer-god of the god-trinity, the god of many functions, the lord of the spirits of music—and, don't forget, the god of dancing.

Autumn 1933. Berlin, Germany. Hitler chooses Albert Speer as his architect. Two years before, Speer heard Hitler speak and joined the Nazi Party. "After years of frustrated efforts," he says, "I was wild to accomplish things—and twenty-eight years old. For the commission to do a great building, I would have sold my soul like Faust. Now I had found my Mephistopheles. He seemed no less engaging than Goethe's." Speer went on to design many buildings, as well as creating the dramatic lighting effect—deemed "a cathedral of ice"—at the Nazi Party rally in Nuremberg. Speer would later rise to the position of Minister of Armaments and War Production, where his technical ability and organizational mastery excelled.

Winter 1933. New York. The problems with Orage and the Prieuré appear to have taken their toll. Gurdjieff looks terrible and has put on a great deal of weight. His *Herald of Coming Good* is misunderstood.

Early 1934. New York. Gurdjieff normally rises at 6–7 a.m. and goes to Childs Restaurant in the Hecksher Building, what he calls his "New York office." According to one witness, "He had grown fat. He looked untidy; time had turned his long, black ringmaster's moustache to grey; but he was unmistakably a personage, and the old, arrogant, undaunted look shone forth from his eyes."

1934. New York. Daly King was asked by Orage to lead a group early on. Among the students are Louise Blinken and William Welch. She had been in an Orage group from the late 1920s. She met Welch at a New York ad agency where they both worked. She and Welch will later marry. It was through her that he was introduced into the Work. Welch later becomes a medical doctor and will be at Gurdjieff's bedside at his death 1949. Welch sees King as one "who considered himself a scientist and who had ample training in that regard, who was at heart a romantic, a lovable, pugnacious, well-to-do semidropout from the world of conventional ideas."

3 March 1934. Leysin, Switzerland. At sixty years of age, Alexander Gustav Salzmann dies of tuberculosis. Earlier, living alone in a hotel in Fontainebleau, with Gurdjieff refusing to visit him, he had gathered all his strength and sought Gurdjieff out at the Café Henri IV. To a student sitting nearby, who has brought him halvah and other delicacies, smuggled from the Prieuré, Gurdjieff is "not very kind" to him.[23]

---

23. Why did de Salzmann leave Gurdjieff? Because Gurdjieff had impregnated his wife Jeanne? Gurdjieff had done the same with Dr. Stjoernval's wife and he had stayed. So was this a test from Gurdjieff's point of view of his seriousness?

1934. Sèvres, France. Madame de Salzmann, who has assisted her husband with the group, moves the meetings to Sèvres. The group will eventually include, besides René Daumal and his companion Vera Milanova, the Orientalist Philippe Lavastine, his wife Nathalie (Madame de Salzmann's daughter, nicknamed "Boussique"), Henri Tracol and his wife, Henriette Lannes, René Zuber and Luc Dietrich.

2 April 1934. New York. Gurdjieff fulfills his three will-tasks. "First," he says, "'puffed' three small booklets into ten substantial volumes. Second, not only understood from all sides different deep-rooted minutiae of the common psyche of man, suspected by me and intriguing me all my life.... Third, my health is now in such condition that I not only, as you may see, live and write such an already ultra-fantastic book, but intend to outlive all my past, present and future enemies."

Spring 1934. New York City. Jean Toomer meets Marjorie Content, the daughter of Harry Content, a wealthy stockbroker. She was a former partner with Jessie Dwight in the Sunwise Turn Bookshop. Marjorie has been married three times previously, the second to avant-garde editor and publisher Harold A. Loeb, best known as Hemingway's model for Robert Cohen in his *The Sun Also Rises*. A photographer and actress and friend of the painter Georgia O'Keefe, Marjorie Content is familiar with Toomer's writing but has no use for Gurdjieff or his teaching. In Toomer she sees someone who "seemed able to see inside me. Seemed to know things about me that I didn't think anybody knew." To win her, Toomer acts as though he is no longer interested in Gurdjieff. Later, Toomer sees Gurdjieff about his impending marriage to her.

Says Fritz Peters, who observed from the Prieuré days onward: "Gurdjieff had an unbelievable (unless you've seen it) awareness of other people. It was nothing so limited as mind-reading or thought-transference. He seemed to know so much about the human processes, about the underlying logic in man, that he was conscious of everything that took place within any human being he happened to observe. It is the same kind of faculty that an occasional highly trained psychiatrist seems to have to a limited degree. Gurdjieff had it to an enormous degree."

14 June 1934. New York. A notice appears in today's *New York Times*: Wallet, pigskin, containing passport, papers, money. George Gurdjieff, 333 West 56th (Apt. H). Reward. COlumbus 5-4956.

30 June 1934. Berlin. Consolidating his power, Hitler orders his chief rival Ernst Röhm, head of the SA (the Brownshirts), and one hundred and fifty of its leaders shot.

Summer 1934. Train from New York to Chicago. Learning that Fritz Peters plans to go to Chicago for a vacation, Gurdjieff decides to go with him and visit the Chicago group. Gurdjieff suggests they take the midnight train. Peters arrives at Gurdjieff's apartment early that evening, and finds Gurdjieff has yet to pack. Leaving the apartment well after eleven they arrive at Penn Station with only ten minutes to spare. Gurdjieff has Peters hold up the train's departure while he bids his New York followers good-bye. "Gurdjieff did not manage to complete his urgent farewells," Peters says sarcastically, "until the train was actually moving and I had to push him through the door of the last car with his six or seven pieces of luggage." With their sleeping berths thirteen cars ahead, it takes forty-five minutes to make their way, luggage and all, through the cars. All the while, Gurdjieff's noisy lamentations about Peters' rude treatment angers the sleeping passengers.

Finally in their seats, the exhausted Peters becomes furious when Gurdjieff refuses to go to bed. Instead he eats, drinks and smokes, still complaining, all in very loud tones, about the shoddy treatment that he, a very important man, is receiving. Peters, in a fit, says he wants to get off the train and away from him. Gurdjieff, with wide-eyed innocence, says he doesn't understand his anger—he "had never imagined that Peters, his only friend, would talk to him in this way, and quite literally, desert him." En route many like episodes follow that annoy, irritate and offend both passengers and Peters. Each time Gurdjieff apologizes profusely then creates new ways to agitate.

At dinner the next evening with his Chicago followers, Gurdjieff publicly praises each follower but berates Peters for how horribly he had treated him. After about an hour of public humiliation Peters bursts into some four-letter words and leaves in disgust.

Peters realizes later that what he called "the nightmare journey" with Gurdjieff has served to "force me out of the pattern of hero-worship which had unconsciously formed in me in relation to him."

22 July 1934. Taliesin. Gurdjieff visits. It has been ten years since Olgivanna and her daughter, Svetlana, last saw him and the first time Frank Lloyd Wright will meet him. Gurdjieff quickly enters into activities, cooking, playing his harmonium, reading from *Beelzebub's Tales,* and discussing Gothic architecture with Wright. Svetlana saw him as "strange, kindly at times, ferocious and violent at other times." She says, "He treats us all like guinea pigs in his laboratory experimenting to see reactions set in." One evening after a reading, Wright, putting himself on a par with Gurdjieff, announces, "Well, Mr. Gurdjieff, this is very interesting. I think I'll send some young people to you in Paris. Then they can come back to me and I'll finish them off." Gurdjieff, furious, shoots back—"You finish! You are idiot. . . . No, you begin, I finish!" With that, whatever thoughts of Taliesin being a center for his teaching went up in flames.

2 August 1934. Berlin. President von Hindenburg dies. Hitler, moving swiftly, abolishes the office of President and combines its power with his own as Chancellor.

20 August 1934. London. In response to Gurdjieff sending him *Herald* to revise, Orage answered: "Dear Mr. Gurdjieff: I've found very little to revise, in view of your unique style; but I have, at least, read every word with care. Unfortunately, 10 pages were missing—from 22 to 32. With my good wishes for your work. Yours sincerely, A. R. Orage."

26 August 1934. Madison, Wisconsin. Though he was absolutely against Gurdjieff creating a center at Taliesin, Frank Lloyd Wright was impressed with Gurdjieff. A long article by Wright appears in the local newspaper, the *Capitol Times*, that begins: "Real men who are real forces for an organic culture of the individual today are rare. I venture to say one might count them on the fingers of one hand with the thumb to spare—unless the thumb were to go to George Gurdjieff of the Prieuré at Fontainebleau, France, and spare the little finger."[24]

1 September 1934. Taos, New Mexico. Jean Toomer and Marjorie Content marry. The painter Georgia O'Keefe, Toomer's lover the year before and a friend of Marjorie's, attends the wedding. What he has been searching for with women, he says, is "a woman who would satisfy all of my needs for love and companionship and at the same time make no unreasonable demands on my time, energies and other interests." He believed this wish "was expressive of the highest ideal of the man-woman relationship."

Late in the year they buy a large farm outside Mechanicsville in Bucks County, Pennsylvania, a center of Quaker activity, about an hour and a half's drive from their home in Greenwich Village. Toomer believes it is the ideal site for the Gurdjieff-like institute he envisions creating, though he has led Marjorie to believe he is no longer interested in the Work.

September 1934. New York. Gurdjieff returns from Taliesin and stays with Fred Leighton who reports that saying "life is hectic is putting it mildly," adding that while Gurdjieff was napping on the sofa two burglars entered the apartment, awakening Gurdjieff who knocked both men unconscious and dragged their bodies out into the hallway, and then went back to sleep on the sofa.

Autumn 1934. Gurdjieff calls in all copies of *The Herald of Coming Good*.

October 1934. London. Nott has a strong feeling that something serious

---

24. See Essay, "Gurdjeef at Taliesin."

is about to happen to Orage. He was sitting with Orage at the A.B.C. café in Chancery Lane when he saw a pale yellow light around Orage's whole head and body. A week before Orage's talk on Social Credit the two are sauntering up Chancery Lane, as they often did, and are speaking of life at the Prieuré when Orage stops and declares in a tone of complete conviction—"You know, I thank God every day of my life that I met Gurdjieff."

5 November 1934. London. Orage gives a speech over the radio on Social Credit. At one point, he pauses for a long time. After the program he says he had not known how clearly the mind can work with severe pain under the breastbone. The next morning when Jessie enters his study she finds him dead.

6 November 1934. Childs Restaurant, New York. Gurdjieff is called to the telephone. The operator has a telegram from Nott in London—Orage has died.

"How you say it in your country?" asks Gurdjieff to the person alongside him who is helping to translate *Beelzebub's Tales*—"May his soul reach the Kingdom of Heaven."

Then Gurdjieff wipes tears from his eyes with his fists.

"This man...my brother," he says.[25]

Just before Nott's telegram, in what Gurdjieff calls a "noticeable coincidence," he has been explaining the difference between the words *voluntary* and *intentional* in the translated text, as the first word has been substituted for the second.

Gurdjieff recalls that this very night exactly seven years before he had dictated a letter to Orage that spoke about suffering and the difference between voluntary and intentional suffering, as well as about "noticeable coincidences."

Orage at that time, says Gurdjieff, "was considered to be, and indeed was, the most important leader in the dissemination of my ideas in the whole northern part of North America." Gurdjieff had advised him to regulate his health by means of intentional suffering "in a form corresponding to his individuality and the condition of his ordinary life." But this Orage would not do.

Gurdjieff must be remembering Orage's great thirst for the truth that was his in the early days, that indomitable desire that was direly tested, as a sixty-two-year-old man with an overweight body forced it all those long days to dig ditch after ditch at the Prieuré. He must have remembered, too, his bright and electric mind, his great warmth and ease with people, and, yes, that sense of humor, that wonderful dry English sense of humor.

He has a letter sent out to all of Orage's students:

> I have just now learned of the death of Mr. Orage, who was for many

---

25. Of no other did Gurdjieff say this except Soloviev.

years your guide and teacher and my inner world essence friend. I invite you to attend a meeting, to pay homage to him and to speak in his memory, on Friday evening, November 9th, at 9 o'clock, in Miss Bentley's studio in Carnegie Hall, at which time, likewise, will be played some of his favorite music and some of those pieces dedicated to him which were composed by me while he was at the Prieuré.

G. Gurdjieff

Later that morning—seven years after the shock of recognizing that *Beelzebub's Tales* was unreadable and had to be rewritten—he begins to write *All and Everything*'s third and final series, *Life Is Real Only Then, When "I Am."*

Yet such was the shock of Orage's death that for two months Gurdjieff says, "in spite of my constant wish, and constant efforts, I was not able to add a single word to what I had written up to half past eleven that morning."

12 November 1934. Hampstead, England. Orage is buried in the churchyard of Old Hampstead Church. On the stone slab covering his grave is a carved enneagram bordered by Krishna's words to Arjuna from the *Gita*, "You grieve for those for whom you should not grieve...."

Of Orage, his longtime friend, Professor Denis Saurat said:

> Orage was a great man who never succeeded in expressing himself, either in life or in letters. He never succeeded because he never came to a clear understanding of himself—that is to say, he never came to a clear understanding of what he wanted.... Of Orage the man much has been written already, for many loved him. To my mind, his chief trait was an unexampled generosity of heart and mind. I have never known him to be bitter in his soul—he was a man who tempted many into betraying him; and also many more played him false on their own initiative—but he found good things to say even of those who had betrayed him.... He tried several Masters. His first attempt was with Nietzsche; but Orage was too like Nietzsche to be a good Nietzschean.... So Orage just kept a Nietzschean veneer all his life, and next betook himself to theosophy and the pretended East from which he never quite came back: to Buddhism, the very opposite of Nietzsche.... Gurdjieff came and took away Orage in 1922. Gurdjieff was Nietzsche *plus* the Buddha: his theory of immortality was that only a few men possess a germ of an immortal soul [all do but few develop it]; and that even those few need the help of a Master, to educate the germ and acquire a really immortal soul: Nietzsche's supermen trained by the Buddha.... Orage put all his great capacity for propaganda at Gurdjieff's service; and years of his life and much of his

strength went into that service; for Gurdjieff was a hard taskmaster. And in the end Orage failed; even as he had failed with Nietzsche, or Annie Besant. . . . A series of failures? No. Orage's life was not a failure, but a series of adventures.

15 November 1934. The New English Weekly. Among those who wrote remembrances of Orage was one of his oldest friends, Holbrook Jackson. Speaking of Orage's external demeanor as "dominant without being dominating," he went on to write:

> I first met Orage in 1901. He was in his late twenties, and restive under the thrall of elementary school teaching, for although he was a born teacher, his setting under the Leeds educational authority was as incongruous as that of Swinburne at Eton, or Shelley at Oxford. . . . Groups formed about him automatically. At one time for the reading and exposition of Plato. At another of Blavatsky. His interpretation of the *Secret Doctrine* and *Isis Unveiled* fluttered the dovecotes of Theosophy. There were excursions also into the *Upanishads* and the *Bhagavat-Gita*. . . . Then came Nietzsche. That was my fault. Orage went over the top and so did the group. We all developed supermania. He wanted a Nietzsche circle in which Plato and Blavatsky, Fabianism and Hinduism, Shaw and Wells and Edward Carpenter should be blended, with Nietzsche as the catalytic. An exciting brew. . . ."

Late 1934. Mill House, Mechanicsville, Pennsylvania. At first, Toomer and his new wife pay visits from the Mill House to their townhouse just above New York's Greenwich Village, but only for weekends. But by the spring of 1935 they will move permanently to the Mill House in Bucks County, lying about halfway between Philadelphia and New Hope, Pennsylvania, an artist colony.

With their houseguests and the flow of weekend visitors, Toomer soon takes the role of the teacher. Often there are a dozen or so people sitting around the dinner table or in a circle around him. Remembers Gorham Munson, who was from time to time a houseguest, "Jean as the host at Mechanicsville was often embarrassing to me. . . . He would actually go into broken English, too, you know, and he would tear loaves of bread apart. He would use bad, vulgar language at times. He would try to shock people by going into these seemingly rambling discourses. He was all imitative of Gurdjieff and bad, bad, bad imitation."

In the end he never manages to establish a Gurdjieff-like institute or permanent commune. Through it all Marjorie, who had paid off all Toomer's numerous debts, most incurred because of his Gurdjieff activities, regarded Gurdjieff "suspiciously as a fraud and a swindler." Although Toomer continued his womanizing, a friend says, "Marjorie didn't want to give up on the marriage. She was very conscious of her own marital failures and determined to stick with it this time around."

At some point Toomer and Marjorie begin to attend meetings of the Religious Society of Friends, a Quaker group. He and his wife become very involved and in time he gives lectures and writes pamphlets for them. His stomach ailments, which he has suffered now and then throughout his life, increase. He has vision problems that at times necessitate his wearing a patch over one eye. He begins drinking.

6 January 1935. New York. Gurdjieff resumes the writing of the *Third Series*.

1935. Lyne Place. Uspenskii now has over one thousand pupils. Maurice Nicoll has a group of over a hundred. The Gurdjieff group in London has perhaps twelve people. With Gurdjieff in Paris there are only a few Americans, English and Russians. In New York, no more than twenty.

January 1935. New York. Toomer goes to Childs restaurant to see Gurdjieff. "He was in a bad way. His health was poor. He looked it, liverish, looked as if he had been drawn through a mill, laboring under a heavy strain, physically, and mentally, and in every way." Gurdjieff again pressures him for money,[26] saying he really needs it this time.

Says Toomer:

> My mind flashed over subsequent happenings, the sure result of which was that I felt a great relief when I left New York and thus left him. To me he seemed like a changed man, changed for the worse. I felt his work was dead. Whether dead or not, there was no place or function for me in it. It was a travesty and hollow mockery of the work I had entered in 1924 with all my heart. I would have nothing to do with what was going on at present. I would have something to do with future work — on the critical basis as if I were meeting him and his work for the first time, taking nothing for granted.

February 1935. New York. Gurdjieff has been staying with Fred Leighton. Jean Toomer visits and gives Gurdjieff $200. Gurdjieff invites him to lunch the following day. After lunch he invites Toomer to discuss business in "my office," which turns out to be the bathroom. He says he needs an additional $350. He is depending on Toomer. He could get the money elsewhere, but due to his policies about different people and aims he doesn't want to. He gives Toomer his essence-word

---

26. Every student thinks himself and his relationship with the teacher special. The demand for money, therefore, is usually painful and difficult not to identify with, as money is so associated with power, status, self-esteem and, hence, the false personality. Though Toomer's wife is quite wealthy, Gurdjieff's apparent 'venality' is, at the very least, distasteful and creates friction and doubts.

to pay him back in four months and to give him a place in his "future creations." Toomer is incredulous that once again Gurdjieff is putting the bite on him for money.

Says Toomer:

> We left the bathroom and took chairs in the main room, the typewriters pounding and clacking [typing *Beelzebub's Tales*]. We smoked and joked. I asked Gurdjieff certain questions about myself. He said I did not deserve to know. I asked, "If I do not deserve, then who does?" His reply was that nobody deserved. I asked [again], "Then for whom are you doing all this work?" [He replied] "I will live for coming generations. It is for them."
>
> Gurdjieff said some things which threw light on his apparently shameful conduct the past months. The gist of what he said was this. That in order to restore himself, particularly his body, it was necessary that he suffer. In order to suffer he had deliberately done things to people and created situations which would enter into his automatic processes and of themselves cause suffering and make him suffer whenever he remembered them.[27]
>
> This did somewhat explain the circumstances related by Leighton that throughout the "worst of it" Gurdjieff had treated him in much the same way as he had always treated him, never mistreating him.

The next day Gurdjieff tells him he is leaving. Toomer gives him another $200, a large sum in those days. Gurdjieff tries to get more.[28] Toomer says:

> What could be in the man's mind? Who and what was he? What were his purposes? What aims did he have for me, if any? What aims for the people of the world? Was I a mere tool? Was I not even that, so nothing from his point of view that he need not even consider the way he used or misused me? Was he the supreme egotist? Was he, as some claimed, insane? ... This is what is so awful about the situation with Gurdjieff. The situations themselves are always taxing—and you can arrive at no sure reconciliation or fixed understanding because for every fact there is a counter fact, for every reason a counter reason, for every bit of "bad" behavior another bit

---

27. Of course Gurdjieff's explanation could be taken as yet another ruse, an arch-clever way of justifying his mendacious and outrageous behavior. What mitigates against it is Gurdjieff's discovery of the special use of suffering—the intentional evoking of blame in others—so that by working to not identify with the anger-charged energy that blame engenders, new energy can be created and refined. As he wrote: "Although it is possible to attain any self-imposed aim, it can only be done exclusively through conscious suffering." See *Third Series*.

28. Webb, Moore and others judge Gurdjieff's actions as if he were an ordinary human being. Therefore, to them he is simply being venal. Gurdjieff's actions should be first seen from the highest possible level. Otherwise we diminish and level his unique being and understanding to that of our own. In so doing, we "psychologize" him and so dismiss him.

of "good" behavior, for every son-of-a-bitching thing a counter saintly thing.... Insane? He was in full possession of every one of his extraordinary faculties. Debauched and slovenly? Nothing of the sort. Afraid of the dark and being alone? It was ridiculous. Whatever he had gone through, the thing that showed plainly was a decided improvement in every respect.

Toomer asks Gurdjieff about his promise many years before that he would make him "ruler of Africa."

"Something went wrong," replies Gurdjieff, smiling.

Toomer presses him to elaborate—"How do you mean?"

"In the very beginning I counted you. You not as I counted."

"How do you mean?"

"You manifest differently at different times, different from what I expected. You not as I counted and I get angry."

"Angry? Why?"

"You not as I counted."

Toomer says, " I thought to myself: my psyche African, American and English, my body with every blood under the sun, my spirit and inner values Oriental, my body and outer aims Occidental, a democrat, an aristocrat, a feudal man, a modern man, my family of the South, I live in the North, what a crock of diverse elements, yet I hang together and am one, I behind the aspects, I through different worlds, I through lives and deaths, I."

He saw Gurdjieff only once after this and that was thirteen years later in December 1948.

9 April 1935. New York. Gurdjieff finishes the prologue to the *Third Series* and begins the chapter "The Inner and Outer World of Man."

10 April 1935. New York. Gurdjieff works and reworks the beginning of "The Inner and Outer World of Man." He becomes stuck when he comes to the expression "problem of the prolongation of human life," which he says among all the questions raised in the *Third Series* is "the basic question, or as one might say, the 'clue.'"

14 April 1935. New York. Gurdjieff buys the Russian newspaper *Rusky Golos*. He reads P. Mann's article, "The Problem of Old Age," and decides to use it in his chapter on "The Inner and Outer World of Man."

Early Spring 1935. Gaddesden. Nott visits Uspenskii for the first time. He finds he is not the forbidding philosopher he expected but a sympathetic person, "warm, friendly and easy to talk to." Madame Uspenskii he describes as small in stature but acting the "Grand Duchess," always maintaining a distance. She does most of the talking. The subject of Orage comes up and Madame Uspenskii, with characteristic directness, says, "There were many things that Mr. Orage did not understand or understood wrongly. Mr. Orage was too formatory for one thing."

Rejoins Nott: "I'm sure Orage would have agreed with you, but you had not seen him for ten years, and he had changed very much in that time. And you know, Gurdjieff himself once said that Mr. Uspenskii himself was too formatory."

Over time Nott and Uspenskii have many talks, with Uspenskii inviting him into his study and opening a bottle of wine. Gradually, Nott develops a real affection for him, though they are at polar extremes about a never-failing subject of discussion—Gurdjieff. Of whom Uspenskii would say:

> You know when Gurdjieff started his Institute in Paris I did everything I could for him. I raised money for him and sent him pupils, many of them influential people. When he bought the Prieuré I went there myself and Madame stayed for some time. But I found that he had changed from when I knew him in Russia. He was difficult in Essentuki and Constantinople but more so in Fontainebleau. His behavior had changed. He did many things I did not like, but it wasn't what he did that upset me, it was the stupid way he did them. He came to London to my group and made things very unpleasant for me. After this I saw that I must break with him, and I told my pupils that they would have to choose between going to Fontainebleau or working with me.

Uspenskii maintained that "Gurdjieff's mind never recovered from his accident."

"I can't accept that," Nott tells him. "We cannot judge Gurdjieff from our level. He lives from essence and, in a great measure, according to objective reason, and a person who lives thus can sometimes appear to our minds spoilt by wrong education and conditioning, as not normal. For me Gurdjieff represents objective sanity.... He lives the Teaching, while we talk about it."

"No," replies Uspenskii, "he lost contact with the source after Essentuki. His behavior goes contrary to his teaching. Then the accident. He drives a car as if he were riding a horse."

"I can't agree that he's lost contact with the source," declares Nott. "For me he is the source."[29]

Sometime after meeting Uspenskii, Nott is in Paris having lunch with Gurdjieff, who makes an unflattering remark about Uspenskii.

"Mr. Gurdjieff," says Nott, always loyal to his friends, "I like Uspenskii and I enjoy talking to him."

"Oh yes, Uspenskii very nice man to talk to and drink vodka with, but he is

---

29. Nott sees in Uspenskii's viewpoint about Gurdjieff an inflexibility that is characteristic of the Russian mentality, and "once they have adopted a mental attitude to a given situation they will stick to it, whatever the cost."

weak man,"[30] replies Gurdjieff.

Nott reflects on this and concludes that Uspenskii's weakness, as with most people, was his emotional center. It was undeveloped and therefore partial and subjective. "Emotionally," says Nott, "I never felt inferior to Uspenskii." But he wonders whether his own emotional center is too strong. He speaks about it to Gurdjieff who tells him—"A strong feeling center is a gift of God."[31]

6 May 1935. Washington, D.C. Gurdjieff has traveled from New York to meet with Senator Bronson Cutting, a Republican from New Mexico, who is interested in giving financial support to repurchase the Prieuré. Cutting is flying to Washington. On the way his plane crashes and he dies.

Several days later Gurdjieff instructs Paul Anderson to go to the Soviet Embassy to ask if he could return to Russia and teach. This isn't entirely surprising in that Gurdjieff had once said, "What started in Russia, finish in Russia."[32]

A day or so later the Soviets inform Gurdjieff that he may return, but only if he will accept work where he is assigned and agrees not to teach.

Midsummer 1935. Lyne Place, Virginia Water, England. Still retaining places at Gwendwr and Warwick Gardens, the Uspenskiis move from Little Gaddesden to Lyne Place, a lightly wooded, much larger country estate on one hundred acres of farmland. The large Regency mansion has the customary English garden, rhododendron walks, ancient trees, small ornamental lake and boathouse. A short walk from the mansion is the farm with barns, outbuildings, greenhouses, stables, pigsties, chicken coops and a walled vegetable garden. Beyond this lay the fields all enclosed by hedges. Lyne Place is not far from Windsor Castle, and only some twenty miles west of central London.

Bennett is allowed to go to Lyne Place but his wife, after one visit, is not. No reason is given.

And of course everywhere Uspenskii is, there are his cats as well. Cats fascinate him. He believes the cat knows and inhabits its body completely; it is aware

---

30. Gurdjieff here is likely referring to Uspenskii's refusal to allow Gurdjieff to work on his emotional center. Uspenskii's life shows he was a man of great integrity, character, and strength with everyone save Gurdjieff.

31. Uspenskii's formulation of Gurdjieff's teaching, as given in the Russian period, is in terms of the intellectual center. But it is just this center that Gurdjieff challenges in *Beelzebub's Tales*. It cannot begin to be understood unless the emotional center of the reader is evoked. Is this why Gurdjieff's *Legominism* is so little read and studied, even by many who practice the Work?

32. In none of the historical records does Gurdjieff make reference to this again. He did not have a high opinion of theosophy or Rudolph Steiner, but perhaps he believed, as Steiner did and as Maria Carlson maintains in her *No Religion Higher than Truth*, in "the importance of the Slavic folk soul as a spiritual bridge between the passive Orient and the active Occident. The religious thought of the Orient belongs to the past; the philosophical-scientific thought of the Occident belongs to the present; the Slavic soul will bridge the two and create a pathway to a spiritual future (in the sixth post-Atlantean age)."

of itself except when, say, a salmon appears. "Everything outside itself it takes for granted, as something given. To correct the outside world, to accommodate it to its own comfort, would never occur to a cat. Maybe this is so because a cat lives more in another world, the world of dreams and fantasies, than in this one."

For exercise, Uspenskii rides his favorite horse, Jingles, around the property. He sits atop an expensive Cossack saddle, a gift from a student, of which he is quite proud. From time to time targets are set up and he practices shooting. He is a crack shot but never shoots anything living. He is fond of Russian prints, a connoisseur of tea and, of course, vodka.

Uspenskii writes a series of five introductory lectures on the teaching which are later published as *The Psychology of Man's Possible Evolution*.

Gurdjieff has copies of *Herald* sent to all of Uspenskii's pupils. Uspenskii has it read to a group of his closest pupils. The general opinion is that it is "almost paranoiac." Uspenskii suggests that Gurdjieff had syphilis, perhaps. Pupils are instructed to hand in their copies and he has them destroyed.

Later, Gurdjieff repudiates *Herald*, calling in all copies.

Looking for a new home for his Institute, Gurdjieff makes another trip to America and asks Mabel Dodge Luhan for the New Mexico ranch she had volunteered eight years before. She refuses, still upset over the $15,000 loan she had given which remains unpaid.

Late Summer 1935. Paris. Gurdjieff is seen again in Paris,[33] taking a flat in the rue du Commandant Marchand.

September 1935. London. Rom Landau's *God Is My Adventure* is published. He gives a positive view of Uspenskii, a very negative one of Gurdjieff.

15 September 1935. Germany. Nuremberg Laws deprive Jews of German citizenship.

17 October 1935. Paris. At Gurdjieff's command, Jane Heap disbands her Montmartre women's group.[34]

---

33. Some, such as J. G. Bennett, believe that Gurdjieff returned to Central Asia between May and July of 1935. There is no evidence to support this. However, of all the years since 1921 when he left Constantinople for Europe, the years 1933–35 had to be the most difficult: the Prieuré lost; *The Herald of Coming Good* misunderstood and recalled; death of Orage; money sources dry up; Senator Cutting, interested in funding a new center in America, dies in a plane crash; Soviet visa all but denied. Gurdjieff then disappeared for three or so months.

34. Heap leaves for London the next day. Not accepted in an Uspenskii group, Heap starts a group of her own. Said Uspenskii, "Only a person who is completely normal as regards sex has any chance in the work. Any kind of 'originality,' strange tastes, strange desires, or, on the other hand, fears . . . must be destroyed from the beginning. Modern education and modern life create an

Georgi Ivanovitch Gurdjieff

18 October 1935. Café de la Paix, Paris. At noon Kathryn Hulme happens to come to the café,[35] sees Gurdjieff, and immediately goes to his table. Three years before, he had met her, but at first he does not remember her. When he does recall their meeting he invites her to sit down and have coffee with him. He talks to her about what he calls "the crayfish club" and how he shears people. "Do you want to be a candidate?" he asks. She does. He tells her it will cost six thousand francs ($400), but as they talk he reduces it to three thousand francs ($200). She agrees and he asks her to accompany him back to his hotel room. There, he asks her to read for him a new translation of his book in English. Afterward, he orders lunch. Later, he tells her they will have a crayfish dinner that night at Brasserie Excelsior. She can bring a friend, if she wishes. Hulme's companion Alice Rohrer, a wealthy milliner from San Francisco, is away, so she asks her friend Louise Davidson, but she won't go without Solita Solano.

At the brasserie Gurdjieff tells the three women, "Drink all you want but in half glasses." They go through a quart of Armagnac. At the end of the dinner, Gurdjieff pays and they leave for the Café de la Paix where he tells Kathryn and Solita they have "Jewish psyche." Solita, he says, is "combination Jewish and canary," and Kathryn is "combination Jewish and crocodile." To Louise he says, "You are sardine and wart. You know how sardine struggle to get back in water when left between sea and sand?" Louise asks, "But what is wart?' He does not reply. Instead he says, "I once knew priest who prayed for one."[36] Of himself—"I now am old idiot; both feet in galosh, moreover old Jewish. I need some church mouse again."[37]

He says he has an eleven o'clock appointment and must leave. When the other two women are out of earshot, he says to Kathryn—"You come back?" "I felt completely lost and stupid," she says. But she goes back and asks if she could reimburse him for dinner. She had borrowed money from the hotel patron. "How much you bring?" Gurdjieff asks. He takes the 500 francs she offers, and tells her, "I take this for you, not for me." He hails a cab and tells her he is going to take her to a place that will astonish her. "But you not show astonishment," he says, "you and me not show astonishment, only inside show astonishment." Kathryn feels

---

enormous number of sexual psychopaths. They have no chance at all in the work." See Uspenskii's "Sex and Evolution," *A New Model of the Universe.*

35. Did Gurdjieff intend to take over her group or is Hulme's coming to the café one of his "noticeable coincidences"? Later, Hulme writes to Heap in England, "When I waved you off two days ago I had no idea that the next step was toward Gurdjieff. You went at 10:17 and at noon, without knowing how it took charge of me, I was walking to the Café de la Paix." Given Hulme's notes, her meeting him in the Café de la Paix looks to be an accident. Given his views on the third sex, was he really interested in teaching lesbians? Or were they the "new guinea pigs" for his experiments? Or was this something else?

36. A year later he says "wart" was not the right word. It was "carbuncle."

37. This apparently is Gurdjieff's way of saying that he needs to become more humble.

paralyzed—"I didn't know if I was riding to doom or what." At the Café Select they leave the cab and walk down Montparnasse. He tells her, "You funny person, I not understand you." Before one house he says, "No, that place too strong for you, we go other place." He stops before a well-known hot spot and says, "Nice house, new house."

"The house was packed with men and naked girls dancing together with only a twist of silk about the loins," says Kathryn. "He was watching me in his way, but I truly was not shocked or astonished; I've seen things in my time and felt nothing inside which would have told itself to him."

They take a small table. Naked girls brush their buttocks past their table, the men nearby reaching out to pet them. Gurdjieff watches everything. Kathryn says, "I've never felt so safe or so secure in all my life."

At one point he asks, "What is your taste? What girl would you pick if you were a man?"

"They all look alike to me, smell alike."

"Choose," he says. "Which one?"

Kathryn, in anguish, finally takes their two Perrier bottles and stands them side-by-side. "It's as if you ask me to choose which bottle, both are the same."

He likes that and smiles and points to his bottle.

"But that have more liquid," he says.

He points to the hostesses dressed in black silk dresses. "If you man and want for animal purpose, you choose any girl on the floor and can have for thirty francs, *but* if you choose hostess she cost fifty francs."

He lets a long time pass. Then he suddenly turns to her and says—"Suppose, example, you out there, no clothes, I here; I choose you, why? Because I see—he puts his hands over his eyes and gestures inward—"I see something else."

He pays the bill and they leave.

He says, "You funny, you not astonished?"

"No," she says.

22 October 1935. l'Écrévisse Restaurant. Gurdjieff and the three women have dinner together and then go to the Hotel Bonaparte, 36 rue Bonaparte, where Kathryn has rented a room and Solita lives. The Bonaparte, though a walk-up hotel on a narrow street on the Left Bank, is well situated. It is near the Seine and opposite the Louvre, and not far from the cafés Deux Magots and Flore. Though five stories tall, it is only two rooms wide, having two on the street side, two on courtside. "A dwarf hotel," Solita calls it. She has lived there for many years with her longtime companion *The New Yorker* writer Janet Flanner. Since Solita and Janet's four permanent rooms are on the fourth floor (the fifth is a communal bathroom), and Kathryn's room is on the second floor, Gurdjieff and the women go to her room to read a chapter of *Beelzebub's Tales*. They read until 2 a.m.

23 October 1935. Fontainebleau. Gurdjieff and the women take the train to his brother Dmitri's house. He has them read the book aloud all the way. At one point, he takes a metal rod from his pocket. He says it is a wand that has a core of platinum. He says he could sell it for millions of francs, if he wished. Once at the house, he shows a machine he has invented. It looks like a radio.[38] He has the women approach one by one. He moves the wand over the machine and it emits music, moans, buzzes or shrieks, changing with each person's vibrations. They have lunch before returning to Paris. He gives Toasts to the Idiots. He gets angry if they don't remember it. Only Solita writes them down.[39]

No one has any money for l'Écrévisse, so they eat dinner at a small Greek restaurant near the Bonaparte. Gurdjieff eats with relish. He says, "First good eating I had since yesterday morning when all upper teeth pulled out." The upper plate that was put in did not exactly fit.

He tells the women he is planning to form a group with them. He tells them: "You very dirty but have something good — many people not got — very special."[40]

Solita begins to cry.

"Must not cry."

"But I *must*."

"Must," Gurdjieff says, "but must not."

"I'm too old [to change], it's too late," says Solita, now forty-seven years old.

"Never too late, but now twice as hard."

Later, he laughs at Solita, telling her, "You have screw loose."

They return to the Bonaparte and read until midnight when Janet Flanner comes down from upstairs to meet Gurdjieff. Solita introduces her — "Old friend, we live here ten years."[41]

---

38. Could the "radio" be based on the Russian Léon Theremin's Etherphone, a high frequency oscillator that originally measured dielectric constant gases with high precision, but was then modified as a motion detector by adding circuitry to generate audio tone impressions registered by a horizontal volume antenna? Theremin gave public performances in 1928 in New York. As Gurdjieff was in New York in January 1929, they could have met then. Also, Hanna Smith, a Gurdjieff student, who attended movements demonstrations at the Prieuré and had acquired an Etherphone in 1927 may have told him or Orage about it. See the documentary video, *Theremin: An Electronic Odyssey*.

39. The toasts rarely go beyond the first four idiots: Ordinary, Super (or Superior), Arch and Hopeless. See Essay, "The Science of Idiotism."

40. In perhaps a contradiction to this, in her notes Solita writes: "Katie told Janet it's plain he feels something special for me. Last night he told the others that I had *will*. I feel so right with him. He hasn't told me yet what he promised to once I was alone with him—just said, 'You very dirty but got something very good—many people not got—very special.'" So is what he said for Solita alone, or is he just reemphasizing this quality of being "very special" to her? In her notes, Solita or someone wrote in pencil above the typing "to SS."

41. In Djuna Barnes' *Ladies Almanack*, a bawdy satire of the American heiress Natalie Barney's literary and lesbian salon, Janet and Solita were named "Nip and Tuck." Barney was referred to as the "Amazon."

"Oh," says Gurdjieff, "sometimes such friendship very bad, great hate comes out, then love, then more hate."

25 October 1935. l' Écrévisse. Gurdjieff and the women dine again at "Madame Crayfish," as he calls the restaurant. He tells Solita, "You are lopsided." Twice when he offers to buy Kathryn and Louise a drink he says to her—"Except you. You cannot have this time." Then he tells her, "I see all your quintessence." Solita and he walk alone back to the hotel for the reading.

"You wonder why I am so good to you?" he asks at one point.

"Yes. Why?" Solita's intense blue eyes sparkle.

"I not tell you yet," and he smiled under the street light like a father. "Is it bad for you that I am so good to you?"

"No, I am sure not."

"I think so too."

Tonight, they read about some of his personal life, the two beings nearest him whom he really loved, his mother and his wife, their deaths, how they sat, he between them, on a bench in the garden, his emotions when they would understandingly whisper together behind his back, how he would see them coming down the path together, one bent with age, the other, once so beautiful she won a beauty contest from Lina Cavalieri[42] in Russia, now bent and yellow with her disease (cancer).

All of this translated with such perfection that Solita weeps. Gurdjieff then speaks about death and the treatment afterward of the dead. Gurdjieff then tells the women he had been four times through the initiate mysteries of Egypt."[43]

Elaine, a friend of Krokodeel's, reads for the first time. At one point, she looks over her shoulder at Solita as if to ask, "How am I doing?" Gurdjieff immediately sees that Solita is the woman's monitor. He says to her, "Ha, you look at her with left eye." Elaine says to Solita, "Left shoulder wing angel." Kathryn says, "Oh, that very bad." Gurdjieff says quietly to Kathryn, "No, not always bad—often very good."

During the reading, he interjects: "Ah, human nature. You give something to someone. First time, he prostrates himself; second time, he kisses your hand;

---

42. Lina Cavalieri (25 December 1874–7 February 1944), an Italian operatic soprano known for her grace and beauty, frequently referred to as the "world's most beautiful woman." She starred opposite Enrico Caruso in the opera *Fedora* in Paris before debuting with it at the Metropolitan Opera in 1906. Her first marriage was to the Russian Prince Alexander Bariatinsky. Returning to Europe, she became a much-loved star in pre-Revolutionary St. Petersburg.

43. This is the first and only specific reference he makes to initiation. It helps in substantiating what Uspenskii reports Gurdjieff saying there being in Egypt "a Christianity before Christ." See *Search*, 302. Odd that this has been overlooked or undervalued by Bennett and others who believe that the origin of the teaching Gurdjieff brings is from Central Asia. Certainly elements of the Egyptian teaching—this from pre-historic Egypt—migrated northward over time and so there are similarities, but the origin is Egypt, brought there, as it says in *Beelzebub's Tales*, by surviving members of the Society of Akhaldans ("Khaldan" means "moon," and "A" means "against").

third time, he gets familiar; fourth time, he merely nods at you; the fifth time he insults you because not enough what you give; and in the end he sues you."

Solita writes to Margaret and Georgette, "He talks all the time and teaches in every sentence only I don't always know what he means. But what a vibration in the air! You learn something just from feeling near him."

27 October 1935. La Coupole. Solita, Louise, Kathryn and Elaine meet Gurdjieff at La Coupole on Sunday afternoon at one o'clock. He suggests they buy food and go back to Kathryn's room.

"He brings a great Sunday spread—caviar, smoked salmon, meat cutlets, Latvian sausage, calves' feet in jelly (a favorite weekly dish at the Prieuré, he tells us), black bread, cheese, olives and pickles, and a bottle of vodka. There is also a small jar of white mustard and one of horseradish which he mixes together in a cup." Gurdjieff waves the women to the table. He tells Solita to begin toasts.

Afterward, he tells her she is a slave to functions and a particular function but he does not name it. "Tonight," he tells her, "I make arise on you one flea—which bite, yes? (To the others.) "And she has had those fleas always—sometime I make arise all her fleas, and all bite, and she never sleep again."

Solita asks a mental question and thunderbolts fall.

"Now you know your illness, your sickness. It is curiosity—American curiosity. Always you want to know more and more without understanding what already I have said to you. For that you will die shit!"[44]

Solita cries.

"You angry?"

"No, it's true."

Miss Elizabeth Gordon, prim and tweedy, comes for the reading. Gurdjieff tells her she has not much time left. It is now or never. She must do something special now. "If you do not, shit you have been, shit you are and shit you will perish, like dog."

Then he announces:

> Miss Gordon will be like Mother Superior for you and you must treat her as such. Now all listen carefully to what I tell. Here is a special exercise, first of seven, and tomorrow Miss Gordon must bring seven questions about this. Think of legs and try to imagine emanations that flow from them. Then try to think you are holding them back so they will not escape. To do this you must remember yourself. This is the beginning, to

---

44. Kathryn says that she and Solita, in taking notes of their experiences with Gurdjieff, substitute *merde* for shit, the word he used. "This word," she says, "so commonly on the tongues of Paris cab drivers, did not convey the horrifying final-waste, end-of-everything sense of its English equivalent as Gurdjieff used it." As this softens its impact and gives a false impression, the word has been changed to what Gurdjieff actually said.

be not dog but part of God. Now Miss Gordon, by telling this I have made myself an obligation to you and I must be your slave, at your service any moment you command me. But if you not do, I have obligation to stop.[45]

Then he talked about emanations of all bodies. "We emanate. This is active function, a dirty process, as dirty as making shit. But sometimes there can be something else but dirt in emanations."
Solita waits to hear what else . . .
"No," says Gurdjieff. "That I not tell."
He goes on then. "The earth emanates. The atmosphere around planet is its emanations." He looks at Solita, hanging breathless in mid-air — "Many more things like this I know but can never tell."
He says curiosity about all this unknown knowledge "Stinks."
He looks at Elaine and tells her: "Two things I like about you — three things I hate." Later, "Sometimes God is unique shit."
Gurdjieff tells the women to work with attention, to accumulate emanations, keep some for oneself, not let all flow out. He raises his hand, index finger pointing up in the teaching pose, gravely evocative, and says:

> This is the beginning. When I tell you this you can do, it makes tonight your biggest moment in life — even more important for you than your birth. Why? . . . because you are born like dog. After tonight you have possibility to die like part of God, you have such responsibility because I tell you this. Your leg . . . emanations go out. Now you think, not all emanations go out of the leg, you save some of them, you accumulate emanations in your leg, not letting all go out. Let some go for necessary reasons, but you accumulate some also.

28 October 1935. Hotel Bonaparte. After dinner at Madame Crayfish, the women return to the hotel. The women sit in a circle around Gurdjieff. Miss Gordon reports on the exercise.
"Where must center of gravity lie, in mind or in leg?" she asks, as she had come to a stop doing the exercise.
Answers Gurdjieff:

> Because too much mind; instead must have attention, association of mind with association of feeling. Attention is the association of mind with association of feeling. Memory working together with sense makes

---

45. Both Solita and Kathryn keep notes of the meetings and personal times with Gurdjieff. Kathryn's are somewhat different but essentially the same, though she doesn't report Miss Gordon being made Mother Superior and that Gurdjieff tells only Gordon to do the exercise. Sometimes dates are different but close to one another.

attention. Important to remember that sense has two meanings—in English there are not two words for it, but it is something like Feeling and Sense, feeling in the solar plexus region and sense in the spinal cord. Feeling has two centers, the solar plexus and spinal cord. Be simple like a monk. Do with Faith, not Knowing [with head] but *sure*-ing [solar plexus region]. Do it when not in life. Lying in bed, sitting in chair. Do not do with psychopathic attention—mental center attention only. Do with totality of memory-sense attention. Keep muscles relaxed. Emanations accumulate and then crystallize. Then there is force. The leg exercise is for the mentation of the inner world. Just as the physical presence of man can arise, so can the soul world of man arise. Between the physical world of man and the soul world there is an intermediate state—the astral body. When the emanations are accumulated, they crystallize and there will be a force that does not pass from you like water.

"How can one know which is sense brain [spinal brain] and which is feeling brain [solar plexus brain]?" Miss Gordon asks.

"Can know that when come to you those stops—maybe you have no spinal brain working at this task—and you can know that by the absence of feeling in the spinal cord." He pauses and reminds everyone, "Memory working together with sense, makes attention."

"How long should I do this exercise? Should one force oneself to do it long, without stopping?"

Gurdjieff shakes his head.

"One third of Man's waking state must be active," he says slowly, "for active mentation, or active in the sense that the real I functions. One third must be actively relaxed; one third must be automatic. You can do this exercise at any time. Example, you go to your kitchen ... you know you have twelve minutes there; then you give four minutes to this exercise. Or, comes a time when you know you have three hours free, know *for sure* you have these three hours; then you give one hour to the exercise."

He adds: "You can *never* stop associations. As long as you breathe, there are associations; these are automatic. Therefore, in this task, you must not try to stop them; let associations flow but *not be active*. With *other* part of mind you work at the new task, and this is active. Pretty soon you find you have beginnings of a new kind of brain—a new one for this kind of mentation. And then that other one becomes entirely passive. Very important that you know the body as a whole, for this work, very important ..."

A look of deep reflection passes over Gurdjieff's face and his voice drops to a rumble as if coming from a cave where an oracle resided.

"Man has three worlds," he says. "One—the outer world, world of impressions, of everything that happens outside us; two—inner world, world of the functioning of all our organs, the totality of organic functioning; and three—the Soul, that is, the world of the soul which was called by the ancients 'The World of Man.' Three worlds man has; this exercise is exercise for the inner world of man—mentation of inner world."

Silence. Then Gurdjieff slowly enunciates the phrase they had heard once before:

"*The arising of the presence of Man*—Just so, as physical presence arises, so can the Soul World of Man arise. Between the physical world—that is, the totality of the physical presence of Man, and the soul world, there is an intermediate world, the astral state."

He nods to Miss Gordon to continue with her questions.

She folds her hands in her lap, looks at them for a moment, then directly looks at him. "Should one do this exercise when *in* life, or when sitting quietly alone?" she asks.

"First, at beginning," Gurdjieff answers, "you do it when *not* in life. When you lie in bed, for example, or sit at home in chair. Important not make mistake in the beginning, not to try it when occupied with outside life. Important to do it first when *outside of life*... then, when sure you are doing it right, do it *in life*. You can make mistakes in beginning by giving only psychopathic attention, only mental center attention—*not* the totality of memory-sense attention. Later, you must do in life, not like monks isolated from life. This must be a full thing."

Later he says that when you start accumulating emanations you find that there is a place in you for them, like the place in automobiles where power is accumulated. "When you have many emanations accumulated, you find that they will crystallize, then you have force. Not force that can go out of you like water, but emanations crystallized. Then can do many things with. And when do this it best to have all muscles relaxed. Weak. Have all muscles weak. *No* tension."

"How can one know which is sense brain and which is feeling brain?" Miss Gordon asks.

"Can know that when come to you those stops—maybe you have no spinal brain working at this task and you can know that by the absence of feeling in the spinal cord."

He repeats again, "Memory working together with sense, makes attention. Important—sense have two meanings—in English no two words—but is something like feeling and sense—feeling the solar plexus region and sense in spinal cord."

Then he speaks about proximity which has to do with atmospheres of the emanations of people physically close together. "I helpless," he says. "You three so close—your emanations *keel* me almost."

When people live in close proximity, he says, their emanations merge and find corresponding emanations in others. Their emanations fuse like the colors of the spectrum and corresponding emanations find one another and mix.

He says to Louise, "You are psychic weak." To Kathryn, "You are like cow who comes home at night and stares at new painted barn door. Not know home because was just painted." To Solita, "I have thought of seven things about you and one I tell now. You have eye of suffering wolf. Only eye, very special thing. I have seen wolf, female wolf, attacked by herd, hungry, tired, bitten; in agony they turn on me, like look in your eye."

Gurdjieff tells them "dirty" means the result of mixed bloods. So does "Jewish" when it doesn't mean stingy. Mixed blood means less chance for individuality. He adds, "My mind not squeamish but my body very squeamish."

Gurdjieff says man has four centers. The fourth is sex. Says he knows what a person is thinking and feeling by the way their muscles are composed—flexed or static.

The meeting ends after midnight and they all go to the Café de la Paix for coffee. "But tonight," he says, "we not be parra-seet (parasite) maybe now we have Armagnac because we not be parra-seet tonight." The toasts begin, "*A la santé des idiots ordinaires.*" Louise, having had chocolate first, is not able to drink the large glass of Armagnac and tries to give Solita and Kathryn half of her glass.

Gurdjieff stops her, saying, "You have more need this than they." He taps his head. "You psychic weak, they have some, maybe only tail of donkey psyche, but better than nothing what you have." He makes her drink the full glass.

Tail of donkey is something very low but nevertheless a little on the way—many things are not tail of donkey to him such as good old Armagnac, crayfish, people, too.

Writes Kathryn, "We listened with the total attention of cats at a rat hole every time he spoke—whether in anger, jest or solemn seriousness...how could one honestly reply? For the first time I was listening to words rooted in reality."

Writes Solita, "I don't know what planet I'm living on, but it's not the old one."

1 November 1935. Hotel Bonaparte. Alice Rohrer, Kathryn's friend, returns to Paris. Gurdjieff promptly invites her to be a "candidate for shearing" at a crayfish dinner and says she is to be included in all of the working sessions.

After dinner they return to the hotel and read aloud for five straight hours until 3 a.m.

Writes Kathryn, "'Wendy' [Hulme's name for Alice] was the country girl from the Cumberland Mountains who had run away from the family farm in her early teens and apprenticed herself to a millinery wholesaler in Baltimore.... (becoming the famous Madame X, the San Francisco milliner). She had made a fortune with her hands. In the cliché of the day she was a 'self-made woman' whose lovely exterior was untouched by her struggles but whose interior, you sensed, was composed of coiled springs and small shiny wheels of business competence geared with the precision of a Swiss watch.... She had married and had dropped off the 'good little man' who had not been able to keep up with her."

Solita writes, "The vibrations chapter was so difficult, the 'dog buried so deep,' that I remember very little. And probably that all wrong. What happened to me was not brain understanding but what I might call stretching of inner man — stirring in its sleep. I felt all organs moving up — in truth I had the most fundamental experience I have ever had. Perhaps I am hypnotized by him, as well as by myself. I can't think of anything but him and his words and all shapes of thought-life have changed their forms. I don't know what he wants of us, but I sense that we are in test tubes now for something he wants to know about his book. He watched us last night as never before and the room was charged with his dynamo and our super-effort. Never have I known or imagined such vibrations... it was really life without a body though our bodies were in extremis."

2 November 1935. Hotel Bonaparte. After dinner Gurdjieff has Solita read the chapter on Time. He says, "Morning sun is best for us, the only time of day when the rays contain certain properties necessary for our understanding."

5 November 1935. Paris. Gurdjieff speaks about the three brains: active or affirming brain in the head; passive or denying brain in the spinal column; and neutralizing brain localized throughout the body. The nerve nodes make up this "Being Brain." These separate functions are nevertheless connected with each other correspondingly so that the sum total of these scattered parts can function in general. Only the active and neutralizing forces serve the *Trogoautoegocratic* process. For the coating of our I only the crystallizations of the denying brain in the spinal column can serve. The majority of people remain with their planetary body alone, do not develop, and when they die are destroyed forever.

Gurdjieff tells them: "Wrong to kill animals. Only planet Earth where beings kill each other. All forms of beings actualize all together the form of process required by our Creator for the existence of Everything Existing. The essences of all beings to Him are equally valuable. All beings only parts of the existence of a whole essence spiritualized by Himself.... The 18th Personal Commandment is love all that breathes." He adds: "God forgives everything." Also, "Every real thought from a conscious being remains in the atmosphere of the planet as long as that planet survives and can be picked up in later ages by other conscious beings."

He says that the informed beings of Atlantis, warned of the second catastrophe to the planet, scattered over the earth. After the catastrophe, they met again in Egypt. They created the pyramids, in which were installed seven tubes for astronomers, and the Sphinx. The Sphinx reminds him of the emblem of the Society of Akhaldans which represents how to become conscious — the body of a bull meaning mighty labors; lion's legs for the might necessary for development; the eagle's wings for pondering; the breast of a virgin for love always; and the head fixed with amber to the neck for impartial love. Amber is one of the seven planetary formations in the arising of which all of its three separate independent and sacred parts are in equal proportions.

He says that the duality of man's general psyche is because of the split between ordinary consciousness—our perceptions of reality—and the subconscious, the normal localization. This daily process of daily existence divides him into two independent personalities. Because of this division man lost the impulse necessary to three-brained beings—*sincerity*. So now the result is deceit. Parents teach this kind of conduct and call it education. The foundation of the whole of man's essence has become the psyche properties of cunning, envy, hate, hypocrisy, contempt, slyness, servility, ambition and double-facedness. He speaks of the five strivings. There are no great Being impulses left in us of faith, hope and love. The only function left is "sacred conscience" which still survives in the subconscious, which, with real work on himself, might pass into the function of man's ordinary consciousness. Only the active and neutralizing forces serve the *Trogoautoegocratic* process. For the coating of our real I only the crystallizations of the denying brain in the spinal column can serve.

Writes Kathryn: "We never knew when Gurdjieff would come, or what he might propose. But, like Wise Virgins, we kept oil in our lamps, and bottled Perrier water on the mantelpiece and were always ready."

6 November 1935. Hotel Bonaparte. Gurdjieff arrives at 8:30 in the evening. They read aloud without a break until 3 a.m. Gurdjieff says he plans to write for two months, finish his last book, then start classes. He tells the women that when the organ *Kundabuffer* was removed, people began to have the same length of life as all normal three-brained beings in the universe. They should have existed until their second being body was completely coated and perfected by Reason up to a certain point. But they ceased actualizing the sacred process of self-development and so the quality of their radiations failed to respond to the demands of the *Trogoautoegocratic* process. Then nature was compelled, for the purpose of equalizing vibrations, to shorten their lives to the length of one- and two-brained beings.

14 November 1935. Café de la Paix. Gurdjieff is having dinner with Solita alone. At one point Gurdjieff tells her: "I make special program now for you. You badly organized—too much here, too little there, one place empty, good physical, fourth center wrong. First will give you piqûres (injections), then initiate exercise for which you must take vow. On what you choose take vow? What is most important to you?"

Kanari says, "My eyes, Mr. Gurdjieff."

"Then let be so, Kanari, would you believe could exist such type man who would give eyes before his arms or legs? Yet it is so."

Krokodeel and her friend Elaine come into the café and sit with them. Gurdjieff was saying something at one point to which Elaine apparently was not listening. He tells her:

"You have zero attention. For ones like you with such dirty life exists special kind of hell. All souls must sit in a lake of shit up to their mouths. They must sit very still, for at the slightest movement, the liquid goes into their mouths. Whenever a newcomer approaches, all the souls call out, 'Get in gently, please, be slow and careful.' Once a year to commemorate Jesus Christ, a great stone is thrown into the lake and all souls receive the liquid in their mouths."

Shocked, Elaine jumps up from the table, and dashes out of the café. A little later, she returns to get her purse. Gurdjieff waves Solita and Krokodeel away. He and Elaine talk for an hour.

Later he tells Solita, "Three time in my life, I have known type like her—my wife, before her another, and now this one. Only my wife changed inside. Very interesting type your friend."

Thereafter, Gurdjieff tries to regain Elaine's interest, but to no avail.

Writes Solita in her diary, "He did everything a man could think of to get Elaine. She won't see him anymore at all. He makes her too nervous. He gave me an exercise to remember myself and prove it myself by making a certain gesture every half hour."

Writes Solita: "If he could have a weakness, I'd say it was for women. Gordon says, 'One never pays any attention to those things or tries to understand.'"

15 November 1935. Café de la Paix. Gurdjieff says he will give Solita piqûres for her nightmares, neurasthenia and anemia. He says he gets them from Germany, as they are the best in the world.

About hypnotism, he said because of the consequences in us of the maleficent organ *Kundabuffer* we are already hypnotized. So that all a hypnotist has to do is to bring together in one place, concentrated, the states of our general hypnosis.

Speaking of Jesus Christ, he says that if an initiate dies without having communicated all his teaching, his astral body may return to Earth for a short time and give his final instructions, or it may be called back to Earth by another high initiate on condition that the second man has taken the precaution before the first man's death to coat his own higher being body with a particle of the same or similar higher body of the first man who has died. The living man can establish a connection with the dead by projecting his astral body connected to himself by a cord whose thickness depends on its distance from him. The astral body rises until it finds its place of gravity in the upper atmosphere and there it communicates with the dead man's body of reason (the time is limited to the completion of a solar revolution). This might be a year or a day, according to when the revolution is due to be completed after his death. Gurdjieff says he has no patience with Christians being "saved" by Jesus, praying and making no being effort of their own. They are all lost forever.

When Solita returns to their hotel, Janet Flanner, jealous of the time she is spending with Gurdjieff, shouts at her—"When is that damned Asiatic bugger going away?"

Writes Solita: "He sees I don't respond to his male principle. He knows more English than we do, though cannot speak fluently. But much better than before."

19 November 1935. l'Ecrévisse. Alice gives the women a luncheon. Miss Gordon came also. She asks Solita suspiciously—"Have you been seeing Mr. Gurdjieff?"

"Yes—every day, sometimes twice a day," Solita says.

Miss Gordon turns red and tells her, "That's a lie."

"Yes—today we've been with him since noon," says Alice.

20 November 1935. l'Ecrévisse. Gurdjieff says the tension between planets causes a feeling of religion—a "being feeling" which, if one is not working on himself, will be a nervous feeling that creates a desire for self-calming—"The only devil in us is self-calming"—and a need of freedom. This often happened with the dynasties in Egypt because that part of the surface of the planet found itself in relation to the common-cosmic-harmonious movement in the position of the center-of-gravity-radiations. That is why the influence of the cosmic law of *Solioonensius* often acts on man abnormally. This is also the cause of Bolshevism. The chief particularity of the beings of the planet Earth is "periodic-reciprocal-destruction."

Kundabuffer, he says, is the assimilation of results of oft-repeated acts. Nature once put in us the organ *Kundabuffer* to make us not see clearly the terror of our situation—then later, when man no longer needed this protection, Nature removed this organ. But we still continue to react as if we had it—because results of oft-repeated acts are assimilated—and we react from this assimilation as if it were caused by the organ (long since done away with by Nature).

24 November 1935. 11 rue Labie, Paris. Gurdjieff moves from the Grand Hotel to a new flat behind the Étoile, just inside the old fortifications of Paris. Every day Gurdjieff cooks lunch for the women at his apartment. Kathryn washes the dishes. Each woman puts fifteen francs in the kitchen box except Miss Gordon. He calls the women "Knachtschmidt," a name that causes him much inner amusement. Asked what it means, he plucks at his clothes and says, "No clothes . . . how

THE HERALD

is that word in English?" Kathryn offered, "Naked?" "Yes, naked ... the Russians say *Knachtschmidt* ... very funny how they mean it. For example, many peasants with no shoes come together in a group. They wish to *make something* together, on a holy day, a feast day ... make something *new* begin. Knachtschmidt and Company ... perfect correspondence for you." And he shakes with laughter.

25 November 1935. 11 rue Labie. Solita and Gurdjieff go to lunch together and return to his apartment. She tells him, "I had a vision of the *Kundabuffer* in the night. Man used to have a tail. In this tail was the continuation of the spinal column containing part of man's 'denying' brain. *Kundabuffer* was not in the tail but at the beginning of the tail."

He says, 'Yes,' and says he would give me his writing on the subject. My reward is the Good and Evil chapter."

2 December 1935. 11 rue Labie. The Good and Evil chapter is read. He said men have never seen angels in the world but always thought they had seen devils. The more "good" men thought they were, the more devils they could see — they see devils where a really good man does not. He said the only devil in us is self-calming.

He is asked if man has evolved from animals. Gurdjieff says, "No, man is a different formula." He stopped drinking three days ago — says he cut off everything — Armagnac, Calvados, Vodka. No more nightly meetings. Only Solita goes to see him twice a day. Miss Gordon is friendlier toward her now.

6 December 1935. 11 rue Labie. Gurdjieff tells Solita, "I know you give me all your heart. Soon you must decide if all give up in world." Solita writes, "How can I not choose him? Janet doesn't know I'm alive — we can't help each other — only make a home for *Kundabuffers*."

9 December 1935. Bonaparte Hotel. Solita writes: "Today I'm keeping out of his way, it's rent day and God help anyone who approaches when he must have money, for he speaks of nothing else. It makes me nervous."

12 December 1935. 11 rue Labie. Gurdjieff says that the only connection our emotions have with our body is through the blood. And the emotions can only be connected with the mind by *Hanbledzoin* — that substance that arises from being-efforts. It is the blood of the *Kesdjan* body.

Solita writes to Margaret Anderson who has written and called her immature (They'd had an affair and Solita was distraught when Margaret broke up with her): "I am completely immature only in a negative emotion. That is true, if you will analyze. That is the strong point you two have [Georgette Leblanc] — you are more mature in negative emotions than practically anyone. In positive emotions,

I have sat aside, mature, while you have leaked energy all over the place on impossible plans and beliefs and stupid hopes and ecstasy. In anything about life and people that requires judgment, you are both immature, and I am not—or so I feel and have proved to myself. Georgette is such a baby that often I have wanted to carry her across the room like one. And you—are you not even called "Baby"? And why do you call me that? Because you of all people in the world have been given the spectacle of all my negative emotions."

1936. London. Though Uspenskii has managed to attract upwards of one thousand people to the teaching, for him, too, life in the mid-1930s now appears to be contracting.

In the early days his lectures were full of inspiration. He became a sort of underground spiritual figure, "a mystery man," according to one follower, "who kept in the background and conducted very secret meetings somewhere in London."

With the passage of time, the energy that Uspenskii had built up from his contact with Gurdjieff began to run down. Says J. H. Reyner, a student of Uspenskii's and a biographer, "The fact was that Uspenskii had lost his way and was living on stale manna." Says C. S. Nott, "The work was too theoretical, too one-centered, intellectual-centered; and often I would leave with a feeling of emptiness, of emotional hunger. . . . I get more from inner work with one lunch with Mr. Gurdjieff than from a year of Mr. Uspenskii's groups."

1936. Lyne Place. According to Bennett, Uspenskii's relations with him have changed. Though Bennett continues to regularly go to Lyne, he says, "I was no longer in his confidence." He gives no reason.

1936. Mill House. Jean Toomer, despite his wife's concerns, again tries an experiment in communal living. "Friends of Being," he calls it, an approach that integrates Quakerism with Gurdjieff's teaching. Toomer's students restore an abandoned gristmill on his property and also farm large tracts of land. Toomer continues to womanize. His wife, determined to make this marriage work, overlooks it.

The Herald

Alexander Nicholayevitch Romanoff who wrote under the pseudonym "Achmed Abdullah"

Jean Toomer

Margery Latimer Toomer

Georgi Ivanovitch Gurdjieff

Mr. Gurdjieff in 1932

René Daumal

Louise Goepfert March

Marjorie Content Toomer

11 rue Labie

Solita Solano

Rom Landau

Alexander de Salzmann was ravaged by tuberculosis

Orage's grave at Old Hampstead Church, London

Uspenskii's country estate, Lyne Place, at Virginia Water, England

Uspenskii seated on his horse, Jingles

Georgi Ivanovitch Gurdjieff

Gurdjieff as the "father" of both Martin Benson & Rita Romilly at their wedding in Bedford, New York, May 1935

Part VII

The Way of the Sly Man

7 January 1936. Café de la Paix. Solita sits alone with Gurdjieff. Kathryn and Alice sit in another room. He tells her they were not "serious." Solita begins to cry. He asks why.

"Afraid to tell you — you will say again I am psychopathic."
"No, no, tell me."
"Today is anniversary of my mother's death and I always have guilt and remorse about her."
"How long ago she die?"
"Fourteen years."

"Then no psychopathic. Very good thing. Mother very important—you get fire from mother. But not think about her only once a year—but think often."

He asks her about the exercise. She tells him it makes her sleepy. He tells her, "This exercise is very important. Your whole future depends from this. It should be even more for you than God. Even get angry, if necessary. You must think of yourself as a baby you take care of and lead by hand. After you do, necessary rest twice as long as exercise done. Be passive afterward."

Solita asks if that means sitting still or could she write on her typewriter.

Gurdjieff laughs. "Oh yes. You passive then. You well asleep then."

Solita writes Margaret: "He forbids associations—emotional especially, all our music, all art, in fact everything we love. Says makes more psychopathic and that force of those emotions must be used to obtain the new being—the second body. So when you say you want to develop you had better think it over. That's why love is psychopathic but sex necessary. When you don't have sex, this force is so strong that it permeates the emotions and almost makes you fall in love. Whereas you wouldn't dream of it if you were living in healthy and satisfied body. You see everything is so against one's emotional nature and ideas that it is terrifying to contemplate the change."

12 January 1936. Café de la Paix. Gurdjieff speaks about things to which man is a slave, and how these slave impulses take their initiative with us because we do not have one strong central aim with one strong corresponding impetus, but many aims, many sources of impetus. "Man is a slave to big things, powerful things like alcohol, sex, drugs and tobacco."

Kathryn admits she had a habit of smoking while writing but never thought she was a "slave" to it. "I can quit any time," she says, and takes another puff, adding—"Man's dogs do not apply to me."

"Why not try ... and *see*," Gurdjieff says.

"You mean *now,* Mr. Gurdjieff?" Kathryn looks at her half-smoked cigarette.

"Why not?" he answers. She leans across the table and presses out what's left of the cigarette into an ashtray.

"I fed on self-esteem for the first week," Kathryn says. "I could look on friends smoking and feel nothing more than pride that I had freed myself from the habit-reflex of lighting up after meals. I even lit their cigarettes for them. But in the second week, all the inner selves that had lain down like dead dogs at my command suddenly rose up and turned into wild animals.

"I spent my waking hours walking in circles around my unused typewriter, crying 'No, no, *no!*' to the craving. In sleep I dreamed of smoking so realistically that I often shocked myself awake, in tears for having failed to keep the pledge. My concentration was reduced to that of a monkey's. The yammering of the thwarted nicotine-slaves started up a kind of interior gang war."

At one point, Gurdjieff teases Solita, "You always have a purpose and you always looking for something unusual or wonderful. I think after you go toilet you look in to see if that was by chance something wonderful." Then he dictates to her a long explanation of the swastika that she had asked him for.

Writes Solita: "Gordon is very jealous of us being with Gurdjieff. I notice every time he calls to me she gets that funny color. She changed from red to green today and back when he dictated to me. I did my best to keep her friendly. I can't cope with such natures."

13 January 1936. 11 rue Labie. The women gather for Gurdjieff's birthday. His manner for the first time is that of a teacher. He sits cross-legged on the big divan. He talks continuously for an hour and a half on "Man's search for a soul," saying:

> If in ordinary life I were asked if man has a soul, I would say no, because in general man has not. Before man can have a soul, he must have an I. Only when he achieves an I can he develop a soul.
>
> There are four ways. Let us compare ordinary man with a three-room apartment. The dining room will represent his organism, his moving center, the place where he eats and attends to the needs of the body maintenance and development. The drawing room represents his feeling center and the bedroom his mental center. But this apartment lacks a bathroom which we will call the I room. In man's ordinary three-room apartment there is disorder. The roof leaks in the dining room or there is no floor in the drawing room or the windowpanes are broken. The building itself may be in the slums.
>
> Man has tried three ways to find the soul. First by living only in the dining room, develop the body, give it great tasks and suffering—Fakirism. In the drawing room, Monks—feeling center and psychic experiences. Bedroom—mental center, via knowledge, Yogism.
>
> I am the Representative of The Fourth Way. And I have no *concurrent* rival. For instance, ordinary yogis who do not know these secrets lie for three hours a day to learn how to use air. With my secret shortcuts they could do this in five minutes—in fact, like magic, drink the active elements they need from air out of a glass.
>
> Man as he is has three or four personalities instead of one I. Each day he is a different person, depends on which center is the day's center of gravity. Only after has made his I can he begin to develop a soul; and unless he does this, he will die the shit he was born.

He gives the example of the rivers again and then concludes:

> Before a man can make a bathroom, his I room, he must first repair his old apartment. Sometimes it is cheaper to make a whole new one, throw out all the furniture, finish each room again, with each new object in its proper place. Then the bathroom can be made and it will be a place to bring up a baby in, with ordered rooms for the purpose of living in order.
>
> I am the architect for apartment—I examine the old apartment, the neighborhood, I tell where reparations must be made and the estimate of the work.
>
> After a certain age this effort is very difficult and often impossible. If each of you decide to continue to work with me, you must now be ready to give up all outside life—no engagements, no cinemas. You must always be ready to be here with me at all times, at any moment I call for you.

Writes Kathryn: "I considered myself a representative of the Way of the Fakir—the 'uneducated' man who had heard somewhere that there was a way but who knew only how to perfect his physical body, make it strong and resistant. Alice, I believed, represented the second line—the Way of the Monk who received through feelings a little knowledge of the other paths but knew, in practice, only his emotional approach of praying and waiting, like an artist. Solita seemed to be our representative of the third, the Way of the Yogi, the 'educated' man who lived in his place of mentation, studying and preparing for the day when a teacher would come along. And Elizabeth Gordon appeared to represent bits and parts of all three ways in her fakir's endurance, her monkish emotions and, occasionally, in her yogi-like response quick with recognition for one of Gurdjieff's references to the early days.... Our friends outside the charmed circle thought we had all lost our minds—which in a sense was exactly what we were trying to do by emptying them of their machine-made contents, their vainglory and false conceptions, an Augean-stable cleanup in the truest sense of that legendary labor of Hercules."

17 January 1936. 11 rue Labie. Gurdjieff gathers Solita, Kathryn, Alice and Elizabeth Gordon. He tells them they will be an active work group. Elizabeth Gordon will be the group's secretary. He tells them they are going on a journey together, one in which he will be their guide. As with a mountain climb, the women must be roped together for safety, where each must think of the others on the rope, one for all and all for one. Only unrelenting hard work on the self, not wishing, would get them where he wanted them to go. Afterward, the women name the group the "Rope."

Gurdjieff gives the women animal names. Solita Solano, because she quivers with animation, he calls "Kanari"; Kathryn Hulme, because of her overflowing sentimentality, is "Krokodeel"; Alice Rohrer is "Theen One"; Louise Davidson, who is added to the group, is "Sardine-Wart." Elizabeth Gordon gets no name, Gurdjieff always referring to her now as "Mees Gordon."

Later, in May, Margaret Anderson and Georgette Leblanc become part of Knachtschmidt and Company but not the Rope. Occasionally, Jane Heap comes from London. He calls her "Mees Keep."[1] All the women, save Miss Gordon, are lesbians.

He tells them it is not going to be easy: "To know the insignificance of self is extremely difficult. It is, for example, like trying to imagine one's own death. You can imagine Mr. Smith being killed, but never can you imagine yourself being killed. So it is with insignificance, with nonentity-ness. You can know this about another person, but not about self."

Later he will speak of their "inner animal." One not only had to contend with their inner animal but make friends with it, so it would help them in their work.

Writes Krokodeel in her diary: "It was a Rope up which, with the aid of a master's hand, we might be able to inch ourselves from the caves of illusory being where we lived. Or, it was a Rope from which, with sloth and lip-service only, we could hang ourselves."

21 January 1936. 11 rue Labie. "Man has wish or desire but not possibility of doing what he wishes or desires. This is not his fault for such he is made. Even if he makes a promise and breaks it, it is not his fault. Either not his fault or we are all guilty.

"For wishing and doing man is made in two separate parts. And such is the law concerning the operation of these parts that the more he may wish to do with one part of him, the less he can do in this doing part, even with constant struggles."

He says there are three kinds of onanism. "Greeks called them onanism, Platoism, Socratism. Each center has its onanism. Man lost his tail because of titillation in three centers."

Krokodeel writes: "Gurdjieff judges you by: attention, impressionability, alertness, intensity, sincerity."

Writes Kanari: "Gordon is now starting to be the general overseer and rebuker and shusher. Alice answered her very well today. He never makes us feel unnatural but she does—sits minding everyone's business but her own and watching, watching."[2]

---

1. Kathryn Hulme said Gurdjieff pronounced *h*'s gutturally and so "Heap" became "Keep," Sometimes "Geep." This seems too literal and ignores Gurdjieff's great sense of humor and deep understanding of language.
2. It doesn't occur to her that Gurdjieff may have told Gordon to act this way.

24 January 1936. 11 rue Labie. "We emanate all the time," Gurdjieff says. "This flows out from us — task is to keep from flowing out. At first, can only *imagine* you not let emanations flow out — but this imagination makes begin data for second body and all this will pass over into the real thing, later. We must have within us *Unchangeable Source.*

"This holding in of emanations will make energy for unchangeable source. Now, as average man, we have many sources instead of just one from which flow all active initiative. Unchangeable source for which we work can be compared to having a real I, but not same thing. Just as we have many "I"s which each day, each hour, take the initiative with us, so we have many sources which give many kinds of impetus and so we have disharmony. We have not one strong central aim with one strong corresponding impetus, but many aims, many sources of impetus. Unchangeable source important, also for harmony. Must have strong wish. Say, 'I wish that the force of my wishing be my own, for Being.'"

Kanari says, "In this work, it's difficult for me to be aware of my body as a whole, it seems the center of gravity for me is always in the solar plexus and so I am more aware of emanation from that part of the body."

"Very important," Gurdjieff says, "you know body as a whole for this work. Must sense body as a *whole.* If divide attention then not good. What you do is this: imagine center of gravity on shoulders — *theenk* it there."

He says ancient science defined attention "as the degree of blending for sameness between the impulses of observation and constation by the processes of one totality with the processes in other totalities."

He speaks about inner vision, something he says is very important in this work. "Look at an object, then suddenly shut eyes and go on seeing it, without any break. Any break in attention when shutting eyes means you must begin again. Must without break in attention go on seeing inwardly exact details of what last saw . . . and this all makes for inner vision, which becomes power in time.

"I give toast, not idiot toast, first time in long time I give such toast — Whom God — not your Jewish God, but God you not know about — and devil — not devil you know about but other devil — Whom God and devil help, *may he return with feeling, all body deserving.*"

Writes Krokodeel: "Behind his multiple kaleidoscopic facades, all roles and all played to the hilt, and with teaching (for those who could seize it) flashing intermittently through his talk like lighthouse beams, I always see a holy man. And often, when he is seriously instructing, whether in the gilded splendor of Café de la Paix or in his dim-lit apartment, I sense the walls of that Upper Room in Jerusalem closing in impalpably about us."

25 January 1936. 11 rue Labie. Gurdjieff tells the Rope, "'Man *must* die to resurrect. But he cannot die until he realizes his nonentity-ness. . . .' The message was the same. Only the Messenger was different . . . and, what was most painfully obvious, the type of material he had to work with."

Krokodeel speaks about her cigarette abstinence. "I discover I have wild animals, I discover 'it' is very crafty, never once has even the word cigarette come up in my mind, imagination never produces a picture of a cigarette, and I can look on friends smoking without feeling anything. All the while 'it' is suffering for a cigarette—but a very cunning crafty animal I have, which spends great craft covering up its desires."

"This can be a thing for power," Gurdjieff says. "I tell you one very important thing to say each time when longing come. At first you say and maybe notice nothing. Second time, maybe nothing. Third time, maybe notice something. Say, 'I wish that the force of my wishing be my own, for being.' [Then he thinks a moment]. No, better another way. Force such as this have special results—make chemicals, have special emanations. Better say, 'I wish result of this my suffering be my own for being.' Yes, can call that kind of wishing suffering, because *is* suffering. This saying can maybe take force from animal and give to being . . . and can do this for many things—for any denial of something that is *slavery*."

Writes Krokodeel: "The discipline under which we put ourselves voluntarily and gratefully was the most intense kind of inner struggle we had ever experienced—simply to discover *what we were*. In short cuts, sometimes merciless, sometimes compassionate, Gurdjieff showed us this every day at his table. He showed up to use one of his most uprooting words—our *nonentity-ness*, thus helping us to die to the artificial selves which our worldly pasts, our materialistic heritage, from a spiritually-stagnant West, had made us."

Writes Kanari: "About this time I saw two examples of Mr. Gurdjieff's power which I have decided to disclose. One day after luncheon, he led me into his room and told me to stand at the window with my back to him. He remained at the door.

"He said, 'Relax your body. If head or any part wishes to move, let move. I wish make experiment and at the same time give you something.'

"In a few seconds, my head began to move from side to side and up and down, slowly. Then a wide hot ray or wave struck my neck with force and moved down, then up my spine. Startled, I said, 'Oh, you're touching me!'"

"'No,' he replied from the door.

"A minute later he said, 'Now enough.'"

"He left the room with no explanation and never referred to this again.

"Another example—I brought him a woman with creeping paralysis who had been given up by all doctors in London and Switzerland. They said she would die within the year. Mr. Gurdjieff said he could not cure her because 'screw' was broken, but he could save her life. Every day he or I gave her injections[3] and he taught me how to treat her with a complicated electric machine that had to be polarized differently on different days. She walked with great difficulty, dragging her feet. One day he told me to bring her into his room. I helped her in a chair and started toward the door.

"He said to me, 'Not necessary go.'

"I turned at the moment his arm stretched toward her and downward in a swift gesture.

"'*Dormez, madame,*' he said.

"Her eyes closed at once. For perhaps three or four minutes he stood before her, passing his hands from her head to her feet, at the distance of two feet, or less. Then he called, 'Madame!' and she opened her eyes. After a question or two about her health, he told me to take her away. I went to assist her, but she rose from her chair and walked quickly to the door, to the front door, down the stairs and into the street. I caught up with her and walked by her side.

"'I wonder why he didn't do anything for me today,' she said. *She did not know she had slept, she did not notice she was walking.*

"In the taxi she scarcely spoke, left it without my aid (usually it was necessary for me and the chauffeur both, to get her in or out of a car) and at her hotel she easily climbed the stairs.

"Finally I said to her, 'You seem to be walking better today.'

"'Why so I am.'

"The next morning she was as before. Part of this mystery is that she never once, then or later, asked me what had happened. She did not ever walk again, nor did she die. She is living in Switzerland today."

26 January 1936. 11 rue Labie. He tells the women:

> We have three tapeworms, one organic, one in feeling center, and one in mental center. We must make preparatory work to have I not in quotation marks, not three "I"s. The work you will do now will give you unchangeable source for achieving single I. Then you will be a different person in every way, but always one person with one aim. Active mentation and later pondering come just from the new processes you are about to exercise and from which you will receive results. Activity of mind cannot be taken without taking this exercise in new feeling. And together with it,

---

3. Gurdjieff has a medical practice with which Kanari sometimes helps. She works part time at the Hospital St. Louis. He has lent her three Russian-Greek anatomical books. He tells her, "Just from these books, I studied for my degree, old German printings and some diagrams, very rare. But, of course, I found much better one Chinese monastery. Such for detail as you could never see even in dream. Only they were hard to learn to read because they not show negative picture, as all other books, but in this case, positive. Must study positive while holding always picture in mind of negative."

the mind. But not mind meditating like monk or philosopher.... Only discussion with yourself on this new activity is important.

You cannot keep out associations. Let them flow on. You can never be without or you would die. But put them in a separate place. Pay no *attention* to them but put your intention on your new activity.

Two kinds of vision we have—outer world and inner, the inner world of man. Like exercise of looking at an object, closing eyes and still seeing it. Thirty years ago I had this force so much that I could split a table in two from a distance, if I so wished, and kill a large animal like a yak.

Religion says believe, and uses words like 'love,' 'hope' and 'faith.' I say to you, believe nothing, trust nothing, hope for nothing, love nothing. Yet I am a very religious man.

Krokodeel writes, "He gave us the 'cinema exercise.' At night, picture the day's events with yourself as the central figure seen impersonally. Do the day from the beginning, not backwards. Engage the mind and leave the emotional center free with its pictures by counting a series of numbers until it becomes automatic. Count 1-2-3-4; 4-3-2-1; 2-3-4-5; 5-4-3-2 up to 10. This is a way of keeping your life from slipping into oblivion. After doing the day's cinema, at some point do the cinema of your life."

Writes Kanari: "He told one half our waking hours should be spent on his exercises. I think perhaps I'll run away—I'm giving out.

"I thought in the night: can this be really I who used to write poetry, who had a great love, who lived and cried and died in this funny room? It was a strange and body-less experiencing—a suspension in time. Then I went on with the exercises. Oh these exercises of intentional suffering—the *Boredom* of sustaining *One* state, *One* activity, *One* fixation, over and over by the hour. Can you imagine the boredom? Try?"

30 January 1936. Café Deux Magots, Paris. Gurdjieff says his work would soon be done and then he would go away, travel, dance the fox trot and they could all suffer as he had suffered. Toward the end of dinner, Kanari casually brings out her compact and powders her nose. Gurdjieff erupts, making himself look terrifying, veins standing out on his forehead as he shouts:

> I am Oriental and man. Never can I see woman making prostitute thing without my insides turning over. Never has woman sat my presence and painted face. I see you make now six times and each time if I had had knife in my hand I wish send it through your heart. This is seven times and finish. At Prieuré no woman ever dare smoke before me. This idiot fashion put paint on face exist only New York and in territory around

Place Opéra. Only prostitute make in other places. If you wish make this thing, you must in water closet go. Now you must remember that you are one of Mr. Gurdjieff's people and pupil. Me, I am Gurdjieff, and compared to me you are shit non-entity.

Then he makes a ceremony of apologizing to Kanari, Mees Gordon, Mees Keep and Theen One. He says, "Now Kanari hate me, she hate me for two days." She kisses him lightly on both cheeks and he cries, "Look, look, she not hate me."
He toasts to Mees Keep, calling her an Arch Idiot.

Writes Kanari: "Afterward Jane told us that 'Gurdjieff is not a single man but a multitude, a crowd of two thousand million men, as many as he is able to incarnate. A developed Being tries to incarnate in himself as many as possible, so that his experience can be complete. Through that multitude there walks a sage. In his talk there is always teaching. You must watch for it, not be put off. In the Bible it says 'Let thine eye be single' and that means we must subjugate all the different personality 'I's to one master essential I. Be, act, feel with the entire being, not under the sway of a multitude of partial personality 'I's."

[No date]1936. 11 rue Labie. C. S. Nott arrives. Speaking of idiots during lunch, Gurdjieff tells Nott he is a hopeless idiot.
"Which you wish to be, objective or subjective [Hopeless Idiot]?"
"Subjective, of course," Nott says. "I don't wish to perish like a dog."
"Every man thinks he is God but a subjective hopeless idiot sometimes knows that he is not God. Objective hopeless idiot is shit. Never can be anything, never can do anything. Subjective hopeless idiot has possibility not to be shit. He has come to the place where he knows he is hopeless. He has realized his nothingness, that he is nonentity."
With that Gurdjieff hands Nott a red pepper and says, "Eat, then will remember."
Nott, like the Kurd in *Beelzebub's Tales*, eats the pepper, which sets his whole body on fire.
Says Gurdjieff, "Can be a reminding factor."
The conversation turns to *All and Everything*, the series of three books. Nott says: "What about people who have never met you, or will never meet you. How will they be able to understand *All and Everything?*"
Answers Gurdjieff, "Perhaps will understand better than many always around me. You, by the way, you see much of me and become identified with me. I not wish people identified with me. I wish them identified with my ideas. Many who never will meet me, simple people, will understand my book. Time come perhaps when they read *All and Everything* in churches."
Nott is concerned that so few people know about *All and Everything*. He speaks

about this to his friend Denis Saurat, professor of French Literature at Kings College, Cambridge, and noted author. Saurat has met Gurdjieff and read the typescript of *Beelzebub's Tales,* which Nott had sent him. Saurat assures him that it is "a great book... there is a very great amount of wisdom and knowledge in it."

Nott, of course, agrees, but if only very few people have the interest, will and attention to read and understand it—what will become of it?

"Nothing much may happen in our time," says Saurat. "We are in too much of a hurry. We have no sense of real time in the West. Perhaps in fifty, or a hundred years, a group of key men will read it. They will say, 'This is what we've been looking for,' and on an understanding of it may start a movement which could raise the level of civilization."

As to Gurdjieff's real identity, Saurat says, "Gurdjieff is a Lohan.... a man who has gone to schools and by incredible exertions and study has perfected himself. He then comes back into ordinary life, sits in cafés, drinks, has women, and lives the life of a man, but more intensely. It was accepted [in the East] that the rules of ordinary man did not apply to him. He teaches, and people come to him to learn objective truths... the West does not understand. A teacher in the West must appear to behave like an English gentleman."

2 February 1936. Café de la Paix. "There are *two* struggles," Gurdjieff tells the Rope—"inner world struggle and outer world struggle. Never can these two make contact. To make data for third world, not even God can give this possibility. Only *one* thing can—must make *intentional contact* between the two struggles, then can make data which crystallize for third world of man, sometimes called world of soul. Understand?"

"Well, not quite," says Kanari, "but get the taste."

"I give taste. You, Krokodeel, for example, give up cigarettes. You have outer world struggle—not to take, not to buy, remember always break habit. But also you have inner world struggle about same thing. Now, with inner world you imagine how it was when you smoked, make it more keen, with more longing, more desirable than it ever could be. This way you make Intentional Contact between two struggles. Even by this small thing you will make data for Third World of Soul. This not exact example. I have chapter on it in *Third Series*, but this enough to give you taste."

Writes Krokodeel: "My cigarette abstinence was indeed a 'small thing,' but because I *was* a slave to tobacco, the silent battle of denial was huge and endless and it drew the lines between the two struggles so sharply that I sometimes fancied I could see them within, a visible demarcation between body and soul, a peculiar no-man's-land across which only one messenger whose name was Chesterfield [a cigarette brand] could pass.

"I became quite thin-skinned as the year progressed. Things seemed to get through to me faster, as if I actually *had* shed one of those seven metaphorical crocodile skins with which Gurdjieff had endowed me. Occasionally he greeted me with the salutation, 'Well, Krokodeel.... and how are the skins today?' When my suffering was too acute for words, I answered in pantomime with a shivering act and woeful face, which seldom failed to arouse his Olympian laughter—a reward that compounded the value of losing one's skins in his work."

6 February 1936. Gare café, Paris. Mees Keep explains to Kanari that in terms of the chapters of *Beelzebub's Tales* they were reading, the raven on Saturn carried Individual Essence to the planet Mars, which represents the head, the earth the body. Venus, on the hot side, cold on the other, is physical love. She says the apes represent the products of the mind we hate—bastard, like product from ape and woman, no legitimate active force. Angels are mirrors of God. China represents higher emotions, Egypt the body. She forgets the meaning of India.

Kanari writes: "I don't understand why a conscious being under an emotion forgets a number three times I have just told him and has to return from the street to the café table to ask and re-ask a two-digit number. Or why he complains of indigestion and gas every day and can't cure a cough after a month."

When Jane Heap[4] hears of this she writes Solita, "You mustn't think of conscious being as an extension of the consciousness you have. And understand, it's on a different plane."

7 February 1936. 11 rue Labie. Gurdjieff says Theen One and Kanari are too complicated and Krokodeel is the most normal of the three. He says he must put them back to their original simple state before he could work as he wished. "I would rather have just simple man,"[5] he tells them.

Kanari writes: "I wanted to say, 'but simple man would not wish your knowledge or have the brain to understand your ideas or the emotion to wish to change his life.' What 'simple' man did he ever have? Uspenskii? Orage? Toomer? Bennett? Jane? Salzmann? All mental emotional types, all lopsided."

10 February 1936. Gare café, Paris. Gurdjieff gives the women a new exercise. "If ever you tell this, terrible punishment for one who tell will happen."

Later, Kanari, reading Xenophon, sees he defines the I as the compound result of consciousness, subconsciousness and instinct. She thinks it is simpler than "a

---

4. Solita later writes to Georgette saying, "Jane irritates him as I used to irritate her in her meetings."
5. Perhaps he is using the word in another way. He has said the same thing to C. S. Nott.

relatively-transferable-arising-depending-on-the-quality-of-the-functioning-thought-feeling-and-organic automatism.

Kanari writes to Margaret and Jane: "He says our subconscious brain *should* be our conscious brain. Everything that has happened to us in life is there, penned up in the cerebellum escaping only in sleep, trances and so forth. In the cerebellum there is a seed, a germ, a possibility of a soul. He calls it the 'representative of God in the essence.'

"The white ray (light) he says is God's communication with everything. Consciousness has three centers. There are three kinds of impressions — mental, feeling and sensing. In the book, Asia is the raven or crow representing essence; Russia is the turkey meaning mixed, and Europe is the peacock or personality."

Writes Krokodeel: "Gurdjieff gave us a pledge to say each time before beginning the new exercise — that we would not use this for the self, but for all humanity. This 'good-wishing-for-all' vow, so deeply moving in intent, had a tremendous effect upon me. For the first time in my life, I felt that I was truly doing something for humanity as I strove to make my own molecule of it more perfect. The meaning of this Work, which at first had seemed quite egotistical and self-centered, suddenly blossomed out like a tree of life encompassing in its myriad branchings the entire human family. The implications of it were staggering. By my single efforts toward Being, I could help sleeping humanity one hairsbreadth nearer to God. I believed this. Every time I said the pledge before beginning my exercise, I believed that if I made something for my own inner world, I would be making it for 'all humanity.' It was my first experiencing of the Mystical Body of Christ of which I knew nothing then, but would encounter many years later like a familiar concept though always shrouded in its immense mystery."

29 February 1936. 11 rue Labie. Kanari tells Gurdjieff she "feels sad all the time." He is delighted, saying, "I have been expecting that from you, is as I thought. This is remorse of conscience and only the beginning. You will be much more sad later, as should be for your shit life you have lived." Later, he tells her, "High sex combined with laziness of organism. Even God cannot tell where will find what lost."

4 March 1936. 11 rue Labie. Mees Keep has come from London again. At lunch, Gurdjieff nodding toward her, says, "My guest here must have so and so."
"I don't want to be a guest," she says. Gurdjieff just smiles.

25 March 1936. Café de la Paix. Kanari is alone with Gurdjieff. He tells her: "You must now live in suffering between two worlds. You must first die in first, be resurrected in second and only then live in both."

"If only I had something solid to build on," says Kanari. "Cannot even explain inner state."

"Yes, no words for these things," Gurdjieff tells her. "But say anything you wish and I will understand from intonation.... I have made first stone foundation. You can be objectively happy now. Look at those people there in street. You have something they not have. Later I will put second gravity stone. Then third, up to seven. You need no longer say you will try. That is over and now you have only to do and do. Imagination has always been your weakness and your enemy. Must now take off quotation marks. Imagination, forget it, hate it. And you will see what your old friends are like. No one who like you before must like you now—must hate you. Seeing their shitness will help you see your own. Only now is being-data being crystallized in you."

At dinner he toasts to her—"Although past was shit, let future not be." Later, he tells her, "The total sum of vibration from all organs in a whole person makes a subjective chord." He talks on objective and subjective satisfaction but Kanari cannot reproduce it, "such was my emotion for its beauty."

"Woman is like leaf—responds to nature in the spring if she is nine years old or ninety-nine," Gurdjieff says. "Do you know first property of a monkey?" he asks Krokodeel.

She says, "Imitation?"

"No. Titillation.... Here is law. If a person is quick in all things he will be slow in one thing; if slow in all things, quick in one. Woman's heart is placed just below navel. Agree with me, Kanari?"

"No."

"Dreaming idiot. To dream in life is shit, but when know consciously of what is good to dream, then good thing to dream."

He speaks of Easter and prayer in old Greek and Russian churches. "Essence through imagination—nature presents life; this truth of all truthfulness."

"Be conscious of your body, aware of emotions and mindful of thoughts.

"We live in sublimated animality, caring for the body, thinking about it, worrying about it and so forth."

And finally—"Everyone in Hollywood is a *Hasnamuss*, and if I were king I would take them all to a dog pound and make them into soap."

1 May 1936. 11 rue Labie. Now the Rope is going to his apartment every day, sometimes twice a day. The midday meal is the big one, served any time between one and three o'clock. They always arrive on the minute Gurdjieff specifies, take their places in his small salon and read from his manuscript.

Krokodeel is a good cook herself and so, she says, knows "what a labor it was to produce the wonderful foods he created, rich with 'active elements' that fueled the body for thought." She is often called to assist him in the kitchen. "Then I saw him 'composing'. Once he was holding his long spice tray while he pinched no less than twelve different herbs into a 'phenomenon soup,' stirring it with a big wooden spoon from which at intervals he tasted, nodding and smacking. 'I compose like symphony' he told me; the spice tray was his keyboard. He waved his long-handled spoon like a baton. 'Three hours after you eat this soup, you will experience I AM — will have sensing of how it is to have I AM.'"

This day at lunch Gurdjieff says: "When you do a thing, do it with the whole self. One thing at a time. Now I sit here and I eat. For me nothing exist in the world except this food, this table. I eat with whole attention. So you must do — in everything. When you write a letter, do not at same time think what will be the cost of laundering that shirt; when you compute laundering cost, do not think about the letter you must write. Everything has its time. To be able to do one thing at a time — this is property of Man, not man in quotation marks."

Writes Krokodeel: "In his at-home attire — shirt sleeves, baggy trousers and carpet slippers, with red fez tilted back on his great shaved head — he appeared the paterfamilias, a deceptive impression unless you rightly interpreted it as high priest of his family with unlimited powers to punish or expose its members. His table talk was as deceivingly simple as his paterfamilias exterior. Often you wondered why he insisted on things you believed you had heard before, or ways of conduct you thought you had always followed . . . until you pondered his advices and realized you had done the exact opposite all your life."

6 May 1936. 11 rue Labie. Margaret and Georgette, who had been living at Vernet, known as the "Cannes of American lesbians," return to Paris. They arrive for lunch. Georgette's great lyric beauty has not survived the rigors of time and three grave illnesses. At sixty-seven she tires easily now and sleeps irregularly. She has given herself wholeheartedly to Gurdjieff's teaching. Margaret, forty-seven years old, who loves argument, holds back sparring and testing; it is her way of relating. Gurdjieff tells Georgette she is still young, it is her liver that is sick and all organs blocked. He would help her.

Gurdjieff expresses a wish for everyone. He is talking about his favorite word, "a good word," he says, and, as Margaret writes, "he has said it again and again to us — *shit*."

"I wish you be not like sheet," he says. "So first I make you feel like sheet, only from there can one begin."

Gurdjieff then tells the women that in order to strengthen the spinal cord brain to "hold out both arms horizontally at an exact angle, at the same time look fixedly at a point before you. Divide your attention exactly before the point and the arms. You will find there are no associations, no place for them. Do this sitting down, standing, then on knees. Do twenty-five minutes each position several times a day, or fewer.

"Do exercise as service, as an obligation," he says, "not for results. Results will come later. Today it is only service. Only that is real."

24 May 1936. 11 rue Labie. Gurdjieff asks Sardine how she likes soup. "I think it is very good," she says.

"*Theenk*—we do not use that word," Gurdjieff tells her—"'I think' is property of onanist."

"Devil and angel have more vanity than man. If you are clever, have cunningness, you can make them your slaves."

About idiots, "Zigzag is high idiot, goes this way, that way, struggles against shit he knows he is."

Turning toward Mees Gordon he tells her—"You superior idiot, have been for years, never change. You are monster."

Theen One and Krokodeel cannot drink that day because of some special medication he had prescribed for them. As he fills the glasses for the toasts and skips theirs, he tells the others that they must now think about Theen One's and Krokodeel's unsatisfaction.

"This is obligation of man toward his neighbor," he says. "You look, you see he had unsatisfaction. Just so much as is his unsatisfaction, so much you must make for yourself, for your inner world. So man makes equilibrium." Krokodeel writes, "This, I thought, was a mortification inconceivable; only saints could do such."

"What you do must be subjective thing?" Mees Gordon asks.

"Yes, of course," Gurdjieff replies, "it is subjective thing. I cannot tell what you must do, I can tell only what I will do to make unsatisfaction for myself today. Every afternoon as you know, I like to lie down for an hour. Today I will not lie, I will stay up and go out later without satisfaction of having had a rest."

"You see, Mees Gordon?"

"All life is a stage and man is one of two things—is meat (for manure), or is actor. To learn role is intelligence, to be able to play role is what intelligence means."

30 May 1936. 11 rue Labie. At dinner, Gurdjieff notices something is wrong with Theen One. He asks Krokodeel what is the matter with her and she says that she has seen a terrible accident in which a young boy on a bicycle was dragged under a bus.

"All things happen around you in life," he says to Theen One, "but you are obliged to take from each. Save such emotions for when thing happen to near one—to Mees Gordon or Krokodeel or Kanari."

"But the boy had such a beautiful young face."

"Ah," Gurdjieff tells her, "*boy is boy*."

5 June 1936. Café de la Paix. It is the day after a general strike has begun that has all but immobilized Paris, everyone making a run on foodstores and gasoline pumps. Krokodeel tells Gurdjieff about seeing the Carrousel bridge workers strike last night, how they walked around, fists in the air, singing the "Internationale."

"In next forty-eight hours," Gurdjieff says, "anything can happen. Everything can broke or burn . . . *as was in Moscow*. Big misunderstanding can be received because of no newspapers—people out in country think something happen here, people here think something happen out there. *Suggestibility*.

"Yes, buy candle. Buy big piece of bread, and water you can find. Then have all that is necessary. I accustom to revolutions, for me is simple thing, all life I have had." In the same intonation as when he says "Bravo Perrier!" he says in an undertone double-barbed with sarcasm—"Bravo Moscow!"

He rags Mees Gordon.

"She not believe I know more about her English than Shakespeare. Long, long ago Shakespeare was my pupil. I teach everything, then one day I 'Tchik'-make. And now history has Shakespeare epoch and nobody know he was mama-and-papa-darling."

He later says that Onan was man who taught doctrine of equal rights. "He say, 'Now we not need woman any more, now can do this thing ourselves, all we need is some soap or oil.'"

"Soap?" says Kanari mystified.

"See Kanari now? All thought stop on *soap*. Soap now her center of gravity."

The word in Russian for die-like-dog, he says, translates exactly to "go into source for stench."

6 June 1936. 11 rue Labie. It is the second strikebound day. Gurdjieff produces a feast. Greeting the women are platters of fresh tarragon, Kurdistan cheese, pastourma, fresh cucumbers, eggplant stuffed with pimento and carrots; two soups—a borscht with sour cream and then his "phenomenon soup" rich with fruits and spices; a special rice steamed with apricots and raisins; a whole roast baby lamb; *fraises des bois* (wild woodland strawberries) with fresh clotted cream; Latvian chocolates, Syrian *loucoum* and Persian melon for dessert, with Turkish coffee. And Armagnac in plentiful supply.

He makes Krokodeel the serving maid of the day, motioning her to stand at his elbow, holding plates. "I named each one for him," she says, "and watched him select pieces and portions corresponding to the needs of the person to be served. This was science in action; the dialogue that accompanied it was equally fascinating . . . always a bit startling to the outsider. For Knachtschmidt and Company it was not only traditional but often personally informative."

She holds out a plate.

"Who is?" he asks.

"This is for First Gravity guest, Mr. Gurdjieff," she says, nodding toward Margaret Anderson who is on his right side.

"Ah, First Gravity guest. You know she is not tail-of-donkey. She must have the *best* piece, also much rice."

Krokodeel holds out another plate, saying, "For Sardine, Second Gravity guest," motioning toward Sardine who is on his left.

"Our Sardine . . . she can swallow ten kilos," Gurdjieff says and heaps the plate.

With the next plate Krokodeel says, "For our Reverence, Mees Gordon."

"Ah-hah, *Mees* Gordon! She likes this meat. Is not frozen Australian beef such as her English eat. She must have two pieces."

Mees Gordon pleads for just one. "No, Mees Gordon, I *know* your tapeworm, he can swallow two pieces."

"Next plate is Kanari, Mr. Gurdjieff."

Gurdjieff says lovingly. "Our sing-ing Kanari. She likes small pieces. Also bones."

Another plate. Krokodeel says, "For Theen One."

"Ah, for Theen One. She must have possibility to grow into Beeg One." He puts much food on her plate while she murmurs that she cannot possibly eat so much, she has stomach trouble.

"I have *pills*," Gurdjieff says.

Krokodeel extends her plate.

"Krokodeel . . . she swallows—everything—except God and Devil."

She extends another plate saying, "For Mr. Gurdjieff."

"Oie, oie . . . Meester Gurdjieff!" He serves himself the fatty lamb's tail while exclaiming—"Look how he comes to me all by himself! He *knows* he is my part."

The plates served, Gurdjieff offers the first toast. Then silence reigns until the next toast.

For Sardine, the official hopeless idiot, he says, "May all the forces from right and left, from up and down, help you to be not the kind of hopeless idiot you are." For Krokodeel's toast, "May God help you change from subjective round Idiot to objective round, after which may you die to this life, to this American life." For Theen One, the official squirming idiot, he commands: "Everyone must drink all remaining in her glass for the health of the Theen One. On her health depend important thing for each one of us, for all the group."

Writes Krokodeel: "His special toasts perhaps look queer when read, giving no indication of the intensity he put into his wishing for us. When he called upon all the Forces, you could almost feel them flying down from the four corners of the universe to converge upon the one for whom he summoned them."

7 June 1936. 11 rue Labie. He gives Theen One and Kanari new names—"Madame Big Pah" is Theen One; Kanari is "Madame Small Pah." He says, "Pah means in Russian 'unfinished.' Can also mean 'brains-in-behind.'"

9 June 1936. Café de la Paix. Gurdjieff names Margaret's animal. He tells her she is a Tibetan yak, cousin of European cow. Later, he tells her that her inner animal is a "tapeworm," a lazy animal that seeks a comfortable place and feeds on the labor and effort of others.[6] Georgette is not given a name.

"But in your case," he says to Yakina, "you not look on door of new paint barn like cow which concerns itself only with question, 'Is that my home, or is it not?' You think like business man about quality of paint, how much cost, if will last, how react in rain—forget self completely."

"But some cows are placid," she tells him. "I don't wish to be a cow."

"Cows not always placid; sometimes yak, this Tibetan cow, go berserk. People run inside house, shut door. Something take psyche of this cow and entire being is wild—try break through wall—could even kill children."

He says, "Yakina has for me Jewish sound," and Sardine laughs saying, "It could be correspondent as Margaret always saves things."

Kanari laughs. He tells her, "You need not laugh, sometimes when I look at you I see in your face an exact Rebecca. You know story of Rebecca?" No one does.

Gurdjieff says, "These Old Testament stories can be more important than all the words of Jesus Christ. I study Bible when I was twelve years old. Little boy, I sit in corner and with one eye I look from window where other boys play and one day my grandmother see me with attention going out window and she did a thing I never forget to this day. She had long beautiful pipe which she always smoke. This pipe she take and throw at me, not at my head but at shoulder here. I can feel it yet. Pipe all broken and was beautiful pipe. This makes terrible impression on me and I understand how much she wish I study Bible. And then I study. I very afraid my grandmother. In village she was the oldest person and had most authority. She had one thousand times more authority than all your kings. She could say to people, 'My grandson not study Bible—kill him.' And they would kill me."

Kanari asks, "But you don't hate her for it now?"

"No," Gurdjieff says with great feeling, "I love her for it."

Gurdjieff fills his glass again, notices Krokodeel's glass is empty and Yakina's half full. "Here is example of strange thing in nature. Krokodeel is small man, should drink small. She," nodding toward Yakina, "is big man and should drink big, but they do just opposite. In my opinion, earth-man not have such un-logic."

10 June 1936. 11 rue Labie. Gurdjieff gives Yakina a toast: "May God help you transformate into other animal. As you are now, any wolf can take."

Later, he tells how when he went to hunt yak, he never shot at the skull, as it was impossible to kill aiming there, but always waited until it turned so that the bullet could be aimed at the heart. Then, he adds, "also can kill by aiming at

---

6. On the face of it, Gurdjieff's words may seem harsh. If it were words only, they might be. But Gurdjieff's emanation, that of pure impersonal love, provides the necessary background. That is, while the personality is shocked by the words, the essence is experiencing a sense of well being. Thus, the student finds herself between a "yes" and a "no."

Mary Jane, the soft part."

An Armenian merchant is at lunch. Gurdjieff heaps his plate with fruit to take home. There follows a discussion in Armenian. Conversation turns to languages. Gurdjieff says, "In the beginning of my actualization I was God of Greek language, then Turkish, Armenian, Russian, in each was God of. Then European languages. Already I *feel* I understand your English better than you."

"But you already use more perfectly, Mr. Gurdjieff," Kanari tells him.

"Excuse, not yet, must have more time for this...."

Yakina says something about charm.

"Charm? What is? No, you not tell. I know what is. I know by inner feeling. Is prostitute word. You not use such word. Only man in quotation marks uses such word. When real man hear, he squirm inside. Moreover, I could tell you hundred such words—all dirty words, make real man feel dirty when he hears. If you wish be friends with me, you not use such word."

11 June 1936. 11 rue Labie. "I create law of *Heptaparaparshinokh*. Everything I do, I do according to this sequence. Even in the water closet my function obeys this law. If you hold watch in your hand, you will see that each amount takes a certain time, all according to law. Not necessary strain or spoil organ. Be patient and all will pass. This is very important thing I tell. If all shit not go out, then body take back through blood. Health of psyche depends from all going out. First time, second time, third time, each time so much. Then fourth time is twice as long and half as much as first time."

Gurdjieff asks Yakina does she understand.

"Yes, in a life sense."

"Is only way—in life! Everything must go back to as is in life, otherwise is psychopathic. In my opinion among all of you is too much psychopathic."

Krokodeel writes: "He said an ancient tradition in the East was that the diatonic scale was originally not associated with music at all; but was a mathematical formulation, in respect of sound, of that series of phases through which all action, physical, psychological, or of any other category, must pass either upwards or downwards in the phenomenal changes of nature. The octave is the mathematical formulation in respect of sound of that series of phases through which all creation, physical and physiological, must pass upward or downward in the phenomenal changes of nature."

12 June 1936. 11 rue Labie. "After roses, roses, come thorns. Only then with thorns can man have possibility for happiness. After thorns comes the branching of the river, the two rivers. If not get on river which continues, you go on other which goes down, down—and into water-closet, moreover public water-closet."

He pauses and then adds: "Only understanding lead to being, while knowledge is passing presence in it. New knowledge take place of old and result is a pouring from empty into void. Must strive to understand; this alone can lead to our Lord God."

He gives Krokodeel a new toast: "Let God help you go Devil through horns of yak."

He says people's understanding of what he says is like "putting horse-saddle on donkey. Even worse is to put on mule, or is when you take this man who punish people, who cut off head, or put in this American chair...."

"Executioner?" says Theen One.

"Yes, executioner. Take executioner and bring him into church and let perform before high altar special service that only the Archbishop performs."

"This picture you make represent what we do when we talk over and try to understand your philosophies."

"No! I never speak philosophy. Philosophy—you know what that mean? From Greek exact meaning is: *logically prove absurdity of absurd*."[7]

"Every chord has accord," after another toast, Gurdjieff says. "In music, many note make accord, but when hear from far, you hear just one note, one chord. Can explain better"—points to Yakina—"as she sit here she have part in her from grandfather, from grandmother, from all past family—but we see only one person, one note. But I can listen"—puts hand to his ear—"and I can know who is her grandfather, her grandmother. In every chord I can hear accord. I can even know if father was banker or keeper of bawdyhouse. She ... in her turn ... will become part of new accord and from new accord will sound new chord, not her any more but some thing else. Every chord has accord, every accord has chord."

Yakina is looking at him.

"Why you look at me?" he says.

"Because I see something in your face, Mr. Gurdjieff. I like to study it."

"Excuse, you not see anything my face. For study me, you are too young. *Three thousand years your America must exist then you can study me*." He points to Sardine-Wart. "In her I make association, I make changes; study her where I make changes come. Her psyche you can learn, you are not able do more."

"But I see you, Mr. Gurdjieff, just now do the same thing in four different ways."

"Could be one hundred and four ... but is not same thing. *Never* I do same thing."

13 June 1936. 11 rue Labie. "My special saint is Saint George. He is very expensive saint. He not interested burning candles to him. He wishes suffering, an inner world thing and only interested when I make something for my inner world. He always knows. This suffering is beyond price."

The women tell him they have been ill from the recent piqûres. Theen One

---

7. That some people level the sacred, seminal teaching of self-development Gurdjieff brought to be a "philosophy" is indicative of the level of their understanding.

and Krokodeel cry and say they considered suicide all day. Kanari thought she was losing her memory and her brain had trembled. Mees Gordon said nothing, just looked on, as Kanari says she usually does.

"Very strong thing," Gurdjieff tells them, "this medicine help your dying, even you can have agony. It make foundation for this series. Now your body, not your mind, must realize its nonentity-ness. There is no word for this feeling you all had."

Kanari tells Gurdjieff: "Sometimes I feel I look on you like dog on master, wait for you to throw stick or order me to sit up."

"No, Kanari, not dog. No dog occupies himself with abstract questions."

Theen One is allowed only one glass of Armagnac and wishes another.

"Well," he said, pouring a few drops, "we can imagine the glass is smaller."

Later, she asks again.

"No. My weakness is always reconciling conscience with logic. In this case with all the combinations I can make, I cannot with clean conscience give you another drop. I am monster; self I can lose but never principle."

18 June 1936. 11 rue Labie. During the meeting with the Rope, Gurdjieff drops many pearls, saying, "I am a small man compared to those who sent me." Then, "The last three portraits in my 'gallery'—Karpenko, Dr. Ekim Bey and Professor Skridlov, from which three full books will flow—represent the astral body of man." And then, "Man has automatic looking [with attention]. Every man has a certain amount. This must be put to work, be concentrated. During a certain exercise, contact must be established with the outer world while inner world attention intensifies. This gradually makes clear the difference between the two worlds, will teach you to separate them, not look on things like monkeys, you all going out to the object and identifying with it. Then you will not live in the outer world."

He says, "Understanding is the essence obtained from information intentionally learned and from all kinds of experiencings personally experienced." Knowledge and Understanding are quite different. Only Understanding can lead to Being, whereas knowledge is a passing presence in it. New knowledge displaced old and as a result there is obtained, as it were, a pouring from the empty into the void.

Further, "One is obliged, as Man, to search for the real knowledge, to find out what really happened on earth—and then to be the bearer of this kind of Understanding."

21 June 1936. 11 rue Labie. "All men with quotation marks are the same. By every proof of science, by every test, such man is exact same—same tempo, same vibration. All, even his shit, is the same. But men without quotation marks are never the same.

"There are many different kinds—seven times seven. I am man without quotation marks.

"Ancient science knows that when there is fat in one place, there will be fat in all places. Clever man knows where to look. He look at Mound of Venus. Is lawable if there is fat there, is fat everywhere. Same for man, woman, and even for middle sex.

"Just now speaking about Mary Jane, remind me of ancient manuscript once I read in which try to prove God is pederast. Such picture of God they make — surrounded by cherubim and seraphim. Which were always boys, all face out and God see always only their backsides. Manuscript says he wish it this way and so he must be pederast.

"Now look, look at how Mees Gordon look on me. She look on me like dog on buterbrot."

"In our country we say bread and butter," Kanari tells him.

"No, is *buterbrot*. Germans are only ones who have kept this expression as it should be. *Buterbrot. Many thousand years necessary for the arising of such a word — was self-created —* and now Americans, with wiseacring make of it bread and butter which is quite another thing. Have broken what was self-created. This is very important thing I tell; for you Americans, it is same in all things."

24 June 1936. 11 rue Labie. Gurdjieff tells the Rope:

> The highest aim of man is to be cunning.[8] The magus is cunning. The magus is the highest that man can approach to God, because only he can be impartial and fulfill obligation to God. In old times the magus was always made chief because he had cunning. I speak of real cunning, not the dirty meaning of the word. Other magus could do either white or black magic but the magus who had cunning and canning[9] (cunning and canning have the same root and in ancient times meant the same thing) could do both white and black and was chief of the initiates. Man with real cunning is man without quotation marks. Angel can do only one thing. Devil can do all. Men like that are nearest man can ever get to God, because only then he has impartial justice.

He then speaks about the ancient sun worshippers and how when Christianity

---

8. For a discussion of the Greek meaning of cunning, or *metis*, taken from the goddess Metis, see *Cunning Intelligence in Greek Culture and Society* by Marcel Detienne and Jean-Paul Vernant (University of Chicago Press, 1991). From the introduction: "There is no doubt that *metis* is a type of intelligence and of thought, a way of knowing; it implies a complex but very coherent body of mental attitudes and intellectual behavior which combine flair, wisdom, forethought, subtlety of mind, deception, resourcefulness, vigilance, opportunism, various skills, and experience acquired over the years. It is applied to situations which are transient, shifting, disconcerting and ambiguous, situations which do not lend themselves to precise measurement, exact calculation or rigorous logic."

9. See *Third Series* for how Gurdjieff uses the word *canning*.

began these sun worshippers were called devil worshippers.

> Yet Christians do *not* change the form—*Christians, why not change? Why always look toward sky?* And not only Christians, but every religion since the sun worshippers.
> You not think strange that now the holy day is called Sunday? Half world calls this seventh day, Sunday, and the other half called it by a word meaning Market Day. The day when man does not work, when he gathers together all results of his labors, he meets, he puts out his things, he looks at what he has done.

When the women left the table he sat for a moment, his chin sunk in his collar, his eyes looking inward, an expression on his face of indescribable sorrow.

Krokodeel writes: "He was gone away from us. We could not even imagine the place. Jane said afterwards that she saw a cross behind him then."

July 1936. 11 rue Labie. Madame de Salzmann introduces her husband's group to Gurdjieff; it includes the avant-garde writer René Daumal.

7 July 1936. Park Café, Vichy, France. At what Gurdjieff calls his "summer office," he speaks to the Rope about his auto accident at Chailly.

"Yes, now all is different since accident," Gurdjieff declares. "Then I die, in truth all died. Everything began then from new, was born that year, 1924. I am twelve-year-old boy now—not yet responsible age." He looks at the women musingly. "But I can remember how I was before . . . how was *me*, then . . . Thought, feeling . . . was heavy, too heavy. Now everything is mixed with light."

Of Madame de Hartmann he says: "She is first friend of my inner life, such thought she had for me. She never think of self, but always of me. In all the years she traveled with me, everywhere she would go into the kitchen and tell exactly how it must be for Mister Gurdjieff. She had much suffering then; but now, after all these years, whenever I go to a place where she was with me, they always remember . . . so well she told! I will give one example, something I did not know about at the time, something one of my people told. You know how woman carry always small valise—once someone of my people see she have in this bag a box of hemorrhoid medicine, because five years before that, just after accident, once I have hemorrhoid . . . and Madame de Hartmann always remember that and she carry just in case. That is why she is first friend of my inner life. Such thought she have for me."

Mees Gordon is very touched by what he says. Seeing this, Gurdjieff says to Theen One, "You know when Mees Gordon was born, small devils, not big ones, but still devils—stand around and prepare her in totality for me. From her, not from your Rockefeller, my future depend. Small devils make, arrange her whole life, not for her, but for me."

This way of thanking Mees Gordon is too much for her. She weeps. Gurdjieff nods toward her, not looking and says, "You know if she were not drunk, she would cry now."

His mood for talk continues throughout the lunch in his hotel. At one point he exclaims: "Strange how the career of man depends from situation!" He had heard there was a Russian doctor in a nearby village, had sought him out to get assistance with the injections he was making on himself, as part of his cure, and had discovered that he and this Russian doctor had studied together in the same medical school in Russia.

"Many years ago," Gurdjieff relates, "he had written across his forehead that he would be a foremost doctor. Now I find him with five children, a wife who was once pretty and now is fat.... and all he thinks about today is how to get bread for six. He is a small man now, big in that small town ... but before me he had shame." He looked at the three of us and added: "And you all are now as he was long ago. Now as I look at you drinking toast to Hopeless Idiot, the word 'hopeless' comes with difficulty. Now you all have possibility. It is written across the forehead of each. *All now depends from situation.*"

9 July 1936. Café de la Paix, Paris. The Rope gathers at the café with Gurdjieff. Krokodeel laughs, telling Gurdjieff that she is "a small man" and Yakina "a big man," but pointing to the size of their drinks, showing they do just the opposite.

13 July 1936. 11 rue Labie. Krokodeel and Theen One remind Gurdjieff that they will sail soon. "I will give you a program for living so you can know how to live in inner life. You must remember when you feel bad you must not lose yourself with mind. Some days you feel bad, then with swing of pendulum, you feel good. On your worst day, prepare for best day. This is the law. What is important is that you never lose self. Let mind be big sister to take care of little sister who is now in the house. Your nature is the little sister."

14 July 1936. 11 rue Labie. It is Bastille Day. Gurdjieff gives Theen One a special toast: "Let God help transform from Squirming to Ordinary Idiot which is very high, next after Unique when sequence begins again." She tells him she hopes with her whole heart she would fulfill his wishing.... He stops her short—"*Not* hope. In my opinion hope is an evil thing, is why man is shit, why he is nearly not man any longer. *Man must use what he has, not hope for what is not.*"

15 July 1936. 11 rue Labie. This is Sardine-Wart's "borning day." Gurdjieff gives a toast: "Today I constate one thing about Sardine. Before, for me, was part of her that was dead, only reason not stink was one small part still alive. Can be so. Today I see this part which was dead begin resurrect—now I begin take interest. Now she not Objective Hopeless—still is Hopeless—but other kind. Is now for us new-arrived baby."

While the women are at table, Gurdjieff speaks of others in the kitchen who also eat. "They destroy the good of nature. Not the good of nature, you know what I mean? In other countries is old understanding—this mean: *They drink my blood.*"

Kanari says, "Is dangerous paraseet, Mr. Gurdjieff, if they drink your blood."

"Truth is so."

"Does blood need special impulse, different from other organ?"

"Blood is only a result—is not important. There is many another thing in man. Look, she have literal understanding for what I say—when I say 'they drink my blood' I speak about their destroying food which I prepare for the people tonight, and for this I am 'nervous' because can't prepare more food. *Five minutes I nervous cost more, objective sense, than three liters of blood.*"

Gurdjieff speaks of active elements and Kanari asks: "Can active elements change bones? Since I have come to you, even the bones in my hands are changed. Everyone has noticed I no longer have the same hands."

"Yes, of course. Can change even tail of man. Active element makes everything. Even the kind of breath you have depend from active elements.... Now my tapeworm sing—not Marseillaise or Internationale. He would only sing God Save King, never would he be communist—only monarchist or republican. Tapeworm of man is lazy and spoiled. He not have, like man, possibility of denying himself or wishing to suffer and make sacrifice for future."

Krokodeel writes, "The Devil's Circle is drawn around Knachschmidt & Co."

18 July 1936. Café de la Paix. Theen One and Krokodeel take money to him. Says Krokodeel, "Here is one pair of group who have strange property—one has cunning, the other canning, and when they work together they have good result."

"You speak in joke but what you say is good thing. Both cunning and canning are necessary in all things. This is why there are two magics. Black magic is cunning—often also is cunning and canness—you understand the difference? Black magic is ideal for being. Cunning and can-ness is like conscious and unconscious, or like two words used in Bible for meaning of two kinds of evil, voluntary and involuntary sin. You, Krokodeel, have cunning; I see possibility for developing big thing. And Theen One have very great canning possibility. What you have now you think is big thing, but compared to how you can be, is like baby made but not born."

Mid-July 1936. 11 rue Labie. Since May Gurdjieff has worked with Georgette to improve her health. The pain in her body has abated, energy has returned, and for the first time in twenty years she sleeps soundly. During lunch, Gurdjieff says, before "she was a candidate for death, she is already a candidate for life."

24 July 1936. 11 rue Labie. Krokodeel asks about prayer. "It is not a question to whom a man prays," Gurdjieff says, "but a question of his faith. Faith is conscience, the foundation of which is laid in childhood. If a man changes his religion, he loses his conscience and conscience is the most valuable thing in man. I respect conscience and since conscience is sustained by man's faith and his faith by religion, therefore I respect his religion and for me it would be a great sin if I should judge his religion or disillusion him in it and thereby destroy his conscience which can only be acquired in childhood."

25 July 1936. Café de la Paix. "Already half the world is Christian," Gurdjieff says, "yet they steal old Jewish God. Like Germans all people begin now hate the Jews yet carry old Jewish God in heart."

28 July 1936. 11 rue Labie. He says the beans in the soup they are eating will have the property of castor oil. Kanari asks if castor oil beans grow in Egypt. He tells her they grow everywhere.
"Is it true," asks Kanari, "that poison can be made from castor oil bean?"
"Yes, of course, can make poison from all things. Even from you can make poison. I tell practically how: first, boil for a while, then marinate—from such process can make poison from you."

29 July 1936. 11 rue Labie. The talk at lunch is of frogs and how they cause warts. Gurdjieff says, "I have eaten everything, but frog I hate—never can swallow such a thing." He never touches eel, though his family sometimes ate it, all except father and him. He speaks about flowers. "Flower is dirty thing—is poison of the Earth—is masturbator thing. In old science, flower evil reputation have. One flower not exist which grows lawable. Flower is black magic material."
"Even roses, Mr. Gurdjieff?" asks Theen One. "The essence of roses for rubbing, and in the Bible they speak often of roses."
"Roses, yes, roses for certain things can have good—but must be in combination. Roses in Bible are always mentioned with thorns. There is an old saying: 'You can understand and love me only when you love—have passion for—my thorns. Then only I am your slave.'"

Krokodeel writes, "He says emotional love is pathologic. The lover is a medium through which uncontrolled power of magnetism passes. Emotional lovers are the victims of their own uncontrolled power. Emotional love always creates hate in the lover, then in the loved one, then back again—an eternal changing of hate. It seldom produces offspring. It is non-biologic. My sex needs were all right, but to be sure I not have fantasia and day-dreaming with them—must be straight sex and not being in love with one person."

30 July 1936. 11 rue Labie. Mees Gordon tells Gurdjieff she regrets what he has said about flowers because she is very fond of flowers and once he said she could be manure for flowers, and she was glad to be able to help them.

"You said I could be manure for lettuce," Kanari says, "even lettuce."

"Not even lettuce. Lettuce is a good thing. Even *might* make manure for lettuce."

In the toasts, Yakina says perhaps she can be candidate for Round idiot.

"How be candidate? Maybe already for a long time you have been round. But you are not round. You are idiot that comes after zigzag—*idiot de naissance* [Enlightened]."

Theen One says she knows she is a boa outside, but what is her interior animal?

"How you know such is your animal?" Gurdjieff asks.

Says Kanari, "Because once, Mr. Gurdjieff, you told us how she was looking at you—like a full boa constrictor, wishing very much to swallow you also but unable to."

"It was easy for me to put serpent in her because she already had by heredity a capacity for great swallowing. And now what suffering she will have. Because I put the serpent in her she will always wish to swallow. And sometimes there will be nothing to swallow and so she will doubly suffer."

31 July 1936. 11 rue Labie. Gurdjieff has the women read the Introduction to *Meetings with Remarkable Men* again.

Krokodeel writes:

> A new understanding arises in us. How great and unforgettable phrases like "the thought that produced my deep thoughtfulness" and "wiseacring-for-the-swing-of-thought" and "tricky-solution-of-a-crafty-problem." The crafty problem is the old saying of ancient people, which he uses as a link between the last chapter of the *First Series* and the first chapter of the *Second Series* of *All and Everything* and the sense of the saying is: Only he is worthy to be called Man and to receive some of that which is prepared for him from Above, who acquires data for preserving intact the wolf and the sheep confided to his care. By wolf is understood the totality of the automatic and reflex functioning of the body. By sheep is understood the totality of the feelings. And the man in this case is understood to be the totality of the mentation—the Reason which directs, guards and guides. In every man there must be the constant striving that "The Wolf–Be-Full-and-the-Sheep-Intact.

1 August 1936. Café de la Paix. Speaking to Krokodeel and Theen One, he looks around the café and sees a few people waiting to speak to him.

"Now I see one or two jackals, you know what is jackal?"

"Like a wolf," Theen One says.

"No, wolf is honor. He come, he take directly. You can see him coming and can take measure, but jackal, you never know from where he comes or which way will jump—he is false.

"You must know a most important thing about man. Man cannot stay long in one subjective state. For subjective state a thousand things depends. You can never know the subjective state of another. It is a typicality of man that no two subjective states can be the same. They are like fingerprints—different in each. No one can explain his subjective state to another. If anyone is angry with you, he does not even know why. You can say, 'It is not with me he is angry. His state is angry with me.' *Never reply with interior. Never revenge associations have.*"

2 August 1936. Gare Saint-Lazare. Gurdjieff, along with the rest of Knachtschmidt and Company, come to see Krokodeel and Theen One off for their return to New York. Gurdjieff gives the women a string bag sagging with the weight of two watermelons and two Persian melons as a bon voyage present. "To eat on train," he says. Theen One becomes nervous and flighty at the sight of a bag of melons added to already excessive hand luggage.

He takes Krokodeel aside and tells her: "One thing you must know, nervousness has a momentum. Mind cannot stop nervousness, it must go on until momentum finishes. Important that you remember this . . . when you see our darling nervous, let her be—soon will pass."

Gurdjieff reminds Krokodeel about not "losing self," not letting the emotions lead into self-forgetting. His final words were so low Krokodeel has to lean across the table to catch them. "*Keep the fire burning,*" he says.

Taking Theen One aside, Gurdjieff tells her, "When you upset not look for reason why upset, but say to yourself, 'I am sick.' This brings positive to negative."

Gurdjieff then walks the two women down the long quay to the railroad coach marked Le Havre, with their Knachtschmidt and Company companions trailing behind. Krokodeel and Theen One look out the train window to see the women formed in a fan-shaped group with Gurdjieff standing forward alone. As the train moves slowly away, he raises his right hand with the palm toward them and gives them a blessing—raising and lowering it three times for Theen One, three times for Krokodeel, whose eyes focus only on Gurdjieff's hand lifting and lowering in the triple blessing and his dark eyes that never left them, sad and forgiving them already, until the train rounds a curve and disappears.

August 1936. 11 rue Labie. Kanari and Mees Gordon at lunch along with a Frenchman and a Russian. Gurdjieff asks the Russian—"How your interior?"

The Russian pats his stomach and says "Very full."

"No," answers Gurdjieff, "that is not your interior. That is your shit."
"Oh, perhaps you meant my heart?" asks the Russian.
"No, that also very dirty."
"My soul?"
"No. He who masturbates can never have a soul."
"Then what is my interior?"
"Man's interior is his psyche," Gurdjieff tells him.

17 August 1936. Rouen. Kanari writes: "An old Russian who lived at Pont de l'Arche with his tiny old wife has just died and Gurdjieff is very upset." He loads the car with food and flowers and takes Kanari, Dmitri and Valya to Rouen. They visit the house and then have dinner. He and Kanari have coffee alone and he talks until half past two.

"I am sometimes God," he says, "and sometimes I have ten thousand devils." Kanari says, "He seemed very upset, and for the first time, talked on and on, manifesting out loud like anybody else."

The next day they follow to the cemetery the villagers and the Russian priest he has engaged to watch and pray for three days. He cheers the grieving wife and calls for a luncheon that includes Armagnac and vodka.

End of August 1936. Vichy. Gurdjieff takes a trip to Vichy with Kanari, his brother Dmitri, and others. Kanari works the windshield wipers, finds the roads, and lights Gurdjieff's cigarettes. He does the roads through the woods at 115 kilometers per hour and through the towns at 90. Four times Gurdjieff stops on the road. Still, they make Vichy in less than five hours, arriving before ten o'clock on Friday evening. They can find no rooms, so they park by a curb. Gloomily, Dmitri looks for rooms. After visiting eighteen of Vichy's many hotels, he finds lodging and at eleven o'clock they have dinner. Saturday, Gurdjieff tells them where to meet him but they cannot find him. It turns out he has given the wrong place, the wrong hour, or his watch stopped. Sunday, he tells Kanari to meet him in the café by the river. For two hours she waits. Finally, someone comes for her and leads her to Gurdjieff sitting in a café in the middle of the park.

On the terrace of a café in Vichy, Gurdjieff says, "Now sitting here reminds me of nine years ago when I was writing the chapter on Good and Evil. I wish know name. I call, what that man name please? . . . Made on Atlantis."

Kanari says, "Man's name was Makari and he made a tablet in two pieces."

"But what was name I call this tablet? Not memory you have. There was name. I made from two names I see on those two shops opposite here. Please you call waiter, ask what name had shop nine years ago."

The waiter says, "*Dé d'Argent.*"

Gurdjieff's face falls. The waiter leaves and returns to say he was mistaken. "*Boule d'Argent,*" he says.

The Way of the Sly Man

"Aha! Now I remember. Name of stones was '*Boolmarshano*' and you sit in galosh. You only remember liquid, Mees."

Monday, they drive seventy kilometers to picnic. Dmitri is in the back seat with indigestion, muttering "*Jamais un peu de repos*" (Never a bit of rest). They have with them only watermelon and Armagnac, so they stop many times for provisions. At Clermont-Ferrand Gurdjieff stops to pick up a Russian nurse and her little boy. They sit on the laps of Dmitri and the other two men in the back seat. The heat is intense but Gurdjieff, because of a sore arm and a cough, insists all the windows be kept closed. For an hour they search for the ideal picnic spot. Passing many wonderful places, Gurdjieff finds the perfect spot—a steep hill—so steep that no one can keep their balance. They sit on sharp rocks, holding on to all the food to keep it from rolling downhill. There is only one glass for everyone. The men tear the chicken apart with their bare hands, wiping their hands on their trousers. Ten minutes later Gurdjieff declares the picnic is over and they leave. Says Dmitri—"Just think, to eat a piece of bread we must come seventy kilometers and spend a thousand francs."

28 September 1936. Darmstadt, Germany. Uspenskii visits Count Hermann Keyserling, author of *The Travel Diary of a Philosopher*, world traveler, and founder of the School of Wisdom. Says Keyserling of their meeting: "Mr. Uspenskii controls himself until he is completely suffocated. Oh yes, I do believe in control, but not in complete canalization. I have never seen so rich a character so controlled and stifled. . . . Mr. Uspenskii is one of the greatest men alive; but I have never seen a man subject so much of himself to *one part of himself*. But he cannot succeed entirely, he is too great." [Emphasis added.]

2 October 1936. 38 Warwick Gardens. Among those attending Uspenskii's lecture are the poet Gerald Heard and his friend, the writer Aldous Huxley. Uspenskii is asked about Krishnamurti.

"Krishnamurti is a strange and a tragic figure," says Uspenskii. "He is not an ordinary man. He is the only man I know at present who is different. But he does not know how he became different."

"Such a thing can happen to a person?" asks Gerald Heard.

"It did not *happen* to him, only partly [did it happen]."

"How does it fit," asks Heard, "with what you said that one cannot attain a higher state of consciousness unconsciously?"

"He knows about his state of consciousness. His being is not ordinary, but not his knowledge."

"He is not conscious of the process of change?" says Heard.

"I think of a part, not of all—knowledge is necessary for that. He says a system cannot awake a man. Certainly it cannot. Mathematics cannot build a bridge. But if bridge is built without mathematics, it collapses. If Krishnamurti keeps to this point of view—he will not be alone. Many people believe in spontaneous awakening, just by realization, without system and without following another man!"

Someone asks about Katherine Mansfield dying at the Prieuré.

"About Katherine Mansfield, what you heard is certainly wrong. Gurdjieff was very good to her. When she came she knew she was dying, and everybody knew it, and he let her die there. So nothing can be said against him in relation to her. Many things, in general, can be said against him, but not in relation to her."

Clive Entwistle, a young English architect, asks about morality and moral values.

"Right and wrong can be defined only from the point of view of aim," Uspenskii answers. "If the aim is to awake, all that helps to awake is good, all that prevents it is bad. No other definition is possible."

"What are the dangers of worldly success?" Entwistle wants to know.

"By itself," Uspenskii replies, "there should be no danger in it. But there is one inclination in us—we are inclined to be hypnotized by things. Success is one of the most hypnotizing things. So success may increase sleep."

Entwistle wants to know about being permanently happy.

"It is all relative," Uspenskii tells him. "How can one be happy if one is in the power of every accidental emotion and desire?"

Someone asks if sleep changes a person and Uspenskii says he does not think the state of man has changed.

"They say people have an increasing sensitiveness to suffering," says Entwistle.

"How can we tell?" answers Uspenskii. "How can we measure it?"

Later Uspenskii invites Heard and Huxley to Lyne Place. He enjoys meeting them, saying, "For the first time I meet what we in Russia called 'intelligentsia.'" The two writers speak about the coming Dark Age and advise Uspenskii to go to America. Neither is interested in joining the teaching.

The biologist Robert de Ropp, who knew both men, does not find this surprising. "Huxley and Heard," he says, "were quite unpractical, could never have managed the physical work, and were too fond of their own opinions to work under the direction of someone else."[10]

(Later, Huxley and Heard, as well as fellow writers W. H. Auden and Christopher Isherwood, and then-theologian Alan Watts emigrate to America.)

When de Ropp personally meets Uspenskii he is much impressed. Uspenskii, he believes, "was probably at the height of his power.... In appearance he was massive and moved with a ponderous intentionality that at times reminded me of an elephant.... The massive body was surmounted by a no less massive head

---

10. The description fits Uspenskii as well, though de Ropp gives no indication that he sees this in his teacher. In the objective language Gurdjieff presents, the word *man* has seven definitions. What de Ropp says of Huxley and Heard seems to be a common obstacle for man number three, those in whom ordinary thinking predominates. See *Search*, 71.

crowned with short-cropped grey hair. The face had considerable strength—an emperor's face, an emperor who was also a scholar and who could very easily become a tyrant."

Uspenskii strikes de Ropp as being Russian to his very core. He so typifies that race's strengths and weaknesses that the saying among his older followers is: "One must distinguish between what is the teaching and what is just Russian." The Russian temperament is to be either a total slave or a complete tyrant. "Uspenskii," says de Ropp, "was authoritarian." At the same time, he finds Uspenskii completely free of sentimentality and pretentiousness. He does not pontificate. "Believe nothing, test everything" are his watchwords.

At Warwick Gardens and in London there is lecture upon lecture, the material first being presented by an older student, often by Lord John Pentland or J. G. Bennett. Then the questions are answered by Uspenskii.

Uspenskii never speaks on the drive back to Lyne Place, but once home he sits in the kitchen, sometimes all night, with male students (Madame Uspenskii will allow no female students),[11] drinking *zoubrovka*, a fiery Polish vodka, and eating lavish spreads of hors d'œuvres. He would often talk about his days in Russia and quote his favorite poet, Lermontov, author of *A Hero of Our Time*. At such times his manner of cold intellectualism falls away and students see Uspenskii's genuine warmth, his sense of humor, his innate honesty and extreme modesty.

"Nearly always," says de Ropp, "we were regaled with tales of Moscow and Petersburg. For this was one of Uspenskii's weaknesses. He could not leave Russia. Nostalgia chained him to that land to which he could never return."

Neither could he ever forget Gurdjieff. De Ropp says that one night he and some others were drinking with Uspenskii. "He was not exactly drunk," says de Ropp, "but he was not sober either. His speech was slurred. He began to talk about what he called the 'Week of Miracles' in Finland. He says, 'I was in another room. I heard Gurdjieff's voice speaking inside me. He told me something, something very important.' Then his eyes glazed and he seemed to go into a trance."

De Ropp tells him, "Gurdjieff must have been a very strange man."

"Strange! He was extraordinary!" Uspenskii declares. "You cannot possibly imagine how extraordinary Gurdjieff was." As to why he broke with Gurdjieff, Uspenskii contends that the "real Gurdjieff" had vanished during the flight from

---

11. Adoration is a stage in the student-teacher relationship when it might be said that the student is most open to the teacher, though unconsciously so. When the student works on himself, attention is being freed from identifications and energy is transformed; what is not absorbed is often projected onto the teacher and, in a male-female context, easily becomes sexual. This is likely the reason behind Madame Uspenskii's decree. What her relationship was with Uspenskii is difficult to determine. All reports are secondhand. It seems clear that their relationship underwent a major shift when Uspenskii left Constantinople alone in August 1921, while his wife left with Gurdjieff and his pupils. The two did not live under one roof again until 1931 when she rejoined him. Perhaps one remark goes to the quick of their relationship. Once the two sat in a Parisian café with a group of students and Uspenskii was particularly withdrawn. "Very hard to make a friend of Mr. Uspenskii," remarked Madame Uspenskii.

Russia. The Gurdjieff of the Prieuré was no longer the real thing; he had either gone mad or switched to the left-hand path and become a black magician. He tells de Ropp and the others: "This new Gurdjieff broke the rules of the Work, took advantage of the weaknesses and credulity of his pupils, and claimed to be personally responsible for the system of knowledge he taught."

Remembering this night many years later, de Ropp still cannot forget the tone in Uspenskii's voice when he spoke of Gurdjieff as being "extraordinary!" De Ropp trenchantly comments, "So many emotional elements entered into that simple statement: wonder, admiration, regret, bewilderment. I had the feeling that in his relationship with Gurdjieff, Uspenskii had confronted a problem that was absolutely beyond his power to solve. He had played the great game with a master and had been checkmated, but he still could not figure out quite how it had happened."

One late evening de Ropp complains that eternal recurrence is not a very encouraging idea.

Uspenskii smiles enigmatically and insists that "there was a way of escaping from the treadmill." De Ropp must realize, he tells him, that time is three dimensional as well as space, and that the time-space continuum had not four dimensions—but six. In four-dimensional time-space, at every moment only one possibility is realized. In five dimensions, time curves back on itself so the pattern of events is repeated. But in six dimensions all the possibilities inherent in a moment could be realized. So by moving into this sixth dimension one could, in fact, change one's fate.[12]

The essence of Uspenskii's teaching, de Ropp says, is to remember one's life.[13] "He himself seemed to go over his life again and again as if to impress on his memory all that had happened."

De Ropp, understanding that part of his duty as a student is to bring others into the teaching, speaks to Rodney Collin. Now twenty-seven years old, Collin first read *A New Model of the Universe* in 1930, the same year he met his future wife, Janet Buckley, who was independently wealthy and eight years his senior. He felt then that he was not ready for the Work, but that later it would be important for him. Collin and Janet Buckley married in 1934. In 1935 they attended some lectures of Maurice Nicoll's. Immediately, Collin recognized that he had found in Uspenskii's system based on *The Fourth Way* the teaching he had been searching for. Meeting Uspenskii, Collin finds him to be vigorous, whimsical and brilliant. He and his wife buy a house close to Lyne Place so as to be near Uspenskii.

8 October 1936. Lyne Place. Uspenskii contemplates forming the

---

12. Uspenskii's understanding of time's period of dimensions and belief in the eternal recurrence of the same likely accounts for his actions in the last months of his life.

13. The idea of linking self-remembering with the remembering, or recapitulating, of one's life, is a powerful practice.

Historico-Psychological Society. The prospectus declares the society's aims:

1: The study of man's true evolution, and the necessity for new systems of thought.

2: The study of esoteric schools in different historical periods and countries and their influences on the development of humanity.

3: The practical attainment of conscious living through the techniques of psycho-transformism.

Through it he also hopes, according to Uspenskii's student, J. H. Reyner, "to organize expeditions to the East in search of the truths with which he felt that Gurdjieff had made only a partial contact."

At tea time, Uspenskii is seated at one end of a long table, his wife at the other end, with students on either side. As her husband adjusts his ever-present pince-nez and begins to read the prospectus aloud, Madame Uspenskii—well trained in Gurdjieff's provocative method of teaching, which works on a person's emotional center—breaks into gales of laughter, so much so that she begins weeping and dabbing her eyes with a tiny lace handkerchief.

30 October 1936. 11 rue Labie. It is Kanari's birthday. Gurdjieff invites her alone to have dinner with him that evening. When she arrives she finds the table set with a clean tablecloth, caviar and a birthday cake. He tells her, "Your name mean Alone, already I know it, existed in Egypt. I know all names from there. One man there was called Holy Shit and from name he swaggered—because meaning was he had fulfilled such transformation with honor, used all active elements according to law. There was ceremony in Egypt for name's day, not for borning day. Day of physical birth is only of domestic interest. Real day was day you were given some great person's name."

Later he speaks of Americans. "Not yet spoiled. Nice burros. Future is donkey, yet at the same time might be something else. Not yet crystallized into turkey who have no future. Now this is your day. You may have what you like—only, of course, not question."

There is old Persian saying, he says—"You must always hold a mirror up to yourself so you can see the devil approaching." He explains that "the emotional center working with the body is the devil."

He speaks about Edward, the English King, and can't believe the gossip that he will marry Mrs. Simpson. "Even such degenerate son of such a degenerate father, and cousin of degenerate Tsar which I knew, would not do such a thing. After all, though degenerate, has something royal in his blood, an heredity that would not permit. All fault of American gossip."

Speaking of a Russian woman whom he had hired to serve them who was laughing at everything, even when he scolded her, he says, "Such empty thing she is—perhaps better she laugh. Even shit can smell sweet. . . . Before I lived with somebody—woman—now I live alone. Live with angel would mean nothing to me—because I live with devils."

Kanari says, speaking of Janet Flanner, "And I live with someone who is always angry."

"Always angry, always laugh, always with lovingness, not make different. All is empty thing."

31 October 1936. 11 rue Labie. At lunch Gurdjieff says his seven-year task which had become nine years' work would end on November sixth. Had it not been for the death of Orage, he would have finished two years ago. "Only a sheep, only an Englishman, would have died just then. Any other man, who was real man, would have waited to die."

1 November 1936. 11 rue Labie. Georgette Leblanc knocks at Gurdjieff's door. She tells him—"I am completely well. I am in a new body."

He steps back and leans against the wall, the light from the little salon illuminating him fully.

"For the first time," Georgette says, "he let me see what he really is. It was as if he had torn off the masks behind which he is obliged to hide himself. His face was stamped with a charity that embraced the whole world. Transfixed, standing before him, I saw him with all my strength and I experienced a gratitude so deep, so sad, that he felt a need to calm me. With an unforgettable look, he said—'God helps me.'"

3 November 1936. 11 rue Labie. Gabo, Gurdjieff's old student from the Russian days, once a professional bridge player known as the "White Wolf," tells Kanari he had told Gurdjieff his stomach was growing too much, that he was eating too much fat. Gurdjieff had looked at him scornfully and said, "Since when egg tell something to chicken?"

Later, he says to Mees Gordon, "Even God make mistake—one big mistake he made."

"But I thought you said He had arranged everything with *Heropass*?" she says.

"All—but not one thing. He made umbrella when he should have made enema. So now he idiot like everyone else and sit in galosh."

5 November 1936. 11 rue Labie. Gurdjieff speaks of the Hopeless idiot. "There are seven aspects of hopeless—dirty hopeless, harmful hopeless, stink hopeless." [The others he does not give.]

"Seven aspects is subjective," Kanari says, "but objective only one?"

"No, is also seven. Everything is seven. Which of arch idiots is worse, do you think?"

"Jerryhund?"

"No, morse (walrus). Yakina, do you know which is morse?"

"Yes," she says, "like Miss Heap."

"Yes. Morse, this walrus sit, look around. In him are all idiots, like in man. Everything like man he have, even brain. And so it goes down to tail part. All parts in him idiot, all idiots in him — except of course unique."

11 November 1936. 11 rue Labie. Krokodeel and Theen One return from America. Gurdjieff gives the Rope a new series of exercises that requires a complex and sustained inner attention beyond anything they had before attempted.

16 November 1936. 11 rue Labie. The women notice changes in each other, Sardine is notably taller. Gurdjieff says to Krokodeel, "You also I make change."
"Not outwardly, maybe," she says.
"I always make picture when I meet a person for the first time — I always imagine him without clothes, naked, this make easy for me recognize next time. You know what picture I make for you?" Turning to the other women, he says, "You remember how she was? Her gesture she make so — formless. The picture I make — in some countries, they have skin for carry water, for milk, butter, but also use such skin for carry away shit and this man do at night when there is moon. This skin, filled with shit, is heavy, man gets tired. So he put down beside road, in moonlight — and you know how such a skin act when put down, almost like living thing, take positions with arms, with legs, move a little, settle down ... put head on it and chapeau and could be man. *Kaki Toolook*,[14] such was my picturing for her."

Writes Krokodeel: "I was home again, in the only place on earth where the truth was painless. His picture of my former self, at once comic and horrible, I knew was exact. I *had* been a skin animated by formless gestures, burning energy in meaningless motion all over the lot — running, crying, hugging, pointing, kissing, exclaiming, throwing both arms wide to the life in a come-to-me frenzy ... until I had learned under Gurdjieff how all things flow into perfect stillness. I gave him a glance of gratitude. I would never forget that goatskin full of 'night soil' settling slowly in the moonlight, taking positions with arms and legs just like man ... the picture of one who on cue thought that exteriorized action proved awareness!"

17 November 1936. 11 rue Labie. Gurdjieff says, "Do your exercises consciously, mechanically and chemically."
They speak of miracles.
He says, "Old Jews believe Jesus Christ fed many people with six, seven fishes, you remember how many was — but *how* was filled, the people, that not tell. Another, believe he turn water into wine, but *who* get drunk on such wine, that they not say. They believe he walk on water, but *how deep was water*, they not

---

14. Russian word for carry off human manure in moonlight.

speak about that."

Krokodeel goes home and consults Smith's *Bible Dictionary*, an analytical and comparative concordance that contained some four thousand questions and answers on the Old and New Testaments. Under the Water index, she finds there are no less than fifty referrals and she had read them all — from Genesis speaking of the Spirit of God moving on the face of the waters, to John — "This is he who came by water." As Peter, preaching to the "spirits in prison," must have looked when he talked of water, of the new baptism that was not only "the putting away of the filth of the flesh, but the answer of a good conscience toward God...."

Later that evening when Gurdjieff asks, "How deep was that water?" she now silently answers him, "As deep as the interior quagmires you teach us to walk over without sinking back into them."

Krokodeel writes: "No great Being impulses left in us of faith, hope, love. The only function left in man to work on (a teacher to arouse) is that 'sacred conscience' still surviving in his subconsciousness which might gradually pass into the function of his ordinary consciousness."

5 December 1936. 11 rue Labie. Gurdjieff gives the Rope, not the Knachtschmidt and Company, a chaplet made of large black beads of a curious lusterless substance. He gives them a special sensing exercise to be done as the beads are passed between the thumb and index finger. Gurdjieff says that in olden times the chaplet was known as the "Inanimate Helper." Many inner world work exercises — more difficult than what he gave — were done with it. "You see such men — Turk, Greek, Arab, Armenian — sit all day in coffee house with chaplet; to you they make picture of lazy man. But what they do with these beads creates inner force you cannot imagine."

When the women leave, Kanari says, "Thank you, Mr. Gurdjieff."
"For what?"
"For...more work."
"Look," he tells the others, "look how she lie, she mean for more Armagnac."

19 December 1936. 11 rue Labie. "Religion is morality," Gurdjieff tells Krokodeel and Theen One. "Morality in English is for you big word, in Russian we have two words: one means morality, ordinary, such as we speak of now — other also means morality but more strong. It means opposite of shameless. Objective shame. This man must have."

22 December 1936. 11 rue Labie. "*Legominism* exists," says Gurdjieff, "what tell until last age no cleaner people exist than Jew. Never they mix. If they marry mixed, then all children from such mixing must die — such law was. Only last hundred years do they mix. But before — they were clean people, very special. In Bible, they tell chosen by God — God not interested such business. Always among many idiots one super-idiot exist, he more idiot than ordinary, therefore he is ober — he is center of gravity: this case Moses could be such, he center of gravity Jewish people, he make chosen. Not God."

23 December 1936. 11 rue Labie. Many new dishes appeared on Gurdjieff's table — a rare Jewish herring soaked five days in milk, a suckling pig which he brought bare, white and uncooked into the salon, holding it like a baby while asking us to note "what sympathetic expression it has!" . . . and many wonderful melons never seen in Paris winter markets — gifts to him from remembering disciples in other, warmer countries.

One melon he serves is especially superb. "I suppose," Krokodeel says, "I had a look of gluttony when the platter of sliced melon, orange-fleshed and dripping aromatic juices, was set before us."

"Krokodeel," Gurdjieff says, "can you imagine that one can imagine that on earth such melon can be?" Krokodeel writes that she shook her head. "He was one imagination ahead of me." Then he watches Theen One take the first bite, and savor it.

"Wonderful, Mr. Gurdjieff!" she exclaims. "I like it because it is sweet." His joking mood changes at once.

"Sweet you must not like, you must use," he says gravely.

"I use for energy, Mr. Gurdjieff."

"*Excuse*, you *not* use for energy, you use because you are slave for sweet." He looks around the table, away from the flustered Theen One, and continues, "One thing I notice about those who like sweet. Always the atmosphere around him is . . . what is opposite of sweet? Sour? No — sour can sometimes be good thing. Bitter . . . yes. Always in atmosphere around him who likes sweet, there is bitter!" He nods at Kanari, who is showing her admiration for his formulation.

"You like how I tell?" he asks her. "You like my mentation?"

"Always you speak objectively. Anybody would like, Mr. Gurdjieff."

"Not anybody," he corrects, "only American. Always you say *anybody*. To *you* it seems wonderful, but not to anybody. It is not my fault that America does not have such idea of mentation."

He pauses for a moment as if choosing his words, then goes on: "Moreover I will tell, in objective sense, I do not have objective mentation, I am not complete Initiate. There are many thousand complete men on earth — not in world, but *on earth*, I tell. Many thousand complete men. I not yet complete. I still have far to go."[15]

---

15. With everything Gurdjieff says the context of who he is speaking with must be considered. As Thomas de Hartmann wrote, "There is a constant temptation for the teacher to show his true self, the way he is in reality. But Mr. Gurdjieff knew full well that then everyone would run after

Says Krokodeel, "With that bombshell launched, he quietly resumed eating his melon."

24 December 1936. Café de la Paix. Gurdjieff tells the women, "I specialist for sand. Never can I get lost in desert. Travel in desert depend from secrets—two—which pass from father to son, a *Legominism*. One I tell. Always big ridges on dunes lie in a certain way, according to winds. Before you start, look how lie these dunes, judge about angles, how you must cross, they never change for small storm, only big can make different. Very important now this, because once you are in fifty meters from starting place, there is no right, no left."

About idiotism, "Is not like law. You know, it takes seven years for creating science idiotism with great knowledge of typicality, polarity. Everything about each is known."

About shit, "For you this word sheet make shock; but it is relative word. For me when I tell, it is nothing, so long and so much I know about it. And you know not always bad thing. Sometimes it can have more vivifyingness than roses. Sheet sometimes more esteemed can be than your teacher."

25 December 1936. Café de la Paix. Gurdjieff, Kanari and Krokodeel have breakfast. When they finish their food, he says, "You know, this is what food is for, for servicing nature. Truth we are slave. Nature not give this good—all life man must work to earn it and when he eat it, is not for him but for servicing Nature. Nature give only one thing, give atmosphere, this air. This is all he give—for all the rest man must work whole lifetime. And that Old Idiot that create such, he swagger now, imagine, for having created such absurdity."

Theen One arrives and tells Gurdjieff that today is the first Christmas that the Dionne quintuplets are allowed to spend with the entire family, as before this they were kept apart in order for scientists to study them.

"With such thing as five from same birth," exclaims Gurdjieff, "there can be nothing to study, no individuality can be there. If people understood what really means this, they would cry. Now man begin breed like mice. Nobody see what this mean—quantity destroying quality."

The subject of languages comes up.

Gurdjieff says, "*I God of Languages.* Only not for such idiot thing as this that anyone can learn. I speak scientific, very simple I speak. Why learn idiot words good only for idiot talks. I not have time."

"What a picture of God that is," says Mees Gordon. "Speaking understood—every word known like leaf on tree going back to the main root."

"Yes, is so," says Gurdjieff.

"Such nose you have," Gurdjieff tells her. "This can be so, only nose is no good

him and become his adoring slave." *Our Life with Mr. Gurdjieff,* 70.

in alien country, only good where in general land is familiar. Imagine yourself in Oriental country where not one syllable, not one word, have for you association. Such is how I am with your English."

30 December 1936. 11 rue Labie. Gurdjieff speaks to the Rope:

> This most important day for you. Twenty-four hours from now when you have assimilated this medicine you will begin be responsible for all your acts, conscious and unconscious. Beginning then, you take position of responsibility. A record is not kept for each soul, as people believe, but only for responsible souls. All you do is written in red or in black ink in the Angel Gabriel's book, not for everyone is this record kept, but only for those who have taken a position of responsibility. There is a law of sinning and you are now subject to this law. If not fulfill all your obligations, you will pay. For every satisfaction, so much dissatisfaction—the Angel Gabriel's books must balance.

Krokodeel writes, "Gurdjieff says everything that has happened to us in life is penned up in the cerebellum, escaping only in sleep, trance, etc. The duality of man's general psyche is because of the split between 'consciousness' (our perceptions in totality) and the 'subconscious' (normal localization). This daily process of his daily existence divides him into two independent personalities. Because of this division man lost the impulse necessary to three-brained beings—sincerity. So now the result is deceit. Parents teach this kind of conduct and call it education. The foundation of the whole of man's essence has become the psyche properties of cunning, envy, hate, hypocrisy, contempt, slyness, servility, ambition, double-faced-ness."

1 January 1937. 11 rue Labie. "Around your body is electrical envelope. On quality, quantity of this material depend if people like or dislike you. Once I had this so strong I could push ship across ocean—and back again.

"A scale will always involute back to its beginning 'do' unless you continue through to 'do' of next scale. Nothing remains half way. This is law. But once you have reached next 'do,' this scale you have gone up is always yours and you can never lose what you have made. If you have gone up scale while transforming your apartment, even if you have no furniture or roof, you have always your doghouse, where you are safe. There are seven times seven scales and formulation for forty-nine is 'You-in-yourself.'

"Now this morning Sardine come disturb me in café. She think because I sit and look out window that nothing I do. But under such lazy exterior is such concentration that no man is capable of. Million things I must think about. There is saying, 'Measure a thousand times before you cut cloth.' Another saying, 'Before you give teaspoon medicine to your neighbor, test a barrel of it.' This is what I do when I sit alone."

"Mr. Gurdjieff, you are spoiling us," says Kanari.

"Spoil? How can spoil what already is spoiled?"

8 January 1937. 11 rue Labie. Gurdjieff returns from three days taking the baths at Vichy. He is very tired at the table. He says he has gone several days without teeth, and now tonight, with them, there is suffering. He says he would not even eat from fingers of godmother, and is too tired to even drink tears of godmother. A moment later he says, "What is it you drink?" (He has forgotten the word *tears*.) They tell him and he says, "How my memory is bad for such idiot thing, only one moment ago I say this word and now when wish say again, I forgot. But can remember a page of writing, such specific have my memory, even where on page come a certain thought, even I can remember mistakes in printing—exact where on page they come. For such thing I have memory, but not for small life thing. Of course this will pass."

12 January 1937. 11 rue Labie. This day marks the completion of Krokodeel's first smokeless year. She now feels she can go on indefinitely. "Yes," Gurdjieff says, "for you this makes a source for force." He looks at her intently and adds, "But at the same time, any man can not smoke. You must smoke. Only not take the habit. You do not wish to do what any man can do?"

"Oh no, Mr. Gurdjieff."

"Smoke then," and he offers her a cigarette from his pack.

Her first puff inhaled deeply makes her head swim. Through the smoke she sees Gurdjieff's face as a mask of cunning. "I knew exactly what he had done as the first dizziness subsided and pleasure expanded; he had attached me again to my 'dog,' only now I must be its master, not its slave. He had set my feet again on the harder way, the golden middle between abstinence and excess. Total abstaining was much too easy."

He has made a dish which he says, "Make melody in mouth." He tells Mees Gordon, "Eat, eat, still remain sweets."

"Ah, but your hospitality is so great," she says.

"Truth, my hospitality so big it is my idiocy. The Jews not have this hospitality—they think it idiotic. Jews of all countries never have friend. Each family stay apart. They not spend money for hospitality because they always see cost of small thing, never big thing. This is one of the aspects of humanity-ness. Not humanity, for word humanity only gives address, while humanity-ness shows a property of humanity."

Kanari is aglow with appreciation.

He says to her, "You like? I not know good your English, I only translate my thought."

The Way of the Sly Man

24 January 1937. London. Mrs. Beaumont, Bennett's wife, tries to commit suicide by taking an overdose of pills. "I have seen a miracle," she says. She went out of her body, heard heavenly music unlike any she had heard on Earth and felt Jesus' presence. She wanted to remain. "You called me back into the body," she tells Bennett. "I did not want to come but your wish was too strong for me.... but I was happy because I knew you really wanted me."

Later, when well, she meets with Uspenskii. She tells him she will speak to him in a year, if she remains convinced of her experience.

7 February 1937. Café in Èze Moyenne-Corniche. Gurdjieff asks if the Rope knows what the word *conjury* is.

"It means 'with swearing,'" says Kanari. "That is, 'con'—with; 'jure'—to swear—with will. But we use, Mr. Gurdjieff, only in sense of magic."

"No," replies Gurdjieff, "conjury *not* magic. Is real English word, real English meaning have. *Wish, not wish, conjury you must believe because all life consist from conjury.* For example, what I do today can be good for me, because *I* do it, but for Mees Gordon would not be good, would be opposite, because is objective conjury and parallel with this is scientific knowledge."

He hears music and says at important moments in life when there was some decision to make there was music. "Long time music center of gravity was, writing was by the way."

Later, he says, "Try this small philosophy understand: who from Paradise go out, he go automatically; who from Hell go out, he go where he wish, he individuality have."

3 March 1937. 11 rue Labie. "You know there is one country called Kafiristan," Gurdjieff tells the women, coming out of the kitchen, "where people one strange custom have, always they begin dinner with the sweet, then roast, then soup, then hors d'oeuvres. Many thousand years a civilized people live here; is high in mountain, those mountain that shut off India. These people very strong. Even I see here two hundred *English people* who are slave, they work like donkey, with my own eye I see. Many traveler try to go this country, even they try make of it what they made of Tibet, but these Kafiri own (control) all the mountain passes and only let pass who they wish pass. Afghanistan, Armenia, Russia, put many thousand man in those mountains, try to pass through, but Kafiri with one stone can kill many thousands because every stone they know. Also they shoot with gun—in one hundred shots they never miss one—can write your name on tree at distance. Yet they are honest people, once say will let pass, you can count on them, only you must pay high. But not money. Money they not wish. You must buy your way with one of three things: women, guns or horses. Only these they like. And always these people stay in own country, they are satisfied, not wish go any other place. This is good country—mountains, high places. So now... we will begin our dinner like them, with sweet." He offers a sweet macaroni dish. "Come, come, *eat. This is kind of people we wish to be.*"

During dinner Gurdjieff tells Yakina that she does not notice one thing that changes his face. He twirls his moustache which is turning black at its roots.

"I see nothing," she says, "except your mustache turns up."

"No," he says. "You have months looked on me, always you look on my eyes and not see anything else. Yet this is crying thing on my face."

Kanari tells Yakina.

"I never see color, only line," she says.

"Excuse, man must not look on one part — is onanist thing you make to see eyes or nose only. Must total see. Man must have normal vision."

"I am not interested in mustaches," Yakina tells him. "I look on a face as I do on sculpture."

"Sculpture. Now you have offended me with this word. I am objective sculptor. I see all — even all of you, I see — even your navel. Crying thing on my face. Good expression, eh? Even your Shakespeare could not write such. He was pederast. Between every line of his poetry I can smell pederastism. Such dirty life he had, not like what he writes."

"You not like or you mean his life did not correspond with what he wrote?" asks Yakina.

"No, not correspond," Gurdjieff answers and begins to leave the room.

Theen One calls out — "Mr. Gurdjieff, Yakina here is still very excited and wishes to ask a question."

Gurdjieff stops at the door.

"Mr. Gurdjieff," says Yakina, "you know that a change in color is not so essential as a change in line!"

"Yes, Mees, I agree that your American art books is written so. But still I am changed man. You know why? A week ago I had not time to waste in discussion with you. But now," he twirls his mustache, "I have auspicious exterior and suspicious interior, so I must do everything corresponding, even titillate with you."

Conversation turns to idiots and Yakina says she thinks she is a zigzag idiot.

"Cannot be," says Gurdjieff.

"But, Mr. Gurdjieff," she says, "that is my condition now."

"Condition? Your condition has nothing to do with inner world, you defile zigzag. Wish to go too high. Zigzag is high idiot, goes this way, that way, struggles against shit as he knows he is. It is as if you, a deacon, put on the archbishop's robes." And he adds, "Slow go ... go far."

4 March 1937. 11 rue Labie. Dr. Stjoernval is at lunch along with the Rope. Among other things Gurdjieff serves boiled chicken. He asks Theen One if she knows what chicken it is.

"Is not fiancée, Mr. Gurdjieff?"

"Is fiancée," he says. "Never satisfaction had. Specially they make so... once each day with such chicken they put in rooster for make play, but never they let do. When wish make mama-papa business, they take off."

"Why torment so?" asks Mees Gordon.

"There is also something else I remember. In Russia is one fish (he names it but Dr. Stjoernval does not know it) even doctor not know name this fish. Every day they take this fish from water and beat him. Then put back. Many many times they do this. This make liver large — the liver very expensive is. Only rich can eat."

"Anger makes the liver big," says Krokodeel.

"Yes, somehow is so. And such liver it is, have active element, like what this chicken have."

"One would have to be sure," says Mees Gordon, "that only a deserving person ate such food, after such cruelty."

Kanari brings up Yakina, who thinks she is in galoshes because of the night before.

"She remember?" he says.

"Oh yes, she knows she was impudent."

"Not *was* impudent. She *is* such. One Russian expression there is"—he nods toward Dr. Stjoernval—"you tell her this."

"A hunchback can't be made straight even in the tomb," he says.

Yakina is much perturbed when Kanari tells her of this, because, she says, "It's a completely false, and certainly unauthorized report, of my reaction. I had said I realized I had been stupid; I could never feel that I had been impudent. Everyone knew my reverence for Gurdjieff. I could never even imagine I could have been impudent to him."

12 March 1937. 11 rue Labie. "Americans ignorant about food," says Gurdjieff. "Body work twenty-four hours to make liquids necessary to digest food, but Americans drink water before they eat which sucks out all these special liquids, dissolves them and when food comes nothing there is for it to mix with, nothing for transformate. They eat only to make shit. Not only this they do but also they eat butter. Butter coats the stomach lining and all the insides and what must pass through the walls cannot pass — they even eat chocolate before meals. Chocolate coats inside and takes away feeling of hunger. Good only for travel, to stop feeling of hunger. Such uneducated people Americans are."

Krokodeel writes: "To give us the proper first food that would transform into the kind of energy required to digest his 'idea foods' is one of the reasons, I believe, why he cooked for his disciples. I swung between anger and pity when cynics declared that our master put too much emphasis on food, that he had not a trace of the wan asceticism of the true mystic and therefore must be a charlatan.

Such critics never assisted him in the kitchen (a laboratory dedicated to the science of dietary law already forgotten in our canned and frozen food age) nor had they ever really listened to him at his table, using food very often as a springboard to his teaching."

16 March 1937. 11 rue Labie. During lunch when fruit comes to the table, Kanari picks up a piece, admiring its color.

"Look," Gurdjieff says, "how she interest take in exterior. For exterior she make imagination, fantasy. She even so far go she opposite sex make present self. "

Gurdjieff asks Mees Gordon if she took her iodine.

"Yes, I have," she says.

"I not ask if have, I know you have in pocket, I ask if you take."

Kanari says, "I would say, 'Did you take your iodine?'"

"No, excuse," Gurdjieff tells her. "This you speak with intonation. Your intonation tell all. Your manipulation make understand, not your word. But I not know your intonation. I strange to your language. For me only word exist. Exact word."

"Language changes with time, Mr. Gurdjieff, we grow careless," offers Mees Gordon.

"Excuse — Life make language change, only Life. But now man go ahead and make change before ready go. For example, English have mentation shepherd, somewhere they learn Greek, so now when they speak even with fisherman they understand only fifty-fifty. Normal man never try change language. Only life can do this."

17 March 1937. 11 rue Labie. Speaking to Mees Gordon, Gurdjieff hyphenates English-Scotch words together as one word. Kanari is admiring of how cleverly he does this, as she did not expect his thought about two separate peoples would go in such a sequence.

"But why astonish? All same is. You know how I call England in book?"

"Albion," says Kanari, "from Latin *alba*, meaning white. Roman name because white chalk cliffs."

"But excuse," answers Gurdjieff, "in book I not spell same. One letter I change and you not see. Even many pages before, I prepare for this when I speak of Khorassan goat, Karabach ass, and people of Albion. But you not see."

"Middle part I cannot remember," says Kanari.

"Middle part not important. Only beginning and end important. Middle part is only bridge. Beginning preparation make. From beginning flow middle, and end flow from beginning. Bridge not interest. Only interest for turkey. *I hate turkey. I write for crow or for peacock.*"

22 March 1937. 11 rue Labie. Gurdjieff speaks about hospitality:

Hospitality, yes. Man not have, in him is atrophied. Hospitality is now only cunningness. Organically man not have. As example, Turkestan. There still exists humanity-ness. From heart. Friend there is when two people buy something together, one sell his part and make money, and this he divide with other, fifty-fifty. Two times he do this and friendship established for always. With Kirghiz, yes, also such people they are. Moreover, they go to Mecca, prove that they are holy men. Simple people with heart. Those places are centrum of humanity-ness.

Once in Russia I lived like gypsy. I had horse, donkey, tent, friends. I make twenty or thirty kilometers one day, then stop, rest two days. Only such travel is real. Then you see how everything is—if each place has three or two stones. Go this way from Paris to Turkestan and will complete education have. Moreover, if you stay a long time with such people, you will gradually become like them, like real man.

To astonish you, I will tell I once go three hundred kilometers on goat—special goat, special training; over the Pamirs to Kashmir. Donkey also good for difficult places. Donkey special psyche has. If he not wish go, he will die first. You can beat, you can kill him, if he not wish, not will do. But if you understand psyche and are friend with, then he will take from you all heaviness and go until he dies. Oh, many friends have I among donkeys.

25 March 1937. 11 rue Labie. "Squirming is only passing state for man. Is state like fish out of sea, man must not long stay or he die and be obliged to be born again.[16] Man can stay squirming two or three months but not a year."

26 March 1937. 11 rue Labie. Gurdjieff serves the Rope small tinned lamb tongues from Tibet, and he tells how he used to have to butter his whole body, then cover with rubber underclothes (made in Germany), then over all that about a six-inch thickness of fur garments—and even then he was cold in Tibet.

"Only part of body have satisfaction was face under hood, warmed by breath. Such cold you never can imagine. Also, such smell from 'booter' after many weeks!"

He says in the Pamirs "there live under snow—have houses under snow and even tunnel connecting each house like streets and so cold was that when you lit fire the solid snow ceiling melted just an instant, then froze over immediately." He says that the wood they burned in their under-snow houses was one black wood, one white.

"Birch," Krokodeel says. "It's what our Indians use for canoes, the 'skin' of the birch—birch bark."

---

16. This, along with what he says when his wife is dying, are the only times, other than to Uspenskii, that he makes reference to eternal recurrence.

Gurdjieff is not sure birch is in Europe. He looks up in his Russian dictionary and sees it is right word. He tells how they made shoes from the 'skin' of it.

He serves Dalai Lama's tea, pouring out the small cups himself, measuring the sugar first, and telling the women how to drink.

"Too bad I not have time make Tibetan tea with butter—boiled, and small amount of flour of roasted wheat—such a drink have *all*.

"You see, not such idiot there in Tibet. There you can find everything, if you know how. Tibet direct communication with *Karatas* has."

30 March 1937. 11 rue Labie. The Rope is there with the exception of Kanari who stayed in the steam baths. Mees Keep has also come from London.

The first half of the luncheon is eaten in silence. Theen One, as Cellaress, refills Krokodeel's glass. Gurdjieff thinks she is drinking false but she tells him she is drinking a new glass. He looks at the glasses of the other women, which are not as full as hers. Mees Gordon has hidden hers.

"Theen One, your obligation you not fulfill. You not see all around you, only ones near like me, Mees Keep, Krokodeel. This is small obligation I give but you not fulfill. If you not can do this, then all you do will be false. You must feel your subjects around you, you for them must be king. Yet even all this is cheap thing beside real man. One man without quotation marks is worth all your kings and subjects."

In the kitchen with Krokodeel he bangs his ladle down into the soup pot, splashing but drawing up each time exactly the same amount of solid and liquid.

After she is seated he says—"Krokodeel, you notice my justness. *Never I give more or less than necessary.* But they not see, they not take what I give for what is."

"Is good food, Mr. Gurdjieff. This must make good for them no matter how assimilate."

"Ahh, that is another question."

Toasts come. "Compassionate not here," Gurdjieff says. "She in bath. She exterior dirt has made clean, but never interior dirt will she make clean, such dirtiness this is."

Writes Krokodeel: "This has been a terrible and grave luncheon, and he in some kind of pitying hidden rage—about us, I feel sure—and his disappointment. All the time I felt tears and Jane said afterwards, 'Today he is sorrowing with Our Common Father. It's because of us, what we have done, we haven't been able to take enough of what he gives, we've failed him somewhere.'"[17]

7 April 1937. 11 rue Labie. At the toasts to the idiots, Gurdjieff says, "My dear Kanari, God help you transformate into crow. Not too much dirt have. If not

---

17. Is it the women in general or is it that Kanari chose the bath over being with Gurdjieff, a taking of the teaching for granted? Of them all, it seems as though he sees in her the greatest possibilities and has given her the most and she is not present, unconsciously devaluing the teaching.

quantity have, quality have." He turns to Theen One, "May God, the Devil and all the people of *Karatas* help you be not Squirming, that you not be in future what you are today." Looking at Krokodeel, "God help you transformate into elephant."

8 April 1937. 11 rue Labie. Gurdjieff gives the beginning of new exercises with *piqûres*. Then he tells the Rope:

> I hope with my whole heart that beginning tonight there will arise in all you the feeling of humanity. You know, I not wish offend, but man is such, especially English and American [only these nationalities were present], that he cannot feel for even one person outside himself, so spoiled is he, so degenerate. This I have proved many years I make study and experiment on psyche of man—this I know for fact even your Negro is not so degenerate—he have twice times more feeling for humanity than you Americans—Negroes I like, I can be friend with, he is not spoiled, so degenerate, he understand tone and gestures.

9 April 1937. 11 rue Labie. During lunch he tips and half spills his coffee and says immediately—"Look," gesturing toward Theen One, "she make black magic, she do this, not I. She is . . ."

"Witch!" the women say.

"Yes, witch, she is witch."

"We even say 'bewitched,' Mr. Gurdjieff, when someone make black magic against you," says Kanari.

"Yes, this exact is. She witch-ness have. You can see it in her nose. Always you must look on nose to know about witch-ness. Also, Sardine have, only not so much as Theen One. First at this table for witch-ness is Theen One; second, Sardine." He turns toward Theen One and says, "any man when see such face, he immediately association have for witch-ness, all he remember from child comes to him by association. [He makes a stooped magician gesture.] Only she not have harmony, because too much one thing she have. Six parts her are empty, one part have too much, this is why her witch-ness not have harmony."[18]

10 April 1937. 11 rue Labie. Gurdjieff tells the Rope: "God is very far—him you can never touch. Tapeworm you can touch. He is in you. He even have his psyche, like man. He knows more than man because he have very fine mentation and imagination. Also has more sense of reality than man. Moreover, if you

---

18. Odd that Gurdjieff does not mention Krokodeel's nose. When in Vichy the year before he had told her: "Question is, why God make such a nose? Because once there was a poor man, he have nothing—no horse, no wagon, no plow—only he have wife with such nose like yours. And he take her, put her feet under his arm, face down on earth, and so walk through field, face dragging, making deep furrow. For such purpose God create nose like yours." He has also said her interior animal is "a baby, naïve, only two and half year. I not blame entirely."

know tapeworm scientifically, you can go up scale."

Kanari says, "You said that even God needs enema."

"Yes, but has umbrella. You know what is umbrella and what is enema. Two ends same stick. This is why I tell always enema-umbrella. You can imagine when need enema, but only have umbrella to put in behind. Then when press button, umbrella opens."

"For six months we tried to think what umbrella could mean," Kanari says.

"Now you see, simple thing is. Everyone knows umbrella—when rain, put up. Such system I put inside. Man even will take in him this thing, because wish exist."

He also says:

"Scotch is concerning material thing. Scotchness is organic thing. Jewishness is psychological thing. Scotch I hate physically, but Jewish I hate more because he psychic dirt have—self-love, vanity, pride. Except for this, I like Jewish, I like for friend. Only he is dirty in objective sense because he had possibility for knowing. Scotch not dirty in objective sense, not guilty, but Jewish born with possibility of knowing, so he is guilty. Such separation I must make for my mentation, and this is why I always tell of all people I meet that they are either Scotch or Jewish. Scotchness have stink, Jewishness have stench."

12 April 1937. 11 rue Labie. At lunch, Gurdjieff says to Kanari, "How are you, what notable change have you felt?"

"I have one small strong place no subjective state can touch," she answers.

"Perhaps you mean that center of gravity is now in your nature, not in your mind."

He asks Theen One if she will have a second helping [they are on a fourth course]. Alarmed, she answers, "Oh no, thank you, Mr. Gurdjieff, I have *no* place for it."

"You are egotist," Gurdjieff tells her. "Speak from head up, you not speak for tapeworm. He is in your presence, you must not make angry, you must be with him indulgent. Who be kind to tapeworm, who satisfy tapeworm, tapeworm help him achieve what he wish."

19 April 1937. 11 rue Labie. The women arrive. Alice has just come from the baths and is nicely dressed.

"I notice one thing today about Theen One," says Gurdjieff. "Look how she is chic."

"You also, Mister Gurdjieff, I noticed yesterday but did not have the chance to speak. Your new green suit, how handsome."

"Look, she is jealous," Gurdjieff answers. "Yesterday she saw me and so today she make self chic. Jealousy, you know, can be good thing—if not just man-woman business. This can be holy impulse. Man see something higher than him and wish be same, and so make effort. Jealousy is a factor for cunning."

Krokodeel writes, "I find jealousy is from a Greek root—'selos,' meaning zeal or eager rivalry—while envy is a Latin root—'invidere'—to see against. So jealousy is active and envy passive."

20 April 1937. 11 rue Labie. Gurdjieff makes the women a "Greek lunch." It consists of seven different courses laid out. Kanari begs off from his special roasted sweet potatoes, saying, "I am afraid will make fat, Mr. Gurdjieff."

"Potato not make fat—potato have in him starch," he tells her.

"But starch makes fat."

"Excuse, not make fat if know what to eat with, with what to combinate. Starch is very important thing, is one of the seven divine things for man. Without it, he could not even breathe. Always this has been known but now nobody know this, now starch is used to make stiff collar for pimp and petticoat for prostitute. And this, one of the seven divine things, people are afraid to eat, afraid make fat."

Mees Gordon says, "Sugar also, Mr. Gurdjieff."

"Excuse, sugar is cheap thing, is *svoloch* thing found everywhere. Everybody can have sugar."

"But sugar makes heat, isn't this bad in the body for making heat?" replies Mees Gordon.

"Sugar gives by the way heat. Starch gives everything—body, heart, material, even God thing."

21 April 1937. 11 rue Labie. Theen One and Krokodeel are to go to America soon. Theen One tells Gurdjieff that Krokodeel is upset, having realized that day that their separation from him will be nearly six months.

He tells Theen One: "Now everyone imagine he can shear me; you for example. But I make naive while you shear and at end I shear you, even of last hair, while you sit like dog in street that have lost hair. You represent yourself what you are not. You not know enough not to trust people. I wish you not be such. Here among us you can be off-guard but not in world where you soon will be. Now you are in scale of nonentity-ness. You will go, but we not will be separated as long as with inside we same idea have. Separation not touch your inner world, because we are together there. Soon again will meet."

He speaks about hopeless idiots. "Two kinds of hopeless idiots, objective and subjective. Objective, he is shit, nothing never he can do. Subjective have possibility not be shit. He already come into place where he himself know he is hopeless, he realize his nonentity. He possibility have not be shit always such as he is. Every man have moment when he can imagine that he is God."

He speaks about newspaper articles and journalists: "They are nothing, but use words to cover their nothingness. This is the fault of your language because no meaning have in its roots, like Greek. Even Russian, which some words come from Greek, have more meaning than languages in Europe which make themselves on dirty Latin. No meaning in roots, so no meaning in words. That is why life is such empty thing."

25 April 1937. Café Gambrinus, Vichy. Two days earlier, Gurdjieff has taken the Rope with him to Vichy. The subject of amber comes up. Gurdjieff says, "Amber is first thing in all incenses. Is base for every kind. Egypt uses amber; in Persia and Turkestan—the rose. In China, 'anasha,' from which come hashish. On Earth this has always been so divided—different base for incenses which produce same results. One other thing also man uses; this poison mushroom, on red cap from pimples one liquid arises—this man freeze and take. This stronger poison than all what exist. More strong even than opium.... Amber is also from sea; when it make so, like cream, like egg white when you beat, sea foam. This foam stay long time then from this two things come; amber, and this what you clean with, what is principal industry of Greece."

May 1937. Lyne Place, England. Boris Mouravieff, the Russian aristocrat, first encountering the teaching in Constantinople in 1920, and hanging around ever since but never joining, pays a visit to Uspenskii. He has helped edit the book Uspenskii has been working on since 1920, *Fragments of an Unknown Teaching*. Mouravieff opposes its publication. "It seemed to me," he says, "that esoteric doctrine, by its very nature, eludes an account described in detail by writing. It must be said that Uspenskii was aware of it. And he ended up agreeing with my way of seeing."[19]

3 May 1937. 11 rue Labie. Krokodeel and Theen One, leaving for America in four days, visit the Russian Orthodox Cathedral in the morning for the Easter ritual. They watch as mound-shaped paschas are carried thrice around the Cathedral in processional and then brought for blessing into the sanctuary where they are laid on a dais surrounded by glowing candelabras wreathed in incense. The sanctuary screen of Byzantine ikons separates the holy of holies from the crowd of believers facing it, crossing themselves with the wide-armed gestures of the Eastern church. Krokodeel then looks up and sees "Gurdjieff, the Teacher who many imagined to be a destroyer of religions."

Later, Gurdjieff has Easter lunch with the Knachtschmidts. He has cooked suckling pigs, couscous curried and peppered to a choking degree, strange tropical fruits, and Russian Easter pudding and cake.

At one point Gurdjieff gives Krokodeel and Theen One a nod of approval. "I am very glad that you, in last days here, went to Russian church to participate

---

19. This will not deter Mouravieff, however, from later publishing his own massive 759-page, three-volume study, *Gnosis*, which puts forth his idea of esoteric doctrine. Interestingly, the material is a compilation of the Gurdjieff teaching from his Russian period—as interpreted by Uspenskii—and mixed with Mouravieff's idea of a tantric "esoteric Christianity." See author's *Taking with the Left Hand*, "The Mouravieff Phenomenon."

in such good thing. For *feeling* experience . . . now Russians feast for forty days until this day when He goes up—Ascension Day. Such custom is. For everything in life there is custom. Only in Europe and America it is not known . . . America has custom only for foxtrot."

Throughout his own Easter feast he goes on talking about churches, how all Christian services derived from the Greek. "Once in Jerusalem, I saw nine different kinds of Christians all together in one place for Christmas. In center was Greek, on right was this very old people Italy now makes war with—Abyssinia. I watched very impartially and I saw that only the Greek was the real thing, and this I do not tell because I am Greek. When you see this Greek Christmas—this *opens up all your feeling*. You forget why is, for who, you forget even Christ—such knowledge they have for composing ceremony for the psychology of people."

"Was the Bible also taken from the Greek?" he is asked.

"Yes, of course," he replies. "Everything Christian came from real old Greek . . . then they spoiled. All, all, comes from Greek, even from before the time when was Bible. Your Bible is *new book,* composed four, five hundred years after by fishermen."

"What happened before?"

"Remember my chapter on Maralpleicie—also Konuzion and poppy seeds. That is what happened before."

"But before the fishermen, what happened to knowledge?" Theen One asks.

"Nothing happened," says Gurdjieff.

"But where was it?"

"Was with initiate people, as always," Gurdjieff replies. "They always go in one stream, it still flows today. You ask question from one stream, I answer from other, then you back your stream with answer. Before there was nothing for man in ordinary stream, but fishermen knew nothing, so nothing could tell but their wiseacrings. You remember the two streams I write about [in *Beelzebub's Tales*]. Difference between two streams is the difference between interpretation of events on earth. One make elephant from fly, the other make fly from elephant. Events have two explanations—one for mankind, one for me. My stream is initiate-ism."

"But there have been messengers before, Mr. Gurdjieff, like you," says Mees Gordon.

"Many such there are," Gurdjieff says, "even you have in America. For English and Americans they are something, but for me they are shit in objective sense. . . . You wish believe in your Bible. Your Bible is one thing but mine is quite another thing. Nobody now believe in Christian thing—not with inner world, especially young ones. Nobody but English old maid and lesbian America. Your Bible is hodge-podge."

He sat back with a great sigh after consuming his pascha and said, "Ach! *Now* my tapeworm thinks what to sing! He wished to sing something more high than your God Save the King."

"Hosannah?" Kanari suggested.

"No, hosannah is dirty word," Gurdjieff said. "This is used only for marriage—only for that business they make after marriage." He flashes a smile at Mees Gordon and says, "I will not say the word."

"Is hallelujah also?" she asks.

"No, Alleluia is a *big* word. It has in it three things..." Gurdjieff then intones them slowly:

"*Amen... God help us... I am you, you are me.* Very *old* word this is. Jewish take but it is not Jewish. Jewish do not understand what this means; not even your Pope understands. It includes all scale—shit to God. A more high expression does not exist because this one is *everything*!"

As they are leaving in a few days, Theen One and Krokodeel go separately to his bedroom to say their goodbyes. Theen One goes first. Then Krokodeel. He tells her, "Let your vow be your left-shouldered angel," and then signs a small cross on her forehead with his thumb. She leaves him with tears in her eyes but with the heart singing alleluias... *Amen... God help us... I am you, you are me...*

7 May 1937. Krokodeel and Theen One sail to America.

14 May 1937. 11 rue Labie. Gurdjieff calls Kanari to come see him. When she arrives she sees he is bruised and his arm is in a sling. "Oh, your arm," she cries. "Is small thing," he says. At lunch he tells her that driving in the Alps he had left the car on a steep slope, engine off, the hand brake holding. He'd gotten out of the car to look the view. Inside the car were children, women, a Russian musician. Suddenly the car moved forward toward the curve and precipice. With one gigantic bound—"Never my brain was so quick"—he leaped onto the running board, put his arm inside and steered the Buick straight off the road down the hill to the only tree in sight. The car was smashed to bits, but the occupants were saved. He was thrown into the air, turned over several times and fell, bruising his shoulder. "Almost all was finished, me, my work, all of you."

Frank Pinder comes for lunch. He has not seen Gurdjieff since January 1924 when Gurdjieff put him in charge of the Prieuré when he left for America. Pinder had rifled through Gurdjieff's papers and then, guilt stricken, fled. Kanari sees him as "a fat, stupid, perspiring old Englishman." Gurdjieff talks a lot to him about food and asks Pinder's opinion of potatoes. His reply is not recorded, but Gurdjieff tells him, "I can see from your answer which way you have gone since you were Prieuré."

Instead of responding, Pinder says, "I want to ask you a question. I want to know why the French cheat one."

"Now more than ever I can see which way you have gone, you ask such question," Gurdjieff tells him.

"What do you mean?"
"Tell, Kanari."
"Elephant from fly," Kanari says.
"What's that?" asks Pinder, confused. "What elephant? What fly?" He pauses and then says, "Don't you think, Mr. Gurdjieff, it's a good thing to learn languages? Wouldn't you advise people to learn Russian? Isn't it worth the effort?"

"*No!* You must have big aim. What you learn is *by the way*. If you cannot learn by-the-way, then you don't fulfill. Not man's center of gravity to learn languages. Either man must *Do*—or have fly business."

Later, he remarks, "Conscious labor and intentional suffering are the same thing—they cannot be separated."

15 May 1937. Café de la Paix. He gives an exercise to Mees Gordon and Kanari in what she says is "nearly perfect English."

> Take any object and put it to your feeling; represent it to yourself with feeling. Then answer these questions. Remember, you must *experience* these feelings. You must stir up your mind and police with feeling. As you continue this exercise, you must diversify your objects. Here are the questions:
> 1. Its nature and beginning
> 2. The reason for its arising, and the aim of its service
> 3. Its dependents and if anything else can be used in its place
> 4. Personal opinion of it and objective opinions
> 5. Its end and its following actualization
> 6. Its legitimate use and the most great and most small use to which it can be put
> 7. Its objective inevitability and its subjective property of services

19 May 1937. 11 rue Labie. At lunch Gurdjieff says "Fruits in your Florida have auspicious exterior but what is interior is another question. There is a reason."

"The soil?" asks Kanari. "Too much artificial manure?"
"No. Reason is emanations from sun. Not come direct."
"Because of the tilt of Earth's axis?"
"Is exact," Gurdjieff answers.
Mees Gordon says, "Such a good lunch today."
"Yes, everything I have, except of course, one thing. Everybody has many wants, I have only one. I need only one thing. This end of stick not correspond and even I can tell reason. Is my organic weakness of mind. I had this even when young. Is because I waste my time trying to make people understand. So everything I have—except. Why I have all except is because I have knowledge. Now about this weakness that consists in trying to give understanding to people—this

weakness is only this much." Gurdjieff raises his hand and measures off a quarter-inch between his thumb and forefinger.

"Then that means you are just that much lopsided, Mister Gurdjieff," says Kanari.

"Yes. Good, good. See, Mees Gordon, how she understand?"

"I'm afraid I didn't understand what Kanari meant," she says.

"Truth, English are hopeless, such sheep, donkey understanding have. Truth, pity you are English. That story about looking at sky for fifteen minutes before replying is for you and all English understanding.

"Reminds me of a story of a cart to which was put a horse, a goat and one tortoise. Of course all could go only as fast as tortoise. The horse very nervous. He said, 'What is this destiny which is written on my forehead?' The goat also spoke his opinion. And the tortoise that nothing understood except that every day the mountain before them seemed as far as ever, became very angry. He cursed and complained, 'Go, go, at all times we go, but stay nearly in same place.'

"So, Mees Gordon, never will you understand two ends of the stick. Now look her face. In one place she love me, in another she hate me. Unconsciously, of course. If it was consciously, long ago I would Tchik-make."

Gurdjieff pauses, "Now why we sit? As for me I have eaten justly. Now, Kanari, why you look on me? Something you notice?"

"Always I notice new word," she says.

"And you, Mees Gordon, you notice? Of course you not. 'Justly' was word."

"I didn't notice," she tells him, "because you always use 'truth'!"

21 May 1937. Along with Mees Gordon and Gabo, Gurdjieff persuades Kanari to drive with him to Vichy, telling her, "Mountains we will pass, and in such surroundings you will have material for third food." They leave at five o'clock, with Gabo beside Gurdjieff, and Kanari and Mees Gordon in the back seat piled high with luggage and odorous food packages. Once out of Paris on the road to Fontainebleau he drives as he usually does, "passing by fractions everything ahead, or when half passing, fell back to the horns and screechings of cars behind." Kanari, terrified, begs him to slow down, but he tells her he has to test the car—"Must make one constatation. Too much money I pay for this car."

"Then stop and let me out," she cries.

He drives a little more slowly. At his brother's house Kanari gets out with her traveling case, telling him, "I'll take the train here and meet you in Vichy."

"No, no, now you sit beside me, slowly I go. Moreover, never I go more than ninety."

"No, you go a hundred and twenty."

"How you know?"

"Because I see on speedometer."

"Impossible, never more than ninety. Now you sit till Montargis and if not like, there you can go and sit in train."

He drives better after that.

He lets some time pass and then says, "Negative emotions difficult because not susceptible to reason. Almost all forms are infantile. We think reason has come but is usually only another emotion that is added. To get rid of a negative emotion say, 'I am sick.' Do not say what or who made you sick. When you say 'I am sick' you establish positive attitude."

They arrive at Nevers at ten, the dining room is closed, but he has them open it and they have a cold dinner.

"Curiosity is a dirty thing," he says. "That is why I am always angry for idiot questions, why philosophizing makes me nervous. In English not exist two words for two kinds of curiosity, as in other languages. Word for other kind of curiosity is needing-to-know. For this needing-to-know you must have material. Then you will not receive something empty."

Later, near Vichy they come to a new lighting system.

"You say in your book," says Kanari, "such use of electricity is a bad thing. Yet more and more is used."

"The more they use, the greater will be the catastrophe."

Just then a cat crosses the road.

Kanari asks, "Why do cat's eyes shine at night?"

"All that family have such property."

"To make other animals afraid?" asks Mees Gordon. "Mesmerize them?"

"Yes."

"Snake also?" she asks.

"Yes, snake also have," says Gurdjieff. "And this same property man can achieve also."

The next day Kanari tells him that she will take the train back to Paris. He is furious and says "terrible things." After lunch she hides and takes the train back to Paris.

Mees Gordon telephones her when she arrives back telling her, "He drove too fast and raced a motorcycle."

29 May 1937. 11 rue Labie. Mees Gordon and Kanari have lunch with Gurdjieff. He tells them, "Two kinds of feeling has man. Physical and another kind for which no name in English or French — feeling-with-sensing. Every day I can tell you difference in this feeling from what was yesterday."

Then he says, "Tapeworm sing 'God Save King.' Like English people. But while this they sing, inside quite another thing they tell, just opposite. They say to the devil with the king. Others sing 'Internationale' and 'Marseillaise' and that makes middle part."

"You mean that neutralizes situation, like safety valve?" says Kanari.

"Of course. Just why such thing is of value. Then can starving people sing 'God Save King' when such nonentity go by. Truth, nobody can have such fruit as this. Take, take, not pity."

"That's what worries me all the time, Mr. Gurdjieff," says Mees Gordon. "To think we have such thing when others have nothing, are starving."

"Mees Gordon, Mees Gordon, may your mentation not be such," interjects Gurdjieff.

"But you tell in your book when some people have much it means others must have nothing," she tells Gurdjieff.

"Yes, I tell how is."

"But why should it be so?"

"I not tell why. Eh, Kanari?"

"You always say fact is fact," she says.

"Is exact. Now, Kanari, explain her."

"It is explained in a chapter of your book—'Idea of Justice Is Man's Most Accursed Mirage,'" says Kanari.

"You see, Mees Gordon," he says, "not enough read my words, also must think about what read, otherwise empty will remain."

30 May 1937. 11 rue Labie. Olgivanna and Frank Lloyd Wright, and their eleven-year-old daughter, Iovanna, come for dinner. Kanari is there and says to Olgivanna, "I saw a friend of yours in America and she told me your place was imbued with a great spirit—that she felt your presence everywhere." Olgivanna smiles with pleasure, but Wright says, "Huh, I wouldn't say that. The spirit there is architecture."

During dinner, trying to be amiable, Wright says, "Mr. Gurdjieff, you're certainly a good cook. You could earn a lot of money cooking somewhere."

"Not so much as I can earn shearing," answers Gurdjieff. Earlier Wright had given him money.

After dinner Gurdjieff brings out a chapter of *Meetings with Remarkable Men* and asks who would read it, as he passes the chapter to Kanari. But Wright takes it, saying—"I read very well."

Gurdjieff gets up and leaves the room as Wright begins to read. After reading a number of pages, Wright whispers to Olgivanna, "Damn, I'm sleepy, I can't take it. Still, I don't want to hurt the old man's feelings."

He begins to read again and Gurdjieff returns and sits down. Wright immediately stops reading—"You know, Mr. Gurdjieff," he says, "this is interesting and it's a pity it's not well written. You know you talk English very well, too bad you can't dictate. Now if I had time you could dictate to me and I could write this for you in good English."

Gurdjieff makes no reply.

Wright reads a few more pages and then says, "Now I must go and take my little daughter home. She's sleepy—and so is her father."

"Yes," Gurdjieff mockingly agrees, "for her sake stop." Then he adds, "She is young. You, of course, old man now and life finish. But she only begin."

Wright's face flames and he tells him—"My life is *not* finished." Pointing to Iovanna, he adds, "I could right now make six more like her."

Olgivanna gets up, tears in her eyes, and leads Iovanna to the door.

Writes Kanari: "Wright is an arch idiot. Sickness from 'art' and besides a mean ego and unconscious conceit to a point I have rarely met. He gave his opinion of idiots, saying he had invented some. G. merely looked on."

1 June 1937. Café de la Paix. Kanari says, "You said the other day that starch is holy thing, God thing." She says she pondered this and now asks, "Is it because, like amber, it has three forces in it—carbon, hydrogen and oxygen?"

"Now I not answer because you go too far," Gurdjieff tells her. "You have one hundred kilos too much curiosity, your enemy. Before you had one thousand kilos, but still too much you have. I advise you recognize enemy and full stop make. Also, another constation I make. Something wrong your sex. Sex very important thing is, like light, like air you breathe, food you eat. If you are in five parts, two of your five parts depend from sex. You must more normal live."

"Cannot even think about such things, Mr. Gurdjieff," answers Kanari. "I do not wish, I have no time. In twenty-four hours I have only four hours for myself and must use them for sleeping."[20]

"Then lopsided you will be and I can nothing do, for this depends only from you."

Later, at lunch, Kanari gives a toast to hopeless idiots.

"Aha, you hear, Sardine?" asks Gurdjieff. "She philological manipulation make. Now I must give her mark. You know what is mark?"

"I think so, Mr. Gurdjieff," says Kanari.

Gurdjieff says, "Among initiates there is always mark. Once in old days there were combats on different days. One day would be cockfights, another day buffaloes, another day man and man, another day scorpion and falanga. Of course no newspapers, so to let people know they would put up flag of different color—yellow for cocks, red for buffalo, white for man and blue for falanga-scorpion. You see, Kanari?"

"I'm afraid so, Mr. Gurdjieff."

"Then what you think about this. What you decide?"

Kanari refuses to answer but later writes in her notes: "I could have said, 'Yes, and nine out of ten times falanga wins.' But not this time. Of course Sardine understood nothing." Gurdjieff invites Kanari and Mees Gordon and Sardine to his apartment for lunch.

---

20. Gurdjieff asked Krokodeel to give up smoking. Now he is asking Kanari to give up lesbian activity. But as connected as she feels to him, she cannot even conceive of it.

Kanari writes, "He was worried, hadn't slept all night. Galoshes in sight. He didn't say much, except, 'Life is not always what you see for a person. Is like the theater.' I supplied, 'Behind the scene.' He said, 'Yes. Also behind fact is always one thousands facts.'"

11–28 June 1937. 11 rue Labie. Kanari has been treating his patients with two electrical machines [presumably "the radio" he first showed the women]. They are very complicated and require different adjustments for each.

"Every person is not polarized alike," Gurdjieff says.

The color in the tubes is beautiful—like neon—even he admires it.

"Something in color *is*—like life. And sometimes in colors, one color something of itself it even has—especially in electricity."

Later, he says, "Usually we constate with the mind. But in the case of constating with feeling instead of with mind, what would such word be in English?"

Kanari doesn't know.

He speaks about a Persian musician. "He is half woman. Such representative of art have too many 'feelings.' We have name for such in Russian, one word, meaning prostitute-in-trousers."

Later, he says, "You must have three states—active, passive, and *life state*."

15 June 1937 11 rue Labie. Kanari has met several times with Rosamund Bland in London. On her return, she writes a long letter to Theen One about their meeting.[21]

8 July 1937. 11 rue Labie. At lunch Gurdjieff says to Sardine, "Today you eat like sparrow. You know sparrow cannot eat much, but peck, peck. Spoil for others."

"Like canary?" asks Kanari, hoping for more details.

"Canary I not know."

"A little you know because once you said is *svoloch* bird."

"I know of course a little but I not know canary *behind* like sparrow. Sparrow I know like myself."

Mees Gordon says, "Yes, you used to paint them to resemble canaries. I always wondered if that was true or a fable like the ladder in the desert. Stilts in sand and ladder."

"No," says Gurdjieff, "those stories true, only ten percent is fantasy. That reminds me how I suffer when Soloviev died. For three months I was not myself. Such friend was—more than brother. I love him more than a mistress."

20 July 1937. 11 rue Labie. "There are three kinds of satisfaction: from the past, after suffering from want or need and you satisfy this waiting place; satisfaction

---

21. See Essay, "Meeting with Rosamund Bland."

of a present need; a satisfaction of something you know is also for your future, that will continue for your future good."

20 July 1937. Avon Cemetery, France. Kanari writes to Theen One in America.

> Sunday was Sardine-Wart's birthday and I came in from Orgeval at noon for it and to give Lolo her piqûre [injection]. I drove Louise to Fontainebleau to the Avon cemetery to see graves of Gurdjieff's mother, wife and Katherine Mansfield. The two Madames Gurdjieff are in a long wide double grave, tall grasses, flowering weeds (he ordered it kept like this), at either end two rough tall uncarved stones—no name, no date. Wife is at mother's feet. Two rose bushes twine about the stones. A white stone bench placed at wife's head—like the one at the Prieuré where he used to sit between the "two beings I loved above all others." Remember in his book? A cypress tree fifteen feet high is by the bench. A strange grave with strange emotions to give. Anyone would know this was not an ordinary resting place.

13 August 1937. 11 rue Labie. Pinder comes to lunch again. Kanari, Sardine and Mees Gordon are there. Gurdjieff says, "Brother very ill, really die three weeks ago, now is only artificial."

Pinder, eating a great deal, says, "I feel I deserve this dish because once for three months in the army I had only a plate of beans three times a day. So I deserve this to make up for that time."

"No, not deserve," Gurdjieff tells him. "If once you unconsciously had such experience and if you consciously again repeat experience, then you could tell you deserve."

Toast is drunk to Compassionate Idiot. Pinder asks exactly what this is.

"Everyone is idiot, even God. But when these idiots see another who is another kind of idiot from themselves, they become angry and curse him. This is very characteristic of these idiots. Now compassionate means that among this company can sometimes exist idiots who know that all are idiots together, so they pity all and not become angry. These are compassionate. I am unique idiot so I am no more this idiot compassionate."

"I am too fat, I eat too much," says Pinder changing the subject.

"Eat, eat, man is not pig. Man has as much room as his valise."

"What valise?" asks Pinder. "You mean leather bag for travelling?"

Gurdjieff pats his sides, saying, "This is man's valise."

"Why do you make me eat so much?" asks Pinder.

"Because I see valise when you come in."

"Because you made me eat too much," Pinder insists.

"You speak only of this moment, but what about past? I not responsible. Pig have stomach, man have rubber. That is why man can eat more than he can."

Mees Gordon gets mad but no one knows why. "I've seen pigs that have eaten more than they could, Mr. Gurdjieff. Such fat stomachs."

"Yes, you've seen," Gurdjieff tells her, enjoying her anger and prodding it—"because pigs not wear clothes. Now you walk around apartment freely, before mirror, without dress, before and after eating—and you look in mirror, Mees Gordon."

Everyone breaks out in gales of laughter.

"Now Kanari," Gurdjieff says, "I can see by smile has idea for two articles, can write and make money. Perhaps you not know, Mr. Pinder, she is writer and moreover famous writer. But with what kind of people she is famous is another question. Is that why you laugh Kanari?"

"I laugh at what you say. I think no question exists in the world that you not examine from all sides."

Asks Pinder, not leaving the subject go, "Why am I so fat? Do I eat too much?"

"Reason you never heard of," Gurdjieff tells him. "Now I go lie" and walks to his room.

Mees Gordon, still mad, says—"I don't understand why Mr. Gurdjieff always says that about pigs. You, Solita, just sit there and listen to him but you haven't seen pigs in the country as I have."

"No," she answers, "but I see the idea that pig eats to his capacity and man beyond."

Kanari writes in her notes: "Pinder was once at the Prieuré, though no one could guess it."[22]

14 August 1937. 11 rue Labie. Gurdjieff's brother has cancer of the stomach and intestines. He is being cared for by two nurses. "By next week," Gurdjieff says, "it will be finished. It is time, in nature, in any case."

16 August 1937. Kanari and Mees Gordon drive to Fontainebleau to meet Gurdjieff and Pinder, who are returning from Vichy. They all picnic in the woods. Kanari is the director. There is a break in the toasts and she thinks Gurdjieff has finished. He looks at her—"If we depend on such director, we could die of thirst," he tells her. Picking up his cup, he says, "To hopeless idiots."

Mees Gordon smiles at him lovingly and says with admiration, "Oh, he remembered this was hopeless."

Gurdjieff casts one look and replies—"But I was here, Mees Gordon."

Later, he says to Pinder, who speaks Russian and French well, that he doesn't

---

22. This luncheon should be enough to dispel the idea that Pinder is a "Patriarch" of the Work, as some believe. (Also included as "Patriarchs" are Orage and C. S. Nott.)

know his own language, but studies another. "Man not know his own nose," he says, "and at same time wish to know God's tail."

31 August 1937. Café de La Paix. Gurdjieff sits with Kanari in the morning. Gurdjieff's brother Dmitri has died of cancer. Gurdjieff tells her he had kept his brother's cancer inactive for twelve years, but when Dmitri quarrelled with him three or four months ago, he went to a German doctor who gave him medicine that was poison for him, made the "flower" grow on the cancer. "When they sent for me at last, it was too late. All could do was give such thing as keep him alive artificially. But he in truth died three weeks ago and if today I joke it is because already I was through experiences of his death. I will put him at Avon—my three near ones, mother, wife, and brother, all one place, and very original place. Nearly all family now dead."

Dmitri lay in the Chapelle Ardente for three days and every night at six o'clock there is a service around the bed. At the Avon cemetery the ground is already prepared beside the small dolmen of his mother. Miss Gordon, Solita, Margaret and Georgette are among the mourners, some coming by car and others, some thirty, in a bus. The service lasts ten minutes. During the priest's reading Solita says, "Gurdjieff's face seemed to be sunken in and of quite another man. He didn't notice when the wind blew out his taper and someone lit it for him."

Later, Kanari tells him, speaking of the Rope, that he has a new family now that loves him, though not the same as his real family.

"No, can never be same," he says. "Blood thing so strong for me. But real; family not love but hate me. Because I am source, it must be so. Never I give them enough and for this they hate me in their hearts. . . . For what you can buy black dress, Kanari?"

She tells him for about one hundred-fifty francs.

"Yet each woman ask me six hundred francs and there are eight women. I gave just half of what they asked. And all angry on me and curse me in heart."

5 September 1937. 6 rue des Colonels Renard. Four years ago Gurdjieff lived here. Now he returns again to what was his brother's apartment in the Russian quarter, near the Arc de Triomphe. Looking around, Gurdjieff says, "What stays of brother is only shit. Brother I knew not here now." On the walls he puts up photos of the Prieuré. He has also brought along the belled clock that was in the study house.

"Now you learn more in one month than in all your past life," he says to Kanari. "From results from last exercise you can now understand what I told six months ago, that what you had done till then was all preparation. Now you can see why. All your life was shit, now can be otherwise and can have hope for future. Think, if for past eighteen years you had worked like now, what could be today."

"Man is such that he can only be egoist. He is so made, but sometimes for an hour or two, what he can do is to look around him, see what is, how is, and make program accordingly. Only this will show him how he should be. I hate man. He is shit. Because he has brain he philosophizes with it. Give him a rose and he thinks it is shit—not recognize. Give him shit and he says it is a rose. He has lost good clean instinct that even animals have. They know the difference between rose and shit. Now because such day I will drink Armagnac. In mornings with such troubles as now, I make nervous, make elephant from fly. But with this Armagnac fly is not elephant. Fly is—fly."

"I hope you are not angry, Mr. Gurdjieff?" says Kanari, though she forgets the reason why she says this.

"Angry? No. Long ago I lost such property. Now I have quite other factors."

22 September 1937. London. J. B. Priestly's play *I Have Been Here Before* opens, marking the first time Uspenskii's ideas on time and recurrence are popularly portrayed on the stage. The main character is the mysterious Dr. Görtler, who intervenes to halt a series of fated misfortunes (if the other characters behave as they have in the past). Priestly acknowledges his debt to *A New Model of the Universe*.

4 October 1937. London. Uspenskii is asked at a meeting about whether the passage of the ideas into general life would be beneficial to humanity and also might help the school, as well. He answers:

> It will happen by itself. There is no need for us to worry about it. Ideas will spread, maybe in our lifetime and maybe after us. Most of these ideas will enter into scientific or philosophic language, but they will enter in the wrong form. There will be no right distinction between doing and happening, and many thoughts of ordinary thinking will be mixed with these ideas; so they will not be ideas we know, only words will be similar. If you don't understand this, you will lose in this way.

19 October 1937. Café de la Paix. Paris. It is two years since Kanari's first evening with Gurdjieff and a year from when he told her to review all her science studies and report to him. She brings her report to the café and he gives her permission to read it. He looks at her chart of head and body systems to which she had applied his law of trimonia (Law of Three) for certain exercises. She finishes reading and he says nothing.

"Perhaps I was impudent to compose such paper for you?" Kanari ventures.

"Not impudent. Even I thank you. You have unconsciously given me answer something I was searching for my book, about future of humanity. If you have found such thing, others of future humanity also can do. This is what you have enlighten for me."

"I can't believe it, Mr. Gurdjieff."

"You can believe. You now may have second degree of initiatism because you have initiated yourself. Today at my table will be like feast day for you—like feast after forty days."

At lunch Gurdjieff toasts her:

"May God and devil both help—not quotation mark devil but real one. With both God and devil helping, you can see what end must be and where—*Karatas*—could not be otherwise. On that planet everyone have tail, so you also. It must grow already and I sure everyone will great curiosity have—look, touch—because they know you are one of my people. Especially in America."

"But Americans will not have eyes to see."

"Excuse, such tail, everyone can see. Even she will be unhappy, nowhere she can go in peace, they will follow in theater, restaurant, try look. You understand, Kanari, what I wish you, what I tell? What we speak this morning?"

"Yes."

Later, he asks Kanari, with Margaret present, if Yakina is her friend, if she would take responsibility for her.

"Yes."

"Good. Better recommendation I could not have."

20 October 1937. 6 rue des Colonels Renard. Payson Loomis shows up for lunch. Gurdjieff tells him, "This is dish of day."

Loomis corrects him. "You can't say 'dish of day'—it's not English."

"Kanari, what is your opinion?" asks Gurdjieff.

"'Dish of day' is good expression."

"But it's not English," Loomis tells her.

"What would you call it, Loomis?" asks Gurdjieff.

"In America we say—ah, ah, uh—well, we say '*plat du jour*.'"

"That is not English either, Mr. Loomis," Gurdjieff answers to great merriment from all. "Let it be 'dish of day,' Loomis."

Loomis turns toward Kanari—"How long have you lived over here?"

"Sixteen years."

Gurdjieff interjects: "She remembers English very good, Mr. Loomis. Kanari is my philological secretary."

Loomis, identified, pays no attention to Gurdjieff.

"Then you are an expatriate!" he tells Kanari.

Later, "This fruit," Gurdjieff says, "you notice, have no seeds. Then how grow tree? Wind blow fruit when small far away, even kilometer. But no seed for growing. How then grow?"

No one speaks.

Kanari finally says, "You not tell?"

"Such secret cost me millions and my time. Why tell for nothing? I not give so cheap. Use your brain. Read book."

Autumn 1937. 6 rue des Colonels Renard. Gurdjieff appoints Kanari as his secretary.

Writes Kanari of the talk they had: "It is the second body which contains not only the nature but also the quality, character and essence of beings. Gurdjieff's is so developed that he can read others like a newspaper. He names the nature part—which we have inherited from the animals—according to what is predominant in us. He sees certain exterior traits that correspond to the salient 'marks' we notice in animals—and our character is also correspondent to the strongest characteristic of whatever he gives for interior animals."

10 November 1937. 6 rue des Colonels Renard. Krokodeel and Theen One return from America and go into kitchen to embrace him. He is preparing a pheasant for the Rope.

11 November 1937. 6 rue des Colonels Renard. "There is voluntary and involuntary sin and there is also voluntary and involuntary goodness, or good deed."
He wanted a word, one verb in English that means "take blessing from above and pass to someone below." Kanari could not find it. He says it exists in Greek in the Gospels. He said that Jesus knew his own nonentity-ness and should he return, he would be very angry that people thought he had said he was God.
Later, Gurdjieff says, "Pray today that God sleeps—then only can devil and his friends help me. I have more friends among devils than angels. When God sleeps is the only time the devil is free to do what he wishes, for good or for evil."

13 December 1937. 6 rue des Colonels Renard. Gurdjieff shows a bit of the inside of an orange. "Is sperm part," he says. "Only one orange in many have this part from which grow new oranges. Sperm is good word for this—sperm can be male or female not only male. Old Turkish word is 'soil' and truth good word is. If all *real* words and meanings in each language were taken, and from them one language created, no more necessary it would be to go to school."

1938. Mill House. Mechanicsville, Pennsylvania. Toomer, now forty-four years old, stomach trouble increasing, his wife's rising ire at the upkeep of a farm that can't pay for itself, forces him to give up his communal experiment "Friends of Being." It marks his last attempt to replicate life at the Prieuré.

January 1938. Lyne Place, England. Uspenskii reminds Bennett's wife that the year is up and she had promised to tell him about her near death experience. They have a long talk. When she returns home, she tells Bennett: "I am deeply sad for him. I had not understood how much he suffered. When I told him all that had happened to me, he was on the verge of tears, and said that since he was a young man he had been waiting and hoping to have for himself the experience which proves the reality of the other world, but it had never come to him."

She says she felt like his mother and knew that he must give up his pride in his own strength.

"He is a great man and I have always respected him, but now I feel differently. I feel warm towards him for the first time. Only I am very sad for him, because I do not believe he will get what he is looking for. It only came to me because I was willing to die. He understood me, but not altogether, and that is why I am sad: because he is terribly lonely."

Upon her leaving, Uspenskii says, "I have neglected you too much; you must come and see me more often."

12 January 1938. 6 rue des Colonels Renard. Gurdjieff looks at the Christmas tree and says, "In general such tree is shit. Any one can make, only when *you* make, is subjective, you lose something of yourself. But when I make, is objective for all humanity. Can be like medicine for you. If you sit and look for two, three hours, you can remember all your childhood. From such shit thing, I make butter. Same thing, what I do with music and my kitchen. I make another vibration from these ordinary things. Truth, after look long time at this tree in beginning of New Year, you can have food for whole year. Man can look and not be just animal.... All I make, if tree, music or kitchen, I make from Law *Heptaparaparshinokh*. Is my law, is Gurdjieff's law.

"When once you are initiated for one thing, it is like a chain—one link flow to another. And then the whole chain flows."

19 January 1938. 6 rue des Colonels Renard. "In Yakina's past, all her can-ness (ability to do) was in her," says Gurdjieff.

Gurdjieff makes a downward gesture—"When first saw, I thought was only such representative of art as have will-lessness in one place. You understand what I tell, Marguerite?"

"Yes."

"No. If understand you would not wear such things." He stares at the row of bracelets she wears on each arm. "Eheu! Life such idiot thing. What good life has dog. He at all times wish only to eat, only one tapeworm has. But biped-man has three tapeworms to satisfy. But some people have two tapeworms atrophied. What was that saying—blessed he..."

The Rope supplies: "Blessed is he who has a soul. Blessed is he who has no soul. But grief and sorrow to him who has its inception."

31 January 1938. Café de la Paix. Late for a meeting, Kanari finds Yakina sitting with Gurdjieff. Her face is so distressed that Kanari waits until she leaves to approach Gurdjieff. The previous day she had said to him, "I see I irritate you, Mr. Gurdjieff, so I will go."

Gurdjieff tells Kanari, "I nervous and your friend come talk empty to empty. So I tell her I explain Kanari who know my language. She too light for this work, too American. In life she perhaps have something good. But not for our work. I thought when she first came that after she had contact with me, something would collect in her empty place, but now I see is not so. Such empty life leave empty place. In fact, I could tell is piece of meat with emanations. Good formulation, eh?"

Kanari says, "I think the reason is result of philosophizing for years with Orage, Miss Heap and all those New York people."

"Yes, like that she is victim of self-observation."[23]

"Perhaps still is hope, Mr. Gurdjieff. She has such wish to work, be different. She knows there is nothing else in life but your work. Don't send her away."

"Well, I will see what I can combinate for her. She must all stop make, wait, begin again another way. She has only automatic mind, she not understand that of mind is two kinds and she quite not have real mind mentation. You explain her, but not use my words."

When Kanari speaks to Yakina, she is stricken and cries and then rebels. She says, "I dislike that man." Then she decides to face him the next day and ask for some task.

9 February 1938. 6 rue des Colonels Renard. At lunch are Yakina, Georgette, Mees Gordon, Sardine and Kanari. Pointing to small black olives, Gurdjieff says: "Is exact like shit of sheep, small, neat, clean. Very convenient for flies to lay eggs in, raise family. Not all is shit and finished, something good remains. Is best manure. But shit of man is worth nothing — is good only for cabbage. All from sheep is good — wool, food, shit — all."

"But you say English are sheep," says Mees Gordon happily.

Scornfully, Gurdjieff says — "But that is for English psyche, Mees Gordon."

Turning to Georgette when squirming idiot toast is given, he says, "God or devil. Choose."

"Both together," answers Georgette.

"Excuse. Cannot have both. How can be Paris and Berlin at the same time? Devil help small things, only so much he can do."

15 February 1938. 6 rue des Colonels Renard. C. S. Nott shows up with a friend of his, a painter from Jane Heap's London group. Mees Gordon is also there.

"Why do you close the shutters and keep out the light?" asks Nott's friend.

"Because sun pass from there in street. And at all times my principle is — all or nothing."

---

23. This is another confirmation that Orage was not given self-remembering. Perhaps because Orage published *Psychological Exercises* in 1927, which made Gurdjieff furious, he realized he could not yet be trusted. Most likely, if Orage had left Jessie, Gurdjieff would have given him the initiation he desired.

"I think you have great patience," Nott tells Gurdjieff.
"I not have patience—I have practice."
"I have patience," says Nott.
"Of course. You are English. All English have patience."

Kanari is taking dishes into kitchen and hears Gurdjieff say, "... careful not be number 18, idiot that has stink coming from him, what I call Harmful Idiot."

"But that's number 19," says Kanari involuntarily.

"Er-er—is number 17."

23 February 1938. 6 rue des Colonels Renard. At lunch are Yakina, Mees Gordon and Kanari. Gurdjieff speaks of Yakina's plumpness and asks Kanari to supply a word. She refuses.

"When have money will find new secretary. Your obligation is to help when I look for word. Yakina, you were perhaps a beautiful child? You can thank this you are now spoiled. You are now receptacle for shit."

"Yes, I know," answers Yakina.

"Must be so with such child. Everyone spoil, parents, young man. Child not study, not learn. If beautiful face have man or woman, always I know is shit. If lawyer or engineer I need, never I choose beautiful face—shit is. I choose monster. He is not spoiled. He study when young, is clever. This is fault of education and parents. Now late, time has passed. You no longer are hard—just liquid now begin. Fault of your past that you are now empty.

"Man is such that he wishes to live until last minute, such is his egoism. Let whole world burn, but let him live.

"Animals and children only have property of pure logicality. They not philosophize. Only a philosopher can understand philosophers.

"Who eats such food will die but who does not eat will perish like a dog. Another kind of man is also—who does not even perish like a dog. If dog perishes in street, there is body, you can see, but cannot even see body of this other kind of man. He neither dies nor perishes—he disappears. Like the soldier of Arc de Triomphe, he is unknown.

"Man is man. He cannot be otherwise. He is such that he can never change his body. He can only be as he is because he is the result of heredity. But his mind he can educate and with this control his animal body and not be its slave. He must at all times struggle and as his mind grows stronger, so will his weakness grow stronger. This is a good thing, it makes for more struggle. It is not good if the body at once lies down. He must command, he must direct. Easy not eat if not see. Only is difficult if he sees before him—and then not take. This will make something for him in another place, something he can use.

"Man's body is shit and shit can never be diamond not even shit of diamond."

[Undated but following previous.] Café de la Paix. Janet Flanner has quarreled

with Kanari bitterly over her devotion to Mr. Gurdjieff. Kanari says: "Please tell me what is Janet's animal?"[24]

"Ah, again, Mees, curiosity you have." He sits with her for five minutes and then says, "Now one secret I will tell. Not only is tapeworm in stomach of man, other worms are also. Perhaps you have seen in shit?"

"No. Only in books as usual."

"Ach! Well, worms, such snakes as I tell about, is different kinds in stomach of man and of them all, one is always chief in this universe of stomach. He commands all and from him, this chief in struggle of stomach universe, from him depends of what consists the psyche of this man and what is his animal."[25]

Gurdjieff then speaks to her for twenty minutes, a monologue of which she says, "I could not understand a single thing, nor retain one sentence." When he finishes she tells him she had understood nothing.

"Of course not. Only I tell you this to give you taste of such thing."

A year or so later he will ask, "Do you understand what I said?"

"I'm trying to," Kanari says.

"Not enough to try. Must understand without trying. He who always try and never do is onanist. Must at once *do* in life, if wish normal man be—in all things. There is no 'nearly' in real understanding, is or is not."

11–12 March 1938. Hitler annexes Austria.

April 1938. London. Uspenskii forms the Historico-Psychological Society. Though some one thousand people attend his lectures, he restricts membership to three hundred people.

2 April 1938. Sotteville-sous-le-Val, Normandy, France. Sixty-six-year-old Dr. Leonid Robertovich de Stjoernval, Gurdjieff's oldest pupil from the St. Petersburg days, long suffering from prostate cancer and a cruel operation as was done at the time, dies of pulmonary tuberculosis. His face is astonishingly serene and relaxed.

Gurdjieff attends the funeral. Stjoernval's wife, Elizabeta, has Father Leperovsky conduct the service. At one point he hammers out: "Doctor de Stjoernval died a true Christian. He regained faith, peace in his soul and the right way, after so many years of servitude and aberrations."

Gurdjieff clears a passage and exits backwards, scowling. Later he reprimands Elizabeta on her choice of Father Leperovsky.

July 1938. Paris. Krokodeel returns for three weeks. "All your filthy fat [psychological] is burned off," Gurdjieff tells her. He makes no mention of Theen One not being there until the third day when he takes Krokodeel aside after lunch and

---

24. If noses are an indication of "witch-ness," as Gurdjieff says, Janet Flanner's is certainly that.
25. Is he telling her that her friend is a snake? It would seem so.

speaks of his disappointment in her failure to appear, if only to show her good wishing for him and his Work.

"She did not know what work I made for her," he says in a sorrowing tone. "Every night, for her, I made special séance. Now, no longer can I make this. *I have not the right.*" He shakes his head and adds, "And about her, now we no longer speak."

September 1938. Sèvres, France. The group that Madame de Salzmann took over after her husband's death continues. Principal members are René Daumal and his wife, Vera Milanova; Henri Tracol and his wife, Henriette Lannes; Philippe Lavastine and his wife, Nathalie de Salzmann; and Luc Dietrich.

September 1938. Munich, Germany. English and French prime ministers Chamberlain and Daladier meet with Hitler and Mussolini and agree to the Munich Pact. Hitler takes Sudetenland.

13 October 1938. Warwick Gardens. Uspenskii gives his last lecture here, as the Historico-Psychological Society has acquired Colet House at 46 Colet Gardens, an imposing and elegant building with a hall that accommodates over five hundred people. With this, together with his magisterial residence at Lyne Place, and some one thousand people now under his tutelage, Uspenskii's future looks exceedingly bright. Even so, his drinking increases, as the Higher Source he hoped to contact had not appeared and his noetic ability failed to offer him the higher mystical experience he sought.

18 December 1938. Germany. General Werner Freiherr von Fritsch, Commander-in-Chief of the Army, writes in his diary: "This man—Hitler—is Germany's destiny for good and for evil. If he now goes over the abyss, he will drag us all down with him. There is nothing we can do."

1939. London. Aldous Huxley's novel *After Many a Summer Dies the Swan* appears. Uspenskii's followers are upset that a main character, Mr. Propter, is thought to be modeled on Uspenskii. Certainly Huxley's Mr. Propter speaks of many Work ideas in the book, such as the liberation from personality, the successive levels of mechanical laws, as well as man's three levels of existence: subhuman, human, and spirit. The first two levels are completely determined and void of God:

> It is in their power to pass from the level of the absence of God to that of God's presence. Each member of the psychological swarm is determined; and so is the conduct of the total swarm. But beyond the swarm, and yet containing and interpenetrating it, lies eternity, ready and waiting to

experience itself.... Let eternity experience itself, let God be sufficiently often present in the absence of human desires and feelings and preoccupations; the result will be a transformation of that life which must be lived, in the intervals, upon the human level.

Most interesting, perhaps, is Huxley's agreement with Gurdjieff that there is no "soul" as such. He writes:

Madness consists, for example, of thinking of oneself as a soul, a coherent and enduring human entity. But, between the animal below and the spirit above, there is nothing on the human level except a swarm of constellated impulses and sentiments and notions; a swarm brought together by the accidents of heredity and language; a swarm of incongruous and often contradictory thoughts and desires. Memory and the slowly changing body constitute a kind of spatio-temporal cage, within which the swarm is enclosed. To talk of it as though it were a coherent and enduring 'soul' is madness. On the strictly human level there is no such thing as a soul.

1939. 54 rue du Four, Paris. Madame de Salzmann's group now meets at the apartment of Philippe Lavastine, who is married to her daughter Nathalie, or "Boussique." Besides those in the original group of 1934, now included are Pauline de Dampierre, Marthe de Gaigneron, Bernard Lemaître and Solange Claustres.

1 March 1939. SS Paris. Gurdjieff and Kanari sail to New York.

3 March. 1939. London. With war imminent, Uspenskii opens the meeting saying, "We know people are machines. How can machines be just? It is not a quality of machines. If they are responsible, Number 5 [types of active force], then you can speak about justice or injustice, but if they just act in a certain way as circumstances and conditions make, how can they be just?"

Question: Did the idea of justice come from higher knowledge or how did man get hold of it?
Uspenskii: It is man's idea. The idea by itself may be quite right, but it does not work. There is nothing you can explain by justice. It is necessary to think how this idea comes. You see you use the word but you do not give account to yourself why you call one thing just and another unjust. One thing is always connected with another, one thing inevitably follows another. All these disturbances that happened in Europe after the war [First World War] create in one country one situation, in another, another. Why take only one and call it injustice?... We cannot speak about injustice as long as we think of it as an exception. When we think of it as

a rule then we think how to escape from it. There can be no justice in our present state, no justice in prison. The only thing one can think seriously when one realizes one is in prison is how to escape, not sit and cry about injustice in prison. Prison is made of injustice, not for justice. . . . So you see this feeling of injustice may be very good by itself but it arises from a very childish view of the world, from the idea that machines can be just.

Q: Where does man come from?

U: We do not know. You see in this system one of the things we must learn is to learn to say "I do not know" if we do not. In ordinary science or philosophy they try to find explanations and find imaginary ideas, theories and so on.

Q: From ideas you give one does get an idea of plan.

U: From that point of view we know we belong to this octave that begins at the Sun; there is an unknown Do, an unknown Si, then on the surface of the earth Organic Life making the three notes La, Sol and Fa. So our origin, according to this, is in the Sun, but what Do means and what Si means we do not know and so we must leave it like that. We must study what it is possible to know.

Q: When I think about it and connect it with other people I see it is as you say but when it affects me then I am negative about it and cannot understand it.

U: You cannot think seriously the way you do. How did the [First World War] war begin? Thirty-six million people died. That was unjust? None of them wanted to die probably. So you see what kind of figures we have to deal with if we begin to think about injustice. With the causes the war created, things cannot be different. When certain causes are created by historical processes, then something happens.

You ask about tasks. You can try to trace this very interesting question. Try to go through your life as far as you can remember, no need to go as far as the very beginning when things really happened to the whole family, but from the moment when things began to happen to you separately from your parents or as a result of your own actions, not necessarily intentional actions. It will be interesting to trace when it began and whether you can find in your life examples of real accident when something happened not as a result of your own action and when something happened as a result of your own action. And compare examples. That makes you think on the right lines; it is a kind of mental exercise and the results are interesting apart from this.

7 March 1939. New York. Gurdjieff arrives and takes a suite at the Wellington Hotel. He meets with people at Childs but the restaurant annoys him, as the manager is not used to a half dozen or so chairs pulled around a table which is soon strewn with lichee nut shells and loucoum. He transfers the meeting to his hotel, midday to two o'clock and six to eight o'clock daily.

He begins making his own coffee, heating it on a Sterno, then Theen One brings a large electric grill. The following day appear some gallon cooking pots as well as forks and knives. Watermelons in the bedroom, cheese on the fire escape, bread on the desk and pickles in the bookcase.

Hearing that Gurdjieff is in New York, Toomer leaves for a Bermuda vacation saying he didn't want to "be on the same soil as Gurdjieff."

12 March 1939. Wellington Hotel. Gurdjieff has Armagnac trouble. His Château de Larresingle is no longer imported.

14 April 1939. Wellington Hotel. Krokodeel sits with Gurdjieff in his bedroom having coffee, only he does not drink. Several days earlier he has sent her out to look for German syringes as he is badly in need of piqûres. She can only find the ordinary ones, the long needles, and these he accepts. He says, "With this you can make injection in brain, through navel."

He asks Krokodeel to sit on the bed and tell a story "with tzimuss." He says the word so it sounds like "quintessence." She tells him this and he says, "Not *tzimess—tzimuss—* nearly same sound have, only quite a different meaning. Tzimess mean sperm."

He asks Krokodeel if she would lie on the bed beside him. He says if she would it would bring *"fulfilling."* She says she does not have the education for understanding such. "Not mama-papa business," Gurdjieff tells her, "you not understand. Man when tired sometimes can fulfill, having passive side beside him. Then *he* can be passive. This very complicate thing I tell. Woman all is same. Man can *be* woman. Just this fulfilling when rest together—without mama-papa business. You not understand. I far go."

15 March 1939. Germany. Hitler invades and annexes Czechoslovakia. A month later forms the Pact of Steel with Mussolini.

19 May 1939. New York. The political situation in Europe worsening—Franco had defeated Republican Spain and Italy had invaded Albania—Gurdjieff's students try to convince him to stay, but he refuses and he and Kanari sail for France on the SS *Normandie*.

June 1939. Paris. Georgette's book *La Machine à Courage* nearly finished, she looks in the mirror and notices a little swelling in her arm. She is diagnosed with cancer. She goes to see Gurdjieff who treats her several times, but the cancer is too aggressive.

19 July 1939. Mill House. Jean Toomer, still suffering abdominal pains[26] and an unarticulated sense of personal and professional failure, leaves for India with his wife, Marjorie, and daughter, Argie. "He thought," his wife recounts, "that maybe through the mystics he could find the answers." The journey will take nine months, much of that time spent in travel to and from India, and will cost five thousand dollars.

1939. New York. Charles Lindbergh, who made the first nonstop flight from New York to Paris to become a national hero, is against America becoming involved in a war with Germany. He writes in an article in the *Readers Digest*: "We can have peace and security only so long as we band together to preserve that most priceless possession, our inheritance of European blood, only so long as we guard ourselves against attack by foreign armies and dilution by foreign races."

In his diaries, he writes: "We must limit to a reasonable amount the Jewish influence.... Whenever the Jewish percentage of total population becomes too high, a reaction seems to invariably occur. It is too bad because a few Jews of the right type are, I believe, an asset to any country."

Summer 1939. England. Madame Uspenskii is stricken with Parkinson's disease.[27] Gurdjieff contemplates a trip to England to help. "If possible I will come," he says. "But she must also make effort." Uspenskii procrastinates. As much as he might reminisce about Gurdjieff during his late night drinking parties, he does not want Gurdjieff in his life.

23 August 1939. Moscow and Berlin. Hitler and Stalin sign a nonaggression pact.

1 September 1939. Poland. The Second World War begins. German troops pour across the frontier.

3 September 1939. England. War is declared on Germany.

12 September 1939. Paris. Georgette has surgery on her arm. "I got it all out," the doctor assures her, but only time will tell. They drive to Georgette's sister's 11th century château at Tancarville built above the river Seine near Saint Romains de Celbus. There they will rest and see what develops.

5 October 1939. Paris. Solita Solano and Janet Flanner leave for New York aboard the SS *Washington*. Miss Gordon, who could easily have returned to England, stays on.

---

26. As a child of ten, Toomer experienced stomach ailments so intense he was confined to bed. In one of his autobiographies he says the ailments were "largely psychosomatic."
27. Madame Uspenskii is also said to have multiple sclerosis. Reyner, *Unsung Genius*, 101.

9 November 1939. Kristallnacht, Berlin. On the anniversary of Hitler's failed putsch of 1923, two hundred synagogues are burned, Jewish stores looted, and Jews beaten and killed.

Late November 1939. Tancarville. Georgette's arm begins to heal, but then the wound opens again and continues to worsen during the Christmas holidays.

1940. 6 rue des Colonels Renard. American followers try to persuade Gurdjieff to go to America, but he insists on staying in Paris. At some point Gurdjieff, Madame de Salzmann and her family leave for Switzerland.

March 1940. Mill House. The Toomers and their daughter return from India. His wife says: "We went here, we went there. Usually I stayed in our lodgings with Argie, but sometimes, if I went, Jean would start talking with somebody inside while we were left sitting out in that God-awful heat. And he would stay as long as it pleased him. It became a very unhappy experience."

Toomer, in search of what he called "The Meeting," traveled to Ramanasramam to meet Ramana Maharshi but was disappointed. Gandhi he sees as "the man of the India of today" but had no interest in meeting him. The German-born Lama Govinda, living on "Crank's Ridge" above the hill-station of Almora, he feels offered "by all odds the most genuine, most impressive, the most promising Way," but still he cannot commit himself.

Finally, it dawns on him: "My experiences thus far in pursuit of new psychological means have continued to make me realize the excellence of the means I already possess. So much is this so that I have sometimes wondered if, in coming here, I were in the queer position of seeking to find that which I already have.... It took India to bring me to my senses.... What hopes I went there with! India did not destroy them; she simply did not fulfill them."

10 May 1940. Major German offensive begins.

29 May 1940. British Army evacuated from Dunkirk.

Early June 1940. Le Cannet. Margaret, Georgette and their Belgian friend Monique, have moved to the Riviera. But now they leave for Bordeaux hoping to sail for America on the SS *Washington,* which is scheduled to depart on June 8. Margaret and Georgette can get visas but not Monique, as Belgium has been overrun by Germans and no longer has the status of a nation. They drive to Bayonne and their passports with the necessary papers are sent to Bordeaux. Days pass. Then word comes. Their passports have been lost.

June 1940. Mill House. Toomer's stomach disorder persists. In the hopes of being free from pain, he has a blocked kidney removed. The operation is not successful. He can no longer sit in a chair. He must either stand or lie down. Arthritis sets in.

12 June 1940. Paris. Gurdjieff and the de Salzmann family leave for Switzerland but shortly thereafter return.

14 June 1940. Paris. The Germans capture the city. The French government retreats to Bordeaux. A large swastika is hoisted onto the Eiffel Tower. Later Hitler arrives to dictate terms of an unconditional surrender.

16 June 1940. Bordeaux. The French Prime Minister Paul Reynaud resigns. Eighty-four-year-old Marshall Pétain, hero of the First World War, forms a new government and the following day orders a ceasefire.

18 June 1940. London. General Charles de Gaulle issues a call for resistance.

22 June 1940. Compiègne Forest, France. Armistice signed, reversing the German humiliation of 1918.

10 July 1940. Bordeaux. French National Assembly votes 569 to 80 to dissolve and cede all powers to the Government of the Republic under the authority of Marshall Pétain.

11 July 1940. Bordeaux. Pétain establishes the Vichy regime. Pierre Laval is appointed vice-premier.

End of July 1940. Bayonne. Margaret, Georgette and Monique decide to return to Le Cannet, taking the back roads that by now they know so well. Coming around a bend, they see the outline of a German soldier, rifle at the ready. Young and bored, he eyes the women cautiously, slowly surveying their luggage and the five canisters of gasoline they have bought. He asks for their papers and makes a show of going through them. Everyone is in stricken silence. Finally, the soldier says to Margaret—"Cinema stars?"
  Margaret was about to say "writers" but stopped herself—"Yes, *cinema stars*."
  Arriving in Le Cannet Margaret rents a little box of a house. It has only three small rooms—two bedrooms and beneath them a studio kitchen. All it lacks is a bathroom. Ernest Hemingway, hearing of their plight from Janet Flanner, wires four hundred dollars. Georgette sings and continues to work on her book. They call the house, situated high on a hillside, its garden overlooking the Mediterranean and filled with roses, "Chalet Rose."

August 1940. Mill House. Toomer, who had studied Quakerism for years, formally becomes a member of the Society of Friends. He becomes a much sought after lecturer.

2 August 1940. France. Stringent food rationing is introduced.

6 September 1940. Lyne Place. Hitler's night bombing of England begins. Uspenskii stands on the roof of the house looking toward London some twenty miles distant. The vast night sky is entirely crimson. Searchlights sweep the night skies in long arcs, streams of tracer bullets shooting heavenward, while thunderous explosions rumble and shake the earth. Over four million pounds of bombs fall onto the docks of London setting them aflame. Uspenskii looks on in amazement, shaking his head, obsessed with his belief in eternal recurrence, murmuring over and over again, "This I cannot remember, this I cannot remember."[28]

With the intensification of the air raids, Uspenskii has to cancel all London meetings and the work at Lyne Place is severely curtailed. He fears, too, the success of Fascism and Communism, both of which he considers to be "criminal" parties dominated by *Sudras*.[29]

27 September 1940. France. First German Ordinance announces Jewish census to be taken. All Jews are to report to the Prefecture of Police before October 20.

Autumn 1940. Lyne Place. Rodney Collin, his wife, Janet, and their three-year-old daughter, Chloe, move in. Uspenskii speaks of his decision to leave for America in January. Shortly after the Collins' arrival, Janet leaves for America with her daughter to prepare for Uspenskii's arrival. She will begin the search for an estate like Lyne from which to conduct the Work.

18 October 1940. France. Second Ordinance prohibits Jews from engaging in banking and other business activities.

19 October 1940. 6 rue des Colonels Renard. Madame de Salzmann formally presents her French group to Gurdjieff. With the Germans patrolling the streets, regular weekly meetings and readings of *Beelzebub's Tales* and movements begin.

3 December 1940. Lyne Place. Uspenskii lectures on self-remembering. He says, "One thought observes another, not I. We observe mechanically through

---

28. This would indicate that Uspenskii has remembered a great deal of the life he has lived.

29. In the Hindu caste system derived from the ancient Laws of Manu, the *Sudras*, laborers, Uspenskii says, "are people without initiative or with wrong initiative, who must obey the will of others." The three other castes are: *Brahmans*, priests; *Kshatriyas*, warriors; and *Vaisyas*, merchants. See *A New Model of the Universe*, 506. A further analysis of the caste system is given in Frithjof Schuon's *Castes and Races* (Perennial Books, Ltd., 1959). Gurdjieff is very much opposed to castes.

external impressions. Our daily bread is wrongly translated—is energy from self-remembering and self-observation. With these you see both 'I' and the 'here' of 'I am here,' both anger and the 'I' that is angry."

Lord Pentland asks, "You have said that one can approach self-remembering through stopping thoughts. Is self-remembering going on all the time and stopping thoughts a way to discovering it?"

"Quite opposite," says Uspenskii. "It is not going on, it has to be produced. Stopping thoughts means [stopping] mechanical thought. Certain kind of thinking also help self-remembering."

1941. New York. Harry Content, Jean Toomer's father-in-law, dies. He had remarried shortly before his death and the expected estate largely goes to his new wife. Says Gorham Munson: "I don't mean to say that they [Jean and Marjorie] were cut off, because they had this place in Mechanicsville, and had a very comfortable income. In general, he did cut them off, cut them down, and so it was now clear that Jean would never have the resources, the considerable resources, needed to set up an institute [like the Prieuré]. That was a gone dream."

Georgi Ivanovitch Gurdjieff

The shuttered windows of Gurdjieff's apartment at 6 rue des Colonels Renard

Café de la Paix, Gurdjieff's "Paris office"

The Way of the Sly Man

Kathryn Hulme

Solita Solano

Elizabeth Gordon

Alice Rohrer

Georgi Ivanovitch Gurdjieff

Margaret Anderson — Georgette Leblanc

Mr. Gurdjieff behind the wheel with students as passengers

Colet House at 46 Colet Gardens acquired by Uspenskii's Historico-Psychological Society

PART VIII

USPENSKII IN AMERICA

4 JANUARY 1941. LIVERPOOL, ENGLAND. MADAME USPENSKII EMBARKS FOR AMERICA ABOARD *THE SS GEORGIC*.

25 JANUARY 1941. COLET HOUSE. USPENSKII, BELIEVING THAT GERMANY WILL WIN THE WAR, WHICH WILL BE A PRELUDE TO A REVOLUTION IN WHICH COMMUNISM WOULD SWEEP EUROPE, ANNOUNCES HE IS EMIGRATING TO AMERICA AND TASKS HIS SENIOR CADRE TO CONTINUE THE WORK. ASKED WHETHER HE WOULD BEGIN GROUPS IN AMERICA, HE SAYS HE COULD NOT FORESEE WHAT WOULD HAPPEN AS HE HAD VISITED AMERICA "ONLY IN PREVIOUS INCARNATIONS."

26 JANUARY 1941. LYNE PLACE. A BOMB FALLS AND EXPLODES WITHIN TEN feet of Uspenskii's home. No one is hurt, nothing destroyed. He puts Dr. Francis Roles, a student of his since the 1920s and his personal physician and a noted authority on tuberculosis, in charge of his groups.

Before Uspenskii leaves, Bennett comes to Lyne Place. He asks three questions: "Is my lack of progress due to lack of effort, or wrong effort, or is it due in part to there being some method or technique we do not know, and have yet to find?"

Replies Uspenskii: "It has nothing to do with methods. Your trouble is that you always make false starts.[1] All your work consists of false starts. And if you keep returning to the starting point, how can you hope to make progress?"

Bennett then asks: "How do I stand in relation to your group here?"

"I can only consider the work at Lyne. The rest, so far as I am concerned, is dissolved. I have given my instructions for continuing the work at Lyne as long as possible. You and your wife can, of course, remain in contact with the work there."

"Have you any objection," inquires Bennett, "to my trying to write out the System as far as I can remember it?"

Answers Uspenskii: "In my opinion, writing is not useful. Mental recapitulation is better. In any case, the System cannot be written in ordinary form. If you do write, it can only be to convince yourself that it is impossible."

For Bennett, Uspenskii's leaving is more than a physical separation. "It is not a sharp break, or any diminution in my respect and deep gratitude towards him," he says. "He has taught me everything, and the contact with his work has had the supreme advantage for me of teaching me my own weakness and foolishness."

Nevertheless, Bennett resolves that he must in the future work independently and sets himself the task of writing all that he can remember of the System.

29 January 1941. Liverpool. Uspenskii, sixty-three years old, embarks for America aboard the SS *Georgic*, the name no doubt causing a grimace.

February 1941. Franklin Farms, Mendham, New Jersey. Rodney Collin and his wife lease the four-hundred acre estate of what was once the home of a former state's governor. Approached by a long circular driveway, the three-story granite residence looks out onto expansive vistas of rolling hills. Behind the mansion sit barns, empty silos and outbuildings, as well as decaying aviaries that once caged ornamental birds. The estate needs a great deal of work, but the idea is that Franklin Farms will be the new Lyne Place.

Meanwhile, Madame Uspenskii lives at Elm Cottage in Rumson, New Jersey, a small community near the ocean and only a half-hour ferry ride to Manhattan. C. S. Nott arrives from England and goes to see her. He says, "Here, by herself,

---

1. Bennett does not explain what is meant by "always make false starts." It would seem to indicate that Bennett begins from his egotism, his self-will, and so no matter the results, the magic circle of the ego is only expanded, not separated from.

away from Lyne Place, a refugee like ourselves, she had no need to surround herself with a protective façade. She was warm, sympathetic and understanding; a highly developed woman with inner power." Soon after, Uspenskii arrives and settles in at Elm Cottage, he writes to Claude Bragdon asking to meet. Bragdon had been instrumental in having the English edition of *Tertium Organum* translated and published, and then sending a copy to Uspenskii in Constantinople in 1921. Over the intervening years, Bragdon sent royalty checks, and two men corresponded about further corrections to the book and about the possible publication of Uspenskii's other books.

Bragdon, now seventy-five years old, a former Theosophist who over the years has become involved with spiritualism, hatha yoga and currently Krishnamurti, says, "After all these years, I wonder what he will be like."

17 February 1941. New York. Bragdon and Uspenskii meet at Bragdon's apartment. Says Bragdon:

> He is portly and distinguished looking, with a big flat Russian face, a little deaf, gentlemanly, a bit derogatory of most things and persons mentioned—the reverse of an enthusiastic person. He manifested no particular interest in me or my affairs but was exceedingly well mannered though not what one would call affable. He spoke approvingly of Krishnamurti and Gerald Heard. He says Gurdjieff is mad. He tried to work with him but found it impossible. All of Gurdjieff's old adherents have left him to a man.

21 February 1941. New York. Some of Uspenskii's Russian students give a party. Bragdon says, "Everybody is all agog to meet him. It was a great surprise to him to find out how well known he was." Bragdon's twenty-eight-year-old friend Carman Barnes is also there. At sixteen she had published a novel, *Schoolgirl*, about her experiences at an all-girls school in the South. It quickly became a best seller that she dramatized for a Broadway play. Both talented and strikingly beautiful, she was brought to Hollywood and known as "Baby Garbo." Strangely, nothing came of her Hollywood career. She wrote a series of novels but none that achieved the acclaim that *Schoolgirl* did. Her interest now is in founding a school for women "such as I should like to go to," she says. The previous June she and Bragdon had met and she convinced him to give a series of lectures at her New York studio. She now offers the studio to Uspenskii for talks and asks that Bragdon introduce them.

27 February 1941. New York. Writes Bragdon to a friend, "There's no vibration between Uspenskii and me." He notes, though, that Uspenskii was "captivated with Carman." Bragdon describes her as "blessed with a lithe figure and a face whose high cheekbones have a strikingly beautiful Egyptian cast." She, as he will later say, is a "femme fatale."

28 February 1941. 170 East 78th Street, New York. Bragdon introduces Uspenskii at Barnes' studio. In the audience are Mabel Dodge Luhan, Georgia O'Keefe, and Miss McLeod, Vivekananda's only surviving American pupil. Bragdon briefly relates the history of the translation and publishing of *Tertium Organum*. Writing to a friend afterward Bragdon says:

> Uspenskii was wonderful in his first public discourse. Cold he was, and a bit inhuman, but a master of clear, logical devastating-because-true thought. His answers to questions were masterly, showing a grasp far beyond that of the questioner. He bewildered most of his audience I think. It's deep strong stuff, way beyond the grasp of most of their minds. I thought it was masterly though there was no *life* in it. They tell me Uspenskii rules his disciples by fear just as Gurdjieff did. It is the Gurdjieff method over again. Self-observation and breaking down of habits. The people who go into it wholeheartedly get something out of it they tell me, but it's all pretty bleak.

12 March 1941. New York. Bragdon is to meet Uspenskii today. He is not looking forward to it. "He'll want me to go to that meeting again but I shan't go. The heart: the heart alone has all the answers: of that I am convinced and all the Gurdjieff and Uspenskii devotees seem to have dried-up hearts."[2]

18 March 1941. 170 East 78th Street, New York. Bragdon, too old for a romantic relationship with Carman Barnes but acting as her mentor, sees what is happening between her and Uspenskii and advises her to see Krishnamurti in Ojai, California. She leaves but rents the studio and apartment to Uspenskii for $175 a month.

22 March 1941. Chalet Rose, Le Cannet. Yakina writes to Kanari about Georgette: "The end is beginning for that human being I love so, who has given me the greatest human blessing—perfect entente. I've just bought her a garden armchair for thirty francs that she loves. Every breath of air, every wild flower, seems unique to us this spring." A few days later she writes again: "She has had three crises—groaning with pain like an animal. We must begin the morphine soon I'm afraid. Could we have ever dreamed that *this* would be her fate? But

---

2. People live in false personality, especially socially. This is the "norm." Self-remembering and self-observing brings a Presence that, seen from false personality, seems dry, flat, impassive. Still, socially, why not, as Gurdjieff says, "Exterior play a role, interior never"?

even if we had known it, years ago, we couldn't have lived more beautifully than we have ... She can't use her arm at all."

April 1941. Chalet Rose, Le Cannet. Georgette's arm has swollen to inhuman proportions. Amputation is considered but refused. Georgette begins corresponding with Jane Heap, telling her of her fear that she would be cut off from Gurdjieff because of the division between the Occupied and Unoccupied Zones of France. Writes Jane from England:

> You can never be cut off, unless you yourself fail to understand yourself in relation to him. It is never an action, an event, a mistake that cuts one off ... it is some non-activity in the verb to be. You remember his chapter on "Good and Evil" there is much talk about serviceability to God, and lacking this serviceability the being does not cease to exist but he ceases to be ... serviceability meaning of value in the design or plan ... As long as we have this as our highest wish, and make efforts to create a positive neutralizing force in ourselves, we are contributing to absolute good and cannot cease to exist in the mind of God. No more can our contacts with Gurdjieff be cut off. One side of him you see manifestations of ordinary man, but the other side you must know is always impartial, timeless ... Give my love to Florence Nightingale Anderson. Bless her heart, I was always afraid I'd be ill and that she would nurse me.

15 April 1941. New York. "I guess when one gets underneath that Russian crust Uspenskii is a regular guy with human feelings and even a sense of humor," says Bragdon.

Spring 1941. Rumsen, New Jersey. C. S. Nott had arrived from England in late January. Now, Uspenskii and Nott have lunch in New York. Nott tells him that people were trying to arrange for Gurdjieff to come to New York. "If he does come," says Uspenskii, "I shall go to California."

Nott arranges for Uspenskii to speak to the group at Muriel Draper's home. Besides Draper and Nott and his wife, Rosemarie, are the Orageans William and Louise Welch, Wim and Ilonka Nyland, and Jessmin Howarth. Fritz Peters also shows up. Peters had met Uspenskii at the Prieuré and considered him Gurdjieff's most objective critic. He asks Uspenskii—"Why did you break with Gurdjieff and publicly disassociate yourself from the Gurdjieff work?"

Uspenskii smiles. "The answer is very simple," he says. "When I had found out that Gurdjieff was wrong I had to leave him."

Recounts Peters, "I replied, with much greater feeling than I would have expected of myself, that I did not need to hear any more. It was a revelation to me to find that I was so fiercely loyal to Gurdjieff and to find that I was so positive that he could not have been 'wrong' about anything."

Like Peters, most of those attending find Uspenskii too coldly intellectual and lacking the emotional authority that they had come to expect from Gurdjieff and Orage.

Later, C. S. Nott assembles a smaller group for Uspenskii; it includes some from the Orage group. Also invited are a number of Uspenskii's English pupils, such as Lord John Pentland, who had sometimes deputized for Uspenskii in England, his wife Lucy, and Christopher and Anne Fremantle.

C. Daly King, from the original Orage group and one of Orage's most loyal advocates, was not invited but learns of Uspenskii's meetings. King attends several meetings; he finds Uspenskii to be a "genuine gentleman in the exact sense." However, he also sees Uspenskii as an "incorrigible mystic, no matter how much or how successfully he may or may not have striven against that tendency after his meeting with and his instruction by Mr. Gurdjieff." Of their discussion King says: "I found nothing of serious interest to me in his formulations and had no further contact with these groups." Later, unable to agree with what he terms "The Uspenskiian Version" of the teaching and fearing Orage's presentation will be lost, King writes a 271-page transcript of what he calls "The Oragean Version."[3] Uspenskii's opinion of King is not recorded.

17 April 1941. New York. Uspenskii sees Bragdon who writes to Carman Barnes in Ojai.

> Uspenskii said everything was going all right with his classes except that the work accomplished in London had to be all built up over again, there he had a fine organization which here he lacks. He is anxious to have me come some evening and I told him I would. Now that there's no chance of my doing anything to commit me to him and his work—I shall. I read him the part of your letter about Krishnamurti at his request. I mean by that—I told him you had seen Krishnamurti and he asked how you

---

3. This is King's understanding of Orage's understanding of self-remembering. "The term Self-Remembering Orage himself used sparingly.... There is thus a division of attention accompanying the observatory act; to the one hand one withdraws from the usual identification with his organism and is aware that he is now a separated 'I' and, to the other, one is aware of the specific organic phenomena taking place, as it were, outside 'I'. Self-Remembering refers precisely to the first of the latter awarenesses, viz., it refers to that part of the attention which at the moment is focused upon the 'I' and not upon the It or organism. This process of division of which we speak, is called Non-identification and in it 'I' is placed apart from the body; the act of Self-Remembering is that included part of the act of Self-Observation which is directed upon 'I' and not upon the phenomena that are the objects of Self-Observation. In fact, Self-Remembering is identical with Self-Awareness." So it is the division of 'I' from 'It' that Gurdjieff first gave at the Prieuré. It lacks withdrawal, sensation, breath, embodiment, stopping of thought, division, and much more.

were impressed by him. "Would you like to hear what she said in her own words?" I asked. "I should. Very much." So I read him these 3 pages. He thought you gave a good picture and expressed yourself very well.

5 May 1941. Coombe Springs, England. Bennett, without a college education and no pedigree in class conscious England, is appointed Director of the British Coal Utilization Research Association, the largest in England, with coal the basic industry of the war effort. He buys a large mansion on seven acres of land.

14 May 1941. France. First *rafle*, or roundup, of Jews.

14 May 1941. 170 East 78th Street. As he did twenty years earlier with Rosamund Bland, Uspenskii invites Carman Barnes for tea, which he makes himself.

31 May 1941. New York. Bragdon writes to a friend:

> Can it be that this great *maestro* is also falling for her charms? It looks so. Few escape. Now she wants to stay on and attend his classes. Carman has completely captivated Uspenskii. He took her to Longchamps the other night and kept her there till 5 a.m. (and drank 12 cocktails) while telling her the story of his life. She's certainly the *femme fatale* and no mistake! Carman goes every night to Uspenskii's classes and has become in effect his secretary and factotum just as she was mine during The Arch lectures [the 18 lectures Bragdon gave at her studio, which he had named "the Arch"]. She says that Uspenskii has still something to learn and she's the one who's going to teach him. And I guess she will and when she can!

2 June 1941. 170 East 78th Street. Uspenskii formally begins his lecture series.

5 June 1941. New York. "Carman told me yesterday," Bragdon writes, "that he is the most fascinating and dangerous man she has ever met and the only man she has ever been afraid of. He is trying his best to beglamour her and enslave her. His wife is intensely jealous."

10 June 1941. New York. At the meeting, Carman asks a number of questions: "Suppose that one does not want to go back and live in the past, does one have to?" "Does one have to keep repeating the same mistakes?" In later meetings, she asks: "Are we attempting to become No. 5? What is our normal line of existence?" "Is there any relationship between the thousands of 'I's and centers?" "Can we make the past occur in a different way?" "Does evil have anything to do with the triad of destruction?" "Suppose that one has power and develops it in the wrong way?" "Do we lead this life over and over again, or do we lead multiple lives?" "How can one tell the difference between imagination and a real experience?" "If a person tries to shut out all these ideas is he escaping?"

21–22 June 1941. Russia. German troops invade Russia. Within ten weeks are at the outskirts of Leningrad, formerly St. Petersburg.

July 1941. Coombe Springs, England. Bennett and his wife move in. Soon, he is holding meetings and teaching movements.

17 July 1941. 170 East 78th Street. At the meeting, Uspenskii is asked about individuality. "Individuality," he answers, "is not a function. Individuality means when the small 'I's come under control of the central I."

A woman, an Orage student, says, "We were taught that individuality was consciousness of will."

"It's only words," replies Uspenskii. "It's not Mr. Gurdjieff. It's Orage. I don't like to say this, but he forgot many things and had to invent."

20 August 1941. France. Second *rafle* of Jews.

30 August 1941. Leningrad, Russia. Germans begin a siege. It will last nine hundred days.

September 1941. Chalet Rose, Le Cannet. "Our fear of death became quieter," Margaret says. "We entered that transition which leads from despair to destiny, from personal grief to impersonal tragedy, and which is like the shift that occurs in art—from stylelessness to form. I knew that our death-in-life was beginning its transmutation into the octave of life-in-death."

Georgette has become obsessed with the idea that Gurdjieff will appear. One evening she cries—"He is coming. I know it, he is already here—he has come in below." That evening an inter-zone card arrives from Paris. The message is from Gurdjieff. He says she has "beaucoup courage" and she is a "friend."

Upon hearing this, Georgette's face transfigures and she says, "He said that? Then . . . we will die without dying."

September 1941. Franklin Farms. The estate readied for occupancy, the Uspenskiis move in. Marie Seton, Uspenskii's secretary in England, arrives. Speaking Russian as well as English, she assumes her duties as she did in England and, slowly the pattern of life at Lyne Place is now resumed at Mendham. Groups are formed and students given farm work and housework. Madame Uspenskii, now walking with a cane, spends more and more of her time in bed but still manages to direct work activities.

For de Ropp and many others, including Lord and Lady Pentland, Madame Uspenskii became *the* teacher. Says Lord Pentland:

> Madame was one of those people who emanates a force which makes them seem larger than they actually are. Her relationship with Uspenskii was much closer and deeper than was apparent to beginners, but she was regarded by us all as an independent source of the teaching.... For many of us, she was the senior teacher. Her instruction, tempered in the hard school of revolutionary Russia, at the kitchen of Gurdjieff's Institute [at the Prieuré], was direct, quite free from moralization and expressed in bad English.

Says another pupil:

> I can still feel the sensation that crept along my spine when I heard Madame approaching, her cane announcing her as she came closer and closer to the terrace or the dining room. Although small in stature, she loomed and towered above us all through the sheer strength and poise that radiated from her presence. When she reached the long narrow tables at which we sat, everyone remained motionless, eyes glued to one spot, simultaneously wishing to draw her attention and yet to become invisible to her.

11 September 1941. Des Moines, Iowa. Charles Lindbergh has joined the 800,000-member America First Committee—those who oppose America entering the World War—and becomes its leading spokesman. In his speech, Lindbergh warns that the three groups pressing us into World War II are the British, Jews, and the Roosevelt administration. He says these war agitator groups are small in number but powerful in their ability to shape public opinion. Of the Jews he says, "The greatest danger lies in their large ownership and influence in our motion pictures, our press, our radio, and our government. We cannot blame them for looking out for what they believe to be their interests, but we also must look out for ours."

Lindbergh[4] is denounced by President Roosevelt as a Nazi sympathizer. J. Edgar Hoover begins an FBI investigation.

15 September 1941. New York. Bragdon writes to a friend:

> Carman is planning to go to Santa Barbara to try to sell the Brahma Temple to Ganna Walska.[5] I hope she gets away because it would mean

---

4. When the United States enters the war, Lindbergh tries to enlist but is denied. He retires to Hawaii. No more is heard from him until the late 1960s, when he begins speaking about dangers to the ecosytem and exhaustion of natural resources.

5. A Polish opera singer and garden enthusiast, Walska buys the Brahma Temple and creates

getting away from Uspenskii who seems to possess an almost hypnotic power over her. He flatters her and tells her how wonderful she is and he evidently has a line of talk of which she never tires for he keeps her up to all hours. Uspenskii is a great man and Carman will undoubtedly get something out of it but I have a feeling she's being used.

Mid-September 1941. Franklin Farms. Rodney Collin, who has been commuting to and from his job with the British government in New York City, increasingly finds himself exhausted by the fifty-mile commute. One night, realizing that fatigue is not the problem, he jumps out of bed and goes to the kitchen. There he finds Uspenskii alone drinking a glass of wine.

"Why am I afraid of you?" Collin shouts.

Uspenskii looks at him calmly and answers, "Why do you say *I*?"

The answer has a profound effect on Collin. Thereafter he spends all his free time with Uspenskii.

23 September 1941. Franklin Farms. Uspenskii writes to Carman Barnes. Given what he says, she has obviously broken through "the hard outer shell" that Anna Ilinishna Butkovskaia felt he had developed after his St. Petersburg days:

> My beautiful darling,[6] please excuse me I did not write you at once. I wired you that we remain at 48th St. but there were some other problems. Now it is all clear. Last week we had a new group—36 new people—and we will have another next Monday, 29. My secretary went to Yale and these are all my news. I hope that there is a letter in N.Y. I am going there in half an hour.
>
> And I also hope that you remember me sometimes. I think about you all the time when I can think anything. If you did not write yet, please write me a few words soon.

29 September 1941. Berlin. The Führer directs his generals "to wipe St. Petersburg off the face of the earth."

October 1941. New York. One day Bragdon meets with C. S. Nott and says, "Uspenskii tells me that Gurdjieff is suffering from paranoia and this accounts

---

the Lotusland Botanical Gardens. She was married six times to a series of wealthy husbands. The lavish promotion of her opera career by her fourth husband inspired aspects of the screenplay for *Citizen Kane*.

6. Uspenskii, seen by Bragdon and others, as cold, indifferent, is really a sensitive romantic as evidenced in his *Strange Life of Ivan Osokin* in which all of Osokin's plights involve a woman. Osokin's night with Tanechka is magical and has no relationship with the physical act of love. Uspenskii's romanticism, shown with his relationship with Anna Ilinishna, really never abated as shown in the chapter on "Occultism and Love" in *Tertium Organum*. Here, at the end of his life, it again emerges.

for his strange behavior. A good many people are saying this."

"Uspenskii has this idea fixed in his head," Nott tells him, "and nothing will change it."

10 October 1941. Franklin Farms. Writes Uspenskii to Carman Barnes:

> My beautiful darling, it was such an unexpected pleasure to hear suddenly that you have already arrived. The question arose immediately, when shall I see you? Certainly I wanted to see you now, immediately. But I am in a funny situation. I am still in my room upstairs and really I am still in the position of an invalid. I hope to become definitely better one of these days and come to N.Y. on Monday, or Tuesday and Wednesday. So on Monday morning I will write or telephone to you. If it happens that I still cannot come then I will ask you to come here. There are so many things I want to tell you and to ask you. But first of all I want just to sit some time and look at you, until I really believe that you came back.
>
> I kiss your beautiful hands and I thank you for all you already have done. Till Monday!
>
> Yours so very much,
> P. Uspenskii
>
> P.S. I am writing this letter and my head is going round and round, so I have to retire to bed at least until lunch time.
>
> Thank you, my darling

12 October 1941. Franklin Farms. Uspenskii writes to Carman Barnes about speaking to Marie Seton, his secretary, at the studio the previous day:

> I found her in a very bad hysterical fit shrieking that she cannot work because that "other woman" tries constantly to put her in the wrong by transferring to her false message from me. I had not the time and no desire to listen to her. Happily she is going away this week and certainly she will not come back to any work. We had enough hysterical ladies in London, but I always managed to keep them apart from any contact with actual organization and work of new groups. . . . The appearance of Miss Seton in the middle of the stage is really an unprecedented fact.

Uspenskii replaces Marie Seton with Miss Romer.

20 October 1941. Franklin Farms. Writes Uspenskii to Carman Barnes:

> What a strange fate that does not give me even a glimpse of you. I feel rather funny again; I mean a little shivering and every moment tired. At

the same time it is not doctors' illness. I know that I am poisoned, but I am poisoned by astral influences. This is the only kind of illness that I have since childhood. Bad astral influences in other languages means negatives [sic] impressions. Negative impressions are not same as negative emotions. Negative emotions can be conquered or even used. But one can do nothing against negative impressions, at least I cannot. At the same time if I go to doctor I could tell him only that I cannot smoke, that a cigarette makes me cough, and that I cannot have a drink because a drink somehow remains outside of me. I cannot describe it better. I think that doctor will send to psycho-analist [sic] and psycho-annalist[7] will try to find out was not I in love with my grandmother or something like that.

Well, I write all this nonsense about myself, but what I really wanted to hear is something about you, about your travels, about people you met and so on.

Tomorrow or the day after tomorrow I will telephone to you and I hope to see you at last.

Please don't forget me completely.

23 October 1941. Franklin Farms. Uspenskii writes to Carman Barnes:

I apologize again for the message I sent to you through Miss Seton. My message was really very short and very innocent. As I wrote you before I expected some furniture to arrive next day and I did not wish to have things mixed. So I told to Miss Seton to ask you when you can remove your furniture. That was all, the rest was her "initiative." When I was writing this message to be telephoned to her, I remembered that we had a spare. In any case I am glad to say that I got rid of Miss Seton finally, and I will try to work the studio with the help of Sherman and Lonia [his grandson] and with your advice.

26 October 1941. Chalet Rose, Le Cannet. Georgette Leblanc, seventy-two years of age, cradled in Margaret's arms, draws her last breath.

Upon learning of her passing, Jane writes to Margaret: "I read and re-read her last days as you tell them, and I think I know what she was trying to do and say, 'As you go, so we come again.' Georgette will never perish. Die we all must, but we can hope that none of us who has 'eaten' of Gurdjieff's food will ever perish."

7 November 1941. New York. "Uspenskii is still ill, poor man," writes Bragdon. "I think he has met his Waterloo in Carman. She is Vivian to his Merlin. The enchanter is enchanted. She showed me a letter from him she said that I might

---

7. Like Gurdjieff, Uspenskii has a poor view of psychoanalysis.

read, but after reading 'My Beautiful Darling' I handed it back to her. He tells her that he came to America solely to meet her, and she tells him that the System makes only monsters out of people, and that he was ruined by becoming the creature of Gurdjieff, and that T.O. [*Tertium Organum*] was his high water mark; to all of which I agree, but Carman got none of these ideas from me. She attended the classes, used her eyes and her brain and her intuition, and came to these conclusions herself."

5 December 1941. Russia. Soviet counteroffensive begins.

7 December 1941. Hawaii. Japanese attack Pearl Harbor.

7 December 1941. 6 rue des Colonels Renard. Gurdjieff tells pupils:

> One needs fire. Without fire, there will never be anything. This fire is suffering, intentional suffering, without which it is impossible to create anything. One must prepare, must know what will make one suffer and when it is there, make use of it. Only you can prepare, only you know what makes you suffer, makes the fire which cooks, cements, crystallizes. Suffer by your defects, in your pride, in your egoism. Remind yourself of the aim. Without prepared suffering there is nothing, for by as much as one is conscious, there is no more suffering. No further process, nothing. That is why with your conscience you must prepare what is necessary. You owe to nature. The food you eat which nourishes your life. You must pay for these cosmic substances. You have a duty, an obligation, to repay by conscious work.

11 December 1941. Germany. Adolf Hitler formally declares war on the United States.

12 December 1941. France. Third *rafle* of Jews.

1942. London. Bennett, with little experience in research, is elected Chairman of the Conference of Research Associations, which represents twenty-five of England's chief industries.

24 January 1942. New York. Bragdon writes: "I addressed Carman's group of eight girls on the subject of Yoga. They meet twice a week. Carman who is by now very expert, teaches them the breathing and the postures. She has never given up the idea that she must do something for her sex."

1 April 1942. Franklin Farms. Janet Collin purchases a parcel of the estate and in September purchases another. In January 1948 she will sell the parcels to

Franklin Farms, Inc., which is owned by Uspenskii's grandson and granddaughter, Lonia and Tania.

18 April 1942. 6 rue des Colonels Renard. Gurdjieff tells pupils to hide Jewish pupils who could not escape.

May 1942. London. Bennett receives a message reminding him that no one is permitted to write anything about the System without Uspenskii's permission. It could not have come as a surprise, as he had asked Uspenskii the previous year. After Uspenskii's departure, Bennett decides to organize the teaching around the triads. He drafts a new chapter of his forthcoming book every week. He reads it to his group of thirty to forty people, then revises it in light of their questions and remarks. Bennett later publishes this as the second in his four-volume *The Dramatic Universe*.[8]

June 1942. Lisbon. Margaret Anderson reluctantly leaves Monique and Chalet Rose to sail to New York aboard the SS *Drottingholm*. Also aboard are Dorothy Caruso and her two daughters. Her late husband was the famed tenor Enrico Caruso. Margaret immediately attracts her attention but she is reluctant to speak to her. Finally, she approaches her, saying—"I hear you published the *Little Review*." And so begins a long lasting companionship between Dorothy Caruso, just shy of fifty years old and Margaret Anderson, six years older.

16 July 1942. France. Fourth and largest *rafle* of Jews.

16 September 1942. New York. Writes Bragdon:

> Uspenskii invited me to dinner at the Lafayette the other night to meet 3 of his English friends and pupils. Carman Barnes was the only other guest. She is doing for him now what she did for me at the time I had the Arch Lectures—attending to all the details of his classes, acting as a sort of hostess and that kind of thing. Being very beautiful and charming as well as an able organizer and manager, she does this uncommonly well. We had a wonderful dinner, washed down with vintage French wine of which I took only the tiniest glass just to be polite, but Uspenskii is a copious drinker and looks to stay up all night. Having been "born in Moscow" he told Carman, which is supposed to give one immunity, I gather.
>
> The party was still going strong when I left, about eleven. Uspenskii

---

8. Bennett in this massive 1,335-page study, begun in 1940 and continually revised till his death Friday, 13 December 1974, focuses on value, will, hazard (uncertainty), and triads. While Bennett contends that much of his work is derived "from sources quite unconnected with Gurdjieff's teaching," the roots, in fact, derive from Gurdjieff.

talks very bad English which grew steadily worse as it became more copious as the evening advanced. Carman plagued him about it. "You say 'bawdy' for body. You never use any articles." He threw her back ponderous Russian compliments. "Whom are you seducing now, Mr. Bragdon?" [He said]. "I ruined Claude's reputation before you ever saw me." [She said]. Whereupon I said that my reputation had been ruined at the age of 17 and one couldn't lose one's reputation twice.

The dinner convinced me more than ever that Uspenskii and I have now very little in common. I do not follow him in his latest flights: He is all *mind*, while I at 77 want only to enrich and perfect my human relations and extend my heart line.

11 November 1942. France. Germans occupy southern France, effectively ending the reign of Vichy government.

25 November 1942. New York. Writes Bragdon: "Carman's birthday was an 'Arabian nights affair.' Uspenskii was there and his 'grandchild' told me it was the first big party Uspenskii had gone to in twenty years."

25 November 1942. New York. Writes Bragdon to a friend: "Uspenskii came to see me on an unknown errand. Carman wants us to be friends. I feel perfectly friendly toward Uspenskii but there is no longer any 'vibration.' He and I now *follow* different paths. He is my superior in every way except one. He is not a *kind* man and I believe in being kind even when I fail in kindness."

26 November 1942. New York. Uspenskii again drops by to see Bragdon. Earlier he had told Bragdon that his original version of *Tertium Organum* was better than the later edition, which was partly rewritten by Bragdon. Writes Bragdon, "He regards nothing he has published as of any real importance except portions of *A New Model of the Universe* compared with the teaching he is now giving because he says it cannot be imparted in books." Earlier, Uspenskii had seen Alfred Knopf about publishing his books and it had gone quite well. He tells Bragdon he will let him read the manuscript of his novel, *Strange Life of Ivan Osokin,* which has just been translated.

11 December 1942. New York. Writes Bragdon: "I am reading Uspenskii's novel and while it is well done and based on a deep metaphysical idea he is no more a fiction writer than I am and I'm afraid I shall have to tell him. It's only fair to say that Carman and other people who have read it like it."

20 December 1942. New York. Writes Bragdon: "I had an amusing visit with PDU as Carman calls him. I told him in as nice a way as I knew how that I didn't think he was a novelist and he took it in good part. He showed me a lot of colored photos of his place in England. There were several pictures of him on horseback, a sport of which in Russia he was very fond he told me."

Christmas Eve, 1942. 6 rue des Colonels Renard. Gurdjieff receives a bilingual French-German passport from the French Department of Immigration. This is fortunate, for his Nansen Identity Certificate[9] wasn't issued after 1938 and his French visa has expired.

29 December 1942. Franklin Farms. Uspenskii writes Carman Barnes:

> My beautiful darling, first of all let me kiss your hands and then let me tell you about my problems and perplexities. The first problem is how I could believe in you more than I did from the first moment I saw you two years ago? Really and truly, it was my strongest feeling when I saw you first time at the Studio. I remember when I went out, I said to myself that you say you are going away, and I don't believe you. So you see this side of the problem presents only technical difficulty how to increase what is already infinite [here Uspenskii inserts an infinity symbol followed by a smaller one higher, like superscript]. . . . Nobody could influence me against you my darling [this perhaps refers to Marie Seton] and who could even attempt it when everybody was admiring you. So you can put lionesses out of your mind completely and absolutely. . . .
>
> P.S. — It is very beautiful what you write about publishing *Osokin*. Personally I think it is quite possible. First of all I must have one day with him quite free from cold and from cough. After that begins a difficult part, i.e. correction of English, and I don't see yet how I can do it without my people who were specially trained for this work. But that we will see later. I promised to show *Osokin* to Alfred Knopf (Mr. & Mrs. Knopf) and I will do it without any promises.

31 January 1943. Stalingrad, Russia. German Sixth Army surrenders.

8 April 1943. 6 rue des Colonels Renard. Group meeting:

> *Question:* Why does the major part of human suffering revolve around love and things of sex?
> *Gurdjieff.* Why this question? It does not concern you personally. Ask it in another way.
> *Q:* Why are the major part of the associations, which interfere with

---

9. Internationally recognized identity cards first issued by the League of Nations to stateless refugees, originally developed for refugees from the Russian civil war.

the work, sexual associations?

G: This question is subjective. It is not so for all men. It is an abnormality which is a result of infantile masturbation.

Q. But what is the connection between this and suffering? There is not a trace of suffering here.

G: Each man has three excrements which elaborate themselves and which must be rejected. The first is the result of ordinary nourishment and eliminates itself naturally, and this must be each day, otherwise there follow all sorts of illnesses. (The physician knows this well.) For the same reason that you go to the bathroom for this maintenance, you must go to the bathroom for the second excrement which is rejected from you by the sexual function. It is necessary for health and equilibrium of the body; and certainly it is necessary in some to do it each day, in others each week, in others again every month or every six months. It is subjective. For this you must choose a proper bathroom. One that is good for you. A third excrement is formed in the head; it is rubbish of the food impressions, and the wastes accumulate in the brain. (The physician ignores it, just as he ignores the important role of the appendix in digestion, and rejects it as wastes.)

It is not necessary to mingle the acts of sex with sentiment. It is sometimes abnormal to make them coincide. The sexual act is a function. One can regard it as external to him, although love is internal. Love is love. It has no need of sex. It can be felt for a person of the same sex, for an animal even, and the sexual function is not mixed up here. Sometimes it is normal to unite them; this corresponds to one of the aspects of love. It is easier to love this way. But, at the same time, it is then difficult to remain impartial as love demands.

Likewise, if one considers the sexual function as necessary medically, why would one love a remedy, a medicine?

The sexual act originally must have been performed only for the purpose of reproduction of the species, but little by little men have made of it a means of pleasure. It must have been a sacred act. Let us hope that if Ashiata Shiemash establishes anew his order on Earth, it will become again a sacred act.

One must know that this divine seed, the sperm, has another function, that of the construction of a second body in us. Happy he who understands the function of the sex for the transformation of his being. Unhappy he who uses it in a unilateral manner.

Q: Why do religions forbid the sexual act?

G: Because originally we knew the use of this substance, whence the chasteness of the monks. Now we have forgotten this knowledge and only remains the prohibition which attracts to the monks quantities of specific disorders and illnesses.

Look at the priests where they grow "fat like pigs" (the concern about eating dominating them), or they are "skinny as the devil" (and have inside little love for their neighbor), the fat are less dangerous and more gentle.

14 April 1943. France. All Jews of French nationality ordered seized.

19 April 1943. Mill House. Jean Toomer writes to the psychic Edgar Cayce about the failure of his kidney operation, his lack of stamina and his continued insomnia. A reading is given, remedies suggested, which help, but only for a time.

22 June 1943. Virginia Beach, Virginia. Toomer visits Edgar Cayce, who recommends a purification of his alimentary canal, X-ray treatments on the sides of the spinal column, and a diet. This helps for a while, but the following year the pain returns.

24 June 1943. New York. Bragdon writes: "Carman has taken Uspenskii's image and is learning Russian, taking lessons in the Russian Ballet from one of the Monte Carlo Ballet male dancers with whom she goes to 'Jacob's Pillow' this summer . . . Uspenskii believes in discipline and that's exactly what Carman needs. She works with the others at gardening, washing dishes, husking corn, digging potatoes, etc. at Uspenskii's community in NJ."

26 July 1943. Franklin Farms. Writes Uspenskii to Carman Barnes:

> My beautiful darling, it is so good of you to write to me. I am very much down and cannot make even an attempt to do something. It may pass. I remember how I have periods when I could not work and then I started again. I will feel lectures and always know to shake people. To tell them something that would awake them for a moment. I know I will look for you on Wednesday.
>
> My darling, who is the next boy friend? How I did miss him? Where he appeared from and when?
>
> About coming to see you? It would be wonderful, but I have no energy ever to think about such strenuous enterprise. I feel really quite worked out, and for several days I had cough and cold. Now I am better, but still I cannot think about travel. Shermans are going away for rest, so Miss Romer will be attached to the studio.

9 September 1943. 6 rue des Colonels Renard. During a meeting at Gurdjieff's apartment, someone says: "You said once that even a cow can work alone."

"Excuse me," interrupts Gurdjieff, "I did not say cow. I said donkey. A cow is a parasite—it only gives milk. The donkey works."

21 October 1943. 6 rue des Colonels Renard. Gurdjieff tells pupils:

> You must accumulate, you have batteries in you in which you must accumulate this substance, like electricity. This substance can only be accumulated by struggle. Therefore create a struggle between your head and your animal. For example, what your body likes, whatever you have the habit of giving it, don't give it any more. The important thing is to have a continual process of struggle, because you need this substance that struggle will give you.
>
> You cannot work interiorly all day. You must make a special time and increase it little by little. To this work you give a half hour of the twenty-four hours. You sacrifice to this time all your occupations, all the work of your exterior functions. Sacrifice everything for your interior work and afterward you can put it aside for the things of ordinary life. You cannot do this work all day.
>
> In *All and Everything* there is everything one must know. Everything is there. All that exists, all that has existed, all that can exist. The beginning, the end, all the secrets of the creation of the world, all is there. But one must understand, and to understand depend on one's individuality.
>
> You have love based on sex; it is a sickness, a weakness. You cannot have love. That which perhaps your grandfather had. Today, for everyone, love is based on sex and sex on polarity. Real love is objective, but in Paris objective love doesn't exist. You have made the word sentiment for sex, for dirty things, you have forgotten real love.... Polarity is a hindrance. You are a slave of this law. Wish or not wish. Your body makes you love or not love. Consciously, you can be no longer the slave of your polarity. But first you must have the taste. All I can say in the meantime is that love exists, objective love.

1943. Coombe Springs. Bennett has sent Uspenskii a paper on five-dimensional physics to which Uspenskii replies—"If successful it will only amount to a new theory of Thermodynamics, and nothing more." He goes on to remind Bennett that "nothing new can be found in intellectual processes alone and that there is only one hope: that we should find the way to work with the higher emotional center. And we do not know how this is to be done."

Uspenskii sends a letter to another pupil [probably Dr. Roles] saying, "All in London should make sure to avoid the smallest departure from the letter of the System as contained in the writings I have left."

Reflecting on this, Bennett says—"It was irrelevant whether Uspenskii was right or wrong in demanding the surrender of all personal initiative on the part of his pupils. The whole point was that I never had surrendered and never could surrender my own independence as others had done."[10]

1944. 170 East 78th Street. Uspenskii speaks about the devil at a meeting:

> Devil is very important. Some people think he is symbolic. I always thought he is very concrete. And I was very glad to hear it was accepted so by the system. . . . He works through considering, negative emotions, imagination. But if you fight against these dangers, you are safe. Devil is the embodiment of evil. But with purpose. . . . No devil can keep you from self-remembering, if you work. If you don't, anyone can prevent you. The devil has so many faces, there are so many legends about him. If you study tales, it would help. The devil has many different ambitions, not only to be God. It is — I don't know — too small. . . . He is real, quite real. It is not the System; it is my opinion. Devil's object is man's soul. Moon feeds on souls only in the sense of life energy. The devil has better ideas. . . . In relation to the devil, or with the help of devil, there is possibility of conscious evil. . . . Can devil have any function in organic life apart from man? No. Animals, insects, fishes, bacteria? No. Devil can manifest only through help of man. Man has possibility of evolution. Devil can stop him; create conditions against it. The devil cannot belong to do [octave] in the sun. But maybe the devil can have his roots in si. Si is bigger than la, sol, fa. Not all si. But maybe when man was invented, the devil was invented also. . . . In no period can he have more power than in this. Now he is in full bloom.[11]

18 January 1944. 6 rue des Colonels Renard. At a meeting someone asks about the injustices of life. Gurdjieff answers:

> "Justice" is a big word. Objective things are not small things like microbes, they go according to law. Remember: as you sow, so you will reap. Not only people reap, but also families and nations. It often happens that that which happens on earth comes from something which was done by a father or grandfather. The results converge on you, the son, the grandson, it is for you who have to regulate them. This is not an injustice, it is a very great honor for you; it will be a means which will allow the past of your father, grandfather, great grandfather to be regulated. If misfortune comes to you in your youth, it means that someone brought them — for this you must reap. He

---

10. And yet he taught. Michel de Salzmann and Lord Pentland saw Bennett giving a talk in New York about the ten-month long teaching he proposed starting at Coombe Springs in the early 1970s. Afterward, de Salzmann told Pentland, "It will come to nothing. Look how he moves about when he talks."

11. Uspenskii believes one only meets the devil at the end of the ascending octave. Also, see his *Talks with a Devil* (London: Turnstone Press, 1972).

is dead, it is another on earth who reaps. You must not look at yourself egotistically. You are a link in the chain of your blood. Be proud of it, it is an honor to be this link. The more you are obliged to repair the past, the more you will have remorse of conscience. You will succeed in remembering all that which you have not done as you should in the past. Those things which you have done contrary to *Justice* have mortified your grandfather. Thus you can have ten times more remorse of conscience and your worth will be augmented in proportion. All your family, past and future, depend on you. Your entire family depends on the way you repair the past. Justice is not occupied with your little affairs, unredeemed pledges, it is occupied with big things. Justice does not touch all that, and at the same time, nothing is done on earth without it. You are obliged to have a position of responsibility in the line of your blood—you must work to repair the past.

1944. 6 rue des Colonels Renard. At a meeting the question of God is raised.

Gurdjieff: If you do not have an ideal, if you do not believe in God, then your father, your mother, your teacher can serve for you as an ideal.

Q: I have an ideal, I have always been a Catholic. But I no longer see Jesus Christ in the same way.

G: In the beginning Catholicism was very good, but not latterly. They searched for midday at two o'clock; they diluted everything. In the beginning it was superior to the Orthodox religion and to all others.

Q: I cannot recapture the faith of my childhood.

G: That is not necessary. You have lost that possibility. You are no longer a child, you are big now. You should have logic and not search automatically. To have direct contact with God is impossible. Millions and millions of nonentities wish to have relations with Mr. God direct. This is impossible. But you can have a relation in this line. What you do here, for instance, has this changed your interior ideal—since you took part in our conversations? (Yes) Then perhaps you have confidence in the person who directs here? (Yes) Then he can serve as teacher in the meantime.

Q: That does not satisfy me entirely. I want something else.

G: Then make a program. You do not know what you want. I wish you to understand that your nearest—father, mother, teacher—can serve as your ideal in place of God. The real God, forget him. As you are, you can never have relations with God. When you have grown, this could be, but you are one among millions of nonentities. Meantime, take as an ideal whoever is nearest and then you can pray to God, because this person has an ideal also, this ideal has in turn an ideal and so on, on to God. God is far, there are many stages before you reach him, do not think about Him. Your ideal will be your God. Later you can have another ideal.

Madame de Salzmann: God is much too far away. You are too small to have direct contact with him. Only he who is immediately above you can be God for you. He is a God who in his turn has a God. It is a ladder, there is always something above. Each degree leads you to another rung and you get your answer by the same chain.

G: You cannot pray directly to God. You imagine so, but you waste your time. It is from there that psychopathy comes. Like a monk. He says directly 'God.' He manipulates like this (gestures) and sixty years later he perishes like a dog without ever having received anything. He wanted God directly. No one has seen Him, for the law of contacts is strict. This law exists everywhere. You will look for your God when you have felt yourself guided in the right direction, on a good road, for instance by Madame de Salzmann. Then she will be your God. She is not God, but she will be your first stage; you can have contact with God through her; make all your prayers and good manifestations pass through her and that itself will make contact with the next stage. Then a third stage and finally it is possible that your prayer will reach the real God. Exactly like the telegraph; a message to a relative in the country near Lyons. First from Paris to Lyons; then to another town, then to the village, then to your relative's house. By stages and it takes some time.

At another meeting, undated, Gurdjieff says, "I will give you a sacred secret. There are two currents, two rivers. You have to cross from one to the other; you are like fish whose natural element is water and who are obliged to live in the water and who are obliged to live in the air. You must now learn to live in both currents at once. There is the habitual current which is ordinary life and then the other current which is your interior life."

In answer to a question about love, Gurdjieff says: "Real love is the basis of all, the foundations, the Source. The religions have perverted and deformed love. It was by love that Jesus performed miracles. Real love joined with magnetism. All accumulated vibrations create a current. This current brings the force of love. Real love is a cosmic force which goes through us. If we crystallize it, it becomes a power—the greatest power in the world."

27 January 1944. Leningrad. German blockade ends. Without food, people have eaten whatever is available in order to live. No pigeons or rats remain. Reports of cannibalism. Of the city's three million inhabitants, an estimated million to a million-and-a-half have died, most of starvation.

8 February 1944. 6 rue des Colonels Renard. At a group meeting Gurdjieff says: "For each man up to a certain age, his father must be his God. God loves him who esteems his father. When the father dies, then there is a place where God can enter in."

"But if the father is unworthy," a student asks. "*Low.*"

"Even if he is the worst criminal, if he is shit, the lowest among men, you must recognize your obligation. You don't know why he has become like that. Here is a law. He created you. You owe your existence to him. And he is answerable for your life in another world. If he is the lowest man in the eyes of everyone, let it be so—but inwardly you must feel your obligation. You have to pay him for your existence."

15 March 1944. New York. Writes Bragdon: "Uspenskii has Luciferian pride and didn't like what I said about him in my autobiography, though I don't see why he should object. He claims he was not helped by Lady Rothermere, whereas I myself cabled him a hundred pounds from her. This he does not acknowledge but I know it to be a fact."

20 April 1944. 6 rue des Colonels Renard. A student says: "I have tried to feel remorse of conscience, but the remorse overwhelms me. I cannot forget that it was from remorse that Judas hanged himself."

"Why do you speak of Judas in this case?" asks Gurdjieff. "What do you know of Judas? He was a great initiate. He was the second disciple after St. John the Baptist. All that is told about him is false. If you wish to know, he was even the master of Christ."

"The search for remorse leads me to depression," says the student. "How should I try to find remorse?"

"In order to experience remorse it is necessary to awaken real will, to remember real aim. You must destroy tranquility."

"I have felt remorse in flashes," the student answers, "two or three times. But I do not know how to make it come. When I look for it intentionally, I do not recapture this quality but find the kind that depresses me."

"When remorse comes without self-love," Gurdjieff says, "it gives us the desire for something better. But when it is mixed with self-love, it weights you down. The effect of true remorse is hatred of yourself, repugnance toward yourself. These two things make up true remorse of conscience."

20 May 1944. Paris. Gurdjieff visits René Daumal on his deathbed, dying of tuberculosis. He places an orange in each hand and tells him, "All your life has been a preparation for this moment." Daumal dies the next day.

22 May 1944. New York. Writes Bragdon: "I have just finished *A New Model of the Universe*, a remarkable book. The last third I do not like as well, but the rest completely fascinated me.... His essay on 'Sex and Evolution' is the greatest thing I have ever read on the subject.... The fifth and sixth dimensions left me behind, completely blank and the Laws of Manu are too horrible. What a mind Uspenskii has. He seems to have read and digested everything, but I wonder toward the last whether or not the use of which has not rather *gotten* him."

6 June 1944. Normandy, France. D-Day landing by Allies.

20 July 1944. Wolfsschanze, East Prussia. Colonel Claus von Stauffenberg plants bomb in a briefcase at Hitler's headquarters. Bomb explodes. Hitler escapes serious injury.

24 August 1944. Paris. Paris is liberated. After liberation, the purge soon begins. Some forty thousand French citizens, taken to be German sympathizers, are killed.

December 1944. 6 rue des Colonels Renard. Janet Flanner visits Gurdjieff.[12] She writes a letter to Solita and Kathryn saying, "... a very wise old man sitting in his rich pantry of foods and thoughts."

28 December 1944. New York. It is Carman Barnes' birthday and she throws herself a large party. Writes Bragdon, "Carman looked beautiful—a Pagan of Greece or Alexandria with vine leaves in her hair. Carman is a Yogin and deeply versed in Ancient Wisdom." She has asked for and received Uspenskii's permission to dramatize *Strange Life of Ivan Osokin.*

1945. 6 rue des Colonels Renard. Gurdjieff's pantry has been full for the entire war. He says shopkeepers gave him credit with the promise of compensation by wealthy Texas oilmen at war's end. Actually, the money is coming from Anna Stefanna, "Anci," wife of François Dupré, a wealthy French hotel owner. In the late 1930s, Anci developed a tumor at the base of her liver which doctors said was inoperable. Gurdjieff had cured her by transmitting *Hanbledzoin* to that area. Devoted to Gurdjieff thereafter, she committed herself to supporting him.

1945. Paris. Elizabeth Gordon dies. According to Ethel Merston, a friend from the early Prieuré days, Gordon was interned at a camp by the Germans after they conquered France; she was released after several months because of her age.

---

12. She came to have an appreciation of Gurdjieff but the teaching eluded her. She was "never a Gurdjieffiete," she says. Near the end of her life she writes, "I have manufactured journalism for nearly a quarter of this century. Nowadays everyone manufactures. Few create. If an individual knows the difference and I do, the failure to create leaves only one conclusion: one has manufactured.... One is old when one no longer believes in the possibility of change. Change won't come true, nor dreams by day, for I never dream at night and so I am wide awake for the rest of my life, eyelids open in shock and tears. I feel not only without faith in my future but I know my past has arrived and that it now becomes inescapable." *Genêt: A Biography of Janet Flanner* by Brenda Wineapple (Lincoln, NE: University of Nebraska Press, 1989), 213.

1945. New York. Carman Barnes marries Hamilton Fish Armstrong, editor of the magazine *Foreign Relations*. He is nineteen years older than Barnes.

1945. Franklin Farms. Nott sees Uspenskii often. The two sit alone as they had in England, talking and drinking. Though Uspenskii, now sixty-seven years old, has become what Nott describes as "a sick man, suffering from the weaknesses and lawful infirmities of old age, as well as from some specific disease [kidneys]," he finds Uspenskii mixing and drinking concoctions that were too powerful for him.

"You must have a stomach of iron!" exclaims Nott, taking a sip. "It's too strong for me."

"It's the only thing that relieves the boredom and depression that comes over me at times," says Uspenskii.

Long ago, in *Tertium Organum*, Uspenskii had written about what he called the secret of the power of alcohol over human souls. "Alcohol," he wrote, "produces the illusion of communion of souls and stimulates fantasy simultaneously in two or more people."

The effects of Uspenskii's long years of self-willed isolation from Gurdjieff, the failure to contact a school, nostalgia for the Russia of his youth, and the increasing amounts of alcohol have all taken their toll.

To the end, Uspenskii never gives any indication that the years without Gurdjieff have brought him to reevaluate his former teacher and their relationship. Denis Saurat, now a professor of French literature at Kings College, believes "Uspenskii could not submit to the pressure Gurdjieff brought to bear on him to break down his particular kind of vanity."

January 1945. New York. Marie Seton, deposed as Uspenskii's secretary but still remaining a student, says that after lectures Uspenskii would sometimes ask a few of the group to go out with him to supper. These gatherings break up later and later, Uspenskii showing a greater disinclination to leave the restaurant, staying sometimes to four in the morning, though never becoming noticeably drunk, talking about his homeland. At one gathering into the early morning when all the others had left except Seton, she says, "he instructed me to cancel the next lecture. I felt the time had come when I must ask him for an explanation as to how he could justify the sudden cancellation of a lecture."

"Where does such action fit into the System?" she asked, "and also where does your violent temper towards some people fit in?"

"They are such fools," Uspenskii said. "I've lost control of my temper."

"But surely," she said, "if we are to try to control our negative emotions, we cannot learn from you, if you can't control yours."

Uspenskii answered bluntly: "I took over the leadership to save the System. But I took it over before I had gained enough control over myself. I was not ready. I have lost control over myself. It is a long time since I could control my state of mind."

"Why don't you give up the lectures and try to gain control over yourself again?"

"The System has become a profession with me," he said.

"One day he said something that was somehow more revealing than anything else as to the way a man becomes entangled in a role, or a vocation."

"In Russia," he said, "there used to be a thousand or two thousand people at my lectures. Here there are a hundred—too few."

One day he said: "I have become dependent on the comfort, the luxury. I can't give it up."

Seton writes: "Here was a man who was at heart honest; a man who was not by any means devoid of compassion for people. But adulation and comfort and the dearth of friends and the terror of a period of war had sapped his will to keep theory and practice united.

"If a man of the undeniable qualities of Uspenskii can go off the track and become absorbed in egotism and dependent on easy living, and become callous as to the effects on himself and on others, what of the gurus who are less basically honest?

"When I went to the country house for practical work, I began to notice what I had not noticed in England: that the people who were the 'old members' and had been living under Madame's direction were drab in clothes, joyless, and strangely closed-up people with one another. All were fearful of her displeasure.... I began to see the pursuit of self-knowledge had to, as it seemed, eliminate an atmosphere of warmth between people and something that might be described as a lack of lovingness."

Spring 1945. Coombe Springs. Bennett, taking things into his own hands now that Uspenskii is in America, has been giving public lectures on Gurdjieff's system. Some Americans had joined his group and, upon returning home, they go to see Uspenskii (Bennett had given them letters of introduction). The Americans believe Bennett's lectures are copied from Uspenskii's pre-war lectures.

30 April 1945. Hitler's Bunker, Berlin. With Russian troops only a block away, Adolf Hitler marries his mistress, Eva Braun. Hitler then issues a last testament blaming international Jewry and the German General Staff for Germany's defeat. Hitler shoots himself in the mouth. Eva Braun takes poison.

May 1945. Franklin Farms. With World War II in Europe concluded, Rodney Collin leaves government service to devote all his time to Uspenskii, driving him to and from meetings in New York and spending long evenings with him in his study. Says Collin: "It struck me very much how Uspenskii, in speaking about his parents, relations or old friends, always recalled their possibilities, their best sides, what they might become, and never recalled anything negative or unpleasant about them."

A frequent subject of discussion is the period of dimensions in time and the idea of different times. "For me," says Collin, "the key to the understanding of this idea up to a certain point lies in Uspenskii's theory of six dimensions—the first, second and third [dimensions] are clearly the length, breadth and thickness of space; the fourth is the line of time that we recognize, the line of individual life; the fifth is infinite repetition of this life and all it contains—the 'eternal now'; the sixth must be the dimension in which all exists everywhere, all possibilities are realized, and all is one. The fourth dimension is 'time,' the fifth 'eternity,' but what shall we call the sixth? For us it is Divinity itself."

7 May 1945. Reims, France. Germany unconditionally surrenders.

May 1945. Coombe Springs. Bennett receives a letter from Uspenskii's solicitor telling him that he is "a charlatan and a thief" and asking for "the return of all Mr. Uspenskii's material, including his lectures." He then hears that a letter had been sent to Lyne Place instructing pupils to break off all relations with him and never again to communicate with him on any subject. Thinks Bennett: "They [referring to the Americans] must have given him very garbled accounts of what I was doing."[13]

Much like Uspenskii when he broke with Gurdjieff in 1924, Bennett convenes a group meeting and reads aloud the solicitor's letter. He then tells the group they can decide either to stay with him or join Uspenskii's group and "never see me again." In August he gives the first of yearly seminars.

Mid-May 1945. 170 East 78th Street. Uspenskii begins to spend more and more of his time in his New York apartment. De Ropp's opinion is that by this time "Uspenskii was no longer a teacher. He had lost his power and wrecked his health by indulgence in two poisons, alcohol and nostalgia." He withdrew more and more into himself, becoming hypersensitive, and perhaps paranoid. "He was apt," says de Ropp, "at the slightest provocation to throw people out of the Work."

Uspenskii revises six introductory lectures which he had published in England shortly before he left. These are later published in 1950 as *The Psychology of Man's Possible Evolution.*

6 August 1945. Japan. The United States drops the world's first atomic bomb on Hiroshima. J. Robert Oppenheimer, head of the project, quotes the Bhagavad Gita, "I am Shiva, destroyer of worlds."

Late Summer 1945. 6 rue des Colonels Renard. Fritz Peters, now thirty-two years old, visits Gurdjieff. Peters had been drafted into the American army and,

---

13. Bennett never gives any indication that he doubts his own actions and motives.

though behind the lines in a clerical job, the horror of the war had thrown him into a deep depression. Many narrow escapes had put him in a highly nervous state—such as when a group he was with at Torquay on the southern English coast was suddenly strafed by six German fighters and many were killed. Faced with hospitalization, Peters convinces a general to give him a pass to go to Paris. When he left for Paris he had not slept in several days, had no appetite, and had lost a great deal of weight. He was, he says, "very close to what I would have to call a form of madness."

He has no idea how to find Gurdjieff but somehow manages to track him down. Gurdjieff is not home when Peters arrives at his apartment and so he waits inside the entrance. After about an hour he hears the sound of a cane tapping on the sidewalk. Presently, Gurdjieff appears and walks up to him. There is no sign of recognition. Peters says his name. Gurdjieff stares at him for a second, then drops his cane and cries out in a loud voice:

"My son!" Gurdjieff says, embracing him. "Don't talk, you are sick," Gurdjieff tells him, and leads him up the stairs to his second floor apartment.

Gurdjieff leads Peters down the hall to a dark bedroom, tells him to lie down and says, "This is your room, for as long as you need it."

Peters lies down but begins to cry uncontrollably, then his head pounds. He gets up and goes to the kitchen where he finds Gurdjieff, who looks alarmed when he sees him. Peters says he wants some aspirin.

Gurdjieff shakes his head, "No medicine. I give you coffee. Drink as hot as you can."

Drinking the coffee Gurdjieff has made, Peters looks at Gurdjieff standing in front of the refrigerator, observing him. Peters suddenly realizes that Gurdjieff looks "incredibly weary—I have never seen anyone look so tired."

Suddenly Peters, slumped over the table, sipping the coffee, becomes aware of an energy rising up within him and he straightens up, staring at Gurdjieff.

"It was as if a violent, electric blue light emanated from him and entered me," says Peters.

All Peters' fatigue drains from his body. He has never felt better in his life. But as his body is renewed, Gurdjieff's body slumps and his massive face turns grey. It is as if Gurdjieff himself, says Peters, "was being drained of life."

"You all right now—watch food on stove—I must go," says Gurdjieff urgently.

In fifteen minutes or so Gurdjieff returns, looking, says Peters, "like a young man again, alert, smiling, sly and full of good spirits."

"Now," Gurdjieff tells him, "you go out and do anything that will amuse you, any kind of play, then come back here at ten o'clock."

10:00 p.m. That Evening. A large group of students assemble at Gurdjieff's apartment. He introduces Peters as his "real son" who had been at his "real school."

During the question and answer period a rich woman speaks of the disadvantages of having money in terms of understanding his work, and that her so-called friends wouldn't like her if she was poor. Gurdjieff says the answer is simple enough. She could give her money to him, that he would make good use of it, and she would soon learn if she had any real friends. Peters and others laugh. The rich woman objects. Gurdjieff says she should learn that laughter was, in truth, a very good medicine. After supper everyone leaves except Peters, who Gurdjieff has asked to help him do the dishes. Then the two drink coffee and Gurdjieff plays on the harmonium much of the music that had been played at the Prieuré. They laugh together and Gurdjieff says that it was a great pleasure to enjoy laughter with someone again—that one of the saddest aspects of his life was that his students were so impressed with him that they could never condescend to anything as low as laughter. The conversation turns to the rich woman. Says Gurdjieff:

> This woman not take me seriously and so will not discover anything. What I tell her is truth. If she could give up money and have to live like poor person she would create possibility for two things. First, would find out what other people like, how they live, and also find out much about herself, that she stupid, shit-person, only have value of her money. Cannot be understanding between rich and poor, because rich and poor, both, only understand money. One understand life with money and despise people without money. Other understand life without money and hate people who have money. This woman now hate self because guilty about being rich. Poor man hate self—or sometimes just life—because feel guilty about not having money or feel cheated by world. With such unreal, false attitude, impossible understand any serious thing like my work. For instance, this woman tell that I most important influence in her life—but would be impossible for her to give me her money—so, very simple, she not tell truth. I not important for her life, but only her money important. With poor man can be same thing. Can believe in me and what I teach only if I first teach how to make money—this what poor man think. Not so. If I teach him how make money, then he will have only other problem—he will not be able to live without this money. But such people can learn important thing if can make effort in self to give up money—or, if poor, to give up desire for money. Impossible to do my work with all energy if also concerned with money. But all these things very difficult for your contemporaries. Not only cannot do. Cannot even understand why this question of money important. Such people will never understand real teaching or real possibility of learning anything . . . You remember Prieuré and how many times I have struggle with money. I not make money like others make money, and when I have too much money, I spend. But I never need money for self, and I

not make or earn money. I ask for money and people always give, and for this I give opportunity study my teaching, but even when they give money still almost always impossible for them learn anything. Already, they think of reward . . . now I owe them something because they give me money. When think of reward in this way, impossible learn anything from me.[14]

Staying at Gurdjieff's apartment, Peters notices that many elderly destitute people visit Gurdjieff, who feeds them and gives them gifts or money. One day as he and Gurdjieff drink coffee, Gurdjieff looks at him reflectively and says:

I play many roles in life . . . this part of my destiny. You think of me as teacher, but in reality, I also your father . . . father in many ways you not understand. I also "teacher of dancing," and have many businesses: you not know that I own company which make false eyelashes and also have very good business selling rugs. This way I make money for self and for family. Money I "shear" from disciples is for work. But other money I make for my family. My family very big, as you see—because this kind old people who come every day to my house, are, also, family. They my family because have no other family.

I give you good example why I *must* be family for such people. You not know, even though you hear about this, what life is like in Paris during war, while Germans here. For such people—people who come to see me every day now—was impossible. But for me, not so. I not interested in who win war. Not have patriotism or big ideals about peace. Americans, with ideals, kill millions of Germans, Germans kill—with own ideals—English, French, Russian, Belgian . . . all have ideals, all have peaceful purpose, all kill. I have only one purpose: existence for self, for students, and for family, even this big family. So, I do what they cannot do, I make deal with Germans, with policemen, with all kinds idealistic people who make "black market." Result: I eat well and continue have tobacco, liquor, and what is necessary for me and for many others. While I do this—very difficult thing for most people—I also can help people.

"But *why* did you do it? Why for *them*?" asks Peters.

Gurdjieff smiles. "Freets, you stupid still. If can do for self and students, can also do for others who *cannot* do such thing." He pauses and then adds, smiling enigmatically: "Ask self why old lady, with very little money, every day feed birds in park. These people—this family—my birds. But I honest: I say I do this *for* people, and also for self. This give me good feeling. Lady who feed birds in park

---

14. In the context of what he tells Peters, it is interesting to review Gurdjieff's actions with Orage, Toomer, and others regarding money.

not tell truth. She tell only do for birds, because love birds. She not tell what pleasure she get."

Peters' question now seems to him somewhat silly and he apologizes for having asked about the "old" people.

Gurdjieff shakes his head. "Not necessary be sorry. Is not bad question you ask me. But one more thing about this question. You notice all such people who come here are already old. Without me not have possibility die properly. Except me, such people not have family, and for future can only look towards death. If I help such people die in right way, this can be very important and very good thing. Someday you understand this better, but you still young."

Autumn 1945. 6 rue des Colonels Renard. Peters wangles another pass from the army, returning to Paris to see Gurdjieff. The two discuss many things and laugh a lot together. The day Peters is to leave, Gurdjieff, seventy-three years old now, tells him he is very tired and that when he finishes the *Third Series*, "my work will be done. So now I can die, because my task in life is coming to an end." He then looks at Peters gravely, saying this also means that he can do nothing more for him.

Gurdjieff says Peters was "necessary" to him for two reasons. One, he came to the Prieuré "as a wounded animal" and suggests he research the meaning of the French word *blesser*.[15] And two, Gurdjieff says that because of his particular heredity and conditioning and the fact that he somehow managed to remain "open" despite his early physical traumas that he, Peters, had been an appropriate receptacle or "garbage can" in which he could "dump" some of the accumulation of his life's work.

They have lunch that day at Gurdjieff's apartment with some twenty other students. Many stories are told and there is much laughter. But at the end of lunch Gurdjieff's mood changes suddenly and he looks very ill. He rises and supports himself by leaning on a chair. He then raises one arm and makes a large sweeping gesture around the room, the act galvanizing everyone's attention.

"Must make announcement," he says dramatically in English. "My last book is now finished, except for work with editor."

He pauses . . . taking in every person individually, as if he is weighing them.

"This mean," he continues, "my work is through—finished. Mean at last I can die . . ." Again a pause, the silence in the room deafening, " . . . but not just because book is finished. In life is only necessary for man to find one person to whom can give accumulation of learning in life. When find such receptacle then is possible die."

He gives a kind smile and continues: "So now two good things happen for me. I finish work and I also find one person to whom can give results my life's work."

Once more he raises his arm, this time with the index finger extended. Slowly

---

15. In English means "wounded." The etymology derives from the medieval French for blood, from the use of blood in consecration.

the arm arcs about the room, the outstretched finger pointing at one person then another.

When the finger points at Fritz Peters, the arm stops.

The silence, the tension, in the room is immense. Gurdjieff and Peters look at one another fixedly. . . . Finally, Gurdjieff drops his arm and leaves the room.

Momentarily, everyone seems transfixed. Peters finally breaks the silence by walking across the room. Near the doorway he is stopped by one of the women instructors. She holds his arm tightly and looks at him with what he says is "a malevolent, sneering smile."

"You will never learn, will you?" she says.

Peters pulls his arm away. "What does that mean?"

She laughs.

"How does it feel to be chosen?" she demands. "From the look on your face, I can tell you exactly what you are feeling. He pointed at you, didn't he? And now—with your colossal ego—you march out of the room . . . the triumphant successor."

Peters returns her smile.

"Your guess is as good as mine," he replies and leaves the apartment.

Peters, overrun with questions and doubts about what Gurdjieff had said, the war in Europe over, visits him one last time. Gurdjieff answers the door, looking sleepy. He gives Peters a cold look and tells him, "Already I tell you good-bye, and already I think you in America. Why you come?"

He says he is on his way to America and has just come to say good-bye. Gurdjieff, without hostility, says: "Cannot say good-bye again—this already done."

He gives Peters a final, impersonal handshake.

Peters turns to leave but Gurdjieff stops him with a gesture, saying sharply, with a smile on his face—"Americans drop bomb on Japan, yes?"

Peters nods.

"What you think of your America now?"

Peters goes to reply, but Gurdjieff closes the door, gently, in his face.

1946. New York. Carman Barnes and her husband separate.

1946. 6 rue des Colonels Renard. Between now and Gurdjieff's death in 1949, Jane Heap sends her students from London three or four times a year. At first they come all together and then, at Gurdjieff's suggestion, in twos and threes. Annie Lou Staveley went often. One of the many things she was struck by was the atmosphere of his apartment. She asked Jane about it. "Haven't you ever heard of the odor of sanctity?" she was told. "For myself," she says, "from the beginning I had with Mr. Gurdjieff a sensation of something that had been crushed and buried in me coming into the light, the stone lifted. It was painful but healing, like the probing of a skilled physician. . . . Of course the lifelong habit of pretending, actually lying, is not so easily shed, but the sense that this is a possibility is liberating and strengthening."

June 1946. 6 rue des Colonels Renard. Krokodeel visits with Marie Louise Habets, a former nun. Later she will write a book about her, *The Nun's Story,* which will be made into a film. Gurdjieff puts Krokodeel in galoshes several times. Then he doses off with labored breathing. He opens one eye, looking sideways at her, his face coming alive with a slow spreading smile that lifted up all its tired lines. He nods and says hoarsely in French, "Sisters of Charity of Jesus and Mary." Says Hulme, "Out of a possible fifty female Orders dedicated to good works and charitable thoughts, he had named point-blank her precise Order."

Summer 1946. New York. Uspenskii, increasingly ill with kidney disease[16] but refusing to submit to treatment, gives his last series of New York lectures. At the end of the final lecture he announces to his sixty-some followers that he will be returning to England.

30 September 1946. Taliesin, Arizona. Svetlana, Olgivanna Lloyd Wright's daughter, dies in an automobile accident.

1947. Spandau Prison, Berlin. Albert Speer, sentenced to ten years in prison, writes in his diary: "The catastrophe of this war has proved the sensitivity of the system of modern civilization evolved in the course of centuries. Now we know that we do not live in an earthquake-proof structure. The build-up of negative impulses, each reinforcing the other, can inexorably shake to pieces the complicated apparatus of the modern world. There is no halting this process by will alone. The danger is that the automatism of progress will depersonalize man further and withdraw more and more of his self-responsibility."[17]

18 January 1947. Grand Ballroom of Steinway Hall, New York. Uspenskii announces that he is leaving for England the next day.

19 January 1947. Franklin Farms. De Ropp, Collin, and other students watch as Pyotr Demianovich Uspenskii, cane in hand, his strong, square face now flabby, the skin pale, slowly makes his way toward the car ready to take him to the New York docks to board the SS *Queen Elizabeth*. Against doctor's orders and the pleas of his wife, he is returning to an England blanketed by heavy snows and whipped

---

16. The kidneys were the seat of the soul, according to Aristotle.
17. When he came to Russia in 1912 Gurdjieff warned against a growth of automatism and personality. "Contemporary culture," he declared, "requires automatons.... Man is becoming a willing slave. He no longer needs chains. He begins to grow fond of his slavery, to be proud of it. And this is the most terrible thing that can happen to a man." *Search,* 309.

by bitter cold, its electricity restricted, food rationed.

23 January 1947. Southampton. Uspenskii arrives and is immediately driven to Lyne Place. Kenneth Walker says, "He was not the Uspenskii of old. There stepped onto English soil a man whom we hardly recognized, a man who had aged by twenty years since we had last seen him, a man on whom Death had already set his mark."

Within days of his arrival, Madame de Salzmann, at Gurdjieff's behest, invites Uspenskii to see his former teacher. Uspenskii refuses. It is sixteen years since they last talked at the Café Henri IV. From Uspenskii's point of view, there is nothing to say. Then Gurdjieff was nearing the lowest point of an outer descending octave and Uspenskii was coming to the highest. Now their situations are totally reversed.

During the six years of Uspenskii's absence, Dr. Francis Roles did as he was instructed and had the groups continue to meet and study the System as Uspenskii had constituted it. Now he calls Francis Roles and tells him to collect three hundred people. "What shall we say to them?" asks Dr. Roles. Says Uspenskii, "Why say anything? Ask *them* what they want."

26 February 1947. 46 Colet Gardens, London. Uspenskii holds the first of what will be six meetings in Colet Gardens, one of the few heated buildings in London. [Bennett is not invited and Bennett's letter asking to see Uspenskii is not answered.] The atmosphere is tense with expectation. Presently, Uspenskii appears. His hand gripping a cane, his every movement obviously a painful effort, he makes his way to the platform's two steps. Dr. Roles sits below, his chair facing the audience. Uspenskii mounts the steps and takes his seat in the same way he has done since his first lecture in England twenty-six years before. Impassively he slowly looks over and takes in the audience. One of the faces his eyes register is that of a school friend mentioned in *Strange Life of Ivan Osokin*. And then the questions begin....

"Do you wish us to continue with the program you gave us in 1940?" someone finally asks.

"Program?" Uspenskii replies. "I don't know program. Which program?"

"Program which you gave in 1940."

"No, I don't remember," says Uspenskii.

Later in the meeting the subject is again brought up.

"We have been trying to follow out the teaching you gave us years ago," someone says.

Declares Uspenskii, "I gave no teaching."

"You told us certain things to help us."

"You misunderstand."

"Where can we begin to work now?"

"I will see what you want to know and where you want to begin," Uspenskii says, "and then we will see first step, and perhaps we will find second step. We don't know first step, that is the question. That you must remember."

"He spoke for nearly two hours," says Fairfax Hall, an early student of Uspenskii's. "There was much emotion in the room. Sometimes anxiety to hear more, and sometimes anger that he would not give material. But Uspenskii still managed to get himself across and give a feeling of great individual attention."

12 March 1947. Colet Gardens. At this meeting someone asks Uspenskii if he has abandoned the System.

"I never taught System," Uspenskii answers.

"What are you going to try to teach us now?"

"That we may see."

Time and again, Uspenskii returns the question to the questioner, saying either he does not know or does not understand. His answers are short, simple. He urges people to make attempts for themselves. But some questions he does answer.

"Is there anything one can do at any given moment now to make sure that one will remember that moment later?"

Replies Uspenskii, "No, we have nothing of that kind—no help in that way. Each one must find chief thing for himself—why one cannot remember."

"I believe that when I want something I only want it because I am selfish and possessive," someone says. "I need an aim which is outside myself."

"Right. Very good."

"How can I make my will come into action as quickly as my desire?"

"Very good—we may see something from that."

Uspenskii is asked, "You said that many of our questions do not refer to you."

"Yes," answers Uspenskii, "quite right."

"Is it because there is no understanding of a purpose other than one's own small purpose?"

"I don't even see small purpose."

"I mean that the questions are based on the inevitable point of view—the personal one—and is it that they lack any idea of a larger purpose? Your purpose, or possible purpose for everyone here?"

Uspenskii: "Well? Further."

"Can we learn to be more humble?"

Says Uspenskii, "I never was humble myself, and I don't know how I can."

"I understood much more what was going on," says Fairfax Hall. "He will not allow any System language and sometimes repudiates knowledge of a System. He was trying to break down the habitual and associative way of thinking and to drive people back and back on themselves to see that they had nothing they could call their own. He seemed to be indicating that each must find for himself the particular personal difficulty that prevents self-remembering. He conveyed that self-remembering was the whole thing and with that everything else was added to the degree in which one could remember. I felt that it was a very simple thing and that we could not be simple. Something like being a little child as it says in the Gospels."

April 1947. Franklin Farms. Rodney Collin leaves for England just before Easter so as to be with Uspenskii. He will spend all summer and autumn with his teacher.

21 May 1947. Colet Gardens. At this meeting Dr. Roles introduces the question of memory.

"People who have been trying to do things," Dr. Roles says, "tell me that they simply don't remember to go on with it. They forget every minute. They do it once a day. Is it possible to start by trying to improve memory in some way?"

"Yes, if it is what I call memory," answers Uspenskii. He adds, "There are many misunderstandings about this."[18]

18 June 1947. Colet Gardens. Uspenskii appears in public for the last time.

A student asks: "I think that what I have learned from these meetings is that I know even less than I thought I did. Is that a desirable result?"

Uspenskii, giving no ground, replies—"Sometimes it may be."

Many were baffled and bewildered by Uspenskii, among them one of his oldest students, the Harley Street surgeon Kenneth Walker. He sees Uspenskii as a "very deeply disappointed man. . . . Something had gone wrong and somebody had failed, but who it was that had failed was never very clear to me."

Others see it differently. Says Rodney Collin, "At Uspenskii's last meetings at Colet Gardens, he reached the deepest level [of sincerity] I ever met in a living man."

Said another:

> Uspenskii seemed very tired at first but I have noticed before how he seems to gain energy as the evening goes on. There were many questions and many answers, but it was from the emotional feeling that I gained the answers and not from the words. He seemed to be indicating that each must find for himself the particular personal difficulty that prevents

---

18. What Uspenskii is likely referring to in regard to memory can be found in Rodney Collin's book *The Theory of Eternal Life*. Collin writes that what we commonly understand can only refer to the denser worlds in which "perception travels through time slowly enough to yield a sense of past, present and future." But in the higher worlds there can be no memory. This is "because everything is now and everything known." Later Collin writes: "For familiar levels of consciousness and for the impulses of memory arising from them death is an absolute insulator. To pass through death in the next life memory would have to be of a far greater force, that is, it would have to arise from an immensely higher intensity of consciousness than any we ordinarily know." *Theory of Eternal Life*, 85.

remembering. I also felt that he conveyed that remembering was the whole thing and that with that everything else was added in the degree in which one could remember. I also felt that it was a very simple thing and that we could not be simple.

Of Uspenskii's return to England, Collin says: "He was a different man. So much of the vigorous, whimsical, brilliant personality, which his friends had known and enjoyed for so many years, had been left behind, that many meeting him again were shocked, baffled, or else were given a quite new understanding of what was possible in the way of development.... He spoke to them in a new way. He said that he abandoned the system. He asked them what they wanted, and said that only from that could they begin on the way of self-remembering and consciousness." Those who understood the way that Uspenskii was now appearing, he says, "realized that in the way of development true knowledge must first be acquired and then abandoned. That exactly what makes possible the opening of one door may make impossible the opening of the next."

Summer 1947. Lyne Place. After the meetings at Colet Gardens, Uspenskii retires to his country home. Concluding that a new start could not be made in England, he instructs Collin and others to prepare for his return to America that autumn. He withdraws from life, sees very few people, and rarely speaks. But his silence is alive.[19]

Says Collin: "He would have two or three people sit with him, not doing anything, just sitting, smoking, occasionally making a remark, drinking a glass of wine, for hours on end. At first it was very difficult—one racked one's brains for what to say, how to start a conversation, thoughts of all kinds of imaginary duties elsewhere. Many people could not bear it. But after a while, these became the most interesting times of all. One began to feel—everything is possible in *this* moment." When Uspenskii does speak, the topic is often eternal recurrence.

4 September 1947. Southampton. Uspenskii has Rodney Collin drive him to the docks and put his luggage on board ship. A few hours before the ship's departure, Uspenskii arrives and tells Collin to unload his luggage and says quietly—"I am not going to America *this time*." [Emphasis added.]

To Collin, the experience "was like the 'stop' exercise on the scale of the whole Work. A stop was made in many lives, everyone's personal plans were turned upside down, and a space made in the momentum of time where something quite new could be done. Then a most extraordinary and indescribable time began...."

---

19. This is reminiscent of the time when Uspenskii visited Gurdjieff's small Moscow apartment on the Bolshaia Dmitrovka and noted that Gurdjieff's pupils "were not afraid to keep silent."

September 1947. Lyne Place. Uspenskii's health worsens. Beset with fever, shivers and a renal abscess, he says, "Give me another month to live." Penicillin injections are given. By the week's end Uspenskii begins to feel better. "He had often told his students," Roles says, "that in his view a man must prepare for death by conquering his physical body. Everyone is amazed at the strength of will he displays at forcing his sick body to the limit." Watching Uspenskii staying up day and night, demanding more and more impossible tasks of his body, Collin says that his teacher is rising "in a crescendo of effort to meet the moment of death."

To impress familiar locations on his memory, Uspenskii has Collin drive him all over the south of England to places he had known, such as his former flat at 55a Gwendwr Road in West Kensington, the house at Gaddesden, and to Alley Cottage, Maurice Nicoll's old seaside cottage in Sidlesham, and Hayes. These excursions often last throughout the night, Uspenskii sitting silently in the back seat, always in the company of his beloved cats.

Says Collin: "When almost unable to set one foot before the other he would make his dying body walk step by step for an hour at a time through the rough lanes; force it to rise in the small hours, dress, descend and climb long flights of stairs; turn night into day; and require of his companions in order to remain with him, such feats of endurance as they in full possession of health and strength were scarcely able to accomplish."

"During his last few days," Dr. Roles says, "he seemed completely changed, to have put aside all the violence innate in his character and to be looking at everything with new eyes in a state of what must have been near 'Cosmic Consciousness.'" By invitation, he saw people who had played a part in his life. One was a fellow much mentioned in his *Strange Life of Ivan Osokin*. "Of all his books," says Dr. Roles, "I believe Uspenskii wanted it to be the one he would most be remembered by."

One night, having spent the whole night forcing his body to stay awake and walk and waking his students in order to make many experiments, Uspenskii says to Collin—"Now do you understand that it has to be done by effort, or do you still think that things come right by themselves?" Says Collin, "At that moment, I saw clearly that if we really understood that everything is done by effort, all our life would be on another basis. We would not be able to hope.... We, ourselves, have to develop our own will up to the highest possible point; that is, the power of putting into practice what we know."

Uspenskii begins to communicate his ideas telepathically.[20] Finally, one of his attendants, fearing that her imagination might overrun her, asks that he speak audibly. He does as she asks. Increasingly, many people at Lyne Place begin to have a sense of the miraculous taking place. (Later, Collin writes about this in an account he entitles "Last Remembrances of a Magician.")

---

20. Where once with Gurdjieff in 1916 in Finland Uspenskii was receiving telepathic messages, he now is generating them.

The coming of death creates an intensity that gives to the so-called ordinary occurrences of life a dimension and significance not usually seen. Sitting with Uspenskii at the dinner table, Collin watches him crumbling a bread roll on the cloth while under the table a cat eats the crumbs. As Uspenskii's love of cats was well known, Collin realizes the animal could have jumped on the table and Uspenskii would have given him the whole roll. He watches the cat eat in the peculiar way well-fed cats have that will eat things they find for themselves but to which, if offered in a dish, they would pay no notice.

Francis Roles speaks with Uspenskii, who tells him, "You must go and find a method by which to remember your Self. If you find the method you may find the source. What you find will help me; somehow it is arranged like that."[21]

1 October 1947. Lyne Place. Uspenskii outlines his plans for the continuation of his work to Dr. Roles, Collin, and two others.

"I had to move you from where you were," Uspenskii says. "There was nobody to help me—nobody strong enough—now it is all arranged and things will be better. But you must speak for yourselves in the language of the future. Don't hang on my soul! You must start again. You must make a new beginning. You must reconstruct everything for yourselves—from the very beginning."[22]

This, Collin feels, is "the true meaning of 'abandoning the system.'" As Uspenskii's use of English was imperfect, Collin believes what Uspenskii meant to say was "reconstructing everything in oneself (instead of for oneself)." Thus, each student was to both create in himself anew the understanding which the system had made possible and achieve its aim of permanently overcoming the false personality and acquiring a new level of consciousness.

Uspenskii sits in silence looking at everyone with an alert penetrating gaze; then he has a final rigor, falls unconscious, and is taken up to bed.

2 October 1947. Lyne Place. At six o'clock, with dawn breaking, Pyotr Demianovich Uspenskii,[23] sixty-nine years old, dies in Rodney Collin's arms. A

---

21. Many years later Dr. Roles is in India and speaks to the Shankaracharya of the North (there are two, one North, one South) about Uspenskii. He is told: "You should not worry about the liberation of such a man, because he seems to have finished his work in this world—in this revolution of the Cosmos. He finds a Divine Body and will be in peace until the creation dissolves in Brahma. Do not worry about him."

22. Uspenskii never doubts his leaving Gurdjieff and so he thinks a "new beginning" has to be made. But the problem is he left too soon. As Shri Anivrân points out in *To Live Within*, 163, "One has access to the Void by four stages. In his book *In Search of the Miraculous*, Uspenskii speaks about the first two stages. He remained silent about the last two because he had left Gurdjieff. In all of his subsequent personal teaching, which is very important, he tells of the development of these two first stages and of his experiences with his Master. The writings of Gurdjieff, on the other hand, open for us the frontiers of the two last stages. These are cleverly hidden in his mythical narrations. The four stages are: plurality of "I"s, a single "I," no "I," the Void."

23. There have been a number of books of varying qualities written about Uspenskii, one even speaks of him as a genius. But Uspenskii was quite adamant about his rejection of this term in

requiem is held at the Russian Church at Pimlico. His body is then buried beneath some shading trees in the churchyard of Holy Trinity Church in the parish of Botley's and Lyne.

Over the years Collin had grown quite close to Uspenskii, who seemed to regard the young man like a son. There appears to be what might be a "heart connection" between the student and teacher. "Uspenskii," he says, "never worked for the moment. It might even be said that he did not work for time — he worked only for recurrence."

Collin returns to the bedroom where Uspenskii had died and locks himself in. There he remains for six days heeding no knocks or calls. Then a bell is heard in the kitchen, the same one that Uspenskii was accustomed to ringing. Collin's wife, Janet, enters the bedroom and finds her husband on Uspenskii's bed, emaciated, dirty, unshaven, sitting in a half-lotus position, looking as though he had been through a tremendous traumatic experience. During this vigil he had taken neither food nor drink. Collin says that when he first sat down he was "in a rather curious, superstitious mood. After a moment or two a voice in me — it could have been a memory of Uspenskii's voice — said with the chuckle which I also remember very well: 'You want a communication from the dead. Well, won't get one!'"

This telepathic communication continued over the days, which Collin says gave the knowledge which he will write about in *The Theory of Eternal Life*.

"Among the many extraordinary impressions at the time of Uspenskii's death," says Collin, "there was — particularly at one period — the immensely strong feeling of some great power or being, some Christ-like being, as far above Uspenskii as Uspenskii was above us, presiding over all that was being done. . . . And I believe the first step to such new nourishment is the realization of Uspenskii as a living force, the permanent intermediary between ourselves and the highest powers, through whom all things can be asked."

Declares Robert de Ropp, "Uspenskii, during the last phase of his life in America, had not lived like a Warrior [but] he certainly died like one."

J. G. Bennett, upon hearing of Uspenskii's death, says:

> Throughout the day I felt a great love towards him, such as I had never known while he was alive. Nevertheless, I was strongly aware of the difference between death after a long life on the earth and a premature departure. Uspenskii's potentialities had been brought into time, and they had undergone an irreversible transformation. There was something

regard to himself. He once explained that a genius is not a being with a higher consciousness, but just a more perfect piece of machinery than ordinary people are. When a student asked, "Don't you think that a man like Beethoven was more than a piece of machinery?" he replied, "I don't; and I am not interested in it, because I am only interested in my own or perhaps your state — that's why we are here."

that I could not understand and should not try to understand. A great cycle of my own life which had lasted twenty-seven years, had closed. I felt love and gratitude towards Uspenskii, but I felt no nearer to him than I had before.

Years before his death, Uspenskii had told Bennett—who was concerned that business ventures would keep him away from meetings for months, if not years—of a Russian fairy tale:

> A knight sets out on a great adventure. He arrives at a place where the road divides into three. Unable to decide which to choose, the knight sees an old man, who tells him that if he goes to the right he will lose his horse, to the left he will lose himself; while if he takes the road in the center, he will lose both himself and his horse. The knight reasons with himself that a knight without a horse is helpless, and a horse without a knight is useless, so he might as well risk losing both. He chooses the middle path, and after desperate adventures, in which the old man's prophecy is fulfilled, he finally reaches his goal.

Uspenskii told Bennett, "You are now in that position. But I may as well tell you that if the knight had chosen either of the other two paths, it would have been the same in the end. Only it was necessary that he should persist and never give up. That is the only condition."

Like the Russian knight, Uspenskii had chosen his solitary path and, wherever it led, he never gave up and, in the eyes of many of his students, he reached his goal.

C. S. Nott was in America and when he read in a newspaper of Uspenskii's death:

> A deep feeling of compassion came over me and I wished that I had been able to have kept in contact with him. He was a good man and helped hundreds of people. His attitude towards the ideas was one of absolute integrity and the evidence is *Fragments of an Unknown Teaching*, a masterpiece of objective reporting, but some kink in him had caused him to reject Gurdjieff as a teacher. Uspenskii always had wanted to found a religious philosophical school; and he had founded a very successful one, with a large organization in England and America. Yet it had not given him real "being satisfaction." At the end of his life he had, it seems, come to realize that a philosophical school was not the basically important thing for him. It may be that he, like others, had had to work out something from the pattern of his life: his philosophical school and all his theories in connection with it, and "next

time" he may be better equipped to understand the real work of the inner Teaching.

Reflecting on Uspenskii and Gurdjieff, Collin says: "I believe that Gurdjieff and Uspenskii were the two chosen agents of at least one stage of a new revelation. They were partners and complements, chosen because they represented and could transmit opposite aspects of the same truth. Two poles have to be separated for electric current to jump between them and make light. This was the reason for the separation of Gurdjieff and Uspenskii—it was by mutual agreement, to create a field of tension in which important preparations could be made."[24]

---

24. Rodney Collin, of course, never met Gurdjieff. Collin's only knowledge of the teaching came through Uspenskii. To compare Uspenskii's *Search* with Gurdjieff's *All and Everything* offers the possibility of seeing, as Orage did, when the two men were on the same platform, who clearly was the teacher and who the student. Collin, like many still, puts them both on the same level and so seals himself off from Gurdjieff's far richer and more profound exposition. The distortion is fundamental and continues to be perpetuated today, not only by students of Uspenskii but students of Nicoll and Bennett as well.

Franklin Farms, Mendham, New Jersey, home of a former state governor

"Chalet Rose," Le Cannet, in the hills above Cannes on the French Riviera

Georgi Ivanovitch Gurdjieff

Pvt. Fritz Peters

Carman Barnes

Last photo of René Daumal

Claude Bragdon

Mr. Gurdjieff prepares for an excursion

Kathryn Hulme & Marie Louise Habets

Georgi Ivanovitch Gurdjieff

P. D. Uspenskii — last days

Madame Uspenskii at Mendham

Maurice Nicoll

Rodney Collin

Part IX

Strike a Big Do

3 October 1947. 6 rue des Colonels Renard. Gurdjieff, told of Uspenskii's death, sits silently, his eyes off in space. Presently, he returns and says—"I am supposed to hate, but he wrote *Fragments* so I love him. It as if I hear myself speaking."

Mid-October 1947. Franklin Farms. Dr. Roles arrives, having been summoned by Madame Uspenskii. Readings are given from *Fragments of an Unknown Teaching*. Near the end of Roles' visit, Madame Uspenskii invites him to come upstairs to her bedroom. She tells him of her plan to publish the book, now to be called *In Search of the Miraculous*.

She asks Roles for his comments.

"No comment Madame," answers Dr. Roles, "Mr. Uspenskii told us you would do that; it's all far above my head and each of us just has to do what we were told."

Returning to England, Dr. Roles becomes the leader of the Uspenskii groups in England.[1]

January 1948. London. Cecil Lewis, airman, author, and cofounder of the British Broadcasting Company, becomes a student of John Bennett's. His initial impressions of Bennett:

> In stature he was a tall, good-looking man [who] had the air of being used to command. He spoke several languages, was widely read and seemed as much at home in philosophy or psychology as he was in higher mathematics. But all this variety was, so to speak, hidden beneath genial conversation and an evident open-hearted generosity of nature. He met all problems with assurance and authority, was never at a loss for an answer and, though, in fact, he had only received a limited part of the Teaching he brought to us, it was quite enough to draw us to it and later, when the source of it all appeared, for him to seem to know it already.

With Uspenskii's death, and the belief that Gurdjieff was dead, Lewis says that Bennett "alone remained as the custodian of these tremendous possibilities, which were Gurdjieff's legacy to the world. How could we preserve them for posterity?"

Bennett, believing the international situation to be unstable enough that a third world war might break out and the teaching be lost, decides the solution is to establish the teaching in a safe haven. Says Lewis: "With practically no further investigation . . . Bennett swept us all off our feet by deciding that something must be done at once. He suggested that South Africa was our best choice."

Presently Bennett, Cecil Lewis and his wife, Olga, and a few others, fly in a converted Lancaster bomber six thousand miles to South Africa. The purpose of the trip is to scout feasible sites to set up the teaching.

Eastern Transvaal is finally chosen. The site, says Lewis, "is in a magnificent lonely valley, unspoiled by any 'civilization' and complete with river and hundred-foot waterfall." The idea is to prepare a commune for some two hundred people.

Bennett, however, begins to have second thoughts. He prays for guidance. Deep into the night, he says, he becomes aware of a Presence that tells him: "You

---

1. Later, Dr. Roles will link his people with the English barrister Leon McLaren's London-based School of Economic Science, which will come to integrate an Indian Advaita Vedanta approach. In the 1960s McLaren and Roles consider turning the school over to the Maharishi Mahesh Yogi and his Transcendental Meditation movement. On stage with McLaren and the Maharishi, Roles is asked by the Maharishi to integrate the teaching with his. He looks upward, as if asking for an answer, and then refuses. For an informative look at these days, see Joyce Collin-Smith's *Call No Man Master* (Gateway, 1988). She also recounts her visit in Mexico City with her brother-in-law, Rodney Collin.

are not meant to stay in Africa. Your place is in London. Trouble will come; not as you imagine, but differently, and you have to be in the midst of it. There is no need for Noah's Ark, for this time there will be no flood. The task before you is quite different from what you suppose."

Later, Bennett sees South Africa's Prime Minister, Field Marshall Jan Smuts, who tells him:

> You think that if European civilization is destroyed, something can still be preserved. I do not believe this. Europe is still, and for at least a century will continue to be, the bearer of the hopes of the human race.... There is nothing like it in the rest of the world.... The crisis in human affairs, as I see it, consists in the premature acquisition by mankind of powers which it cannot use wisely. But this crisis cannot be solved by running away from it. If you have understood the situation a little better than others, then your place is at home. Go back and preach the supreme importance of our European heritage.

Bennett returns to London, and the Lewises and a handful of other students stay behind to build the commune. Bennett apparently never tells Lewis of his experience with the Presence.

7 June 1948. Franklin Farms. Bennett visits Madame Uspenskii. Previously, he had tried to find Gurdjieff in Paris but without success. Gurdjieff, he thinks, has either died or gone mad. "Gurdjieff is not mad. He has never been mad," Madame Uspenskii tells Bennett. "He is living in Paris now. Why don't you go to him?"

Earlier, she had also told her more mature students, such as Lord Pentland and Christopher Fremantle,[2] that Gurdjieff is alive—"Hurry, don't waste a moment. Go to him."

1948. 6 rue des Colonels Renard. Jessie Orage knocks on the door. The last time she saw Gurdjieff was in 1933. She has lost her husband and her son, her daughter is still alive. Everyone is already eating lunch and a place is set for her. After a short conversation, Gurdjieff says to her:

"Miss Jessie, you have my plate, my dinner."

"No, I've had it," she replies.[3]

Gurdjieff then begins to speak about a certain man who knew everything but lacked "the simple understanding.... He tried for such and was too intelligent to grasp it."

Jessie begins to cry.

---

2. Christopher Fremantle would later play a significant role in helping to establish the Work in Mexico and later America. See his book *On Attention* (Indications Press, 1993).
3. An interesting reply, given what has happened between her, Gurdjieff, and Orage.

Georgi Ivanovitch Gurdjieff

Gurdjieff never takes his eyes off her.

1948. England. Maurice Nicoll, told that Gurdjieff is living in Paris, still under Uspenskii's spell, shows no interest in seeing his former teacher. However, Kenneth Walker, who began with Uspenskii in 1924, does visit. Gurdjieff reminds him of "a Lohan figure with his clean-shaven head rising to an unusual height above the level of the ears, reaching its zenith at a point midway between the frontal region and the occiput. The most remarkable feature about this head of his was that although he claimed to be over eighty years of age, his face was smooth and serene and devoid of wrinkles, and at the same time charged with virile power."

Walker continues to visit and says, "The more I saw of Gurdjieff the more convinced I became of his uniqueness. He had qualities which I had never seen in anybody else: profound knowledge, immense vitality, and complete immunity from fear. He was old but he was still capable of working for a longer time than anybody else."

June 1948. Southampton, England. Following Uspenskii's death, Rodney Collin appears, to a number of people, to have come to a new level of being and authority. Now he and a small party leave for New York en route to Mexico, which he feels is his place for a new beginning of the teaching. They spend six months in Guadalajara, where Collin finishes *The Theory of Eternal Life*, and then move to a large house in Tlalpam, outside Mexico City, where they will be joined by others, mostly from England. Translations are then begun of Uspenskii's books into Spanish and a large site in the mountains is acquired. A building is erected which becomes the center of Collin's work with students. Called "Planetarium of Tetecala," meaning in Aztec "Stone House of God," it is named for the field on which it lay. Groups are formed in South America. In 1954 Collin publishes his major work, *The Theory of Celestial Influence*. Two years later in Cuzco, Peru, 11,800 feet above sea level, he said he felt "rather strange," but he climbed the ninety-eight steps to the belfry of a cathedral where a crippled Indian beggar boy he had befriended several days before was allowed to sleep in a corner under the bells. Looking out at the vista of the city, Collin had a heart attack and fell from the cathedral to the street below. The date was 3 May 1956. Rodney Collin was forty-seven years old.[4]

30 June 1948. 6 rue des Colonels Renard. Margaret and Dorothy Caruso visit Gurdjieff. Says Margaret:

> Gurdjieff's small dingy familiar apartment had not changed—details of destruction only emphasized its changelessness: the colors had faded, the

---

4. Before she died, Joyce Collin-Smith told this author that she had heard that the crippled boy, when an aging man, confessed that he had pushed Collin from the belfry in anger because Collin had given another boy a new pair of shoes but not him.

furniture was shabbier, the dining room carpets had worn through and now had big patches on it. Nine years and a war brought new people to the remembered table, but the quest was the old quest, the same as ours. The pictures on the walls were new, but they had the same quality as the old ones—"everything but art," as Jane said long ago.

Gurdjieff himself seemed to me unchanged. He was a little older, he was a little tired, but he was still as lavish as ever with his existence and his ceremony. He sat at the side of the table, instead of at the end, and he was more silent than in the years before. But there was teaching in all that he did or said, only its form had changed: he was teaching now chiefly through his presence—from his "being," he might have said. . . . We listened with all our force to his rapid or elaborated, terse or kindly, criticism of human egoist; he let no slight failing pass without signal or correction. Most of the old pupils felt that he was gentler than in the old years. I could only feel that his weariness with the human condition had reached the breaking-point. But we knew that he would fulfill to the end his obligation to life.

There were now so many new pupils—English and American and French—that he transmitted much of his instruction through a person we had known in the old Prieuré days. After years of work with him her stature was now visible to everyone. Her name was Jeanne de Salzmann.

After lunch Gurdjieff invites them to return for the reading at nine o'clock. Dorothy finds the book boring and his interactions with students confusing, berating them and then smiling and offering a sweet. She doesn't know what to make of it all. She returns with Margaret for several days but has such strong reactions. "There was no continuity in the reading—chapters read the week before were repeated the following week, or sometimes a chapter read half through was never resumed. After a while my attention wandered, but that of the pupils did not. The concentration of those motionless bodies began to irritate me. What were they concentrated on?" says Caruso. She stays away for five days. She remembers that he had told her—"Inside you are a rabbit." She begins to understand he is telling her what Margaret had told her—instead of acting honestly, she covers her emotions with good manners. The shell of her false personality begins to crack.

7 July 1948. 6 rue des Colonels Renard. Caruso returns with Margaret. Gurdjieff pretends to be surprised to see her. She tells Margaret that "during lunch I felt a glow as if there had been established between us a new and special bond—a kind of unspoken sympathetic understanding." Gurdjieff invited her afterward into the pantry full of fruits and sweets and wines, with slender sausages of camel's meat, bunches of scarlet peppers and sprays of rosemary and mint suspended like a canopy above. Gurdjieff pours coffee out of a battered old thermos bottle. He offers her a piece of sugar. "You want to ask me something," he says.

"Everyone here seems to have a soul except me. Haven't I any soul?"

"You know what means consciousness?" he asks.

"Yes, it means to know something."

"No. Not to know something—to know yourself. Your I. You not know your I for one second in your whole life. Now I tell and you try. But very difficult. You try to remember to say 'I am' once every hour. You not succeed, but no matter—try."

She speaks about her childhood and her father with whom she had a difficult time.

"You must help your father," he says.

"But my father is dead."

"I know," Gurdjieff says. "You tell already. But because of your father you are here. Have gratitude for this. You are your father and you owe to him. He is dead. Too late to repair for himself. You must repair for him. Help him."

4 August 1948. Coombe Springs. Bennett writes to Cecil Lewis in South Africa: "We are writing this on the eve of our journey into the unknown. At this time tomorrow Polly and I will be in Paris and we shall see G. on Friday. . . . Today, I feel like a new boy creeping timidly into the Great Hall of some ancient school—where even the other boys seem to be supermen and all about is a mystery. Somehow I cannot bring myself to realize that, at last, I have come to the possibility of real guidance and help. . . . I will write you from Paris."

"We think of you battling with Nature in the distant South and we here struggling to keep our minds clear. . . ."

6 August 1948. 6 rue des Colonels Renard. It is twenty-five years to the month when fifty-one-year-old John Godolphin Bennett, now a powerful business executive and leader of his own groups, rings the bell. With him is his seventy-five-year-old wife, Winifred, whom he calls "Polly."

Madame de Salzmann answers and motions them inside. They walk down the dark, dingy hallway, every inch of the walls covered with paintings, either ugly, bizarre or decidedly amateurish. They enter a small sitting room on the right. Its walls are also covered with paintings of the same dubious quality. Though it is early afternoon, the windows are shuttered and the only illumination is provided by electric lights.[5] Bennett notices the furniture is shabby and the carpets threadbare. On either side of the fireplace hang representations of the enneagram, made from mother-of-pearl and sewn to fabric-covered black disks. In the corners of the room abutting the street sit two odd glittering artifacts. One is a sort of stylized Christmas tree, made out of some gold-colored metal or gilded wood. It gleams from light

---

5. For why Gurdjieff always keeps the windows shuttered, see *Views from the Real World*, 37.

reflected from countless prisms of glass. The other is a cabinet containing a large collection of dolls dressed in different national costumes, as well as an assortment of keepsakes, pipes, musical instruments, Orientalia. When the room is properly lit, the cheap materials scintillate and sparkle, giving the feeling of being in Aladdin's cave.

Presently Gurdjieff appears in the doorway. Quite heavy now, he holds himself as erect as ever. The moustaches are white now and the face has lost its firm outline, but the skin is still smooth. He wears a tasseled magenta fez, open shirt, and rumpled trousers. He moves into the room with the same grace and economy of gesture as when Bennett first saw him at the Prieuré.

Madame de Salzmann introduces the Bennetts to Gurdjieff. But he does not remember them. He takes Bennett in for a few moments. Then tells him—"You are Number Eighteen. Not a big Number Eighteen but small Number Eighteen."[6]

Soon, others arrive and are standing about. It is nearly two o'clock. Gurdjieff suddenly growls, "Chain. Chain."

People form a line from the kitchen to the dining room. Plates of food are passed. Gurdjieff motions Bennett to sit at a seat on his right, Bennett's wife on his left. Lunch is eaten. With his fingers, Gurdjieff slowly eats morsels of lamb, hard bits of goat cheese and fresh tarragon leaves. At one point, he nods and the toasts to the idiots begin. The meal and toasts do not end until nearly five o'clock.

Gurdjieff invites Bennett into the pantry for coffee. Though food is still rationed, the shelves are stocked with tins and jars of food. Gurdjieff pours some coffee out of a battered old thermos bottle, takes a piece of sugar, puts it into his mouth, and sips coffee through it. He suddenly looks at Bennett and says, "You know what is the first Commandment of God to man?"

Bennett fumbles for an answer.

"Hand wash hand!" Gurdjieff barks.

He pauses to let Bennett absorb that. Then he says in a low voice, "You need help and I need help. If I help you, you have to help me."

Bennett tells him he is ready to do whatever Gurdjieff wants.

Gurdjieff speaks about his money difficulties, then asks Bennett what he wants from him.

"Will you show me how to work for my Being?"

"It is right," Gurdjieff declares. "Now you have much Knowledge, but in Being you are a nullity. If you wish, I will show you how to work, but you must do it as I say."

Bennett is amazed. It is an exact continuation of the conversation they had twenty-seven years before in Constantinople.

"I know my situation is hopeless," admits Bennett. "That is why I have come back to you."

Gurdjieff repeats: "If you will do as I say, I will show you how to change. Only

---

6. Gurdjieff at one point said Number Eighteen was a Harmful Idiot, a stink idiot. Bennett will later become a Round Idiot.

you must stop thinking. You think too much. You must begin to sense." He asks if Bennett understands the distinction between sensing and feeling.

Bennett gives an intellectual definition.

"More or less. But you only know this with your mind. You do not understand with your whole being. This you must learn."[7]

8 August 1948. Gurdjieff sets out on a trip to Cannes with a large sum of money that Bennett has given him. Driving through the town of Montargis, a small truck, its driver drunk, shoots out of a side road and smashes into Gurdjieff's 15-horse-power Citroën. The impact is so great that the drunken driver and his passenger are instantly killed. Gurdjieff is pinned against the steering column, his ribs broken, skull fractured, sternum broken and lungs choked in blood. Bennett is on hand when he returns from the hospital a day later.

It is dusk when Gurdjieff arrives back at the apartment. Bennett, who had not gone on the trip, holds the car door open. Gurdjieff slowly gets out. "His clothes were covered with blood," says Bennett. "His face was black with bruises. . . . It was a dead man, a corpse, that came out of the car; and yet it walked."

Somehow, Gurdjieff gets to his room and sits down.

"Now all organs are destroyed. Must make new," he says.

"Tonight," he tells Bennett, "you come dinner. I must make body work."

With that the pain gives his body a great spasm and blood flows from his ear. Bennett thinks he has a cerebral hemorrhage, and if he continues to force his body to move, he will kill himself. But then he realizes Gurdjieff must do this. "If he allows his body to stop moving, he will die. He has power over his body."

Late August 1948. Café des Acacias. C. S. Nott is having coffee with Gurdjieff. Nott says, "Mr. Bennett and his organization and all these pupils [he had brought sixty] could be a very good thing for the Work; they seem to have money, too."

Gurdjieff replies laconically, "Bennett is small thing. Useful for money, yes. He will bring me a thousand pupils and out of these I shall choose perhaps ten."

Daily lunches continue. One of Bennett's pupils says:

> We all eat jammed around the table with our elbows in each other's tummies almost. The meal always starts with so-called "salade" too disgusting, floating about in a little bowl. "Not such salade never was"—and indeed I hope so. Then there is usually meat or bird with rice and a big dish of radishes, onions, etc. passed round to eat with it. Then a sweet—always very sweet and syrupy—and fruit, melon, grapes, etc.

---

7. This would seem to indicate that Bennett knew little to nothing about self-remembering. Gurdjieff never told him when he came to the Prieuré and left after a month or so, and apparently Uspenskii never told him either. So all these years Bennett has been working and teaching from the head.

> Sometimes coffee, sometimes not. Throughout the meal he [Gurdjieff] passes round oddments of food—apparently quite indiscriminately, so that one may easily find oneself eating sprats or bear meat with one's sweet, sheeps' meat from Bokhara, camel sausage from Kayseri—one never knows what to expect. Once he broke up fish in his fingers and then held out a fistful across the table, saying benevolently "Who not squeamish?" The last evening we were there one of Brynn's goat cheeses was handed round which Gurdjieff described as "special Scotch cheese from Scotland" and enveloped us all with a baleful stare, defying us to deny it. All this is washed down with, mainly, bread or white vodka for the toasts, but there is also Marc, Calvados, Armagnac....

Another comments on the music:

> After the meal is over we go into the salon and settle ourselves on the chairs, the divan, the stools and the floor. Gurdjieff sits in his chair and Lise [Tracol] brings him his little portable organ which he rests on his knee playing with one hand while he works the bellows with the other.
>
> He then makes the strangest music—the most wonderful music. He says it is "objective"—that is, the vibrations he produces have a definite affect on people, both organically and psychologically. It affects people in different ways, tough business men and scientists sit with the tears streaming down their faces, others are merely bored or puzzled, others again are moved but do not know why.
>
> He is asked about this music. A woman says she found she did not listen to it with her ears. He said: "Ears are no good for this music, the whole presence must be open to it. It is a matter of vibrations." Then he added, "But tears must come first." He also said he had to put the whole of himself into these vibrations, it was very difficult for him. He is always exhausted after playing. Often he does not play. Then we play the records of the music.

The lunch sessions usually last from 1:30 to 4:30 or later; the evening sessions from 10:30 to 2 or 3 in the morning. Gurdjieff sometimes reminds guests: "When I eat, I self-remember." Of those who insist on talking he says, "Idiot God made only one mouth. Should have made two."

Very late August 1948. Lascaux, France. Gurdjieff visits the caves with the Bennetts and several others. He tells Bennett that the enneagram, like the Sphinx, is not a symbol but an emblem of an esoteric society. He explains further that the composite animal near the cave's entrance is no more than eight thousand years old, from the time of the loss of Atlantis. Bennett tells him that pre-historians date the cave paintings between fifteen to twenty-five thousand years ago. Gurdjieff says nothing but later he makes it clear he does not want Bennett to travel with him.

"I go left," Gurdjieff tells him, "you go right."[8]

"Then we must say good-bye to you?" asks Bennett, hoping to keep an opening.

"Yes, good-bye!"

Back in Paris, Bennett experiences again being out of the body and separate from the mind as he had during the First World War.

When he meets Gurdjieff again he is treated "like an outcast." Gurdjieff complains to him that he had not been able to eat on the drive back from Lascaux for lack of company.

"But you sent me away," Bennett exclaims.

"But you tell me you have to go fetch wife," says Gurdjieff, "but she here all the time. You not honest. Your manifestations disgusting."

4 September 1948. Café des Acacias. Bennett goes to the café Gurdjieff frequents. Gurdjieff is there but ignores him. Much time passes. Bennett prods but there is no response. Finally, Bennett says, "I cannot thank you for what you have done for me. That I can never repay."

Gurdjieff somewhat acknowledges Bennett's existence but says nothing. People come and go from the café. Finally, Gurdjieff turns toward Bennett and, speaking slowly, tells him—"What you say about never repay—this is stupidity. Only you can repay. Only you can repay for all my labors. What you think is money? I can buy all your England. Only you can repay by work. But what you do? Before trip I give task. Do you fulfill? No, you do just the opposite. Never once I see you struggle with yourself. All the time you occupied with cheap animal."

Later, at lunch Gurdjieff speaks of conscience. "When conscience and consciousness are together, then you will not make such mistakes. Objective conscience not yet atrophied, exists in subconscious."

Bennett drives Madame de Salzmann home after lunch. He tells her he has a sense that he has failed Gurdjieff.

"The work changes," she tells him. "Up to one point, one gets fairly clear guidance. Then comes a time when it is made so confusing that you can easily do exactly the wrong thing in the conviction that it is right."

Early September 1948. 6 rue des Colonels Renard. Lord John Pentland arrives in Paris. "One day," says Pentland, "I wormed my way into having lunch with Mr. Gurdjieff and some others, though I had not been invited. Mr. Gurdjieff said nothing at the time, but the following day he took me to a Turkish bathhouse on the outskirts of Paris. The sense was that this was a reward for something I had done that had

---

8. One of Gurdjieff's father's subjective sayings was: "If the priest goes to the right, then the teacher must without fail turn to the left." *Meetings with Remarkable Men*, 46.

been in his eyes especially praiseworthy. I was, of course, elated. While I undressed, Mr. Gurdjieff took the owner of the bathhouse aside to whisper something but, in fact, he spoke quite loudly, telling the man that his 'special friend' was to be given 'the best treatment.' Thereupon, a masseur was summoned, a huge man, who proceeded to beat me to a pulp while of course Mr. Gurdjieff looked on, not being above showing a certain sly satisfaction. Afterward, on the way back to his apartment, a policeman stopped him and he blamed me to the policeman for distracting him. Can you believe it?" Later, Gurdjieff appoints Lord Pentland as his chauffeur.

At Gurdjieff's invitation, Lord Pentland, his wife, Lucy, and young daughter, Mary, come for lunch. In the early 1930s he had been Uspenskii's chief deputy and during the 1940s he worked under Uspenskii's and Madame Uspenskii's guidance at Franklin Farms. Mary sits by her mother's side and just across from Gurdjieff. She becomes bored. Gurdjieff suddenly speaks to her, saying—"In life it is never possible to do everything."

The child is puzzled. Having her attention, Gurdjieff points to the table in front of her where she has crumbled her bread. "On my table you cannot make this mess," he says. "Perhaps at home Mother permits. Then if you want to do this thing, you must stay at home. But if you stay at home, you will not be able to come here and see me. So you see, you can never do everything."

In the evening at the end of the dinner, Gurdjieff asks Mary, "Who do you respect most?"

She doesn't understand the question.

"Who do you think is the most important person here?" her mother asks.

Without hesitating, Mary declares—"My Daddy."

Gurdjieff beams. "I not offended," he says. "God not offended either."

Gurdjieff explains that a person who loves his parents loves God, and he says, "If people love their parents all the time that their parents are alive, then, when their parents die, there is a space left in them for Him to fill."

As the Pentlands prepare to leave, Gurdjieff pats Mary on the shoulder, saying to everyone present: "For my aim, I want twenty such. If I had twenty like her, I get my aim. Not because she special, but because she not spoilt."

September 1948. 6 rue des Colonels Renard. Gurdjieff says he needs a new place like the Prieuré. Some forty miles southeast of Paris and about sixty miles from the Prieuré, near the forest of Rambouillet, lies Château de Voisins. Gurdjieff says he has heard its owner, a millionaire sugar baron, is looking to lease it.

18 November 1948. South Africa. Cecil Lewis receives another letter from Bennett:

> The truth is that everything is so exciting here [London] at the moment that hardly anyone can bear the thought of being separated from it. At the

same time if and when disaster strikes, the very people who are reluctant to do anything to share in building up a home for us to go to, will be only too ready and anxious to take advantage of what has been done.... I am equally certain that within two or three years we shall enter that period of acute nervous tension which Gurdjieff called *Solioonensius*. Such periods induce intense incentive to work in those who are capable of it, but they engender madness in those who have lost touch with the real aim of life. Whenever the process of *Solioonensius* occurs on earth, a state of tension is created in which it is impossible for people to exist quietly like cows. They have either to work on themselves or they begin "to destroy everything within sight." As I understand it, the next *Solioonensius* will be the most intense of all. As an outcome, either mankind will change to a different mode of existence or there will occur the most terrible process of mutual destruction.... So our decision to seek a place in SA remains just as valid as it was three years ago.

30 November 1948. France. Gurdjieff sails for America with Madame de Salzmann, Lord Pentland and Aubrey Wolton. On the boat train there is a large luncheon. Bennett, director of the toasts, breaks the ritual by proposing a toast to Mr. Gurdjieff's health.

"No," says Gurdjieff, "I will propose myself health of English. Thanks to the English I sail to New York free from all debts. Pure *comme bébé*."

At the end of the toasts he tells everyone: "Before I return I hope with all my being that everyone here will have learned the difference between sensation and feeling."

17 December 1948. Hotel Wellington, New York. Gurdjieff arrives from France and takes a large suite, stocking it with food and drink. Luncheons and dinners begin. He is preparing to buy a large château for his headquarters and he says his health is even better than before his accident.

At one point Alice Rohrer from the days of the Rope bursts into the suite. "What, Theen One!" Gurdjieff shouts. "You not afraid to come?"

"No, Mr. Gurdjieff," she answers.

"Why you not afraid?"

"Well—because I have known you many years." She tells him she has changed from squirming idiot to square idiot.

"Ha! Was automatic change," he tells her and points out a seat.

Toasts begin. Gurdjieff formulates a second series of mesoteric toasts. He gives the first two.

"To the health of all hopeless idiots, both subjectively and objectively; that is, to the health of all candidates for perishing like dogs."

"And to health of all candidates for all kinds of idiots."

He then says to all at the table—"If you wish to help me, every hour you must say *I AM*; *I* with feeling, *AM* with sensing."

18 December 1948. Hotel Wellington. At lunch Gurdjieff says, "Scale is from shit to God." About the toasts he says, "Unique Idiot is highest thing and in stone or static thing is the lowest; between the two is our scale or measure. First time, one starts up the scale they automatically proceed as far as #1. Easy to go up. For going down is difficult because go down with consciousness. Second time go up, can go beyond #16—even to Stink Idiot. This Idiot not harmful. Sometimes can be made clean. But harmful never, in objective sense."

Donald Whitcomb, a student of many years, says, "I need help, Mr. Gurdjieff. No use to struggle without help."

"You shall have help," Gurdjieff tells him. "Now you have thousand 'I's; each weakness is an 'I' that is master of you. To have your own I it is necessary for it to be born. It has been conceived—now by feeding it, it will accumulate substance and one happy day take form. Then it can develop and be born.

"This substance of I comes only from intentional suffering. When, for instance, you wish strongly for a cigarette and deny yourself you will suffer inwardly. Then say, 'I wish to make this inward force my force.' 'I wish to receive this substance of my intentional suffering for my I.' By this means, you can become an individual.

"Now you have a name but it is empty. Then Mr. Whitcomb will *be* Mr. Whitcomb."

Later on, Gurdjieff visits Madame Uspenskii at Franklin Farms. He wants to begin to consolidate the groups, putting the "Uspenskii people"—Lord Pentland and his wife, Lucy, Christopher and Anne Fremantle, William and Cora Segal, Paul and Naomi Anderson, Tom Forman, Basil Tilley and Clive Entwistle—in contact with the dozen or so "Gurdjieff people"—including Dr. William Welch and his wife, Louise, Wim Nyland and his wife, Ilonka, and Peggy Flinsch, all of whom are from the original Orage groups. Jean Toomer is invited but does not attend. Before Gurdjieff leaves, Madame Uspenskii gives Gurdjieff chapters of *Fragments of an Unknown Teaching*.

Back at the Wellington, during one luncheon Bennett arrives from England. He promptly announces himself as Mr. Gurdjieff's oldest pupil. Gurdjieff tells him he is a Round Idiot.

Louise Goepfert [March], one of Gurdjieff's secretaries from the Prieuré days, is astounded to hear her idiot is the same as Bennett's. "It sat badly with me," she says. (Round Idiots were "those that never stop, but day-night-year-round continue," Gurdjieff had told her.)

After the toasts, a chapter from *Fragments* is read aloud to the group. "Is too liquid. Lost something," Gurdjieff says about one passage. He praises another. "Very exact is. Good memory. Truth was so."

1948. New York. Jean Toomer meets Gurdjieff. After the meeting Toomer writes: "I do not really know myself, who I am, my selfhood, my spiritual identity, or what I am. I have some information about it, but also some misinformation, some understanding, but much illusion. Real knowledge, real recognition, realization? No. What are my complex motivations? What is my aim, assuming that I have but one aim? I do not really know my wife, my child, my closest friends. I do not really know anyone or anything."

1949. New York. Once again Carman Barnes and Hamilton Fish Armstrong separate. They divorce in 1951. She then leaves for Austria. With Uspenskii's permission, she has dramatized *Strange Life of Ivan Osokin* and hopes that Greta Garbo will play Zinaida, the woman Osokin knew "in the future that had already been—before he met her in the present."

1949. New York. Reflecting on Jean Toomer, Louise Welch says:

> It's an interesting thing that some people are either born, or however it comes about, magnetic; and they have an influence over people, sometimes long before they're wise enough to make the right use of this influence. Also having that quality makes one wish to be worthy of the admiration and so on that one gets from others. I think in Jean's case it began with a magnetic quality and it continued with his really wishing to find his way to being as wise as those people thought he was.... I think he realized at a certain point that he needed to understand more himself.

Early 1949. New York. During a dinner conversation, Gurdjieff says when Hitler came to power a critical phase of history had begun. In terms of the teaching, he had been obliged to wait until it became clear how mankind would react.

January 1949. New York. Frank Lloyd Wright, Olgivanna and their daughter Iovanna visit. Gurdjieff seats Olgivanna beside him at dinner and the two speak together in Russian the entire evening. Wright had heard the rumor that women followers had to have sex with Gurdjieff if they really wanted to be initiated into his work. The babies were to be "seekers of truth." When Wright raises this with his wife she tells him, "But, Frank, he was my teacher. It was completely different from two lovers."

13 January 1949. New York. It was in the year 223 after the creation of the World, by objective time-calculation, or, as it would be said here on the "Earth," in the year 1921 after the birth of Christ.
Twenty-five years after having first dictated these lines, Gurdjieff decides to

publish the *First Series* of *All and Everything—Beelzebub's Tales to His Grandson.*⁹

In the morning at Childs on Fifth Avenue, Gurdjieff's "New York office," he tells Bennett to write a circular letter to all his students telling of his decision to publish *Beelzebub's Tales.*

Says Bennett: "I asked for a sheet of paper, and wrote without knowing how or what I should write.... The manner of writing was completely foreign to me. I had used the word 'adept' instead of pupil. This both surprised and annoyed me, as the word 'adept' grated harshly on my ear as savoring too much of occultism."

At lunch that day, Gurdjieff's rooms at the Hotel Wellington are jammed wall to wall with his students, overcoats piled four feet deep the length of the foyer. Early arrivals are seated cross-legged on the floor around the sofa, everyone else standing, Gurdjieff sits on the sofa with one leg characteristically tucked under him, parting his moustaches with the thumb and index finger of his hand. Finally, he takes a letter from his pocket and hands it to Bennett, sitting near him.

"Read, read—is for everybody," Gurdjieff says in a low voice. He listens as if weighing each word.

Bennett, who says Gurdjieff handed him the letter as if he had never seen it before, reads: "This circular is addressed to all my present and former adepts and to all who have been directly or indirectly influenced by my ideas and have sensed and understood that they contain something which is necessary for the food of humanity. After fifty years of preparation and having overcome the greatest difficulties and obstacles, I have decided to publish ... "

Following the reading, Gurdjieff says three representatives are needed: for France, England, and America. For America he appoints Lord John Pentland;¹⁰ for France, René Zuber; and for England, J. G. Bennett. Sometime later he appoints people to certain tasks: Lord Pentland, Figurehead; Wim Nyland, Comptroller; Donald Whitcomb, Recorder; Rita Romilly Benson, Reader; Edith Taylor, Custodian of the Books; Jessmin Howarth, Director of Movements; and Carol Robinson, Movements Pianist. In the afternoon there is a children's party at

---

9. This is Orage's English edition with edits Gurdjieff made over the years, having chapters read aloud from its completion until his death. In 1992 a revised edition was published, the reasons given were that Gurdjieff did not know English well enough to know that his Russian was badly translated and that the Russian version of Lili Galumnian's was more exact; though this could be an amalgamation of the 1925 version and the reedited English version of post-1927. However that is, it has been amply demonstrated here that Gurdjieff, a serious philologist concerned with the roots of words, knew English and spoke it well when he wished to. The book did not sell well. Perhaps this was the reason that in 1957 Madame de Salzmann had the revision of the 1950 edition begun. The revision was not published until some two years after her death. Many of the 1992 revisions, albeit in a handsome edition, diminish the original. For example, there are no hyphens between strings of words Gurdjieff wanted to be taken as one thought form, as in 'first-degree-initiated-beings'; "Arch-Preposterous" is now "Archfantasy"; the name "Jericho Ass" is "idiot"; and the refrain "Let her with the saints repose/ Now that she's turned up her toes" becomes "she was not a simple human being."

10. For an account of his unique capacity to teach and his understanding of leadership, refer to the author's book *Eating The "I"* (Arete Communications, 1992).

Gurdjieff's hotel room. At the party's end everyone leaves. Bennett finds himself alone with Gurdjieff, who sits on a low couch at the end of a long drawing room. Bennett goes up and kneels beside him, thanking Gurdjieff for all that he has done for him. Says Gurdjieff:

"What I have done up to now for you is nothing. Soon I return to Europe. You come to me, and I will show you how to work. If you do what I tell, I will show you how to become immortal. Now you have nothing, but if you will work you can soon have soul."

He wants six young women, "the calves"—his two daughters, Dushka Howarth and Petey (Eve) Taylor, Iovanna Wright, Tania Savitsky, Patty Welch and Marian Sutta—to come to Paris to train as the first row for future movements demonstrations.

11 February 1949. New York. Gurdjieff sails for Paris aboard the *Queen Mary*. It was apparent that his coming had been at great physical expense. The auto accident the previous summer had left him with a serious bronchial congestion, cirrhosis had developed quite alarmingly, and he also suffered from dropsy, his belly and legs swollen, but he resisted all attempts to have the fluid drained off.

Once Gurdjieff sailed, Lord Pentland put into motion preparations for his return in the fall and then contacted Harcourt, Brace about publishing *In Search of the Miraculous* and *Beelzebub's Tales*. They agreed to publish Uspenskii's book but demanded a $25,000 subscription for Gurdjieff's. E. P. Dutton was then contacted; they demanded a prepublication subscription of $400 a copy each with an inscription.

26 May 1949. New Jersey. C. Daly King completes *The Oragean Version*.[11] He does so because he feels Orage's understanding was different from both Gurdjieff's and Uspenskii's and was on "the verge of being irrecoverably lost." In a later book, *The States of Human Consciousness,* King says of Gurdjieff:

> With one exception the writer has never encountered anyone of whom he felt assured that the latter was living permanently in a state of Awakeness. The exception was Gurdjieff himself. In these respects [the mode of living and the manner of contact with other persons, friendly, hostile or neutral] and many more, Gurdjieff manifested himself in ways never encountered by the writer, in ways so different from those of others that

---

11. In the book (privately published), King faithfully records the teaching, as he received it from Orage. He makes some interesting points concerning self-observation and his book is worth studying. But, just as Gurdjieff pointed out eighteen years before to Orage and his groups, he doesn't see what is missing in the practice and appears to misunderstand its intent. C. Daly King will die in 1962 at the age of sixty-seven, not once in his published work questioning his viewpoint about Gurdjieff or the teaching.

they constituted a plain and perceptible difference in level of existence upon his part. His famous reputation as an enigmatic rested largely upon this circumstance. He is the only person ever met by the writer who gave the indubitable impression that all his responses, mental, emotional and practical, were mutually in balance and thus the further impression that everyone else was out of step, but not this man himself.

The writer has no hesitation in calling him [Gurdjieff] one of the hundred, perhaps one of the fifty, most remarkable men known to us in our history. Although he did not claim personally to have discovered all of it, the mere range of his knowledge was so far beyond that of others as to make comparisons not merely invidious but impossible. His methods of instructing his pupils were highly individual and highly unusual and one of his principles seems to be to guard against their acquirement of too much knowledge prematurely; a corresponding degree of understanding was to be demanded and, until it had been attained, additional knowledge was inadvisable.

6 July 1949. New York. A notice appears in *The New York Times*:

P. D. Uspenskii, physicist, philosopher and author of two philosophical books, *Tertium Organum* and *A New Model of the Universe,* has a new book set for October 13 publication by Harcourt, Brace. *In Search of the Miraculous* is a story of his quest for a teaching that would penetrate to the real meaning of life and of his eight years of study under George Gurdjieff.

3 August 1949. 6 rue des Colonels Renard. At lunch Gurdjieff speaks of starting up again, as he had with the Prieuré. He says he is thinking about acquiring the Château de Voisins at Saint-Hilarion, near Rambouillet, saying it will be "center world [for] Beelzebub." Clive Entwistle, an English architect who had been with Uspenskii, and whom Gurdjieff calls "Mephisto," becomes very interested in the project and holds many consultations with Gurdjieff.

That evening, while reading aloud at the evening meal, Bennett suddenly has the experience of leaving his body. "I found myself several feet away from my body," he says. "My voice was still speaking, but it was not 'my' voice any more, but a stranger's. . . . The sense of separation from the body persisted for several hours, although I remained inside it."

Later, at another mealtime, Gurdjieff speaks to Bennett in a low voice on the Last Supper and the role of Judas. He tells Bennett that Judas was Jesus' best and closest friend and that he alone understood why Jesus was on the planet. By his selfless action Judas had saved the work of Jesus from being destroyed.

Then Gurdjieff asks him: "You know what I say of Judas and how differently the church teaches. Which do you believe is true?"

To Bennett it seems that somehow the crowded dining room and time disappears and he finds himself back in the Jerusalem of 33 AD. He becomes aware of the good and evil forces at war and sees that Judas was unmistakably on the good side.

"You are right," Bennett answers. "Judas was the friend of Jesus, and he was on the side of good."

In a voice so low as to be almost inaudible Gurdjieff says: "I am pleased what you understand."

Several times during the coming days Gurdjieff tells Bennett that his relationship with him is the same as that between Judas and Jesus.

Bennett says that once he and Lord Pentland were sitting next to one another and Gurdjieff said "Mr. Bennett is like Judas; he is responsible that my work is not destroyed. You," he said to Lord Pentland, "are like Paul; you must spread my ideas."[12]

During these last days, Bennett says Gurdjieff "never spoke of death, but of going far away."

September 1949. Taliesin, Wisconsin. After some nine months studying the movements in Paris, Iovanna Wright returns home and tells her mother Gurdjieff has asked her to start a movements group at Taliesin. Olgivanna has wished for this for twenty-five years. The Gurdjieff Work is officially launched at Taliesin on her fifty-first birthday.

October 1949. London. Bennett gives a series of lectures in London that he calls "Gurdjieff: The Making of a New World."

October 1949. 6 rue des Colonels Renard. Kanari arrives from New York and visits Gurdjieff as often as she can.

14 October 1949. Salle Pleyel, Paris. Gurdjieff collapses during a movements class and is taken back to his apartment where he is nursed by Lise Tracol. Throughout the coming days, his condition fluctuates.

18 October 1949. New York. A notice appears in *The New York Times:*

> *In Search of the Miraculous* by P. D. Uspenskii, an account of the Russian philosopher's quest for a teaching that would solve for him the problems of man and the universe, will be published Thursday by Harcourt, Brace. Mr. Uspenskii, author of *Tertium Organum*, describes his meeting with

---

12. Lord Pentland would be instrumental in creating and establishing the Gurdjieff Foundations in New York and San Francisco and helped with the forming of many groups. He was president of the New York Foundation from its inception in 1954 until his death 14 February 1984.

the Russian mystic Gurdjieff in Moscow on the eve of the revolution and his eight-year search in St. Petersburg, the Caucasus, Constantinople and London.

19 October 1949. Mill House. Jean Toomer, who has fallen away from his involvement with the Quakers after having given the prestigious William Penn Lecture, and who is now seeing a Jungian therapist, writes a letter to Paul Anderson, who is helping Lord Pentland with the publication of *Beelzebub's Tales to His Grandson:*

> I said yes to the idea of having lunch with you and Lord Pentland because I had interest in such a meeting and also because I wanted to convince you that I have no interest in doing anything about either Uspenskii's or Gurdjieff's books at this time. My life and needs run in other directions.... Gurdjieff and his projects are, for me, nothing to touch unless you want to get deeply involved in them.... For some reasons known to me, and some unknown, I am, for better or worse, out of it—and I want to remain out, quite out—until such time, if and when that time comes, that I again move towards it by impulses arising within myself. As you know, some drinks mix; some don't. I must not mix what I am doing now with the world and works of Mr. Gurdjieff.... You are in the work. I know the feeling. You want to leave no stone unturned in your efforts to fulfill your function in the work. Splendid. It is a grand active sense of purpose. When I was an active agent I liked it too. It was meat and bread and life. So I, from my side, say more power to you. And do you then, from your side, understand that I do not like being on the passive end.[13]

21 October 1949. 6 rue des Colonels Renard. Gurdjieff sees the first proofs of the American edition of *Beelzebub's Tales*. As he said in 1945, "I now very tired and I know that when I finish this last book my work will be done. So now I can die, because my task in life is coming to an end."

Kenneth Walker visits. The Gurdjieff he sees is quite sick. "The eyes told me that he was far from well; his breathing was difficult, his lips were blue, and his ankles were swollen. His girth had increased, and I believed that there was a great deal of fluid in his abdomen... it was obvious that the fluid should be removed

---

13. Finally, in 1953, he returns to the Gurdjieff Work with Madame de Salzmann and Louise Welch. Several years later, his physical condition deteriorating, he is forced to withdraw. His longtime friend and somewhat jealous critic Gorham Munson said: "Jean pretended to be more than he was. He assumed the development and psychology beyond the point that he had ever reached.... Jean would not accept his being a nonentity. Instead of that, he stepped across to being somebody, to accepting the claim to himself." But the courage of such sincerity signals a new start. However, Toomer's physical condition steadily grows worse. After 1955 he is unable to take care of himself and his wife must put him in a nursing home, where he dies 30 March 1967.

as soon as possible by puncture." Walker told him this and Gurdjieff said a new drug was coming from America. "We shall try this medical treatment first and if it fails I will do what you say. Thank you for your advice."

22 October 1949. Paris. Bennett finds Gurdjieff at his café in the rue des Acacias. He is dressed in his coat with the astrakhan collar, sheepskin boots, a brown and red woolen scarf folded over his chest and his black astrakhan cap covering his head. His appearance—that of a sick old man—is shocking. He looks ill, his face very dark, the eyes sunken with black rings around them. Gurdjieff speaks of the future.

Bennett tells him that in his lectures he is saying that *Beelzebub's Tales* contains the key to understanding what mankind needs.

Gurdjieff nods in agreement and says, "There is a war between the old world and the new. The next five years will decide. It is the beginning of a new world. Either the old world will make me 'Tchik' [squash me like a louse], or I will make the old world 'Tchik.' Then the new world can begin. From now on I need soldiers who will fight for me for the new world."

24 October 1949. 6 rue des Colonels Renard. Still seriously ill, Gurdjieff oversees the toasts to the idiots. Four people sit in the salon throughout the night—Madame de Salzmann, Vera Daumal, Russell Page and Gabo. Gurdjieff sits down and looks at them for a long time, uttering not a word. They believe he is saying goodbye.

26 October 1949. 6 rue des Colonels Renard. Early this morning the American doctor William Welch, who has flown in from New York, is led to the little room where Gurdjieff lies. Says Welch:

> I was shocked to hear his labored breathing, to see his gray color, and the gaunt wasting of the body, except for his swollen belly and legs. The mark of death was on his face.
>
> "Bravo, America! Bravo, *docteur*!" His guttural voice had lost none of its rich timbre. He turned warmly to me, and his smile brightened his face with an almost childlike gaiety, so characteristic of him when he was pleased. I said little and set about examining him slowly and thoroughly.
>
> As I began, he settled himself expectantly.
>
> "Doctor," he said, "you do your business." And he only spoke again when he saw that I was leaning near his mouth to smell his breath, which was faintly tinged with the aroma of his failing kidneys.
>
> "Not stink?" he inquired, his eyebrows arched, a trace of his old smile on his lips.
>
> "No, Mr. Gurdjieff," I assured him, "not stink."

The decision is made to take Gurdjieff to the American Hospital in Neuilly-sur-Seine, a suburb of Paris.

While waiting for the ambulance to come I went into the little dining room. I told the people that Gurdjieff was mortally ill and there was little hope of recovery. Where I sat I faced the corridor to his room, and as I was speaking I looked up and saw him walking toward me, slowly in a kind of caricature of his old vital stride. It was as if he had picked himself up by the scruff of his own neck and was hoisting himself along by a naked will. He turned into the watercloset down the hall and disappeared from my view.

I do not know why he took this merciless attitude toward his body, but all his life he had scorned its complaints and put it to tests that would have done in a lesser man. Now its resources were nearly exhausted and it would at last have its way.

A stretcher is brought to his bedroom but he refuses to use it. Instead, Gurdjieff gets out of bed and appears in the hallway wearing his pajamas and a red fez. On seeing the stretcher he says, "Oy!" He sits on it upright, his fez at a rakish angle, and lights a cigarette. Outside, as the stretcher is carried to the ambulance, the cigarette between his lips, Gurdjieff makes a sort of wave and says, *"Au revoir, tout le monde!"*

27 October 1949. American Hospital, Neuilly-sur-Seine. Welch prepares to perform an abdominal puncture to tap and drain the bloated abdomen. Gurdjieff sits up in bed wearing his old red fez and cloaked by his camel hair coat, holding a cup of coffee and wooden cigarette holder. Welch asks if he is ready. Gurdjieff, the old fox, replies—"Only if you not tired, Doctor." His breathing was labored and his sad eyes looked down on Welch warmly. "You carry on."

Twelve to thirteen liters of fluid are taken from him.

Gurdjieff gives his last instructions to Madame de Salzmann. "Publish as and when you are sure that the time has come. Publish the *First* and *Second Series* [of *All and Everything*]. The essential thing, the first thing, is to prepare a nucleus of people capable of responding to the demand which will arise.

"So long as there is no responsible nucleus, the action of the ideas will not go beyond a certain threshold. That will take time . . . a lot of time, even.

"To publish the *Third Series* is not necessary. It was written for another purpose. Nevertheless, if you believe you ought to do so one day, publish it."

28 October 1949. American Hospital. Gurdjieff falls unconscious.

29 October 1949. American Hospital. Georgi Ivanovitch Gurdjieff takes his last breath at 10:30 a.m. The cause is cancer of the liver.[14] Besides the tumor, his

14. See the Solita Solano papers, Library of Congress. His followers did not admit the real cause of Gurdjieff's death in that he himself had said that cancer and heart disease "were almost always

heart was dilated and his lungs were riddled from bouts of bronchitis, which he had suffered for thirty years. A French doctor examines him. He raises Gurdjieff's eyelids. His impression is that Gurdjieff is looking back at him. Four hours after his death his forehead and neck are still warm. It is a curious phenomenon the doctor says he cannot understand. Later, Dr. William Welch, sitting in the kitchen of Gurdjieff's flat, says that Gurdjieff died peacefully, all the sickness disappearing from his face. "I have seen many men die. He died like a king."

2 November 1949. Alexander Nevsky Cathedral, 12 rue Daru, Paris. Gurdjieff's body is too large for the coffin; a larger one must be found. In absolute silence, the congregation stands for an hour waiting for the coffin to arrive. The priest who will perform the service is dressed in the old tradition with robe, silver cross and chain, long black hair and beard. In a honeyed voice he asks:

"What did this man Gurdjieff teach? For my whole life I've wanted a congregation like this."

The chapel is lit with candles. Gurdjieff's body is dressed in his best suit, bought for the forthcoming American trip. It is covered with a pale cloth piled high with red roses, pink orchids and white flowers. On either side of his head are two enormous bouquets of violets.

Says one pupil: "The face is like a statue's. Yesterday he looked alive still, a slight smile made him seem so; his skin had a most curious lavender tinge. Today he is darker, the smile has gone, he is already far away, the eyes have begun to sink, the lips are in a grave line, though not quite stern.... He looks as if he had just said: 'Now I go away with all my secrets and my mystery. My work is finished here.'"

Says another pupil:

> I was overwhelmed by the force that came from him. One could not be near his body without feeling unmistakably his power. He looked magnificent; composed, content, *intentional*, for want of a better word. Not simply a body placed by someone else. He was undisguised, nothing was concealed from us. Everything belonging to him, his inner and outer life and all the circumstances and results of it, were there to be seen, if one could see. What force there was in him then! I have never seen anything in any way like it. This, I think, was what I had dreaded: I could not bear to see him with the force gone from him. Yet in fact I saw his power for the first time unobscured.

the inevitable results of living in an unharmonious atmosphere under constant strain and pressure." (See Fritz Peters, *Gurdjieff Remembered*, 62.) But this was Gurdjieff's great sacrifice: his own life. It must be remembered that he took a vow on 14 September 1911, "to live an *artificial* life" in order to establish the ancient, esoteric teaching of The Fourth Way in the West. [Emphasis added.] Given the abnormal conditions and customs and deviations of our contemporary world, a constant and unflagging super-effort would be demanded that must, of course, be paid for in terms of continual strain and pressure. What was taken as a negative was really quite otherwise when truly seen.

Just as the service ends, the electric lights in the church and in that entire quarter of Paris fail.

3 November 1949. Alexander Nevsky Cathedral. The day is cold but sunny. At eleven o'clock there is a high requiem mass. Five white-and-gold-robed Russian priests and a cantor perform ceremonies, chanting and praying and singing, all in Russian.

The Russian "Service for the Dead" begins for Georgi Ivanovitch Gurdjieff.

> *Give rest eternal in the blessed falling asleep,*
> *O Lord,*
> *to the soul of thy servant departed this life,*
> *and make his memory eternal.*
> *Memory eternal!*
> *Memory eternal!*
> *Memory eternal!*

The priest reads the eulogy that Thomas de Hartmann had written.[15] He wrote it in such a way that the last words pronounced by the priest in front of the coffin are the words from Gurdjieff's ballet scenario *The Struggle of the Magicians*:

> *Lord Creator and all you His assistants, help us to be able to remember ourselves at all times in order that we may avoid involuntary actions, as only through them can evil manifest itself.*

One by one all those assembled pass by the coffin, making a genuflection at his head, stepping up to the icon at his feet, kissing it and walking off to the left.

At two o'clock Gurdjieff's coffin, still topped by flowers, is carried out and put into the large black funeral carriage. His family rides with him. Private cars and four large buses carry his students. The streets around the church are closed to traffic for blocks. The funeral cortege drives through Gurdjieff's street, through all the old familiar streets of Paris, the outlying roads and forest until it comes to the gates at Avon Cemetery.

Braving an icy wind, hundreds walk through the gates to the family plot. Gurdjieff's grave lies beside the large dolmen under which he buried his wife. At the opposite end is a smaller dolmen under which his mother lies buried. The dolmens, with time, have begun to bend toward one another. At sunset the coffin, a golden cross at its head, is lowered slowly into the rocky, watery, dark earth of the grave. The long pale coffin in place now, a great sigh involuntarily issues from the people—the only sound they have made. The priest now begins to chant as, one

---

15. He had not seen Gurdjieff since 1930, but he obviously carried him in his heart.

by one, in accordance with the old Russian custom, people begin to approach the grave of their teacher, kneeling, making the sign of the cross, throwing a handful of earth on the coffin, and passing on. Some throw a few red and white roses along with a handful of dark earth.

Lord Pentland said the feeling was:

> It was impossible to go on. Because up till a few days before he died, he was seeing everybody and appearing at meals . . . and refusing to allow various feelings to start [that he was going to die]. Fortunately, there were people who understood enough to help us all once he did die. Of course there were very few people. . . . Fortunately, somebody was able to show the way to go on without at once trying to manifest everything that they understood. In other words, to go on learning from each other, and in a way not too obvious.

That evening, following Gurdjieff's burial, Madame de Salzmann speaks with her French students and a few English people.

"When a Teacher like Mr. Gurdjieff goes, he cannot be replaced. Those who remain cannot create the same conditions. We have only one hope: to make something together. What no one of us could do, perhaps a group can. Let us make this our chief aim in the future."

Bennett, having witnessed the friction between Gurdjieff's close pupils and marveling at Madame de Salzmann's optimism, says: "I was bound to agree that in unity lay our only hope."

Declares Frank Pinder:

> Gurdjieff came to strike a big Do, to help the upflow of the Law of Seven against the current of mechanical life. . . . Gurdjieff came to give us a New World, a new idea of God, of the purpose of life, of sex, of war. But who are "Us"? "Us" are those who accept him and his teaching and help to carry out this work. This world of ours cannot be saved in our measure of time. Had it been possible it would have been "saved" long ago by prophets and teachers who have been sent. Those who look for the world to be saved by a single teacher in a given time are shirking their own responsibility. They wait in hope of a "second coming" with no effort on their part—indulging in the disease of tomorrow.

Finis

STRIKE A BIG DO

Mr. Gurdjieff and Madame de Salzmann confer

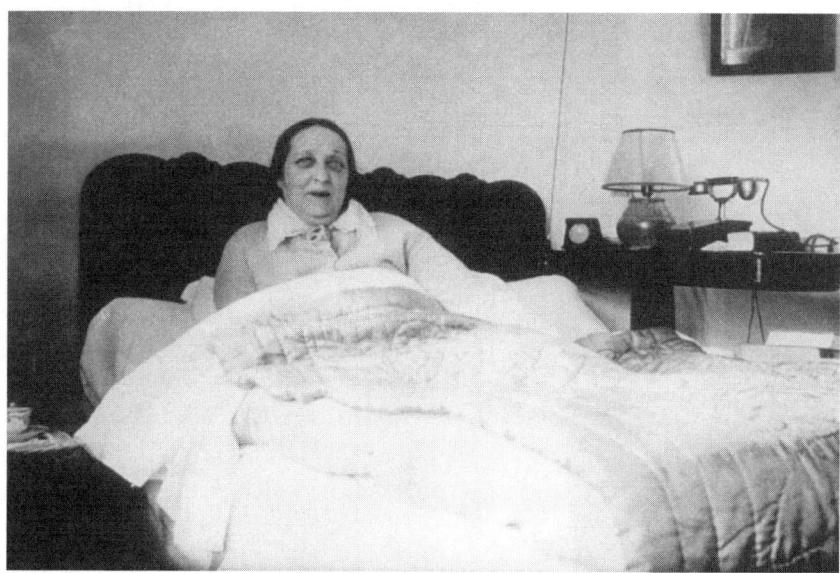

Madame Uspenskii, bedridden, dispenses teaching at Franklin Farms

Georgi Ivanovitch Gurdjieff

Mr. Gurdjieff at lunch

Dr. Francis Roles

*Madame de Salzmann, Tanya Savitsky,
Lise Tracol & Mr. Gurdjieff*

Strike a Big Do

Lobby of the Salle Pleyel in Paris

Mr. Gurdjieff supervises preparations for an excursion

Mr. Gurdjieff at his table in Childs during his last trip to America

Georgi Ivanovitch Gurdjieff

Mr. Gurdjieff lying in state at the Alexander Nevsky Cathedral

Funeral cortege at the cemetery in Avon

Russian Orthodox priest presides over the last rites for Mr. Gurdjieff

It would be a blessing for all: to God, to the deceased and to you and me, and even to the whole of humanity, if there proceeded in you because of someone's death the process of realization about your own forthcoming death instead of the manifesting of meaningless words.

Only a full realization by man of the inevitability of his own death can destroy in him those factors for the manifestation of the different aspects of egotisms which is the root of all evil in our reciprocal existence.

Only such a realization can again regenerate in people the data formerly already in them for the divine impulses of Faith, Love and Hope.

G. Gurdjieff

Afterword

Who is this man Georgi Ivanovitch Gurdjieff? There is P. D. Uspenskii after spending a week with Gurdjieff exclaiming—"I have found the miracle!" The Finnish psychiatrist Dr. Leonid Robertovich Stjoernval saying—"Yes! I believe Georgi Ivanovitch is not less than Christ himself!" And A. R. Orage, called "the finest literary critic of his day" by no less than T. S. Eliot, declaring, Gurdjieff is a "solar god" and his Beelzebub's Tales to His Grandson is "an objective work of art of the highest kind; it is in the category of scripture." And there are others, of course, calling him a fraud and a charlatan.

Georgi Ivanovitch Gurdjieff

Unlike Mr. Gurdjieff's students, who experienced him directly and in many settings and situations, our estimate of him is limited to his writings, his students' personal accounts, and our own level of understanding. Those who think they know Gurdjieff will relegate him to one end of the stick or the other. For most others the word most likely used will be *enigmatic*, which, interestingly, is defined by *Webster's* as having three meanings. The first, "to speak in riddles" or "an obscure speech or writing." The second, "something hard to understand or explain." And the third, "an inscrutable or mysterious person." Accordingly then, Georgi Ivanovitch Gurdjieff is "an inscrutable or mysterious person who speaks in riddles and obscure speech or writing and is hard to understand or explain." The title of Margaret Anderson's book puts it more simply, *The Unknowable Gurdjieff*.

For those who believe they can know who Gurdjieff is if they know the facts of his life, the problem is, as Jane Heap warned the Rope: "You mustn't think of conscious being[1] as an extension of the consciousness you have. And understand, it's on a different plane." Or as C. S. Nott pointed out: "We cannot judge Gurdjieff from our level. He lives from essence and, in a great measure, according to objective reason, and a person who lives thus can sometimes appear to our minds spoilt by wrong education and conditioning, as not normal. For me Gurdjieff represents objective sanity.... He lives the Teaching, while we talk about it."

Whoever Gurdjieff was he was always teaching. And often that meant "acting." Acting against what? Against the self-limiting belief in everyone's knowing. His aim was to keep students between a "yes" and a "no," keep them in question, and thus not knowing, for knowing is closure. In a like way he always scorned adulation,[2] as it is a definite obstacle to self-awakening.[3] For in idolizing the teacher the student unconsciously minimizes his own responsibility to awaken. Yet of course, as Gurdjieff often declared, a teacher is absolutely necessary (a central tenet many dismiss) because if everyone is an assemblage of "I"s, which "I" is going to awaken them? It's only the self-love and vanity of a lunatic, tramp or rock hard egotist who thinks he or she can awaken themself.

But given Gurdjieff's power — "What a vibration in the air! You learn something just from feeling near him," says Solita Solano — and given the immensity of his esoteric knowledge, it is difficult not to fall into adulation (or hatred). To diminish this Gurdjieff created questions, even belittled himself. "In objective sense," he once told the Rope, "I do not have objective mentation, I am not

---

1. What would we think of the other primary figures, Moses, Buddha, Jesus and Mohammed, if we really knew their lives in full rather than the sanitized versions handed down to us?

2. This is one of his primary criticisms of Orage.

3. "I not wish people identified with me, I wish them identified with my ideas," Gurdjieff says. "Many who never will meet me, simple people, will understand my book. Time come perhaps when they read *Beelzebub's Tales* in churches."

complete Initiate. There are many thousand complete men on earth — not in world, but on earth, I tell. Many thousand complete men. I am not yet complete. I still have far to go." But at another time, he said, "I have no concurrent rival." At another, he had "seven zeros," meaning his soul had been fully coated.

While he often taught in ways that were purposely confusing, there was one subject he was always definite about: *the question of the soul*. Where once it was believed only the pharaoh had a soul, then the aristocracy, now everyone has a soul. This keeps people in imagination worrying about not losing what they don't have rather than working with the possibility they do have — that of developing a soul. Gurdjieff was unequivocal — "A man is born without a soul, with only the possibility of acquiring one, and he has to earn it during his lifetime. For those who have not acquired a soul, nothing happens to them. They live and they die."[4] He then added, *"But even immortal souls exist in different stages. Full immortality is quite unique."*

This idea is often missed: that the process of development does not end after a soul is first coated. This newly coated soul, an embryonic soul, is still in the process of further perfecting toward *full* immortality.[5] And presumably, given the octave do to si that shows the process of all development, there would be seven additional stages, from embryonic to full immortality. Therefore, embryonic to old souls exist at different stages of Reason, of understanding, a word Gurdjieff defined as comprised of both self-knowledge and being. We see a mention of this when his wife, Madame Ostrowska, lay dying — "She live many lives," he says, "is very old soul;[6] she now have the possibility to ascend to other world."[7]

[4]. Gurdjieff says, "No one has yet been born with a fully developed soul. Before we can speak of reincarnation, we must know what kind of man we are speaking about, what kind of soul and what kind of reincarnation. A soul may disintegrate immediately after death, or it may do so after a certain time. For example, a soul may be crystallized within the limits of the earth and may remain there, yet not be crystallized for the sun." *Views from the Real World*, 87.

[5]. See Chapter XXXIX, where the *Choot-God-litanical* period is first mentioned, and also the "admixture of any extraneously caused arisings whatsoever with their own subjective properties" with the sacred *Theomertmalogos* issuing from the Most Most Holy Sun Absolute, along with what is revealed and admitted in Chapter II, *Beelzebub's Tales* can be realized as a confession which deservedly culminates in Chapter XLVII.

[6]. Souls, then, live many lifetimes in this world, or a higher one. Or, is it the same world but lived at a higher rate of vibration? And are these lifetimes *different*? Or does the soul live the *same* lifetime over again? Or, is there a *spiral of lifetimes*, one and the same lifetime, but different in the sense of occurring at different levels of vibration? That is, experiencing the same lifetime but at different levels of consciousness and understanding. The questions are intriguing for the curious mind, but impossible of resolution at our stage of development.

[7]. Gurdjieff speaks at length about the many meanings of *world* in *Search*, 75–77, one of which is that we live in several worlds, one world contained within another. The world nearest us is the organic life. The world for organic life is our planet, and the world for our planet is the planetary world of the solar system, etc. In Kathryn Hulme's raw notes of talks with Gurdjieff, not dated, she writes: "Reincarnation presupposes incarnation. Stress falls first on Incarnation. Is it a completed factor or a fact in process? Not yet subject to a repetition until completed process. (G.'s method is a technique for a speeding-up of process in activity — not to be identified with the process itself.) 'Being' is incarnation. Analogy: Tree, seed = reincarnation. Leaves = incarnation. Gurdjieff speaks of 'blocks of essence' = tree. Blocks of essence = human life, and leaves = each life. Leaves recur — not

Now, it is commonly presumed that Gurdjieff's students, his Idiots, were working toward creating a soul, that none had as yet coated one. But *what if they had already coated an embryonic soul?* Then what we read of their lives and interactions with Gurdjieff is seen as an even deeper and more complex revelation. We get some taste of this with Uspenskii who often foresaw what was, or would, happen. Yes, everything happens, as Gurdjieff says, but one who already had coated a soul would often experience their life as recurring. Watching the German bombing of London, Uspenskii says again and again—"This I do not remember. This I do not remember." As he reminds J. G. Bennett, "You are like Madame Uspenskii. Both of you have young souls. You have not the experience of living many times on earth."

If we accept that Uspenskii is an old soul who has lived many lifetimes on the earth, how old a soul is Gurdjieff? A key to this is what Gurdjieff calls himself—"Teacher of Dancing."[8] That is, one who embodies, understands and teaches the principles and laws of consciously receiving and transmitting energy in order to coat a soul. Uspenskii always acknowledged that Gurdjieff was higher than he was, and so Gurdjieff must be a very old soul indeed. And Beelzebub, who Gurdjieff sometimes called himself, what is his degree of Being? Read *Beelzebub's Tales,* chapter XLVII, "The Inevitable Result of Impartial Mentation." Some hint of this is given by Jane Heap, herself an old soul: "Gurdjieff is not a single man but a multitude," she says, "a crowd of two thousand million men, as many as he is able to incarnate, so that his experience can be complete. Through that multitude there walks a sage. In his talk there is always teaching. You must watch for it. You must not be put off."

Provisionally, if we accept that some of Gurdjieff's early followers, be they Russian, English or American, already had embryonic souls, had "seven zeros," but not fully developed ones,[9] then the question arises: will their rebirth be to a new human life, or to a reliving of the previous one? Uspenskii's understanding of eternal recurrence (Gurdjieff used the word "repetition") was that, if we develop sufficiently, when we die we are reborn on the exact day of our previous birth. If this is true—and remember Gurdjieff said, "The idea of repetition

to be confused with reincarnation. But seed falls from tree and entire cycle is repeated = principle of reincarnation. Every one of us recurs, not a reincarnation of previous leaf or a continuation—does not inherit any of the virtue or experience. Issues recur like leaves—no continuity of progress except as (tree) human essence has undergone development. Individual can pass from wheel of recurrence by identifying himself with another part of tree—seed, relative freedom. But oak to oak—type, etc. If we were to pass from 24 to 12 laws, that is gaining relative freedom."

8. The capitalization of "Teacher of Dancing" means this should be taken in its highest form and meaning. Gurdjieff said that in his youth he had been taken into the service of the Lord God on the Sun Absolute. That he mentions Gilgamesh, the hero of his early life, is quite telling.

9. Madame de Salzmann, who became a student in 1919 and assisted Gurdjieff in meetings in the 1940s and led the teaching after his death, could certainly be considered an embryonic soul, if not older.

is not the full and absolute truth, but it is the nearest possible approximation of the truth"—could it be that some of Gurdjieff's primary students had lived the *same life* many times before, *but at different degrees of development*? That is, with each recurring lifetime, they developed their understanding and will, but still were as yet not able to subdue their chief weakness to accept and help their teacher in his mission?

Certainly several of these students were magicians; that is, they had cunning, in Gurdjieff's use of the term, and could inspire and galvanize people, but their chief feature, or chief weakness, was strongly embedded. Uspenskii's chief feature Gurdjieff named as "extreme individualism." Of the others, given what is known of their lives, we might hazard the opinion that Orage's was a feminine element; Bennett's, inordinate self-will; Toomer's, a desire for power; and so forth. Imperfectly perfect they were, yes, but all extraordinary in their own right.

Given eternal recurrence, could it be then, that in their next life Uspenskii, Orage, Bennett, Toomer and others will work, as it says in *Beelzebub's Tales*, so that they "will consciously assist the non-desires to predominate over the desires, behave in accordance with the essence of our COMMON FATHER CREATOR HIMSELF," and so "lighten as much as possible the Sorrow of our COMMON FATHER," and help Gurdjieff to accomplish his great mission of introducing the teaching in the West?

Gurdjieff accepted his mission because he recognized—more than a hundred years ago now—that "Unless the 'wisdom' of the East and the 'energy' of the West could be harnessed and used harmoniously, the world would be destroyed." A major shock had to be given to avert the world's destruction—the revelation of a heretofore esoteric teaching[10] known only by its initiates—and so he took a vow to live an artificial life for twenty-one years to introduce and establish in the West the ancient seminal teaching of self-development and transformation he called The Fourth Way. As he told his students at the Prieuré in the mid-1920s:

> We should look at the world in the same way that we look at a man, or at oneself. Each individual is a world, of itself and the globe—the big world in which we all lived—was, in a sense, only a reflection or an enlargement of the individual world in each one of us. Among the purposes of all leaders, messiahs, messengers from the gods, and so forth, there was one fundamental and very important purpose: to find some means by which the two sides of man, and, therefore, the two sides of the earth, could live together in peace and harmony.
>
> *The time is very short*—it is necessary to achieve this harmony as soon

---

10. All the authentic religions and teachings are reflections of the Truth, but which have the scale and depth, the laws and processes revealed in The Fourth Way? Furthermore, most assume everyone already has a soul, one that can only be lost—hence the emphasis on sin and good and evil, the root identification with duality.

as possible to avoid complete disaster. Philosophies, religious and other such movements have all failed to accomplish this aim, and the only possible way to accomplish it is through the individual development of man. As an individual developed his own, unknown potentialities, he would become strong and would, in turn, influence many more people. *If enough individuals can develop themselves—even partially—into genuine, natural men, able to use the real potentialities that are proper to mankind*, each such individual would then be able to convince and win over as many as a hundred other men, who would, each in his turn, upon achieving development, be able to influence another hundred, and so on.

History has already proven to us that such tools as politics, religion, and any other organized movements which treated man 'in the mass' and not as individual beings, were failures and that *the separate, distinct growth of each individual in the world is the only possible solution.* [Emphasis added.]

What is the origin of this teaching of soul creation that Gurdjieff introduces? In the early days in Russia when Gurdjieff was asked, "What is the relation of the teaching you are expounding to Christianity as we know it?" He answered unequivocally: "I do not know what you know about Christianity. . . . But for the benefit of those who know already, I will say that, if you like, *this is esoteric Christianity.*" [Original emphasis.]

Later, Gurdjieff expands on its origin, saying, "The teaching is completely self-supporting and independent of other lines and it has been completely unknown up to the present time." So not only is the teaching esoteric Christianity but it is complete, independent and, until now, not publicly known. Further, Gurdjieff says:

> The Christian church, the Christian form of worship, was not invented by the fathers of the church. It was all taken in a ready-made form from Egypt, only not from the Egypt that we know but from one which we do not know. This Egypt was in the same place as the other but it existed much earlier. It will seem strange to many people when I say that this prehistoric Egypt was Christian many thousands of years before the birth of Christ, that is to say, that its religion was composed of the same principles and ideas that constitute true Christianity. . . . The Christian church is a school. . . .

Therefore, without question, the origin of the esoteric Christian teaching he brings is prehistoric Egypt.[11]

---

11. Why, then, one might ask, for some people does the idea persist that the teaching is a mixture of Eastern teachings? Gurdjieff was against mixtures in that they do not "possess full knowledge and therefore attempts to bring them to practical realization give only negative results." But, yes,

That the teaching he brings is solely Christian is explicitly shown at the opening of the Institute for the Harmonious Development of Man at the Prieuré, when Gurdjieff defines its purpose.

> The program of the Institute, the power of the Institute, the aim of the Institute, the possibilities of the Institute can be expressed in a few words: the Institute can help one to be able to be a Christian. Simple! That is all! It can do so only if a man has this desire, and a man will have this desire only if he has a place where constant desire is present. Before being able, one must wish.
> Thus there are three periods: to wish, to be able, and to be.
> The Institute is the means.

It is important to recognize—as it is often dismissed or missed—that the teaching of The Fourth Way originates not from a secular foundation but a religious foundation,[12] and is therefore *sacred* in that word's deepest meaning.[13] But many called to this ancient, seminal teaching of self-awakening, rebels all, seem to have an unconscious, even deliberate, bias against religion.[14] For them the word *religion* automatically, as Gurdjieff says, "evokes data from memory that reacts to impressions producing impulses which in turn affect associations and gradually disharmonize the whole of one's functioning." That needs to be observed and verified, its origin recognized, if we are to step beyond the attributions and accretions that have distorted the word-symbol "religion" into what it unfortunately has devolved to today. We need to ponder what *religion* is in itself, *purely*. The genuine definition of the word is "wholeness," as Gurdjieff first experienced it, "the whole sensation of myself." When asked what his whim was, his true desire in life, Gurdjieff answered unequivocally—"To live and teach so that there should

---

Gurdjieff's writings do reveal his knowledge and experience with a variety of practices of various religions, but, while there may be certain correspondences, the teaching he brings, the Science of Being, predates all of these.

12. Denis Saurat, who while not a student had a deep understanding of the teaching and saw Gurdjieff as a Lohan, says, "Some parts of Gurdjieff's teaching could not be of terrestrial origin. Either Gurdjieff had revelations vouchsafed only to prophets or he had access to a school on a supernatural level."

13. Gurdjieff explains the difference between the two kinds of religious-teachings: "One kind was invented by those three-brained beings there themselves, in whom, for some reason or other, there arises the functioning of a psyche proper to *Hasnamusses*; and the other kind of religious-teaching is founded there upon those detailed instructions which have been preached, as it were, by genuine Messengers from Above, who indeed are from time to time sent by certain nearest helpers of our COMMON FATHER, for the purpose of aiding the three-brained beings of your planet in destroying in their presences the crystallized consequences of the properties of the organ *Kundabuffer*."

14. It is essential to remember that The Fourth Way is a two-headed snake. It gives great power and knowledge but when divorced from its sacred religious foundation, however serious one's intent, the practice remains fundamentally that of the "esoteric I," the jealous god. It is only when it is lawfully rooted in being-Partkdolg-duty for God-the-Father, God-the-Son, God-the-Holy-Ghost that it leads to a full flowering of the consciousness and conscience of the perfected soul.

be a new conception of God in the world, a change in the very meaning of the word." If there is to be a new conception of God, then it follows that there must be a new conception of religion.

And just who are we who will institute this new conception? "We are the images of God," Gurdjieff tells us. "Of everything known to most people concerning cosmic truths," he says, "this expression of theirs is the only true one of them all."[15] But what is not commonly recognized is that we are *undeveloped* images, negative images, of God. Like camera film of old, negative images have to be put through a solution and dried, until the inherent positive image emerges, the seed becoming a tree. We either develop the positive or die in the negative.

This eternal truth is inborn in every World-Time, be it Hunter-Gatherer, Agrarian, Industrial, Post-Industrial, and now the Technological. But as was warned in *Spiritual Survival in a Radically Changing World-Time*:

> Technology is not neutral. It seeks, though unknowingly, as it knows nothing in our sense of the word, to remake and redefine everything in its own image. Relentlessly, it is reordering how we live and think and who we take ourselves to be. It poses a direct challenge to our identity and purpose as human beings. Are we facing a kind of Faustian bargain in which for unimaginable material powers we are exchanging our possibility of spiritual transformation? . . . Technology is not us. And yet it is us. This is what makes it so difficult to understand. Aristotle spoke of man as "the rational animal." Technology is man's rational part—the logical part of our power of binary reasoning—developed to an extraordinary degree through millennia of experience and experiment. Thus, we are its parents and like all parents had no idea of what we were conceiving. . . . Our situation is this: We are born bioplasmic machines and have developed through the millennia the logical, binary part of ourselves to such an extraordinary degree that we have 'created' ourselves in machine form—the 'Son of Man,' the 'Robo-sapien' which returns us anew to the primordial question that has always been at the center of our being—*Who am I?* And deeper—*Why am I?*

Yes, Technology shrinks time and distance, opens new vistas high and low, and penetrates realms of thought and perspective and control heretofore unknowable. The Faustian question, not bargain, is how we relate to and control and for what purposes do we employ these powers. The hazard of not relating to it rightly is not only to forfeit our very identity and spiritual possibility, but to open the Gates of Hell to a certain planetary destruction that will erase the human experiment.

---

15. See Essay, "Images of God or Machines?"

Afterword

The seminal and sacred teaching Gurdjieff brought is in essence scientific in that it is centered in continual questioning, verification, exploration, and faith of Consciousness, not belief or dogma. The Fourth Way reunites the two teachings of Christianity, the exoteric and the esoteric, the "Be Christians" with "How to Be Christians."[16] It is *the religion for our time* so directly attuned is it to this World-Time. Only The Fourth Way can stand against the scientific entrancements of Technology, as it itself is founded in a scientific technology, albeit a sacred one, of self and soul development by inner practices based on the knowledge of chemical processes and laws. The only foundation that can adequately carry this is the awakening to and acceptance of the truth that the teaching Gurdjieff brought is an esoteric school united with its true and original Christian origin.

---

16. See Gurdjieff's talk 5 March 1923 at Warwick Gardens, London. Also *Search*, 304. He was saying the same thing in Russia 1916–17 as he was later in England in 1923.

The Struggle of the Magicians

G. I. Gurdjieff

Scenario of the Ballet

Act One

The action takes place in a large commercial town of the East.

The market square where various streets and alleys meet: around it, shops and stalls with every variety of merchandise—silks, earthenware, spices; open-fronted workshops of tailors and shoemakers.

To the right, a row of fruit stalls; flat-roofed houses of two and three stories with many balconies, some hung with carpets and others strewn with washing.

To the left, on a roof, a tea shop; further on, children are playing; two monkeys are climbing on the cornices.

Behind the houses are seen winding streets leading to the mountain; houses, mosques, minarets, gardens, palaces, Christian churches, Hindu temples, and pagodas.

In the distance, on the mountain is seen the tower of an old fortress.

Amongst the crowd moving about the alleys and the market square, types of almost every Asiatic people are to be met with, clad in their national costumes: a Persian with dyed beard, an Afghan all in white, with proud and bold expression, a Baluchistani in a white turban with a sharp peak to it and short white sleeveless coat with a broad belt, out of which stick several knives; a half-naked Hindu Tamil, the front of his head shaved and a white and red fork, the sign of Vishnu, painted on his forehead; a native Khiva wearing a huge black fur cap and a thickly wadded coat; a yellow-robed Buddhist monk, his head shaved and prayer-wheel in his hand; an Armenian in black 'chooka' with a silver belt and a black Russian forage cap; a Tibetan in a costume resembling the Chinese, bordered with valuable furs; also Bokharis, Arabs, Caucasians and Turkomans.

The merchants cry their wares, inviting customers; beggars with whining voices beg for alms; a sherbet-vendor amuses the crowd with a witty song.

A street barber, shaving the head of a venerable old 'hadji,' recounts the news and the gossip of the town to a tailor who dines in the adjoining eating house. A funeral procession passes through one of the alleys; in front is a 'mullah' and behind him the corpse is borne on a bier covered with a pall, followed by the women mourners. In another alley a fight is in progress and all the boys run there to watch. On the right, a fakir with outstretched arms, his eyes fixed on one point,

The Struggle of the Magicians

sits on an antelope skin. A rich and important merchant passes along ignoring the crowd, his servants follow him carrying baskets laden with purchases. Then appear some exhausted beggars, half-naked and covered with dust, evidently just arrived from some famine area. At one shop, Kashmir and other shawls and materials are brought out and shown to customers.

Opposite the tea shop, a snake-charmer seats himself and is at once surrounded by a curious crowd. Donkeys pass by, laden with baskets. Women walk along, some wearing the 'chuddar' and others with unveiled faces. A humpbacked old woman stops near the fakir and, with a devout air, puts money into the coconut alms bowl standing near him. She touches the skin on which he is seated and goes away, pressing her hands to her forehead and eyes. A wedding procession moves by; in front are gaily dressed children, behind them buffoons, musicians and drumbeaters. The town crier passes, shouting at the top of his voice. From an alley is heard the din of the coppersmith's hammers. Everywhere there is noise, sound, movement, laughter, scolding, prayers, bargaining—life bubbling over.

Two men separate themselves from the crowd. Both are richly dressed. One of them, Gafar, is a handsome, well-built, wealthy Parsi about thirty or thirty-five years of age, clean shaven except for a small black mustache and close-cut hair. He wears a light yellow silk coat with a pale rose-colored scarf and blue trousers, over this a brocade robe, the skirt, cuffs and facings of which are embroidered in silver; on his feet are high boots of yellow leather, the legs embroidered in gold and precious stones; his head is covered with a turban of a figured Indian material, its predominating color is turquoise blue; on his fingers are rings with large emeralds and diamonds. The other man is his confidant, Rossoula, dressed equally richly, but carelessly. He is short, stout, subtle and cunning, the chief assistant of his master in all his love affairs and intrigues. He is always in a sly and merry mood. On his head he wears a red skull-cap with a yellow turban wrapped round it; in his hand is a short red rosary.

Gafar looks at some of the wares and stops occasionally to speak with some of his acquaintances, but evidently nothing interests him. In all his movements one can see the pride of a man satiated with pleasures. To his equals he is patronizingly civil, but on everyone else he looks with contempt or aversion. He has experienced everything, seen everything, and the things for which other people struggle and exert themselves no longer exist for him.

At this moment, two women come out of a side street on the left, into the square. One of them, Zeinab, is young, about twenty or twenty-two years of age, of an Indo-Persian type, more than average height and very beautiful. She is dressed in a white tunic with a green scarf round her waist; her smoothly-dressed hair parted in the middle is bound with a gold fillet; thrown over her head she wears a 'chuddar,' but her face is uncovered. The other is her confidant, Haila. She is a short, plump, middle-aged, good-natured woman. She is dressed in a blue velvet coat under a violet 'chuddar.' Her mouth is covered with a handkerchief.

Zeinab holds a roll of parchment wrapped in a silk handkerchief. She passes along the square, graciously giving alms to the beggars whom she meets. Gafar notices her and follows her with his eyes. Her face interests him because it seems, at the first glance, to remind him of someone or something. He enquires of Rossoula and other acquaintances who she is, but no one knows.

Just then, Zeinab goes up to a beggar woman near whom stands a half-clad boy about eight years old with an open sore on his naked arm. As she gives him alms, Zeinab notices the sore and bending over him she speaks sympathetically to the beggar woman about him. Finally she says something to her, pointing to one of the side streets and then to the boy. It is evident from her gestures that she is advising the woman to take the boy where he can be cured.

All this time, Gafar does not cease to observe Zeinab. Zeinab wishes to bind up the boy's arm, but she has nothing to wrap round it, so she unfolds the silk handkerchief in which the rolls of parchment are wrapped and binds it round the sore. Then, accompanied by Haila, she leaves the square by a side street.

Gafar quickly consults Rossoula. It is evident that he is giving him instructions to follow Zeinab and to find out what he can about her. When Zeinab has disappeared, Rossoula follows by the same street. Gafar stands looking after him, then slowly goes up to the beggar woman and begins to talk to her. Recognizing the handkerchief on the boy's arm as the gift of Zeinab, he, without knowing why, desires to buy it. He offers the woman some money, but she refuses to sell it. Gafar, thereupon, throws down a handful of money and takes the handkerchief almost by force from the boy, then slowly walks towards the middle of the square. The astonished woman excitedly picks up the money and raising her hands to heaven, thanks Gafar. Then, taking the boy by the hand, she goes down the alley pointed out by Zeinab.

Rossoula returns and with deprecating gestures, tells Gafar that he has discovered that Zeinab is not a woman whom it is possible to approach casually. Then, still talking together, Gafar and Rossoula go out by one of the streets on the left.

Evening draws on. In one of the alleys there is much movement, and out from it comes a dervish accompanied by a crowd amongst whom are many women and children. This dervish has been much honored in the country of late, and he enjoys great respect amongst all the different nationalities. He recites some sacred verses and to the rhythm of the verses he makes certain movements resembling gymnastics or a dance.

The meaning of the verses is:
God is one for all.
But he is three-fold.
Men err, because he is seven-fold.
In his totality he is one-sounding.
In his division he is many-sounding.
And in another division he is contradictory.

The Struggle of the Magicians

He is everywhere in all forms.
When men see him
It depends on their qualities
Which part they touch.
But who touches, if he is ignorant,
Sees in the part he touches, all of him,
And not doubting, preaches about him.
He sins already
Because he acts against
The laws laid down
In the commandments of the Most High.
The commandment is this:
I am truth.
Your unbelief draws you
Into nearness with me
Because he who sees me…

The end of the verses is lost in the loud beating of drums round a charlatan selling medicines.

The twilight deepens. One by one the merchants collect their wares and close their shops. At the moment when the movement of the crowd is at its height, the curtain falls.

Act Two

In the school of the White Magician.

A spacious room which looks like a laboratory or an observatory with here and there shelves on which stand boltheads, glasses and objects of fantastic shape recalling modern apparatus, also several parchment rolls and books.

At the back, an enormous curtained window. To the left, a door leading to an inner room. To the right, a door leading outwards.

In the right-hand corner stands an hour-glass. At the left-hand side stand low tables on which there are more boltheads, glasses and open books.

In front of the window stands a telescope of strange form, and to the left, on a small table, is an apparatus similar to a microscope.

To the right stands a large throne-like chair, with a high back on which is portrayed the symbol of the enneagram, and at the left side is a small chair for the Magician's assistant.

When the curtain rises there are several pupils, both men and women, already on the stage and others are seen to enter from time to time. They are well-built, nice-looking young people with good and pleasing expressions on their faces. They are dressed in white tunics; those of the girls are long, those of the men, to the knee. On their feet are sandals. The girls have their hair dressed smoothly and bound with gold fillets, the men wear silver ones. All have scarves round their waists; those of the girls are yellow, orange and red, those of the men are green, dark blue and light blue.

They are all occupied. Some are arranging and cleaning the apparatus, some are reading and others are shaking certain liquids in glasses. By now, the number of pupils has increased.

Through the outer door the Magician's assistant enters. He is an old man of medium height, wearing spectacles and with a short thin grey beard. He wears a robe of yellow over a short white under-garment with a violet-colored scarf round his waist. On his feet are sandals; on his head a white skullcap with a violet-colored scarf wound round it. In his hands he holds a long rosary of mother-of-pearl, and on his breast, hanging from a silver chain, is the symbol of the heptagram — a seven-pointed star in a circle.

The pupils greet the Magician's assistant who responds graciously while going from one to another examining and correcting the work. The pupils continue to assemble. It is evident that the relationship between them all is kindly, gracious and friendly.

A servant enters through the inner door and says something, and from the movements of those present, it is obvious that they await someone,

The White Magician enters. He is a tall well-built old man with a benign and pleasant face and a long white beard. He is dressed in a long white robe with broad sleeves and facings beneath which is seen a cream under-garment. On his feet are sandals. In his hand is a long staff with an ivory knob, and on his breast, hanging from a thick gold chain, is the symbol of the enneagram worked in precious stones.

To the deep bows of the pupils the Magician replies with a kind smile as he blesses them. Then walking slowly to the throne, and after again blessing the pupils, the Magician sits down. (At this moment the symbol on the throne lights up.) The pupils each in turn, come forward and kiss his hand, after which they return to their places and resume their interrupted occupations.

At this moment Zeinab enters. She is late and out of breath from hurrying. She goes up to the Magician and also kisses his hand. By the way in which the Magician greets her, it is evident that she is one of his favorite pupils. She then goes to the other pupils and apparently imparts to them her recent impressions of the beggar woman with the boy.

One of the pupils goes up to the Magician, who is talking with his assistant, and asks him to explain something. Evidently the Magician's answer interests everyone, for gradually they all collect round him and listen. Continuing the explanation the Magician rises (at this moment the symbol on the throne is extinguished) and going to the microscope he starts some demonstrations. The pupils in turn go up to the microscope and look through it. Afterwards, the Magician goes to the window and draws back the curtain. The clear starry sky is seen. The Magician directs the telescope towards the sky. The pupils in their turn go to the telescope and look through it, at the same time listening to the explanation of the Magician.

The chief idea of the exposition is as follows: What is above is similar to what is below, and what is below is similar to what is above. Every unity is a cosmos. The laws which govern the Megalocosmos also govern the Macrocosmos, the Deuterocosmos, the Mesocosmos, the Tritocosmos and others, inclusively down to the Microcosmos. Having studied one cosmos, you will know all the others. The nearest cosmos of all for our study is the Tritocosmos, and for each one of us the nearest subject of study is oneself. Knowing oneself completely one will know all, even God, since men are created in his likeness.

Having said this, the Magician slowly returns to his throne.

The servant enters, and approaching the Magician, informs him that someone is asking leave to enter. Having received permission, the servant brings the beggar woman with the child. She throws herself at the feet of the Magician and begs for help, pointing to the boy. Zeinab also goes up to the Magician and intercedes for the boy.

The Magician, after looking at the wound, speaks to two of the pupils who then go into the inner room and return, one carrying a cushion on which lies an ivory wand with a large silver ball at one end, and the other carrying a handkerchief, a cup and a jar containing some liquid. The Magician takes the jar and pours the liquid into the cup, steeps the handkerchief in this and lays it on the wound. Then with great care he takes the wand and, without touching the wound, passes the wand several times over the boy's arm. When the Magician takes the handkerchief off, the sore is no longer there.

The beggar woman, struck dumb with astonishment, falls on her knees and kisses the edge of the Magician's robe. The Magician strokes the boy's head caressingly, and then dismisses them.

The pupils disperse to their places and resume their occupations. The Magician walks about the room, going to some of the pupils to examine their work and give suitable instruction. After some little time, he says something to all of the pupils and returns to his throne.

Immediately the pupils leave their work and place themselves in rows, and at a sign from the Magician they go through various movements resembling dances. The Magician's assistant walks up and down and corrects their postures and movements.

These 'sacred dances' are considered to be one of the principal subjects of study in all esoteric schools of the East, both in ancient times and at the present day. The movements of which these dances consist have a double purpose; they express and contain a certain knowledge and, at the same time, they serve as a method of attaining a harmonious state of being. Combinations of these movements express different sensations, produce varying degrees of concentration of thought, create necessary efforts in different functions and show the possible limits of individual force.

During an interval, one of the pupils points to the hour-glass, whereupon the Magician tells them all to finish their previous occupations and prepare themselves for what is to follow. Meanwhile he himself goes to the window and raises the curtain.

It is early morning and the sun is rising on the horizon. As the first rays appear, the White Magician with his assistant and his pupils behind him fall on their knees. They pray.

The curtain falls slowly.

Act Three

In the house of Gafar.

A room with an alcove in the right-hand corner, in which—behind carved columns—can be seen a fountain with a marble basin.

To the left, a door leading to the inner apartments, and at the back, another door leading to the garden.

The room is arranged in the Perso-Indian style. At the right, benches covered with rugs and cushions are placed in several tiers against the wall Mindari. In the left-hand corner is a low divan near which are several fretwork tables. On one stands a kalian and other smoking appliances, on another a sherbet set, on a third a small gong and on a fourth a jug and basin of exquisite and costly workmanship for washing the hands.

Gafar is walking about the room. He is without a robe but on his head is a skullcap adorned with precious stones. His every movement, his every glance show that he is waiting impatiently. Occasionally he sits on the divan and becomes absorbed in thought. He feels that quite new things are happening to him. He who has always been so haughtily calm and indifferent is now agitated and worried by trifles which before would not even have attracted his attention. Of late he has become irritable, suspicious and impatient.

Just now he is waiting for Rossoula who is to bring him news concerning Zeinab, the woman whom they met in the bazaar a month ago, and whom Rossoula—in spite of all his skill and experience in such matters—has not yet succeeded in enticing into Gafar's harem. Yesterday Gafar ordered Rossoula to arrange this at any cost and what disturbs him so much now is the expectation of the result of Rossoula's final efforts. But at the same time, he feels that all this is simply ridiculous. Many times before he has been attracted by some woman, but while Rossoula has been busying himself in the matter, either he forgot about the woman or she ceased to interest him. But now, not only does he not forget, but every day he thinks more and more about Zeinab.

Rossoula enters by the door at the back. He seems very distracted—and this is quite unnatural for him. He brings very discouraging news. He tells Gafar that all his efforts to fulfill his orders have failed and even he does not know what more to attempt.

They both reflect deeply. Every means of enticing Zeinab has been tried; everything has been done that can be done in such a case. They have sent her the most varied gifts: ancient Indian fabrics embroidered in gold; the finest horses—Arab, Chinese and Persian; Siberian furs; such a rarity as a priceless emerald necklace—the gift of the Rajah of Kolhapur to Gafar's grandfather; Gafar's famous blue pearl, the 'Tear of Ceylon'; and lastly, they have offered her for her very own—as a separate a harem with menservants and maidservants—the renowned castle of the Gafar's, the pride of their family, the 'Breath of Paradise.' But all has been in vain. Zeinab has refused everything and will listen to nothing.

Gafar is perplexed. He becomes more and more convinced that he has not the strength to reconcile himself to Zeinab's incomprehensible stubbornness and he understands that, in truth, she has been the cause of his unusual mental state during this time. It is evident that in this woman there is something exceptional. The way in which he, Gafar, receives all Rossoula's failures amazes himself. In any other case he would simply have been indignant, but now although he is unable to suppress his anger, in his heart he is almost glad that in this case all Rossoula's ordinary methods are insufficient.

The strange things which he observes in himself turn his attention to his relationship with women in general.

Thanks to his riches, his eminence and the circumstances of his birth, his life has been so arranged that, even at seventeen, he was already surrounded by women and—in accordance with the custom of his country—he had his own harem. At present he is thirty-two but still unmarried, in spite of the fact that for a long time he has wished to marry, especially to please his old mother who is always dreaming of his marriage. But, until now he has never met any woman who, according to his views, is suited to be his wife. Many women have attracted him and in the beginning have seemed devoted and deserving of his trust, but in the end all have shown that their love and devotion have only been masks beneath which have lain petty egotistical feelings. With some it had been the passion for a young and handsome man, with others the thirst for the luxury which he could procure for them, with others again, the vanity of being the favorite of a nobleman and so on.

All that he has seen has utterly disenchanted him. He has never known a woman for whom he could feel the trust and esteem which, according to his views, should belong to his wife. He has become accustomed to look on all the fine words about love and the sympathy of souls as the mere fantasy of poets, and gradually women have become more or less alike for him, differing only in their types of beauty and in their varying manifestations of passion. His harem has become part of his collection of precious things. He could no more live without his women than he could live without smoking, without music, or without all the luxury which has always surrounded him. But he has long ceased to look for anything more in woman than the momentary enjoyment of a beautiful thing.

And now, suddenly there has arisen within him this strange curiosity towards this incomprehensible woman. Can it be possible that she is in truth so utterly different from all others? Zeinab's appearance had impressed him at the first glance, but what more does he know of her? According to the information obtained by Rossoula, Zeinab is the only daughter of a rich khan of a distant town. She is twenty-one years old and completely free, not betrothed to anyone, and she lives alone very quietly, with some servants and an old woman called Haila. At home she occupied herself with sciences and she came here in order to study at the school of a celebrated magician. This school she visits every day and the remainder of the time she spends at her house engaged in her studies. In all this there is much that is strange, unlike anything to which he has ever been accustomed. But the thought of Zeinab gives him no rest; he cannot stop thinking of her and he is prepared for any sacrifice to gain possession of her.

Still thinking deeply, Gafar gets up and walks about the room. Then, evidently in the grip of a new thought, he seats himself once more on the divan.

It is now clear that it is impossible to seduce Zeinab by means which attract other women and conquer their resistance. This being so, there remains but one thing to do — to marry her. Sooner or later he must take a wife, and a more beautiful one than Zeinab he will never find. And if she should prove to be such a wife as he has dreamed of, then it will be happiness for him and joy for his mother.

Gafar thinks thus for some time and finally speaks of his decision to Rossoula. Then he summons a servant and gives him an order. The servant goes out by the door on the left.

Soon after an elderly woman enters by the same door. She is one of Gafar's nearest relatives. He explains his decision to her and begs her to undertake the part of matchmaker. The old lady says she will carry out his commission with pleasure and has no doubt of success. It is well known that all the most famous beauties of the country would count it a happiness to become his wife, knowing of his wealth and position. She goes back to the inner apartments and presently returns accompanied by two other women. All three, veiled in 'chuddars,' then set out for Zeinab's house.

Gafar, with a thoughtful expression, still sits on the divan. Rossoula walks about the room and from time to time turns to Gafar suggesting various distractions. But Gafar's thoughts are far away and nothing attracts him. He listens to Rossoula in an absent-minded way and finally, only to get rid of him, agrees to one of his suggestions.

Immediately on Rossoula's orders, musicians enter forming an orchestra of assorted Afghan, Indian and Turkestan musical instruments. These instruments are: a zitera (a kind of balalaika with a long finger-board with seven strings, played on with a bow), an adoutar (a kind of balalaika with two strings, played with the fingers), a rabab (with three gut strings and three copper strings, played on with a small wooden pick), an atarr (a kind of mandolin with a long finger-board with seven strings, played as a mandolin), an asaz (also a kind of mandolin with three silk and three gut strings, played as a mandolin), a caloup (a kind of zitera with many strings of steel and copper, played on with a bone pick worn on the thumb), a zourna (a kind of pipe), a gydjabe (a kind of violin), a daff (tambourine), a galuk (a kind of clarionet), and others. The musicians seat themselves on the Mindari and begin to play.

As soon as the music starts, the dancers of the harem make their appearance entering by pairs, dancing.

These dancers have all been brought from different countries. For their beauty, as well as their skill and agility, they are considered to be the finest in the land. People have come from afar simply to see them, No stranger seeing their group dances could help being enraptured by them, and when each one dances the dance of her own country, the cleverest judges are moved to ecstasy.

There are twelve dancers, all of them dressed in their national costumes. Today, either because they feel the mood of their master or because it is long since they have danced before him, they dance with exceptional abandon.

First, a Tibetan performs one of the dances of her mysterious fatherland. Next, an Armenian from Mousha dances to the accompaniment of slow music an amorous dance of her country, almost drowsy, but full of hidden fire. She is followed by an Osetinka of the Caucasus in a dance light as air. Then a Gipsy, a daughter of the people who have forgotten their homeland, in a burning, whirling dance seems to speak of the freedom of the steppes and the distant fires of the camp. After her, an Arabian, beginning slowly then quickening and quickening her movements, attains a mad pace, then suddenly relaxes and gradually swoons in ecstasy. Then a Baluchistani, a Georgian, a Persian, an Indian Nautch girl—each one by her movements manifests the soul, the nature, the temperament and the character of her country.

Gafar, indifferent to everything else, has always delighted in his dancers, but today he looks at them almost without seeing them so completely is he immersed in his thoughts and feelings.

During one of the group dances the women envoys return. With a contrite look the old lady tells Gafar that his proposal is not accepted. Gafar become mad with rage, chases everyone out of the room and remains alone with Rossoula. They are both silent.

Gafar strides up and down the room. He could have expected anything, but not this. It is beyond everything. Never in his life has he had to experience such a humiliation. Rossoula is no less thunderstruck than Gafar. He stands in deep thought, and is evidently racking his brain. Presently his face clears and he goes up to Gafar and speaks to him.

Gafar listens with a gloomy face. What Rossoula proposes goes against his deepest feelings, but he is insulted and indignant and wishes at all costs to have his own way. His desire for Zeinab has almost turned to hatred, and the wish to have revenge for his humiliation overpowers him. Rossoula continues to persuade him. Finally, after a short struggle with himself, Gafar consents.

They call a servant and send him with a message.

Gafar again seats himself on the divan with a morose and wrathful expression. Rossoula wanders about the room rejoicing in his inventiveness and resource.

After a short time, an old sorceress enters accompanied by the servant.

She is short and bent with a large hooked nose, tousled grey hair and lively roving eyes, swarthy-faced with a large hairy wart on the left cheek, her long, thin sinewy hands have long dirty nails. She is dressed in a short soiled coat of violet color and black trousers; on her feet are old Turkish slippers; she is covered with a dirty black 'chuddar' patched in many places with colored scraps; in her hand is a plain stick.

Gafar asks the sorceress whether she can bewitch a woman into falling in love with him. The sorceress, with self-confident expression, replies affirmatively, but when she hears the name of the woman, she trembles with fear and says that in this case she is powerless. They offer her gold, but his time gold does not help.

The sorceress is unable to do anything herself, but she tells them that there is one person who, if he wishes, can bewitch Zeinab. It may be possible to persuade him, but it will be necessary to give him much, much gold.

Gafar and Rossoula consult together; they question the sorceress and evidently decide to set forth at once. The sorceress consents to guide them.

The servant enters and helps them on with their outer garments. Meanwhile, by Gafar's order, servants bring from the inner apartments bags filled with gifts. Then, accompanied by the servants carrying the bags, Gafar and Rossoula go out by the door at the back. Curtain.

Act Four

The school of the Black Magician.

A large cave. The back wall has a projection in the middle; to the right is an ascent to the entrance, to the left, a passage leading to an inner cave.

At the left-hand side in a dark recess is a kind of hearth or stove in which a fire is blazing. On the stove is a cauldron out of which clouds of greenish smoke escape occasionally. In front of the stove sits a shaggy half-naked creature who stirs the fire with a three-pronged fork of strange shape and now and then throws wood into the stove. In a niche above the stove is a human skeleton and more curiously shaped forks project from one side. In the center of the cave, towards the back, stands a large stone shaped like a throne-couch. On a pole above it is a symbol of the pentagram.

Hanging from the ceiling are various stuffed animals—an owl, a toad, bats, also human and animal skulls.

Here and there stand low tables with various objects scattered on them, and boltheads, glasses, books and rolls of parchment are lying in disorder about the cave.

A boa-constrictor glides around at liberty and black cats walk to and fro.

This is the school of the celebrated Black Magician.

When the curtain rises some of his pupils are moving about the cave; others are sitting down. A few are laying out cards as though telling fortunes; some are studying the lines of each other's hands, and some—collected in a corner—are preparing potions.

The pupils are men and women of varying ages, some young, others older, but all of unpleasing appearance. One or two are deformed, thin with disagreeable shifty eyes, disheveled hair and warts. The movements of all are sharp, angular and jerky. Their attitude towards each other is hostile and derisive. They are dressed in a slovenly fashion in short violet-colored coats and black trousers. On their feet are Turkish slippers. The only difference between the dress of the men and the women is that the women wear belts of black cord and have black handkerchiefs on their heads. Some of them are tattooed on the face and hands.

One of the pupils near the throne begins slowly to make strange, rhythmic movements which apparently please the others, for one by one they leave their various occupations and join him. As their number increases the movements quicken and become more and more varied and gradually they form themselves into a ring and begin to revolve madly round the throne. At the moment of greatest frenzy a noise and a knocking are heard at the left of the cave.

Instantly the ring breaks up. Disordered movements and bustle follow. Jostling one another with fear, the pupils rush back to their places and snatch up their former occupations trying to give the impression that they have never interrupted them.

From the inner cave the black Magician enters. He is a man of medium height, lean, with a short half-grey beard, black eyes with long eyelashes and thick unkempt hair. His movements are jerky with a characteristic manner of his own, his glance is contemptuously piercing. He is dressed in a short black silk coat beneath which is seen a glowing crimson under-garment a little longer than the coat. On his feet are Turkish slippers; on his head a black skullcap. In his hand is a long whip, and on his breast, hanging from a black silk cord, is a golden pentacle.

At the Magician's entrance all fall on their faces. He goes to the throne without looking at anyone; on the way he even steps on one of the pupils. He seats himself. (The symbol above the throne lights up at this moment.) He throws open his coat, baring his breast and his belly. The pupils in turn go up and kiss him on the belly. With a kick he knocks one of them over. The others with cowardly malevolence mock at the fallen one.

When the ceremony of kissing the belly is ended, the pupils at the Magician's order, place themselves in rows to right and left of him and at a sign from him they begin to perform various movements.

During one of the intervals the old sorceress comes in through the outer entrance with a candle in her hand. She goes slowly and fearfully up to the Black Magician, kisses him on the belly and says something to him in a cringing manner, pointing towards the entrance.

After a moment of reflection the Magician nods his head in consent. The old woman goes out backwards and quickly returns with Gafar, Rossoula and the two servants carrying the sacks of gifts. The servants come in trembling with fear and looking about them with astonishment and horror. When they reach the center of the cave they throw down the sacks and rush headlong away. Rossoula and even Gafar feel almost as much fear as the servants.

Gafar goes up to the Magician and tells him what he wishes. The Magician listens but when Gafar mentions the name of Zeinab, he absolutely refuses to do anything whatever, knowing, like the sorceress, that Zeinab is a pupil of the White Magician.

Gafar persists. Pointing to the sacks he pulls out his purse, draws a ring from his finger, takes off precious jewels and throws all before the Magician.

At the sight of the gold and jewels the Magician hesitates, and finally consents to cast the spell if Gafar can obtain something that has recently been in contact with Zeinab's person. Gafar reflects, then suddenly remembers the silk handkerchief which he bought from the beggar woman, and drawing it out he gives it to the Magician. The Magician points to the corner of the cave and bids him wait. Then in a powerful voice he gives some orders to his pupils.

Some of them move a table into the center of the cave and cover it with a black cloth bordered with the signs of the Zodiac and Kabalistic symbols, worked in red. Others go into the inner cave and bring out various objects including an ebony wand with a gold ball at the top and lump of soft clay which they place on the table. Next to the clay they place, opened, a thick book with strange hieroglyphics and the symbol of the hexagram and an urn, out of which projects a human thigh bone.

The Magician takes off his garment, receives some unguent from one of the pupils, smears it over his body, resumes his garment and over his usual dress puts on a robe with very wide sleeves. The robe is bordered all round with the signs of the Zodiac; on the back is embroidered the symbol of the pentagram, on the breast a skull and crossbones. On his head he places a high pointed head-dress embroidered with large and small stars.

Then he takes Zeinab's silk handkerchief and crumpling it up places it in the middle of the lump of clay, from which he models the likeness of a human figure. This he places on the table. Next, on the floor around the table, he draws a large circle within which all the pupils collect. The Magician stands near the table and gives a certain order to the pupils. They immediately form themselves into a chain, men and women alternating. The man standing on the Magician's right and the woman on his left, take hold of his elbows with their free hands. Some of the pupils remain outside the chain.

The Magician takes the wand in his right hand and with his left he makes certain movements and whispers incantations.

It is seen that the pupils in the chain contort themselves, making convulsive movements; some of them become weak and even fall. Their place is speedily taken by other pupils outside the chain who try to do this as quickly as possible so that the chain may not be broken.

The clay figure on the table gradually begins to light up, at first faintly, then more strongly and more brightly.

Two pupils are working at the stove; one constantly throws wood into it, the other stirs it up. The fire in the stove grows fiercer, long tongues of flame shoot out from it. As time goes on, the movements of the pupils in the chain become ever more violent and terrible; they are evidently exerting their utmost strength. The Magician himself is making an intense effort.

The clay figure lights up ever more and more strongly when the wand passes near it, and at intervals it gives out bright flashes. Above the cauldron a noise is heard which gradually increases, and at the moment when the noise becomes very loud, the light in the cave becomes dim and suddenly — above the stove — the shadow of Zeinab appears and slowly lights up. As the shadow brightens the steam escaping from the cauldron decreases. The flame in the stove burns even more fiercely. The sphere on the wand and the clay figure give out strong intermittent flashes. The Magician and all the pupils in the chain are terribly convulsed. The noise in the cave increases and becomes like claps of thunder and, at one of the terrible explosions, the cave is plunged in darkness.

Little by little the light re-appears. The shadow of Zeinab above the cauldron can no longer be seen. The flame in the stove has died down. The pupils utterly exhausted lie on the ground. Even the Magician is half-lying on his throne, weak and spent. One by one the pupils begin to rise. The less exhausted among them give the weaker ones something to drink and help them to rise.

The Magician having partially recovered, takes the clay figure, wraps it in a rag and gives it to Gafar with some instructions.

All that has happened has produced such an overwhelming impression on Gafar and Rossoula that at first they cannot move. However, after a while, with dragging footsteps they go out, accompanied by the old sorceress.

The Magician, by now fully recovered, takes the sacks with the gifts and scatters them on the ground. The pupils with wild rejoicings fling themselves on them and snatch them up, after which they dance in a ring round the Magician.

In the midst of the wildest dancing the curtain falls.

Act Five

The same scene as the Second Act.

When the curtain rises the White Magician and all his pupils with the exception of Zeinab are present.

The Magician and his assistant with whom he is talking are watching the pupils who, placed in groups, are performing movements resembling dancing.

Suddenly Haila rushes in, falls on her knees before the Magician and with excited gestures hurriedly tells him what has happened to Zeinab.

What she relates is so unexpected that at first the Magician can scarcely understand what she is trying to tell him. He is amazed. Reflecting deeply he rises and walks about the room. The pupils, too, are astounded. From time to time the Magician turns to the old woman in order to ask more details of the situation.

Finally he comes to a decision, and turning to his pupils he makes a proposal to them. Several of them express agreement. The Magician, having chosen one of them, places him on a chair, takes both his hands and looks into his eyes. It is seen that the pupil gradually falls asleep. When his eyes are closed the Magician makes several passes over him from head to foot. The pupil is now in a hypnotic sleep. The Magician puts several questions to the sleeping man. By the movements of his lips it is seen that the pupil answers. The room becomes half-dark.

The purport of the sleeper's answers is reproduced in a series of pictures which appear on the back wall.

Zeinab's room. She is alone. Each of her postures and movements, every expression of her face, bears witness to some powerful struggle within her. Sometimes she springs up and walks nervously about the room; at one moment she appears to conquer what torments her, at the next, overcome by something stronger than her reason, she falls helpless on the divan. She is suffering terribly; this is evident from her gestures which are full of grief and despair. At times it seems as though she were defending herself against something; her mind is stubbornly resisting a strange feeling or desire which has entered into her.

Haila, on entering, does not recognize her mistress, so entirely has Zeinab changed towards her. She hardly notices Haila, and to the old woman's words and entreaties she either pays no attention at all, or else replies with impatient gestures. The old woman goes out with a crestfallen expression.

Zeinab's torture has no end; the struggle within her increases and increases. Mixed feelings of fear, desire, curiosity, shame, alternate more and more rapidly within her. Now becoming very excited, then suddenly growing weaker, she hurries from spot to spot and can find no resting place for herself.

At the moment of her greatest agitation, Rossoula enters, bearing a tray of

The Struggle of the Magicians

jewels from Gafar. Zeinab is not in the least astonished at this unusual visit, on the contrary, it seems as though she had expected it.

Rossoula, after presenting the gifts, speaks to Zeinab, who with nervous agitation, questions him. She takes the jewels, and in an excited and automatic manner tries them on before the mirror. Rossoula, meanwhile, is trying to persuade her to some course to which she finally consents.

Haila again enters. She is amazed and can understand nothing, so unusual is all this for her. Realizing at last what is happening, she throws herself on her knees before Zeinab, imploring her not to consent to Rossoula's entreaties. But Zeinab appears completely changed. Impatiently tapping with her foot, she orders the old woman to be silent. Then rapidly throwing a cloak round her, she goes out with Rossoula.

Haila remains distracted, not knowing what to do. Suddenly she comes to a decision, puts on her shawl, and goes out hurriedly.

The picture vanishes. The ordinary light returns.

The Magician moves away from the sleeper and walks about the room, greatly perplexed. His assistant, making several passes over the sleeper from foot to head, awakens him and one of the pupils gives him a drink.

The Magician now realizes what has happened. He is indignant and at the same time alarmed. Having walked agitatedly up and down the room several times, he seats himself on a chair and reflects deeply. Suddenly he gets up and gives an order to the assistant and to the pupils.

They carry out his instructions rapidly. They move a table into the center of the room and clear the space around it. From the inner room they bring various things: certain vestments, various appurtenances, and the wand on its cushion. They cover the tables with a white cloth on the border of which are embroidered astronomical signs and chemical formulas.

The Magician robes himself. He draws maniples over his hands; puts on a special girdle and a peculiar kind of covering on his feet, resembling rubber. On his head he puts a kind of crown, a broad fillet with three cones, the sharp ends pointing upwards. Over his coat he puts a robe resembling a chasuble. Meanwhile the pupils, under the direction of the Magician's assistant, also get ready, putting similar coverings on their feet and girdles round their waists. They wash their hands, shaking them downwards a few times, and then take some kind of drink.

The Magician is now ready. He takes a vessel like a large bowl and places it in front of him; another vessel of similar shape, but smaller, he puts at the opposite end of the table. The two vessels are connected by a copper bar. The pupils hand him a liquid which he pours into the vessel. Around the first vessel stand nine candles, six are alight and three are unlighted. Having taken the wand in his left hand, the Magician makes certain movements with his right hand, and pronounces some unknown words. At the same time four of the pupils, two men on the right and two girls on the left, make passes above the smaller vessel.

It is noticeable how soon they become exhausted doing this. Immediately they are replaced by other pairs. Gradually the larger vessel begins to emit light from within. At the moment when this light first appears, the three unlighted candles light up. Every time the Magician brings the wand near to the vessel a spark appears, and as time goes on the spark grows stronger and stronger. The candles and the symbol above the throne burn more brightly. The ceremony continues. The movements of the Magician become ever more energetic and intense. The noise within the vessel increases, and, at the moment of greatest uproar, there is a terrible crackling within the vessel, and a fearful explosion takes place.

Immediately there is complete darkness, after which, by degrees, a half-light returns, and on the back wall a picture appears showing a portion of the cave of the Black Magician, who, seated on his throne, contorts himself, making convulsive movements. The White Magician continues his manipulations. Again there is a terrific explosion, followed by an echo from behind the scenes, and accompanied by shrill whistling sounds and great uproar. The Black Magician falls in convulsions from his throne. There is again a moment of complete darkness and oppressive silence, after which the light returns and the picture of the cave disappears.

The White Magician is greatly exhausted; the pupils who assisted him are no less spent than he, but the work continues. Quickly they take away the vessels and candles from the table. They remove the table and in its place they put an armchair in which the Magician seats himself. Around him stand the pupils. The Magician, holding the wand in his hand, closes his eyes and whisper some words with concentration. Gradually the light grows dim again. Another picture appears. It shows a part of Gafar's room. He is half-lying on the divan and with an expression of joy and self-satisfaction looks towards the inner room. Apparently he expects someone.

Zeinab enters with a woman, who bowing low before Gafar, motions with her hand towards Zeinab and immediately goes out backwards.

Gafar rises, takes Zeinab by the hand and is about to seat her on the divan, when all at once, with a sudden start, they both become rooted to the spot in exactly those postures in which they were standing. After a short pause, they turn, like automata, and go out of the room.

The streets and alleys through which they pass like sleeping people, flash by. The picture vanishes. The former light again returns, and at this moment Gafar and Zeinab enter. Both are in a somnambulistic state. At their appearance the Magician, with a sigh of relief, gets up and begins to disrobe. The assistant with some of the pupils place Gafar and also Zeinab on chairs, and awaken Zeinab.

Zeinab, on coming to herself, asks those around her what is the matter. They explain what has happened, pointing to the sleeping Gafar. She suddenly remembers, bursts into sobs, and with gestures of penitence, throws herself at the feet of the Magician.

He, having finished his disrobing, bends down to her, and stroking her hair, raises her from the ground. Then he goes to Gafar who has already come to himself. Gafar is at first dumbfounded, but, learning what has happened, he grows excited and almost threatens the Magician. The latter with a calm smile answers him. Gafar listens and gradually becomes more composed. The Magician continues to talk, accompanying his words with gestures and pointing to the back of the room where once more a picture appears.

A street with a crowd of people is seen; there are women, children and old people. From a side street comes Gafar; he is old, bent and feeble. He is followed by some bright being. In spite of his age, Gafar is evidently very happy and cheerful. In the crowd he is greeted by everyone, women and men bow low to him and children bring him flowers. All is joy, happiness and blessing.

The Magician goes on speaking. The picture changes.

The same street with a crowd of people. Again Gafar appears, but this time he is accompanied by a terrible being of dark red hue. Gafar is an old man with an evil and dissatisfied face. Those who meet him turn aside with aversion and spit in his footsteps; the boys throw stones at him; their disgust is plain, and it is obvious that everyone is revolted by the sight of him.

The picture vanishes. The Magician continues to speak. Gafar is evidently perturbed and overwhelmed by some inner struggle.

The chief point of what the Magician has said is this: As you sow, so shall you reap. The deeds of the present determine the future, all that is good and all that is bad; both are results of the past. It is the duty of every man in every moment of the present to prepare the future, improving on the past. Such is the law of fate. And 'May the source of all laws be blessed.'

At this moment the light again becomes dim; some movement is seen. When the light returns, the assistant is standing on the Magician's right and Zeinab on his left; she is kissing the hand of the Magician. Gafar is at his feet in an attitude of reverence. Around the throne and about the room the pupils stand in various attitudes.

The Magician raises his right hand aloft. He looks upwards and whispers these words as if in prayer:

'Lord Creator, and all you His assistants, help us to be able to remember ourselves at all times in order that we may avoid involuntary actions, as only through them can evil manifest itself.'

All sing, 'Forces become transformed to be.'

The Magician again blesses them all with both hands and says, 'May reconciliation, hope, diligence and justice be ever with you all.'

All sing, 'Amen.'

Curtain

Essays

P. D. Uspenskii

Why I Left Gurdjieff (1926)

IN CONNECTION WITH MY LEAVING THERE ARISES A WHOLE SERIES OF QUESTIONS:

1. If G.'s system is true in my eyes, if I admitted it to be "esoteric," how could it come to pass that I left him?
2. Is G. the "teacher" of whom he himself speaks, and if so, again how could I leave him?
3. Can a "teacher" cease to be a teacher if he is a true teacher? And, can the attitude of the pupil toward the teacher change?
4. Did G.'s circles and his work represent an esoteric "school" and in particular a "school of The Fourth Way" of which he spoke?

I will endeavor to answer these questions.

First of all the question of whether G. was the teacher of whom he himself speaks.

I consider that G. was my teacher in exactly this sense during the period of time from the autumn of 1916 to the middle of 1918. After this however, some very essential change took place between G. and myself.

Then the second question, whether a teacher can cease to be a teacher and whether the attitude of the pupil toward the teacher can change.

In my opinion a teacher cannot cease to be a teacher and the attitude of the pupil toward the teacher cannot change. But this does not mean that a man has no right and no possibility, without abandoning his work, to leave the particular teacher with whom he had begun work, if there are changes in the teacher's work.

The right attitude toward both the teacher and the work cannot mean that a man is once and for all tied to the particular school (or attempt at a school) with which he had come into contact or into which he had been drawn. There exists however a general rule of which I was aware even before I met G., and namely, that a man who leaves one teacher because he could not overcome certain difficulties or refuses to submit to certain demands, meets under another teacher (if he succeeds in finding one) *literally* the same difficulties and *literally* the same demands, possibly even in an intensified form. There cannot be the slightest misunderstanding, because the character of the demands made upon him and the nature of the difficulties on his way are determined by the man's own features and qualities. But this rule is valid only in the case of a perfect school. If a man was forced to leave through lack of organization in the school or through wrong demands made upon him, this does not at all mean that the same demands will arise again.

For some people all the questions enumerated and examined above are rendered still more confused and complicated by the question as to whether G.'s groups and his work constituted a "school" and in particular a "school of The Fourth Way," of which he spoke. To this I can answer quite definitely that the question is simply naive.

All that G. said about "schools" was simply an elucidation of the principles which render the existence of a school possible. G. never called his groups an esoteric school. And to understand all I have said earlier concerning schools in the sense that it definitely referred to our groups, would be certainly wrong. G. brought with him many new ideas, and particularly many new ideas about schools. This fact explains why it had seemed at first as though his activity could lead to the foundation of a school. But it would be utterly wrong to see in everything that took place *an already existing school.*

Such an interpretation would distort the fundamental idea.

Returning to the question of leaving a school one may say that to leave even a perfectly organized school may sometimes be quite right and legitimate. A man always approaches a school with his eyes closed. At school his eyes open and he may see that this school is not for him. Moreover, his eyes may open both in a right and a wrong school, for a wrong school is always an imitation of the right one.

At the same time one must bear in mind that a "school" in the true sense of the word is a phenomenon so rare that to use it in the plural that is to say "schools," is almost impossible. If a man happened to come into contact with one school and then left it, it is almost certain to be that he will never find another school. It can never happen that a man's field of vision contains two schools between which he may choose. To believe that it is possible for a man to leave one school and to enter another is in itself "pseudo-occultism."

And of course, when I decided to leave G. I knew no other school and no other G. More than that, I knew for certain that I would never find anything of its kind or even if I ever happened to meet something like a school, it would be after many years, in quite different surroundings, in quite different circumstances, which I could neither foresee nor foretell. Consequently it was not at all easy for me to leave G. and I did not deceive myself with false expectations and hopes. I knew that something had failed. Why it had failed was another question, and I preferred to leave it unanswered.

The formal reason of my leaving G. in 1918 was the fact that I could not accept certain demands which he made on me. I have spoken before about many of his demands which were very hard for me to accept, but which I nevertheless accepted.

The first of these demands was the fact that I had to work in a group with people who seemed to me quite unprepared for work; then, the fact that I had to accept theories which seemed absurd at first; the next was the fact that I had to introduce people to G. and to take upon myself the responsibility for doing so without the slightest idea of what he intended to do with them. Further, my work with G. actually demanded that I should abandon my own work, that I should remain in Russia after the revolution, in spite of my thinking it absurd, and so on. Besides this, at a certain definite moment in 1916 I had to accept a series of demands of a very difficult personal character. All this was not at all easy, but I realized perfectly that everything I received from G. was only due to my submitting to his demands.

Yet, in spite of this I decided to leave him, because later his demands acquired a character to which I could not agree.

Unfortunately I can say nothing about the demands which determined the character of my subsequent relations with G. Any attempt to describe these demands or to explain why I refused to accept them would inevitably acquire a character of self-justification and a desire that G. was in the wrong. Neither the one nor the other enters my intention. But the fact remains that I did not find it possible to accept certain demands, which were either directly made upon me as a condition of my further work with G., or followed from his actions. As a result of all this I drew apart from G. and his work.

Apart from these demands which I refused to accept there were two kinds of demands which I also resisted although for different reasons.

The first category included all demands which were insignificant in themselves, but which forced me to do things that went very much against my nature. At times my resistance to these demands may perhaps have seemed ridiculous to anybody not concerned, but on several instances these demands touched upon those sides of my nature which I was unable to overcome.

"One must ridicule oneself," said G. once, not directly referring to these demands, but in connection with them. I understood his idea, I understood that submission to these demands would have given me a remarkable chance of "acting." And yet, I did not submit to them. The question as to whether G. was right or wrong in making upon me these demands never even entered my head. Of course he was right in principle; although on the other hand I must say that the two particular demands which I refused to accept and which excited most comment contained sides which fully justified my refusal to submit to them. Besides, in relation to these demands I was never quite sure whether G. was serious in demanding one or another thing or whether he only wished to test me and to see what my resistance was based on and whether I could, and knew how, to resist him without losing my temper and without it interfering with the general trend of my work.

Then there were other demands about which I can say candidly that I never understood them and do not understand them even to this day.

These demands appeared firstly in several instances of my literary work with G. when I was editing some of his writings; and secondly in conversations with new people who came to us. In the first instance, that is, in literary work, G. definitely demanded *bad work* and this especially amazed me for there were moments when he showed very fine taste and a great understanding of form. But at times his demands were ridiculous, illiterate and absurd—and it was quite impossible to convince him of this.

All great men have their weaknesses. G.'s weakness was his conviction that he could write if he wished—the very thing he could not do. Very soon after my first meeting with him I knew that although owing to his birth and education in a polyglot country between the East and the West he could speak seven or eight languages, he knew none of them thoroughly and his writings in Russian were full of impotent efforts to express things for which he had no forms, were unnecessarily long, and full of endless repetitions and platitudes. In a word they rather reminded me of the literary efforts of provincial amateurs with which I had to deal in my youth in the editorial offices of various newspapers and periodicals. His speech was incorrect but full of life and force. His writings were impotent and lifeless. Fortunately he never attempted to publish any of them. Although at the same time he always refused to admit that he could not write and, for instance, in correcting his already edited manuscripts, he was wont to insert in a long paragraph some new word which spoiled the whole meaning and demanded that I should adapt the whole paragraph to this new word, or else insisted on some quite impossible combination of words. At other times he was completely unable to understand the hidden meaning of a given combination of words and stood up for the meaning which he ascribed to them.

In Constantinople in 1920 he gave me the text of his scenario of the ballet called "The Struggle of the Magicians" to correct. Later I shall speak of the idea of this ballet. But the scenario was written in the language of Armenian anecdotes. "The stage is in complete darkness . . . noise, rumbling, movement . . . the darkness increases. . ." and so on.

And G. argued with me about every little correction which I made and insisted that I should preserve his text. One scene had a sentence with an unmistakable double meaning which he could in no way wish but he could not understand why I protested. His demands concerning conversations with the new people were still worse. He often demanded that these people should be told strange, exaggerated and absurd things which made them smile uncertainly and look away. Moreover he often said himself perfectly incredible things and demanded that I or the others should support him and corroborate what he said.

This, however, related to his "acting." After "demands" the most difficult point was G.'s "acting." He confused and muddled people so much that they finally lost all sense of the right and the left side. This was the system. And sometimes G. even explained it. He said that a man ought to be so sure of his right and his left sides that it should be quite impossible to confuse him. And so long as he could be confused, he must be confused. But it was strange that in many cases he evidently could not stop himself and continued to "act" even when his "acting" had become too obvious and produced results directly opposed to the ones he expected.

It was still more strange when his "acting" extended to people who had nothing to do with our work who crossed our path by accident or who joined us for a short time and, having left, protested loudly and unequivocally against this "acting" which they called by quite a different name. Altogether, G.'s "acting" was the most difficult point. Many people remained with him so long as they believed in "acting" and left when they ceased to see "acting" and began to see the "genuine thing" and many things that passed as "acting."

On the whole people around G. fell into two categories—those who saw "acting" in all G.'s strange actions and those who did not see it. I do not propose to decide which of them was right.

Now, speaking of G.'s "demands" and his "acting" together, I come to the most interesting point.

The point is that no matter whether G. was right or wrong in everything he did and demanded, my arguments remain the same. In other words, what I want to say is that it is quite impossible in this particular case to establish by means of argument who was right and who was wrong. Both the one who is right and the one who is wrong would say exactly the same thing. I remember cases when people who protested against G. and his methods were unquestionably wrong. And yet I also remember other cases when from my point of view people were right. This is very difficult to understand in words but it must be understood. In this particular case truth cannot be discovered through arguments, it lies deeper than words and facts.

At the same time this does not mean that there were no criteria for distinguishing the right from the wrong, but expressed in words these criteria cease to be at all convincing.

One of the criteria for judging about the given moment of the work was for me personally the character of the people who were following G. at that particular moment. People always changed around him. One moment one kind of people gathered around him, another moment—another kind. And at times G. was surrounded by a very strange crowd.

The characteristic feature of the summer of 1918 was the appearance together in our work and in our house of a great number of new people many of whom knew nothing about the ideas of our work and who temporarily followed G. simply driven to it by the force of circumstances, such as the revolution, the famine in Moscow and St. Petersburg, etc.

Of course the presence of these people in our midst made life in the big house very difficult for those who wanted to work in accordance with the principles with which we had begun.

Partly in this connection we once had a conversation which remained in my memory of some of the people in the work.

"It is very easy to make everybody's life here pleasant and comfortable" said G. once, "but then where would the work be, work consists in surrounding difficulties. Everybody knows it, everybody has agreed to it. And yet, when I create difficulties, people refuse to accept them and accuse me of not making their work lighter. I can easily arrange a very pleasant life for everyone here. What is the sense of doing this? I thought you wanted to work!"

These words were often repeated later by some of the people who remained with him. But I never could bring myself to agree with them.

First of all I could not agree that there was but one alternative, that it was to be either a "pleasant life," or the difficulties we had in the big house. In my opinion there was a fundamental mistake at the very root of such a proposition. "Work," the work I wanted, contained many more difficulties, demanded much more resolution, much more courage and more readiness to risk and to suffer, than the work which was going on in the big house. The work we wanted did not at all mean an easy life. On the contrary, compared with the difficulties of this work the hardships of the work in the big house seemed to me very small. At the same time these difficulties of the new directions which G.'s work had taken were somehow aimless and led nowhere. The new work, as I saw it, lost touch with the *search for the miraculous,* sank into an everyday life, became a kind of "existence." All the difficulties were difficulties of a work-a-day character. This everyday life absorbed everything. Completely obscured all sense of the aim. It made us forget where we were going and why. And of course some people in the work very soon conceived the idea that merely through this "existence," through submission and obedience, without any other strivings, they would be able to attain something.

And later when the center of gravity of G.'s work was transferred to "movements," which were extremely interesting in themselves but which give rise to an enormous amount of false interpretations, there appeared a theory that without the help of any intellectual effort, the study of movement should in itself change a man's essence and lead him to another plane of being.

All this was of course pure fantasy, and a fantasy of a very cheap character, depriving G.'s ideas of all value, making them heavy and blurred, and in its turn giving rise to a whole series of other vague guesses and suppositions.

And finally (this happened in 1923 in Fontainebleau) I heard from one of G.'s new pupils an extraordinary phrase:

"We do not ask *why*."

I remember thinking at the time that if in St. Petersburg, seven or eight years previously, we were to define the meaning and significance of all the work which we were beginning, we would have said that we begin it precisely in order to ask "Why?"

At Essentuki in 1918 such a phrase was still impossible, but as I have already said the demands which G. put before me, in my opinion, contradicted the fundamental aims and forced me to refuse to work with him and to leave his house.

My leaving G. and everything I said at the time as well as later did not and does not show any distrust of G. or any doubt in him. I did not see anything actually negative and did not look for it. And this looking for negative sides which seemed to be the chief object of some of the people who joined us was always incomprehensible to me and seemed to be a strange peculiarity in a definite type of people.

Even during the first years of my acquaintance with G. there came to us from time to time people who very quickly discovered in G.'s ideas and actions what they thought to be negative sides. Many of them were clever people. They saw these negative sides and left. But who lost by it? Naturally only they. I saw this quite well and endeavored to remain with G. as long as it was possible. When it became too opposed to my fundamental aims and intentions I left.

However, I understood from the very first that a critical or a negative attitude toward G. himself and his ideas would be essentially wrong. And not only would it be wrong, but it would also be *impossible* owing to the fact that I admitted his ideas to have an "esoteric" origin.

"Esotericism" excludes all possibility of criticism. One may accept esoteric ideas and methods, or one may refuse to accept them, but one cannot criticize them, because it is impossible to find anything on which this criticism could be founded.

This criticism cannot be founded on scientific thought, because esotericism repudiates scientific thought. It cannot be founded on logic because esotericism does not recognize logic. It cannot be founded on common sense, because esotericism denies common sense. It cannot be founded on anything, because esotericism denies all the foundation of our thought, it rejects all the recognized values and establishes in their stead its own values which one may accept or not accept, but against which one can say nothing.

Esoteric system, esoteric methods, esoteric school, all this either becomes straightaway inaccessible to all criticism or ceases to be esoteric.

Suppose that you see an incongruity in a system the origin of which you recognize as esoteric. You say that this is an absurdity, that it contradicts everything, that it is even opposed to all we know about esotericism. And in answer to this you are told:

"What after all do you know of esotericism? Have you not admitted that you know nothing? Perhaps all this is done on purpose in order to see in what way each person takes it?"

And you realize that there is nothing more to be said to this.

Or suppose that you see the failure of the work which was planned and began. You say: "This is an obvious fiasco, an obvious failure."

And in answer you are told: "Did you know the aim? Perhaps what you call 'failure' was actually the aim."

It is clear that nothing more can be said to such arguments. One must either accept them as a possible interpretation or abandon all attempt to unite things that could not be united.

As I have said before, I realize this from the very first. I understood that this constitutes one of the principles of an esoteric school's existence. An esoteric school does not concern itself with proofs of its rightness or its origin. Its proofs are its ideas. If it does not produce new ideas, it cannot be recognized as esoteric. The person who does not recognize the very idea of esotericism will never see an esoteric school.

On the other hand, however, if a school is accessible to observation, be it only in its outward form, and if it is outwardly open, its work cannot be concealed from those who wish to see it. If there is nothing that can be called "work," one cannot speak of a school. But this again can be understood many different ways and people may call "work" anything they please.

OPSL, Original draft of ISOM, Folder 1688
The Gurdjieff Journal, Vol 16, No. 1

THE STRUGGLE OF THE MAGICIANS: WHERE I DIVERGE FROM GURDJIEFF

STRANGELY ENOUGH, TWO OR THREE FEATURES IN THIS AND ESPECIALLY ONE SCENE WENT A LONG WAY IN EXPLAINING TO ME THE REASON IN PRINCIPLE OF MY DIVERGENCE WITH GURDJIEFF.

The chief dramatic element lies in the scenes of the two magical ceremonies of the Black Magician and the White Magician. The whole struggle between the two magicians is contained in these two ceremonies. And here the first thing that struck me unpleasantly was the realization that the ceremony of the White Magician was too much like the ceremony of the Black Magician. In both cases, allowing for slight differences in the ritual, it was what is known as "envoutement"—deprivation of will power. However according to my ideas, "deprivation of will power" was the very thing that could not be practiced in the school of the *White Magician*. I may even go so far as to say that for me this impossibility constituted the difference between the schools of the White Magician and Black Magician. "Envoutement" could be practiced in the school of the White Magician only as an experiment. In the school of the Black Magician it could be practiced for the purpose of attaining a certain definite object. The whole idea of the White Magician's school ought to have consisted in the development of will and consciousness, and forcible removal of will and consciousness, even temporarily and prompted by the best intentions, could never lead to this. From the standpoint of a rightly understood idea of "school" it would have been much better for Zeinab if she were left in the hands of Gafar to go through all the consequences of the spell and later through repentance, regret and the realization of her fall to return unaided to the right path, perhaps, even bringing Gafar with her. This would have been esotericism, this would have been a true "struggle of the magicians." The White Magician ought to have been strong in his very passivity in relation to evil. But in Gurdjieff's scenario there was actually no difference between the White and Black Magicians except in the staging of the ceremonies. Both employed the same means, that is, violence, forcible removal of will.

Gurdjieff evidently attached a great importance to this scene of the White Magician's magical ceremony and the scenario contained a very minute description of how Gafar and Zeinab, suddenly plunged into a trance, walk in the streets like automatons, neither seeing nor noticing anything. This was to be staged with the help of cinematograph, the pictures succeeding one another on the back wall of the White Magician's school after the ceremony. In other words, when the ceremony of envoutement is over, the pupils see Gafar's house and Gafar with Zeinab. All at once both become frozen in their postures, then turn about like automatons, leave the house and walk through the streets but when I read the description of this scene and of this automatic movement of Gafar and Zeinab, and when at the same time I remembered all that Gurdjieff had said about the division of the dances into dances of the White Magician and dances of the Black Magician I suddenly said to myself—"But this is the Black Magician's dance!" and all those who took part in these dances and with whom I talked about it later agreed with me that only among the dances (or exercises) of the Black Magician were their movements similar to those which Gafar and Zeinab were supposed to do in this scene.

This fact made me think and explained much to me. It also helped me to formulate to myself the cause of my divergence with Gurdjieff.

Gurdjieff began by demanding consciousness in work, and passed to the demand of submission. He lowered the standard of his demands, became satisfied with mechanical submission. As he failed to keep up with the style of the White Magician in his scenario so he failed to keep up with the style with which he began his work. The future proved that at least in certain respects I was right. The new style of work began to attract to G. and to gather around him people of quite another type than before. And later it became so accentuated that at times it was quite impossible for people who came to Gurdjieff with ideas similar to mine, to work with him.

Naturally I do not want to say that I believe in a real existence of White and Black Magic. This idea is purely artificial. By its very nature magic can only be of one kind, there can be no two opposite magics. And before, in St. Petersburg, Gurdjieff often said that if there could be at all such a thing as a Black Magician he was known to be nothing but a half educated person, a man who has been in a school, but has not finished it and who has begun to practice magic as he understood it, on his own risk and on his own responsibility. Moreover, it clearly followed from Gurdjieff's words that such a Black Magician could not obtain any results except purely subjective ones, that is, hypnosis, and self-hypnosis and could never and on no condition be placed on the same level as a man who had actually gone through a school, a man who could "do." Moreover, and this was a very interesting point in Gurdjieff's explanations, Black Magic was not created by the motive. In other words, the Black Magician could be prompted by the very best intentions; his actions could be actuated by the idea of good, of knowledge, of light and so on, as he understood them. What made him a Black Magician was first of all the fact that he had not finished his education and consequently acted with incomplete knowledge (even if he knew anything at all); secondly that he was acting on his own having broken his connection with the school; and thirdly that he used (or attempted to use) mechanical means in circumstances where the "school" would not have allowed mechanical means to be used.

However, in his scenario of the "Struggle of the Magicians," Gurdjieff appeared to renounce these definitions and his "White Magician" differed from the "Black Magician" only in motives.

OPSL, Original draft of ISOM, Folder 1688

WILLIAM PATRICK PATTERSON

GURDJIEFF IN EGYPT: THE ORIGIN OF ESOTERIC KNOWLEDGE

THE SEARCH FOR THE SOURCE OF THE ANCIENT TEACHING OF HARMONIOUS SELF-DEVELOPMENT THAT MR. GURDJIEFF BROUGHT HAS ALWAYS BEEN TO THE EAST. Certainly elements can be found in such diverse places as Safed, Bokhara, Kurdistan, Azerbaijan, Mt. Athos and Sheikh Adi. But the knowledge that dwells in these areas, even if all linked together, does not resonate with the depth and richness, the completeness, of Gurdjieff's Fourth Way teaching. An area that has been given little attention is Khem or Khemet (meaning "black earth"), or Egypt, as it is presently known.

But when Gurdjieff first spoke of the origin of the teaching he spoke not of the East but of Egypt. Uspenskii reports that during the short Essentuki period from mid-July to August 1917, with the mass psychosis of the impending civil war becoming more feverish, Gurdjieff "unfolded to us the plan of the whole work. We saw the beginnings of all the methods, the beginnings of all the ideas, their links, their connections and direction." It was then, according to Olga de Hartmann, that he also answered the question all his students wanted to know: how did the teaching begin?

"The beginning," said Gurdjieff, "was a prearranged meeting in Egypt at the foot of one of the pyramids. There three persons met after long years of separate work in places where initiation centers were still maintained."

One man was a man of science, the second a connoisseur of religions and their histories, and the third "could be called a 'man of being.'"

In the late 1920s, when writing *Meetings with Remarkable Men*, Gurdjieff described this meeting in richer detail. Having recently come across a map of presand Egypt, he was just outside Cairo at the Giza Plateau, the site of the Sphinx and the Pyramid of Cheops, where he worked as a professional tour guide. It was here that he first met Professor Skridlov, an archaeologist, and Prince Lubovedsky. The Pyramid of Cheops, or Khufu, as the pharaoh of that period was known, is thought to have been erected between 2551–2528 BC. The earliest pyramids are believed to date to Egypt's Early Dynastic Period (3050–2575 BC). It should be noted that Gurdjieff told Uspenskii that Christianity came "in ready-made form from Egypt." And not from historical Egypt but from prehistoric Egypt "many thousands of years before the birth of Christ." In other words, about 2500 BC or earlier.

Some, most notably the Egyptologist and symbolist R. A. Schwaller de Lubicz (1891–1962), believe the Sphinx to be even older than all of Egypt's 5,500 years of estimated history—much older than the pyramids. Schwaller de Lubicz observed that the severe erosion of the body of the Sphinx of Giza is due to the action of water, not of wind and sand. This viewpoint is gaining scientific credibility because of recently discovered watermarks on the Sphinx. In agreement is the noted Egyptologist John Anthony West, who says:

> If the single fact of the water erosion of the Sphinx could be confirmed, it would in itself overthrow all accepted chronologies of the history of civilization; it would force a drastic reevaluation of the assumption of "progress"—the assumption upon which the whole of modern education is based. It would be difficult to find a single, simple question with graver implications. The water erosion of the Sphinx is to history what the convertibility of matter into energy is to Physics.
>
> An abstract of our team's work was submitted to the Geological Society of America, and we were invited to present our findings at a poster session at the GSA convention in San Diego in October 1992—the Geological Superbowl. Geologists from all over the world thronged our booth, much intrigued. Dozens of experts in fields relevant to our research offered help and advice. Shown the evidence, some geologists just laughed, astounded ... that in two centuries of research, no one, geologist or Egyptologist, had noticed the obvious—that the Sphinx had been weathered by water.

Egypt, the Sphinx and the pyramids were also of great interest to Uspenskii. Traveling in Egypt some fourteen years after Gurdjieff, Uspenskii felt it "as extraordinarily real, as though I was suddenly transferred into another world, which to my own astonishment I seemed to know very well. At the same time I was aware that this world was the distant past. But here it ceased to be past, appeared in everything, surrounded me, became the present. This was a very strong sensation and was strangely definite." Uspenskii recognized the pyramid as an observatory which was also "a whole library on physics, mathematics and astronomy; or, to be still more exact, it was a 'physico-mathematical faculty,' and at the same time a 'depository of measures.'" In *Beelzebub's Tales* Gurdjieff also speaks of pyramids as astronomical observatories.

Coming from Cairo, as Gurdjieff did, there are only two possible entrances to Giza. One is to enter by way of the Pyramid of Cheops, as Uspenskii would some years later, and the other is by the Sphinx. Gurdjieff, apparently, entered by the Sphinx and was hired as a guide by Professor Skridlov. "We were walking from the Sphinx towards the Pyramid of Cheops," wrote Gurdjieff, when they were hailed by the Russian Prince Lubovedsky, an old friend of the Professor's.

Gurdjieff writes on many levels, each having its own meaning. Thus, exactly where Gurdjieff places the scene of the first encounter between himself, Professor Skridlov, and Prince Lubovedsky may have important symbolic significance—a site used for the scientific purposes of a prehistoric civilization that may have predated the ancient Egyptians. Given the emphasis on the scientific in the teaching that Gurdjieff brought to the West, his placing the men's first awareness of one another in this location is not surprising.

Interpreting symbolically, Gurdjieff, the man of being, and Skridlov, the man of science, are walking from the prehistoric period into the historic—from the Sphinx to the Pyramid of Cheops—when they hear Prince Lubovedsky call out. The first part of "Lubovedsky," interestingly enough, in Russian means love. So, in effect, Cheops is the location of the first encounter between being, reason, and love, and from this sacred triad springs what will be a modern reformulation of an ancient teaching. Note that Gurdjieff will tell Uspenskii "The teaching whose theory is here being set out is *completely self-supporting* and independent of other lines and it has been *completely unknown* up to the present time." [Emphasis added.]

Recognizing one another, the Professor and the Prince sat down at the foot of Cheops with Gurdjieff, the guide, not far away listening and eating a chourek (traditional Greek bread). The two men speak in a style reminiscent of two other Seekers After Truth, Pogossian and Yelov, though their remarks are not as biting. In the conversation, which most readers are likely to pass up because of its deprecatory nature, each man defines the other's chief desire, or idée fixe. The Prince asks the Professor if he is still "collecting the utterly worthless rubbish supposedly once used in their stupid lives?" And the Professor, for his part, attacks the Prince, saying he is looking "for truth invented once upon a time by some crazy idler." In this disguised manner, Gurdjieff informs the reader of what he himself is doing in Egypt.

Finally, the Professor and the Prince leave one another, "arranging another meeting in ancient Thebes." Because Gurdjieff has dark skin and converses with them in Italian, both men take him to be an Italian, that is, not one of them, which is to say that neither 'sees' him. Thus, there is no real meeting yet between the three. Several days later, Gurdjieff writes, he was at the site spending all "my free time walking among these places like one possessed, hoping to find, with the help of my map of pre-sand Egypt, an explanation of the Sphinx and of certain other monuments of antiquity." One such monument must be the Pyramid of Cheops.

Deeper than Gurdjieff's and the Prince's ancestry or language is their interest in pre-sand Egypt. It is the map of pre-sand Egypt which brings them together. The map, therefore, has a significance beyond itself. Gurdjieff writes that he was at one of the pyramids, most likely not the Pyramid of Cheops or he would have mentioned it, and looking at the map in an emotional state, when "suddenly," he says, "I felt that someone was standing over me." The sight of the map has produced in the Prince a like emotional state. "Pale and in great agitation, he asked me in Italian how and where I had obtained this map," says Gurdjieff. He "at once guessed" that this was the same prince the Armenian priest had described at whose house he had secretly copied the map. The two men speak for a while and then the Prince invites Gurdjieff back to his apartment in Cairo to "quietly continue" their conversation. Why quietly? Because what they were discussing should not be discussed openly. The word must be given this meaning, as earlier in the same sentence Gurdjieff reports, "the prince had become quite calm again."

Later, Gurdjieff reports that he traveled with the Prince to the ancient city of Thebes where the Prince and Professor Skridlov had arranged to meet. Originally known as Uast or Waset, City of the Scepter, the Greeks gave this city the name Thebes (Thebai). The Romans called it Diospolis Magna, "the Great City of the Gods." Correctly so, in that Thebes is the site of the Temple of Karnak and Temple of Man, and just across the Nile lies the mountainous and majestic Valley of the Kings where the pharaohs were entombed. It is interesting that Gurdjieff never uses the modern name for Thebes, which is Luxor (from the Arabic *al-qusur*—The Palaces—as it was called by Arabs). Though this meeting is taking place in contemporary time, Gurdjieff may be directing the reader to understand that the meeting is really ancient, beyond ordinary psychological and calendar time, and therefore archetypal. It may be important, as well, to remember that Gurdjieff has not traveled to Thebes with Professor Skridlov, whom he met first, but with Prince Lubovedsky—this is the first of many such expeditions with the Prince. Interpreting this symbolically, it could be said that, in effect, the Prince and Gurdjieff have traveled from the prehistoric being of the Sphinx to the scientific observatory of the pyramid of Cheops, to ancient Egypt's most sacred site, Thebes. A journey then of being in the company of love to meet science.

Thebes lies some four hundred miles south of Cairo. It was certainly a long enough trip for the two men to form a firm and lasting bond. Thereafter, Gurdjieff says, "We met often, and our correspondence continued uninterruptedly for almost thirty-five years."

At Thebes, Gurdjieff reports his second meeting with Professor Skridlov: "Soon after this I met him again in ancient Thebes, where I ended my first trip with Prince Yuri Lubovedsky and where the professor joined us to make some excavations." It is here, on the sacred ground of Thebes, not the scientific ground of Giza, that the men become "such intimate and good friends."

The principal and largest structure in Thebes is Karnak whose two-hundred-fifty acres of temples, chapels, obelisks, columns and statues comprise "the most remarkable religious complex ever built on earth." Thebes, and especially Karnak, is dedicated to the god Amon, who was known in earlier eras but attained preeminence during the New Kingdom (1550–1070 BC) in which Thebes became the capital of Egypt. The name Amon means "hidden." He figured in the Hermopolitan myths associated with the dynamic force of life. Hermopolis was the capital of Upper Egypt and a cult center for Thoth, the god of learning and wisdom. Thoth has a strong association with the moon and is the protector of priest-physicians. He was skilled in magic and was depicted in every age as the god who "loved truth and hated abomination." These traits correspond strongly with Gurdjieff. He was an esoteric, or hidden, priest-physician in whose teaching the moon and the life force play primary roles and who, in the *First Series* of his magnum opus, *Beelzebub's Tales*—a testament to his love for truth and hatred for abomination—names his spaceship Karnak. It may be of some interest, as well, given Gurdjieff's use of horns in *Beelzebub's Tales*, that one must pass through a long line of ram-headed sphinxes in approaching the first pylon, or outer wall, of Karnak.

When the Prince left, Gurdjieff and Professor Skridlov decided to live together for three weeks in one of the tombs of the Valley of the Kings. They then traveled up the Blue Nile to its source, and "went on into Abyssinia, where we stayed about three months, and then coming out to the Red Sea we passed through Syria, and finally reached the ruins of Babylon" where they stayed together for four months. Skridlov stayed on and Gurdjieff went off, taking a circular route through Meshed to Isfahan, in northeastern and western Persia, which is today Iran. Sometime later, Gurdjieff reunited with the Prince in Constantinople.

Interestingly, Gurdjieff mentions Abyssinia, or modern day Ethiopia, for when asked where he would go to spend the rest of his days, he mentions Ethiopia. One generally retires to a place that is most congenial to one, be it their home, where they were born, or some place of significance. What is Gurdjieff telling us here?

The Origin of The Fourth Way

In the early days in St. Petersburg, Uspenskii asks Gurdjieff about the origin of the teaching he brings. Gurdjieff tells him the teaching is complete in itself and wholly independent of the other major teachings. Its origin, Gurdjieff says, is "pre-historic Egypt." If that was Gurdjieff's only reference, then our inquiry into the teaching's origins would have to stop there. But, fortunately, Gurdjieff provides many further clues in the *First* and *Second Series* of *All and Everything*.

Egypt, Gurdjieff tells us in *Beelzebub's Tales*, was the second home of the learned Society of Akhaldans, which was first formed on the continent of Atlantis 17,735 years before the second Transapalnian perturbation. The name Akhaldan means "The striving to become aware of the sense and aim of the Being of beings." This, of course, is also the aim of ancient historic Egyptian religion, whose essential perception one noted archaeologist describes as viewing "their living universe as a rhythmic movement contained within an unchanging whole." That is, within Being, the unchanging whole, there is becoming, recurrent change. What was important was only that which had always been and would never change.

The emblem of the Society was called "Conscience." Like the Sphinx, it was an allegorical being with the trunk of a bull and the four legs of a lion. On its back were the two large wings of an eagle. Where its head should have been there were what are called "breasts of a virgin," which were attached to the bull body by a piece of amber that "signifies," wrote Gurdjieff, "that this Love (represented by virgin breasts) should be strictly impartial, that is to say, completely separated from all the other functions proceeding in every whole responsible being."

Akhaldans, Egypt, & the Pyramids

Following the catastrophe caused by the second Transapalnian perturbation, the surviving members of the Society of Akhaldans first settled in the center of the continent of Grabontzi, or Africa. Later, in searching for another area to inhabit, they met a number of beings of Beelzebub's tribe. Good relations between the two groups had been established much earlier in the Atlantean capital city of Samlios where general meetings of Beelzebub's tribe had been held in one of the sections of the Society's principal cathedral. Forewarned of the coming catastrophe by their medium, Beelzebub's tribe had left the continent of Atlantis to settle at the source of the Nile. That is to say, the tribe settled in Ethiopia. (Interestingly, they did not warn the Akhaldans.)

The tribe might have settled in the Ethiopian Highlands, the source of the Blue Nile. Issuing from Lake Tana, the origin of the Blue Nile is a spring, which feeds a stream locally believed to be the Gihon, which in the Book of Genesis is said to flow through the Garden of Eden. Or perhaps they settled in the region of the White Nile somewhere between Lake No and Khartoum where the White and Blue Niles converge. Or they might have gone even farther south to Lake Victoria in Tanzania. Lake Victoria is the second largest body of fresh water in the world. Its outlet is the Victoria Nile at Jinja, Uganda, which is the uppermost region of the White Nile. Wherever the meeting between Beelzebub's tribe and the Akhaldans occurred, the Akhaldans were advised to migrate northward to Egypt, which they did. As Egyptians, the descendants of the Akhaldans became priests.

Among the results of the Akhaldans settling in Egypt were the invention of the telescope and the building of pyramids, what Beelzebub calls "observatories." A telescope was placed deep within the pyramid. From there specialists observed other suns and planets of the universe and also determined and intentionally directed "the course of the surrounding atmosphere in order to obtain the 'climate' desired." Still another result was the knowledge of preserving the physical body through mummification. As much knowledge as the Egyptians had, they could not prevent terrifying processes of self-destruction proceeding there. According to Beelzebub, Egypt "found itself in relation to the common-cosmic Harmonious-Movement in the position of what is called 'center-of-gravity-radiations', and that is why the influence of the cosmic law *Solioonensius* often acted on the presence of the three-brained beings." By the time of Beelzebub's sixth descent, he finds most of the pyramids have disappeared—either destroyed by war or buried under sands.

Akhaldan Influence

Through their scientific and spiritual contributions, the Society of Akhaldans has had a great influence on individuals and society. Among those influenced by Akhaldan learning were such seminal individuals as Pythagoras and Moses. Members of the Society, according to Gurdjieff, included the scientist Makary Kronbernkzion who wrote the *Boolmarshano*, "The Affirming and Denying Influences on Man." It was he who created the words *good* and *evil* to describe the primordial action of the *Sacred Triamazikamno*, its involution and evolution, the one force in three, words later badly misunderstood and the cause of many troubles. Also, the princely brothers Choon-Kil-Tez and Choon-Tro-Pel—who rediscovered the knowledge of the *Sacred Heptaparaparshinokh*—were Akhaldan descendants of King Konuzion, one of the chief members of the Society. The principal laws elucidated by The Fourth Way, then, are directly derived from those of the Society of Akhaldans.

Not only did the Society have a significant influence on historic Egyptian culture and history but on that of Hebraic, Greek and European, as well. Even a first reading of Gurdjieff's *Beelzebub's Tales* shows the paramount role the Society plays in his objective history of the world. It is interesting, too, that Beelzebub's tribe settled in Samlios, the capital of Atlantis, before relocating to Ethiopia and environs. In terms of Objective Reason, then, these two groups—one whose origins are terrestrial, the other extraterrestrial—form the basis for the evolution of consciousness and conscience among humankind.

However that may be, the origin of The Fourth Way as it relates to other teachings is clear.

Although many teachings claim The Fourth Way as their own, pointing to this or that likeness, Gurdjieff is quite emphatic that the teaching he brings is different from all others and in no way a derivative of any of them. He speaks of the four principal lines, Egyptian (historic), Hebraic, Persian and Hindu, and two mixtures of these lines, theosophy and occultism. Both of these mixed lines, he said, "bear in themselves grains of truth, but neither of them possesses full knowledge and therefore attempts to bring them to practical realization give only negative results."

Christianity & The Fourth Way

Many years later, in Paris, Gurdjieff was again queried about Christianity and The Fourth Way. "I find the system at the base of the Christian doctrine," said Boris Mouravieff, a Russian expatriate and intellectual. "What do you say to this subject?"

"It's the ABC," replied Gurdjieff. "But they didn't understand at all."

In Gurdjieff's view, not only did the Church fathers not understand but also they were confused about their own origins. Uspenskii reports that Gurdjieff said Christianity was "not invented by the fathers of the church. It was all taken in a ready-made form from Egypt, only not from the Egypt that we know but from one, which we do not know. This Egypt was in the same place as the other but it existed much earlier... prehistoric Egypt was Christian many thousands of years before the birth of Christ."

In *Beelzebub's Tales*, Gurdjieff shows what happened to Christianity: "And into this teaching [Christianity] of truth and verity, they began also to mix for various egoistic and political reasons, fragments taken from other religious teachings already existing there, but fragments such as had not only nothing in common with the teaching of Jesus, but which sometimes even flatly contradicted the truths this Divine Teacher taught." And because of what he calls "criminal wiseacring" the "genuine faith in all this Divine and uniquely accomplished teaching of salvation of the All-Loving Jesus Christ was totally destroyed."

Seeing Everything Topsy-Turvy

If it is true, as Gurdjieff says, that the origin of The Fourth Way is prehistoric Egypt, then it follows that The Fourth Way is the source of the Egyptian religion. And so, too, the source of Judaism and Christianity. Everything is turned on its head. Gurdjieff often stated that we see things "topsy-turvy." This is usually taken in a psychological way. How startling then to consider that we also have everything upside down historically. In *Beelzebub's Tales*, he declares that his intention is to "destroy, mercilessly, without any compromises whatsoever, in the mentation and feelings of the reader, *the beliefs and views, by centuries rooted in him, about everything existing in the world."* [Emphasis added.] Of everything said to be a cosmic truth, he says, the only one that's true is that we are the images of God, with 'God' defined by Gurdjieff as our Megalocosmos, represented in our location on the Ray of Creation by the solar system with its planets and, of course, the sun. The Egyptian religion that we do know about is also focused on the sun and the solar system. But what of the prehistoric Egyptians?

What we know of Egypt is confined to the history of the Dynastic Period—the thirty-one dynasties which extended from 3100 BC to 332 BC. Hieroglyphics were invented at the very beginning, simply appearing, fully developed. The hieroglyphic system of writing did not evolve over the centuries, as was the case with the cuneiform system. Some linguists think the impetus may have come from the Sumerians whose clay tablets with cuneiform writing date from 3300 BC. But Egyptian hieroglyphs and Sumerian pictograms show profound differences. Moreover, there is a correspondence between hieroglyphs and the designs and signs painted on pottery, amulets and weapons from the pre-dynastic period. That hieroglyphs suddenly appear, full blown, as do a carefully established calendar, a social order, census, and a well-developed mythology and cult, gives ample testimony to a long-civilized epoch that must have preceded the historical period.

What is known of the kingships of the Dynastic Period derives from Manetho, an Egyptian high priest of Heliopolis (a city now buried under a suburb of modern Cairo), in the third century BC. His dynastic history is supported by other documents, such as the Abydos King-List and the Royal Papyrus of Turin. All these sources, however, also speak of three different eras of kingship. While Menes, or Narmer, circa 3000 BC, is generally acknowledged by most Egyptologists as the first of the historical kings, they deny the historicity of the two preceding eras of kingship. The first of these is Zep Tepi, or the First Time of the Gods, whose kings were the Neteru (Neters or Gods). This era ended with the kingship of Horus. The second of the eras is the Shemsu Hor, the era of the Followers of Horus, which led up to the beginning of the Dynastic era and the kingship of Menes. As one renowned Egyptologist stated, "The Egyptians believed that in the beginning their land was ruled by a dynasty of great gods, of whom Horus, the son of Isis and Osiris, was the last. He was succeeded by a dynasty of semi-divine beings known as the 'followers of Horus,' who, in turn, gave place to the historical Kings of Egypt."

Zep Tepi is spoken of in the hieroglyphs known as the Building Texts, inscribed on the Temple of Edfu, located in Upper Egypt midway between Thebes and Aswan. The temple is built, like all Egyptian temples, on hallowed ground. Dedicated to Horus, it is the best preserved of all the temples of Egypt. The texts are the only preserved references to Seven Sages who were "divine beings who knew how the temples and sacred places were to be created." Says E.A.E. Reymond, a noted Egyptologist who has carefully studied the Edfu texts: "[This is] the first era known by our principal sources as a period which started from what existed in the past." The texts convey "an ancient world, [which] after having been constituted, was destroyed, and as a dead world it came to be the basis of a new period of creation which at first was the re-creation and resurrection of what once had existed in the past." The Sages were divine survivors of a previous cataclysm who made a new beginning. Originally, they came from an island—the Homeland of the Primeval Ones—the majority of whose divine inhabitants were drowned.

Arriving in Egypt, the survivors became "the builder Gods, who fashioned in the primeval time, the Lords of Light ... the Ghosts, the Ancestors ... who raised the seed for gods and men ... the Senior Ones who came into being at the beginning, who illumined this land when they came forth unitedly." The correlation with Gurdjieff's description of the second Transapalnian perturbation which caused the island of Atlantis "to enter within the planet," and with the surviving members of Beelzebub's tribe and the Society of Akhaldans who resettled in the region of Ethiopia and Egypt and restarted civilization is, of course, exact. It would be interesting to undertake a detailed study of correspondences between The Fourth Way teaching and what we know of Egyptian religion, but space does not permit. (One can say with certainty that both are rooted in and directed toward Being.) And no matter how well that task succeeded, we would still be working with only a reflection of the religion of prehistoric Egypt.

The Sphinx's Telltale Marks

The historical watershed of 3300 BC has appeared as an impenetrable buffer, which forbids all crossing. The indefatigable labors and insightful strikes of intuition of R. A. Schwaller de Lubicz kept open the desire and questioning to penetrate further. Of the thousands of scholars who have studied the Sphinx, it was he who saw watermarks on the limestone from which it has been carved and so realized that the Sphinx was older than the pyramids of Giza. As de Lubicz noted: "A great civilization must have preceded the vast movements of water that passed over Egypt, which leads us to assume that the Sphinx already existed, sculptured in the rock of the west cliff of Giza, that Sphinx whose leonine body, except for the head, shows indisputable signs of aquatic erosion." It wasn't until June 1990 that John Anthony West, an authority on de Lubicz and for many years a member of a mainstream Gurdjieff group in London, tested this theory. He convinced Dr. Robert M. Schoch, a paleontologist and a specialist in the weathering of soft rock, to validate or rebut the aquatic erosion theory. Schoch indeed found the Sphinx to be water-eroded, but he believes the cause is not a flood but precipitation, or rainwater. Schoch puts the tentative date for the carving of the Sphinx at 5000 to 7000 BC as a minimum. Egyptologists continue to rigorously dispute such findings, believing that the Sphinx was built around 2500 BC with Egyptian history beginning at 3000 BC.

The Sphinx may be the repository of the answers to where we came from and when we began. Building on Robert Bauval's *The Orion Mystery* and Graham Hancock's *Fingerprints of the Gods*, the two authors collaborated on *The Message of the Sphinx*. By means of computer simulation, the authors scroll back through astronomical heavens to show how the prehistoric skies of 2500 BC and 10,500 BC appeared. In effect, they deduce—and marshal a great many facts to prove—that a priestly elite they call "The Followers of Horus" used the heavens as a *Legominism*, a conscious means of passing and preserving knowledge down through time's inherent, law-conformable distortions. By ingenious reckoning and reasoning, Hancock and Bauval not only theoretically solve the riddle of the Sphinx but also determine that the much heralded but never discovered "Hall of Records"—which is said to preserve the knowledge and wisdom of "a highly advanced antediluvian civilization that was destroyed by a 'Great Flood'"—lies just one hundred feet below the hind paws of the Great Sphinx.

It seems we live in a time when we will learn more and more about prehistoric Egypt. If so, evidence to support Gurdjieff's declaration that the origin of The Fourth Way was prehistoric Egypt will likely be in the offing and enable the teaching to take its rightful place among the sacred ways of self-transformation.

The Gurdjieff Journal, Vol. 3, Nos. 2, 3, 4

Notes

1. *Unfolded to us.* P. D. Ouspensky, *In Search of the Miraculous*, 346.
2. *'A man of being.'* Thomas and Olga de Hartmann, *Our Life with Mr. Gurdjieff*, definitive edition, 68.
3. *We were walking.* G. I. Gurdjieff, *Meetings with Remarkable Men*, 119.
4. *Many thousands of years. Search*, 302.
5. *A whole library.* P. D. Ouspensky, *A New Model of the Universe*, 350, 355. It is his theory that the meaning and significance of these ancient monuments was "quite incomprehensible" to the people we call the "ancient Egyptians," that they found them lying half-buried in the sand and restored them, but didn't construct them.
6. *If the single fact.* John Anthony West, *The Serpent in the Sky* (Quest, 1993), 186, 229.
7. *The teaching whose theory. Search*, 286.
8. *Pre-sand Egypt.* According to Gurdjieff, it is the third and fifth planetary catastrophe that covered Egypt with sand. See *Beelzebub's Tales*, 312.
9. *I felt someone. Meetings with Remarkable Men*, 75.
10. *We often met. Meetings*, 121.
11. *Soon after. Meetings*, 225.
12. *The most remarkable.* Margaret Bunson, *A Dictionary of Ancient Egypt* (New York: Oxford University Press, 1991), 133.
13. *Amon.* Bunson, 20.
14. *Loved truth.* Bunson, 264.
15. *Went on into Abyssinia. Meetings*, 225.
16. *Gurdjieff mentions Abyssinia.* J. G. Bennett, *Gurdjieff: A Very Great Enigma*, 20–21. Speaking of Abyssinia, Bennett describes it as a place "where there are strange contacts with lost traditions." He says: "I do know that Ethiopia was very important to him because to the very end of his life he spoke of his great love for Ethiopia. Once he said that he thought of going

to spend the rest of his days there. He said that the two places where he felt he had ties were Central Asia, that is, Bokhara, and the other Ethiopia."
17. *Independent of other lines and unknown up to the present time.* This statement means that Sufism, Christianity, the Cabala, etc., are *not* the origin of The Fourth Way, as it *comes before*, not after them. There are certain similarities (as there are similarities between all true ways), yes, but that proves nothing. Perhaps the real question is why do proponents of these ways try to appropriate The Fourth Way for themselves? What is the attraction? And, further, why do so many use the teaching that Gurdjieff brought to supplement their own teaching? It would seem that their chosen teaching is in some way lacking, or not enough for them.
18. *Continent of Atlantis.* Plato was the first to speak of Atlantis in his *Timaeus*, which are his religious and teleological accounts of the world's origin and the phenomena of nature. "There have been," said Plato, "and will be many different calamities to destroy mankind, the greatest of them by fire and water ... there is at long intervals a variation in the course of the heavenly bodies and a consequent widespread destruction by fire of things on the earth." Then Plato mentions, 38, that "there were earthquakes and floods of extraordinary violence, and in a single dreadful day and night all your fighting men were swallowed up by the earth, and the island of Atlantis was similarly swallowed up by the sea and vanished...." Plato went into more detail in *Critas*, 131 (Penguin, 1971) mentioning that Atlantis "was an island larger than Libya and Asia put together" and, 145, that the Atlanteans were no longer able to sustain their prosperity with moderation "when the divine element in them became weakened by frequent admixture with mortal stock, and their human traits became predominant." It has been suggested that the island of Thera, or Santorini, lying some ninety miles north of Crete in the Mediterranean, may have many ties to Atlantis. See *Unearthing Atlantis*, Charles Pellegrino (Vintage Books, 1991). In *Meetings with Remarkable Men*, 37, Gurdjieff speaks of Atlantis being "where America is now." In his *First Series*, Gurdjieff referred to Atlantis as "the chief continent of that ill-fated planet."
19. *Their living universe.* Henri Frankfurt, *Ancient Egyptian Religion* (Harper and Row, 1948), 13.
20. *Breasts of a virgin.* G. I. Gurdjieff, *Beelzebub's Tales*, 310. "The Breasts of a virgin express that Love should predominate always and in everything during the inner and the outer functionings evoked in one's consciousness, such a Love as can arise and be present only in the presences of concentrations formed in the lawful parts of every whole responsible being in whom the hopes of our common father are placed." Do the breasts symbolize the two hemispheres of the brain?
21. *Amber. Time* magazine, 1996 February 68. Because it sometimes contains

dead [fossilized] animals, amber was strongly associated with death in ancient times. "It was believed to serve as a ray of light for the dead person in the afterlife," says Faya Causey, a historian of ancient art at the National Gallery of Art in Washington. Many of the amber figurines carved during the classical period relate either to death or to fertility and rejuvenation. Egyptians may have used amber in the mummification process, possibly because it is a powerful desiccant, or drying agent. It was also valued as a medicine. According to Pliny the Elder, Roman peasants used it to cure diseases of the neck and head. In the New World, the Maya burned it as incense to treat a variety of ailments. Most significant, amber is also a nonconductor of electricity. In *Beelzebub's Tales*, 311, it says "Amber is one of those seven planetary formations in the arising of which the Omnipresent Active Element *Okidanokh* takes part with all its three separate, independent, sacred parts, in equal proportion" and which serves the 'impeding' of the independent flow of these three parts.

22. *Tribe settled in Ethiopia.* Ethiopia has many interesting associations. It is here, for example, that the Ark of the Covenant is rumored to reside. See *The Gurdjieff Journal*, "Gurdjieff & Abyssinia," Vol. 13, No. 4.
23. *The course. Beelzebub's Tales*, 308.
24. *Found itself. Beelzebub's Tales*, see chapter XXX.
25. *Bear in themselves grains of truth. Search*, 286.
26. *The teaching. Search*, 286.
27. *Esoteric Christianity. Search*, 102.
28. *I find the system.* Boris Mouravieff, "Uspenskii, Gurdjieff et les fragments d'un enseignement inconnu," *Revue Syntheses*, Brussels, 1957, 8. For more, see "The Mouravieff Phenomenon," in Patterson, *Taking with the Left Hand* (Fairfax, CA: Arete Communications, 1998), 63–95.
29. *Images of God.* G. I. Gurdjieff, *Beelzebub's Tales*, 775. "We are the images of God.... These unfortunates do not even suspect that, of everything known to most of them concerning cosmic truths, this expression of theirs is the only true one of them all. And indeed, each of them is the image of God, not of that 'God' which they have in their bobtailed picturings, but of the real God, by which word we sometimes still call our common Megalocosmos."
30. *Hieroglyphics were invented.* Andrew Robinson, *The Story of Writing* (Thames and Hudson, 2007), 93.
31. *Watermarks on the limestone.* Selim Hassan, *The Sphinx: Its History in the Light of Recent Excavations* (1949).
32. *The first era known.* E. A. E. Reymond, *The Mythical Origin of the Egyptian Temple* (Manchester University Press, 1969), 106–107.
33. *An ancient world.* Reymond, 798–803.
34. *Temple of Edfu.* The Rosetta stone was first discovered in Egypt in 1799

and, using its clues, Champollion was the first to decipher Egyptian hieroglyphs in 1823. Gurdjieff says in *Meetings with Remarkable Men* that he and Professor Skridlov spent three weeks in Thebes and "From Thebes we traveled up the Nile to its source, and went on into Abyssinia, where we stayed three months." As the Temple of Edfu was on the way up the Nile, it seems likely they would have visited it. Gurdjieff gives no indication, written or verbal, that either he or Skridlov could decipher hieroglyphs.

35. *A great civilization.* R. A. Schwaller de Lubicz, *Sacred Science* (Rochester, VT: Inner Traditions, 1988), 96. "It is maintained that this erosion was wrought by desert sands, but the entire body of the Sphinx is protected from all desert winds coming from the West, the only winds that could effect erosion. Only the head protrudes from this hollow, and it shows no signs of erosion."

GURDJIEFF & CHRISTIANITY

WAS GEORGI IVANOVITCH GURDJIEFF A CHRISTIAN?

THE ORIENTATION OF THE TEACHING—IS IT CHRISTIAN? ENTERING THE NEW MILLENNIUM, SOME FIFTY YEARS AFTER MR. GURDJIEFF'S PASSING, IT IS IMPORTANT TO BEGIN TO UNDERSTAND THE PART THAT CHRISTIANITY PLAYED IN HIS LIFE AND IN THE TEACHING HE BROUGHT.

Certainly, as Gurdjieff makes clear in *Meetings with Remarkable Men,* he was raised as a Christian—"I know the rituals of the Greek Church well," he would say many years later, "and there, underlying the form and ceremony, there is real meaning." His first religious tutor was seventy-year-old Dean Borsh, the highest spiritual authority of the region. As Dean Borsh aged, he asked the young priest Bogachevsky to tutor Gurdjieff and to confess him every week. For two years, Bogachevsky tutored the young Gurdjieff and then, when the priest was posted elsewhere, he had Gurdjieff continue his confessions by mail.

It is interesting to note, regarding Bogachevsky's caliber, that later he went to Mount Athos as a chaplain and a monk. Soon, however, he renounced monastic life as practiced there and went to Jerusalem where he joined the Essene Brotherhood and was sent to one of its monasteries in Egypt. He was given the name Father Evlissi and later became one of the assistants to the abbot of its chief monastery. According to Gurdjieff, the Essenes had preserved the teaching of Jesus Christ "unchanged" and, as it passed from generation to generation, it "has even reached the present time in its original form."

The depth of the relationship Gurdjieff felt for this man was expressed when, in his maturity, Gurdjieff declared, "Father Evlissi, who is now an aged man, happened to become one of the first persons on earth who has been able to live as our Divine Teacher Jesus Christ wished for us all." This choice of words would seem to indicate that for himself Gurdjieff accepts the divinity of Jesus Christ. In addition to "Divine Teacher Jesus Christ," he speaks of Jesus Christ as "a Messenger from our endlessness," and "Sacred Individual Jesus Christ."

Although Gurdjieff speaks highly of Christianity and of Jesus Christ, there are also many stories of his making fun of Catholic priests, even shouting at them on occasion. For example, his niece Luba reported in her *Luba Gurdjieff: A Memoir with Recipes,* "My Uncle never taught us how to go to church, or pray, or anything like that. And he never liked priests or the nuns. When we were out driving and he saw a priest, he would say, 'Shoo! Son of a bitch.'"

Gurdjieff had intended to found the Institute for the Harmonious Development of Man in Russia but the revolution precluded this. It was not until eight years later, in 1921, that he was able to establish the Institute in France. At the time, he stated the Institute's aim unequivocally: "The program of the Institute, the power of the Institute, the aim of the Institute, the possibilities of the Institute can be expressed in very few words: the Institute can help one to be able to be a Christian." He spoke of a Christian as being "a man who is able to fulfill the Commandments ... both with his mind and his essence." St. George the Victor was proclaimed as the Institute's patron saint.

The Original Christianity

The opening of *Beelzebub's Tales* begins with a prayer: "In the name of the Father and of the Son and in the name of the Holy Ghost. Amen." And within, Gurdjieff speaks of Christianity as based on "resplendent love," saying also that among all of the ancient religious teachings none had so "many good regulations for ordinary everyday life." He believed that Christianity is the best of all existing or future religions "if only the teaching of the Divine Jesus Christ were carried out in full conformity with its original." It is not clear what he means by the words "its original" but presumably a religion or teaching that came before Christianity. Something of the same sort happens with the aforementioned prayer, for he says in introducing it that this "definite utterance ... has been formulated variously and in our day is formulated in the following words. ..." He is quite clearly, then, pointing to something that was Christian but which *predates* Christianity.

It is clear he believes that Christianity — the religion — was mixed with Judaism, and that Judaism by that time "had already been thoroughly distorted." During the Middle Ages, Christianity was further distorted by the fantastic doctrines of hell and heaven imported from Babylonian dualism by the Church Fathers. Christianity, Gurdjieff says, had been "the religion and teaching upon which the Highest Individuals placed great hopes" — note how he separates religion from teaching — but, as a result of what he calls "absurdities" and "criminal wiseacring," genuine faith in Christianity was "totally destroyed."

Messengers from Above

Perhaps more significant for determining whether or not Gurdjieff was a Christian is that, while he obviously held Jesus Christ in very high regard, he does not take him as the only Son of God. Rather, Jesus Christ was but one of a number of Messengers from Above, though of these He apparently holds a special place. Although Gurdjieff speaks of Jesus as a saint, as he does of Saint Buddha, Saint Mohammed, Saint Lama and Saint Moses, it is only Jesus and Buddha that Gurdjieff also speaks of as being "Divine."

Gurdjieff's view of the resurrection of Jesus Christ differs radically from accepted doctrine. He holds that if a person dies and is buried, "this being will never exist again, nor furthermore will he ever speak or teach again." However, in seeming contradiction he views the Last Supper as being a preparation for the sacred sacrament *Almznoshinoo* on the *Kesdjan* body of Jesus Christ. *Almznoshinoo*, he says, is a means of materializing and communicating with the higher-being bodies of a deceased physical body by the *Hanbledzoinian* process of intentionally coating its *Kesdjan* body. In order to accomplish this, a particle of an individual's *Hanbledzoin* must be taken while he is alive and either kept in a corresponding surplanetary formation or taken in and intentionally blended with the *Kesdjan* bodies of those who will afterward participate in the *Almznoshinoo* process.

Because Jesus Christ did not have the necessary time before he was crucified to explain and instruct his apostles in certain cosmic truths, he had to resort to a magical ceremony so that he might complete his mission while still in a cosmic individual state. It was at that moment, according to Gurdjieff, that Judas put forward an ingenious plan — the conscious betrayal of Christ — that would gain them the necessary time. Gurdjieff refers to Judas as a saint who, of all the disciples, was the most devoted and had the highest degree of reason.

Concerning religion per se, Gurdjieff tells us there are seven levels. The religions of the first three are subjective and correspond to people who are primarily instinctual, emotional, or intellectual. It is at the fourth level that religion begins to become objective, free from the distortions of personality. At this level, the practitioner is beginning to emerge from the hypnotism of ordinary life and engaging in a struggle with what it means to be a Christian. Only at the fifth level does one have "the being of a Christian," for only at this level can life actually be lived in accordance with the precepts of Christ, because one has now achieved a commensurate unity and will that is free from external influences.

No *External* Good & Evil

Concerning good and evil Gurdjieff is quite clear. "The fantastic notion," he says, "namely, that outside of them [outside of people] there exist objective sources of 'Good' and 'Evil' acting upon their essence" is without foundation — there is no external good and evil.

Our present notion of good and evil, Gurdjieff believes, is based on misunderstanding. He says that long ago Makary Kronbernkzion, a terrestrial three-brained being, who was a full member of the Society of Akhaldans, an esoteric brotherhood, was the first to employ the words. In an essay he wrote, entitled "The Affirming and Denying Influences on Man," he spoke of the trinity of forces in the conscious evolution of human beings. The first force he characterized as arising from the causes proceeding in the Sun Absolute, and issuing from it by momentum. This force, like the other two, is totally independent. Kronbernkzion called this force "Good." When the momentum of this force is spent, there is then a striving to reblend with its source, the Sun Absolute. This fundamental World Law is characterized as, "the effects of a cause must always re-enter the cause." This second backward-flowing force, which must continually resist the momentum of the first force, he called "Evil." (When activated in terms of real evolution and not involution, it is just the opposite from the way commonly thought. The forward-flowing force, that of continual creation, is passive, 1-2-3; the denying force is now active in its passive but conscious acceptance, 2-3-1 or 3-1-2.) From the clash and friction of these two forces is formed the resultant which in relation to the two other forces is considered neutralizing. This trinity of forces issues from one cause, the Prime Source of all creation. As long as people project a good and evil having some objective existence outside of themselves, spiritual evolution becomes curtailed.

Gurdjieff, raised as a Christian and no doubt baptized, had a deep understanding of Christianity and held its regulations and commandments in high regard, as he did its Divine Messenger from Above, Jesus Christ. However, he would not be accepted by either the Roman Catholic or Eastern Orthodox Churches as a practicing Christian. Nevertheless, Gurdjieff, it is quite clear, would insist that he was a Christian—a genuine Christian.

Clearly, for Gurdjieff, the word *Christianity* has a meaning different from that of contemporary churches. After his arrival in St. Petersburg, the subject was broached when Gurdjieff was first asked, "What is the relation of the teaching you are expounding [The Fourth Way] to Christianity as we know it?"

"I do not know what you know about *Christianity*," answered Gurdjieff, emphasizing this word. "It would be necessary to talk a great deal and to talk for a long time in order to make clear what you understand by this term. But for the benefit of those who know already, I will say that, if you like, *this is esoteric Christianity*."

In the account it is important to note that the word *Christianity* is italicized. The word is given even greater stress by making clear that he himself emphasized the word when he spoke. Saying he does not know what the questioner understands by the term Christianity, Gurdjieff adds that in any case he will answer but "for the benefit of those who know already." On the basis of these remarks some have believed, such as Boris Mouravieff and Robin Amis, that Gurdjieff was referring to Eastern Orthodoxy as it is practiced at Mount Athos. But this is simply an external reading, which, even at that, contradicts itself.

In continuing the discussion, in the very next paragraph, Gurdjieff speaks about "the desire to be master of oneself, because without this nothing else is possible." Then he addresses the subjects of love of mankind and altruism, and concludes with "In order to help others one must first learn to be an egoist, a conscious egoist. Only a conscious egoist can help people. Such as we are we can do nothing."

In sum, one must strive to become a true individual and to do that one must practice esoteric Christianity.

Rediscovery of the Original Christianity

From the remarks discussed previously, it is quite clear that Gurdjieff, in his quest for the origin of esoteric knowledge, rediscovered in Egypt what he called a Christianity before Christ. "The Christian church," said Gurdjieff, "the Christian form of worship, was not invented by the fathers of the church. It was all taken in ready-made form from Egypt, only not from the Egypt that we know but from one which we do not know.... This prehistoric Egypt was Christian many thousands of years before the birth of Christ, that is to say, that its religion was composed of the same principles and ideas that constitute true Christianity."

After being initiated four times into ancient Egyptian Mysteries and rediscovering the essential principles and ideas, Gurdjieff, realizing that over time segments of the teaching had migrated northward, made a second journey travelling to Persia, the Hindu Kush, and Tibet reassembling the elements he found and reformulating the teaching for modern times. He called the teaching The Fourth Way to distinguish it from the three classical ways of body, heart and mind, as it works on all three at once. In first speaking of its origin he declared, "The teaching whose theory is here being set out is *completely self-supporting* and *independent of other lines* and it has been *completely unknown* up to the present time." [Emphasis added.] It is "completely unknown" because its origin is prehistoric—predating the ancient Egyptian religion, Judaism, Zoroaster, the Avesta and the Hindu Rig Veda.

So, in sum, Gurdjieff is, and is not, a Christian. The Fourth Way teaching is, and is not, Christian. It depends on what we know about Christianity, our definition of it.

For Gurdjieff, there are two forms of Christianity, its original form and its contemporary form.

The Fourth Way, for Gurdjieff, is esoteric Christianity in its highest form. That is, if it is so recognized and practiced. Otherwise... ⚔

Telos, Vol. 6, No. 2 [Later retitled *The Gurdjieff Journal*]

Notes

1. *Greek Church.* G. I. Gurdjieff, *Views from the Real World,* 86.
2. *Passed from generation to generation.* G. I. Gurdjieff, *Beelzebub's Tales,* 703.
3. *"Divine Teacher Jesus Christ." Beelzebub's Tales,* 703.
4. *"Messenger from our endlessness." Beelzebub's Tales,* 99, 701.
5. *"Sacred Individual." Beelzebub's Tales,* 701.
6. *"Shoo! Son of a bitch."* Luba Gurdjieff, *Luba Gurdjieff: A Memoir with Recipes* (Berkeley, CA: Ten Speed Press, 1993), 64.
7. *English.* Did Gurdjieff speak English? Madame de Salzmann told James Moore that Prince Ozay was Gurdjieff. Paul Dukes reports that the prince's friends spoke in Russian. "Ribald stories made up part of the conversation, some of which my host [the prince] translated to me with gusto." *The Unending Quest* (Cassell & Co. Ltd., 1950), 104. Dukes, an intelligent young man with a fine ear, makes several references to the prince speaking English. As Dukes said he visited with the prince off and on from 1913 until February 1917, it is inconceivable that Dukes could have been misled. By making reference to Gurdjieff speaking English, was Dukes protecting Gurdjieff? As Dukes published his book after Gurdjieff's death, there was no reason to protect him. Did Gurdjieff feign not being able to speak English to make it harder for his English and American students to understand him? Solita Solano says he spoke "near perfect English" when giving an exercise. Jean Toomer also heard him speak English. Gurdjieff as a linguist with a great interest in words and their roots, and having come to America so often, staying for months, that he didn't speak and understand English is highly unlikely. Therefore, the revision of *Beelzebub's Tales* to supposedly improve its English, chapters of which he had read aloud to him again and again from 1931 until his death in 1949, simply has no factual support.
8. *Prayer.* Ozay told Dukes that a greater measure of the mantric art survived in the Greek Orthodox Church, especially in its Russian branch, because of its devotion to pure song without instrumental interference; the Orthodox Church has never allowed its singing to be crippled or debased by organ 'support,' and indeed does not permit organs to be placed in churches. Dukes, 110.
9. *The Institute and Christianity.* G. I. Gurdjieff, *Views from the Real World,* 152–54.
10. *Relation of The Fourth Way to Christianity.* P. D. Ouspensky, *In Search of the Miraculous,* 102–103.
11. *Resplendent Love. Beelzebub's Tales,* 702.
12. *"Full conformity with its original." Beelzebub's Tales,* 1009.
13. *"Definite utterance." Beelzebub's Tales,* 3. Given this, it is wondered whether Gurdjieff's admonition "Do not do to others what you would

not wish them to do to you" is an example of an original formulation, later changed.
14. *Makary Kronbernkzion. Beelzebub's Tales*, 1,138.
15. *"Thoroughly distorted." Beelzebub's Tales*, 703. Mouravieff and Amis. See Patterson, *Taking with the Left Hand*, "The Mouravieff 'Phenomenon.'"
16. *"All taken in ready-made form from Egypt."* Ouspensky, *Search*, 302.
17. *"Completely unknown." Search*, 286.

Gurdjieff, Uspenskii, Orage & Bennett

Uspenskii, Orage and Bennett were not ordinary men, not ordinary seekers. Each was blessed with a rare and strong intellect, a deep occult understanding, great will, and an enduring thirst for self-knowledge. Each could hold and direct the attention of a great many people, many quite powerful in ordinary life. Though none could take that final step beyond themselves, each took many steps, passed many tests, made many sacrifices. Each had developed, were embryonic souls—or souls—in Gurdjieff's sense of the term. Yet none could totally sacrifice himself to Gurdjieff's mission. Uspenskii could not sacrifice his independence of mind; Orage, his feelings; Bennett, his thirst for adventure, his self-will.

Despite their time and training with Gurdjieff, none of the three seemed to really understand the idea, monumental in its implications, that Gurdjieff had brought an ancient teaching, reformulated for our time, and was as he said "completely self-supporting and independent of other lines and completely unknown up to the present time"—a teaching, he said, that could save the world from destroying itself. Like all seekers, understandably, what they searched for was a teaching for themselves, not for mankind. In this way only were these men ordinary. What Gurdjieff searched for was a man or men, who would help to step-down the teaching. Gurdjieff's aim in founding the Institute for the Harmonious Development of Man, as he states quite clearly in *Beelzebub's Tales,* was to prepare helper-instructors who would help him disseminate and establish the teaching in the major capitals of the world. His Institute, which he once described as a "hatching place for eggs," had a very short life. Within twenty-three months of its purchase, Gurdjieff disbanded the Institute. What precipitated this was his near-fatal car crash. But well before, he likely realized that no "eggs" would hatch—that none of his pupils could make the necessary transformation in so short a time. Despite Gurdjieff's awesome powers, the immensity of his will and understanding, and the quality of his students—their egoism, the deep identification with themselves, was too hardened. The car crash was the shock he needed to admit the hard truth to himself—in terms of his mission, the Institute was a dead end.

Looking back, it seems that what Gurdjieff had to do was what he never could do: convince Uspenskii, Orage and Bennett of the full authenticity of his message and his authenticity as its messenger.[1]

It was not difficult back then to miss the mark...to miss the amazing fact and grace that a teaching so practical and powerful, and a man as unique as Gurdjieff, could appear at all.

So it was then, so it is now.

Of the three pupils, Uspenskii seems the oldest soul. Certainly, of the three, he was the first to meet Gurdjieff—and the depth of his understanding appears much deeper then either Orage's or Bennett's, both of whom had been Uspenskii's pupils. If Gurdjieff's idée fixe was the purpose of man's existence on earth, Uspenskii's was time in its fullest dimension.

Early on, Uspenskii had felt the gnawing emptiness of death. In his bones he realized that life was about dying. Growing up, he saw through the sham of ordinary life, its deceits and absurdities. He knew that all the carrots life offered were only dream carrots. He was the black sheep that could not be tempted with being a lion or eagle—or even a man. He had left the herd long before he met Gurdjieff, searching for a way to break out of life's magic circle. He realized that to break out took time and that each human being had only so much time. "I formulated my own aim quite clearly several years ago," he told Gurdjieff, "I want to know the future." He had come to the conclusion, he said, that "the future can be known." And, further, that a man "has the right to know the day and hour of his death...for what is the good of beginning any kind of work when one doesn't know whether one will have time to finish it or not."

Uspenskii's great and singular achievement was his objective reporting[2] in many instances of the ancient teaching Gurdjieff brought. His ability to absorb and so cleanly communicate the teaching shines with intelligence and integrity. The pity was, knowing the teaching, he could not fully live it. Two factors stood in his way. One was what he called his "extreme individualism." This, Uspenskii himself admitted, was the fundamental feature of his attitude toward life. The other was the emotional scarring caused by the death of his father when Uspenskii was not yet four years old, followed the next year by the death of his beloved grandfather. "I didn't play with toys as a child," he said. "From an early age I knew what life was about."

---

1. It is not surprising, for how many—even these many years later—would agree that Gurdjieff brought an ancient teaching that would save the world from destroying itself and that he, yes, this kaphir, was a Messenger from Above? Though no one has met one, and thus has no real basis of comparison, we are influenced and unconsciously judge by the sanitized versions passed down to us. There were many, of course, who did have a direct revelation, most notably Dr. Stjoernval, Thomas and Olga de Hartmann, Jeanne de Salzmann and Louise March. But Stjoernval, the de Hartmanns and March were not equipped for the role Gurdjieff needed to be played and Madame de Salzmann would come into maturity only in his life's final phase.

2. After many years of editing his original manuscript of subjective interpretations; see Essays for two examples.

It wasn't until he was twelve or thirteen years old, he says, speaking of his wonderment upon reading a book on levers, that "For the first time in my life, my world emerged from chaos." However, death continued to dog his footsteps. At sixteen his mother died and at twenty-nine his sister. That he fathered no children of his own seems significant. Protecting himself against feeling the grief of these losses was the isolation, the alienation that must have been the background of his "extreme individualism." These two factors—individualism and death—entwined within him like two snakes, the one feeding the other.

"Wraps up the Thought." That was Gurdjieff's early nickname for Uspenskii. (Nicknames, Gurdjieff said, often point toward a pupil's chief feature or chief fault.) Gurdjieff saw that when Uspenskii was asked a question, he would answer so completely that nothing would be left of the question. In effect, he demolished it. Answering in this way not only demonstrated, one could say showed off, his great intellectual capacity, but also pointed to a need to control, a word he used quite often. What Uspenskii was likely controlling was his emotional center. Later, Gurdjieff said that some people's chief feature was so buried beneath its formal manifestations that it was incapable of discovery. "Then," wrote Uspenskii, "a man can consider himself as his chief feature just as I could call my chief feature 'Uspenskii,' or, as Gurdjieff always called it, 'Pyotr Demianovich.'"[3]

One wonders, in this regard, if Uspenskii actually felt Gurdjieff's presence. Virtually everyone, friend or foe, who encountered Gurdjieff remarked on the rare quality of *Hanbledzoin* he emanated. As detailed as Uspenskii's account of his first meeting with Gurdjieff is, he does not speak of it. Nor does he ever mention it later. Unlikely though it seems, could it be that Pyotr Demianovich was so armored and so identified with knowledge that he did not experience it? How was it he could withstand Gurdjieff's many direct attacks to break through his chief feature and to set him right? Did Uspenskii register it but in some way discount it? These can only remain questions.

We do know that his Pyotr Demianovich began to weaken as a result of Uspenskii's work on himself and the telepathic experiences Gurdjieff induced in him in Finland. As a result, he began to feel his community more with other

---

3. A possible deduction might be that Gurdjieff could not discover Uspenskii's chief feature. It was too hidden. Which would mean that Gurdjieff, at root, didn't understand Uspenskii. This would account perhaps for Gurdjieff's failure, or inability, to change roles, or at least refrain from playing a role with Uspenskii to a point of no return. More likely, Gurdjieff understood that for Uspenskii to be of any real use to him, he had to work directly on Uspenskii's emotional center. Though the odds against a breakthrough were great, Gurdjieff's mission and the urgency of the time meant that he had no time to coddle Uspenskii. It was all or nothing. Moreover, if the personality, that is, Pyotr Demianovich, was the chief feature it meant that it was thick enough to resist any penetration, any discovery. In psychological terms the "armor" of personality was the chief feature—that which was always protecting, controlling, interpreting. Pyotr Demianovich did weaken, become penetrable. Uspenskii did achieve a new level of being with Gurdjieff, but then Pyotr Demianovich reappeared. It wasn't until his chief feature played its last card and Uspenskii faced death that he finally came to the clarity and will to make the super-effort necessary to free himself.

people. Uspenskii did not see, however, that—because of his insincerity[4] with Gurdjieff—his rapport with his teacher was also weakened. Within a year and a half of first meeting Gurdjieff, Uspenskii was already distancing himself psychologically. Though he would relive his days with Gurdjieff until the end of his life, the fact is he remained blind to the real significance of the events in Finland, thus giving testimony to the incredible power of buffers, regardless of the quality of the pupil.

The seed of premature separation which Uspenskii planted in himself in Finland grew and festered, until in Essentuki he began to divide Gurdjieff from the teaching. Once sufficiently divided, Uspenskii, of course, was in a position (another of his favorite words) to judge Gurdjieff, who, he convinced himself, was a "tainted channel." This was not surprising. Next to "time," the subject of "good and evil" seemed to be Uspenskii's major interest, likely stemming from his feelings about having his loved ones taken away from him. "Good and evil" was one of the chief contexts through which he saw life. It was the subtle interpretation coloring all his impressions. For Uspenskii to have kept the good end of the stick for himself, transferring the bad end to Gurdjieff (whose seemingly erratic behavior, it may be said, gave ample room for doing so) was in the cards from the start. From what Uspenskii reports, Gurdjieff invited, even fostered, such negative attitudes, intentionally creating division in his pupils. It was up to his pupils to see and work with it. A powerful and dangerous way to teach, but time, Gurdjieff knew, was short.

In breaking with Gurdjieff, Uspenskii made his incomplete understanding of the teaching the basis of a new line. "I took over the leadership to save the System," he said. There is no reason to doubt that this is what he believed. But to save it from what? To save it from Gurdjieff! From the very first, Gurdjieff's "play" had upset Uspenskii, made him wary. Gurdjieff's "play" was like that of no holy man, no teacher or guru known to Uspenskii. That Gurdjieff seemed to go out of his way to create negative and false impressions, that he cultivated people's worst fears about himself, Uspenskii could not fathom. It was the doubt—that Gurdjieff was irrational—that would continue to grow in Uspenskii. In Essentuki, Gurdjieff's stern and seemingly pitiless handling of Uspenskii's friend Zacharov, together with Uspenskii's concern over where he believed Gurdjieff was leading them, ultimately led Uspenskii to admit: "I gradually began to see that there were many things I could not understand and that I had to go."

Interestingly, Uspenskii deletes from the published manuscript of the retitled *In Search of the Miraculous* not only his long and rather confused explanation

---

4. Speaking of his telepathic experience, Uspenskii wrote: "I knew that he [Gurdjieff] would not believe me and that he would laugh at me if I showed him this other thing. But for myself it was indubitable and what happened later showed that I was right." *Search*, 263. What happened later is most likely his break with Gurdjieff in Essentuki. In that case, "this other thing" would relate to why he broke with him, i.e., "Gurdjieff was leading us in fact towards the way of religion." *Search*, 375.

of why he left Gurdjieff, his divergence from Gurdjieff regarding *The Struggle of the Magicians* (see Essays), but also deletes what he termed the "St. Petersburg conditions." The agreement, from his point of view, put them on the same level, or almost the same level, in that it gave Uspenskii responsibility for who was accepted and not accepted into groups. Using this in an irrational way—telling him he was responsible for the Moscow groups as well as the St. Petersburg groups—Gurdjieff worked on his emotional center. Opening this center would do what Uspenskii most feared—plunge him into the feelings of death and chaos he once felt as a child. This was the 'wound' he carried, his burden, and, it was dressed in irrationality. Ironically, he used his power of rationality to protect his irrationality.

Though he was quite successful in establishing his version of the teaching in England, and later America, Uspenskii's divorce from Gurdjieff would dog him for the rest of his life. It was a wound upon a wound. When asked in a meeting "if the line [of teacher to student; the passage, or octave, of the teaching] was broken when you left Gurdjieff?" Uspenskii answered huffily: "What has all this to do with Gurdjieff and me? I was working with Gurdjieff until I saw a difference in him. This has nothing to do with esotericism." But, of course, it does. It was a lie that this very honest man had to live with.

If he refused to suffer emotionally with Gurdjieff, one German bombing of London was all it took to convince Uspenskii to sail for America. The reasons he left England are rational enough, but the fact is Uspenskii did what Gurdjieff never did: *he left his pupils*. Gurdjieff brought his pupils through a raging civil war, took responsibility for them in Constantinople, Berlin, at the Prieuré and stayed on in Paris during the Nazi occupation.

At Franklin Farms in Mendham, the grand estate-farm in New Jersey that his followers had provided for him, Uspenskii gave his lectures as always, but grew increasingly reclusive. He began to see, in part, what had happened. "I took it [the leadership of the Work] over," he admitted, "before I had gained enough control over myself. I was not ready. I have lost control over myself. It is a long time since I could control my state of mind." And later: "The System has become a profession with me."

Not only did the teaching, or "the System" as Uspenskii called it, become a profession for him, but his interpretation of it became—and still is to this day—the most widespread and influential representation of it. Gurdjieff is spoken about, of course, but it is largely the "Gurdjieff" and the "teaching" as Uspenskii saw them. Not only do his books dwarf Gurdjieff's in terms of readership, but many more people study them than they do the *Legominism* Gurdjieff created, *All and Everything*. They thereby base their practice entirely upon Uspenskii's version of the teaching, which is comprised of his understanding of Gurdjieff's Russian and early French periods (1915–1924) and his later interpolations. In terms of students, whereas Uspenskii was teaching upwards of a thousand people at Lyne

Place, perhaps not more than a hundred or so passed through the Prieuré before it was disbanded in 1924. Afterwards, Gurdjieff worked only with small groups of people. It was not until 1948 that people came to him in any numbers, and most were from Uspenskii's and Bennett's groups.

So what has largely been taught is Uspenskii's version of the Work, a version which stresses intellect, work with negative emotions, pessimism, 'good' and 'evil,' perfectionism and, most of all, psychology. When once asked if he had altered the teaching much, Uspenskii said he had not altered it at all [as he understood it]. "But I prefer," he said, "to start with the psychological side." It might be recalled that during their first meeting Gurdjieff reminded Uspenskii that "in his work, which was chiefly psychological in character, *chemistry* played a big part." Uspenskii spoke at length about psychology in his *A New Model of the Universe*. He took a dim view of psychoanalysis, as did Gurdjieff. But many people do not carefully distinguish between it and what Uspenskii means by psychology as he explains it in *The Psychology of Man's Possible Evolution*. Uspenskii's emphasis on psychology from Gurdjieff's Russian period has come to dominate many of the forms of the teaching and has led to some of these being unduly psychologized.

In his *Beelzebub's Tales* Gurdjieff speaks of psychoanalysis as being a maleficent means of distorting the psyche, calling it one of the "pseudo teachings." This is especially true of New Age psychologists who fold the teaching into their professional practice and who even, with little to no Work experience, start their own groups. Others, having never been in an authentic Gurdjieff group, like Robert Burton and A. H. Almaas, even create their own teaching, giving off an eclectic mix of Fourth Way, Sufi and Buddhist ideas. In any case, such has been Uspenskii's imprint on the Work that it might be said that the full development of the teaching as given by Gurdjieff has yet to be fully appreciated and practiced. The sense of the sacred, of community, in particular, often seems to be missing.

Plagued with depression and kidney problems, and against the advice of his wife and doctors, Uspenskii left America after the war to return to England. Though nearly sixty-nine years old, he hoped to make a new start with the pupils who had stayed behind. So in his lectures upon his return, time and again, he turned questions back on the questioners, trying to break them free of their doctrinal reliance on the teaching. He had taken the teaching, that is, his version or understanding of the teaching, as far as he could and had reached a dead end. He needed to begin anew. For his pupils, he saw that was not possible. In one of his last public meetings, he was asked: "Can we learn to be more humble?" Uspenskii answered: "I never was humble myself, and I don't know how I can." But, in fact, he was becoming humble through the means by which, unfortunately, most of us become humble—humiliation. His life, his search, had come to nothing. Yet he had the self-sincerity, no small thing, to admit this to himself. And so, at the last minute, his bags already aboard a ship that would return him to America, he ordered them to be unloaded. "I am not going to America *this time*," he said. [Emphasis added.]

What did he mean—this time? It must mean that he remembered...remembered having gone to America before in his previous life in the great wheel of eternal recurrence. It was now, having reached the nadir of his life, that he began his valiant climb to the zenith and his ultimate triumph of stepping through time, of dying a conscious death. His last days, his great struggle with his body and emotions, and his breakthrough, are all recorded by his pupil and spiritual friend, Rodney Collin. So, at the very end, Uspenskii was able to return to where he began, to find the miraculous, to penetrate "beyond the thin film of false reality." In his thirst for the truth, his self-sacrifice, his faults, confusion and rebellion, we can all perhaps see aspects of ourselves and know, too, through the testament of his life, that there is always the grace of redemption, no matter how far we stray, if we are open to it.

It is not recorded what idiot Gurdjieff ascribed to Uspenskii, but one that must be considered is 'enlightened' idiot. Nor did Alexander de Salzmann[5] paint Uspenskii's animal on the wall of the Study House of the Prieuré. Had he done so, the animal would have been highly intelligent, visionary, mystical, stubborn, fiercely independent to a fault. Perhaps a 'white,' or even a 'black' swan.

Orage was altogether a different type of animal. De Salzmann painted him as an elephant. But Orage was also part fox—clever, possessed of breadth of intellect, charm and benevolence. He wanted to be loved and so he was. He was the classic 'white knight,' a 'St. George' in a tweed jacket.

Of Uspenskii, Orage and Bennett, the dynamic of relationship with Gurdjieff was deepest with Orage. Orage could, as only Alexander de Salzmann and Fritz Peters could, make Gurdjieff laugh. It is no small thing that upon hearing of Orage's death, Gurdjieff, wiping the tears from his eyes with his fists, declared: "How you say it in your country? May his soul reach the Kingdom of Heaven! This man...my brother."

With an impartial self-honesty—not often found in Uspenskii or Bennett—Orage, brother of Gurdjieff, pinpointed the problem. He said he lacked (like Uspenskii and Bennett) the absolute faith. The difference was—and this is considerable—Orage recognized it. He did not foist his problem off on his teacher. As Orage wrote to a friend:

> I cannot go more than half a hog, let us say. I can regret it and wish that I had been different; but the fact remains that I cannot "sell all"—and everybody—to follow G. in person. His method I continue to regard as the Word of God; I practice it to the best of my powers. His system I regard also as probably the very latest word of truth; but, as I cannot verify it myself, and have lost hope that I ever shall be able; and as, furthermore, I cannot merely believe and, still less, try to persuade others

---

5. In Tiflis, Georgia, when he was born, his name is registered as Salzmann.

of just my beliefs—I see no probability of my resumption of G. groups or teaching for the rest of my life.

It is significant that the figure of Orage, the 'superior idiot,' dominates Gurdjieff's *Third Series*.[6] Orage, in a sense, symbolizes the teacher-student problem even more than Uspenskii and Bennett. He was closer to Gurdjieff than either of the others and so, perhaps, well knew Gurdjieff's human side and his weaknesses. Orage's remark to Gurdjieff, for example, about the harmonium being a "sacred relic" was a pulling of the Messenger from Above's tail. Both Uspenskii and Bennett wanted to set up their own teaching. Orage simply wanted to remain a 'human being.' He was blind to why he could not have his Jessie and his Gurdjieff, too.[7]

Gurdjieff tried to warn him but Orage was not listening. How deaf he had become plays out in the scene between Gurdjieff, Orage and Nott in which Gurdjieff speaks to the two men about his auto accident. Gurdjieff told them that he habitually picked an apple from a tree when driving from Paris to Fontainebleau. To do this, he drove with only one hand. On this particular day, he said, the wheel of his car must have bumped into something for afterward he could remember nothing. He was found with his head lying on a car cushion.

Having told this story, Gurdjieff continued, "You know, Orage," addressing him directly. Then he related to Orage how a man reacts when you do something for him. A man's attitude, he declared, would go from "kneeling and kissing your hand" to "suing you for not giving him enough." Gurdjieff ended by again repeating, "You know, Orage … we must pay for everything." After Gurdjieff leaves, Orage comments: "He was probably getting at us for not knowing how to give …"[8]

To understand the true import of what has transpired we must know the issue between Orage and Gurdjieff. Gurdjieff, he felt, "regarded me as someone who had come with him from another planet with a task to carry out. But I had fallen in love with a native, and this interfered with his aim." Like all students, Orage had a desire for knowledge but he'd become entranced with a young, beautiful, intelligent and strong-willed woman who loved him passionately—an 'apple' in any man's eye—but who had little sense of or feeling for the Work, much less Gurdjieff's mission. Everything she saw and interpreted in an ordinary, formatory way. Orage, given his many affairs with Rosamund Bland, Beatrice Hastings,

---

6. It is said that in the original version Gurdjieff was much harder on Orage.

7. Gurdjieff's great generosity and compassion are seen in the *Third Series* where, along with the skewering of Orage and the reason for his failure, Gurdjieff revealed a great deal about himself and his own failures. Of the four books Gurdjieff wrote, it is the author's opinion, contrary to present opinion, that it is his greatest testament and that the text is complete, not incomplete, but it is for us to complete it by understanding what the ellipsis the book ends with refers to.

8. The importance of this, not only for Orage but for every seeker, is indicated by Gurdjieff having repeated it as a saying of popular wisdom in the prologue to his *Life Is Real Only Then, When "I Am,"* 56.

Kathryn Mansfield and nameless others, thought, if with regard to this subject he was thinking at all, that he could have his 'native'[9] and Gurdjieff, too. He didn't see the force of the descending octave she unconsciously represented—younger, beautiful, intelligent, self-confident, well-bred, and passionately identified with him. Just as in Gurdjieff's story when his vehicle hit an unexpected bump when he was not in full control of the car, Gurdjieff was warning Orage that his body would receive so great a shock from her that he would lose control over himself, i.e., lose his head. The result would be that Orage would remember nothing of his intention to awaken and the mission Gurdjieff has given him. Orage would self-calm himself from the spiritual catastrophe he will have brought upon himself by resting his head on a cushion; that is, no longer thinking but enjoying creature comforts. It might be worthwhile, too, to consider the apple as the symbol representing knowledge in the Garden of Eden. (And for this, the serpent must be included as well.)

Gurdjieff had given Orage a great deal and demanded the same in return. But with the giving, Orage's attitude changed. His self-love convinced him that he deserved and had assimilated what he had been given, and so he had no qualms about asking for more. As for Orage's remark that he and Nott don't know "how to give" (interesting how Orage includes Nott in this when Gurdjieff was clearly speaking to him), the real issue was not giving but that Orage was taking without paying. In effect, he was spiritually stealing. That he might have been "paying" in other ways was of no import. Only the teacher, the giver, can say what payment must be for what he gives.

Bennett's animal, had de Salzmann painted it, would likely have been a chameleon, or perhaps a lion, "lord of the beasts," as Bennett himself said. Certainly, of the three men, Bennett was the most elusive. With time, the lives of Uspenskii and Orage took definite shape and proceeded along established lines, but Bennett's seemed to carom erratically from cushion to cushion, like a cue ball stroked with too much English. Where Uspenskii was focused on finding "the new or forgotten road," the teaching that would release him from the circle of eternal recurrence . . . where the aim for Orage was becoming an elder brother of the human race . . . for Bennett the two constants throughout his life were the fifth dimension and making his own "contribution" to the teaching. Of the three, Bennett left behind the largest body of writing. Certainly in terms of sheer volume he published more books on the teaching, or his version of it, than Gurdjieff, Uspenskii and Orage combined. His books *Gurdjieff: Making a New World*, *Gurdjieff: A Very Great Enigma*, and *Talks on Beelzebub's Tales* offer many important insights into Gurdjieff, his mission and his teaching, though strangely he places its origin as an offshoot of Sufism completely deaf and blind to what Gurdjieff says regarding Egypt. Others, such as *The Dramatic Universe*,

---

9. A 'native' is a person asleep in and totally identified with materialism.

give Bennett's own interpretation and interpolation of the teaching. He introduced his work with the enneagram and systematics to the corporate business world, where these once esoteric concepts began to be applied to organization, design and manufacturing.

Gurdjieff recognized Bennett's capabilities, his brilliance, but thought his students, and therefore Bennett as well, "lunatics," that is, having unreliable values. Bennett appeared quite candid about his shortcomings. For example, he confessed he had the "particularly irritating habit of telling lies, either from the desire to please people or from the impulse to avoid awkward situations." "I was well aware that I had no stable attitude," he wrote. "I had often compared myself to a chameleon that takes the color of every background." He admitted: "My exasperating habit of agreeing upon a course of action and then doing something quite different is tolerable only for those who can value a little gold even when mixed with much dross. I could make real sacrifices for the sake of unity and then destroy all the good-will I had gained by following a course of action I had agreed to forswear." That, intellectually at least, Bennett saw a great deal about himself cannot be doubted. But did his admissions ever really reach his essence? Did he ever come to realize his own powerlessness, nothingness, in the face of his weaknesses? Or, did he buffer himself by admitting his weaknesses, but not suffering them?

One prevalent weakness he does not admit is his need to be in control. This may stem from his problematic relationship with his father. Whereas Uspenskii's and Orage's fathers died early in their lives—each son becoming at that time the 'man of the family'—Bennett was an adult when his father died. However, Bennett gives the impression in his memoir *Witness* that his father was absent from the home. He characterized his father as being "incurably optimistic...constantly making plans for new journeys and new undertakings to make us all rich." Bennett's mother,[10] coming from a puritanical New England family, likely held her husband in contempt for, as Bennett framed it, his father had an "inability to behave properly either in sexual or in financial matters." In effect, although for different reasons, Bennett became, like Uspenskii and Orage, his household's surrogate father. The archetypal role of the father in the family is that of a king, and all three men were 'kings' before they were adults. They became accustomed to being adored, having their own way and leading others.

Kings do not lightly become princes. This is aptly demonstrated when the twenty-seven-year-old Bennett first came to the Prieuré in August 1923, and Gurdjieff gave him what he called his "great experience." Gurdjieff infused Bennett with his *Hanbledzoin*—"I was filled with the influx of an immense

---

10. Their relationship must have been problematic in that he only makes a brief mention of her in his memoir, *Witness*, 326, and admits of "the need to hide from myself my deep fear of women." Where Orage has a "feminine element," Bennett has a fear. Uspenskii seems centered here, given his experience with Anna Ilinishna Butkovskaia and Carman Barnes.

power," said Bennett. Gurdjieff told him: "There are some people in the world, but they are very rare, who are connected to a great reservoir or accumulator of this energy.... Those who have this quality belong to a special part of the highest caste of humanity.... What you have received today is a taste of what is possible for you." Gurdjieff then asked Bennett to stay on at the Prieuré. But Bennett was wary. His life was a long string of 'great experiences.' It was Bennett's blessing and curse. Always in motion, he feasted on experience. A 'young king,' he was wary of coming under another man's will and direction.

Looking for a way to decline Gurdjieff's invitation, Bennett asked Gurdjieff—"If I should stay with you, how much time would be needed?" He said he expected Gurdjieff would tell him twenty years. Instead Gurdjieff answered—"If you will devote all your energies to the task, it may take two years before you can work alone." Gurdjieff saw Bennett's chief feature and spoke to it.

To no other pupil is it recorded that Gurdjieff ever gave such a promise. Whether Gurdjieff was serious is another matter. Speaking even more explicitly, Gurdjieff said he would take Bennett with him to America to act as his interpreter. Bennett insisted he must leave, he had debts to pay off. Gurdjieff, under heavy financial burdens and cash-strapped himself, said he would pay all Bennett's bills. (From Bennett's description, one gets the sense that Gurdjieff was almost pleading with Bennett to stay on.) But Bennett was having none of it. In *Witness,* Bennett obscures the real reason for his leaving by saying that "It was much rather as if Gurdjieff himself had withdrawn from me, and would not let me follow him."

It would be twenty-five years before Bennett would reunite with Gurdjieff. Though Bennett was now fifty-one years old, Gurdjieff found Bennett immature and ignorant.[11] Even so, Gurdjieff realized his possibilities and, according to Bennett, on several occasions likened their relationship to that between Judas and Jesus. "Mr. Bennett," says Gurdjieff, "is like Judas; he is responsible that my work is not destroyed...." Bennett's critics, given the eclectic teaching he later put together, wonder if he strayed into the more ordinary meaning of the word.

Of all the ideas Bennett put forward, two in particular need to be noted. One was the idea that Gurdjieff sent students away for their own development, thus taking the onus from those who left Gurdjieff. This idea along with its companion idea of 'graduating'[12] from the Work, has created much confusion. Gurdjieff was preparing "helper-instructors" who would be instrumental in enlarging the Work and who could take part, as he expressed it, "in God's government." Certainly, some people were sent away. But this was because they were either unsuitable, or could be of no further use, or needed to withdraw from the world for a time.

---

11. Perhaps what he was really pointing to was that Bennett was a young soul, much younger than Uspenskii or Orage.

12. In no place does Gurdjieff mention graduating, but he does speak of initiation. "A change of being," he says, "cannot be brought about by any rites....There is not nor can there be, any outward initiation. In reality only self-initiation, self-presentation exist." *Search,* 314–15.

Both of Bennett's ideas—being sent away and graduating—appear self-serving. Both support his own leaving of Gurdjieff, his disobeying of Uspenskii, and, later establishing his own "line" of teaching.

Throughout his life Bennett, a creative, mercurial and willful man, always posed problems for other people. For Uspenskii, Bennett became a problem as early as the spring of 1928 when he was jailed in Athens. Upon Bennett's return to London later that year, Uspenskii vowed never to speak with him. So Bennett, always the consummate political chess player, formed his own group. Slyly, he made what is called in chess a "forking" move, that is, a move that attacks in two directions simultaneously. He sent Uspenskii transcripts of his meetings, implying that if Uspenskii disapproved of what he read, then, as Bennett said, "I would stop." As Bennett had been a pupil of Uspenskii less than five years at best, it was indeed presumptuous of him to start, unauthorized, his own group. At the very least it revealed a lack of valuation. Moreover, exactly what he meant by saying "I would stop," Bennett left, quite characteristically, ambiguous. Would he stop speaking about whatever Uspenskii objected to? Or did he mean he would disband his group? In any event, Bennett would have forced Uspenskii to do what Uspenskii had decided not to do—to make a move, that is, to break his vow and communicate with him. No matter Uspenskii's response, whether he moved or didn't move, communicated or remained silent, Bennett 'won.' For if Uspenskii made no reply (and he didn't reply) Bennett could then interpret this lack of response favorably—as Uspenskii's tacit approval of his activities.

However, only two years later in 1930, Uspenskii, seeking to expand his Work and needing able helpers, made his peace with the 'devil.' He invited Bennett to join him. Toward the end of the decade, concluding that Bennett was too erratic to be trusted, Uspenskii moved him outside his inner circle. "All my life I had acted willfully," said Bennett of himself, "with little regard for the opinion of others, but I never trusted myself.... My way of acting had always been exasperation to my best friends because of this constant vacillation between self-will and self-effacement."

In January 1941, with Uspenskii leaving for America, Bennett asked him about the reason for his own lack of progress in the Work, wondering if it was because of a lack of a certain method or technique.

Uspenskii told him straight away: "It has nothing to do with methods. Your trouble is that you always make false starts. All your work consists of false starts."

Bennett then shifted the conversation to the subject of group work; that is, Bennett's own groups. Again, Uspenskii was quite direct.

"I can only consider the work [groups] at Lyne. The rest, so far as I am concerned, is dissolved."

The clear implication is that Uspenskii was telling Bennett to dissolve his groups.

Bennett, however, did not follow up on this, but again shifted to another subject. "Have you any objection to my trying to write out the System as far as I can remember?" he asked, making it sound as if this would be an outline for his own purposes, and not the four-volume study he planned to write.

Uspenskii told him: "In my opinion, writing is not useful."

Bennett makes no mention of how he views what Uspenskii said concerning his "false starts," but a characteristic of Bennett's, if not his chief one, is his willfulness. Even nine years after his conversation with Uspenskii, Bennett is still in its grip, for as his wife, Elizabeth Bennett, says: "So certain that he knew how to work, so blind to the opportunities in front of him, so humorless, so determined that force—physical, mental and moral—would bring him to the gates of heaven! In that month of August 1949 he was obsessed with himself and his own subjective states, to the point of distorting Gurdjieff's instructions so that they would fit his own preconceived picture of what was needed to bring about liberation."

Following Uspenskii's embarkation for America, Bennett began writing his book—contrary to Uspenskii's instructions—drafting one chapter every week. Hearing of this, Uspenskii sent a message to Bennett telling him no one was permitted to write anything about the System without his permission. Bennett neatly sidestepped this by evolving his own philosophy, or teaching, centering it on will, hazard and the triads. Later, in 1945, Bennett gave public lectures. This caused Uspenskii to break completely with Bennett. Uspenskii demanded Bennett return all his materials and instructed his pupils to have nothing to do with him. Bennett was also charged with being "a charlatan and a thief."

After Gurdjieff's death, Bennett crusaded for the Work, but his ideas and actions met with resistance from Madame de Salzmann in France and Lord Pentland in America. Stymied, he turned to Subud. Having a number of experiences with Subud which he felt opened his heart, he travelled the world proselytizing in its behalf. By 1962, seeing the limitations of Subud, he came under the influence of Idries Shah who professed that he, Shah, was a messenger from the "Guardians of the Tradition." Eventually, Bennett became a believer. In 1965, after much pressure from Shah, he offered Shah his own home and meeting place, Coombe Springs (at that time valued at $300,000). Shah accepted but insisted that "his hands be perfectly free." He told Bennett "the gift must be absolute, irrevocable and completely voluntary." As soon as Shah took possession of Coombe Springs, he made Bennett feel unwelcome and banned all Bennett's students. Shortly thereafter Shah had Coombe Springs bulldozed and sold off for development.[13]

Shah's demolition was a tremendous public humiliation. It shocked Bennett, as he said, into "the idea of self-effacement and withdrawal." For his seventieth birthday in 1967 his friends collected a large sum of money as a gift. Said Bennett: "In a very boorish and unkind way, I refused everything...and said I did not even want a birthday party. This uncivil behavior was attributable to my inner turmoil."

---

13. J. G. Bennett, *Witness*, First Edition, 359–62.

Six years passed. An inner voice—one Bennett said had always spoken to him in moments of crisis—told him "You are to found a school." He said there "then entered my awareness the significance of the 'Fourth Way.' There was a task for me to do and I had to prepare people who could help me in it. The school to be founded was a school of the Fourth Way."[14] And so on 15 October 1971, envisioning a coming crisis for humanity,[15] Bennett opened his own school in England, the International Academy for Continuous Education. Student residency was limited to ten months. Thus, Bennett proposed to do in less than a year what Gurdjieff himself had failed to do at the Prieuré in two years—prepare a core of helper-instructors. His experiment in accelerated development was called by his critics the "Bennettron." Bennett introduced his students to an eclectic sampling of exercises and ideas taken from many different ways. They studied Gurdjieff's books, as well, heard lectures by Bennett that ranged far and wide over esoterica, practiced the movements and zikr, fasted, staged theatricals, and did community service. Thus, The Fourth Way—which Gurdjieff had said "is completely self-supporting and independent of all other lines and completely unknown up to the present time"—was mixed with others. From this emerged the Bennett version.

Of Bennett's critics, it is perhaps biologist and author Robert de Ropp who offered the most balanced insight into the complexity of the man.

> The man was a Warrior of the first order, but ambitious. That was his problem. There were two men in Bennett. The first was a very sincere Seeker After Truth, who would spare no expense, no trouble, to learn more about the great game [transformation]. That aspect of Bennett I admired. But there was a second aspect. I called it the Arch-Vainglorious Greek. It was a Gurdjieffian term and referred to Alexander of Macedon, the strutting hero who had spread havoc all the way from Greece to

---

14. Here Bennett assumes the role of the Teacher by putting himself, unconsciously or not, on a level with Gurdjieff and his mission. A Fourth Way school emanating directly from Gurdjieff already existed. What was the need for another? Gurdjieff had told Bennett to take The Fourth Way teaching into the world. Instead, Bennett took a teaching of his own formulation into the world and called it The Fourth Way. Had he been able to resist such an impulse, or 'voice,' he would not have contributed to the present day confusion of Fourth Way tongues. It is because of this that Bennett's most militant critics charge him with being a Judas who betrayed Gurdjieff and his mission.

15. It is interesting to consider Uspenskii, Orage, and Bennett in terms of their perception of the future. Uspenskii, given his theory of eternal recurrence, is looking backward in time. Orage gives little indication of what he thinks but seems to believe that Social Credit, a barter system, would help the world. Of the three men, Bennett is the most future-oriented. His insights and assessments are mostly on target and his recognition of what was needed following Gurdjieff's death seems now, in hindsight, to be largely true. Many of his ideas could have been helpful. But he was not as developed as he thought he was and could not subsume himself for long to any group effort which he did not lead. He was a slave to his own brilliance. He left perhaps three hundred or so students who had taken his ten month course, some of whom are still connected with communities that he envisioned would act as "arks" in what he saw as the certain collapse of society, a collapse he believed would come about in the 1980s.

India and then expressed regret that there were no more worlds to conquer.... The Seeker After Truth was basically humble and sincere, content with little, modest and retiring. But the Greek was ambitious, full of great schemes, always liable to overextend himself, to attempt too much.

Robert de Ropp, a student of Uspenskii's since 1936, had also started a center to teach the Work. Some of his pupils left to study with Bennett. Upon their return, de Ropp says he "had expected well-trained, obedient, ready-for-service disciples." Instead he received "rebellious, starry-eyed, self-opinionated 'adepts.'... They were, as they put it, 'Messengers of the Higher Powers.'"

However one looks at Bennett, the feeling is that one has no sure footing. What can be said is that Bennett mixed the teaching. Naively 'democratic' in his thinking, Bennett never seemed to understand or value the Work's need to be hermetic. Others, however, might argue that he only did what Gurdjieff asked him to do and, further, that the rapidly increasing "terror of the situation" confronting humankind demanded all gates be opened. For all the dross, Bennett does have his gold. Many of his ideas are thought-provoking, potent and visionary.

More importantly, in terms of the line of the teaching, the octave of the Work, its force, as it had been with Uspenskii, was again halved with Bennett. Today there is still talk of the "Bennett Work," as if it were a teaching in its own right and Bennett were on the same level as Gurdjieff, or, for that matter, Uspenskii and Orage. With the passage of the current generation of Uspenskii's and Bennett's students, these versions of Gurdjieff's teaching are likely to play themselves out. Then the original teaching, the teaching that Gurdjieff paid so dearly to bring to those of mankind for whom it was prepared, might regain its original force and play the role in the world for which it was destined.

Of course Gurdjieff more than anyone understood how in *Heropass* all things, particularly a teaching as potent as The Fourth Way, are subject to deflection, distortion, and finally deviation. That is why he labored so to bequeath to the world *All and Everything*. Of the significance of Gurdjieff's *Legominism*, one can fully agree with Professor Denis Saurat's vision in the 1930s:

> Nothing much may happen in our time. We are in too much of a hurry. We have no sense of real time in the West. Perhaps in fifty, or a hundred years a group of key men will read it. They will say, "This is what we've been looking for," and on an understanding of it may start a movement which could raise the level of civilization.

Notes

1. *Hatching place for eggs.* MNP, 89.
2. *I want to know the future.* ISOM, 99.
3. *Extreme individualism.* ISOM, 266.

4. *I could call my chief feature 'Uspenskii.'* ISOM, 267.
5. *Gurdjieff and me.* RM, 15–17.
6. *The psychological side.* THC, 398.
7. *Chemistry.* ISOM, 8.
8. *Psychoanalysis.* AE, 577–78.
9. *Pseudo teaching.* AE, 249.
10. *This man . . . my brother.* OGA, 137.
11. *I cannot go more than half a hog.* OGA, 124–25.
12. *Lunatic.* W, 252.
13. *Incurably optimistic . . . constantly making plans.* W, 9.
14. *Connected to a great reservoir.* W, 121.
15. *As if Gurdjieff himself had withdrawn from me.* W, 126.
16. *Is like Judas.* W, 262.
17. *You always make false starts.* W, 178.
18. *So certain that he knew.* IP, xi.
19. *Turmoil.* W, 362.
20. *A Warrior of the first order, but ambitious.* WW, 327–28.
21. *Key men.* JTW, 46–47.

Personas & the Inner Animal

A preliminary exploration concerning Gurdjieff's teaching of the inner animal.

SITTING AT THE CAFÉ DE LA PAIX WITH THE ROPE, GURDJIEFF POINTED OUT THE PERSONAS, THE SOCIETAL MASKS, OF THE PEOPLE PASSING. THE PERSONA IS A primary image, along with subordinate images, rooted in personality—that which one has acquired and learned in life. Identity and persona are usually confused. When people say someone is "looking for their identity, who they really are," more often than not what is being sought is a persona mask. The young and inexperienced crave experience, but all experience leaves its mark. To avoid that "marking"—to have the experience but not be marked by it—the young often try on a number of masks. Whatever the mask, one thing is certain: in no case do they want to look like or be like their parents.

There is confusion here in that there is no discrimination between image and being. Gurdjieff says, "Exterior play role, interior never." The persona is adopted in reaction to experience, be it fear, or a resistance; or in desire, a full-blooded drive to be, participate in, the experience. With most people, image and being become so entwined over time that image, like a sybaritic vine, sucks the life out of being. A person becomes all persona, no substance.

The concept and experience of the inner animal is quite different. Gurdjieff speaks of scratching a person to see what they are like. Scratch the persona image and reaction is usually instant. That which reacts is one's inner animal. It doesn't live in the head but in the instinctual center. It would seem to be a part of, or closely connected to, essence—what a person is before they acquire, learn from, and react to experience. One's inner animal wants what it wants when it wants it. It has no higher aspiration. Its desires are basic, primitive. In this sense, one is ever in contention with it. But, as Gurdjieff says, one must make a friend of it, for without its motive force one cannot make a soul. One must know one's animal, work with it, feed it when it performs well, pet it—but keep it always under watch.

When one hears their inner animal named it often evokes a strong reaction, as was the case with Solita Solano—"Canary? Oh, Mr. Gurdjieff...not canary!" Or Kathryn Hulme's confusion. One simply doesn't think of oneself as an animal. We are human beings, "three-centered beings," as Gurdjieff said. But if the three centers are occupied only in a mechanical way, then do we really represent the species? Unawakened to our full potential, asleep, we are perhaps subhuman, something between human and animal. Not an endearing idea but how else to account for the continual wars, savagery and crime that mark human history—how else to account for, as it was once formulated, "the ghost in the machine"?

Whatever one's inner animal, according to Gurdjieff it has seven aspects.

"Kanari," he said, "one of your seven aspects is fly-mice (bat). Even exterior is such for me, can see even when look at your face."

"Oh, dear, bat is a squeamish animal," said Solita.

"Bat squeamish? Or man?"

"Man, of course. All mankind hate bat."

Replied Gurdjieff, "Not when I tell what means."

Which, of course, in true Gurdjieffian fashion he never does.

Along with the seven aspects, there seems to be a hierarchy of inner animals. The animals evolve—he says transformate—with our understanding. Gurdjieff told Solita that while her inner animal started as a Kanari (canary), it could become a crow, perhaps even a peacock. (Or, conversely, devolve into a turkey.) He said a small crow was better because it has shit of a better quality. His use of the word shit is shocking, crude. That he is speaking to women in this way offends. But could Gurdjieff also be indicating something deeper?

Shit represents the negative distillation of the three foods one has digested—physical food, air and impressions. The condition of one's Shit is a concrete example of the state of one's digestive process. The science of scatology deals with this. And shit, of course, isn't just physical, but mental, emotional and instinctual as well. The popular phrase "Don't give me any of that shit" is a personal statement, as opposed to the maxim "Shit happens," which is impersonal. The first is psychological, the second, cosmic. So shit itself is suggestive of three categories of meaning—functional, psychological, cosmic. To write off Gurdjieff's use of the word as simply obscenity and not as a possible teaching in itself is a limitation.

One might suppose that whatever one's inner animal it will evolve within its species. However, Gurdjieff told Kathryn that her crocodile might become an elephant, so that presupposition is not necessarily true. There also appears to be some confusion between inner animals and tapeworms. When Alice asked, "Is my animal really boa constrictor?" Gurdjieff replied speaking to Kathryn: "Yes. It was easy for me to put serpent in her because she already had by heredity a capacity for great swallowing. Now what suffering she will have. Because I put the serpent in her, she will always wish to swallow. And sometimes there will be nothing to swallow and so she will double suffer."

But earlier, Gurdjieff had said her interior animal was a tapeworm, the dictionary definition of which is "any of various cestode flatworms that live in the intestines." Later, at one of the luncheons, he will say, "We have three tapeworms. One organic, one in feeling center and one in mental." If we think of all three centers having "digestive functions" then in each there would be these parasitic "worms" which eat our impressions and energy. And later, "When tapeworm is satisfied it have beautiful smile like bird of paradise. When angry and wants something, he makes so—angry face, angry noise."

Fortunately, tapeworms, as adjuncts to the inner animal, or as the inner animal itself, can evolve. For example, when Solita asked—after noticing that the bones in her hands had changed—"Can active elements change bones?" Gurdjieff said, "Yes, of course. Can change even tail in man. Active element makes everything. Even the kind of breath you have depend from active elements.... Now my tapeworm sing—not 'Marseillaise' or 'Internationale.' He would only sing 'God Save King,' never would he be Communist—only monarchist or republican. Tapeworm of man is lazy and spoiled. He not have, like man, possibility of denying himself or wishing to suffer and make sacrifice for future."

Gurdjieff said also that tapeworms are of two kinds. "One—eat all but no satisfaction have. Other, eat all—but have satisfaction." And then there is this statement: "Not only is tapeworm in stomach of man, other worms also. Well, worms, such snakes as I tell about, is different kinds in stomach of man and of them all, one is always chief in this universe of stomach. He commands all and from him this chief in struggle of stomach-universe, from him depends of what consists the psyche of this man and what is his animal."

So the psyche of man and his inner animal are the products of the chief tapeworm that lives in his gut. Reciprocal maintenance is a key part of Gurdjieff's teaching, but who ever would suspect that it could be so personally applied? Besides the "tapeworm" and "inner animal," there is an "interior animal" also. So there are four levels. One is psychological, the persona, or mask. Then on an instinctive level (and each center is divided into intellectual, emotional and instinctive), there is the inner animal, interior animal and tapeworm.

Apparently, as with animals per se, there is no "peaceable kingdom." When Solita brought Janet Flanner's lover, Noel Murphy, to meet Gurdjieff, he told her:

"You are combination camel and sparrow. I not understand why Kanari call you friend. I know very well psyche Kanari. Also I have made special study of camel properties during 40 years. Never can two such animals be friends—is not basis of friend. Now I look to see if you are male camel or female camel. I not know yet. But I know even what kind of shit you make. You ever see camel shit? Small hard rounds, no scientist ever understand why shit like that. But I know. I also study strange sex organ female camel have." So friendships, rivalries, attractions and repulsions, predator and prey would seem to all be based on one's inner animal, or combination of animals. Which, in turn, is based on one's chief tapeworm.

Did Gurdjieff's inner animal teachings have an extension beyond what he gave? The relationship of animals and human beings in an initiatory context is quite ancient. In Siberia, for example, where Gurdjieff made a number of expeditions, the shamanic use of animals as "helping spirits" is quite common. As Mircea Eliade points out in *Shamanism: Archaic Techniques of Ecstasy*, "The presence of a helping spirit in animal form, dialogue with it in a secret language, or incarnation of such an animal spirit by the shaman (masks, actions, dances, etc.) is another way of showing that the shaman can forsake his human condition, is able, in a word, to 'die.'" Joseph Epes Brown in *Animals of the Soul* says that for the Lakota Indians "When the word for an animal is placed within a human's personal name, the name has then the power to establish for the bearer a kind of relationship with the qualities of that animal. This relationship is personal, private, and takes on the character of the sacred." Henri Frankfort in *Ancient Egyptian Religion* says that "In human beings individual characteristics outbalance generic resemblance. But the animals exist in their unchanging species, following their predestined modes of life, irrespective of the replacement of individuals. Thus animal life would appear superhuman to the Egyptian in that it shared directly, patently, in the static [being] life of the universe. For that reason recognition of the animals' otherness would be, for the Egyptian, recognition of the divine." When Gurdjieff speaks of maintaining a friendship with one's animal, for one cannot create a soul without its help, perhaps there are many levels on which his statements can be taken.

There is a great deal more that might be touched upon, but this should provide a brief introduction to the subject of the inner animal.

The Gurdjieff Journal, Vol. 16, No. 4

The Science of Idiotism

Gurdjieff first spoke about "The Science of Idiotism" at the Prieuré. He said it is a symbolical representation of human destiny. It was known in Babylon and later preserved in Central Asia. The monastery of a brotherhood at which he spent some time used the symbolism as a way to express and preserve for initiates important knowledge about Man and his Destiny. Because he saw in it a special power which did not exist in other ways of expressing the secrets of the inner life of Man, Gurdjieff decided to use it for the uninitiated.

Anyone having any contact with reality is called an Idiot—most people, immersed in fears, dreams and ambitions have no real contact at all. The word has two meanings. The first, according to ancient sages, is to be oneself. If he is, then to others living in the illusory world, he will look like a madman. "Everyone who decides to work on himself," says Gurdjieff, "is an Idiot. No one can make you an Idiot, you must choose it for yourself." The root of the word in Greek means "I make my own."

All individualized essences are Idiots, including very High Sacred Individuals. In another sense Idiots are contrasted with Wise Men and Intelligent Men. Only Idiots are to be toasted with alcohol; Wise Men with pure water; Intelligent Men with water with something added. The Idiot is someone who strives toward something—he is the Being in process of Becoming. That is why those who are stationary, such as "Wise Men," cannot be Idiots. Idiots eighteen, nineteen and twenty occupy a special place. Gurdjieff gives eighteen a number of definitions, pro and con. Bennett was this, though small, before becoming a Round Idiot. Nineteen and twenty, Gurdjieff says, are Sacred Individuals who perform functions in relation to the whole Megalocosmos. Twenty-one is God, the Unique Idiot.

The special force of the Science of Idiotism as a method of instruction lies to a great extent in the ordering of the series. Looking at the first ten—those most commonly toasted—there appears to be an ascending order from Ordinary to Enlightened. The next seven move in a direction which does not seem to be upward or downward but rather of greater helplessness and dependence on influences out of their control.

There are two directions of movement—"downwards" toward the Ordinary Idiot, experiencing one's nonentityness, and "upwards" toward number Twenty-one. If the aspirant does not first move downwards but attempts to move upwards then he will soon become stuck and the identifications can no longer be shed, and become an insurmountable obstacle. Those identifications that are objectively real, in essence, cannot be realized as such until they are discovered from their results.

Therefore, wherever one finds oneself, whatever Idiot one is, one must first "descend consciously" to the Ordinary Idiot, that is the Idiot with no distinguishing features, no personality, no special powers or properties.

"Necessary consciously descend to Ordinary Idiot—then consciously ascend," said Gurdjieff. This is closely connected with his insistence on the necessity of "realizing one's own nothingness" before one can hope to move toward anything real.

Ascending, Gurdjieff said, is automatic for everyone who works on themselves. Every two or three years they move up one stage. This automatic ascent is the result of life experience, of increasing self-knowledge. It does not come without effort and sincere striving, but it lacks something essential, it is the way of knowledge and not being.

The way of knowledge leads only to the stage of the Enlightened Idiot. "I pity Enlightened Idiot," says Gurdjieff. "More unhappy person not exist." The Enlightened Idiot has struggled and climbed, finally reaching the stage of knowledge where he knows everything (or thinks he does). He can say exactly what he must do—but can he do it? Is he all just words? Is it his fault, or a defect in his heredity? The only way for him is to give up his "knowledge" and descend to Ordinary Idiot and begin again. Yakina is an example. When she tells him that she hopes with her whole heart to fulfill his wishing for her, he stops her short—"*Not hope. In my opinion hope is an evil thing, is why man is shit, why he is nearly not man any longer. Man must use what he has, not hope for what is not.*"

After Ordinary Idiot is Super Idiot. He appears to have "something." If he has to descend to Ordinary Idiot, this "something" is an encumbrance, a relic of his self-importance, from which he must divest himself. If he is already moving upward on the right hand side of the scale, this "something" has a certain real value if it has been acquired in the ordinary world. According to Gurdjieff, Moses and Orage were examples of such. The next in the scale is the Arch Idiot. They are those who occupied positions of importance in the realization of their immediate plans. Jane Heap and Dr. Stjoernval were Arch Idiots.

Next comes the Hopeless Idiot. There are two kinds, Objective and Subjective. Says Gurdjieff, "Objective, he is shit, nothing never he can do. Subjective have possibility not be shit. He already come into place where he himself know he is hopeless, he realize his nonentity. He possibility have not be shit always such as he is." He says there are "seven aspects of Hopeless, dirty Hopeless, harmful Hopeless, stink Hopeless." The others he does not name. "Every man thinks he is God," Gurdjieff says, "but a Subjective Hopeless Idiot sometimes knows that he is not God. Objective Hopeless Idiot is shit. Never can be anything, never can do anything. Subjective Hopeless Idiot has possibility not to be shit. He has come to the place where he knows he is hopeless. He has realized his nothingness, that he is nonentity." Sardine was originally such an Idiot in the Objective sense, C. S. Nott in the Subjective.

Next is Compassionate Idiot, either Sympathetic or Antipathetic. The one sees a man lying in the gutter and goes to help him immediately; the other does so as well, but only because his fiancée's father is looking out the window. A third category is someone who sometimes is compassionate and sometimes not. Gurdjieff says, "I am Unique Idiot so I am no more this Idiot Compassionate." He also said he was Number Seventeen.

Squirming Idiot doesn't know left from right; one should not remain long in this Idiot. Theen One is an example. Square Idiot, which has breaks at corners of the square, is where something may momentarily enter. Round Idiot is an Idiot on all sides, is never to blame. Whatever they do, they have a good excuse. Krokodeel is an example. "Zigzag is high Idiot," says Gurdjieff, "goes this way, that way, struggles against shit he knows he is." Jessie Orage was an example.

Gurdjieff once said to Solita Solano, "Scale is from shit to God." About toasts, he said, "Unique Idiot is highest (thing) and in stone or static thing is the lowest; between the two is our scale or measure. First time, one starts up the scale automatically proceeds as far as #16. This is easy, easy to go up. For going down is difficult, because go down with consciousness. Second time go up, can go beyond #16—even to Stink Idiot."

Solita asked, "Is Stink Idiot same as Harmful?"

"No. Sometimes Stink Idiot can be made clean. But Harmful never, in objective sense."

In giving the "Toasts to the Idiots," the Director, usually a man, always seated to Gurdjieff's left, begins at the beginning of the scale. Everyone was given a small tumblerful of Armagnac or vodka. Men were supposed to drink the glass in three toasts, one-third per toast; women in seven. The toasts usually stopping at four or five and only rarely going beyond twelve. The first four toasts were to Ordinary Idiots, then Super, Arch and Hopeless. The Objective Hopeless Idiot is satisfied with himself and does not see that he is a candidate for perishing like a dog. The Subjective Hopeless Idiot sees his own complete nothingness and does not realize that this death of self is the guarantee of his resurrection. From this stage he becomes a Compassionate Idiot whose reason has opened to the suffering of others. The Squirming Idiot is not ready for help. The geometric Idiots are Square, Round and Zigzag; they represent states in the establishment of true reason, at first momentarily, then comes the discovery of one's own identity and third the desperate struggle to break free. The next series is Enlightened, Doubting and Swaggering Idiots. The Doubting Idiot doubts he is an Idiot, he is "shit of shit." But there are two kinds. One is Antipathetic—he only wishes to appear clever. The other is Sympathetic, one who doubts sincerely. Beyond these are Idiots whose characteristics are deep in their essential nature. At each stage there is a death and resurrection before a new gradation of reason is attained. Very difficult for these three.

There are 21 gradations of reason from ordinary man to that of our ENDLESSNESS. No one can reach the Absolute Reason of God, and only sons of God like Jesus can have two gradations of reason that are 19 and 20. Therefore the aim of every being who aspires to self-perfection it would seem is to develop to the 18th gradation.

Scale of Idiots

1. *Ordinary*
2. *Super/Superior*
3. *Arch*
4. *Hopeless—Subjective and Objective*
5. *Compassionate—Sympathetic and Antipathetic*
6. *Squirming*

7. *Square*—Sometimes not an Idiot as there are corners where something can get in
8. *Round*—Idiot on all sides, morning, noon and night
9. *Zigzag*—Have five Fridays a week; hysterical people
10. *Enlightened*
11. *Doubting*—Sympathetic and Antipathetic
12. *Swaggering*
13. *Born Idiot*—Remorseful from Birth
14. *Patented*—Also Born Dreaming
15. *Psychopathic I*
16. *Polyhedral*—A Stinking Idiot (one of stinking heredity)
17. *Not named*
18. *Highest development of human reason and being*
19. *Sons of God*
20. *Sons of God*
21. *Unique Idiot (our God)*

The Gurdjieff Journal, Vol. 16, No. 2

Images of God or Machines?

MR. GURDJIEFF SAYS WE ARE "IMAGES OF GOD." BUT HE ALSO SAYS WE ARE "MACHINES." HOW COULD WE BE BOTH IMAGES OF GOD AND MACHINES? HOW TO UNDERSTAND THIS? THE GULF BETWEEN THE TWO SEEMS SO IMMEASURABLE THAT THE CONTRADICTION LOOKS IRRESOLVABLE.

It is difficult to think of ourselves as being a machine. Something in me just rebels at the thought. I associate the word to the machines I know, those made of plastic, iron or steel. But if we modify the word machine with *bioplasmic*—that is, that we are *bioplasmic machines* that is more digestible. But, still, something in me rejects this. Bioplasmic or not, I don't feel like a machine.

Before examining this "I" that we all base everything on, let's first focus on the meaning of the word *machine* itself. What is a machine? It is that which has been created to do something, to accomplish a given task or tasks. It is programmed to perform as efficiently as possible.

Now are we programmed?

This word, too, something in me immediately rejects—we don't like to think of ourselves in this way. But if we say "conditioned" that is more acceptable. It's a primary term of psychology and sociology. So there is agreement that we are conditioned by our heredity, our parents, peers and society, and by the World-Time, the context in which we live. The conditioning involves our memory, which is based on our experiences, real and imagined, some of which we remember and much of which we don't. The most fundamental conditioning happens between our birth and about the age of nine years. Our parents, for example, are the primary male and female images. The difference between father and mother we take in very early. One feeds and comforts and the other—well, what does the other do? The image is there but how we experience and thereby relate to what will be called "father" develops more slowly.

But what is it that is perceiving and receiving these images of mother and father and all the succeeding ones? I take the images in sensorially, instinctively, and then through feeling and, as the head brain develops, mentally.

Now, exploring the idea of our being bioplasmic machines, let us say that each of these—instinctive, feeling and intellectual—is a bioplasmic brain. That is, the machine is composed of three different brains. Each operating and processing at different speeds and refining different qualities of energy. Each of these brains is conditioned by experience. At one and the same time, then, I can say feeling-wise, I like someone, mentally be impressed with them, but instinctively distrust them. So, then, which brain is the most powerful, which brain am I?

Now, what is this "I" that you and I and everyone keeps referring to? We commonly take this to be the unchanging, indivisible center of all my experience. Given our life experiences and how we interpret them, the "Story of I," the world each of us creates, is who take ourselves to be. On one end of the human spectrum are the megalomaniacs among us either falling totally in love with themselves as a Master of the Universe (albeit, in miniature form, if confronted); on the other end the professional victims forever tarring themselves with guilt and self-loathing. The rest of us? If we sincerely observed ourselves, wouldn't we find ourselves, given the moment, yo-yoing somewhere along that spectrum?

Now what about this World-Time we live in as a conditioning agent? Certainly there have been many world-times before us. Just a quick journey back in time shows us that our ancestors lived in a hunter-gather society, which was succeeded by the agrarian, and then, in the early 1800s, came the industrial, followed in the early 1900s by mass production and scientific management, which established modern industrialization. With the 1940s came computers, then semiconductors and the breaking of the DNA code in the 1950s, followed by microprocessors and artificial intelligence and biotechnology. These, and many other discoveries and inventions, are the foundations of the World-Time we live in now, which I call the Technological.

The Technological World-Time has given birth to many marvels, but most primary and threatening is the "Son of Man," that is, binary computerization and robotization. Its exponential acceleration of power has many experts predicting that human intelligence will be totally outstripped by the year 2020. This, they believe, will very shortly lead to a human-machine interface in which the human brain is ported into robots. This is not a sci-fi fantasy.

So while we revel in all the powers of computation, communication and worldwide and interstellar travel that Technology offers us, there is, as with everything, a downside — that is, that Technology will render human beings nothing but bar codes, worker ants, in a great and interlocking and self-regulating computerized and robtoticized world in which the "oil" of this time will be electricity to run the machines and water to cool them down.

Should this happen, human beings will lose what is most precious and unique — our possibility to evolve, to spiritually awaken. If we remain at the machine level and so identify with machines we will simply want to become better machines, to do it faster, better, more accurately, yet because we do not run on electricity and can only be programmed to a point, we will never overcome the "Son of Man" in any of its myriad forms. Thus, we will self-reduce to the level of a machine — just cogs in a vast wheel of production, used as nothing more than a part of the raw materials and resources — and thus forfeit spiritual self-transformation.

To understand the challenge we face we must first understand Technology, its essence — *what it is in itself*. It is not something alien but a part of us. Aristotle defined man as "the rational animal." Technology is simply our rational part developed to an extraordinary degree. Back in the hunter-gatherer World-Time, the First Man (or woman) observed lightening striking a tree and igniting it. Over and over she or he observed this — the Gita says that intelligence is a feminine attribute you know — and suddenly an intuitive leap was made and two sticks were rubbed together and presto — a spark of new life. The First Observer was the rational part and from there to here simply gives us "The Son of Man," we who are potentially "The Sons of God."

Sons always challenge fathers and so Technology challenges us to awaken to a new level of ourselves or to suffer the consequences. We must strive to understand the essence of Technology. As it is a part of us, to understand it we must first know our own essence.

What are we? Are we bioplasmic machines or not? If we deny this question, then we begin on too high a level; that is, we assume our oneness, that we have free will, an ability to do. We need to know whether or not, and in what way, we are machines. But to know ourselves as machines — *what is it that will know it?* Computers and "robo-sapians," as some call them, can never truly know what they are. Self-consciousness they can never have. Self-consciousness is only possible for a human being.

But our consciousness has become so identified with the working of our three brains — intellectual, emotional and instinctive — that it is one with them; there is no differentiation. If we can rightly learn to observe ourselves impartially we will see that our functioning is that of a machine. And as we suffer this — and what is suffering is our self-image, the "I-of-the-moment" we take ourselves to be — our consciousness, that which we truly are and why we are images of God, separates from the functioning of the machine. All things gross and subtle appear and disappear within consciousness, but consciousness is *not* these impressions, it is only their receiver. And so, through serious and unflagging work on ourselves to awaken. We gradually realize that I am both a machine and not a machine. The *I Am* is something far greater. As Mr. Gurdjieff titles the most esoteric of his three series of books, *Life Is Real Only Then, When "I Am."*

Now, how to awaken?

Images . . . the mind lives in images, either those of perception or memory. Our senses are like a camera constantly recording the environment, whether consciously or not. If we think of these images being recorded on a kind of bioplasmic camera film, then as we know, at least before the day of the digital camera, there are two images: a negative image, one yet to be developed; and a positive image, one which is developed. To be developed, the image had to first pass through a solution, exposed to light, then dried. With time, like magic, the negative image becomes positive. The positive image is not different than the negative. It was latent in the negative, like the tree in the seed; it only has to be developed. And so, as long as we remain undeveloped we remain negative images, that is, machines. Developed—truly awakening to our real self—we cease to be a machine and, to the degree that is consciously realized, become an image of God.

As with developing a negative image—where is the solution? Where is the light? The light and the solution is the seminal, esoteric and sacred teaching that Mr. Gurdjieff brought to the West called the The Fourth Way. The teaching begins by admitting the very danger that confronts mankind—that man is a machine; that we are bioplasmic machines in terms of our identification with the mechanicality of our three centers—mental, emotional, instinctive. Our consciousness, as we've said, has been so attracted by the activity of these centers that it has lost itself in them. We only cease to be machines when we learn to observe impartially the truth of the facticity of our mechanicality, our conditioning.

But how to see this if I am a machine?

How can a machine see itself? It can't. But the consciousness which we fundamentally are can. Each of us has a certain small amount of freedom to choose—if we choose to become awake and have the knowledge to do so—then an inner space will be created and the consciousness that is our true identity will gradually separate from the mechanical activity of the machine. This knowledge is fundamental to The Fourth Way. And it is why The Fourth Way is the teaching for our time.

The Gurdjieff Journal, Vol. 16, No. 4

GEORGI IVANOVITCH GURDJIEFF

JESSE DWIGHT ORAGE

ELSIE AT THE PRIEURÉ

Elsie found the Prieuré a most extraordinary place. When she drove up to the gate set in a high stone wall which surrounded the entire estate her impulse was to turn and fly but Stephen had told her that she was having a taste of conscious suffering, and so—she rang the bell 'très fort' as letters on the gate directed. A young Russian clad in working clothes opened the gate and brought in her bags and showed her to her room, a large room in the best part of the chateau. Then she was taken to greet Allah [Gurdjieff]. He was in the forest at the end of the garden and when they met said, "Very good, miss, you come."

Elsie wandered about the grounds and went to sit on the terrace. She took out a cigarette and began to smoke. A pupil who passed informed her that it was against the rules for women to smoke unless in their rooms. Elsie laughed. It amused her to break their silly rules. She didn't want to be there anyway and she didn't much care if she was thrown out but Stephen would care and that kept her from doing many things she otherwise would have done.

Allah certainly worked Elsie. If there was something a bit difficult to do, "Here you, miss," screamed Allah and Elsie did it if she could. After all she was there for a purpose and all such tests should add strength. Some things she refused to do. It might be argued that with such a man as Allah it took more courage and was more difficult to refuse than accept. However Elsie was a very stubborn young person, also to be driven aroused her quicker than anything else and the sheepish attitudes of the majority of the pupils was degrading to an American girl brought up to have her own way in almost everything reasonable. Some of the things which were so abjectly accepted by the other pupils seemed anything but reasonable to Elsie. For example, when the bell rang for meals if Allah were not there, picks, shovels, wheelbarrows were flung aside and a rush was made for the house, but if Allah were overseeing, everyone worked steadily on until he either left or said "Enough." Sometimes they worked on until it was an hour after the bell. Elsie also stayed on for a few days but finally she revolted. "What's the idea?" she said to Allah. "I want my dinner," and she walked off alone. Allah dismissed the others then. Allah came to her and said, "Very necessary go work at once—no rest after dinner today."

"Nonsense," said Elsie. "You not allow women smoke. I smoke in room after dinner. No smoke, no work." And she laughed.

Allah looked a little nonplussed—he compromised. "Walk to work with me," he said. "I give you cigarette." And he did.

Elsie & Allah

Stephen was very keen for Allah to see the baby. Elsie was not but then that was as much Stephen's [choice] as hers. Still she would have to go too as she knew Allah's methods of stuffing children with all sorts of horrible sweets. She had seen Allah but once since he had arrived. It was at a group meeting she had attended not expecting him to be there. He was already there when they arrived and yelled at Stephen "Where you been damn fool."

"Damn fool yourself," said Elsie in a rage walking up to him.

He looked at her astounded "Who are you?" Allah asked as though he did not recognize her.

"And who are *you*?" retorted Elsie blazing at him. In her hand was a packet of matches and she threw one at him.

"Oh," said he after a pause, "It is Elsie" and held out his hand.

After another pause on Elsie's part she took it. She had made scene enough.

The next day Allah told Stephen that although Elsie had hurt him very much it was an odd thing that of all the sheep present she was the only dog. To a friend of hers, Martha, a woman he had long tried to unsuccessfully attach to his train, he said "Elsie over love me—I turn her out—now she hate me and very funny now I desire her very much. Love and hate very like."

So naturally Elsie did not wish to see him again but for Stephen's sake she went with him and Martha taking the baby.

Allah appeared to take pains about his reception of them. He tried to inveigle the baby with candy to come to him. The baby refused—he simply stood and looked at Allah and would not be coaxed. He was not frightened, he just looked.

When he had an opportunity, Allah came over to Elsie and said, "You come sit here. I wish talk to you."

"Perhaps," said Elsie.

"You come here—my bed," said Allah and his look made his meaning clear.

Elsie did not reply. What was the use. His methods were always so crude.

When they were leaving, Martha took the baby and went ahead with Stephen. Allah laid his hand on Elsie's arm and detained her. If he tries to kiss me what shall I do thought Elsie inwardly, shuddering, and to cover her nervousness she said, "You like my baby?"

"No," said Allah. "I don't like that baby," implying to Elsie if it were mine I would.

"You don't like *him*?" she said drawing away. "Goodbye."

"Goodbye," said Allah and taking her hand he kissed it. "You phone me—come see me."

Elsie left in a fury.

That evening Allah asked Martha, "You think Elsie pleased this afternoon?"

"Very pleased, I think," said Martha. The line of least resistance was always

Martha's line but it was hardly friendly of her as she was perfectly aware of Elsie's reaction to the afternoon's episode.

Stephen and Elsie had a violent quarrel about the whole business. Elsie maintained that if any other man but Allah had behaved so to her Stephen would have considered it an insult. That he condoned Allah or preferred to ignore the incident she could not understand. "He'll be coming down here, Stephen. You'll see," she said.

That very day a large package of sweets was left at the house for Elsie. "Of all the fools! Does he think I can be bought with Turkish delight?" said Elsie. "It goes straight back to him and that will be a little surprise for Allah!"

So it proved. That evening in the midst of Stephen's lecture a henchman of Allah's appeared with a message that Allah desired his presence. As soon as possible, Stephen went. On his return he told Elsie that for once he had seen Allah truly disconcerted. He had asked why his gift was returned.

"You insult my wife," Stephen said to him.

It was then that Allah was taken aback but he tried to justify himself by saying the candy was for the baby.

"It was not so addressed," said Stephen.

Allah then rushed into an explanation of the hand kissing. He did not know that Elsie had related the whole story including the bedroom invitation. His explanation was that Elsie was so naïve as to be hurt when he, in fun, said he did not like the baby and so, seeing she was hurt, he did something quite unusual for him—he kissed her hand and poor Elsie was so naïve she had even misunderstood that.

Stephen had said no more but no other advances were made and Elsie did not see Allah again.

Solita Solano

Meeting with Rosamund Bland

Rosamund was tallish, heavy, 51, strange sad face, dark masses of short hair, beautiful feet and ankles, hands, arms. Friend, companion, Uspenskii, Orage, once was at Prieuré, knew [Miss] Gordon from early days, also Katherine Mansfield. Well, I saw her diary from the Prieuré... when I knew her better she told me her story and showed me all Orage's letters.... First about her. She was born a Cockney (titular) you know, and she discovered at the age of seventeen that she was illegitimate. Her mother Edith Nesbit had not been her mother at all, but accepted the baby of the family governess to keep its father, her husband [Hubert Bland] in the house and later had to bring in the governess [Alice Hoatson, Rosamund's birth mother] as well. So four children, two wives and one man lived and quarreled for twenty years. Rosamund was engaged to [Clifford] Sharp. Orage, Sharp's great friend, made her marry him, since he could do nothing. They were moral, too, in those times and struggled against this love (I saw the letters) which went on for 16 years on her part and longer on his [Orage's]. They lunched together the week he died. In those years Orage was looking always for a man without quotation marks. He picked up psychoanalysts, mind readers, freaks of all kinds, only to drop them and continue the search. Then Uspenskii came to London.... Orage met him, was wildly enthusiastic, "At last, a *Man*," telephoned Rosamund, she had to come. Rosamund wrote in her diary that the meeting was, much of it, over her head—apart from the universal laws—but that there seemed to be a lot of sense in what Uspenskii said but no sense in the people there. Uspenskii noticed her, asked her to tea at the old Chinese restaurant near Piccadilly (men have always fallen for her, and always the most important men). I don't know if Uspenskii was in love, but she was his "secretary" for years.... Rosamund was fascinated, her mind was fed, she kept on meeting Uspenskii and listening and learning.

Orage's jealousy was terrific. He had for years considered himself as a guide and mentor to her interests. His "bitterness welled up," she wrote in her diary, "and shows in public." Hard for him to be dethroned by the Work, as he is. "I am not learning from him now and that is a position he does not want. He wants from me a sort of adoration and belief in him that I cannot possibly give any longer." Later Uspenskii forbade them to speak or see each other, or even write.... Seemed to me so strange to hear her call Orage "Andrew," to see his letters so signed. The other side of Orage we have never heard of, the man-woman jealousy. I took one note on "identifying." Uspenskii said there was a word in Russian for this that means "flowing into" or "merging into." This is what takes all our energy.... Our Gurdjieff said at last picnic, "take impressions in such place—shock in the scale at 'si.'"... I said to him "Bearers of new direction?" And he nodded. "'Si' is where impressions came in on the food chart." He said "Yes, if not too late in place where you are—if still you are young enough."

Orage was not the man then he was years later. Used to torture Rosamund. For instance at their meeting place, the old Café Royal, he would often say, "Well, since you won't sleep with me, pick out a woman for me here. Anyone you like, I don't care, I'll take her off for the night."... Then, how I don't know, Uspenskii and Orage and Rosamund went to the Prieuré. Times were difficult, no money after Lady Rothermere and some others went away from the Work. Rosamund was quite ill and Gurdjieff promised her a "little" cure because he had no time. He told her that what she had was serious, she would realize it many years later. That was in 1922 and today she is dying. Tube contracted, hardly any food can pass into stomach and contraction continues. If he [Gurdjieff] hadn't had his accident and she hadn't gone off with Uspenskii after the split with Gurdjieff—well, who can "if" these matters.

In spite of all [at the Prieuré], Rosamund's terrific physical exercise, hardship from cold and insufficient food and fatigue, never hearing him [Gurdjieff] say anything as we do, having to share a room with *three* Russians, she wrote at the time she would rather be there than anywhere else in the world. She was never afraid of him [Gurdjieff], she just looked into his eyes when he seemed angry and felt perfectly safe.... When I think what roses, roses we have, all his attention, instruction, the book, exercises, food-medicines, music, friendship, intimacy—well, I just can't believe it. Wish to or not, we must thank his accident that broke up the Prieuré and made him free for other experiments.

Uspenskii's situation in London now is what I call pitiable. Uspenskii has become lazy and increasingly doubtful about the book he wrote about Gurdjieff [*Fragments of an Unknown Teaching*]. Changes it constantly, has even made Gurdjieff talk like normal man in English. Now Uspenskii only has classes on Monday nights in which he reads chapters (like "Purgatory") he stole from Gurdjieff through renegade pupils of Gurdjieff's and waits for intellectual questions. If he ever had anything, except desire to find out what Gurdjieff knows, he has lost it.... Regrets bitterly she obeyed Gurdjieff when he told her he could do nothing for her from lack of time so to stay in London with Uspenskii. (That was before Gurdjieff threw Uspenskii out.) If she had followed Gurdjieff around in spite of everything, she would be with him today perhaps. Now too late, can't travel.... I made a special point of telling Gurdjieff when I returned that I had seen Rosamund and that she is dying. How she was full of remorse she hadn't followed. He said, "Always they cry when too late."

The Gurdjieff Journal, Vol. 13, No. 1

Initiation

(KANARI WRITES TO MARGARET) ONE OF THESE DAYS I REALIZE I AM AND SHALL REMAIN FOREVER A WEAKLING. ALTHOUGH FROM THE MINUTE I WAKE UNTIL I SLEEP I make one continuous effort—probably I don't—there is no advance made in will or brain. I can still be conquered by subjectivity even when on my guard. What to do? Just go on struggling, I suppose.

What secret do these men bear with them to the tomb? Why are they wondered at without being understood? Why are they acquainted with things of which others know nothing? Why do they conceal what all men burn to know? Why are they invested with a dread and unknown power?

There existed in the past and there exists in the present a potent and real magic. There is indeed a formidable secret.... This secret constitutes the fatal science of 'good and evil' and the consequence of its revelation is death.... There is one sole, universal, and imperishable dogma, strong as the supreme reason; simple like all that is great; intelligible like all that is universally and absolutely true;

and this dogma has been the parents of all others. There is a science which confers on man powers apparently superhuman. They are enumerated as follows in a Hebrew manuscript of the 16th century:

"The powers and privileges of such a man—he beholds God face to face without dying and converses with the seven genii who command the entire celestial army. He is above all afflictions and all fears. He reigns with all heaven and is served by all hell. He disposes of his own health and life and can equally influence that of others. He can neither be surprised by misfortune nor overwhelmed by disasters nor conquered by his enemies. He knows the reason of the past, present and future. He possesses the secret of the resurrection of the dead and the key of immortality (you will interpret all this in the method—naturally not a real resurrection of the planetary body). To find the philosopher's stone (Self-development). To enjoy the universal medicine (Probably air and impressions). To be acquainted with the laws of perpetual motion (this means always making the second and third bodies to go on with after body death). To subdue the most ferocious animals (our awful emotions). To speak learnedly on all subjects without preparation and without study. To force nature to make him free at his pleasure. To foresee all future events. To conquer love and hate. To know how to enjoy poverty."

Gurdjieff says in sum, "When I make use of the consecrated terms God, heaven and hell, let it be understood that my meaning is as far removed from that which the profane attach to them as initiation is distant from vulgar thought. Magic is composed of two things—a science and a force; without the force the science is nothing. To give knowledge to power alone, such is the supreme law of initiation." "The kingdom of heaven suffereth violence and the violent only shall carry it away." The door of truth is closed; he must be a man who would enter. All miracles are promised to faith but what is faith except the audacity of a will which does not hesitate in the darkness but advances in spite of all ordeals, surmounting all obstacles. Unnecessary to repeat here the history of ancient initiations; the more dangerous and terrible they were, the greater was their efficacy. Ordeals of courage, discretion and will. (Do you wonder I am so weak and discouraged? Gurdjieff went through the fire and water and God knows what else four times in Egypt. I won't even get into an automobile with him.) ❋

CARMAN BARNES

MUSIC OF THE SPHERES

*"Seek him that maketh the seven stars and Orion,
and turneth the shadow of death into the morning...."*
Amos 5: 8

"VERY INTERESTING," SAID THE GREAT PHILOSOPHER, AS HE HANDED BACK TO THE YOUNG WOMAN HER NOVEL, WRITTEN WHEN SHE WAS ONE-HALF HER PRESENT YEARS.

"I was very young when I wrote it," faltered the Young Authoress.

"No, but it's very interesting," said the Great Philosopher, his small, gray eyes peering at her through his unrimmed spectacles, "You must write more on the same subjects."

The gaze of the Young Authoress widened. "You're the first man who ever said that to me," she said. "Usually men think I should write on subjects that are more—more solid. 'A solid reputation'—that's what they want me to have. A textbook, maybe."

The Great Philosopher smiled indulgently.

"Nonsense," he said. "There are only two important things in the world: sex and magic. You know nothing about magic, so you can't write about it. Leave solidness to others." He waved it away.

"Really," said the Young Authoress, from force of habit, for she was still suffering from the effects of her career as a sensational child prodigy. "None of the things that happened to my heroine happened to me."

"Of course not," said the Great Philosopher. "You never would have written about them, if they had. But your young lady had curiosity. A most important thing. You must write a book where the girl goes to her father and tells him she has lied about her experiences in school; nothing ever happened to her. Your young lady had her experiences in school; nothing ever happened to her. Then you must write what she found out afterward. Your young lady had curiosity, and you have curiosity. What she found out...."

"Do you really think I should write that book?" asked the Young Authoress, still timidly.

"Of course. What else?"

The Great Philosopher turned back to his blackboard with an air of finality, and began drawing a marvelous and apparently incomprehensible diagram, a representation of the universal creation.

The Young Authoress sighed, and sat down with the other members of the class. She took out her notebook and began to copy the diagram before her.

This is what she drew:

[Large circle with three smaller circles inside it. Inside one of the inner circles are five successively smaller circles drawn concentrically. The large outer most circle is labeled World I Absolute. The inner circle with the enclosed circles is labeled, from the outmost to the innermost:

World	3	All Galaxies
World	6	Our Galaxy
World	12	Sun
World	24	All Planets
World	48	Earth
World	96	Moon]

"Each world," the Philosopher explained, "has three forces of its own, and three of the preceding world, except the Absolute, where the three forces are one. Our mechanical laws begin in World 6. That is: time, birth, death, accident. But the Absolute reaches only World 3. It does not reach us."

"Don't you believe in God, Sir?" asked someone in the class.

The Great Philosopher shrugged. "God is the architect who went on vacation to the Riviera after completing the general cosmic plan. He delegated the rest of the work to his engineers, designers, decorators."

"You mean the Suns, Moons and Planets?"

"Naturally."

"But if the forces of the absolute do not reach us"—there was a desperate look in the eye of the questioner, The universe had collapsed beneath him.

"Only energies from the Sun, Moon, and Planets reach us directly," shouted the Philosopher, impatient at such formatory thinking. "We live in a very bad place of the universe—toward the end of the line, where things are more mechanical; there are more laws. We can draw this diagram another way."

do	World	1	Absolute
si	World	3	All Galaxies
la	World	6	Milky Way, Our Galaxy
sol	World	12	Sun
fa	World	24	Planets
mi	World	48	Earth
re	World	96	Moon

"You must understand that this is an octave of radiation of cosmic energies from the Absolute to the Moon. We use a musical notation to establish the progression of radiation, or vibrations. It is said that the musical scale was used as a system of cosmological notation, long before Pythagoras used it for music."

"If the earth is in a bad place in the universe, how can we get off the earth?"

asked an ambitious student.

"We can't get off the earth," said the Philosopher. "But we can — in time, and with work, and knowledge — live under fewer mechanical laws."

"How can we do that, Sir?"

"Ah — that is what we are here to study. In time, we may be able to receive higher influences — impressions from higher worlds."

"From the planets and the moon?" asked the Young Authoress.

"From the planets and the sun," said the Philosopher. "The moon is at the end of the line. The moon isn't born yet."

"Not born yet! Why the moon is supposed to be dead. How do you know it isn't born, Sir?" asked the Frightened Young Man.

"Somebody told me," said the Philosopher.

"How can we receive higher influences — from the planets?" persisted the Young Authoress. "Is this astrology?"

"Astrology, no. Astrology may be accepted only as language for psychological types. This is chemistry, or better — alchemy."

"That means turning base metals into gold, doesn't it?" asked another student.

"Time. It takes time," said the Philosopher. "All this will be repeated. You see, Organic Life is a sensitive film around the Earth." He drew it.

"It fills up the interval or gap between mi and re. Organic life was created to help vibrations or radiations to pass between the Sun, Planets, Earth and Moon. Man is part of organic life."

The expression on the face of the Frightened Young Man clearly indicated that he believed himself to be in a den of heretics.

"You mean man was created only to help some radiations pass between worlds?" he gasped.

The Great Philosopher shrugged again. "It looks that way."

"But the stars" — said the Young Authoress, and they were in her eyes. "You mean we can go to the stars?"

"That's a poetic way of putting it," replied the Great Philosopher.

After the lecture, the Young Authoress walked down the avenue on the sidewalk along the dark park. Overhead, the green leaves of late spring canopied the night sky. The moon was sailing overhead. She looked at it with new wonder. The moon was not a dead world, but waiting to be born! The stars seemed very far away, whirling in their orbits, like the dreams in her own head; dancing a stately saraband, mathematical as Bach, out in the dark reaches of space. Trailing the moon was a giant star, blue in color, and more brilliant than the rest.

"That is Venus," mused the Young Authoress. And immediately she thought of love.

It was spring. She stretched up her arms to the green, leafy trees overhead, and to the night world of the sky; to the unborn moon, and the phosphorescent dust tracks of the stars.

"What am I?" she asked herself; for all students of philosophy ask themselves this question. "I, too, like the other worlds, like the stars, am a musical note. Part of something—organic life—that fills an interval in a great universal symphony. Something musical, something mathematical, something mystical—boiled down to an infinitesimal invisibility. But I'm part of the harmony. I can dance like the stars in their spheres. I can almost reach to the moon. And perhaps, perhaps some night, I shall go to the planets. He didn't say how to go there, but already I begin to see. Already I think I know."

She glanced up overhead at the brilliant Venus.

The Gurdjieff Journal, Vol. 15, No. 4

Miracles Can Happen

A NEW RELIGION IS OFFERED TO THE WORLD. THE 20TH CENTURY MAY WELL BE REMEMBERED BY FURTHER GENERATIONS—IF THERE ARE TO BE ANY—BY THREE momentous events: the atom bomb, the flight to the moon, and this teaching. It is not a new doctrine nor a new cult nor a new philosophy but actually a whole new religion, the first one since Mohammed and probably the last one before our civilization ceases to exist. This new religion, the most important since the Gospels, has the inherent power to postpone the destruction of our society; indeed, if anything can prevent the coming world catastrophe, it can.

Man is a machine and no evolution is possible for him unless he becomes other than a machine; that is, unless he acquires Consciousness, Permanent I, Unity and Will. If Man knew himself for what he really is—a helpless puppet in the mechanical repetition of happenings with no hope of changing things—he might go mad.

Uspenskii, convinced that he had fallen upon the great and terrible truth, abandoned all his previous conclusions. He began to tell his pupils that with the exception of the last two chapters of *New Model of the Universe* he no longer believed his books led to anything.

When he came to America in 1941, like others whose ideas had been radically affected by his two great books, *Tertium Organum* and *A New Model of the Universe*, I became one of his pupils. I found it disconcerting when he said that now he felt them useless. He offered, in their stead, what seemed, to begin with, an obscure and confusing system of thought, the origin of which we did not know, the end of which we could not foresee, the methods of which we doubted, and the pursuit of which seemed abstract and incapable of realization.

"Modern scientific man has forgotten how to believe in the possibility of miracles," Uspenskii once said. "We must not allow ourselves to forget that they *can* happen. The possibility exists for man gradually to free himself from mechanical laws."

Perhaps the miracle that can happen for the world is that, through the publication of this hitherto esoteric knowledge, our deteriorating civilization will be shown—and accept—before it is too late, "the way out." ⚔

The Gurdjieff Journal, Vol 16, No. 2

Frank Lloyd Wright

Gurdjeef at Taliesin

Real men who are real forces for an organic culture of the individual today are rare. I venture to say one might count them on the fingers of one hand with the thumb to spare—unless the thumb were to go to George Gurdjeef of the Prieuré at Fontainebleau, France, and spare the little finger.

Only One

There is only one Gurdjeef. His career is as unique as is the man himself. Rarely going out of his way to visit anyone during his brief stay in the United States, he honored us at Taliesin by coming out from Chicago to stay 24 hours with the Fellowship. He is a Greek who has roamed about Asia and western Europe in search of the temple rituals of Oriental culture. He has from this data by way of the genius that is his, developed new rhythms in the dance and new music so designed as to integrate the human faculties and prepare the man for a more harmonious development than any we can show by way of our current ideas of education.

In his sardonic fashion, with his tongue in his cheek a good deal of the time, he has crystallized his philosophy in nine fat volumes and has in manuscript form, as yet unpublished, some 8000 pieces of music of such quality that undoubtedly when he permits their publication, he will be best known as the author of a new school of "objective" music; that is to say, music that does not mean one thing to one man and another thing to another man but music so crystal clear and simply related to human feeling that all men will weep or smile or dance as the music itself does. And when one of our young men played from the Gurdjeef manuscripts 25 or 30 of his compositions this seems to be true. A prayer, a solemn dance, a gayety—all were emotionally true and organically beautiful.

Three Classes

His writing is to be had by translation only and so his involved oriental style comes out in some confusion but no humbleness. The thought is there, however, addressed to "idiots" by way of Beelzebub. Beelzebub has his fun with the idiots. Gurdjeef, declaring all mankind idiots, divides them into three classes—those who take what they can get; those who get what they can take; those who get what they get.

There is enormous ego in this man. Always deliberate in movement, not large although he seems so—with the skull bald and tall behind—forceful humorous luminous eyes. In him we see a massive sense of his own individual worth. A man able to reject most of the so-called culture of our period and set up more simple and organic standards of personal worth and courageously, if outrageously, live up to them. He affected us strangely as though some oriental Buddha had come alive in our midst. With perfect unconsciousness of self he would deliberately walk to the piano and adjust his glasses to correct the player. Or, his bulk seated at ease in his chair, he smiled about him when his readings were read, watching the different faces and recognizing the feelings behind the various expressions.

Nothing Escapes Him

A kind, solid, fatherly man. All that went on about him seemed to impress him little and yet he would later give evidence that nothing escaped him, so highly are his powers of observation and concentration developed. He would appraise a character in a remark. He has rejected them and perhaps the personality of Gurdjeef is somewhat similar to that of Gandhi only, of course, more robust, aggressive and venturesome in nature. Now a man of perhaps 85 looking 55, he has some 40,000 "followers"—he will not call them students or disciples—has 104 sons of his own and 27 daughters for all of whose education he has made provision and to which he has given his attention.

He rather impressed me as being something of a Walt Whitman in Oriental terms, which neither describes nor explains him. He is an interesting study in himself, defying such analogy. He would resent such study and in no uncertain terms would put the observer back into his proper place.

Knowledge Seems Perfect

His knowledge of human nature and all its foibles seems perfect, and he does not hesitate to use this knowledge for his own ends although with a conscience that sees to it that they get something worthwhile out of his meeting them. Not caring at all for America or Americans, he has come over here, as he frankly put it, "to shear the sheep." He will turn the wool into some kind of good work for humanity. His hypnotic powers have served him well in this connection, but he is more careful now in exercising them. American fruits and foods he finds unfit to eat—likes only our tomato juice and our dollars. But eats enormously just the same. The style of our money he approves. But the shearing I imagine is not so good. The wool is now so short. Notwithstanding a superabundance of personal idiosyncrasy, George Gurdjeef seems to have the stuff in him of which our genuine prophets have been made. And when prejudice against him has cleared away, his vision of truth will be recognized as fundamental to the man men need.

Georgi Ivanovitch Gurdjieff

Count Bobrinskoy

Peacock from Heaven

THE GIGANTIC, BARREN CLIFFS THAT LOOM ALMOST VERTICALLY FROM THE RIVER ARAXES WHICH FLOWS INTO THE CASPIAN SEA DIVIDING RUSSIA FROM PERSIA, ARE favorite haunts of a wild mountain goat known as Capra Sibirica or Asiatic Ibex. The head of this swift and amazingly sure-footed creature is a trophy much coveted by all keen sportsmen. It was to try my youthful luck in shooting an ibex that I ventured to brave the desolate and perilous region which is its habitat. This was at the southernmost tip of Transcaucasia between Nakhitchevan and Ordubad.

My friends in St. Petersburg had never tired of warning me beforehand that it was a spot infested by snakes, scorpions, and Kurds. "And," they added with malicious relish, "as everyone knows, a Kurd is a cut-throat and a robber. If you return from these parts alive or at best without a half-a-dozen knife wounds and as much as a single rouble in your wallet — it will be a miracle...."

Concerning the snakes and the scorpions my friends were indeed right for never before had I seen so many of these. However, I soon discovered that they had been grossly unfair to my guides and fellow hunters, the Kurds, with whom I got on well. I certainly would never have had any success in my quest without the expert advice of my burly companions. I found them to be a strong, fine people, helpful to a young sportsman without expecting an exorbitant recompense for all their toil on my behalf.

Stalking ibex is no easy matter, for no creature on earth is more shy and wild than are these mountain goats. They possess such a keen sense of smell that the slightest change in the wind's direction will set the whole herd galloping off at full speed over the precipitous crags, never to be seen again. Day after day we stalked and pursued, and evening after evening returned to camp disappointed.

My fellow hunters, though helpful enough in the chase, did not prove to be very entertaining companions when the day's work was over. They sat around the campfire in almost complete silence, and sometimes they would scarcely answer me when I spoke. This taciturnity was particularly noticeable if I plied them with questions about religious matters. I was always eager to learn about the various tribes inhabiting Russia. They had each their own particular from of worship, and I was glad to have this opportunity to add to my knowledge.

I noticed with surprise that my new friends apparently observed no religious ritual of any kind. I was puzzled by this more especially as I had only recently returned from a visit to a village in the North Caucasus where the inhabitants were extremely devout Muslims. Their calls to prayer had seemed to me to be never-ending.

"Are you not Muslims?" I asked them one evening, I apologized for my ignorance, and requested to be enlightened as to what religion they did follow if they were not disciples of Mahomet. They looked at one another darkly, and curtly replied: "We are not Muslims."

As time went on I became increasingly curious. Surely, I said to myself, these somber, serious looking people must have some form of faith, but try as I might, I could not get a single one of them to reveal it.

Meanwhile the difficult quest for ibex continued, and my time was fast drawing to a close. I began to face the prospect of having to make an ignominious return to St. Petersburg empty-handed. On the very last day, however, I was lucky enough to kill a couple of the elusive ibex with good heads. That evening my friends and I sat at the mouth of a cave and enjoyed a hearty meal. Under us lay a deep gorge, through which, far below, swirled the muddy waters of the Araxes.

In the hollow basin of a rock the Kurds had made a fire of heaped charcoal over which they had strung upon iron skewers chunks of freshly killed meat. To my delight, as time went on, my companions became a little more communicative. Gradually the mystery of their religion was divulged.

"We call ourselves *Yezidi*," said one of the men.

"Yezidi? What does that mean?" I asked. Battai, the man who had first spoken, hesitated for a moment, then said very solemnly: "The Yezidi are those who worship Yasdan."

"And how do they worship him?" I asked. "Is your way very different from the way of the Muslims or the Christians. . . . ?"

"It is very different," replied Battai.

After this remark there was a long silence. My companions looked at each other uneasily, as though secretly wondering how far they should go in revealing their sacred doctrine to a young Russian stranger. The meal was over now, and to the charcoal embers my friends added a great pile of logs and twigs. The firelight flickered eerily over their swarthy faces, and plunged the surrounding landscape into mysterious darkness. I longed to know more but I restrained my inquisitive tongue and waited.

At last Battai spoke again. "It is not our custom to explain our religion to those outside the Faith, but we like you and trust you. Since earliest times," he went on, "we Kurds have lived in these hills, some on this side of the river, some on the other bank. We were here even before your Prophet Jesus came into the world. Our ancestors came from Iran, and their teacher was Master Zoroaster who said that Ormuzd and Ariman, the Spirit of Good and the Spirit of Evil, were the twin sons of the mighty fundamental principle called Zarvana Arakana or Limitless Time. It is the eternal conflict of these two Spirits in the Universe, and in the soul of Man, which creates life. Both are equally important. The Master said, 'Without Good how can Evil be recognized? Without Evil how can we know what is Good?' Each needs the other as that fire needs fuel . . ."

Battai looked deeply into the embers as he spoke, as though contemplating his own symbol, and weighing it up in his mind.

I was amazed at the unsuspected wisdom and erudition of this simple, uncouth looking hunter...

From where did he get his knowledge, I wondered. Was he a priest in disguise?

Battai, however, was unaware of my surprise.

"Yes, that is the way of it," he continued, "sometimes the Good conquers, sometimes the Evil. So it has ever been and so it always must be: for these twin sons are truly the one double face of the God Yazdan. We believe that in recognizing, understanding, and appeasing the Evil, we can better deal with its influence both within ourselves and in others. We do not like the legend of St. Gurgi perpetually spearing the Dragon..." By this Battai meant St. George. "You will never find a Yezidi called Gurgi. The Dragon must be tamed, not speared. One cannot kill such a Dragon with a man-made weapon. In this way we only anger him."

Battai paused for a moment, and gazed once more into the heart of the fire. "Perhaps you may have noticed," he went on, suddenly looking at me, "that we, Yezidi, never wear blue...?"

"I had not realized it," I answered, " and what is the reason?"

"Because it would offend the Fallen Angel," Battai replied, "blue is the color of Heaven out of which he was flung."

"So that legend comes into your religion too?" I asked.

"It is not a legend," corrected Battai, "it is a true fact. Furthermore it is a great privilege conferred upon us, the Yezidi, that we are descended directly from the shepherd who saw him fall. Yes, yes, one evening it was, many, many hundreds of years ago, when our shepherd ancestor was bringing his flock home to the mountain cave where he lived. Suddenly the sky was torn asunder by a blinding flash of lightning while, almost simultaneously, there followed such a roar of thunder as would have deafened a giant. The shepherd flung himself down upon the bare rock, and hiding his face, prayed to the great Power of Life and Death that he might be spared. Then, looking up, he saw an Angel standing in the middle of the Heavens with an enormous spear in his hand.

"There followed another horrifying clap of thunder, and something was hurled from the sky down onto the crags below. A great gust of wind arose and swept over the mountaintops. The valley shook. Then all was quiet again.

"Gradually recovering from his great shock the shepherd rose from the ground and looked around. He saw that a huge cedar had been struck by the lightning and was lying across a deep ravine.

"On the further bank lay a beautiful peacock badly hurt but still alive. The shepherd crawled across the fallen tree trunk and took the dying bird in his arms. After washing its wounds in a nearby stream, he carried it into the cave which was his home. Without any thought of sleep he tended it throughout the long night. When the morning came the peacock had completely recovered and spoke to the shepherd in a human voice, saying: "Be not afraid, man, you were kind to me in my misfortune, so I will reward you and all your descendants. I am the

Spirit of Evil thrown out of Heaven by my twin, the Spirit of Good. But I am not conquered. On earth, as in Heaven, I shall continue the struggle. Amongst men I shall spread sorrow and instill my poison into their hearts so that the great conflict will be implanted within them. Teach your descendants to accept Evil as you have accepted me. Be compassionate towards Evil both in yourselves and in others. Delight me with songs. Placate me with prayers. Tend me as you have tended me last night."

"So saying, the Angel Peacock, Melek Taus as we call him, spread his wings and flew away over the inaccessible mountaintops. That is why," concluded Battai, "we Yezidi, the descendants of that compassionate shepherd, sing hymns to appease and glorify the Spirit of Evil to this very day. Our hymns are scorned by the rest of the world. Both Christians and Muslims alike hate and persecute us. They call us 'Musaddun'—Infidels and Devil-Worshippers. Our priests, Quawals, travel secretly and do not wear priestly robes. They carry with them, hidden away from Muslim and Christian eyes, the effigy of a peacock. When we pray we do not turn towards Mecca like the Muslims but towards the Polar Star, the immovable source of light in darkness, the point of the axis round which the whole universe revolves. We honor Wednesday as our day of rest, not Friday like the Muslims, nor Sunday like the Christians. A quarter of all that we earn we give to the poor. Churches we have none, for if we built them they would be at once destroyed by either Muslims or Christians. But we are not angry. We do not hate our persecutors because our religion bids us to be tolerant." As he finished his story Battai's harsh voice grew silent.

I sat spell-bound. The old man suddenly got to his feet, and the party broke up. It was nearly midnight when I retired to my bed of leaves and grass in the mountain cave.

The stars were shining brilliantly. Across the valley I thought I heard a distant rumble of thunder...

The following day, laden with the two splendid ibex heads, I took leave of my good friends and made my way on horseback down a narrow mountain path to the nearest railway station, a journey which took many hours. In the train I happened to share my compartment with a woman and her small daughter. The mother was telling her child a story, but my thoughts were still with the Yezidi and I only half listened.

Suddenly, as though from far away, I caught these words:

"And so, my little pigeon, Beauty kissed the Beast right on its dirty hairy snout, and *then* what do you think happened...? That dreadful, hideous monster simply shriveled away, and in his place stood a handsome young prince, and..."

With a start I woke from my brooding recollections, and looked at the woman in amazement. Beauty and the Beast!... What a remarkable coincidence! Fresh from the philosophy of my friends the Yezidis, the well-known fairy-tale seemed alight with a new and profound meaning. To kiss the Beast, to realize, to accept completely the ugly and the hateful in life, instead of eternally denying, resisting, fearing it, as we all do. Was not this exactly the Yezidi ideal? And did not the fairy-tale prove that it was a good one?

The little girl thought so, at least. With her head nestled against her mother's arm, she seemed entirely satisfied by the result of Beauty's courageous kiss; but she would have been equally appeased, no doubt, by the more ruthless methods of St. George towards the dragon.

I settled back into my corner and closed my eyes. Assuredly both of these ways are necessary when dealing with the mighty powers of darkness.

Anyway my holiday was a fruitful one. I was able to tell my friends in the Capital that I returned with no wounds in my flesh and with a great spiritual fortune in my heart.

Notes

A Hero of Our Time. Uspenskii speaks about the author Mikhail Lermontov in the chapter "Eternal Recurrence and the Laws of Manu" in his *A New Model of the Universe,* 472–73. "The feeling of the repetition of events was very strong in Lermontov," wrote Uspenskii. "He is full of presentiments, expectations, 'memories.' He constantly alludes to these sensations, especially in his prose. 'The Fatalist' [a chapter in *A Hero of Our Time*] is practically written on the theme of repetition and of remembering that which seems to have happened in some unknown past. Many passages in 'The Princess' and in 'Bela,' especially the philosophical digressions, produce the impression that Lermontov himself is trying to remember something that he has forgotten.... In our time the idea of recurrence and even the possibility of half-conscious remembering becomes more and more pressing and necessary. In *The Life of Napoleon* (1928), D. S. Merejkovsky constantly alludes to Napoleon in the phrases 'he knew' ('remembered'). And later, in dealing with Napoleon's last years in Europe, 'he forgot' ('he ceased to remember').... I wished only to show that the idea of repetition and recollection of the past which is not in our time is far from being foreign to Western thought." Translated by Vladimir and Dmitri Nabokov, Lermontov's novel is published by Everyman's Library (Alfred A. Knopf, Inc., 1992). For a review of the book see *Telos,* Vol 1, No. 8.

Ahl-i Haqq. Sharing many characteristics with Yezidism are the Ahl-i Haqq (People of Truth) tradition, which seems to have originated among speakers of Western Iranian languages and has its oldest center in Kurdistan. In the *Second Series* of *All and Everything,* Father Giovanni of the World Brotherhood tells the story of Brother Sez and Brother Ahl. Could Gurdjieff be pointing in this direction? Among their beliefs before Heaven and Earth existed, God created a Pearl from his own pure light and came to dwell in it. The Heptad of Angels was created with a Covenant between God and them, the role of each of the Angels was defined and they would obey His law and become manifest on earth at certain times. The name of Satan is forbidden to be spoken. According to Ziba Mir-Hosseini, "Inner Truth and Outer History: The Two Worlds of the Ahl-I Haqq," they believe in "The successive manifestations of Divine Essence which act as a link between the inner world (*ālam-i bātin*) and the outer world (*ālam-i zāhir*) without ever bringing them together. Human life is nothing but the transmigration of souls during which the soul migrates from one world to the other. In each of these journeys, the soul takes on a different body, likened to putting on a new garment. Death is only an interval in the inner world during which one is confronted with the sum total of one's deeds in the outer world. Suffering and good fortune can only be understood in relation to one's deeds and thoughts in the course of one's previous incarnations. The whole purpose of all these comings and goings, whose number and duration are already fixed at 1,000 incarnations in the course of 50,000 years, is for the soul to gain perfection. Those who have completed the journey become perfect souls, part of the *bātin*, and if they come back to the world of *zāhir*, it is always for a purpose of a mission."

According to J. G. Bennett in *Gurdjieff: A Very Great Enigma*, "Ahl-i-Haqq was founded in 1316 A.D. by Sultan Sahaq, but this was more a fresh start or reform than a new beginning. They preserved, through the coming of Islam, not only Nestorian Christian traditions but also much earlier Chaldean or Zoroastrian traditions that had belonged to the time of the greatness of Babylon.... This knowledge is chiefly concerned with the transformation of energies." Bennett says that at some point when he visited Gurdjieff in Paris that he saw in his kitchen twenty or thirty little sacks of Persian rice, all with labels and Persian stamps. They were mailed from Kirmanshah, a town near the center of the Ahl-i-Haqq. "This may mean anything or nothing," he writes. Odd, that for all his erudition and research, Bennett never saw the significance of Egypt in the teaching Gurdjieff brought. Perhaps, as Martin Bernal argues in his three-volume work *Black Athena*, Bennett never saw that the African and Semitic lineage of Western civilization had been deleted from the record of ancient Greece by the bias of 18th- and 19th-century historians. For additional information, see "Yezidism," *The Gurdjieff Journal*, Vol. 5, No. 2 & 3; for Ahl-i-Haqq, see Vol. 5, No. 4.

Anderson, Margaret (1889–1973). A woman of high energy, great beauty and sensitivity, Margaret Anderson lived a large portion of her life by her feelings and emotions, trying to attain one of three states: liberty, ecstasy, and peace. The way many live out of the intellectual center, Margaret lived out of the emotional. Wrote Hugh Ford, in his *Four Lives in Paris*, "Feeling, emotion, sensation, nuance, fine distinctions, and emanations were the qualities Margaret pursued and celebrated, none of which, in her opinion, intellectuals comprehended or considered useful. She prided herself on knowing what they did not know or did not care about." When Orage advised her, "Remember you're a pianist, not a piano," a recodification of Gurdjieff's "Act, don't be acted upon," she came to learn, as she phrased it, "The quality of every life is determined exclusively by its position in relation to acting or being acted upon." Her longtime companion Georgette Leblanc, a singer and great beauty herself, never felt comfortable with intellectuals for, as she said, "We live for emotions ... they live for events. In our relations with people, we wait on the development of personal atmosphere; they don't wait, they crouch.... They become critics." Margaret Anderson wrote one book about her years with Gurdjieff which she titled *The Unknowable Gurdjieff*. Of her three-volume life story which concluded with *The Fiery Fountains*, she wrote:

> I wonder why I have wanted to write this story of my life. I know it at first hand, but so incompletely that it has little meaning. It has been so happy

and so sad, as happy as flowers, as sad as moonlight—a happy life that loves the saddest music. It has been a striving and a failing; a development and a diminution; it has been proud, and egotistic, and modest; aggressive and unassuming; alert and unconscious; hopeful and, I fear, lost. It has overflowed with thankfulness and remorse—a life like any other, but which has seemed to me so different, so special, and so blessed as to be unique. The blessings I wanted were love and music, books and great ideas and beauty of environment. I have had them all, and to a degree beyond asking, even beyond my imagining.

Barnes, Carman. Born 20 November 1912 in Chattanooga, Tennessee, Carman Barnes was intelligent, magnetic, with a lithe figure and a face having a strikingly beautiful Egyptian cast. When only sixteen, Carman Barnes published her first novel, *Schoolgirl,* which became an international best seller. Two years later, having dramatized her novel with A. W. Pezet, it ran for a short time on Broadway. Paramount Pictures bought the rights for $30,000, but it was never made into a film.

In the next four years, Barnes published four more novels before finally being lured to Paramount. Barnes, immediately nicknamed "Baby Garbo" in Hollywood, says she was "photographed 700 times in the first week." Wrote Mollie Merrick, 10 June 1931, in the local paper:

> There are bets going the round that Carman Barnes will never see the light of day as a star.
>
> Carman Barnes is the blond, brown-eyed, white-skinned schoolgirl prodigy who broke upon Hollywood some months ago as author. She was retained as one of the writing staff of Paramount, but, after a tryout in that department, was announced as a forthcoming star.
>
> This announcement came at a time when Clara Bow was in serious trouble and when Warner Brothers had made a raid on Paramount talent. The raid carried out many of the established names of the firm. So what better than to throw in a few new ones.
>
> Enter then, Carman Barnes—"Carman spelled with an a," she told you in a high fluting voice. Carman Barnes, a slim sprout who chatted volubly of her "play," her "novel," the "picture" she was writing and in which she was to star. It sounded like a child's dream of artistic heaven.
>
> Then Carman Barnes was put into the cast of another picture—not the one she was writing for her own talents. And that story was forgotten for the time being.
>
> Now those who nod wisely and narrow their eyes a bit over their Scotch glasses do be saying that there will be no Carman Barnes starring this year—or any other year.

Her future once so bright now suddenly dimmed. The questions it raised caused her interest in a range of esoteric subjects. Theos Bernard, a leading yoga and tantric practitioner who called himself "the first white lama," became a strong attraction. With the passing years, she became interested in creating a school "such as I would like to go to." (*Schoolgirl* hints at lesbian relationships and perhaps this was why she was expelled from Nashville's Belmont School for Girls.) In New York in June 1940 she contacted the architect and writer Claude Bragdon, whom she had met at a party. Bragdon, like most men, is instantly smitten. He writes to her:

> Believe it or not the moment I set eyes on you I knew that you were somehow mixed up with my destiny, no, perhaps not the first time which was at Mabel's [Dodge Luhan] party though then I noted you out of a great number of women, but the *second* time surely, in the Rainbow Room when I looked into your Egyptian eyes.

Then he writes:

> Your letter this morning—as before—pleased and excited me. Yes. I think it is more than likely that we have known one another, as Henry James would have said, 'from far back.' Of the people who are factors in one's destiny this is probably always true.

Despite Bragdon's seventy-four years of age and flagging health, Barnes convinced him to give a series of his lectures on art and mathematics in her New York studio, which he named "The Arch." He agreed to give a series of eighteen lectures, "The Arch Series." Bragdon became her mentor and she related to him the sexual experiences that shamed her. He consoled her and tried to lead her to forgive herself but his approach was mental.

In 1941 Bragdon introduced her to Uspenskii. Barnes captured Uspenskii's attention as perhaps no one had since Rosamund Bland twenty years before. He agreed to give lectures in her studio. As he did with Bland, he soon began to see the twenty-nine-year-old Barnes privately as well as in the group, the private meetings going on well into the early morning, the sixty-three-year-old Uspenskii drinking heavily and telling of his life. A number of his letters give a sense of their relationship, which was intense but not likely consummated as Uspenskii was in failing health. His last letter extant is 26 July 1943 in which he asks "who is the next boy friend?" This was likely Hamilton Fish Armstrong, editor of *Foreign Affairs*, whom she married in 1945. Before Uspenskii's and Barnes' relationship ends she will dramatize his *Strange Life of Ivan Osokin*.

Married to Armstrong, Barnes and he together wrote a play, *Passionate Victorian*, about the English actress Fanny Kemble. It was never produced. Following more than ten years of publishers' rejections of various works, Barnes' novel *Time Lay Asleep* was published in 1946. After a few years, Barnes and Armstrong separated, formally divorcing in 1951. Barnes travelled to Europe that year, settling finally in Austria. She suffered the first of several breakdowns in the summer of 1952 and was treated with insulin shock therapy and psychotherapy, among other methods. She died in Salzburg, Austria, on 19 August 1980 at the age of sixty-eight.

Butkovskaia, Anna Ilinishna. In her book *With Gurdjieff in St. Petersburg and Paris* she twice writes that she first met Uspenskii in 1916. Later, she mentions his going to India and then returning. But we know from *In Search of the Miraculous* that he returned to Russia in November 1914. She also writes that she first heard of Uspenskii through his book *Tertium Organum*, which was published in 1912. She writes her book in 1975 at ninety years of age and is likely to have been confused about dates. With James Moore, we take her first meeting with Uspenskii to be in 1912. However, Moore has Uspenskii first speaking to Anna about Gurdjieff when he returns from Moscow after a week of meetings with Gurdjieff in April 1915. In Anna's book, however, she writes: "You remember I told you [says Uspenskii] the time I went to Moscow . . . Well, that man is here now, in Petersburg. I've just come from him this moment." On the preceding page she writes: "Now that Uspenskii was back in Petersburg we resumed our morning meetings . . ." Clearly, a good deal of time had elapsed.

Chief Feature. According to Kathryn Hulme's notes, Gurdjieff tells the women that they must learn where their chief feature lies and what it consists of. It is the pattern of our wishes and motives. It is mechanical, of the essence but in the emotions. In bowling balls there is a pellet of lead added, so that the ball must be thrown with a special quirk to make it go straight. Look for it in five things: greed, self-pride, lying, fear, and sex. It can often be a combination of one or many of these five things. There is in each of us a "special little quirk" which makes us do things as we do them, not like anyone else. It is imaginary, not real, and is not ever a good thing. But once found it can be used consciously. Chief feature is an outgrowth of our *emotional attitude toward ourselves.*

Devil according to Uspenskii. "'The Devil,' that is, the slanderer or tempter," wrote Uspenskii, "was in the original text [of the New Testament] simply a name or description which could be applied to any 'slanderer' or 'tempter.' And it is possible to suppose that these names were often used to designate the visible, deceptive, illusory, phenomenal world, 'Maya.' But we are too much under the influence of mediaeval demonology. And it is difficult for us to understand that in the New Testament there is no *general idea* of the devil. There is the idea of evil, the idea of temptation, the idea of demons, the idea of an unclean spirit, the idea of the prince of the demons; there is Satan who tempted Jesus; but all these ideas are separate and distinct from one another, always allegorical and very far from the mediaeval conception of the Devil." Speaking of the biblical phrase where Christ says, "get Thee hence, Satan," Uspenskii says that in this case Satan "represented the visible, phenomenal world, which must not 'get hence' by any means, but must only serve the inner world, follow it, *go behind it.*" *A New Model of the Universe,* "Christianity and The New Testament," 154–55. For a serious study of this area, see *The Old Enemy: Satan & the Combat Myth* by Neil Forsyth (Princeton University Press, 1987).

Enneagram. It is clearly the primary symbol of Gurdjieff's Fourth Way teaching of self-development. Words can take one only so far. There is too much that has been written and too many who have appropriated the symbol for their pseudo-teachings to add to the general confusion and misunderstanding. For one misrepresentation, see "The Many Worlds of Oscar Ichazo," *The Gurdjieff Journal,* Vol. 16, No. 1.

Evil. Uspenskii quotes Gurdjieff in *Search* as saying that there can be no conscious evil. But in a deleted passage from the original draft he writes: "I said, 'Do you wish to say that there can be conscious evil, and he [Gurdjieff] certainly said it can be. Anything that produces big phenomena can have mind and intelligence behind it. Then I remember he said—'Why are you upset?' I was upset because it meant changing all I thought before. He said, 'It becomes even more interesting—it is one thing to have against you only mechanical forces and quite another to have intelligence; it is one thing to struggle with intelligence, and another to struggle with mechanical forces.'" Gurdjieff added that, "If in a full sense conscious evil is possible, it is only possible in a very elaborate way and a very rare case." In *Beelzebub's Tales,* Gurdjieff gives another perspective on the word *evil,* 1139.

Ferapontoff, Boris. The notes of Boris Ferapontoff, which extend from February 1920 through the summer of 1921, give an impression of how the teaching was presented at that time. It was said, for example, that "sol 12 can sometimes pass to la 6, if the shock was sufficiently strong, for instance, with the help of artificial, or sometimes, natural breathing." Ferapontoff stayed with Gurdjieff through the early Prieuré period and was appointed along with five others, including Sophia Uspenskii, Jeanne de Salzmann, Olga Hinzenberg, Elizabeta Galumnian and Dr. Konstantin Kiselev, as an Assistant Instructor of the Institute of Harmonious Development of Man. He taught movements at the Prieuré and, of all the Russian pupils, spoke the most fluent English. Ferapontoff died in 1930.

Fourth Dimension. In 1898, at the age of twenty, Uspenskii published his first book, *The Fourth Dimension.* The two books by the Englishman C. H. Hinton, *A*

New Era of Thought (1910) and *The Fourth Dimension* (1912), were a great influence on Uspenskii's later thought on the subject.

Gurdjieff's Birth. In February 1930, before going to America Gurdjieff burned all his private papers and documents. The passport he used says 1877, and so, many have taken this as his birth date. But the Russian Orthodox Church of which Gurdjieff was a member and where he sang in the choir was not established until after the conquest of Kars by the Russian army in 1877, so this could not be his date of birth.

Olga de Hartmann felt Gurdjieff was considerably older than the birth date of 1877 but was unable to prove it. As her passport gave her birth date as 1896 when she was actually born in 1885, she dismissed the 1877 date given on Gurdjieff's passport. Louise Goepfert March, Gurdjieff's secretary for many years, in an unpublished essay she wrote within a year of his death, "Gurdjieff: An Indication of His Life and Work," gave his birthday as 1872. J. G. Bennett perhaps made the most intensive search into Gurdjieff's background. In his *Gurdjieff: A Very Great Enigma*, 8, he stated: "So far as I myself can make out from various sources, from what he himself and his family have told us, it does seem probable that he was born in 1872, in Alexandropol." Lastly, the first edition of *All and Everything* gave the year of his birth as 1872 on the dust jacket. In later editions, at his younger sister's insistence, the year was changed to 1877.

James Moore argues for 1866 being Gurdjieff's date of birth. He bases this largely on *Meetings with Remarkable Men* where Gurdjieff remarks that he was "about seven years old" when a cattle plague happened. Moore found evidence that in 1872–73 a rinderpest cattle plague developed in the area where Gurdjieff lived, thus he believes Gurdjieff was born in 1866. This date seems plausible until one more deeply examines what happens in 1888 and 1886, the dates Gurdjieff gives in *Meetings with Remarkable Men*.

It was then that Gurdjieff has a "silent romance" with a girl twelve or thirteen years old, and risked his life on an artillery range duel with Karpenko, the other rival for her affections. If born in 1866, Gurdjieff was twenty-two years old when he risks his life for a girl nine to ten years his junior. At twenty-two Gurdjieff was a fully grown man responsible for his acts as taught by Dean Borsh, whom he calls "my second father ... the founder and creator of my present individuality." He was also the eldest of his siblings and so responsible to a degree for them. If born in 1877, Gurdjieff would have been eleven in 1888; if in 1872, he would have been sixteen. Both dates are feasible, though logic tends toward 1872.

Further, in 1886 Bogachevsky, or Father Evlissi, arrived in Kars and Dean Borsh asks him to be Gurdjieff's teacher. Using Moore's 1866 birth date, Gurdjieff would be twenty years old when Bogachevsky arrived; if 1872, fourteen; if 1877, nine years old. Again, the 1872 birth date seems the more reasonable.

One last note: sometime after Father Evlissi arrives, Gurdjieff becomes interested in the supernatural and Dean Borsh, disagreeing with him, says "Come, you little garlic-head...." Gurdjieff is twenty years old and is being called "little garlic-head"?

Given this reasoning, I had no doubt that Gurdjieff's birth was 1872. But then in researching this book I happened to read a 28 October 1943 meeting in Paris in which Gurdjieff says, "Myself I am old, I am seventy-six, I play my part." If this is true, then the birth date is 1867. But then on 16 December 1943, just a few months later, he says he is seventy-eight, meaning he was born in 1865. Then when his life is nearing its ending he says he is eighty-three, so born in 1866. As Gurdjieff came to differ with his teacher, Dean Borsh, I now must respectfully differ with him, given the aforementioned reasoning. All dates related to Gurdjieff's age given here are based upon an 1872 birth. Like so many things concerning him, we are left in wonderful, lasting question. Joppa!

Gurdjieff's Mother. Evdokia and her husband wanted very much to have children, and twice she gave birth. The first child died after several months. It is unclear what happened and when, but the second child also died. She saw this as a punishment and proof of her unworthiness to be a mother. Thereafter, she refused all social events, adopted the simplest clothing, ate frugally, no longer took care of herself and always acted in a sober and modest way. She gave herself to humble prayers imploring the Divinity to grace her with a child. One of the deepest humiliations of ancient times was to fulfill a vow by begging and offering the collected sum to a good work. As the family was rich at that time, this increased the sense of humiliation. To beseech forgiveness and kill in herself maternal pride, she humbly made a vow to buy wax equal in weight to the child she hoped for. With this wax she would make candles and give them to the poor to light for their favorite saints during religious ceremonies. She further committed herself, after childbirth, to go begging, barefoot and unkempt, without hat or shawl.

When she arrived at the Prieuré in December 1923, Tchekhovitch says, "I will not say a word about the feelings that united son and mother for I feel unworthy of approaching this subject. I will only say that having done nothing towards my own parents, I saw in the conduct of Georgii Ivanovitch an example which, for me, was unfortunately no longer feasible." She was known as Babushka, grandmother, and Gurdjieff would often sit with her and his wife in the garden, the two women he so deeply cared for. She contracted liver cancer and began praying, as she wished to remain conscious in the face of death. This continued for several days. Sensing her last day had come, she washed and prepared her body, chose and dressed herself in the garment that would serve as her shroud, lay down and awaited death. Already her body began getting cold. She spoke the words of her favorite prayer, "Our Father who art in Heaven," repeating ceaselessly, sometimes looking at the people present, as if to assure herself that she was still here, sometimes pronouncing more loudly, "Thy Kingdom come...hallowed be Thy name

...," as if to hear the words herself. Her last words were an Armenian proverb, which, translated into French unfortunately loses all meaning in our Western life.

The translation is a little like this:

> The flower has faded ...
> It leaves life ...
> The wind sows its seeds ...
> The bird being you
> Flew away ...
> To live in another country.

And looking at those around her, she added, "And you ... laugh or cry ... do as you wish. I am already indifferent. I am already beyond."

With these words, she closed her eyes, never to open them again.

—Tcheslaw Tchekhovitch, *Tu l'aimeras: Mémoires sur Georgii Ivanovitch Gurdjieff*

In the English edition the title is *Gurdjieff: A Master in Life*. The above, edited here, did not appear in the French edition.

Gurdjieff in Russia. The general consensus is that Gurdjieff arrived in Moscow in 1912. However, he is remembered to say in "The Material Question," an addition to *Meetings with Remarkable Men*, 270, that he arrived in Moscow the late part of 1913. In the Institute's prospectus circulated in 1922 it says, "Only a small number of them [Seekers of Truth] returned to Russia in 1913, with Mr. Gurdjieff at their head."

Ideas. Uspenskii's appreciation for the ideas that Gurdjieff brought never wavered (though at the end he wondered if there was a simpler way). Though he recognized that "some separate fragments of it [the teaching] could be found elsewhere, but not connected and put together" in the form that Gurdjieff presented, he always understood that their origin was beyond ordinary life. In 1926 he wrote, "The system is waiting for workers. There is no statement and no thought in it which would not require and admit further development and elaboration.... [However] ordinary intellectual study of the system is quite insufficient; and there are very few people who agree to other methods of study who are at the same time capable of working by these methods." He understood that the power of the ideas and the course of involution would have them eventually entering into scientific and philosophic language. "But," he says, "they will enter in the wrong form. There will be no right distinction between doing and happening, and many thoughts of ordinary thinking will be mixed with these ideas; so they will not be ideas we know now, only [the] words will be similar." He makes no mention of the pseudo-esoteric eclectic teachings of the so-called "New Age," for this perhaps was a later development, so *Hasnamussian* even he, who foresaw many things, did not foresee it.

Intelligentsia. The word first entered the English language through Russian émigrés. It had been adopted from French and German, where in the 1830s–1840s the term was used to designate educated citizens with progressive interests. Having a university education was not enough; one had to also have a strong interest in the public good. The word, then, referred to academics, men of letters, journalists, writers, and professional revolutionaries. With the twin emergence of scientific advances and secular societies, European intellectuals appeared in the sixteenth century as a distinct group who considered traditional philosophical questions outside the clerical and theological bulwarks. Dominating thought in the sixteenth and seventeenth centuries was the Socratic idea of innate ideas, which had entered Western thought through St. Augustine. The immutability of human nature posited in such thought meant that people's behavior was also immutable. In 1690 John Locke's *Essay on Human Understanding* rejected the concept of innate ideas, declaring that all ideas had their genesis in sensory experience (thus, the beginnings of Behaviorism). In 1758 Claude Helvétius, the French philosopher, siphoned off the political ramifications of Locke's theory of knowledge and made a great leap of reasoning, arguing that since all of man's knowledge and values were the result of sensory experience, then if that experience can be controlled, it is possible to affect and determine people's thought and behavior. Says Richard Pipes in *The Russian Revolution*, "This is one of the most revolutionary ideas in the history of political thought: by extrapolation from an esoteric theory of knowledge, a new political theory is born with the most momentous practical implications." The control of sensory data, i.e., environment, is to be through reason, through rationality, which is of course the province of the intellectuals, the intelligentsia, or what we today would call the "cognitive elite." Unlike in England, the intelligentsia in Russia (as in France) were not allowed to participate in public life, a fact observed by de Tocqueville, and so they tended to run aground in extreme ideologies based on reason alone.

Only in an open and egalitarian society in which independent opinion can flourish can the intelligentsia have influence. The Russian intelligentsia came into being in the 1860s as the result of the Great Reforms of Tsar Alexander II. "To understand the [Russian] intelligentsia," writes Pipes, "it is imperative to keep in mind at all times its deliberate detachment from reality: for while the revolutionaries can be ruthlessly pragmatic in exploiting, for tactical purposes, the people's grievances, their notion of what the people desire is the product of sheer abstraction." There could be no belief in God or the immortality of the soul or accident in human affairs if one was to be a 'pure' Russian intellectual.

King, C. Daly (1895–1962). King believes Orage, and not Uspenskii, taught the true Gurdjieff canon. Uspenskii he sees as having introduced into the Work "a sort of overlay of religious enthusiasm and of mystical atmosphere." In particular he finds Uspenskii's characterizations of self-remembering and self-observation as fuzzy, saying they lack "rigorous and conclusive definition" and finds them "far more introspective than genuinely objective." He also disagrees with the concept that man has many "I"s. Wrote King in his last book, *The States of Human Consciousness* (1963), "In the waking state, as elsewhere, there can be only a single 'I'-entity involved." Earlier, wishing to preserve the teaching as he had received it from Orage, King had written *The Oragean Version* (1951), which is privately published. His other books include: *Integrative Psychology* (1931), *The Psychology of Consciousness* (1932), and "Heritage: A Social Interpretation of the History of Ancient Egypt," unpublished, as well as six published detective novels.

Lenin. Brilliant, compulsive and secretive, Lenin's chief feature was hatred. Says Peter Struve, who had frequent dealings with Lenin in the 1890s: "His principal *Einstellung*—to use the new popular German psychological term—was hatred. Lenin took to Marx's doctrine primarily because it found response in that principal Einstellung of his mind. The doctrine of the class war, relentless and thoroughgoing, aiming at the final destruction and extermination of the enemy, proved congenial to Lenin's emotional attitude to surrounding reality. He hated not only the existing autocracy (the Tsar) and the bureaucracy, not only lawlessness and arbitrary rule of the police, but also their antipodes—the 'liberals' and the 'bourgeoisie.' That hatred had something repulsive and terrible in it; for being rooted in the concrete, I should say even animal, emotions and repulsions, it was at the same time abstract and cold like Lenin's whole being." According to Lenin the decisive influence on him as a young man were the writings of Nikolai Chernyshevskii. A leading radical of the 1860s, Chernyshevskii was the author of *What Is to Be Done?*, a novel portraying the existing world as corrupt and doomed. Its hero, Rakhmetov, is the "new man" of iron will who is totally dedicated to radical change. Lenin borrowed the novel's title for his first political tract. Born in April 1870 to a well-off bureaucratic family, Lenin was expelled from the university for revolutionary activity. In 1893 he moved to St. Petersburg where he studied Marx's *Das Kapital* and agitated the workers. He was consequently jailed in 1895 and later given a Siberian exile from 1897 to 1900. After he was deported, he lived in a number of European capitals before finally taking residence in Switzerland. In appearance, Lenin was quite provincial looking and not at all attractive. Pipes writes in *The Russian Revolution*: "His strength of will, indomitable discipline, energy, asceticism, and unshakable faith in the [revolutionary] cause had an effect that can only be conveyed by the overused term of 'charisma.'" But he alone, of everyone, whatever side they were on, proved himself the grand master at revolutionary chess. His analysis was far deeper and more realistic. At all times he knew exactly his position on the 'board,' its strengths and weaknesses in terms of material force and time, and that of his opponents. Without illusion, he was an implacable foe. His will to win was absolute. No costs were too large. Tactics he could adapt to the moment, but the overall rightness of his strategy was never in doubt. He had long studied the French Revolution and would not make the mistakes of Robespierre, whose cardinal mistake, according to Lenin, was its "excessive generosity—it should have exterminated its enemies." He would seem to be a classic prototype for the Gurdjieffian *Hasnamuss*. "The question of power is the fundamental question of every revolution," said Lenin. And in his most famous remark, he says, "Kto kogo?" or "Who-whom?" that is, "Who masters whom?"

Mercourov, Sergei Dmitrievich. Sixteen years younger than Gurdjieff, his cousin Mercourov was born on 21 October 1888, in Alexandropol. Mercourov's family were next-door neighbors of Gurdjieff's family. Growing up, he developed somewhat of an interest in the occult and Hindu philosophy, but his passion was sculpting. His first commissions were of the Khan of Nakhichevan's concubines. Well regarded in Moscow circles before and after the Revolution, he took the death mask of Leo Tolstoi in 1910. Later, in 1924 he took Lenin's death mask, executed a number of statues of him, and in 1939 was awarded the Order of Lenin. The first mention of Mercourov as the "M" to which Uspenskii alludes appears in James Webb's 1980 biography, *The Harmonious Circle*, 93.

Mouravieff, Boris Petrovitch (1880–1966). Born in Kronstadt, the naval base at St. Petersburg, his father was Graf Piotr Petrovitch Mouravieff, admiral of the Russian fleet and vice minister of the Russian navy of the last imperial government before Tsar Nicholas II's abdication. An ancestor, André Mouravieff, was chamberlain at the Russian Imperial Court and a member of the Holy Synod of the Russian Orthodox Church; he founded the monastery of St. Andrew on Mount Athos. In 1917 when Kerensky took office as the second prime minister of the new Russian Republic, Boris Mouravieff became his principal private secretary. Meeting Uspenskii in Constantinople, Mouravieff then, through Uspenskii, was introduced to Gurdjieff. Mouravieff later emigrated to Paris where Uspenskii asked that he help in editing his manuscript *Fragments of an Unknown Teaching*. Always on the fringe of the Gurdjieff circles, casting doubt, criticizing, he apparently could never get Gurdjieff and the teaching out of his system. In 1944 he and his wife moved to Switzerland where, studying at the University of Geneva, Mouravieff obtained a Ph.D. He then taught Russian history and Eastern philosophy at the Institute of International Studies in Geneva. In 1958 he lectured on "An Introduction to Esoteric Philosophy," which was eventually expanded into his three-volume work *Gnosis*. He then opened the Center for Christian Esoteric Studies. When he died in 1966 the institute closed and his books went out of print. Recently they have been republished.

Mouravieff's intention is to cut the teaching from its Fourth Way and Gurdjieffian mooring and link it to what he calls a "fifth way," a Christianity of his own design (many of his views being heretical). Interestingly, Mouravieff's fifth way, basically tantric, is clearly an amalgamation of Uspenskii's Gurdjieff-Eastern Christianity-Catharism. The material he presents in *Gnosis* is a rewriting of Uspenskii's *Search,* which, of course, is from Gurdjieff's Russian period and lacks the fuller development that Gurdjieff gave the teaching in *All and Everything.* Mouravieff's perspective, as well as his writing, is at a level far below that of Uspenskii and, of course, does not even begin to approach Gurdjieff's. For a detailed study of "The Mouravieff Phenomenon" see *Telos* [retitled *The Gurdjieff Journal*] Vol. 3, No. 4, and Vol. 4, No. 1, and my book *Taking With the Left Hand.*

Munson, Gorham. As many of Munson's perspectives concerning Jean Toomer have been quoted, this is how Jean Toomer (writing about himself in the third person) saw Munson:

> He is always uneasy in his presence. He wishes to be Jean's equal. He can convince himself that he is when Jean is absent. But even Jean's absence does not bring real peace. For he is never absent altogether. Somewhere on the horizon he looms up (what things he might be doing over there!) a dark, unpredictable object which at any moment may sweep near, burst in, and upset the chairs and tables. Even were the things just narrated to be canceled, still Gorham would be uneasy in Jean's presence. For Gorham feels Jean to possess an essential energy that displaces his own and which he is unable to cope with. If it were not that Gorham is a literary critic, needs literary material, and has stated his belief that Jean is a significant potential, he could be well rid of him. He sincerely likes Jean personally, but their affection would not have a ghost of a chance against his need of security and peace of mind. Gorham thinks that all of Jean's silences are critical, and that, for the most part, they are destructively critical of those about him, Gorham himself included. But Gorham does not wish therefore that Jean should speak, for his spoken thought might prove to be more disturbing than his silence. Jean's quickness, power, and command of words and thought in discourse is in an unpleasant contrast to his own slowness. Moreover, Gorham can never tell when Jean will break out with an opposition to some pet theory or prejudice which he, Gorham, has been laboriously building and hence does not wish demolished in a moment, particularly by Jean. Nor can Gorham tell when Jean will narrate some strange, unusual effect or experience. Such things are in unfortunate contrast to Gorham's commonplaces. They give evidence too vividly of Jean's greater range in life. And whether Jean is silent or otherwise, Gorham always feels in him an assumption of greater maturity, an attitude which says that he, Jean, is on the one right road, and that he has already achieved a degree of calm mastery. In short, Gorham thinks

that Jean always feels himself to be superior. Gorham greatly resents this feeling, he would like to disrupt it, but he fears to attempt it.

Quest Society. Formed in 1909 by G. R. S. Mead, Madame Blavatsky's secretary and a leading theosophical writer and gnostic historian, because of the readmittance of C. W. Leadbetter into membership in the Theosophical Society by Annie Besant, its president. Leadbetter, accused of pedophilia, was later disowned. The Quest Society still followed the theosophical teachings and so the link between Uspenskii and theosophy continued when Uspenskii arrived in London.

Russian Revolution. Lenin understood the crucial importance of timing. Writes Trotsky: "If we had not seized power in October we would not have seized it at all. Our strength before October lay in the uninterrupted influx of the masses, who believed that this party would do what the others had not done. If they had seen any vacillation at this moment on our part, any delay, any incongruity between word and deed, then in the course of two or three months they would have drifted away from us.... It was just this that made Lenin decide to act."

Russian Theosophy. Though theosophy had its adherents in Russia, it took root only through the efforts of Anna Alekseevna Kamenskaia (1867–1952), who organized the Russian Theosophical Society in 1908, lectured endlessly, and edited the Society's journal *Vestnik Teosofii*. The Society's headquarters was in St. Petersburg and Uspenskii was considered one of the leading theosophical thinkers and writers. A detailed history of the theosophical movement in Russia is given in Maria Carlson's *No Religion Higher Than Truth* (Princeton, NJ: Princeton University Press, 1993).

Sārmoung Brotherhood. Gurdjieff spent a good deal of time in Tibet, apparently married and had a son who was in charge of a monastery. Among Tibet's best known monasteries is Surmang which belongs to the Ka-gyü school, the basic teaching of which was from the great adept Marpa the Translator. Marpa had studied with Naropa, whose classical work *The Ornament of Precious Liberation* is the leading manual of the Ka-gyü School. Chögyam Trungpa, Rinpoche, the eleventh Trungpa Tulku, became its head, and when he came to America in 1970 became very much interested in Gurdjieff's teachings. So one wonders if Sārmoung might really point us to Surmang and its teachings.

J. G. Bennett, *Making a New World*, 56–57, says the pronunciation of Sārmoun or Sārman Society:

> is the same for either spelling and the word can be assigned to old Persian. It does, in fact, appear in some of the Pahlawi texts to designate those who preserved the doctrines of Zoroaster. The word can be interpreted three

ways. It is the word for bee, which has always been a symbol of those who collect precious 'honey' of traditional wisdom and preserve it for future generations. [The symbol of the bee appears in the Hypostyle Hall of the temple complex of Karnak, at Thebes, modern day Luxor, Egypt. It stands for the nada sound heard when attention has developed beyond the formatory mind; the sound of the bee is the first of many subtle sounds.] A collection of legends, well known in Armenian and Syrian circles with the title The Bees, was revised by Mar Salamon, a Nestorian Archimandrite in the thirteenth century. The Bees refers to a mysterious power transmitted from the time of Zoroaster and made manifest in the time of Christ.

A more obvious rendering is to take the *man* in its Persian meaning as the quality transmitted by heredity and hence a distinguished family or race. It can be the repository of an heirloom or tradition. The word *sār* means head, both literally and in the sense of principal or chief. The combination of *sārman* would thus mean the chief repository of the tradition, which has been called 'the perennial philosophy' passed down from generation to generation by 'initiated beings,' to use Gurdjieff's description.

And still another possible meaning of the word Sārman is 'those who have been enlightened'; literally those whose heads have been purified. This gives us a possible clue to Gurdjieff's intention. In the chapter "Beelzebub's Opinion of War," in the *First Series*, he refers to a fraternity existing in Central Asia under the name of the 'Assembly of the Enlightened. . . .' This is the nearest Gurdjieff comes to specific mention in his own writing of a group that could correspond to the 'Inner Circle' of Humanity.

Seabrook, William. An adventurer, journalist and author, Seabrook lived as a member of the Bedouin tribe. He joined the Druze in the Arabian mountains, and later moved into a monastery in Tripoli. He lived with Yezidi devil worshipers and dervish mystics, writing a book *Adventures in Arabia*. Of Gurdjieff he said, "He knows more about dervish mysticism and magic than any man I have ever met outside a dervish monastery." This is said in his *Witchcraft: Its Power in the World Today*, where Gurdjieff is portrayed as a white magician.

Seekers of Truth. (Sometimes referred to as Seekers of the Truth, or Seekers After Truth) Gurdjieff tells the names of thirteen members of the group: Prince Yuri Lubovedsky; Professor Skridlov, anthropologist; Dr. Ekim Bey, hypnotist; Piotr Karpenko, mining engineer; Abram Yelov, linguist; Sarkis Pogossian, priest; Dashtamirov, astronomer; Baron X, ardent occultist; Vitvitskaia; Soloviev; Prince Nijeradze; Dr. Sari-Ogli; and Samsanov. Thomas de Hartmann, in his and his wife's book, *Our Life with Mr. Gurdjieff*, 72, reports Gurdjieff saying there were fifteen members of the group, and that "There were also women...." So the last and unnamed member of the group must have been a woman. Three of the fifteen died during their expeditions. In terms of religion they were Orthodox, Catholic, Muslim, Jewish and Buddhist.

In the original manuscript of *Meetings with Remarkable Men*, Gurdjieff devoted a chapter to Prince Nijeradze. Several times Gurdjieff rewrote this chapter but never completed it. Writes Bennett in *Gurdjieff: Making a New World*, 178, "We gather that Prince Nijeradze had been concerned in some embarrassing episode connected with the difficulty Gurdjieff came up against, through having broken some of the rules of one of the Brotherhoods, where he had been receiving help and teaching. One who heard the chapter read in 1933, recounts that it produced a profound impression by its account of the state of man who wakes up after dying and realizes that he has lost the chief instrument of his life, his body, and recalls all he could have done with it while he was still alive."

Sincerity. "I remember Uspenskii speaking very interestingly once in New York about sincerity. We think we have only to decide to be and we can be. But sincerity has to be learnt, slowly and painfully. Takes a long time. And when one finds sincerity on one level, one realizes that there is another completely different level of sincerity hidden beneath."—Rodney Collin, *The Theory of Conscious Harmony*, 77.

Said Gurdjieff in a meeting:

> Many things are necessary for observing oneself, the first is being sincere with oneself. It is much easier to be sincere with a friend. Man is afraid to see something bad, and if by accident, looking deep down, he sees his own bad, he sees his nothingness. We have the habit of driving away thoughts about ourselves because we fear remorse. Sincerity may be the key which will open the door through which one part can see another part. With sincerity man may look and see something. Sincerity with oneself is very difficult, for a thick crust has grown over essence. Each year man puts on a new dress, new mask, one after another. All must be gradually removed, for until they are removed, man cannot see.

This is somewhat different in emphasis from what he writes in *Views from the Real World*, 145–46.

Strange Life of Ivan Osokin. Did Uspenskii self-publish the book before or after his April 1915 meeting with Gurdjieff? The likelihood is afterward, and if so, then he most likely would have rewritten the scenes in which the magician appears. The magician then is Gurdjieff. And Zinaida may be Anna Butkovskaia.

Zinaida asks Osokin, 131: "Well, are you going to Australia soon?" In Butkovskaia's book, *With Gurdjieff in St. Petersburg and Paris,* 30, Uspenskii talks to Anna about going to Australia.

Theosophy. Originated with Helena Blavatsky, a Russian occultist, medium, and author of *Isis Unveiled, Voice of Silence,* and *The Secret Doctrine.* Blavatsky's teaching draws heavily on esoteric Buddhism. In Gurdjieff's view theosophy, and Western occultism represent "a mixture of fundamental lines. Both lines bear in themselves grains of truth, but neither of them possesses full knowledge and therefore attempts to bring them to practical realization give only negative results." *Search,* 286.

Triads. We see the functioning of the triads, or three forces, active, passive, reconciling, in the Table of Hydrogens, its twelve categories of matter descending from the Absolute to the moon. They can also be seen in the Food Diagram where physical food, second and third being food are processed by the organism, either unconsciously or consciously.

Study of triads must begin with study of second force. If we could have our plans actualized without struggle, there could be a chance we would get what we wanted. Struggle changes everything. Each triad has two important points—beginning and end. If it ends with first or third force, active or reconciling, it will produce good results. If the second, passive, the result will be worse than the beginning. Every triad has different levels. Each force in each place has a special meaning. There are no wrong triads in themselves. First force in first place always means effort or even violence, or something unexpected from what has happened before. In the second place the same first force means either the use of some hidden energy specially designed or stored. In the third place it gives good results. Second force in first place means raw material that can be worked on or natural state of things that has possibility of change or improvement. Second force in second place means the same as in first place. But work has already begun or action has evoked resistance. In the third place, second force means decline, loss, destruction. Third force in first place always indicates emotional element, like curiosity, desire to know, feeling of beauty or desire for power, cunning, envy, jealousy. Third force in second place means either same as first, only when action has already begun, or when resistance has made itself felt, or use of some hidden energy or hidden principle—only different from first force. Maybe clever acting, use of lies. Third force in third place is very near to first force in third place, but sometimes better. Violence is 1-3-2. Expansion 1-2-3. Crime is 3-1-2, while 2-3-1 and 3-2-1 are self-remembering, the latter is also art. Effort in the case of self-remembering is 3; it is the creation of mental image or sensation of self-remembering. Can only be done with neutralizing force.

Uspenskii's mother and his wife. It is unclear when Uspenskii's mother died. In J. H. Reyner's biography, *Ouspensky: Unsung Genius*, he has the twenty-year-old Uspenskii and his mother visiting Paris in 1898 and her dying "shortly afterwards." Colin Wilson in his *The Strange Life of P. D. Ouspensky* says she died in 1894. Neither cite sources. Reyner, oddly, speaks of Uspenskii meeting Sophia Grigorievna about 1905, well before his 1917 meeting with her. Wilson says nothing of when they met. James Webb's *The Harmonious Circle* ignores Uspenskii's early life, as does James Moore's *Gurdjieff: An Anatomy of a Myth*.

Yezidis. William Seabrook, who established a close relationship with Gurdjieff, writes in his *Adventures in Arabia* that he visited the Yezidis' sacred temple of Satan and the shrine of the religion's founder, Sheik Adi, in Mount Lalesh valley which lies in the mountains north of Baghdad, on the Kurdish border, near Mosul. The Yezidis believe that God created seven spirits and the first of these spirits was Satan, whom God made supreme ruler of the earth for a period of ten thousand years (we are now in our three thousandth year). And because Satan was supreme master of the earth, those who dwelt on it could prosper only by doing him homage and worshipping him. The name of Satan, or Shaitan, is forbidden to be spoken, so the reference is to Melek Taos (Angel Peacock). In their scripture, Khitab al Aswad (Black Book), Shaitan says: "Speak not my name nor mention my attributes, lest ye be guilty, for ye have no true knowledge thereof; but honor my symbol and image." He is worshipped in the form of a brass bird. This occurred, Seabrook was told, because "Jesus was a spirit who came to earth and took the form of a man, to wage war on Melek and wrest the earth from his dominion. When Jesus hung on the cross, being crucified, the magic was such that if he had been able to carry out his purpose and die in the form of a man, it would have given him power and dominion. Melek thwarted this with his greater magic by taking Jesus from the cross alive, expelling him from earth, and hung on the cross in his stead a figure without substance which seemed to the watchers to be Jesus. When this figure without substance seemed to die and was laid in a tomb, it dissolved and disappeared. The two Marys came to the tomb, found it empty, and were astonished. Melek Taos then appeared to them as an angel and told them to have no fear, for their friend Jesus had been taken from the cross and sent safely away to other worlds. They refused to believe Melek Taos. In order to convince them of his power, he slew a peacock which was in the garden, took out its entrails, cut it into pieces, and then brought them all together again to make a living bird more glorious and beautiful than the one which he had seen. Then he himself entered the body of this bright bird and flew away. Therefore he is called Angel Peacock, and the bird is his symbol." At the end of ten thousand years Shaitan will reenter paradise as the chief of the Seven Bright Spirits and all his true worshippers will enter with him. The Yezidi priest meets Seabrook at the sacred temple and tells him, "We believe in God but our difference with all other religions is this—that we know God is so far away that we can have no contact with Him—and He, on his part, has no knowledge or interest of any sort concerning human affairs, it is useless to pray to Him or worship Him. He cares nothing about us." They believe that they are made from Adam, not Adam and Eve, as everyone else is.

E. S. Drower, who like Seabrook visited the temple and spent time with the people, says in her book *Peacock Angel* that apart from the fact that Shaikh (or Sheikh) Adi bin Musafir, their principal saint, was recognized in his time as an orthodox Moslem, that her personal impressions are contradictory. "I cannot believe that they worship the Devil or even propitiate the Spirit of Evil . . . the Peacock Angel is a Spirit of Light rather than a Spirit of Darkness. . . . The Peacock Angel is, in a manner, a symbol of Man himself, a divine principle of light experiencing an avatar of darkness, which is matter and the material world. The evil comes from man himself, or rather from his errors, stumblings and obstinate turnings down blind alleys upon the steep path of being. In repeated incarnations he sheds his earthliness, his evil, or else, if hopelessly linked to the material, he perishes like the dross and illusion that he is. . . . One Yazidi [her spelling] propounded to me the curious theory that the accumulated experiences of various earthly lives was, on the Day of Resurrection, gathered into one over-soul, but that the individuals who had once lived those lives continued as separate entities, but how this was possible he did not explain." Concerning their drawing a circle on the ground, Philip G. Kreyenbroek, *Yezidism—Its Background, Observances and Textual Tradition*, says the Peacock Angel was not given birth and has never been born. He is the king of the world. The lord of men and jinn's, He made Adam eat forbidden food, thus helping him to live in the world. He sees God three times a day. Oaths are administered by drawing a circle on the ground. The inside of the circle is declared to be the property of Melek Tawus [another spelling], an observance which has a parallel in Zoroastrianism.

Chronology[1]

Dates prior to 1918 are according to the Julian calendar. After 31 January 1918 Russia changed to the Gregorian calendar.

1872[2]

1 January Georgi Ivanovitch Gurdjieff, born on this date (Julian old style calendar) near Alexandropol. He celebrates his birthday on 13 January (Gregorian new style calendar). He will be the eldest, with a brother, Dmitri, born soon after, then a sister, and later two more sisters

1873

Rinderpest, or cattle plague, outbreak devastates herds of cattle throughout Asia Minor. Gurdjieff's father loses his large cattle herd, and he opens a lumberyard

1877

24 April Russians declare war on Turkey
18 November Russians capture Kars
The father's lumberyard fails and he opens a carpentry shop

1878

Gurdjieff's family moves to Kars. Dean Borsh, of the Kars Military Cathedral, friend of Gurdjieff's father, agrees to tutor Gurdjieff

1879–80

Dean Borsh appoints Bogachevsky to become Gurdjieff's teacher; he confesses Gurdjieff every week for two years. Ordained as Father Evlissi, he becomes a monk. At Holy Athos for a short time, he renounces monastic life. He then becomes an assistant to the abbot of one of the branches of the Essene Order in Egypt, an order thought to have been founded 1200 years before the birth of Jesus Christ. Gurdjieff and Pogossian discover reference to the "Sārmoung Brotherhood" in an underground monastic cell

1888

Summer Gurdjieff, sixteen years old, frees Yezidi boy inside Yezidi magic circle by rubbing out part of the circle. Has his first taste of alcohol. Falls in love with twelve- or thirteen-year-old girl, and on a challenge risks his life on an artillery range and comes to "the whole sensation of myself"

1892

Staying at a Dervish monastery, Gurdjieff begins to collect written literature and oral information on "*Mehkeness*," hypnotism

---

1. All dates are provisional up until 1912. The remainder are based on archives and various authors, notably Thomas and Olga de Hartmann, C. S. Nott and Fritz Peters.
2. See Notes, "Gurdjieff's Birth."

Chronology

1893

Meets Professor Skridlov and Prince Lubovedsky at the Giza Plateau outside Cairo. They share Gurdjieff's desire for "hidden knowledge" and form the Seekers of Truth

1895

Summer Gurdjieff's friends Piotr Karpenko, Sarkis Pogossian and Ekim Bey join Seekers of Truth

1896

Gurdjieff begins to heal people
Gurdjieff wounded by accidental gun shot in Crete

1898

Soloviev dies in Gobi desert

1900

The Seekers of Truth make an expedition to cross the Himalayas from the Pamir region to India and lose their guide in an avalanche on the northwestern slopes of the Himalayas

1902

Gurdjieff wounded by a stray bullet in Tibet, while working in the employ of the thirteenth Dalai Lama

1905

22 January St. Petersburg's Bloody Sunday. Uspenskii's sister imprisoned in Moscow's Butyrskaya prison

1908

Uspenskii's sister dies in prison. Uspenskii and his best friend plan a trip to the East. The friend dies and Uspenskii leaves alone on the trip

1911

14 September Gurdjieff takes twenty-one-year vow to lead an artificial life

1912

Gurdjieff arrives in Moscow.[3] Uspenskii meets Anna Ilinishna Butkovskaia

1913

June Uspenskii leaves on second trip to India and Ceylon
Gurdjieff, in the guise of 'Prince Ozay,' meets Paul Dukes in St. Petersburg. In Moscow Gurdjieff establishes a group that meets at the apartment of well-known Jewish lawyer Alexei Yakovlevich Rachmilievitch. Members include Gurdjieff's cousin, the sculptor Sergei Dmitrievich Mercourov, the composer Vladimir Pohl,

---

3. In *Meetings with Remarkable Men* the date is "near the end of the year 1913."

Alina Fedorovna and Alexander Nikorovich Petrov

1914

19 July[4] Germany declares war on Russia
2 November Russia declares war on Turkey
13 November Uspenskii, having returned from his trip to the East, reads newspaper notice for the ballet *The Struggle of the Magicians*

1915

Easter Week Gurdjieff and Uspenskii meet
Autumn Gurdjieff travels to St. Petersburg and meets Uspenskii again, who introduces him to Anna Ilinishna Butkovskaia

1916

February Gurdjieff makes the 350-mile train trip from Moscow to St. Petersburg every fortnight
Spring St. Petersburg Group formed consisting of Uspenskii, Anna Ilinishna Butkovskaia, Dr. Stjoernval,[5] Anthony Charkovsky, Andrey Andreivitch Zaharoff and Nicholas R.
April Gurdjieff gives his first lectures on the seven cosmoses
August The group meets in Finland at the home of Madame Maximovitch, a wealthy patient of Dr. Stjoernval
Late October Uspenskii meets Sophia Grigorievna Maximenko
Mid-December Thomas de Hartmann meets Gurdjieff[6]

1917

9 February Thomas de Hartmann introduces his wife to Gurdjieff
14 February 90,000 strikers demonstrate against the war and government
End February Gurdjieff leaves for Alexandropol
2 March Tsar Nicholas II abdicates in favor of his brother, who refuses the position. Provisional government formed with Alexander Kerensky as its head
3 April Lenin arrives in St. Petersburg
21 April First Bolshevik demonstrations occur in St. Petersburg and Moscow
Early June Gurdjieff sends Uspenskii a telegram from Alexandropol. Uspenskii makes the journey to see him
Early July Gurdjieff and Uspenskii leave for St. Petersburg, but Gurdjieff stops in Essentuki and sends Uspenskii on alone to St. Petersburg
Mid-July Gurdjieff's pupils from St. Petersburg and Moscow begin to arrive in Essentuki
28 August Thomas and Olga de Hartmann join Gurdjieff
September Dr. Stjoernval receives a telegram from Gurdjieff telling him to

---

4. The New calendar date is 1 August.
5. It is not clear whether Dr. Stjoernval's wife, Elizabeta, was a member.
6. De Hartmann gives no actual date.

"Terminate all your affairs" and join him
24–25 October Bolsheviks seize power

1918

March Some forty pupils are now in Essentuki. Gurdjieff gives the group a name, "International Fellowship for Realization Through Work"
15 May Gurdjieff's father killed in Turkish massacre defending his home in Alexandropol
Mid-July Gurdjieff's family and relatives—twenty-eight people—have fled Armenia and arrive in Essentuki.
16–17 July Tsar Nicholas II, family and servants are murdered by Bolsheviks
6 August Gurdjieff and pupils begin trek to cross the Caucasus mountain range to Tiflis. Uspenskii stays behind saying Gurdjieff is leading the group "towards the way of religion" and "it is not my way"
November First World War ends. Russian civil war continues

1919

Mid-January Gurdjieff, Madame Ostrowska, the de Hartmanns and Stjoernvals arrive in Tiflis
Easter Gurdjieff meets Alexander and Jeanne de Salzmann, Lili Galumnian and Olga Hinzenberg[7]
Autumn Gurdjieff reestablishes Institute in Tiflis

1920

Late January Uspenskii and his family arrive in Constantinople. Begins to give lectures on the teaching
7 July Gurdjieff and his students arrive in Constantinople
July–August Gurdjieff meets Tcheslaw Tchekhovitch and Boris Ferapontoff. Uspenskii reunites with Gurdjieff, works with him on the ballet scenario *The Struggle of the Magicians*. Gurdjieff also meets J. G. Bennett at Prince Sabaheddin's home
October Institute is reestablished
November End of Russian civil war
December Gurdjieff receives letter from Jacques-Dalcroze inviting him to come to Hellerau, Germany

1921

14 May Uspenskii receives telegram from Lady Rothermere inviting him to come to London
Mid-May Gurdjieff closes Institute
13 August Gurdjieff and his students, including Madame Uspenskii, take train for Hellerau, Germany. Uspenskii leaves for London

---

7. She may have met Gurdjieff before in Moscow.

22 August Gurdjieff arrives in Berlin
September Uspenskii arrives in London
21 October Uspenskii begins to lecture on the teaching
24 November Gurdjieff gives his first lecture in Berlin

1922

13 February Gurdjieff's first talk in London. Meets A. R. Orage
5 March Gurdjieff's second talk in London
15 March Gurdjieff's third talk in London
Late Spring Prospectus of proposed Institute issued
14 July With Germany inhospitable and an English passport denied, Gurdjieff arrives in Paris
28 September A. R. Orage sells *The New Age*
30 September Gurdjieff purchases Château du Prieuré in Avon, France. Establishes the Institute for the Harmonious Development of Man
17 October Katherine Mansfield arrives at Prieuré
27 October Digging of Turkish bath begins
End of November Building of Study House begins

1923

9 January Katherine Mansfield dies at the Prieuré
15–19 February Series of articles published on teaching and Prieuré in the *London Daily News*
March Two articles on the teaching and Prieuré published in the *New Statesman*
4 April Gurdjieff speaks with Uspenskii. Tells him to give up the Work in London
August J. G. Bennett arrives at the Prieuré
23 August Bennett leaves, telling himself, "I will go away and make money, and then I will return"
December Gurdjieff's mother, brother and younger sister and their families arrive from Russia
December Maurice Nicoll rejects Gurdjieff's offer to go to New York and he and his family leave Prieuré
16 December Demonstration of movements at Théâtre des Champs-Élysées, Paris
23 December A. R. Orage and Dr. Stjoernval arrive in New York

1924

Early January Gurdjieff and his troupe of dancers leave for New York
9 January Orage gives talk at Sunwise Turn in New York
Mid-January Uspenskii gathers his key group and tells them: "I have decided to break off all relations with Mr. Gurdjieff"
13 January Gurdjieff and his dancers arrive in New York

Chronology

23 January First movements demonstration at Lesley Hall
2 February Demonstration at Neighborhood Playhouse, Greenwich Village
3 March Movements demonstration at Carnegie Hall
1 April Adolph Hitler convicted of treason. Sentenced to five year imprisonment
8 April New York branch of the Institute created
23 April Gurdjieff says the Feast Day of St. George the Victor, Warrior of God, Knight of Christ, is to be regarded as the Institute's "Coronation Day"
June Gurdjieff returns to the Prieuré
29 June Jessie Dwight arrives at the Prieuré
2 July Jane Heap, Margaret Anderson and Fritz and Tom Peters arrive at the Prieuré
8 July Gurdjieff has auto accident.[8] Calls it result of *Tzvarnoharno*
Late July Jean Toomer arrives at the Prieuré
Summer Hitler begins dictation of *Mein Kampf* to his cell mate Rudolph Hess
26 August Gurdjieff disbands Institute
28 August Orage arrives at the Prieuré
17 October Orage and Jessie return to New York
2 November Orage begins a new round of public lectures
16 December Gurdjieff begins dictation[9] to Olga de Hartmann of *Beelzebub's Tales to His Grandson*
20 December Hitler released from prison

1925

Orage gives Toomer permission to form a Harlem group, but it comes to nothing
March Orage receives several translated chapters of the manuscript of *Beelzebub's Tales*. He sends chapters back saying "completely unintelligible"
Spring Uspenskii finishes introduction to first draft of *Fragments of an Unknown Teaching*
Late June Gurdjieff's mother dies
July Orage and Jessie return to the Prieuré. Orage edits the manuscript while Jessie types
29 July Gurdjieff begins intensive work and collaboration with Thomas de Hartmann on music for the movements
Mid-November Orage and Toomer dine with Mabel Dodge Luhan, a wealthy heiress interested in Gurdjieff's teaching
3 October Orage and Jessie leave for New York
Winter Madame Julia Ostrowska's cancer becomes more acute

8. The exact date is in question. Olga de Hartmann in *Our Life with Mr. Gurdjieff* says it is 5 July; J. G. Bennett, 6 July; Jane Heap, 8 July. Bennett was not there in 1924. In the *Third Series*, Gurdjieff says it is 1 January 1925.
9. She definitely states this but others believe he began after he disbanded the Institute in August.

1926

January Mabel Dodge Luhan tells Toomer she is offering her Taos ranch in New Mexico and a loan of $15,000 for a Gurdjieff center in America
28 May Jean Toomer arrives at the Prieuré
9 June Jessie arrives at the Prieuré
17 June Orage arrives at the Prieuré
26 June Madame Ostrowska, thirty-seven years old, dies
Mid-July Aleister Crowley visits the Prieuré. After showing him hospitality, Gurdjieff tells him—"You filthy, you dirty inside!"
Autumn Jean Toomer forms a Gurdjieff study group in Chicago
27 November Orage writes Jessie saying, "The book is too colossal"

1927

January Payson Loomis arrives at the Prieuré. He is to help with the English translation of *Meetings with Remarkable Men*
14 January Orage sails for New York
March Orage publishes his book *Psychological Exercises* without Gurdjieff's permission
1 May Gurdjieff ends music collaboration with de Hartmann
August Orage arrives at the Prieuré for a month
9 September Orage's divorce decree becomes final
24 September Orage marries Jessie Dwight
6 November Gurdjieff finishes and decides to rewrite first draft of *Beelzebub's Tales*

1928

7 January Orage and Jessie arrive at the Prieuré
29 February Orage and Jessie return to New York
23 April A. Y. Rachmilievitch's toast to Gurdjieff at the feast of Saint George at the Prieuré
Spring Bennett accused of bribing an official imprisoned in Athens
Late Summer Gurdjieff finishes first revision of *Beelzebub's Tales*

1929

23 January Gurdjieff visits New York for the second time
5 April Gurdjieff leaves for France
19 April Jessie Dwight gives birth to a son, Richard
Autumn Bennett returns from Greece to London. Not accepted into a group by Uspenskii, Bennett, unauthorized, forms his own study group

1930

15 February Gurdjieff burns personal papers and makes third visit to America
11 April Gurdjieff leaves for France
30 October Uspenskii decides to expand his work
13 November Gurdjieff makes his fourth trip to New York

28 November Gurdjieff gives the first of five talks to Orage's students
1 December Gurdjieff demands Orage's students sign oath denying any relationship to Orage
10 December Orage arrives from England. He signs oath not to associate with 'Orage'
12 December Orage attends fourth meeting

1931

January Gurdjieff asks author William Seabrook to arrange party of New York intelligentsia
13 March Gurdjieff leaves for France
April Mimeographed copies of *Beelzebub's Tales* offered to the New York group for $10 each
3 July Orage and family leave for England
Mid-Summer Gurdjieff and Uspenskii meet for last time at the Café Henri IV
Summer Uspenskii's *A New Model of the Universe* published
Late Summer Toomer stages communal living experiment based on teaching. Later writes "Portage Potential"
9 September Uspenskii tells Nicoll to "go away and teach the System"
30 October Jean Toomer marries Margery Latimer
November Gurdjieff's fifth visit to America
16 November "Achmed Abdullah," at a New York dinner party that Gurdjieff also attends, says he recognizes him as Dalai Lama's chief tutor and the main Russian political agent for Tibet. Gurdjieff later tells Orage he was not a foreign agent, but was appointed collector of dues from the monasteries for the Dalai Lama

1932

16 January Gurdjieff returns to France
February Kathryn Hulme sees Gurdjieff
21 April Orage publishes *The New English Weekly*
11 May Gurdjieff closes Prieuré and moves to Paris
13 September Gurdjieff begins writing *The Herald of Coming Good*
Autumn Payson Loomis leaves Gurdjieff

1933

30 January Adolph Hitler becomes Chancellor of Germany
27 February Reichstag fire
April Alexander de Salzmann and Gurdjieff meet at Café Henri IV
7 March Gurdjieff writes the supplemental announcement to *The Herald of Coming Good*
May Unable to meet mortgage payments, Gurdjieff loses Prieuré. All contents auctioned
26 August Gurdjieff publishes *The Herald of Coming Good*

September Jessie gives birth to a daughter, Ann
Autumn Gurdjieff makes sixth visit to America

1934

3 March Alexander de Salzmann dies. His wife takes over his group
2 April Gurdjieff says he has fulfilled his three will-tasks
22 July Gurdjieff visits Taliesin in Wisconsin
Autumn Gurdjieff calls in all copies of *The Herald of Coming Good*
5 November Orage dies

1935

6 January Gurdjieff resumes writing the *Third Series*
Spring Gurdjieff meets with Toomer. Pressures him for money. Gurdjieff tells him he is "not as I counted"
9 April Gurdjieff finishes prologue to *Life Is Real Only Then, When "I Am"*
6 May Gurdjieff and Senator Bronson Cutting are to meet. Cutting is interested in giving the funds necessary to repurchase the Prieuré. Flying to the meeting Cutting's plane crashes and he dies
8 May Gurdjieff applies for a Soviet visa. Admission is based on the condition that he not teach
Summer Gurdjieff's whereabouts unknown
September Rom Landau's *God Is My Adventure* published
17 October Gurdjieff tells Jane Heap to disband her Montmartre ladies group and go to London
18 October Gurdjieff meets with Kathryn Hulme, Solita Solano, Louise Davidson
26 October Gurdjieff reveals he has been initiated into Egyptian Mysteries four times
24 November Gurdjieff moves from Grand Hotel to 11 rue Labie

1936

Early January Gurdjieff forms the Rope, composed of Solita Solano, Kathryn Hulme, Alice Rohrer and Elizabeth Gordon. All are lesbians except for Gordon, who is made their "Mother Superior"
Spring Toomer again experiments with communal living. Calls it "Friends of Being"
May Gurdjieff accepts Margaret Anderson and Georgette Leblanc as "Knachtschmidt and Company"

1937

24 January Bennett's wife, Polly, tries to commit suicide
31 August Gurdjieff's brother, Dmitri, dies of cancer
5 September Gurdjieff moves into his brother's apartment at 6 rue des Colonels Renard

Chronology

Autumn Solita Solano replaces Elizabeth Gordon as Gurdjieff's secretary

1938

April Uspenskii founds the Historico-Psychological Society
2 April Dr. Leonid Stjoernval dies in Sotteville-sous-le-Val, Normandy

1939

1 March Gurdjieff and Solita Solano sail to New York, his seventh visit. Toomer refuses to see him, leaves for Bermuda, saying "I don't want to be on the same soil as Gurdjieff"
19 May Gurdjieff and Solita depart for France
July Toomer and family leave for nine-month trip to India. He is in search of "The Meeting"
Summer Madame Uspenskii stricken with Parkinson's disease
September Germany attacks Poland. France and England declare war
5 October Solita Solano leaves France for New York. Elizabeth Gordon elects to stay in France

1940

21 March Paul Reynaud replaces Daladier as French Prime Minister
10 May German offensive begins
13 May German army enters France
End of May French and British armies defeated. British troops evacuated from Dunkirk
12 June Gurdjieff and de Salzmann family leave Paris for Switzerland
14 June Germans occupy Paris. French government moves to Bordeaux
16 June Reynaud resigns as Prime Minister. Marshal Pétain forms new government
17 June Pétain orders cease fire
18 June General Charles de Gaulle, speaking from London, issues call for resistance
22 June Pétain and Hitler sign armistice agreement
28 June British recognize de Gaulle as leader of Free French
10 July French National Assembly dissolves itself
11 July Pétain establishes Vichy government
August Gurdjieff and de Salzmann family return from Switzerland to Paris
2 August Stringent food rationing introduced
19 October Jeanne de Salzmann presents pupils to Gurdjieff

1941

4 January Madame Uspenskii leaves for America
29 January Uspenskii leaves for America. Shortly beforehand he meets with Bennett who asks about his lack of progress in the Work. Uspenskii tells him, "Your trouble is that you always make false starts"

February Uspenskiis take up residence at a cottage in Rumson, New Jersey
17 February Uspenskii meets Claude Bragdon
21 February Uspenskii meets Carman Barnes at a party in New York
28 February Uspenskii gives talk at Barnes' New York studio. Claude Bragdon introduces him
5 May Bennett buys Coombe Springs
September Uspenskiis move to Franklin Farms, Mendham, New Jersey
11 September Charles Lindbergh, against America becoming involved in World War II, warns against Jewish ownership and influence of motion pictures, press, radio and government
20 October Georgette Leblanc dies of cancer
5 December Soviet counteroffensive begins
7 December Japanese attack Pearl Harbor
11 December Adolf Hitler formally declares war on the United States

1942

18 April Gurdjieff tells pupils to hide Jewish pupils. Group has grown to some forty people
11 November Germany incorporates occupied zone of France, effectively ending reign of Vichy government
Christmas Gurdjieff is classified as a bilingual French-German Caucasian emigrant and thus was issued a *carte d'identité* from the French Department of Immigration,[10] which qualified him for a French passport after the war

1943

31 January German Sixth Army surrenders at Stalingrad
14 April All Jews of French nationality ordered seized

1944

27 January German blockade of Leningrad (St. Petersburg) ends. An estimated million to a million and a half have died, most of starvation
14 April Food scarce in Paris. Rations cut from 1200 to 1000 calories a day
21 May René Daumal dies of tuberculosis
6 June D-Day landing by Allies at Normandy, France
25 August Paris liberated. Purge soon begins. Some 40,000 French citizens, taken to be German sympathizers, are killed
December Janet Flanner visits Gurdjieff

1945

Elizabeth Gordon dies. Released from a German internment camp for the British, she dies in Paris shortly thereafter
Spring Bennett gives public lectures on Gurdjieff's teaching

---

10. The Nansen Identity Certificates he carried weren't issued after 1938 and his French visa had expired.

30 April Adoph Hitler commits suicide
May Uspenskii's solicitor writes Bennett saying he is "a charlatan and a thief" and asking for "the return of all Mr. Uspenskii's material, including his lectures"
7 May Germany unconditionally surrenders
July Kathryn Hulme and Fritz Peters, at different times, visit Gurdjieff
6 August United States drops the world's first atomic bomb on Hiroshima
14 August Japan surrenders

1947

19 January Uspenskii leaves America to return to England
26 February Uspenskii holds the first of six final meetings
2 October P. D. Uspenskii dies
3 October Gurdjieff says, "I am supposed to hate Uspenskii, but he wrote *Fragments* so I love him"

1948

Bennett, fearing another war, flies to South Africa to set up teaching
Maurice Nicoll learns Gurdjieff is alive but refuses to see him
7 June Bennett visits Madame Uspenskii at Franklin Farms
30 June Margaret Anderson and Dorothy Caruso visit
6 August Bennett visits Gurdjieff. It's been twenty-five years to the month since he last saw Gurdjieff
8 August Gurdjieff has another auto accident
Early September Lord John Pentland and his family arrive
30 November Gurdjieff sails to New York with Madame de Salzmann, Lord John Pentland and Aubrey Wolton
17 December Gurdjieff arrives in New York, his eighth visit. Meets with English and American pupils, including Jean Toomer

1949

11 February Gurdjieff departs for Paris
26 May C. Daly King completes "The Oragean Version." Privately published in manuscript form
June Lord Pentland, his wife, Lucy, and daughter, Mary, C. S. Nott, Jane Heap, Margaret Anderson, Dorothy Caruso, Peggy Matthews, Kenneth Walker and others visit Gurdjieff
Late August Gurdjieff visits Lascaux
14 October Gurdjieff collapses during movements class
21 October Gurdjieff sees proofs of *Beelzebub's Tales*. Says, "Now I can die"
26 October Gurdjieff is taken to the American Hospital
29 October Gurdjieff, seventy-seven years old, dies at 10:30 a.m.
3 November Service is held at the Russian Orthodox Church. At 4:30 p.m., Gurdjieff is buried at the Avon Cemetery.

References[1]

Guide to References

Each quotation or significant fact is designated by the code for the source material and the page upon which it appears. Thus:

I waited all these years. W, 154

means the material will be found in the book *Witness* on page 154.

Key to Titles

A&E	*All and Everything.* G. I. Gurdjieff
AEF	"An Experiment at Fontainebleau." James Carruthers Young
AFR	*A Further Record.* P. D. Ouspensky
AIA	*Adventures in Arabia.* William Seabrook
ALF	*A Lasting Freedom.* Francis Roles
AMDS	*After Many a Summer Dies the Swan.* Aldous Huxley
AMY	*All My Yesterdays.* Cecil Lewis
AROPL	Orage Papers, Leeds University, England
ARO	*A. R. Orage: A Memoir.* Philip Mairet
AWW	*A Woman's Work.* Mary Ellen Korman
BGT	*Being Geniuses Together.* Robert McAlmon and Kay Boyle
BL	Beinecke Library, Yale University
BM	*Balanced Man.* Fritz Peters
BWG	*Boyhood with Gurdjieff.* Fritz Peters
CHA	*The Crisis in Human Affairs.* J. G. Bennett
CLKM	*Collected Letters of Katherine Mansfield.* Vincent O'Sullivan & Margaret Scott, eds.
CPO	"The Case of P. D. Ouspensky." Marie Seton
DC	*Dorothy Caruso: A Personal History.* Dorothy Caruso
E	*Essentials.* Jean Toomer
JF	Janet Flanner Papers. Library of Congress
FLP	*Four Lives in Paris.* Hugh Ford
G	*Gurdjieff.* Louis Pauwels
GAB	*Gurdjieff: An Annotated Bibliography.* J. Walter Driscoll
GAM	*Gurdjieff: Anatomy of a Myth.* James Moore
GGE	*Gurdjieff: A Very Great Enigma.* J. G. Bennett
GKM	*Gurdjieff and Katherine Mansfield.* James Moore
GMA	*God Is My Adventure.* Rom Landau
GML	*Gurdjieff: A Master in Life.* Tcheslaw Tchekhovitch

1. For Foreword, Main Text and Afterword only

REFERENCES

GO	*Gurdjieff and Orage.* Paul Beekman Taylor
GR	*Gurdjieff Remembered.* Fritz Peters
GY	*The Gurdjieff Years: 1929–1949.* Recollections of Louise March. Beth McCorkle
HCG	*The Herald of Coming Good.* G. I. Gurdjieff
ID	*Invisible Darkness.* Charles Larson
IDR	*In Denikin's Russia.* Carl Bechhofer Roberts
IUO	*It's Up to Ourselves.* Jessmin and Dushka Howarth
IP	*Idiots in Paris.* J. G. Bennett
ISOM	*In Search of the Miraculous.* P. D. Ouspensky
JKM	*Journal of Katherine Mansfield.* J. Middleton Murry, ed.
JTOG	*Jean Toomer's Years with Gurdjieff.* Rudolph P. Byrd
JTW	*Journey through this World.* C. S. Nott
KHP	Kathryn Hulme Papers, Beinecke Library, Yale University
KMAB	*Katherine Mansfield: A Biography.* Jeffrey Meyers
KMB	*Katherine Mansfield: Biography.* Antony Alpers
KML	*Katherine Mansfield: Selected Letters.* Vincent O'Sullivan
LDKM	"The Last Days of Katherine Mansfield." Olgivanna Lloyd Wright
LFR	*Letters from Russia 1919.* P. D. Ouspensky
LG	*Luba Gurdjieff: A Memoir with Recipes.* Luba Gurdjieff
LJT	*The Lives of Jean Toomer.* Cynthia Kerman and Richard Eldridge
LL	*Lives and Letters.* John Carswell
LOR	*Ladies of the Rope.* William Patrick Patterson
LRIA	*Life Is Real Only Then, When "I Am."* G. I. Gurdjieff
M	*Mosaic.* Lincoln Kirstein
MAP	Margaret Anderson Papers. University of Wisconsin
MBS	*Martin Benson Speaks.* Carl Lehmannn-Haupt, editor
MDL	*Mabel Dodge Luhan: New Woman, New Worlds.* Lois Palken Rucnick
MEPS	*Diary of Madame Egout Pour Sweet.* Rina Hands
MLO	*More Lives than One.* Claude Bragdon
MN	*Maurice Nicoll: A Portrait.* Beryl Pogson
MNW	*Gurdjieff: Making a New World.* J. G. Bennett
MOG	*Memories of Gurdjieff.* A. L. Staveley
MRM	*Meetings with Remarkable Men.* G. I. Gurdjieff
MTYW	*My Thirty Years War.* Margaret Anderson
NL	*Nine Letters.* Rosamund Bland
NMU	*A New Model of the Universe.* P. D. Ouspensky
NRT	*No Religion Higher than Truth.* Maria Carlson
OGA	*Orage with Gurdjieff in America.* Louise Welch
OGF	"Ouspensky, Gurdjieff et les Fragments d'un Enseignement Inconnu." Boris Mouravieff
OL	*On Love.* A. R. Orage

OLWG	*Our Life with Mr. Gurdjieff*. Thomas and Olga de Hartmann
ONC	*Orage and The New Age Circle*. Paul Selver
OPSL	Ouspensky Papers, Sterling Library, Yale University
OUG	*Ouspensky: The Unsung Genius*. J. H. Reyner
RM	*A Record of Meetings*. P. D. Ouspensky
RPDO	*Remembering Pyotr Demianovich Ouspensky*. Merrily E. Taylor
SLO	*Strange Life of Ivan Osokin*. P. D. Ouspensky
SLP	*The Strange Life of P. D. Ouspensky*. Colin Wilson
SOC	*The States of Human Consciousness*. C. Daly King
SOH	*Shadows of Heaven*. Paul Beekman Taylor
SS	*Spiritual Survival in a Radically Changing World-Time*. William Patrick Patterson
T	*Telos*. William Patrick Patterson, editor
TA	*Tu l'aimeras: Souvenirs sur Georgii Ivanovitch Gurdjieff*. Tcheslaw Tchekhovitch
TAT	*The Awakening Twenties*. Gorham Munson
TCH	*The Theory of Conscious Harmony*. Rodney Collin
TCI	*The Theory of Celestial Influence*. Rodney Collin
TE	*Time Exposures*. Waldo Frank
TF	*The Fellowship*. Roger Friedland and Harold Zellman
TEL	*The Theory of Eternal Life*. Rodney Collin
TFF	*The Fiery Fountains*. Margaret Anderson
TGJ	*The Gurdjieff Journal*. William Patrick Patterson, editor
THC	*The Harmonious Circle*. James Webb
TMO	*Talks by Madame Uspenskii*. Robert de Ropp
TO	*Tertium Organum*. P. D. Ouspensky
TOG	*Teachings of Gurdjieff*. C. S. Nott
TOV	*The Oragean Version*. C. Daly King
TPBL	Toomer Collection. Beinecke Library, Yale University
TWD	*Talks With a Devil*. P. D. Ouspensky
TWH	*Taking with the Left Hand*. William Patrick Patterson
TWS	*The Wayward and the Seeking: A Collection of Writings by Jean Toomer*. Darwin T. Turner, editor
UC	*Undiscovered Country*. Kathryn Hulme
UG	*Unknowable Gurdjieff*. Margaret Anderson
UQ	*The Unending Quest*. Paul Dukes
VID	*Voices in the Dark*. William Patrick Patterson
VWI	*Venture with Ideas*. Kenneth Walker
VRW	*Views from the Real World*. G. I. Gurdjieff
W	*Witness*. J. G. Bennett, First Edition
WF	*What For?* Olga de Hartmann, unpublished manuscript
WGP	*With Gurdjieff in St. Petersburg and Paris*. Anna Butkovsky-Hewitt

References

WHB	*What Happened in Between.* William J. Welch
WPT	*Witchcraft: Its Power in the World Today.* William Seabrook
WW	*Warrior's Way.* Robert de Ropp
Y	*Yezidism — Its Background, Observances and Textual Tradition.* Philip G. Kreyenbroek

List of References

Foreword

1. Teacher of Dancing. A&E, 50
2. You are like Paul; you must spread my ideas. W, 262, first edition; omitted in editions thereafter
3. I do not pretend to understand Georgi Ivanovitch. W, 158
4. The present period of culture. MRM, 8
5. Completely self-supporting. ISOM, 286
6. The world would be destroyed. GR, 122
7. Genuine, natural men. BWG, 161
8. Bon ton literary writing. A&E, 6, 14
9. P. Uspenski. MLO, 262

Search for the Miraculous

10. Whole sensation of myself. MRM, 205
11. What is the sense. MNW, 184.[2]
12. The legend of the Babylonian hero. MRM, 35
13. A 'spiritualizing factor.' MRM, 34
14. His father would get him up. MRM, 45
15. Elder brother. MRM, 39
16. Eldest of my grandsons! A&E, 27
17. My second father. MRM, 57
18. The founder and creator. MRM, 34
19. Was a tall, thin. MRM, 51
20. Very mischievous. MRM, 50
21. Learning came very easily. MRM, 53
22. Priest and a physician. MRM, 54
23. Ever-continuing interest. MRM, 59
24. Agitated me so profoundly. MRM, 60
25. Come, you little garlic-head. MRM, 61
26. There was not a single book. MRM, 70

---

2. Gurdjieff formulates the aim in *The Herald of Coming Good*, 13, as: "To understand clearly the precise significance, in general, of the life process on earth of all the outward forms of breathing creatures and, in particular, of the aim of human life in the light of this interpretation."

27. This so dumbfounded me. MRM, 65
28. They are devil-worshippers. MRM, 68
29. Master of all trades. MRM, 61
30. Acolyte of the famous Father Yevlampios. MRM, 79
31. The whole sensation of myself. MRM, 205
32. Have possessed great knowledge. MRM, 9
33. Map of pre-sand Egypt. MRM, 99
34. A real bond. MRM, 121
35. Christian many thousands of years. ISOM, 302
36. The pyramids are much more ancient. NMU, 350–61
37. The teaching whose theory. ISOM, 286
38. Empty and abortive interval. MRM, 8
39. The whole of our progress. ISOM, 299
40. Unless the 'wisdom'. GR, 122
41. Sacred vow. HCG, 11–12
42. Necessary to be independent. MRM, 249
43. A man would be. MRM, 270
44. Prince Ozay. UQ, 99–113
45. You believe in ventilation! UQ, 100
46. You are a musical instrument. UQ, 107
47. God is achieved not through activity. UQ, 108
48. Are you afraid of risks? UQ, 113
49. Several quite clear mental pictures. RPDO, 9
50. I did not play with toys. RPDO, 14
51. It is only when you realize. RPDO, 14
52. Dead wall everywhere. RPDO, 3
53. Very anarchistically inclined. RPDU, 10
54. Suicide must build a strong momentum. OPSL
55. I mistrusted and disliked. RPDO, 10
56. I found theosophical literature. RPDO, 12
57. Unbroken line of thought. NMU, 5
58. Schools of the distant past. ISOM, 4
59. The most independent and talented. NRT, 74
60. Here was a book. WGP, 16
61. These ordinary members are sheep. WGP, 17
62. A prolonged self-consciousness. TO, 277
63. Must always feel equal. WGP, 19
64. I came across your orbit like a comet. WGP, 24
65. Almost boyish enthusiasm. WGP, 22
66. A driving force and a will to seek. WGP, 19
67. As extraordinarily real. NMU, 309–10
68. I did not exist, that there was no I. NMU, 321

69. Uspenskii Fourth Dimension. OUG, 19
70. I was watching the play. TO, 258
71. But why don't you go. WGP, 30
72. Nietzsche was the greatest. ARO, 31
73. Speaking sincerely with myself. OPSL
74. Everything was beginning to totter. ISOM, 29
75. Why on earth did I ever go to India. WGP, 31
76. You must realize. OPSL
77. A new or forgotten road. ISOM, 3
78. Thin film of false reality. ISOM, 3
79. A more rational kind. ISOM, 5
80. P. D. Uspenskii's lectures. NRT, 75
81. Indian raja. ISOM, 7
82. Narcotics cannot. ISOM, 8–9, 162, 195; TO, 278
83. Chemistry. ISOM, 8
84. To do this, a great knowledge. ISOM, 8
85. Feline grace and assurance. ISOM, 10
86. At once, without delay. ISOM, 11
87. I saw without hesitation. OPSL
88. Some are dead. ISOM, 16
89. If you understood. ISOM, 20
90. I have found the miracle! WGP, 35
91. You will find me here. WGP, 112
92. A *man* is responsible. ISOM, 20
93. His journeys from Moscow. OPSL, Box 39, Folder 1887
94. The situation in its essence. OPSL, Box 039, Folder 1820
95. Listen, Georgi Ivanovitch. OPSL, Box 39, Folder 1887
96. Predominant emotion in me. RPDO, 8; OPSL, Box 40, Folder 1721
97. Extreme individualism. ISOM, 266
98. St. Petersburg conditions. OPSL, ISOM, draft
99. People do not value a thing, if they do not pay for it. ISOM, 12, 165
100. A business-like man. WGP, 66–75
101. He was kind and good to everyone he met. WGP, 75
102. People are machines. ISOM, 52
103. Not one of you has noticed you do not remember yourselves. ISOM, 117
104. I remembered that I had forgotten. ISOM, 121
105. We are undoubtedly moving. NRT, 77
106. Man has no permanent and unchangeable I. ISOM, 59–60
107. A man's life and its conditions. ISOM, 49
108. A very great quantity. ISOM, 38
109. Our ordinary European logical method. OPSL
110. I began to realize what an immense value. OPSL, Folder 1726

111. Appreciated and understood. OPSL, Box 39, Folder 1887
112. Sometimes there was too much of it. OPSL, Box 39, Folder 1887
113. Did not see me. OPSL, Box 39, Folder 1887
114. I began to realize what an immense value. ISOM, Box 39, Folder 1726
115. It is with this that science. OPSL, Box 39, Folder 1886
116. It is not merely a coincidence. ISOM, 205
117. In speaking of man's different 'I's. OPSL, Box 39, Folder 1887
118. Time is breath. ISOM, 213
119. You must not be afraid. OPSL, Box 39, Folder 1887
120. Whatever is this rubbish you're talking. WGP, 79
121. Sense the struggle. WGP, 69
122. Another time, doctor. WGP, 69
123. Uspenskii's is Wraps up the Thought. WGP, 103
124. 'Piotr Demianovich.' ISOM, 267
125. Give rise to perplexity. OPSL, Box 40, Folder, 60–65
126. "Play" is not necessary in itself. OPSL, Box 40, Folder 60–65
127. Gurdjieff's "play." OPSL, Box 40, 60-65
128. We saw spread out before our eyes. MRM, 245
129. A revaluation of all values. MRM, 246
130. *This is esoteric Christianity.* ISOM, 102
131. It will seem strange to many people. ISOM, 302
132. The teaching whose theory. ISOM, 286
133. Some of those who attended. OPSL
134. It is all hypocrisy. OPSL, Box 39, Folder 1887
135. Yes! I believe that Georgi Ivanovitch. WGP, 67
136. There is no business. I used to buy souls. AFR, 55–56
137. People around Gurdjieff. OPSL
138. What he had been born with. OPSL
139. Every man's personal work. ISOM, 226
140. A state of unusual tension. ISOM, 260
141. Alexander Technique. TAT, 206
142. I saw this man in motion. THC, 282
143. The miracle began. ISOM, 262
144. But I had found something else. ISOM, 263
145. I can only say. ISOM, 266
146. It is difficult to climb the hill. ISOM, 271
147. Not afraid to keep silent. ISOM, 271
148. A man will renounce. ISOM, 274
149. The only way is by suffering. OPSL, Box 392, Folder 1705
150. So how to awaken feelings? OPSL
151. "Play" is indispensable. OPSL
152. There are usually more whores here. OLWG, 8

153. From the start. OLWG, 9
154. Contemporary culture requires automatons. ISOM, 309
155. What is the main thing that hinders. OLWG, 11
156. When you live among wolves. OLWG, 12
157. What do you expect from me? WF, 55–57
158. You are an officer. OLWG, 13–14
159. Faith in his teaching is not required. OLWG, 14
160. We had all been sitting together. WGP, 104
161. Oil king. ISOM, 325–26

Higher Dimensions

162. What a great and all-encompassing. NRT, 171
163. I certainly myself heard. MNW, 99
164. There is no sense. ISOM, 328
165. If you want to rest. ISOM, 340
166. Comrades, do not worry. LFR, 21
167. Very old and peculiar culture. ISOM, 340
168. A robust old man. ISOM, 342
169. How shall I put it? MRM, 43–44
170. Events are against us. ISOM, 342–43
171. How can one strengthen the feeling of "I"? ISOM, 343
172. Tell them I am beginning a new work. ISOM, 343–44
173. Now all responsibility towards myself. ISOM, 344
174. I am a difficult, pretentious man. WGP, 105
175. Gurdjieff tells them. OLWG, 70–72
176. Schools are imperative. ISOM, 347
177. I always have a very strange feeling. ISOM, 346
178. Began to waver. ISOM, 368
179. She was tall of stature. OLWG, 17
180. What the matter was. ISOM, 368
181. A very absurd quarrel. ISOM, 370
182. I am a *svolotch*. OLWG, 54
183. I have now already spent. ISOM, 371
184. At this critical moment. NRT, 80
185. Julia Osipovna Ostrowska. GAM, 66
186. The Society for Struggle. OLWG, 58
187. If we didn't study attention. OLWG, 45
188. Chief feature. OLWG, 65
189. [soul] has to be awakened in us, OLWG, 41
190. I can lift you to heaven. OLWG, 55
191. Where did you acquire this knowledge. OPSL, Folder 1892
192. The plan of the whole. ISOM, 346

193. Man of being. OLWG, 68
194. Why always a suggestion. OLWG, 74
195. As the basis of Mr. Gurdjieff's Work. OLWG, 69–70
196. There is a constant temptation. OLWG, 70
197. Under the mask of bad personality. OLWG, 55
198. When the personality is made to suffer, OLWG, 55
199. He wanted to make me submit to his will. OPSL
200. In fact towards the way of religion. ISOM, 375
201. It became perfectly clear. OPSL,
202. You are right in one thing. OPSL, Box 39, Folder 1884
203. For me personally. MRM, 271
204. Besaraboff visits. MLO, 260
205. The expedition intends. OLWG, 78
206. Meanwhile, Gurdjieff had the women. OLWG, 79–81
207. Miracles were performed. MRM, 274
208. Faith is the knowledge of feeling. OLWG, 109
209. In my opinion, we got out safely. MRM, 274–75
210. He is a fine man, and she — is intelligent. OLWG, 122
211. Eat bacon every morning. WF, 121
212. I gathered together. OPSL, Box 39, Folder 1688
213. The prices of all products, LFR, 6
214. I honestly pity. LFR, 1
215. Very characteristic. ISOM, 38
216. In the face of the weakness of the intelligentsia. LFR, 33
217. The ground had fallen away behind me. NMU, 388
218. Some of them are very nice people. SLIO, 140,
219. Strange confidence. ISOM, 380
220. Gurdjieff astonished us. OPSL
221. The armies consisting of Chinese. LFR, 14
222. People don't understand. LFR, 23
223. In the autumn of 1917. LFR, 27
224. One of Russia's richest towns. LFR, 41–42
225. Negative frame of mind. ISOM, 381–82
226. Why are you so astonished? OLWG, 147
227. It struck something deep in me. TF, 47
228. I wish immortality. TF, 52–53
229. A curious individual. IDR, 65
230. How could you do this to me? TF, 424
231. A very dangerous book. MLO, 262
232. *Tertium Organum* published. MLO, 262
233. A city rapidly acquiring a Western. NMU, 388
234. The ancient wisdom of the East. GML, 4

235. What is needed today. GML, 4–6
236. I finally gave up wasting my time and energy. MRM, 281
237. Spencer Kellogg, Jr. MLO, 263
238. Could be bought cheaply. OLWG, 152
239. Everyone must help. GML, 13–18
240. I have spent nearly all my money. GML, 14–15
241. But Georgi Ivanovitch. GML, 17
242. In the interests of the work. ISOM, 382
243. Three ideas lying at the basis. OPSL
244. As one of the very few men. W, 55
245. I met the strangest eyes. W, 55
246. I can personally confirm. MNW, 90
247. His coming to Constantinople. CHA, x.
248. Nothing but dirty jokes. OPSL
249. I gradually arrived at the same difficulties. OPSL, Folder 1688
250. "*Davay! Davay!*" he shouts. TF, 57
251. There are not three. GML, 42–46
252. Even if you knew what to do. OPSL
253. I personally consider that subconsciousness. GAM 168
254. With Mr. Gurdjieff there are only two 'I's. OPSL
255. There, now make one line out of that. ISOM, 383
256. Problem of this 'play.' OPSL
257. In former Russia. NMU, 388
258. I related to him in detail. OPSL, Folder 1688
259. Excellent translation. MLO, 263
260. Deeply impressed. GAM, 152 MLO 263
261. Gurdjieff himself in the beginning used this word. OPSL

Magicians at War

262. The finest critical intelligence. ARO, 121
263. Not so impressed by his features. ARO, 24–25
264. Orage was shocked and hurt. ARO, xxi
265. He rang me up. NL, 1
266. There were none of the usual mannerisms. GMA, 167
267. Quite monumentally boorish. ONC, 72
268. When sitting in reflection, LL, 172
269. I may find. LL, 172
270. This man, Uspenskii. NL, 1
271. Finally, I decided. NL, 5
272. I went to see Uspenskii again yesterday. NL, 23
273. This is going to lose me. NL, 31
274. I told Uspenskii this afternoon. NL, 34

275. I have lost him. NL, 39
276. He was awfully nice to me. NL, 45
277. Yes, and he will have a worse time. NL, 46
278. A. tried to be easy and rather flippant. NL, 47
279. I found it difficult to follow him. VWI, 8, 12, 57
280. You must come and hear Uspenskii. MN, 71
281. Uspenskii seemed rather depressed. NL, 63
282. I have lost him absolutely. NL, 73
283. He had developed a hard outer shell. WGP, 22–23
284. I want to tell you how sensible. LL, 180
285. All the former obstacles. OPSL
286. When we speak of ourselves. VRW, 75
287. One center of our machine. VRW, 79
288. Everything more vivid. MNP, 72
289. I *knew* Gurdjieff was the teacher. TOG, 27–28
290. He was working on the wrong lines. JTW, 98–99
291. Normal human beings. GAM, 164
292. I had decided. ISOM, 385
293. Orage knew it but he told me a lie. OPSL, Box 017, Folder 0818
294. Even that? TF, 59
295. *New Age's* circulation. LL, 144, 173
296. "The Ordinary Home Life of Women." LL, 80
297. Aphrodite amusing herself at our expense. LL, 28
298. Orage was tall, slim, with a feline face. LL 20
299. Orage named Mansfield *marmoset*. ARO, 75
300. I received some very strange letters. OPSL, Box 55, Folder 1839
301. I knew that Gurdjieff was the teacher. TOG, 27
302. I wish above anything. GO, 24
303. 250 pounds. LL, 138
304. 100 pounds for it. AOPL, Leeds
305. I felt he was weighing me up. AWW, 3
306. An extraordinarily sympathetic person. JKM, 311
307. I don't feel influenced. KMB, 345
308. This child I had conceived. MWM, 292
309. He looks exactly like a desert chief. JKM, 250.
310. If she dies here. GML, 82
311. I learned that a great many prominent sanatoria. LDKM, 6
312. I want to learn. KML, 275
313. Mother-in-law, digestion. A&E, 343
314. He constantly manipulated people. TOG, 54
315. Mr. Gurdjieff makes several movements. GML, 95–96
316. Try to sew the rest of the carpets. GML, 107–108

References

317. It is not a center. TOG, 59
318. Until I came here. CLKM, 319
319. The air was supposed to be good for her. LDKM, 8
320. By the way I have had a great talk. CLKM, 322
321. The life of a person. OLWG, 191
322. In the Institute you have to learn. OLWG, 179–83
323. For the average person. GR, 126–27
324. Very motley company. ISOM, 385
325. I know that this is true. ISOM 386
326. I am going to find God. ARO, 88
327. "The Quest for God." ONC, 78
328. I had had no real exercise for years. TOG, 28
329. A hatching place for eggs. MNP, 8
330. It was precisely the complete. ARO, 93
331. When I was in the very depths of despair. TOG, 28
332. Now, Orage, I think you dig enough. TOG, 28
333. House of devotion. ARO, 93
334. Her face shone. KMB, 356
335. *Child of the sun.* JKM, 254
336. An opportunity. KMB, 356–357
337. Your body is only a medium. TF, 68
338. She was tall, beautifully proportioned. Olgivanna Lloyd Wright, "The Last Days of Katherine Mansfield," *The Bookman*, March 1931
339. He looks very surly. CLKM, 332
340. They live in one smallish room. CLKM, 328
341. He is the only man who understands. KMAB, 244
342. We are going to celebrate Christmas. KML, 280
343. Marked with the symbol of goodness. TF, 71
344. I got the gold coin. TF, 71
345. You see, my love. KML, 282
346. I have been leading a very tame. KML, 284
347. Failed in the Work. OPSL, Folder 0818
348. Temptation. ISOM, 389
349. I could find no place. ISOM, 389
350. Her eyes wide with terror. TF, 69
351. I have heard enough about that place. GKM, 3
352. I have asked you to come. OPSL, Box 17, Folder 821
353. Uspenskii could never forget. JTW, 91
354. When the work was organized. OPSL, Box 17, Folder 821
355. Uspenskii was a brilliant. MNW, 141
356. But is there one righteous person. WGP, 81
357. She made out this big case. OPSL. Folder 0818

358. It is said in some ancient teachings. OPSL
359. When I say "I fear." JKM, 255
360. Thin, almost gaunt. G, 168
361. What results are you trying. G, 176–80
362. Extraordinarily highly developed. ARO, xxvii
363. He found a kindred spirit. Bowyer, London Daily News 15–19
364. It was quite evident. OPSL, Box 017, Folder 0818
365. The Institute can give very little. VRW, 152–54
366. People talk of union with God. OPSL, 840, Series 1, Box 17
367. How could she say such a thing. OPSL
368. Many wrong types came to your Work. OPSL, Box 017, Folder 0818
369. There are definite. OPSL, Box 017, Folder 0818
370. All that Uspenskii had of value. JWT, 90–91
371. Anything that produces. OPSL, ISOM, 157–58
372. He drove like a wild man. UC, 56–57
373. Man has three powers. VRW, 159
374. There are two kinds of love. VRW, 251–52
375. When you return to Institute. MNP, 89
376. Whether the difficulties. MNP, 89
377. Now only your mind is awake. W, 108
378. You have the possibility of learning. W, 121
379. With too much knowledge. W, 121
380. I am not interested in your money. W, 121
381. A student's son was hit by a bus. OGA, 6
382. Teacher who would indulge. G, 201–213
383. For one section of the people here. VRW, 107
384. I will go away and make money. W, 122
385. It was much rather as if. W, 126
386. The cult has been spreading. BGT, 95–96
387. Uspenskii was grim. OPSL, Box 054, Folder 1838
388. I expect to be sailing. MLO, 321
389. Adam and Eve. OPSL, Box 017, Folder 0820
390. My father used to help my Uncle George. LG, 19, 28
391. His family had suffered much. TOG, 34–35
392. I found myself at the last minute. MRM, 293
393. Expensive brooch. IUO, 426, MRM, 294–95
394. What occurred was one of those interventions. MRM, 293
395. All that was connected with it. ISOM, 389
396. I have asked you to come. OPSL, Box 17, Folder 821
397. Uspenskii could never forget. JTW, 91
398. I wanted to save the System. CPO, 34
399. Uspenskii was a brilliant and dedicated exponent. MNW, 141

400. But is there one righteous person among you? WGP, 81–83

Tzvarnoharno

401. The life of our time. TOG, 1–3
402. Orage is the most persuasive man. THC, 281
403. How did you enjoy the talk? ARO, 79
404. None at all. I could not get the hang of it. TOG, 6
405. I was taken to meet him. WPW, 179–80, 182
406. With ordinary love goes hate. TOG, 22–23
407. The demonstrations, I imagine. WPW, 180
408. At once I sensed I was a mere youth. TOG, 20
409. I saw this man in motion. THC, 282
410. Power—something more than. JTG, 71–72
411. I had an opportunity. MLO, 323
412. The sensation in New York. ID, 35–36
413. I had just time to look. TFF, 111–12
414. Mr. Uspenskii, there is no love in your system. W, 87
415. It was Orage, the perfect disciple. MLO, 324
416. I felt that this man's note. TAT, 253–54
417. I felt his alertness. TAT, 253
418. I have ventured to come to this 'dollar-growing country. MRM, 248
419. The famous prophet and magician. GMA, 185
420. African-American. LJT, 55
421. His sex nature. ID, 24
422. Long after the liability. THC, 214
423. The acute sensibility. ARO, 79
424. Here were true intellectuals. TE, 151
425. Prose that ranks with Shaw's. TE, 153
426. You have to choose. TOG, 31–32
427. You must remember. TOG, 32
428. Gurdjieff says the attitude to finance. TOG, 35
429. Uspenskii sat at Gurdjieff's left. UG, 83–84
430. He resided on the earth. UG, 136
431. No greater contrast can be imagined. MAP
432. In the power of a despot. TF, 86
433. Very important you come Prieuré. GO, 64
434. I want to know everything. BWG, 5
435. You see, I am dedicated to this. GO, 64–68
436. I unfortunately did not go. GO, 83
437. No, I will tell you nothing. WF, 168–69
438. Eoung-Ashokh Mardiross. MRM, 61, 64
439. He has a severe concussion. GML, 142

440. A bit of live meat. A&E, 1186
441. Gurdjieff lost contact. JTW, 98
442. I'm frightened. THC, 294
443. Their usual superficial. LRIA, 80–81
444. The law of accident. THC, 294–95; GIOA, 102–103
445. You do not understand. ISOM, 249
446. A deep-seated unwillingness. JTOG, 72
447. Damnation! TOG, 83
448. Things begin to hum. JTOG, 75
449. Manual work. JTOG, 74–75
450. When you work the way we did. TPBL
451. The saying took instant. TPBL
452. I had been strong. TWS, 74
453. Each day was a full day. JTOG, 75
454. I was very ill. OLWG, 233
455. I had to die. OLWG, 233
456. In my conscience to lead. HCG, 12
457. Most of us were shot straight into the air. JTOG, 77
458. He certainly was under some special. GGE, 98–99
459. Impact which his work and ideas. MNW,
460. Gurdjieff's work failed. OPSL
461. I do not pretend to understand. W, 158
462. Working in a woman's lavatory. TF, 90
463. Totally unusual and impressive. TOV, 4
464. Fanatics meeting privately. TOV, 4
465. Jean had a lot of nerve. ID, 42
466. Work hard while you feel like it. TPBL
467. I have taught you everything. TF, 90
468. I went to my room. TAT, 279
469. God had heard my earnest wish. TF, 97–98

All and Everything

470. It happened in the 223rd year. A&E, 51
471. Since I had not. LRIA, 4
472. Introduces "The Science of Idiotism." TOG, 101
473. One of them always adored by me. LRIA. 31–32
474. Uniquely nearest to my inner life. LRIA, 36–38
475. Would like to learn from you. THC, 339
476. It is completely unintelligible. TOG, 92
477. It is really an objective work of art. TOG, 93
478. I've never encountered. TOV, 14
479. The desire for power. LJT, 141

References

480. Orage thought that this came pretty close. LJT, 141
481. He is also radiating more light. TOG, 99
482. The sign of a perfected man. TOG, 112
483. All the time I am sitting there. TOG, 100
484. I can't see two inches ahead. LJT, 150
485. Freets, because I try to do thing. BWG, 78
486. You know, Orage, when you give something. TOG, 100–101
487. Orage, a tall man, seemed withered. BWG, 31
488. My feelings were completely reversed. BWG, 33
489. Instinctive love. OL, 7–17
490. If you want something, must ask. BWG, 33
491. I was aware that her life had been full of suffering. OLWG, 249
492. It leaves all philosophy behind. TPBL
493. Some very essential change took place. OPSL, Folder 1688
494. I haven't plumbed the depths. THC, 360
495. Gurdjieff proposes in the book. AROPL
496. Successful in getting people to support him. ID, 25
497. Do not come, I do not wish to see you. MBS, 169
498. What we say is personality. TPBL. Box 68, Folder 1544
499. The only types of sexual relations. TPBL, Box 68, Folder 1544
500. What you not understand. BWG, 60–62
501. I got really drunk. GO, 110
502. For whom are you doing all this work. TC, Box 46, Folder 954
503. When I live with blacks. SOH, 48
504. African nature. SOH, 88
505. Writing, real writing. JTOG, 63–64
506. Toomer convinces him. SOH, 89
507. If she alone, already she be long time dead. BWG, 78,
508. We are not entitled to entertain. LJT, 230
509. She had been ill for sometime. WF, 193
510. You have seen that I helped her. WF, 194
511. Monsieur Gurdjieff had succeeded. LJT, 221
512. Few knew better how to joke and have fun with him. TOG, 121
513. I found nobody of much authority. TOV, 5
514. No doubt for many years to come. TOV, 11
515. Orage spoke of Eliot's. MTYW, 268–69
516. "Act," said Orage. "Don't be acted upon." MTYW, 268–69
517. Borne above the body into a world. LJT, 156–58; ID, 46
518. I was startled by an uncommon. ID, 46
519. There was no filter. LJT, 156
520. Four-day-old jar of caviar. THC, 363
521. Edith restrains Jessie just in time. GO, 113

522. The Great Beast, TOG, 121–22
523. You filthy, you dirty inside. THC, 315
524. It's really a 'Bible'. AROPL
525. A good deal of Jean's life. ID, 45–46, LJT, 382
526. I got a blow in the middle of my forehead. TF, 117–18
527. The book is too colossal, AROPL
528. Strictly corresponded. LRIA, 41
529. Watching the children. LRIA, 42
530. Do you still love yourself as much as ever. Luhan, 229–30
531. You see, Jean. LJT, 148
532. Will see not one man. UG, 28
533. I hoped for a demigod. UG, 29
534. Gurdjieff is quite extraordinary. THC, 360
535. Dubious messiah. TOV, 13
536. I could never properly deceive myself with toys. MN, 102
537. He was sometimes silent. MNP, 98–102
538. It was like a match struck. M, 139
539. The man was no beauty. M, 138
540. A classic prototype of an American farmer. M, 140
541. So, Little Father, you go? M, 147–51
542. Deliberate... to speak broken English. TAT, 267
543. "Health—candidates for idiots." TAT, 267–70
544. What angry man say? I not understand. GAM, 221
545. I ran out on my first wife. OGA, 49
546. If only you'd admit that you're a squirming idiot. THC, 362
547. That abnormality as the basis of family life. LRIA, 92
548. He regarded me. OGA, 49
549. I fell in love with a native. OGA, 42
550. The sole means now. A&E, 1183
551. I must confess. OLWG, 251
552. Our language. OLWG, 252
553. God give you the strength. THC, 321
554. Nujol. BWG, 141–43
555. Gurdjieff became very angry. BWG, 97–100
556. You are now half mine. THC, 362
557. He was superb. SOH, 126
558. If you keep my super-idiot from coming back to me. THC, 363
559. It must be all to the good. GO, 87
560. Become a threat... of the Western world. BWG, 172
561. Squirming idiot and candidate for harmful. SOH, 127
562. Sympathy to Bennett. W, 149
563. I wrote to say that if he disapproved. W, 153

References

564. Women collaborators of men. SOH, 143–44
565. To remove from my eyesight. LRIA, 45
566. Ten million people. SOH, 130–31
567. It has to be read from the real heart. TOG, 126
568. The book destroys existing values. TOG, 193
569. Only such a sensation. A&E, 1183
570. I had become more adroit. MRM, 7
571. How dare you say we can't think. AOPL, Leeds
572. Jesus Christ was not a Californian. OGA, 76
573. Board with nails. BM, 62
574. Compulsive melodrama. BM, 60
575. She had the most stimulating. JTW, 78
576. Gurdjieff is more himself. THC, 364
577. I'm not really a woman. JTW, 78
578. The whole trouble is. SLIO, 17
579. A man's whim. ARO, 115
580. "Thank God I'm free again!" THC, 365
581. I saw my husband. WF, 204–206
582. Take time, wash off American dirt. TGY, 17
583. May I say something to you. TOGY, 30
584. I am overwhelmed. TOGY, 21
585. I always work in cafés. GY, 25
586. So you decide to go? BWG, 171–74
587. The essence of the document. GR, 10
588. Bennett telephones for an appointment. W, 149
589. You are quite blind. WF, 206–07
590. If you acknowledge your sin. JTW, 8
591. You can only understand evil. RM, 568–69
592. Mr. Gurdjieff began to speak. OLWG, 64
593. Wonderful talk. OLWG, 256
594. Come in a week's time. OLWG, 257
595. If love not dissipated. GAM, 235
596. Confess, Orage. JTW, 21
597. Interesting thing Orage. GO, 162
598. You remember Prieuré. GR, 89
599. And what are your conditions. JTW, 19
600. Allah. See Essay, "Elsie & Allah"
601. "Jessie not sheep—she dog." GO, 162
602. "Sacred relic." OGA, 95
603. Americans more receptive. GR, 127
604. The latter meet for themselves. OGA, 103
605. The third center of gravity. OGA, 103–07

606. Elders. OGA, 103–07
607. We had a farewell meeting. OGA, 107
608. I told Gurdjieff that I'd come to the end. OGA, 108–09
609. I waited all these years. W, 154

The Herald

610. A candidate for the madhouse. LRIA, 70
611. All the questions not accessible to the average man. LRIA, 77
612. Exaggerated importance. LRIA, 81
613. That abnormality at the basis of family life. LRIA, 92
614. Saleswoman of the 'Sunwise Turn. LRIA, 95
615. Manipulate in every way. LRIA, 96
616. If Orage made a mistake. OGA, 111
617. The charge against Mr. Orage. TOV, 9
618. While I have received. TOV, 13
619. I, the undersigned. LRIA, 100
620. I came to New York. OGA, 115–17
621. Tails between their legs. LRIA, 127
622. "Philosophizing." LRIA, 123
623. Loving father. LRIA, 119
624. Enjoy an Arabian Nights collation. WPT, 187
625. Mr. Gurdjieff was more brilliant. WPT, 188
626. Orgy. GR, 30–36
627. Wish to fuck. GR, 34
628. "I am Beelzebub." *New York Herald Tribune*, 28 January 1931
629. Gurdjieff sailed last night. JTW, 14
630. Toomer I couldn't bare to look at. ID, 124
631. Ten dollars apiece. JTW, 19
632. New methods of work. MNW, 175
633. Mr. Gurdjieff has a very big plan. JTW, 38
634. Uspenskii does not understand. JTW, 37
635. *New Muddle of the Universe*. JTW, 37
636. I needed rats for my experiments. JTW, 38
637. A man named Rom Landau. JTW, 39
638. Sly and jovial, arrogant and clownish. T, Vol. 2, No. 4
639. I am satisfied that it is entirely possible. ID, 125
640. What has all this to do with Gurdjieff and me? OPSL
641. As I understand it. RM, 15–17
642. Nicoll, you had better go away. MNP, 109
643. Since the writings. GR, 17
644. There is a new race in America. TPBL, Box 17, Folder 9
645. When Gurdjieff entered the room. GMA, 189

References

646. As to Gurdjieff. GMA, 203
647. Madame Alexandra David-Neel, THC, 50
648. In Tibet he was not a foreign agent. TOG, 153
649. He gave his name and papers. MNW, 95–96
650. A former dervish. THC, 434
651. I was astonished at the change. JTW, 24
652. We can never understand. JTW, 31
653. Like a battlefield. MBS, 193–95, 239
654. I'm disappointed that you and others. OGA, 124
655. There are very definite reasons. TPBL
656. I have been hoping. JWT, 201
657. Jane Heap in appearance. UC, 40
658. With one leg pulled. UC, 64
659. I could not resist a rapid reading. TPBL
660. I wish I could work up. TPBL
661. You are very kind. GY, 61
662. A sharp electric spark. GY, 61
663. There was a time. THC, 371
664. Take this and shoot me. M, 158
665. Time was. JTW, 37
666. You not wish. GR, 25
667. Fertilizer. GR, 24
668. You must learn to look right side up. GR, 24
669. America is still very young, strong country. GR, 27
670. When you come Prieuré. GR, 28
671. Toomer's own writing. ID, 233
672. As I spoke I went quite outside myself. W, 169
673. You are like Madame Uspenskii. W, 207
674. This idea of repetition. ISOM, 250
675. At the end I was the only one there. MBS, 244
676. I began to feel queer. GMA, 191–92
677. I washed them. GMA, 195
678. The little book. GMA, 196
679. Even to me certain things. GMA, 202
680. Everything outside itself. TO, 76
681. He had grown fat. THC, 421
682. Considered himself. WHB, 48
683. Not very kind. THC, 435
684. First 'puffed' three small booklets. LRIA, 46
685. Seemed able to see. JTW, 215
686. Gurdjieff had an unbelievable awareness. GR, 127
687. Nightmare journey. GR, 37–43

688. Strange, kindly at times, ferocious. TF, 240–44
689. Dear Mr. Gurdjieff. GO, 184
690. Woman who would satisfy all of my needs. LJT, 142
691. You know, I thank God. JTW, 51–52
692. This man ... my brother. OGA, 137
693. Was considered to be. LRIA, 153
694. You grieve for those. JTW, 53
695. I first met Orage. ONC, 87
696. Jean as the host. ID, 144
697. He was a gentle man. ID, 144
698. Suspiciously as a fraud. ID, 141
699. Marjorie didn't want to give up. ID, 152
700. He was in a bad way. TPBL
701. My mind flashed over. TPBL
702. We left the bathroom and took chairs. TPBL
703. What could be in the man's mind? THC, 422–23
704. You not as I counted THC, 424
705. I thought to myself. LJT, 221
706. There were many things. JTW, 95
707. You know when Gurdjieff. JTW, 98
708. Gurdjieff's mind never recovered. JTW, 98
709. Many things Orage did not understand. TOG, 107
710. You known when Gurdjieff started his Institute. JWT, 97
711. I like Uspenskii and enjoy talking to him. JTW, 107
712. A strong feeling center is a gift of God. JTW, 108
713. What started in Russia, finish in Russia. MNW, 108
714. Everything outside itself. TO, 76
715. Wendy was a country girl. UC, 23–24
716. Drink all you want but in half glasses. For all references between Gurdjieff and the Rope, see Solita Solano Archives and Janet Flanner Archives, Library of Congress, Washington D.C., and the Hulme Archives at the Beinecke Library, Yale University.
717. The fact was Uspenskii had lost his way. UG, 94
718. The work was too theoretical. JTW, 110
719. I was no longer in his confidence. W, 173

The Way of the Sly Man

720. Which you wish to be. JTW, 76–77
721. We are too much in a hurry. JTW, 46–47
722. A great book. JTW, 46–47
723. We discovered early. UC, 109
724. Count Keyserling. OPSL.

725. Krishnamurti is a strange. OPSL.
726. Probably at the height of his power. WW, 99
727. Strange! He was extraordinary! WW, 103
728. Gales of laughter. WW, 109
729. This new Gurdjieff broke the rules. WW, 103
730. He himself seemed to go over his life. WW, 104
731. I have seen a miracle. W, 174–75
732. It seemed to me that esoteric doctrine. OGF
733. It will happen by itself. RPDO, 36
734. I am deeply sad for him. W, 176
735. All your filthy fat. UC, 162
736. It is in their power. AMDS, 304
737. We know people. OPSL, Box 27, Folder 1221
738. Didn't want to be on the same soil as Gurdjieff. JTW, 244
739. He thought that maybe through the mystics. ID, 149
740. I can only say. ID, 149–150
741. If possible I will come. JTW, 123
742. I got it all out. TFF, 165–66
743. We went here, we went there. ID, 150
744. It took India to bring me to my senses. ID, 151
745. Cinema stars. TFF, 216
746. It's an interesting thing. LJT, 282
747. This I cannot remember. WW, 138
748. One thought observes. OPSL
749. I don't mean to say. ID, 157

Uspenskii in America

750. Is my lack of progress. W, 178
751. It is not a sharp break. W, 179
752. Here, by herself. JTW, 158
753. After all these years. For all correspondence between Claude Bragdon, Carman Barnes and Uspenskii see University of Rochester Library, Rochester, New York
754. The end is beginning. MAP
755. You can never be cut off. MAP
756. If he does come, I shall go to California. JTW, 158–59
757. Why did you break with Gurdjieff. GR, 72
758. Genuine gentleman in the exact sense. TOV, 284
759. The term Self-Remembering. TOV, 149
760. Director of British Coal Utilization. W, 181–82
761. Individuality is not a function. RM, 492
762. I don't like to say this. RM, 492

763. Our fear of death. TFF, 231
764. Madame was one of those people. Lord Pentland's personal papers
765. Why am I afraid of you? T, "Beloved Icarus," Vol. 3, No. 1
766. I read and reread her last days. TFF, 239
767. Uspenskii has this idea fixed in his head. JTW, 160
768. One needs fire. TGJ, Vol. 5, No. 3
769. With little research experience. W, 191
770. I had never surrendered. W, 196
771. Devil is very important. RM, 568–70
772. It will come to nothing. Personal conversation with Lord Pentland
773. Anci. GIA, 264–67
774. A very wise old man. UC, 257
775. Gordon was interned. AWW, 34
776. You must have a stomach of iron. JTW, 161
777. Uspenskii could not submit. JTW, 47
778. Where does such action fit the system? CPO, 34; OPSL, Box 1832a, MS 840
779. It struck me very much. TCH, 81
780. Charlatan and a thief. W, 207
781. Uspenskii was no longer a teacher. WW, 152
782. My son! GR, 81
783. This woman not take me seriously. GR, 88
784. I play many roles in life. GR, 92
785. So now I can die. GR, 110
786. He was very close to what I. GR, 70
787. It was as if a violent. GR, 82
788. Must make announcement. GR, 112
789. How does it feel to be chosen? GR, 113
790. What you think. GR, 116
791. Gurdjieff is not a single man. MOG, 51
792. Haven't you ever heard. MOG, 35
793. For myself. MOG, 69–70
794. Sisters of Charity. UC, 260–61
795. He was not the Uspenskii of old. VWI, 137
796. What shall we say to them? OPSL
797. Program? I don't know program. Which program? RM, 585
798. He spoke for nearly two hours. OPSL, Box 54, Folder 1838
799. I never taught system. RM, 616
800. I never was humble myself. RM, 624
801. I understood much more. OPSL, Box 54, Folder 1838
802. Yes, if it is what I call memory. RM, 634
803. Sometimes it may be. RM, 642
804. Absolute insulator. TEL, 85

805. Very deeply disappointed man. OPSL
806. He was a different man. TCI, xx–xxi
807. He would have two or three people. TCH, 64–65
808. I am not going to America this time. TCH, 179–80
809. Give me another month to live. OPSL
810. When almost unable to set one foot. THC, 6
811. Of all his books. OPSL
812. At that moment. TCH, 7
813. Now do you understand. THC, 6–7
814. You must go and find a new method. OPSL
815. I had to move you. TCI, xxi
816. Uspenskii never worked for the moment. TCI, xix
817. Reconstruct everything. TCH, 110
818. Genius — a more perfect piece of machinery. GAM, 177
819. You want communication from the dead. TCH, 131–32
820. Collin returns to the bedroom. T, "Beloved Icarus," Vol. 3, No. 1
821. Among the many extraordinary impressions. TCH, 152
822. Uspenskii, during the last phase. WW, 159
823. Throughout the day. W, 219
824. A knight sets out. W, 128–29
825. A deep feeling of compassion. JTW, 238–39
826. Gurdjieff and Uspenskii were two chosen agents. TCH, 133

Strike a Big Do

827. I am supposed to hate Uspenskii. W, 252; JWT, 243
828. No comment, Madame. OPSL
829. I believe that Gurdjieff and Uspenskii. TCH, 133
830. In stature he was tall. AMY, 136
831. Bennett alone remained as the custodian. AMY, 137–38
832. You are not meant to stay in Africa. W, 223
833. You think that if European civilization. W, 226–27
834. Gurdjieff is not mad. W, 232
835. Miss Jessie, you have my plate. THC, 372
836. Lohan figure. VWI, 159
837. The more I saw of Gurdjieff. VWI, 176
838. I do not really know myself. TPBL
839. En route to Mexico. TCH, x–xi, 187–88
840. Gurdjieff's small dingy. UG, 171–73
841. There was no continuity in the reading. UC, 174
842. During lunch I felt a glow. UC, 176
843. I am writing this on the eve of our journey. AMY, 142
844. It is twenty-five years to the month. W, 236–40

845. His clothes were covered with blood. W, 241
846. Bennett is small thing. JTW, 241
847. We all eat jammed. AMY, 145–46
848. When I eat, I self-remember. IUO, 246
849. I go left, you go right. W, 265
850. Only you can repay for all my labors. W, 267
851. One day I wormed my way into having lunch. ETI, 53
852. For my aim, I want twenty such. MEPS, 54
853. The truth is. AMY, 142–43
854. Gurdjieff sails. GIA, 270
855. I will propose myself health of English. W, 249
856. You will tell stories about me. TF, 424
857. It was the same as me. GY, 75
858. Is too liquid. GY, 74–75
859. It's an interesting thing. LJT, 282
860. When Hitler came to power. MNW, 216
861. But, Frank, he was my teacher. TF, 424
862. I asked for a sheet of paper. W, 253
863. Gurdjieff appoints people. IUO, 210
864. Great physical expense. IUO, 280
865. One day, I read in the paper. JTW, 238–39
866. With one exception the writer. SOC, 5–6
867. Mephisto. IP, 17,79
868. I found myself several feet away. W, 261
869. You know what I say of Judas. W, 262
870. You [Lord Pentland] are like Paul. W, First edition 262, (deleted thereafter)
871. I said yes to the idea. TPBL
872. I now very tired. GR, 110
873. The eyes told me. VWI, 190
874. There is a war between the old world and new. MNW, 261
875. The next five years will decide. W, 270
876. Jean pretended. LJT, 382
877. I was shocked. WHB, 137–39
878. *Au revoir, tout le monde!* IP, 104
879. Only if you not tired, Doctor. GAM, 315
880. The essential thing is. LRIA, xi–xii
881. He died like a king. IP, 104
882. What did this man Gurdjieff teach? GY, 89
883. Eulogy. OLWG, 259
884. I was overwhelmed by the force. IP, 134
885. Lord Creator. TSOM, 47–48
886. It was impossible to go on. T, #7

887. When a Teacher like Mr. Gurdjieff goes. W, 274
888. I was bound to agree that in unity. W, 274
889. Gurdjieff came to strike a big Do. TOG, 224

Afterword

890. I have found the miracle! WGP, 35
891. Yes, I believe that Georgi. WGP, 67
892. Solar god. JTW, 31
893. Objective work of art. TOG, 93
894. We cannot judge Gurdjieff from our level. JTW, 31
895. I not wish people identified with me. JTW, 77
896. A man is born without a soul. OLWG, 183
897. But even immortal souls. OLWG, 183
898. She live many lives. BWG, 91
899. Reincarnation presupposes incarnation. Hulme Archives
900. Idea of repetition. ISOM, 250–51
901. This I do not remember. WW, 138
902. You are like Madame Uspenskii. W, 207
903. Teacher of Dancing. A&E, 50
904. Had in his early youth. Orage Lectures 1927–28
905. Gurdjieff is not a single man. MOG, 51
906. The idea of repetition. ISOM, 250
907. Extreme individualism. ISOM, 266
908. Consciously assist the non-desires. A&E, 373
909. Lighten the Sorrow. A&E, 372
910. Unless the 'wisdom' of the East. GR, 122
911. We should look at the world. BWG, 160–61
912. "This is esoteric Christianity." ISOM, 102
913. The teaching is completely self-supporting. ISOM, 286
914. The Christian church. ISOM, 302
915. The program of the Institute. VFRW, 152–54
916. Some parts of Gurdjieff's teaching. MNW, 82
917. God-the-Father. A&E, 752
918. To live and teach. ARO, 115
919. One kind was invented. A&E, 233
920. We are the images of God. A&E, 775
921. Technology is not neutral. SS, 4–7
922. Be Christians. 5 March 1923 . See text.

Georgi Ivanovitch Gurdjieff

Gurdjieff Students

	Born	*Met Gurdjieff*	*Died*
Sergei Dmitrievich Mercourov	1882	1882	1955
Alina Fedorovna	xxx	1913	xxx
Julia Osipovna Ostrowska	1889	1913	1926
Alexander Nikorovich Petrov	xxx	1913	xxx
Vladmir Pohl	1875	1913	1962
Alexei Rachmilievitch	xxx	1913	xxx
P. D. Uspenskii	1878	1915	1947
Anna Ilinishna Butkovskaia	1885	1915	xxx
Madame Bashmakova	xxx	1916	xxx
Anthony Charkovsky	xxx	1916	xxx
Thomas de Hartmann	1885	1916	1956
Nicholas R.	xxx	1916	xxx
Lenotchka Savitsky	xxx	1916	xxx
P. V. Shandarovsky	xxx	1916	xxx
Elizabeta Grigorievna Stjoernval	xxx	1916	1972
Dr. Leonid Stjoernval	1872	1916	1938
Sophie Grigorievna Uspenskii	1874	1916	1963
Andrey Andreivitch Zaharoff	xxx	1916	1919
Gabo	xxx	1917?	xxx
N. F. Grigoriev	xxx	1917	xxx
Olga de Hartmann	1885	1917	1979
Zukov	xxx	1918	xxx
Elizabeta Galumnian (Chaverdian)	1896	1919	xxx
Nina Lavrovna	xxx	1919	xxx
Frank Pinder	1882	1919	1961
Alexander de Salzmann	1874	1919	1934
Jeanne de Salzmann	1889	1919	1990
Nathalie de Salzmann (de Etievan)	1919	1919	2007
Nikolai Stjoernval (Nicolas de Val)	1919	1919	2010
Olgivanna Hinzenburg Wright	1898	1919	1990

Gurdjieff Students

	Born	Met Gurdjieff	Died
J. G. Bennett	1897	1920	1974
Boris Ferapontoff	1891	1920	xxx
Tcheslaw Tchekhovitch	1895	1920	1958
Jessmin Howarth	1892	1921	1984
Rosemary Lillard (Nott)	1897	1921	1979
Dr. J. A. M. Alcock	xxx	1922	xxx
Dr. Mary Bell	xxx	1922	xxx
Rosamund Bland (Sharp)	1886	1922	1950
Léonor Champion-Jones	xxx	1922	xxx
Elinor Crowdy	xxx	1922	xxx
Elizabeth Gordon	xxx	1922	1945
Maud Hoffman	xxx	1922	1953
Adèle Kafian	xxx	1922	xxx
Rowland Kenney	xxx	1922	xxx
Katherine Mansfield	1888	1922	1923
Ethel Merston	1882	1922	1967
Bernard Metz (aka Bernard Mayne)	1896	1922	1981
Catherine Nicoll	xxx	1922	xxx
Maurice Nicoll	1884	1922	1953
A. R. Orage	1873	1922	1934
Mrs. Page	xxx	1922	xxx
Ralph Philipson	xxx	1922	xxx
Lady Rothermere	1874	1922	1937
Dr. Kenneth Walker	1882	1922	1966
Dr. James Young	1888	1922	1950
Michel de Salzmann	1923	1923	2001
Margaret Anderson	1889	1924	1973
Martin Benson	1898	1924	1971
Rita Romilly (Benson)	1900	1924	1980
Louise Blinken (Welch)	1905	1924	1999
Melville Cane	1879	1924	1980
John O'Hara Cosgrave	1908	1924	1968
Muriel Draper	1886	1924	1952
Jessie Dwight (Orage)	1901	1924	1985
Peggy Flinsch	1907	1924	2011

Georgi Ivanovitch Gurdjieff

	Born	Met Gurdjieff	Died
Waldo Frank	1889	1924	1967
Blanche Grant	xxx	1924	xxx
Jane Heap	1887	1924	1964
Schuyler Jackson	xxx	1924	xxx
C. Daly King	1895	1924	1963
Georgette Leblanc	1875	1924	1941
Fred Leighton	xxx	1924	xxx
Sherman Manchester	xxx	1924	xxx
Larry Morris	xxx	1924	xxx
Elizabeth Munson	1893	1924	2000
Gorham Munson	1896	1924	1969
C. S. Nott	1887	1924	1978
Ilonka Karasz (Nyland)	1897	1924	1981
Willem Nyland	1890	1924	1975
Fritz Peters	1913	1924	1979
Nick Putnam	xxx	1924	xxx
John Riordan	xxx	1924	xxx
Mavis Riordan	xxx	1924	xxx
Carol Robinson	1889	1924	1979
Juliet Rublee	1876	1924	1976
Israel Solon	1874	1924	1949
Stanley Spiegelberg	xxx	1924	xxx
Edith Taylor	1896	1924	xxx
Jean Toomer	1894	1924	1967
Donald Whitcomb	xxx	1924	xxx
Edwin Wolfe	1893	1924	1983
Caesar Zwaska	1897	1924	1972
Payson Loomis	xxx	1927	xxx
Solita Solano	1888	1927	1975
Carl Zigrosser	1891	1927	1975
Dorothea Dooling	1910	1929	1991
Louise Goepfert March	1900	1929	1987
Paul E. Anderson	1897	1931	1999
Pamela L. Travers	1889	1931	1996
Katherine Hulme	1900	1932	1981

Gurdjieff Students

	Born	Met Gurdjieff	Died
Alice Rohrer	1885?	1932	1958
Dr. William Welch	1907	1934	1997
Louise Davidson	xxx	1935	xxx
René Daumal	1908	1936	1944
Vera Daumal	xxx	1936	1962
Philippe Lavastine	xxx	1936	xxx
Pauline de Dampierre	xxx	1938	xxx
Luc Dietrich	1913	1938	1944
Marthe de Gaigneron	xxx	1938	xxx
Henriette Lannes	1899	1938	1980
Bernard Lemaître	xxx	1938	xxx
Henri Tracol	1909	1938	1997
Solange Claustres	1921	1940	xxx
Michel Conge	1912	1940	1984
René Zuber	1902	1943	1979
Hubert Benoît	1904	1944?	1992
Elspeth Champcommunal	xxx	1946	xxx
Michael Currer-Briggs	1922	1946	1980
Dr. John Lester	1919	1946	1999
Annie Lou Stavely	1906	1946	1996
Russell Page	1906	1947	1985
Irmis B. Popoff	xxx	1947	xxx
Jean Vaysse	1917	1947	1975
George Adie	1901	1948	1989
Helen Adie	1909	1948	1996
Dorothy Caruso	1893	1948	1955
Dr. Bernard Courtenay-Mayers	xxx	1948	xxx
Clive Entwhistle	1916	1948	1976
Christopher Fremantle	1906	1948	1978

Georgi Ivanovitch Gurdjieff

	Born	Met Gurdjieff	Died
Rina Hands	xxx	1948	xxx
Reginald Hoare	xxx	1948	xxx
Dushka Howarth	1924	1948	2010
Elizabeth Mayall (Bennett)	1918	1948	1991
Cynthia Pearce	xxx	1948	xxx
Lord John Pentland	1907	1948	1984
Lady Lucy Pentland	1916	1948	2005
Mary Sinclair (Rothenberg)	1942	1948	
Dorothy Phillpotts	1916	1948	2008
Hugh Ripman	1909	1948	1980
William Segal	1904	1948	2000
Marian Sutta	xxx	1948	xxx
Henri Thomasson	1910	1948	1996
Basil Tilley	xxx	1948	xxx
Aubrey Wolton	xxx	1948	xxx

Note: If there is information on these students' births or deaths, or others whom we may have overlooked, please get in touch with us.

Selected Bibliography

Alpers, Anthony. *Katherine Mansfield: A Biography*. New York: Alfred A. Knopf, 1953
Amin, Kamal. *Reflections from the Shining Brow*. Santa Barbara, CA: Fithian Press, 2004
Anderson, Margaret. *The Unknowable Gurdjieff*. New York: Arkana, 1991
 —*The Fiery Fountains*. New York: Rider & Co., 1953
Appelbaum, David. *Disruption*. Albany, NY: State University Press, 1996
Bennett, J.G. *The Crisis in Human Affairs*. New York: Hermitage House, 1951
 —*A Very Great Enigma*. New York: Samuel Weiser, 1973
 —*Idiots in Paris*. York Beach, ME: Coombe Springs Press, 1980
 —*Witness*. First Ed. Charles Town, WV: Claymont Communications, 1983
 —*Gurdjieff: Making a New World*. Santa Fe, NM: Bennett Books, 1992
Benson, Martin. *Martin Benson Speaks*. Edited by Carl Lehmann-Haupt. New York: Codhill Press Books, 2011
Berman, Louis. *The Glands Regulating Personality*. New York: Macmillan Co., 1921
Bernal, Martin. *Black Athena: The Afroasiatic Roots of Classical Civilization*. vol. 1. *The Fabrication of Ancient Greece*. New Brunswick, NJ: Rutgers University Press, 1987
 —*Black Athena: The Afroasiatic Roots of Classical Civilization*. vol. 2 *The Archaeological and Documentary Evidence*. New Brunswick, NJ: Rutgers University Press, 1991
Bland, Rosamund. *Extracts from Nine Letters*. Cape Town, South Africa: The Stourton Press, 1952
Bragdon, Claude. *More Lives than One*. New York: Alfred A. Knopf, 1938
Brewster, Jerry. *Spiritual Physics*. Raleigh, NC: Lulu Enterprises, 2013
Bryce, James Bryce. *Transcaucasia and Ararat*. Miami, FL: HardPress Publishing, 2010
Bullock, Alan. *Hitler and Stalin*. New York: Alfred A. Knopf, 1992
Butkovsky-Hewitt, Anna. *With Gurdjieff in St. Petersburg and Paris*. New York: Samuel Weiser, 1978
Byrd, Rudolph P. *Jean Toomer's Years with Gurdjieff*. Athens, GA: University of Georgia Press, 1990
Carlson, Maria. *No Religion Higher Than Truth*. Princeton, NJ: Princeton University Press, 1993
Carswell, John. *Lives and Letters*. New York: New Directions, 1978
Caruso, Dorothy. *Dorothy Caruso: A Personal History*. New York: Hermitage House, 1952
Claustres, Solange. *Becoming Conscious with G. I. Gurdjieff*. Utrecht, Holland: Eureka Editions, 2005
Cobb, Ivo Geikie. *The Glands of Destiny*. London: William Heinemann Ltd., 1936
Collin, Rodney. *The Theory of Eternal Life*. London: Stuart & Watkins, 1950

— *The Theory of Celestial Influence.* London: Vincent Stuart & John M. Watkins Ltd., 1954
— *The Theory of Conscious Harmony.* London: Robinson & Watkins Books Ltd., 1958
Collin-Smith, Joyce. "Beloved Icarus." *Telos,* nos. 9 & 10
Conge, Michael. *Inner Octaves.* Toronto: Dolmen Meadow Editions, 2004
Daumal, René. *Mount Analogue.* Baltimore, MD: Penguin Books, Inc., 1974
Drowser, E. S. *Peacock Angel.* London: John Murray, 1941
Dukes, Paul. *The Unending Quest.* London: Cassell & Co. Ltd., 1950
Everitt, Luba Gurdjieff. *Luba Gurdjieff: A Memoir with Recipes.* Berkeley, CA: Ten Speed Press, 1993
Fisher, Louis. *The Life of Lenin.* New York: Harper & Row, 1964
Ford, Hugh. *Four Lives in Paris.* San Francisco: North Point Press, 1987
Frank, Waldo. *Time Exposures.* New York: Boni & Liveright, 1926
Fremantle, Christopher. *On Attention.* Denville, NJ: Indications Press, 1993
Friedland, Roger, and Harold Zellman. The Fellowship. New York: HarperCollins, 2006
Gurdjieff, G. I. *All and Everything.* 1st Ed. New York: Harcourt Brace & Co., 1950
— *The Struggle of the Magicians.* Cape Town, South Africa: The Stourton Press, 1954
— *Meetings with Remarkable Men.* New York: E. P. Dutton & Co., 1963
— *Life Is Real Only Then, When "I Am."* New York: Triangle Editions, Inc. 1975
— *Views from the Real World.* New York: E. P. Dutton and Co., 1975
— *The Herald of Coming Good.* Edmonds, WA: Surefire Press, 1988
Hands, Rina. *Diary of Madame Egout Pour Sweet.* Aurora, OR: Two Rivers Press, 1991
Hartmann, Thomas de, and Olga de Hartmann. *Our Life with Mr. Gurdjieff.* definitive ed. New York: Arkana, 1983
Hartmann, Olga de. "What For?" Unpublished typescript
Hastings, Beatrice. *The Old "New Age": Orage and Others.* London: Blue Moon Press, 1936
Heap, Jane. *Jane Heap/Notes.* Aurora, OR: Two Rivers Press, 1983
— *The Notes of Jane Heap.* Aurora, OR: Two Rivers Press, 1994
Howarth, Jessmin, and Dushka Howarth. *It's Up to Ourselves: A Mother, a Daughter, and Gurdjieff.* New York: Gurdjieff Heritage Society, 2010
Hulme, Kathryn. *Undiscovered Country.* Boston: Little, Brown and Co., 1966
Huxley, Aldous. *After Many a Summer Dies the Swan.* Chicago: Ivan R. Dee, 1993
Ivanov, W. *The Truth Worshippers of Kurdistan.* Leiden, Holland: E. J. Brill, 1953
Kerman, Cynthia Earl, and Richard Eldridge. *The Lives of Jean Toomer.* Baton Rouge, LA: Louisiana State University Press, 1987
King, C. Daly. "The Oragean Version." Unpublished typescript, 1951
Kirstein, Lincoln. "A Memoir: At the Prieuré des Basses Loges, Fontainebleau." *Raritan* 2 (Fall 1982): 33–50

—*Mosaic*. New York: Farrar, Straus & Giroux, 1994
Korman, Mary Ellen. *A Woman's Work With Gurdjieff, Ramana Maharshi, Krishnamurti, Anandamayi Ma & Pak Subuh*. Fairfax, CA: Arete Communications, 2009
Kreyenbroek. Philip G. *Yezidism—Its Background, Observances and Textual Tradition*. Lewiston, NY: The Edwin Mellen Press, 1995
Landau, Rom. *God Is My Adventure*. London: Ivor Nicholson and Watson, 1936
Larson, Charles. *Invisible Darkness*. Iowa City, IA: University of Iowa Press, 1993
Lewis, Cecil. *All My Yesterdays*. London: Element, 1993
Mairet, Philip. *A. R. Orage*. New Hyde Park, NY: University Books, 1966.
Mansfield, Katherine. *Journal of Katherine Mansfield*. Edited by J. Middleton Murry. New York: Alfred A. Knopf, 1927
—*Katherine Mansfield, Selected Letters*. Edited by Vincent O'Sullivan. New York: Oxford University Press, 1989
—*The Collected Letters of Katherine Mansfield, 1922–1923*. Edited by Vincent O'Sullivan and Margaret Scott. London: Oxford University Press, 2008
March, Louise Goepfert. *The Gurdjieff Years: 1929–1949*. Edited by Beth McCorkle. Walworth, NY: The Work Study Association, Inc., 1990
Martin, Wallace. *The New Age Under Orage*. Manchester, England: Manchester University Press, 1967
May, W. Marshall, ed. *Rita Romilly Benson: Pupil of Gurdjieff, Teacher to Some of Us*, Raleigh, NC: Lulu Enterprises, 2013
McAlmon, Robert, and Kay Boyle. *Being Geniuses Together 1920–1930*. New York: Doubleday, 1968
Meyers, Jeffrey. *Katherine Mansfield: A Biography*. London: Hamish Hamilton, 1978
Mir-Husseini, Ziba. "Inner Truth and Outer History: The Two Worlds of the Ahl-I-Haqq of Kurdistan." *International Journal of Middle Eastern Studies*, 26, no. 2 (May 1994)
Moore, James. *Gurdjieff and Mansfield*, London, Routledge & Kegan Paul, 1980
—*Gurdjieff: Anatomy of a Myth*. London: Element, 1991
Mouravieff, Boris. "Ouspensky, Gurdjieff et les Fragments d'un Enseignement Inconnu." Brussels: *Revue Synthesis*, no.138 (1957). All quotes of Mouravieff, unless otherwise indicated, derive from this article
Moynahan, Brian. *Comrades: 1917—Russia in Revolution*. Boston: Little, Brown and Co., 1992
Munson, Gorham. "Black Sheep Philosophers: Gurdjieff, Ouspensky, Orage." *Tomorrow*, 9 (1950), 20–25
—*The Awakening Twenties*. Baton Rouge, LA: Louisiana State University Press, 1985
Murry, J. Middleton, ed. *Journal of Katherine Mansfield*. New York: Alfred A. Knopf, 1927
Needleman, Jacob. *A Sense of the Cosmos*. New York: Doubleday & Co., 1975

—*Lost Christianity.* New York: Penguin/Tarcher, 2003
Nicoll, Maurice. *The New Man.* Baltimore, MD: Penguin Books, Inc., 1950
 —*Psychological Commentaries.* vols. 1–5. London: Watkins Publishing, 1952
 —*Living Time.* London: Vincent Stuart, 1952
Nietzsche, Friedrich. *Thus Spake Zarathustra.* Cambridge, England: Cambridge University Press, 2006
Nott, C. S. *Teachings of Gurdjieff.* London: Routledge & Kegan Paul,1961
 —*Journey Through This World.* London: Routledge & Kegan Paul, 1966
Orage, A. R. *Nietzsche in Outline and Aphorisms.* London: T. N. Foulis, 1907
 —*Commentaries on All and Everything.* Aurora, OR: Two Rivers Press, 1985
 —*On Love & Psychological Exercises.* York Beach, ME: Red Wheel/Weiser, 1998
O'Sullivan, Vincent, ed. Katherine *Mansfield: Selected Letters.* New York: Oxford University Press, 1989
O'Sullivan, Vincent, and Margaret Scott. *The Collected Letters of Katherine Mansfield 1922–1923.* London: Oxford University Press, 2008
Ouspensky, P. D. *A New Model of the Universe.* New York: Alfred A. Knopf, 1934
 —*In Search of the Miraculous.* New York: Harcourt Brace and Co., 1949
 —*The Psychology of Man's Possible Evolution.* New York: Alfred A. Knopf, 1954
 —*The Fourth Way.* New York: Vintage Books, 1971
 —*Talks with a Devil.* London: Turnstone Press Ltd., 1972
 —*Letters from Russia.* 1919. London: Routledge & Kegan Paul Ltd., 1978
 —*Conscience.* London: Routledge & Kegan Paul Ltd., 1979
 —*Tertium Organum.* New York: Vintage Books, 1982
 —*A Further Record.* New York: Arkana, 1986
 —*Strange Life of Ivan Osokin.* New York: Arkana, 1987
 —*A Record of Meetings.* New York: Arkana, 1992
Patterson, William Patrick. *Eating The "I".* Fairfax, CA: Arete Communications, 1992
 —*Struggle of the Magicians.* Fairfax, CA: Arete Communications, 1996
 —*Taking with the Left Hand.* Fairfax, CA: Arete Communications, 1998
 —*Ladies of the Rope.* Fairfax, CA: Arete Communications, 1998
 —*The Life & Significance of G. I. Gurdjieff.* Documentary trilogy. Film. Fairfax, CA: Arete Communications, 1999–2003
 —*Voices in the Dark.* Fairfax, CA: Arete Communications, 2000
 —*The Life & Teachings of Carlos Castaneda.* Fairfax, CA: Arete Communications, 2008
 —*Spiritual Survival in a Radically Changing World-Time.* Fairfax, CA: Arete Communications, 2009
 —*Adi Da Samraj—Realized or/and Deluded?* Fairfax, CA: Arete Communications, 2012
 —*From Selves to Individual Self to The Self.* Film. Fairfax, CA: Arete Communications, 2012
 —*Spiritual Pilgrimage: Visiting Gurdjieff's Father's Grave.* Film. Fairfax, CA:

Arete Communications, 2014
Pauwels, Louis. *Gurdjieff*. Paris: Editions du Seuil, 1954
Pentland, John. *Exchanges Within: Questions from Gurdjieff Group Meetings with John Pentland in California* 1955–1984. New York: Continuum, 1997
Peters, Fritz. *The World Next Door*. New York: Farrar, Straus and Young, Inc., 1948
— *Finistère*. New York: Farrar, Straus and Young, Inc., 1951
— *Gurdjieff Remembered*. New York: Samuel Weiser, 1971
— *Balanced Man*. London: Wildwood House Ltd., 1978
— *Boyhood with Gurdjieff*. Fairfax, CA: Arete Communications, 2006
Phillpotts, Dorothy. *Discovering Gurdjieff*. Central Milton Keynes, England: AuthorHouse, 2008
Pipes, Richard. *The Russian Revolution*. New York: Alfred A. Knopf, 1990
Pogson, Beryl. *Maurice Nicoll: A Portrait*. London: Globe Press Books, 1987
— *Unforgotten Fragments*. Edited by Lewis Creed. York, England: Quacks Books, 1994
Popoff, Irmis, *Gurdjieff: His Work on Myself, with Others, for the Work*. 1978
Reymond, Lizelle. *To Live Within*. Garden City, NY: Doubleday & Co., 1971
Reyner, J. H. *Ouspensky: The Unsung Genius*. London: George Allen & Unwin, Ltd., 1981
Roberts, Carl Eric Bechhofer. *In Denikin's Russia and the Caucasus, 1919–1920*. W. Collins Sons & Co., 1921
Roles, Francis. *A Lasting Freedom*. London: Society for the Study of Normal Psychology, 1972
Ropp, Robert de. *Talks by Madame Ouspensky*. San Francisco: Far West Press, 1974
— *Warrior's Way*. New York: Dell Publishing Co., 1979
Rudnick, Lois Palken. *Mabel Dodge Luhan: New Woman, New Worlds*. Albuquerque, NM: University of New Mexico Press, 1984
Salzmann, Jeanne de. *The Reality of Being*. Boston: Shambhala Publications, Inc., 2010
Saurat, Denis. "Visite à Gurdjieff." *Nouvelle Revue Française*, 1 November 1933, 686–98
Seabrook, William. *Adventures in Arabia: Among the Bedouins, Druses, Whirling Dervishes & Yezidee Devil Worshippers*. New York: Paragon House, 1927
— "Our Modern Caliostros," in *Witchcraft: Its Power in the Modern World Today*. New York: Harcourt Brace, 1940, 204–16
Segal, William. *Opening*. New York: The Continuum Publishing Co., 1998
Selver, Paul. *Orage and The New Age Circle*. London: George Allen and Unwin, 1959
Seton, Marie. "The Case of P. D. Uspenskii." *Quest*, no. 34 (July–Sept. 1962)
Shirer, William L. *The Rise and Fall of the Third Reich*. New York: Simon and Schuster, 1960
Silva. Andrew J. da. *Do from the Octave of Man Number Four*. New York: Borderline Press, 1985
Speer, Albert. *Inside the Third Reich*. New York: The Macmillan Co., 1970

Staveley, A. L. *Memories of Gurdjieff.* Aurora, OR: Two Rivers Press, 1978
"P. D. Uspenskii Commemorative Issue," *The Bridge,* no. 12, London: The Study Society, 1997
Taylor, Merrily E., ed. "Autobiographical Fragment." *Remembering Pyotr Demianovich Ouspensky.* New Haven, CT: Yale University Library, 1978, 9–13
Taylor, Paul Beekman. *Shadows of Heaven.* York Beach, ME: Weiser Books Inc., 1998.
— *Gurdjieff and Orage.* York Beach, ME: Weiser Books Inc., 2001
Tchekhovitch, Tcheslaw. *Tu l'aimeras: Souvenirs sur Georgii Ivanovitch Gurdjieff.* Paris: Editions Charles Antoni L'Originel, 2003
— *Gurdjieff: A Master in Life.* Toronto: Dolmen Meadow Editions, 2006
Tereshchenko, Nicolas. *Mister Gurdjieff and the Fourth Way.* Austin, TX: Kesdjan Publishing, 2003
Thring, M. W. *Quotations from G. I. Gurdjieff's Teaching.* Oxford, UK: Luzac Oriental, 2002
Toomer, Jean. *Essentials.* Athens, GA: University of Georgia Press, 1991
— "Portage Potential." Unpublished typescript. Beinecke Library, Yale University
Turner, Darwin T., ed. *The Wayward and the Seeking: A Collection of Writings by Jean Toomer.* Washington, DC: Howard University Press, 1982
Ukhtomsky, Esper. *Travels in the East of Nicholas II, Emperor of Russia, 1890–91.* 2 vols. London: 1896 and 1900
Val, Nicholas de [Nikolai de Stjoernval]. *Daddy Gurdjieff.* Geneva: Georg, 1997
Vaysse, Jean. *Toward Awakening.* San Francisco: Far West Undertakings, 1978
Walker, Kenneth. *Venture with Ideas.* New York: Pellegrini & Cudahy, 1952
— *A Study of Gurdjieff's Teaching.* London: Jonathan Cape, 1957
Webb, James. *The Harmonious Circle.* New York: G. P. Putnam's Sons, 1980
Welch, Louise. *Orage with Gurdjieff in America.* London: Routledge & Kegan Paul Ltd., 1982
Welch, William J. *What Happened in Between.* New York: George Braziller, 1972
Wellbeloved, Sophia. *Gurdjieff: The Key Concepts.* London: Routledge, 2003
Wilson, Colin. *The Strange Life of P. D. Ouspensky.* London: Aquarian Press, 1993
Wineapple, Brenda. *Genêt: A Biography of Janet Flanner.* University of Nebraska Press, 1989
Wright, Olgivanna Lloyd. "The Last Days of Katherine Mansfield." *The Bookman* (March 1931)
Young, James Carruthers. "An Experiment at Fontainebleau: A Personal Reminiscence." *New Adelphi* (September 1927): 26–40
Zuber, René. *Who Are You, Monsieur Gurdjieff?* London: Routledge & Kegan Paul Ltd., 1980

Bibliography

Collections

Margaret Anderson, University of Wisconsin, Madison, WI
Carman Barnes, University of Rochester Library, Rochester, NY
Claude Bragdon, University of Rochester Library, Rochester, NY
Muriel Draper, Beinecke Library, Yale University, New Haven, CT
Janet Flanner, Library of Congress, Washington, DC
Thomas de Hartman, Music Library, Yale University, New Haven, CT
Kathryn Hulme, Beinecke Library, Yale University, New Haven, CT
Maurice Nicoll, Sterling Library, Yale University, New Haven CT
Alfred R. Orage, Special Collections, Leeds University, Leeds, UK
Florence Reynolds, University of Delaware, Newark, DE
Solita Solano, Library of Congress, Washington, DC
Jean Toomer, Beinecke Library, Yale University, New Haven, CT
P. D. Uspenskii, Sterling Library, Yale University, New Haven, CT

Index[1]

A

"Abdullah, Achmed" 262–63. *See also* Romanoff, Alexander Nicholayevitch
Adam and Eve 147
Afghanistan 351
Akhaldans, Society of 6, 291, 297
Alexandropol 2, 4, 39, 58, 60, 61, 74, 148
All and Everything 169, 193, 223, 230, 265, 273, 280, 318–19, 411–12, 434, 453, 459
    Beelzebub's Tales seen as
        Bible 212
        Legominism 223
        Scripture 196
    use of language 229
    intended effects 222
Alleluia 362
Allemand, Jeanne. *See* Salzmann, Jeanne de
amber 298, 360, 367
Anderson, Margaret
    arrives at Prieuré 173
    as "Yakina" 327–30, 336, 352–53, 373, 375–76, 396, 544
    on Gurdjieff 167
    on Orage 162
    on Uspenskii 173
Ani 4
animal, inner and outer 240, 312, 315, 317, 322, 326, 327, 336, 357, 365, 374, 375, 378, 410
Arabian Nights party 253–55
Armenian 328, 346, 351, 499
associations 20, 123, 163, 229, 294, 317, 409, 508

B

Barnes, Carman 14, 395, 396, 398, 402, 403, 407, 408, 410, 416, 424, 452, 533
Beaumont, Winifred "Polly" (Mrs. Bennett) 86–87, 88, 90, 195, 351, 374
Bennett, Elizabeth 536
Bennett, John Godolphin 86–87, 88, 95, 101–102, 121, 195, 242, 257, 264, 441, 447–48, 456
    and fifth dimension 86, 90, 411
    and Gurdjieff
        at Prieuré 143–46
        death 462
        English representative 453
        final meeting 458
        first meets 89
        Judas 455–56
        Paris meeting 444
    and Uspenskii
        first meets 86
        joins teaching 151
        of his death 432
        sees as 151
    arrested in Athens 227
    assumes role of teacher 227
    business success 399
    confidence withdrawn 302
    deputized 261
    known or seen as
        air of command 440
        a nullity in Being 445
        charlatan and thief 419
        not honest 447
        round idiot 451
        small Number Eighteen 445

---

1. For Foreword, Main Text and Afterword only

young soul 272
only you can repay 448
out-of-body experience 90–91, 448, 455
South Africa 440–41, 449–50
Benson, Martin 203–204, 217–18, 220, 221, 265, 273
Benson, Rita Romilly 453
Bessaraboff, Nicholas 73–74, 84, 95
Bey, Ekim 330
Bland, Rosamund 105, 106–109, 111, 139, 368, 399
Blavatsky, Helena Petrovna 12, 17, 215, 281
Blinken, Louise. *See* Welch, Louise
blood 179, 270, 296, 301, 334, 343, 371, 383, 413
Bogachevsky 3
Borsh, Dean 230–31
Bragdon, Claude 73–74, 84, 87, 95, 168, 184, 263, 395, 398–99, 401, 402, 404, 405–406, 407, 410, 415
Butkovskaia, Anna Ilinishna 13–17, 19–20, 26, 28–29, 30–31, 31–32, 37–38, 47–48, 51–52, 63, 67–68

C

Caruso, Dorothy 406, 442
Catholicism 413
Cavalieri, Lina 291
chaplet 346
Charkovsky, Anthony 15, 30, 68
Christ 40, 137, 169, 176, 202, 299, 327, 415
Collin, Rodney
  and Uspenskii
    at Franklin Farms 394, 405
    death 431
    first meets 342
    last public talks 428
    on final days with 430–31
    relationship with 402, 418, 428, 429
  establishes Uspenskiian version 442
Collin-Smith, Janet (née Buckley) 342
Constantinople 12, 16, 85, 86–96, 103
Crowley, Aleister 210, 211
Cutting, Senator Bronson 286

D

Dalai Lama 263–64, 356
Daumal, René 264, 276, 332, 379, 415
Daumal, Vera 379
Davidson, Louise 288, 295
  as "Sardine-Wart" 313, 329, 333
Denikin, General Anton Ivanovitch 65, 67, 74, 78, 79, 81, 82, 85
devil 8, 41–42, 134–35, 147, 222, 237, 261, 301, 314, 324, 326, 329, 331, 338, 343, 373, 374, 376, 412
Djartklom 64
Draper, Muriel 144, 168, 170, 397
Dukes, Paul 7–8, 46, 263
Dwight, Jessie
  and Gurdjieff
    at the Prieuré 172–73
    last sees 441
    short stories 175
    warned by 226
  known or seen as
    a native 223
    dog 239
    drinking 204, 210
    left-shoulder Angel 248
    pampered 223
    squirming idiot 223

E

Egypt
  Mysteries 291
  pre-sand map 4–6
  pyramids 5, 16

Georgi Ivanovitch Gurdjieff

Sphinx 5, 39
Teaching 5, 40–41
electricity 365, 368, 411
emanations 134, 163, 292–93, 295–96, 314, 315, 363, 376
Entwistle, Clive 340–41, 451, 455
eternal recurrence 9, 10, 16, 93, 198, 257, 272, 342–43, 355, 386
Evreinoff, Nicholas 14, 17, 63

F

Fairfax Hall 147, 427
Fakirism 311
fate 89
Ferapontoff, Boris 88, 104, 140
Flanner, Janet 216, 267, 289, 290, 344, 377, 383, 385, 416
fourth dimension 9, 16, 36, 118, 419
Fourth Way 5
  characteristics of 32–33, 40–41, 93
Frank, Waldo 104, 166, 168, 169, 171, 184, 221–22
Freemantle, Christopher and Anne 441, 451
Freud, Sigmund 40, 91, 105, 122

G

Gabo 344, 364, 458
Galumnian, Elizabeta "Lili" (m. Chaverdian) 86, 104, 121, 140, 194, 212, 216, 453
Giovanni, Father 39, 230, 567
"Glimpses of Truth" 24
Gobi (desert) 6
Goepfert, Louise 234, 248, 251, 268, 451, 573
Gordon, Elizabeth
  exercise 293–94
  Mees Gordon 313
  Miss Gordon 301, 311
  Mother Superior 292
  Rope formed 312
  Superior idiot 324–25, 332, 361, 363–64, 368–69, 383, 416
Gurdjieff, Georgi Ivanovitch
  arrives in Russia 7
  death 459
  discoveries
    letter to Sārmoung 4
    map of pre-sand Egypt 4
  early influences
    artillery range 1, 4
    Bogachevsky 3
    Dean Borsh 2–3
    father 2
    Gilgamesh 2
    Yezidis 3
  family
    Giorgiades, Evdokia (mother) 2, 61, 197, 231
    Giorgiades, Ioannis (father) 2, 61, 74
    Gurdjieff, Dmitri Ivanovitch (brother) 2, 74, 148, 210, 290, 338, 371
    Ostrowska, Julia Osipovna (wife) 7, 61, 65, 68, 75, 87, 120, 121, 129, 176, 178, 198, 208
  known or seen as
    a devil 222
    a Lohan 319, 442
    a prophet 174
    Christ 41
    Dr. Black 70
    Joshua Gurdjieff 253
    Lama Dordjieff 263
    Messenger from Above 167, 227
    Prince Ozay 7, 8, 24, 46, 263
    Teacher of Dancing xvii
  later influences
    Egyptian Mysteries 5, 291
    Esoteric Christianity 6, 136, 318–19

INDEX

Father Giovanni 39, 230
Prince Lubovedsky 5
Professor Skridlov 5, 39
Society of Akhaldans 6
mission
   begins Moscow group 8
   begins Petersburg group 30
   establishing Institute
      aim in founding 136
      at the Prieuré 121
      Caves of Lascaux 447–48
      in New York 168
   his stream 361, 414
   money 30, 169
   recruits Bennett 143–45
   recruits Uspenskii 20, 22–26
   sacred oath 6
   tells his whim 232
   "will tasks" 276
on Orage's death 279–80
selected events
   accident at Chailly 175
   accident at Montargis 446
   Egyptian initiations 291
   first talk in London 112
   Prieuré leased 117
   Prieuré sold 273
teaching ideas and methods
   associations 294
   attention 293
   being 37, 124
   bodies 32, 314
   breathing 68
   centers 31, 47, 113
   chief feature 43, 69
   confession 68
   conscience 298
   conscious egoism 145
   cosmos 35
   creating conditions 119
   crystallization 69
   devil 41, 301, 374

emanations 314
esoteric Christianity 40–41, 136, 414
essence 114
everything happens 31
evil 141
faith 50, 76–77
feelings 62–63, 365
group work 33
habits 92
Hasnamuss 322
identification 113
individuality 125
inner animal 313
inner vision 314
'I's 112, 152
knowledge 33, 37, 144
love 41, 50, 142–43, 163–64, 184, 411
man is a machine 26
materialism 33, 50
money 30
movements 68
negative emotions 122, 365
nicknames 37
onanism 313
personality 113
"play" 38
power(s) 141, 315
presence 295
relaxation 68
Religion 92
sacrifice 46
self-calming 300
self-observation 31, 92, 248, 256, 266, 376, 396, 398
self-remembering 31, 92, 143, 250, 386, 396, 398, 427, 429
shit 270, 312, 328, 371, 377
sincerity 298
soul 42, 69, 126, 135, 311, 375
struggles 319

subconscious 321
submission 36
substance 411
suffering 47
super-efforts 52
tapeworms 316
telepathy 44
time 36, 59
understanding 330
valuation 38
vibrations 297
whim 232, 475
will 135
writings
  Beelzebub's Tales to His Grandson 136, 194, 196, 198, 201, 202, 212, 223, 224, 227, 228–31, 229–32, 239, 257, 259, 318, 452
  "Glimpses of Truth" 24–25
  Life Is Real Only Then, When "I Am" 280, 282, 284–85, 319, 423, 459
  Meetings with Remarkable Men 198
  The Herald of Coming Good 269, 273–75, 278
  The Struggle of the Magicians 20, 24, 83, 88, 461

H

Habets, Marie Louise 425
Hall, Fairfax 427–28
Hanbledzoin 301, 416, 520, 526, 533
Hartmann, Olga Arcadievna de
  and Gurdjieff
    and lease of Prieuré 117
    as his translator 135
    dictation of *Beelzebub's Tales* 193, 194, 230
    "first friend of inner life" 332
    first meets 50
    leaves Prieuré 238
    on Uspenskii 49
Hartmann, Thomas de
  and Gurdjieff
    collaborates on music 199
    collaboration ends 216
    first meets 48
    on his roles 71
    writes eulogy 461
    leaves Prieuré 233–34
    on life at Prieuré 121, 125, 130
Hastings, Beatrice 115, 116, 171, 531
Heap, Jane
  arrives at Prieuré 173
  Mees Keep 170, 318, 320, 321
  perspectives 321, 397, 404
  sent to teach by Gurdjieff 215, 266, 287
Heard, Gerald 167, 339–40
Heptaparaparshinokh 328, 375
Heropass 344, 538
Hinzenberg, Olgivanna. *See* Wright, Olgivanna Lloyd
Hinzenberg, Svetlana 83, 86, 92, 104, 115, 183, 277, 425
Hinzenberg, Valdemar 83, 104, 141, 146
Historico-Psychological Society 343, 378
Howarth, Dushka 182, 454
Howarth, Jessmin 111, 182, 228, 397, 453
Hulme, Kathryn
  and the Rope 312–13
  as "Krokodeel" 313, 315, 322, 325, 334, 345–46, 382–83, 425–26
  cigarettes 319–20, 350
Huxley, Aldous 167, 339–40, 379

I

Idiots
  science of 195, 259

arch 318, 367
compassionate 369
eighteen 445
enlightened 336
harmful 377, 445, 451
hopeless 318, 326, 333, 334, 344, 359, 450
round 326, 336, 451
square 450
squirming 223, 326, 333, 355, 357
stink 344, 445, 451
superior 170, 324
unique 369
zigzag 324, 352

J

Jacques-Dalcroze, Émile 77, 95
Judas 141, 415, 455, 456, 520, 534, 537
Jung, Carl 105, 110, 122, 457

K

Kafiristan 39, 351
Kamenskaia, Anna Alekseevna 13, 31, 58, 67, 68, 580
Karatas 356, 357, 373
Karma 93, 177
Karpenko, Piotr 330, 573, 581
Kars 2, 3, 4, 573
Kesdjan 301, 520
Keyserling, Count 339
King, C. Daly
  defends Orage 249
  impression of Gurdjieff 249
  "The Oragean Version" 398, 454
Kirghiz 355
Kirstein, Lincoln 217–21
Knachtschmidt and Company 300, 313, 325, 337, 346, 360
Krishnamurti 339, 395, 396, 398
Kundabuffer 181, 298, 299, 300, 301

L

Landau, Rom 105, 258, 262, 263, 273, 287
Lannes, Henriette 276, 379
Lascaux cave paintings 447
Lavastine, Philippe 276, 379, 380
Leblanc, Georgette 173, 267, 301, 313, 344, 404, 568
Legominism 193, 223, 286, 346, 348, 514, 528
Leighton, Fred 273, 278, 282
Lenin, Vladimir Ilyich 11, 58, 59, 60, 61, 65, 76, 96, 577, 578, 580
Lewis, Cecil 444, 446, 449
Lillard, Rosemary 111, 121, 184, 221
Lindbergh, Charles 383, 401
Loomis, Payson 215, 217, 218, 219, 220, 221, 269, 373
Lubovedsky, Prince Yuri 5, 7, 39, 87, 238, 506, 507, 508, 509, 581
Luhan, Mabel Dodge 168, 200, 201, 203, 206, 215, 253, 287, 396, 570
Lvovitch, Lev 7, 8

M

magus 331–32
Maharishi Mahesh Yogi 440
Mairet, Philip 128, 170, 241
Mansfield, Katherine 112, 115, 116, 118, 120, 122, 124, 125, 127, 129, 130, 132, 133, 146, 171, 257, 340, 369, 532, 552
March, Louise. *See* Goepfert, Louise
Mardiross, Eoung-Ashokh 175
McAlmon, Robert 146
McLaren, Leon 440
Mercourov, Sergei 8, 21
Merston, Ethel 118, 121, 194, 200, 204, 206, 212, 416
Metz, Bernard 182, 194, 218
Mitrinović, Dmitri 105, 128
Moore, James 7, 10, 21, 30, 61, 94,

283, 523, 571, 573, 584
Moses 40, 253, 347, 511, 520, 544
Mount Analogue 264
Mouravieff, Boris 86, 151, 176, 177, 360, 512, 517, 521, 524, 578
Munson, Gorham 166, 168, 170, 183, 184, 207, 211, 221, 262, 267, 281, 387, 457, 579
Murry, John Middleton 116, 118, 120, 133

N

Naumburg, Margaret 168, 169, 177, 197, 203, 206
Nicoll, Maurice 105, 110, 118, 122, 141, 142, 146, 151, 217, 261, 282, 342, 430, 434, 442
Nietzsche, Friedrich 10, 12, 17, 83, 88, 104, 280
Nijeradze, Prince 231, 581
Nott, C. S. (Charles Stanley)
  and Gurdjieff
    apple story 198
    at the Prieuré 178, 196, 221
    first sees 165
    hopeless idiot 318
    on judging his teacher 285
    on sign of perfected man 197
    on understanding *First Series* 318
    rats for experiments 258
  and Orage 163, 239
  and Uspenskii 284–85, 302
    assembles group around Uspenskii 397–98
    weakness of 417–18
Nyland, Wim 203, 204, 397, 451, 453

O

obligolnian strivings 241
octave
  octave and 'life' or 'death' 241, 400

of Work deflected 150, 151, 251, 528, 532, 538
shock points 258, 381, 426
O'Keefe, Georgia 276, 278, 396
Orage, Alfred Richard
  and *Beelzebub's Tales* 201, 202, 214, 229, 257
  and C. Daly King 183, 196, 216, 232
  and Gurdjieff
    American stomach 112
    at Prieuré 128–29
    de facto mandate to teach 199
    edits writings 194, 196, 198, 202, 212, 214, 229
    must pay for everything 199
    Orage's death 279, 280
    relations with 233, 238, 252–53, 256, 265, 269, 279
    sent to New York 146
    whim 233
  and *Herald* 278
  and Jean Toomer 183, 195, 200, 204, 214
  and Jessie Dwight Orage
    marries 223
    secretary 171
    Sunwise Turn 161
  and Uspenskii
    first meets 17
    publishes Uspenskii's Letters 79
    sees him as teacher 105
  authorizes King to teach 232
  breaks from Gurdjieff
    ambition 233
    John the Baptist 252
    lacks absolute faith 252
    "loving father" and philosophizing 251
    needs new initiation 229, 232, 238, 242
    sexual relations 204
    super-idiot 226

early life 104, 148, 281
feminine element 170
I love the group 241
impressions of 115, 116, 128, 134, 162, 168, 171, 196, 199, 280
The New Age 115, 118, 119
women—first meets
   American women 172
   Beatrice Hastings 115
   Jean Walker 206
   Jesse Dwight 162
   Katherine Mansfield 116
   Rosamund Bland 105

P

Page, Mrs. 117, 132, 139, 458
Pentland, Henry John Sinclair, Lord xvii, 341, 387, 398, 401, 412, 441, 448–49, 450, 453, 456
  and Gurdjieff
    appointed representative 453
    chauffeur 449
    Turkish bathhouse 457
    "you are like Paul" 456
  and Madame Uspenskii 401
  and Uspenskii
    deputized 261
  helps publish *First Series* 454
  on Gurdjieff's death 462
Pentland, Lucy Elisabeth Smith, Lady 401, 451
Sinclair, Mary (daughter) 449–50
Peters, Fritz 126, 174, 198, 199, 204, 224, 232, 234, 242, 253, 261, 270–72, 276, 277, 397, 419–20
  and Uspenskii 397
  arrives at Prieuré 174
  as triumphant successor 422
  leaves Prieuré 235
  on Chicago group 261
  on Gurdjieff 276, 422–23
    as born troublemaker 204
  as caretaker 198, 224–25
  as concierge 224
  as son 420
  as wounded animal 423
  first meets 174
  nightmare journey 277
Petrov, Alexander Nikorovich 8, 68, 70, 74, 75, 83
Philipson, Ralph 119, 149
philosophy 6, 18, 21, 35, 70, 83, 85, 145, 201, 203, 258, 272, 329, 351, 381, 440, 536, 559, 578, 581
Pinder, Frank 80, 87, 112, 113, 122, 124, 139, 141, 144, 150, 172, 182, 233, 363, 369, 370, 462
Pogossian, Sarkis 4, 5, 507, 581
Pohl, Vladimir 8, 21
Pound, Ezra 122, 219–20
psychopathic 256, 294, 295, 309, 310, 328

R

Rachmilievitch, Alexei 8, 68, 77, 121
Rasputin, Grigori 19, 30, 45, 49
Roberts, Carl Bechhofer 84, 121, 145
Rohrer, Alice 266–67, 450–51
  as "Theen One" 313, 324, 326, 334, 334–36, 336, 337, 347, 356, 357–59, 358, 378–80
Roles, Dr. Francis 261, 394, 411, 426, 428, 430, 431, 440
Romanoff, Alexander Nicholayevitch 262–63
Romilly, Rita. *See* Benson, Rita Romilly
Ropp, Robert de 340, 342, 401, 419, 425, 432, 537, 538
Rothermere, Lady Mary 95, 104, 105, 107, 109, 110, 114, 119, 122, 415, 553

S

Sabaheddin, Prince 86, 89
Saint George 329
Salzmann, Alexander de
 "a very fine man" 77
 dies 275
 early life 77
 jokes with Gurdjieff 238
 leads group 264
 painter 78
 Pierre Sogol 264
 René Daumal 264
Salzmann, Jeanne de
 and Gurdjieff
  assists at meetings 414
  first movements performance 78
  last instruction from him 459
  meets Gurdjieff 77
  presents group to him 332, 386
  translating *First Series* 234
 early life 77
 leads group 276
 on Gurdjieff's death 462
Salzmann, Michel de 149, 174
Sārmoung Brotherhood 4, 5, 580
Saurat, Denis 134, 136, 280, 319, 417, 538
Savitsky, Lenotchka 68
Savitsky, Leonidas ("Lonia") 77
Savitsky, Tania 406, 454
Seabrook, William 163, 164, 184, 253, 254, 581, 584
Seekers of [After]Truth 25, 39–40, 161
 origin of 5
Segal, William and Cora 451
Seton, Marie 400, 403, 408, 417
sex 8, 164, 170, 194, 204, 219, 255, 260, 270, 287, 296, 310, 321, 331, 367, 405, 408, 409, 411, 415, 452, 462, 542, 556, 571

Shandarovsky, P. V. 68, 74
Sharp, Clifford 105, 139, 553
Skridlov, Professor 5, 39, 330, 506, 507, 508, 509, 518, 581
Solano, Solita
 American curiosity 292
 and Janet Flanner 290, 300, 344, 377, 383
 and the Rope 312
 as Gurdjieff's secretary 374
 as "Kanari" 312, 314, 315–16, 321, 364, 372, 383
 eye of suffering wolf 296
 first impression of Gurdjieff 216
Solioonensius 300, 450, 511
Solon, Israel 184, 195
Soloviev 368, 581
soul 6, 8, 23, 32, 40, 42, 69, 126, 135, 198, 280, 286, 294, 295, 299, 311, 319, 321, 338, 349, 375, 380, 412, 417, 425, 444, 461, 471, 473, 474, 530, 534, 540, 542, 567, 576, 585
Stalin, Joseph Djugashvili 57, 231, 383
Stavely, Annie Lou 424
Stefanna, Anna ("Anci") 416
Stjoernval, Dr. Leonid
 acts as group's leader 49
 dies 378
 how Gurdjieff teaches 234
 "Mean" 37
 nursing Gurdjieff 176
 on Uspenskii 258
 psychiatrist 30
 sees Gurdjieff as 41
 sent to America 148
Stjoernval, Elizabeta Grigorievna 30, 41, 65, 68, 75, 83, 378
Stjoernval, Nikolai 82, 174
St. Petersburg conditions 29, 64, 139, 150–51, 256, 528

Index

T

Taylor, Edith 203, 205, 214, 226, 231, 453
Taylor, Eve (Petey) 84, 454
Tchekhovitch, Tcheslaw 64, 88, 123, 209, 574, 575
Theremin, Léon 290
Tilley, Basil 451
Toomer, Jean 169, 200, 201
   and Gurdjieff
      and money 203, 269, 281, 282
      assumes role of teacher 183
      at Prieuré 177, 181
      desire for power 196
      final meeting 452
      first impression of 165–66
      manual work, transformation 178–80
      racial identity 205
      "ruler of Africa" 205, 284
   and Orage
      helps with translation 200
      jealousy 214–15
      learn from you 195
      sex 204, 206
   Friends of Being 302, 374
   out-of-body experience 209–10
   Portage experiment 260, 262, 266, 267
   racial identity 261, 267
   Society of Friends 386
   "The Meeting" 384
Toomer, Margery Latimer 256, 260, 261, 262, 268, 269
Toomer, Marjorie Content 266, 276, 278, 281, 383, 387
Tracol, Henri 276, 379
Tracol, Lise 447, 456
Trogoautoegocratic 297, 298
Trotsky, Leon (Lev Davidovich Bronstein) 13, 65, 231, 580
Tzvarnoharno 177, 248

U

Ukhtomsky, Prince Esper Esperovitch 7
Uspenskii, Pyotr Demianovitch
   abandons the System 427
   admits System a profession 418
   and Bennett
      first meeting 86–87
      invited to return 242
      on false starts 394–95
      Sympathy to Bennett 227–28
      Uspenskii's death 432–33
      young soul 272–73
   and Bragdon 395–96, 399–400, 401, 404, 406
   and Orage
      confrontations 108–109
      first meeting 17
      lies and betrayal of 114–15, 139–40
      The New Age letters 79, 81–83
   authorizes Nicoll 261
   challenged by students 260–61
   contacts with Gurdjieff
      chemistry 23
      chief fault
         extreme individualism 37, 45
         Pyotr Demianovitch 46
         Wraps up the Thought 37
      dirty jokes 91
      early impressions of Gurdjieff 27–28, 34–35, 42
      editing ballet scenario 20, 88, 92
      final meeting 257–58
      first meets 22
      forming a group 33
      found the miracle 26, 341
      "Glimpses of Truth" 24–25
      hypocrisy 41–42
      impression of Prieuré 42, 132
      London Daily News articles 136

    miracle and resistance in
        Finland 44–45
    Moon and suffering 48
    new or forgotten road 23
    not my way 72–73
    plan of whole work 69–70
    "Play" 38–39
    predominant fear 29
    principal of seniority 141
    psychology 25
    real confession 68
    reunites with Gurdjieff 88–89
    sacrificing knowledge 36
    saving the System 149
    schools are imperative 63–64
    separates teacher from teaching
        65–66
    St. Petersburg conditions 29, 64
    strange confidence 81
    The Fourth Way 32
    the two Gurdjieffs 94
    this is esoteric Christianity
        40–41, 49
    time is breath 59
    told to stop teaching 113, 139
  death 431
  drinking 417
  expands System 242
  final break with Gurdjieff 149
  first meetings in London
    impressions 105–106
  his life and family
    A Hero of Our Time 9
    early life and death 9–11
    eternal recurrence 9–10
    fourth dimension 16–17, 36
    Nietzsche & Overman 10, 17–18
    search for a school 12, 16
    Theosophy 12, 13, 21
  Historico-Psychological Society
    343, 378
  Lady Rothermere's telegram 95
  letters to Orage 79, 81, 82
  makes super-efforts 430–31
  meetings in New York 396
  speaks on evil and devil 237, 412
  too formatory 285, 302
  women, first meeting
    Anna Ilinishna Butkovskaia
        13–15
    Carman Barnes 395
    Madame Uspenskii 47
    Rosamund Bland 106
  writings
    A New Model of the Universe 36,
        72, 258, 372, 415
    "Fragments of an Unknown
        Teaching" 96, 151, 196
    In Search of the Miraculous 439,
        456
    Strange Life of Ivan Osokin 11,
        36, 37, 430
    Symbolism of the Tarot 26
    Tertium Organum 12, 25, 36, 95,
        239, 395, 407
    The Fourth Dimension 16
    *The Psychology of Man's Possible
        Evolution* 287
Uspenskii, Sophia Grigorievna
  and Gurdjieff
    at Prieuré 139
    follows to Berlin 103
    For me he is X 182
    gives "Fragments" to 451
    in Constantinople 93
    in Essentuki 76
    sends students to him 441
  and her husband 341, 343, 401
  at Franklin Farms 400
  at Lyne Place 341
  embarks for America 393
  first meets Uspenskii 47
  her allegiance 94
  known or seen as

emanates a force 401
Grand Duchess 284
warm, sympathetic 395
young soul 272
Parkinson's disease 383
settles in England 228, 261

W

Walker, Dr. Kenneth 110, 150, 151, 428, 442, 457
Walker, Jean 206, 215
Watson, John B. 253, 254
Webb, James 7, 21, 283, 578, 584
Welch, Dr. William 275, 397, 451, 458, 459, 460
Welch, Louise 249, 275, 397, 451, 452, 457
Welch, Patty 454
Whitcomb, Donald 451, 453
Wilder, Thornton 259–60
Wolfe, Edwin 168, 184, 253
Wright, Frank Lloyd 73, 184, 277, 366, 452
Wright, Iovanna 84, 201, 366–67, 452, 454, 456
Wright, Olgivanna Lloyd
  and Frank Lloyd Wright 184, 201, 231, 277, 366–67, 452, 456
  and Gurdjieff
    demands 92, 182
    Do you have a wish? 83
  and Katherine Mansfield 120, 124, 129, 133
  and Madame Ostrowska 129, 212
  early life 83
  new life 131, 183

Y

Yevlampios, Father 4
Yezidis 3, 163, 332, 584
Young, Dr. James 119, 139

Z

Zaharoff, Andrey Andreivitch 30, 37, 44, 48, 66, 68, 75, 83
Zhukov 68, 75, 104
Zigrosser, Carl 168, 184, 221
Zuber, René 276, 453

THE GURDJIEFF STUDIES PROGRAM

*"Awakening begins when a person realizes
that they are going nowhere
and they do not know where to go."*
— G. I. Gurdjieff

G. I. Gurdjieff, circa 1930s

Deeply rooted
in the fundamental ideas
and practices of
Gurdjieff's teaching
of The Fourth Way,
the Program is grounded
in an immediate
exploration of what is real,
and not real, through
genuine self-remembering,
self-observation and verification,
which guide the student
to the self-knowledge and being
that comprise real understanding
and conscience.

To inquire about
The Gurdjieff Studies Program,
please contact:

Inquiry@GurdjieffStudiesProgram.org